S Quiller
407- 482- 6694

Philosophical Issues in Art

PATRICIA H. WERHANE
Loyola University of Chicago

PRENTICE-HALL, INC., Englewood Cliffs, New Jersey 07632

Library of Congress Cataloging in Publication Data
Main entry under title:

Philosophical issues in art.

    Includes bibliographical references.
    1. Arts—Philosophy—Addresses, essays, lectures.
2. Aesthetics—Addresses, essays, lectures. I. Werhane,
Patricia Hogue.
BH39.P473 1984   700'.1   83-19225
ISBN   0-13-662288-7

Editorial/production supervision and
    interior design: Barbara Alexander
Cover design: Ben Santora
Manufacturing buyer: Harry P. Baisley

Printed in the United States of America

10   9   8   7   6   5   4

ISBN 0-13-662288-7

PRENTICE-HALL INTERNATIONAL, INC., *London*
PRENTICE-HALL OF AUSTRALIA PTY. LIMITED, *Sydney*
EDITORA PRENTICE-HALL DO BRASIL, LTDA., *Rio de Janeiro*
PRENTICE-HALL CANADA INC., *Toronto*
PRENTICE-HALL OF INDIA PRIVATE LIMITED, *New Delhi*
PRENTICE-HALL OF JAPAN, INC., *Tokyo*
PRENTICE-HALL OF SOUTHEAST ASIA PTE. LTD., *Singapore*
WHITEHALL BOOKS LIMITED, *Wellington, New Zealand*

Contents

Preface *ix*

Introduction *1*

PART I: THE WORK OF ART

1

Representation in Art: Mimesis *5*

PLATO Imitation *13*
R.G. COLLINGWOOD Art and Craft *22*
ARISTOTLE Mimesis and Catharsis *32*
E.H. GOMBRICH Truth and the Stereotype *41*
NELSON GOODMAN Reality Remade *56*

MIMESIS IN THE ARTS

ALEXANDER POPE An Essay on Criticism *68*
SIR JOSHUA REYNOLDS Discourses on Art *73*
CHARLES BIEDERMAN Constructionism and Mimesis *79*

Illustrations

1. GREEK, C.100 B.C. *Vénus de Milo* *82*
2. SIR JOSHUA REYNOLDS *Lady Elizabeth Delmé and Her Children, 1789* *82*

3. **JOHN CONSTABLE**   *Wivenhoe Park, Essex, 1816*   **83**
4. **CHARLES BIEDERMAN**   *Construction 10/39 (9), 1939*   **83**

2

Didacticism   *84*

SIR PHILIP SIDNEY   The Purposes of Poetry   **86**
LEO TOLSTOY   The Moral and the Spiritual in Art   **90**

Illustrations

5. **SIR PHILIP SIDNEY**   Thou Blind Man's Mark   **97**
6. **PABLO PICASSO**   *Guernica, 1937*   **98**

3

Formalism   *99*

CLIVE BELL   Significant Form   **102**
BERYL LAKE STEELE   The Irrefutability of Bell's Aesthetic Theory   **106**
T.S. ELIOT   Tradition and the Individual Talent   **109**

FORMALISM IN THE ARTS

ROBERT A.M. STERN   The Doubles of Post-Modern   **116**
LEONARD MEYER   Emotion and Meaning in Music   **123**
DONALD SHERBURNE   Meaning and Music   **131**
JOHN CAGE   The Future of Music: Credo   **137**

Illustrations

7. **PHILIP JOHNSON and JOHN BURGEE**   A.T. & T. Corporate
                                                    Headquarters   **139**
8. **JOHN CAGE**   *Concert for Piano and Orchestra*   **141**

4

Marxist Aesthetics   *142*

KARL MARX   Creativity and Alienation   **144**
ADOLFO SANCHEZ VÁZQUEZ   Marxist Aesthetics   **150**

MARXIST PERSPECTIVES IN THE ARTS

BERTOLT BRECHT   The Modern Theatre   *158*
ANTONIN ARTAUD   No More Masterpieces   *167*

Illustrations

9. BERTOLT BRECHT   The Measures Taken   *173*

PART II: THE CREATIVE PROCESS

5

Expressive Theories of Art   *191*

IMMANUEL KANT   The Imagination   *196*
SAMUEL TAYLOR COLERIDGE   Fancy and Imagination   *210*
SAMUEL TAYLOR COLERIDGE   Organic Form   *214*
HAROLD OSBORNE   Organic Unity   *216*
R.G. COLLINGWOOD   Emotion and Imagination   *220*

6

Contemporary Theories of the Imagination   *226*

JEAN-PAUL SARTRE   The Psychology of Imagination   *227*
GILBERT RYLE   Imagination   *231*
EDWARD CASEY   Imagination and the Image   *243*
MONROE BEARDSLEY   On the Creation of Art   *251*

EXPRESSION AND IMAGINATION IN THE ARTS

WASSILY KANDINSKY   Concerning the Spiritual in Art   *261*
MAURICE MERLEAU-PONTY   The Film and the New Psychology   *268*

Illustrations

10. SAMUEL TAYLOR COLERIDGE   Kubla Khan   *279*
11. WASSILY KANDINSKY   *Large Study, 1914*   *280*
12. PAUL VALERY   Le Cimetière Marin   *281*
13. NATHANAEL WEST   The Movie Set   *285*

7

Expression and Symbolism *290*

RUDOLF ARNHEIM   Art and Visual Perception *291*
SUSANNE LANGER   The Art Symbol and the Symbol in Art *297*
ELISEO VIVAS   Animadversions on Imitation and Expression *304*

SYMBOLISM IN THE ARTS

HERBERT READ   Hieronymus Bosch: Symbolic Integration *311*

Illustrations

14. MICHELANGELO   *The Creation of Man, 1509–1512* *315*
15. HIERONYMUS BOSCH   *The Garden of Earthly Delights, 1500* *316*

8

Art As a Psychological Phenomenon *317*

FRIEDRICH NIETZSCHE   Apollo and Dionysus *319*
SIGMUND FREUD   Oedipus and Hamlet *328*

Illustrations

16. WILLIAM SHAKESPEARE   Hamlet *332*
17. WILLIAM BUTLER YEATS   The Second Coming *339*
18. RICHARD SALIARIS   *The Second Coming* *340*

PART III: BEAUTY, TASTE, AND AESTHETICS

9

Historical Perspectives *341*

PLOTINUS   The Idea of the Beautiful *345*
SAINT THOMAS AQUINAS   Beauty and Art *352*
FRANCIS HUTCHESON   The Universal Sense of Beauty *356*
IMMANUEL KANT   The Analytic of the Beautiful *359*
GEORGE SANTAYANA   The Sense of Beauty *367*

BEAUTY AND THE AESTHETIC IN THE ARTS

WALTER PATER The Aesthetic *374*
OSCAR WILDE The Decay of Lying *376*
OSCAR WILDE Preface from The Picture of Dorian Gray *380*

Illustrations

19. JAMES JOYCE A Portrait of the Artist As a Young Man *381*

10

Contemporary Theories of Beauty and the Aesthetics *389*

EDWARD BULLOUGH "Psychical Distance" As a Factor in Art and As an Aesthetic Principle *391*
VIRGIL ALDRICH Prehension *399*
ROMAN INGARDEN Aesthetic Experience and Aesthetic Object *403*
FRANK SIBLEY Aesthetic Concepts *412*
GEORGE DICKIE Psychical Distance: In a Fog at Sea *422*

THE AESTHETIC IN THE ARTS

EDUARD HANSLICK The Beautiful in Music *430*

Illustrations

20. George Seurat *Sunday Afternoon on the Island of La Grande Jatte, 1884–86* *434*

PART IV: CONTEMPORARY ISSUES IN ART THEORY

11

Can a Work of Art Be Defined? *435*

LUDWIG WITTGENSTEIN Lectures on Aesthetics *439*
MORRIS WEITZ The Role of Theory in Aesthetics *447*
MAURICE MANDELBAUM Family Resemblances and Generalizations Concerning the Arts *454*
GEORGE DICKIE Defining Art *464*

GEORGE DICKIE   The Return to Art Theory   *469*
TED COHEN   The Possibility of Art   *477*

Illustrations

21. **FRANZ KLINE**   *White Forms, 1955*   *488*
22. **e.e. cummings**   when god lets my body be   *489*
23. **JAMES JOYCE**   Molly's Monologue from Ulysses   *489*
24. **MARCEL DUCHAMP**   *The Fountain, 1915*   *491*
25. **SUZANNE HARDING,**   *A Piece of Driftwood, 1980*   *491*

12

The Ontology of Artworks   *492*

NICOLAS WOLTERSTORFF   Toward an Ontology of Art Works   *493*
JEFFREY MAITLAND   Identity, Ontology, and the Work of Art   *503*

Illustrations

26. **ARNOLD SCHÖNBERG**   *Verklärte Nacht*   *517*

13

New Approaches in Art Theory   *518*

ALLEN CARLSON   Appreciation and the Natural Environment   *519*
LUCY LIPPARD   What Is Feminist Art?   *531*
A PANEL DISCUSSION   What Is Female Imagery?   *533*
ESTELLA LAUTER   Moving to the Ends of Our Own Rainbows: Steps
                         Toward a Feminist Aesthetic   *537*
ALAN TORMEY   Aesthetic Rights   *543*

Illustrations

27. **SUZANNE HARDING,**   *Door Country, 1977*   *553*
28. **NTOZAKE SHANGE**   sorry   *554*

Preface

This book grew out of my experiences in teaching courses in the philosophy of art. In offering these courses to undergraduate students I was struck by three things. First, students need a mix of traditional and contemporary theory. To examine contemporary ideas in the absence of their historical content deprives students of a philosophical background necessary to study aesthetics properly. Likewise, exclusively studying traditional theories of art fails to satisfy the student's curiosity about the latest developments in aesthetics. Second, I discovered that students are interested in what artists have to say about art. Artist's comments are seldom included in aesthetics courses. And sometimes an artist's view of art theory contributes significantly to that theory. Third, today's students seldom have at hand good art examples to which they and their professors can refer as illustrations with which to test a particular theory.

This anthology, then, is an answer to these needs I see in teaching aesthetics. A large collection of essays could not hope to do justice to all of these works in one quarter or one semester. However, I hope to have included enough material to appeal to the philosophical preferences of many teachers of aesthetics and to invite examination by students interested in the subject.

Many people have contributed to the form of this volume. I want to mention especially Raymond and Toni Johnson, who were influential in its inception, and Estella Lauter, who evaluated each selection and criticized the structure of the anthology. Other people who assisted in this text include Arthur Bloom, Ted Cohen, Suzanne Gossett, Suzanne Harding, Joe Pirri, and Brenda Shapiro. Special mention should be made to Eliseo Vivas, my first professor of aesthetics. I am deeply obliged to Loyola University for its continued support of this project, and to Kenneth Thompson and Robert Harvanek, S.J., chairpersons of the department of philosophy, for their encouragement. My tireless secretaries Cynthia Rudolph and Ruby Murchison deserve special thanks. Three blind reviewers at Prentice-Hall contributed enormously to the volume. Finally, the editors at Prentice-Hall, Raymond O'Connell and Doris Michaels, have provided invaluable editorial assistance.

PATRICIA H. WERHANE

Chicago, Illinois

Introduction

This is a book about art. It concerns many facets of art: the artist, the work of art, the audience, the critic, ideas of the aesthetic and, finally, philosophies of art.

Philosophy of art is neither art appreciation nor art criticism. In art appreciation one qualitatively evaluates specific works of art and compares certain aspects of these works with qualities of other works. In art appreciation it is assumed that the viewer knows what art is and that the viewer accepts certain kinds of descriptive and evaluative criteria as valid for an analysis of art. Critics, too, make these sorts of assumptions, and they assume their readers understand their interpretive schemes. In philosophy of art, on the other hand, we examine assumptions made by three groups: the artists, the appreciators of art, and the critics. Philosophers try to define art. They assess what is the proper subject matter for art appreciation and criticism. They establish general criteria for distinguishing what is important or unique in artworks. Philosophers of art might also develop an idea of the aesthetic wherein certain qualities of artworks, the activities of the artist/creator or the reactions of the experiencer of art, are set apart as unique "aesthetic phenomena" or "aesthetic experiences."

Philosophy of art, or aesthetic theory as it is viewed in the Western world, has a long tradition. The ancient Greek philosophers of fifth-century Athens were fascinated with art. They were concerned with the artistic process of representation in art (which they called "mimesis"), and they were also concerned with the possible effects, both positive and negative, that a work of art could have on its viewers. It was not until the Renaissance, however, that the contemporary notion of art was fully developed. Until that period art was by and large considered a form of craft created for some utilitarian, decorative, or religious purpose, and the artist was thought of as a kind of craftsman. The Renaissance germinated the idea that the artist might be a special sort of professional person, that the artistic process takes a special sort of talent and the results of this process, artworks, have a unique cultural status different from other man-made things or artifacts. The professionalization of the artist and the recognition of art as a valuable cultural phenomenon led to the acceptance of the study of art as a worthy intellectual enterprise. Consequently, it was only after the Renaissance that aesthetic theory was singled out as a worthwhile philosophical endeavor.

The first aesthetic theories to emerge after the Renaissance—often called Classical theories of art—concentrated on the work of art itself as a unique creation developed for no other purpose than its own being. That is, it was recognized that works of art were sometimes made for no utilitarian or religious purpose, but simply for their own existence. This led to questions such as, "What is a work of art?" and "What is the definition of art if it is a unique sort of cultural phenomenon?" Part I of this volume contains some of these theories.

In the eighteenth century philosophers of art became explicitly concerned with an element in the aesthetic situation heretofore recognized but not always singled out: the response of the audience or the viewer to art. And during this period, aestheticians developed specific theories about the nature and the quality of this response which they termed "aesthetic response," or simply, "taste." The aesthetic response was characterized as a disinterested contemplative experience or a pleasure triggered by works of art, an experience having no particular value or benefit to the contemplator beyond the sheer aesthetic character of the experience itself. Thus the response of the viewer, as well as the work of art, were considered as unique and important cultural phenomena. More will be said about the aesthetic response in Part III. What is most important is to notice that what was defined as a unique and disinterested reaction of the viewer—and later of the critic, the philosopher, and the community at large—became a singularly important notion in aesthetic theory.

Another shift in focus in aesthetic theory occurred in the nineteenth century. Beginning in the late eighteenth century some aestheticians became fascinated with the role of the artist in the process which produces artworks. From this fascination emerged the idea that the artist is a unique, unusual, imaginative genius who pours his or her emotions and imaginative energies into the creative work. Exploration of this image became a nineteenth-century preoccupation, as we shall see in Part II.

Thus as the twentieth century began there were at least three different kinds of aesthetic theories: those which focused on the work of art, those which concerned themselves with the creative process (the artist), and those which analyzed the unique effect of art on its audience: the aesthetic response. There were common elements in all of these theories. First, there was a strong conviction that works of art are unique, that they are created for aesthetic contemplation, and that art has no other explicit function. How artworks are unique can be discovered, and the nature of art can be defined. Secondly, it was believed that the creative process is a function distinct from other human activities and that this process, too, can be defined. Thirdly, the aesthetic response is a peculiar contemplative response triggered by art, or by great works of art. It is a human activity which is unlike other human activities and it, too, can be exhaustively described by aesthetic theory.

In the twentieth century, as we shall see in Part IV of this volume, aestheticians have become more cautious. With the influx of new styles, new art forms, and the questioning of traditional conventions in art, one wonders whether art *can* be described in terms of a unique set of defining characteristics. The introduction into museums of "ready-made" art—such as shovels and urinals—brings into question the claim that artistic creation necessarily involves the play of genius or unfailingly presupposes originality. Philosophers in this century have also questioned the existence, peculiarity, and importance of the aesthetic response.

Nevertheless, despite these questions, the fascination with art, with artists, and with the enjoyment of art remains. This fascination continues, I think, because it is surely the case—at least in Western civilizations—that a certain class of phenomena are created simply for the pleasure (or pain) of creating them, by persons whose full-time occupation is making works which have no other use or value except to be viewed, to be read, or to be listened to. Many of us in this culture indulge hours, even years, in contemplating, viewing, listening to, and studying these works for no other reason than the enjoyment—or the horror—of the experience. Putting all theoretical questions aside, we in the Western cultures spend a great deal of energy and time indulging in nonutilitarian aesthetic activities. Thus the study of that to which we devote such energy, art, is worthy of our serious attention.

This anthology studies art, artists, and aesthetic theory by organizing the subject matter according to three facets of art: the work of art, creativity, and the aesthetic response. We begin the volume with a study of the work of art, the subject matter of aesthetic theory. But the role of the artist, too, is an essential component in art, and Part II concentrates on various aspects of creativity and the creative process.

Some works of art are created with a possible audience in mind. This is particularly true of theatre, music, and dance, which are created to be performed. Other art forms may or may not have the viewer or the reader in mind. Nevertheless, unless one paints in a cave and buries one's works from the world, art is something to be seen, read, heard, and experienced. Thus audience responses are an important part of art in any social context. Part III analyzes this aspect of art.

Part IV of the volume is a potpourri of new developments in aesthetic theory, ones not easily classifed elsewhere in the book. Readings in Part IV raise challenging new questions, the most important being, "Can art be defined?" These last selections will serve as stimuli to whet the curiosity of the student in aesthetics.

The four parts of this book are each organized into topics, or themes, relevant to the facet of art under discussion. And each topic is treated from an historical as well as a modern perspective. The historical selections have been chosen not merely to give the student background for a particular aesthetic issue, but also because what that particular philosopher has to say is still relevant to contemporary aesthetic theory. Many of the modern selections are criticisms of the historical article so that the reader can evaluate each position from at least two points of view. The philosophical readings are supplemented with selections from art critics and artists. Often these persons shed philosophical light on an issue heretofore overlooked even by careful analysis. Again, these readings have been selected carefully to insure that they draw attention to the aesthetic issue at hand in a new and illuminating way. Each section of the book is illustrated with art examples which give substance to the essays. For the student new to the study of aesthetics this should seem natural and normal. After all, this book is about art. Inexplicably, however, almost no book on aesthetics, to date, has used art illustrations to make its points. More importantly, each illustration is mentioned in the text of at least one of the readings in the volume. Thus each work of art is an example of an art form important to at least one philosophical view. And each work exemplifies at least one aspect of art crucial to a particular theory. Students should use illustrations from all sections of the book when examining theories in any one; the illustrations can function as "tests" for the strength or weakness of any particular theory in question.

1

Representation in Art: Mimesis

The study of art should begin with a crucial element of art: the work of art itself. In Part I, we shall examine theories which focus on the analysis of artworks as the most important aspect of aesthetic theory. These theories attempt to define art and to spell out its most universal, essential, and pervasive qualities. These qualities, it is argued by each philosopher in Part I, define what is unique and significant in artworks. Some are what are called "exhibited" qualities of art: perceived characteristics of the work itself. For example, the color of the marble, the shape of the sculpture, the representation of a female figure, and even the fact that the arms are missing are all qualitative exhibited features of the statue *Venus de Milo* (Illustration 1). Other characteristics are what are referred to as the "nonexhibited" or relational qualities of artworks, features by which a work of art is related to an audience or to society in general. According to Part I's theorists, certain exhibited characteristics of artworks set apart art from other things, and these qualities establish what is unique in a work of art. The qualities then become standards for distinguishing good works of art from other art, because works which do not exhibit these characteristics are not unique or great works.

Chapter 1 discusses mimetic theories, theories which emphasize the representational quality of art. What is important in art according to these views is the way in which the work represents its subject matter. The use of proper art media and rules which govern the patterns or the formal structures an artist employs are also important. But, according to these theories, the idea of representation or mimesis is the most essential feature in defining and evaluating art.

Almost every work of art in some way reflects the world in which the artist lives and works. The subject matter for the work, the raw materials from which it develops, its content—each is in some way related to what the artist perceives and what he idealizes from those perceptions and from his experiences, environment, feelings, and emotions. In many works of art, the subject matter represents a world or a universe external to the personal or subjective feelings of the artist. But even if the artist is trying merely to reflect or express his or her own private ideas, the artist usually does this through a subject that, by communicating these ideas, in some way represents or reflects experiences or situations accessible to or understood by his or her audience. Therefore, it is important in the philosophy of art to examine the possible relationships between a work of art and the world, or nature, or human experience. But how does the process of representation—or mimesis—take place in art? Is *all* art essentially mimetic?

The notion of mimesis in art probably originated with the ancient Greeks. The famous Greek philosopher Plato, one of the first aestheticians, felt that art was mimetic. What we might call the "artistic" process was held to be somewhat like the process of the craftsman. The artist, according to Plato, copies, imitates, or reproduces nature in works of art, just as the craftsman reproduces chairs or beds. Good artists reproduce nature as if the reproduction itself were real, just as fine craftsmen reproduce almost perfect beds. Most artists consider what they do more original and creative than so-called craft. But Plato did not concur with this view. In his well-known work, the *Republic*, Plato goes so far as to claim that the artist is an imitator of the craftsman. Thus the artist is less creative than the craftsman and the artist's importance in society is slight indeed.

Plato bases this conclusion on his idea of nature and on what is called his theory of Forms. Plato argued that what we call "nature" or "experience" is a world of appearances. The world as we experience it is in constant flux or change. One never perceives the same thing in the same way more than once. Objects of perception, the perspective of the perceiver, and even the perceiver him or herself change over time so that each perception is a new awareness of a slightly different thing. However, Plato noticed that despite these changes we identify similar or like objects in all our experiences. There are then, in nature, similarities which persist throughout change and things which share the same characteristics. Moreover, for any set of similar things which have the same properties, such as beds or triangles for instance, we have, or can develop, an idea of a perfect example of that bed or triangle, even though we never perceive that perfect example. But how can one conceive of such perfections if none exists in nature? Plato proposes what he calls the theory of forms to account for the appearance of a multitude of similar but not identical things in nature and to explain the source of our idea of a perfect triangle or an ideal bed for which there are no existing examples. According to Plato there must exist, besides nature, an intelligible real world which consists of perfect examples (Forms) of the things we perceive in nature.

The world of Forms cannot itself be perceived, but it can be understood intellectually. The world of Forms is truly the real world because it is eternal and does not change. And nature, consisting of imperfect changing likenesses of the Forms, is less real than, and thus one level below, the world of Forms. Therefore the Forms are the source of true knowledge while nature, which is an imperfect changing copy of this world of Forms, is only, at best, the source of true beliefs.

Plato applies this theory to the craftsman and the artist. The good craftsman, according to Plato, conceives of a mental ideal, a Form, from which he crafts beds, tables, and so on. The crafted article, like nature, is an appearance, a copy of a Form. The artist, on the other hand, procures images from nature, that is, he or she copies individual appearances or crafted articles. Therefore, Plato argues, "the work of the artist is a third remove from the essential nature [the Form] of a thing." Works of art are merely copies of appearances, and the artist in the *Republic,* as an imitator of imitations, a copier of copies, is less respectable than the craftsman.

Despite his opinion of artists Plato recognized that some artists are very good at imitating nature in such a way as to give it the appearance of reality. Artists can be supurb propagandists, portraying their view of the world of appearances as if it were truth. Thus art can arouse persons to immoral or evil action. And Plato's fear of the artist remains an issue in contemporary times. In the 1930s a well-known German producer, Leni Riefenstahl, made what has proved to be technically and aesthetically one of the finest films of that era, *The Triumph of the Will.* However, the subject matter and the intent of the film are morally questionable. The film portrays the glorification of the Nazi party, the beauty of the Aryan race, and the supremacy of anglo-saxon racism. These portrayals are so well-executed that when watching the film one sometimes forgets the values they embody. How should one treat an artist who portrays banality or evil in a positive and even a beautiful way?

Plato's pupil, Aristotle, was both an admirer and a critic of his teacher. While staying within the mimetic tradition, Aristotle questioned Plato's criticism of art as a copy of a copy, and responded to Plato's worry about the dangers of art. Using drama as an example, Aristotle, in the *Poetics,* argues first that, while the essential characteristic of art is its mimetic function, the artist does not merely imitate particular phenomena or simply report experiences. This would be a job for an historian. Rather, the artist depicts general types of human character and human action rather than particular historical persons or events. And the artist represents nature not as it is but as it should or could be. Drama and poetry, for example, represent what might happen generally; they depict possible universal characteristics of human nature rather than individual occurrences. Thus the mimetic process is more complex than Plato suggests.

Second, the artist does not copy naively. Rather, Aristotle argues that because the essential characteristic of art is its mimetic function, the medium of representation (the art form) and the manner of imitation (the formal elements employed by the artist) are of utmost importance for proper representation of nature. For example, Aristotle considers tragedy the proper medium for depicting noble human action. The form of the tragedy is prescribed to achieve these ends. A proper tragedy should be written in four parts: prologue, episode, exode, and choral song. The characterizations should be appropriate to the role they are to play in the plot, lifelike, and consistent. There should be unity of plot and action where the action itself is complete during the time span of the play. Plot, action, and language of the play should specifically represent the thought content of the play and its effect on the audience. This seems circular, but Aristotle's point is that proper depiction of complete, unified, noble human experience can only be correctly executed through a well-constructed four-part tragic drama which itself is formally unified so that plot is noble and complete. Thus great artists should employ certain rules and methods which govern the mimetic process.

According to Aristotle,

> A tragedy, then, is the imitation of an action that is serious, and also, as having magnitude, complete in itself—with incidents arousing pity and fear, wherewith to accomplish its catharsis of such emotions.

What Aristotle meant is that a good work of art such as a well-structured tragedy should represent deep, noble human feelings such that these same feelings are aroused in the audience. But the arousal is an aesthetic experience, not, as Plato feared, an arousal to action. By experiencing these emotions second-hand through a work of art, the audience is freed from the harmful effects of similar emotions when experienced in actual life. There is a sort of "cleansing of the souls" of the audience through the communication of emotion in the work of art, and art thus has what is called a "cathartic" effect. Great works of art, then, do not stir people to action as Plato thought. Rather, according to Aristotle, aesthetic emotions are felt during a performance of a play, and these emotions are then purged rather than activated by the work of art. Thus art has a positive rather than a negative social effect by exhibiting and cleansing persons of emotions without leading persons to violent action.

Although Aristotle concentrates on drama and poetry, by extrapolation his views form a general thesis about all art. Aristotle's theory of catharsis, for instance, evaluates positively the artist and the role of art in society. His definition of drama sets up certain criteria for evaluating what should count as good art: that it depicts the possible, that it depicts the universal type rather than a particular character, and that art follows certain formal rules. These criteria became the norms of what are called Classical theories of art, theories which have become the paradigm of the mimetic ideal.

Classical theories of art are represented in this section by the writings of Alexander Pope and Sir Joshua Reynolds as well as Aristotle. A Classical theory of art assumes mimetic principles. What is important for this theory is the process and nature of selectivity in mimesis. According to the Classical theories of art, what is to be represented in a work of art is some form of nature. But the subject matter of art should not be nature in its specifics, but rather in its essentials. In each of its limitations or representations the work of art mirrors some selected, generalized, typical, average, possible, or ideal aspect. Idiosyncrasies, individualities, malformations, and distortions are deliberately left out. By avoiding extremes and irregularities the work of art is intended to represent the possible, the universal, or the ideal. By freeing the artwork from irregularities, what is depicted appears as a norm by which the natural world can be measured.

A major spokesman for Classical theories of art, the eighteenth-century painter and aesthetician Sir Joshua Reynolds claims:

> . . . the usual and most dangerous error (in art) is on the side of minuteness. . . . The general idea constitutes real excellence. All smaller things, however perfect in their way, are to be sacrificed without mercy to the greater. . . .

Reynold's work, *Lady Delmé and Her Children* (Illustration 2) exemplified his view of art. Lady Delmé is the ideal of an English lady with immaculate children portrayed in a flawless landscape. No detail of this scene is peculiar. Each item in the painting is a generalized representation of an ideal British landscape. *Venus de Milo*, too, illustrates a perfect example of the Classical ideal in art.

Also important to any Classical idea of art is the claim that an artist must work within specific formal structures which are sometimes called "rules of imitation." For example, during the Renaissance it was deemed that a proper drama was a play in five acts. Time, place, and action were to be unified. The action of a proper drama is a complete action occurring in one location during a twenty-four-hour period. A poet wrote only according to established rules of rhyme scheme, length of line, and rhythmic organization of words. As late as the nineteenth century Emily Dickinson's poetry was criticized and at first not accepted because of its imperfect meter. The poet Alexander Pope goes so far as to claim that the rules or formal patterns the artist employs in a work of art parallel the order and harmony in nature which are being represented:

> Learn hence for ancient rules a just esteem;
> To copy Nature is to copy them.

While this is probably an exaggeration of the importance of formal structure, philosophers of art from Aristotle until at least the nineteenth century have emphasized the importance of proper form as one of the distinguishing elements of art.

At the extreme, Classical theories of art have sometimes been labeled "technical" theories of art by contemporary philosophers such as R. G. Collingwood. Because—according to Classical theories of art—the subject matter for art is defined or limited, and because predefined rules governing the structures of art forms constrain the way in which artists can express their ideas externally in artifacts, Collingwood argues that according to Classical theory the artist is merely a kind of impersonal craftsman or technician who has a particular talent for transcribing his or her perceptions or idealizations of nature into the formal structure of defined art forms.

If the distinction *can* be made between an art work and a craft article, some Classical theories of art make this distinction on the basis of the idea of inspiration: the artist is an inspired craftsman. Inspiration is sometimes thought of as "natural genius," inherited at birth. Alexander Pope, in *An Essay on Criticism* (reproduced in Chapter 1), conceived of inspiration not necessarily as divinely inspired, but as "nameless graces" beyond ordinary human skills and reason, the endowment of which distinguishes the work of the poet from that of the craftsman. The idea of inspiration or genius is not taken so seriously in our century, but for Classical theories of art it distinguished the artist from the craftsman, because it is the inspired artist who can transmit representational subject matter through well-defined rules of imitation to express a new or fresh view of nature.

The concept of mimesis is not limited to Classical theories of art. Because many art works appear to represent, reflect, or imitate nature, the role of the mimetic features of art is of continuing philosophical interest. This role is of particular concern in drama and in the novel where at least minimal representational subject matter is always necessary. Recently the playwright Samuel Beckett presented his controversial work, *Breath*. This is a short play in which the curtain opens on an empty stage, a few sighs are heard from offstage, and within thirty seconds the curtain closes. Although there is a minimum of staging and no one appears on stage, even this play has an element of representation of the emptiness (and shortness!) of the human experience as breathed, that is, lived, by anonymous persons.

To respond to the charge that mimetic theories of art are merely technical theories, some contemporary defenders of mimesis claim that *mirroring*, not copying, is the aesthetic principle upon which the concept of mimesis in art is grounded. According to a true mimetic idea of art, a work of art does not merely reproduce a natural or human experience. The notion that one of the functions of a work of art is to mirror or imitate is not the same idea as that of copying. The artist is not a Xerox machine, nor the work of art a photocopy. The notion of imitation implies that a selection of what is to be imitated by the artist has taken place. That process is not merely the reduction of three-dimensional nature to two dimensions, or visual experience to audible experience in the case of music. The process is also a limiting, defining, or isolating process. Just as the frame confines what is reflected in the mirror, so too the work of art selects, isolates, confines, and discriminates its subject matter within the frame of the canvas or length of the poem. The concept of mimesis, then, does not mean the idea that a work of art is a copy. Rather the artist selectively imitates or "re-presents" his subject matter, translating and transforming it into something new: a work of art. To illustrate, the modern Constructionists, represented in this section by Charles Biederman (Illustration 4) claim that Structurist art, which creates and assembles multi-colored three-dimensional geometric forms on canvas, is mimetic. This is because Structurist art imitates the basic three-dimensional structure of nature by forming it into a more abstract form on canvas.

Other contemporary views of mimesis claim that all art is in some sense mimetic, but the subject matter of mimesis is not limited to nature. Rather, art can reflect any reality an artist deems suitable, including the activities of the artist's mind, his dreams, or images. Even abstract art, such as Kline's *White Forms,* is mimetic (Illustration 2) according to this view because abstract artworks reproduce another reality stranger but more real to the artist than nature.

As our discussion has already indicated, the theory of mimesis has remained important far beyond the Classical period. In Chapter 4 we shall read about Marxist theories which emphasize the mimetic feature as a necessary element of all great art. And Susanne Langer's theory of art, included in Part 2 of this book, is often called a mimetic view of art. This is because Langer argues that a work of art is an expressive form which symbolically "re-presents" the nondiscursive, inarticulate feelings and emotions of the artist. Langer's theory is often criticized by philosophers such as Eliseo Vivas because of this mimetic emphasis, which, according to Vivas, neglects the creativity of the artist.

The section on mimesis concludes with two papers strongly critical of mimetic theories of art: "Truth and the Stereotype" by well-known art historian and aesthetician E. H. Gombrich, and "Reality Remade" by Nelson Goodman. Gombrich, who is influenced both by the eighteenth-century philosopher Immanuel Kant and by Ludwig Wittgenstein, raises the question, "Does the painter paint what he sees?"—as mimetic theorists claim—"or does he see what he paints?" Gombrich argues that even if art is in some sense mimetic, the representational process takes place only through the preconceptions of the artist. Through a series of examples Gombrich demonstrates that every artist begins with a model, a vocabulary, or a conceptual scheme through which the artist views and models his or her images. Without a set of stereotypes or categories one could never sort out the mirage of impressions nor organize one's perceptions into orderly experiences. The history of art is the history of evolving styles and stereotypes. Art tells us little about reality but a great deal about the ways in which artists have conceived of reality. The artist, then, according to Gombrich, "tends to see what he paints." John Constable's so-called naturalistic painting, *Wivenhoe Park* (Illustration 3), demonstrates how many artistic conventions are involved in what appears to be a naturalistic depiction or imitation of a landscape taken from nature.

One of the conventions an artist may use in depicting nature is that of perspective. During the Renaissance artists discovered and perfected the scientific technique of transforming the appearance of three dimensions onto a two-dimensional flat canvas. And even Gombrich admits that this technique enables the painter to represent nature as a three-dimensional and truly representational image.

On the other hand, Nelson Goodman, the widely respected contemporary philosopher, argues that even the so-called science of perspective cannot produce a faithful representation of nature. This is in part because there is no such thing as a "normal perspective" or a "faithful representation." How one sees an object—"perspective"—depends on one's vision, the light, one's position in relation to the object, and so on; that is, perspective is variable. But moreover, the ideal of true mimesis also fails because the so-called object to be representated is itself not one object, but a series of objects as viewed from different points of view.

The problem, as Goodman sees it, is that, traditionally, representation was assumed to be equated with resemblance. Goodman points out, however, that representation is by and large symbolic—anything can symbolize almost anything else in art. For example, the peace sign is (resembles) two fingers in the air, but no one thinks literally of "two fingers" when someone makes the sign. Rather, the sign reminds the viewer of what it symbolizes—peace—which two upraised fingers scarcely resemble in any way. One need only look at the figures in Picasso's *Guernica* (Illustration 6) to see how little they resemble lifelike figures, but how much they *represent* (symbolize) them. All art, then, even that which seems most to resemble nature, is at the least, a symbolic presentation of the subject matter from a particular point of view. That the viewer understands what is being represented or symbolized in a work of art is not because of a lifelike resemblance. Rather it is because, as human viewers, we are able to symbolize and thus understand the symbols of the artist. The student should examine Goodman's views carefully. Is his theory a form of the mimetic view of art?

Imitation[1]

PLATO

Indeed, our commonwealth has many features which make me think it was based on very sound principles, especially our rule not on any account to admit the poetry of dramatic representation.[2] Now that we have distinguished the several parts of the soul, it seems to me clearer than ever that such poetry must be firmly excluded.

What makes you say so?

Between ourselves—for you will not denounce me to the tragedians and the other dramatists—poetry of that sort seems to be injurious to minds which do not possess the antidote in a knowledge of its real nature.

What have you in mind?

I must speak out, in spite of a certain affection and reverence I have had from a child for Homer, who seems to have been the original master and guide of all this imposing company of tragic poets.[3] However, no man must be honoured above the truth; so, as I say, I must speak my mind.

Do, by all means.

Listen then, or rather let me ask you a question. Can you tell me what is meant by representation in general? I have no very clear notion myself.

So you expect me to have one!

Why not? It is not always the keenest eye that is the first to see something.

True; but when you are there I should not be very desirous to tell what I saw, however plainly. You must use your own eyes.

Well then, shall we proceed as usual and begin by assuming the existence of a single essential nature or Form for every set of things which we call by the same name? Do you understand?

I do.

Then let us take any set of things you choose. For instance there are

From *The Republic Of Plato* trans. by F. M. Cornford (1941). Reprinted by permission of Oxford University Press.

---

[1]*The Republic,* like all of Plato's writings, takes the form of a dialogue. Socrates is traditionally the main speaker. This dialogue is between Socrates, Glaucon, and Adeimantus.

[2]Plato seemed to exclude all dramatic poetry because this contains no narrative but involves the impersonation (*mimesis*) of all types of character, good or bad; whereas epic, for instance, can limit speeches in character to the representation of virtuous or heroic types. He will now argue that all poetry and other forms of art are essentially *mimesis*. The meaning of the word is obviously enlarged where he speaks just below of "representation in general."

[3]The plots of Greek tragedy were normally stories borrowed from epic poetry. Hence Homer was spoken of as the first tragic poet.

any number of beds or of tables, but only two Forms, one of Bed and one of Table.

Yes.

And we are in the habit of saying that the craftsman, when he makes the beds or tables we use or whatever it may be, has before his mind the Form[4] of one or other of these pieces of furniture. The Form itself is, of course, not the work of any craftsman. How could it be?

It could not.

Now what name would you give to a craftsman who can produce all the things made by every sort of workman?

He would need to have very remarkable powers!

Wait a moment, and you will have even better reason to say so. For, besides producing any kind of artificial thing, this same craftsman can create all plants and animals, himself included, and earth and sky and gods and the heavenly bodies and all the things under the earth in Hades.

That sounds like a miraculous feat of virtuosity.

Are you incredulous? Tell me, do you think there could be no such craftsman at all, or that there might be someone who could create all these things in one sense, though not in another?[5] Do you not see that you could do it yourself, in a way?

In what way, I should like to know.

There is no difficulty; in fact there are several ways in which the thing can be done quite quickly. The quickest perhaps would be to take a mirror and turn it round in all directions. In a very short time you could produce sun and stars and earth and yourself and all the other animals and plants and lifeless objects which we mentioned just now.

Yes, in appearance, but not the actual things.

Quite so; you are helping out my argument. My notion is that a painter is a craftsman of that kind. You may say that the things he produces are not real; but there is a sense in which he too does produce a bed.

Yes, the appearance of one.

And what of the carpenter? Were you not saying just now that he only makes a particular bed, not what we call the Form or essential nature of Bed?

Yes, I was.

---

[4] "Form" does not mean "shape" but the essential properties which constitute what the thing, by definition, is.

[5] The divine Demiurge of the creation-myth in the *Timaeus* is pictured as fashioning the whole visible world after the likeness of the eternal Forms, which he does not create but uses as models. He is thus the maker of natural objects, corresponding to the carpenter who makes artificial objects; and both, as makers of actual things, are superior to the painter or poet, who makes all things only "in a way," by creating mere semblances like images in a mirror.

If so, what he makes is not the reality, but only something that resembles it. It would not be right to call the work of a carpenter or of any other handicraftsman a perfectly real thing, would it?

Not in the view of people accustomed to thinking on these lines.[6]
We must not be surprised, then, if even an actual bed is a somewhat shadowy thing as compared with reality.

True.

Now shall we make use of this example to throw light on our question as to the true nature of this artist who represents things? We have here three sorts of bed: one which exists in the nature of things and which, I imagine, we could only describe as a product of divine workmanship; another made by the carpenter; and a third by the painter. So the three kinds of bed belong respectively to the domains of these three: painter, carpenter, and god.

Yes.

Now the god made only one ideal or essential Bed, whether by choice or because he was under some necessity not to make more than one; at any rate two or more were not created, nor could they possibly come into being.

Why not?

Because, if he made even so many as two, then once more a single ideal Bed would make its appearance, whose character those two would share; and that one, not the two, would be the essential Bed. Knowing this, the god, wishing to be the real maker of a real Bed, not a particular manufacturer of one particular bed, created one which is essentially unique.

So it appears.

Shall we call him, then, the author of the true nature of Bed, or something of that sort?

Certainly he deserves the name, since all his works constitute the real nature of things.

And we may call the carpenter the manufacturer of a bed?

Yes.

Can we say the same of the painter?

Certainly not.

Then what is he, with reference to a bed?

I think it would be fairest to describe him as the artist who represents the things which the other two make.

Very well, said I; so the work of the artist is at the third remove from the essential nature of the thing?

Exactly.

The tragic poet, too, is an artist who represents things; so this will apply

---

[6]Familiar with the Platonic doctrine, as opposed to current materialism, which regards the beds we sleep on as real things and the Platonic Form as a mere "abstraction" or notion existing only in our minds.

to him: he and all other artists are, as it were, third in succession from the throne of truth.[7]

Just so.

We are in agreement, then, about the artist. But now tell me about our painter: which do you think he is trying to represent—the reality that exists in the nature of things, or the products of the craftsman?

The products of the craftsman.

As they are, or as they appear? You have still to draw that distinction.[8]

How do you mean?

I mean: you may look at a bed or any other object from straight in front or slantwise or at any angle. Is there then any difference in the bed itself, or does it merely look different?

It only looks different.

Well, that is the point. Does painting aim at reproducing any actual object as it is, or the appearance of it as it looks? In other words, is it a representation of the truth or of a semblance?

Of a semblance.

The art of representation, then, is a long way from reality; and apparently the reason why there is nothing it cannot reproduce is that it grasps only a small part of any object, and that only an image. Your painter, for example, will paint us a shoemaker, a carpenter, or other workman, without understanding any one of their crafts;[9] and yet, if he were a good painter, he might deceive a child or a simple-minded person into thinking his picture was a real carpenter, if he showed it them at some distance.

No doubt.

But I think there is one view we should take in all such cases. Whenever someone announces that he has met with a person who is master of every trade and knows more about every subject than any specialist, we should reply that he is a simple fellow who has apparently fallen in with some illusionist and been tricked into thinking him omniscient, because of his own inability to discriminate between knowledge and ignorance and the representation of appearances.

Quite true.

Then it is now time to consider the tragic poets and their master, Homer,

---

[7]Jowett and Campbell quote from Dante Virgil's description of human art as the "grandchild of God," since art is said to copy nature, and nature is the child of God: *si che vostr' arte a Dio quasi è nipote*, Inferno xi. 105.

[8]The distinction is needed to exclude another possible sense of *mimesis*, the production of a complete replica.

[9]Knowledge of carpentry is the essence of the carpenter, what makes him a carpenter. The painter could not reproduce this knowledge in his picture, even if he possessed it himself. This may sound absurd as an objection to art, but Plato is thinking rather of the application to the poet, for whom it was claimed that he both possessed technical and moral knowledge and reproduced it in his book.

because we are sometimes told that they understand not only all technical matters but also all about human conduct, good or bad, and about religion; for, to write well, a good poet, so they say, must know his subject; otherwise he could not write about it. We must ask whether these people have not been deluded by meeting with artists who can represent appearances, and in contemplating the poets' work have failed to see that it is at the third remove from reality, nothing more than semblances, easy to produce with no knowledge of the truth. Or is there something in what they say? Have the good poets a real mastery of the matters on which the public thinks they discourse so well?

It is a question we ought to look into.

Well then, if a man were able actually to do the things he represents as well as to produce images of them, do you believe he would seriously give himself up to making these images and take that as a completely satisfying object in life? I should imagine that, if he had a real understanding of the actions he represents, he would far sooner devote himself to performing them in fact. The memorials he would try to leave after him would be noble deeds, and he would be more eager to be the hero whose praises are sung than the poet who sings them.

Yes, I agree; he would do more good in that way and win a greater name.

Here is a question, then, that we may fairly put to Homer or to any other poet. We will leave out of account all mere matters of technical skill: we will not ask them to explain, for instance, why it is that, if they have a knowledge of medicine and not merely the art of reproducing the way physicians talk, there is no record of any poet, ancient or modern, curing patients and bequeathing his knowledge to a school of medicine, as Asclepius did. But when Homer undertakes to tell us about matters of the highest importance, such as the conduct of war, statesmanship, or education, we have a right to inquire into his competence. "Dear Homer," we shall say, "we have defined the artist as one who produces images at the third remove from reality. If your knowledge of all that concerns human excellence was really such as to raise you above him to the second rank, and you could tell what courses of conduct will make men better or worse as individuals or as citizens, can you name any country which was better governed thanks to your efforts? Many states, great and small, have owed much to a good lawgiver, such as Lycurgus at Sparta, Charondas in Italy and Sicily, and our own Solon. Can you tell us of any that acknowledges a like debt to you?"

I should say not, Glaucon replied. The most devout admirers of Homer make no such claim.

Well, do we hear of any war in Homer's day being won under his command or thanks to his advice?

No.

Or of a number of ingenious inventions and technical contrivances, which would show that he was a man of practical ability like Thales of Miletus or Anacharsis the Scythian?[10]

Nothing of the sort.

Well, if there is no mention of public services, do we hear of Homer in his own lifetime presiding, like Pythagoras, over a band of intimate disciples who loved him for the inspiration of his society and handed down a Homeric way of life, like the way of life which the Pythagoreans called after their founder and which to this day distinguishes them from the rest of the world?

No; on the contrary, Homer's friend with the absurd name, Creophylus,[11] would look even more absurd when considered a product of the poet's training, if the story is true that he completely neglected Homer during his lifetime.

Yes, so they say. But what do you think, Glaucon? If Homer had really possessed the knowledge qualifying him to educate people and make them better men, instead of merely giving us a poetical representation of such matters, would he not have attracted a host of disciples to love and revere him? After all, any number of private teachers like Protagoras of Abdera and Prodicus of Ceos[12] have succeeded in convincing their contemporaries that they will never be fit to manage affairs of state or their own households unless these masters superintend their education; and for this wisdom they are so passionately admired that their pupils are all but ready to carry them about on their shoulders. Can we suppose that Homer's contemporaries, or Hesiod's, would have left them to wander about reciting their poems, if they had really been capable of helping their hearers to be better men? Surely they would sooner have parted with their money and tried to make the poets settle down at home; or failing that, they would have danced attendance on them wherever they went, until they had learnt from them all they could.

I believe you are quite right, Socrates.

We may conclude, then, that all poetry, from Homer onwards, consists in representing a semblance of its subject, whatever it may be, including any kind of human excellence, with no grasp of the reality. We were speaking just now of the painter who can produce what looks like a shoemaker to the spectator who, being as ignorant of shoemaking as he is himself, judges only by form and colour. In the same way the poet, knowing nothing more than how to represent appearances, can paint in words his picture of any craftsman

---

[10]Thales (early sixth cent.) made a fortune out of a corner in oil-mills when his knowledge of the stars enabled him to predict a large olive harvest, thus proving that wise men could be rich if they chose (Aristotle, *Politics*, i. II). Anacharsis was said to have invented the anchor and the potter's wheel (Diog. Laert. i. 105).

[11]Creophylus' name is supposed to be derived from two words meaning "flesh" and "tribe." He is said to have been an epic poet from Chios.

[12]Two of the most famous Sophists of the fifth century. Plato's *Protagoras* gives a vivid picture of them on a visit to a rich patron at Athens.

so as to impress an audience which is equally ignorant and judges only by the form of expression; the inherent charm of metre, rhythm, and musical setting is enough to make them think he has discoursed admirably about generalship or shoemaking or any other technical subject. Strip what the poet has to say of its poetical colouring, and I think you must have seen what it comes to in plain prose. It is like a face which was never really handsome, when it has lost the fresh bloom of youth.

Quite so.

Here is a further point, then. The artist, we say, this maker of images, knows nothing of the reality, but only the appearance. But that is only half the story. An artist can paint a bit and bridle, while the smith and the leather-worker can make them. Does the painter understand the proper form which bit and bridle ought to have? Is it not rather true that not even the craftsmen who make them know that, but only the horseman who understands their use?[13]

Quite true.

May we not say generally that there are three arts concerned with any object—the art of using it, the art of making it, and the art of represent-ing it?

Yes.

And that the excellence or beauty or rightness of any implement or living creature or action has reference to the use for which it is made or designed by nature?[14]

Yes.

It follows, then, that the user must know most about the performance of the thing he uses and must report on its good or bad points to the maker. The flute-player, for example, will tell the instrument-maker how well his flutes serve the player's purpose, and the other will submit to be instructed about how they should be made. So the man who uses any implement will speak of its merits and defects with knowledge, whereas the maker will take his word and possess no more than a correct belief, which he is obliged to obtain by listening to the man who knows.

Quite so.

But what of the artist? Has he either knowledge or correct belief? Does he know from direct experience of the subjects he portrays whether his rep-resentations are good and right or not? Has he even gained a correct belief by being obliged to listen to someone who does know and can tell him how they ought to be represented?

---

[13]In the *Parmenides* Plato's half-brother Antiphon, who had transferred his interest from phi-losophy to horses, is discovered instructing a smith about making a bit. Ancient craftsmen were far less specialized than ours. A blacksmith and a cobbler today might need instructions from a jockey.

[14]This recalls the association of a thing's peculiar excellence or "virtue" with its function, 352 D, p. 37 f [of Cornford, *Republic*].

No, he has neither.

If the artist, then, has neither knowledge nor even a correct belief about the soundness of his work, what becomes of the poet's wisdom in respect of the subjects of his poetry?

It will not amount to much.

And yet he will go on with his work, without knowing in what way any of his representations is sound or unsound. He must apparently, be reproducing only what pleases the taste or wins the approval of the ignorant multitude.[15]

Yes, what else can he do?

We seem, then, so far to be pretty well agreed that the artist knows nothing worth mentioning about the subjects he represents, and that art is a form of play, not to be taken seriously. This description, moreover, applies above all to tragic poetry, whether in epic or dramatic form.

Exactly.[16]

. . . the heaviest count in our indictment is still to come. Dramatic poetry has a most formidable power of corrupting even men of high character, with a few exceptions.

Formidable indeed, if it can do that.

Let me put the case for you to judge. When we listen to some hero in Homer or on the tragic stage moaning over his sorrows in a long tirade, or to a chorus beating their breasts as they chant a lament, you know how the best of us enjoy giving ourselves up to follow the performance with eager sympathy. The more a poet can move our feelings in this way, the better we think him. And yet when the sorrow is our own, we pride ourselves on being able to bear it quietly like a man, condemning the behaviour we admired in the theatre as womanish. Can it be right that the spectacle of a man behaving as one would scorn and blush to behave oneself should be admired and enjoyed, instead of filling us with disgust?

No, it really does not seem reasonable.

It does not, if you reflect that the poet ministers to the satisfaction of that very part of our nature whose instinctive hunger to have its fill of tears and lamentations is forcibly restrained in the case of our own misfortunes. Meanwhile the noblest part of us, insufficiently schooled by reason or habit, has relaxed its watch over these querulous feelings, with the excuse that the sufferings we are contemplating are not our own and it is no shame to us to admire and pity a man with some pretensions to a noble character, though his grief may be excessive. The enjoyment itself seems a clear gain, which

---

[15]Living in the world of appearances, the poet reproduces only "the many conventional notions of the mass of mankind about what is beautiful or honourable or just" (479 D, p. 188 [Cornford]).

[16]It should now be clear that this chapter is not concerned with aesthetic criticism, but with extravagant claims for the poets as moral teachers. It may leave the impression that Plato has been irritated by some contemporary controversy, and is overstating his case with a slightly malicious delight in paradox. At p. 341 [Cornford] he speaks of all this Part as a "defence" of his earlier exclusion of poetry.

we cannot bring ourselves to forfeit by disdaining the whole poem. Few, I believe, are capable of reflecting that to enter into another's feelings must have an effect on our own: the emotions of pity our sympathy has strengthened will not be easy to restrain when we are suffering ourselves.

That is very true.

Does not the same principle apply to humour as well as to pathos? You are doing the same thing if, in listening at a comic performance or in ordinary life to buffooneries which you would be ashamed to indulge in yourself, you thoroughly enjoy them instead of being disgusted with their ribaldry. There is in you an impulse to play the clown, which you have held in restraint from a reasonable fear of being set down as a buffoon; but now you have given it rein, and by encouraging its impudence at the theatre you may be unconsciously carried away into playing the comedian in your private life. Similar effects are produced by poetic representation of love and anger and all those desires and feelings of pleasure or pain which accompany our every action. It waters the growth of passions which should be allowed to wither away and sets them up in control, although the goodness and happiness of our lives depend on their being held in subjection.

I cannot but agree with you.

If so, Glaucon, when you meet with admirers of Homer who tell you that he has been the educator of Hellas and that on questions of human conduct and culture he deserves to be constantly studied as a guide by whom to regulate your whole life, it is well to give a friendly hearing to such people, as entirely well-meaning according to their lights, and you may acknowledge Homer to be the first and greatest of the tragic poets; but you must be quite sure that we can admit into our commonwealth only the poetry which celebrates the praises of the gods and of good men. If you go further and admit the honeyed muse in epic or in lyric verse, then pleasure and pain will usurp the sovereignty of law and of the principles always recognized by common consent as the best.

Quite true.

So now, since we have recurred to the subject of poetry, let this be our defence: it stands to reason that we could not but banish such an influence from our commonwealth. But, lest poetry should convict us of being harsh and unmannerly, let us tell her further that there is a long-standing quarrel between poetry and philosophy. There are countless tokens of this old antagonism, such as the lines which speak of "the cur which at his master yelps," or "one mighty in the vain talk of fools" or "the throng of all-too-sapient heads," or "subtle thinkers all in rags." None the less, be it declared that, if the dramatic poetry whose end is to give pleasure can show good reason why it should exist in a well-governed society, we for our part should welcome it back, being ourselves conscious of its charm; only it would be a sin to betray what we believe to be the truth. You too, my friend, must have felt this charm, above all when poetry speaks through Homer's lips.

I have indeed.

It is fair, then, that before returning from exile poetry should publish her defence in lyric verse or some other measure; and I suppose we should allow her champions who love poetry but are not poets to plead for her in prose, that she is no mere source of pleasure but a benefit to society and to human life. We shall listen favourably; for we shall clearly be the gainers, if that can be proved.

Undoubtedly.

But if it cannot, then we must take a lesson from the lover who renounces at any cost a passion which he finds is doing him no good. The love for poetry of this kind, bred in us by our own much admired institutions, will make us kindly disposed to believe in her genuine worth; but so long as she cannot make good her defence we shall, as we listen, rehearse to ourselves the reasons we have just given, as a counter-charm to save us from relapsing into a passion which most people have never outgrown. We shall reiterate that such poetry has no serious claim to be valued as an apprehension of truth. One who lends an ear to it should rather beware of endangering the order established in his soul, and would do well to accept the view of poetry which we have expressed.

I entirely agree.

Yes, Glaucon; for much is at stake, more than most people suppose: it is a choice between becoming a good man or a bad; and poetry, no more than wealth or power or honours, should tempt us to be careless of justice and virtue.

Your argument has convinced me, as I think it would anyone else.

Art and Craft

R. G. COLLINGWOOD

The Meaning of Craft

The first sense of the word "art" to be distinguished from art proper is the obsolete sense in which it means what in this book I shall call craft. This is what *ars* means in ancient Latin, and what τεχνη means in Greek: the power to produce a preconceived result by means of consciously controlled and directed action. In order to take the first step towards a sound aesthetic,

From *The Principles of Art* by R. C. Collingwood (1938). Reprinted by permission of Oxford University Press.

it is necessary to disentangle the notion of craft from that of art proper. In order to do this, again, we must first enumerate the chief characteristics of craft.

(1) Craft always involves a distinction between means and end, each clearly conceived as something distinct from the other but related to it. The term "means" is loosely applied to things that are used in order to reach the end, such as tools, machines, or fuel. Strictly, it applies not to the things but to the actions concerned with them: manipulating the tools, tending the machines, or burning the fuel. These actions (as implied by the literal sense of the word means) are passed through or traversed in order to reach the end, and are left behind when the end is reached. This may serve to distinguish the idea of means from two other ideas with which it is sometimes confused: that of part, and that of material. The relation of part to whole is like that of means to end, in that the part is indispensable to the whole, is what it is because of its relation to the whole, and may exist by itself before the whole comes into existence; but when the whole exists the part exists too, whereas, when the end exists, the means have ceased to exist. As for the idea of material, we shall return to that in (4) below.

(2) It involves a distinction between planning and execution. The result to be obtained is preconceived or thought out before being arrived at. The craftsman knows what he wants to make before he makes it. This foreknowledge is absolutely indispensable to craft: if something, for example stainless steel, is made without such foreknowledge, the making of it is not a case of craft but an accident. Moreover, this foreknowledge is not vague but precise. If a person sets out to make a table, but conceives the table only vaguely, as somewhere between two by four feet and three by six, and between two and three feet high, and so forth, he is no craftsman.

(3) Means and end are related in one way in the process of planning; in the opposite way in the process of execution. In planning the end is prior to the means. The end is thought out first, and afterwards the means are thought out. In execution the means come first, and the end is reached through them.

(4) There is a distinction between raw material and finished product or artifact. A craft is always exercised upon something, and aims at the transformation of this into something different. That upon which it works begins as raw material and ends as finished product. The raw material is found ready made before the special work of the craft begins.

(5) There is a distinction between form and matter. The matter is what is identical in the raw material and the finished product; the form is what is different, what the exercise of the craft changes. To describe the raw material as raw is not to imply that it is formless, but only that it has not yet the form which it is to acquire through "transformation" into finished product.

(6) There is a hierarchical relation between various crafts, one supplying

what another needs, one using what another provides. There are three kinds of hierarchy: of materials, of means, and of parts. (*a*) The raw material of one craft is the finished product of another. Thus the silviculturist propagates trees and looks after them as they grow, in order to provide raw material for the felling-men who transform them into logs; these are raw material for the saw-mill which transforms them into planks; and these, after a further process of selection and seasoning, become raw material for a joiner. (*b*) In the hierarchy of means, one craft supplies another with tools. Thus the timber-merchant supplies pit-props to the miner; the miner supplies coal to the blacksmith; the blacksmith supplies horseshoes to the farmer; and so on. (*c*) In the hierarchy of parts, a complex operation like the manufacture of a motor-car is parcelled out among a number of trades: one firm makes the engine, another the gears, another the chassis, another the tyres, another the electrical equipment, and so on; the final assembling is not strictly the manufacture of the car but only the bringing together of these parts. In one or more of these ways every craft has a hierarchical character; either as hierarchically related to other crafts, or as itself consisting of various heterogeneous operations hierarchically related among themselves.

Without claiming that these features together exhaust the notion of craft, or that each of them separately is peculiar to it, we may claim with tolerable confidence that where most of them are absent from a certain activity that activity is not a craft, and, if it is called by that name, is so called either by mistake or in a vague and inaccurate way.

The Technical Theory of Art

It was the Greek philosophers who worked out the idea of craft, and it is in their writings that the above distinctions have been expounded once for all. The philosophy of craft, in fact, was one of the greatest and most solid achievements of the Greek mind, or at any rate of that school, from Socrates to Aristotle, whose work happens to have been most completely preserved. . . .

. . . Plato and Aristotle . . . took it for granted that poetry, the only art which they discussed in detail, was a kind of craft, and spoke of this craft as ποιητικὴ τέχνη, poet-craft. What kind of craft was this?

There are some crafts, like cobbling, carpentering, or weaving, whose end is to produce a certain type of artifact; others, like agriculture or stock-breeding or horse-breaking, whose end is to produce or improve certain non-human types of organism; others again, like medicine or education or warfare, whose end is to bring certain human beings into certain states of body or mind. But we need not ask which of these is the genus of which poet-craft is a species, because they are not mutually exclusive. The cobbler or carpenter or weaver is not simply trying to produce shoes or carts or cloth. He produces these because there is a demand for them; that is, they are not ends to him, but means to the end of satisfying a specific demand. What he is really aiming at is the production of a certain state of mind in his customers, the state of having these demands satisfied. The same analysis applies to the second group. Thus in the end these three kinds of craft reduce to one. They are all ways of bringing human beings into certain desired conditions.

The same description is true of poet-craft. The poet is a kind of skilled producer; he produces for consumers; and the effect of his skill is to bring about in them certain states of mind, which are conceived in advance as desirable states. The poet, like any other kind of craftsman, must know what effect he is aiming at, and must learn by experience and precept, which is only the imparted experience of others, how to produce it. This is poet-craft, as conceived by Plato and Aristotle and, following them, such writers as Horace in his *Ars Poetica*. There will be analogous crafts of painting, sculpture, and so forth; music, at least for Plato, is not a separate art but is a constituent part of poetry. . . .

The technical theory of art is . . . by no means a matter of merely antiquarian interest. It is actually the way in which most people nowadays think of art; and especially economists and psychologists, the people to whom we look (sometimes in vain) for special guidance in the problems of modern life. . . .

Break-down of the Theory

(1) The first characteristic of craft is the distinction between means and end. Is this present in works of art? According to the technical theory, yes. A poem is means to the production of a certain state of mind in the audience, as a horseshoe is means to the production of a certain state of mind in the man whose horse is shod. And the poem in its turn will be an end to which other things are means. In the case of the horseshoe, this stage of the analysis is easy: we can enumerate lighting the forge, cutting a piece of iron off a bar, heating it, and so on. What is there analogous to these processes in the case of a poem? The poet may get paper and pen, fill the pen, sit down and square his elbows; but these actions are preparatory not to composition (which may go on in the poet's head) but to writing. Suppose the poem is a short one, and composed without the use of any writing materials; what are the means by which the poet composes it? I can think of no answer, unless comic answers are wanted, such as "using a rhyming dictionary," "pounding his foot on the floor or wagging his head or hand to mark the metre," or "getting drunk." If one looks at the matter seriously, one sees that the only factors in the situation are the poet, the poetic labor of his mind, and the poem. And if

any supporter of the technical theory says "Right: then the poetic labor is the means, the poem the end," we shall ask him to find a blacksmith who can make a horseshoe by sheer labor, without forge, anvil, hammer, or tongs. It is because nothing corresponding to these exists in the case of the poem that the poem is not an end to which there are means.

Conversely, is a poem means to the production of a certain state of mind in an audience? Suppose a poet had read his verses to an audience, hoping that they would produce a certain result; and suppose the result were different; would that in itself prove the poem a bad one? It is a difficult question; some would say yes, others no. But if poetry were obviously a craft, the answer would be a prompt and unhesitating yes. The advocate of the technical theory must do a good deal of toe-chopping before he can get his facts to fit his theory at this point.

So far, the prospects of the technical theory are not too bright. Let us proceed.

(2) The distinction between planning and executing certainly exists in some works of art, namely those which are also works of craft or artifacts; for there is, of course, an overlap between these two things, as may be seen by the example of a building or a jar, which is made to order for the satisfaction of a specific demand, to serve a useful purpose, but may none the less be a work of art. But suppose a poet were making up verses as he walked; suddenly finding a line in his head, and then another, and then dissatisfied with them and altering them until he had got them to his liking: what is the plan which he is executing? He may have had a vague idea that if he went for a walk he would be able to compose poetry; but what were, so to speak, the measurements and specifications of the poem he planned to compose? He may, no doubt, have been hoping to compose a sonnet on a particular subject specified by the editor of a review; but the point is that he may not, and that he is none the less a poet for composing without having any definite plan in his head. Or suppose a sculptor were not making a Madonna and child, three feet high, in Hoptonwood stone, guaranteed to placate the chancellor of the diocese and obtain a faculty for placing it in the vacant niche over a certain church door; but were simply playing about with clay, and found the clay under his fingers turning into a little dancing man: is this not a work of art because it was done without being planned in advance?

All this is very familiar. There would be no need to insist upon it, but that the technical theory of art relies on our forgetting it. While we are thinking of it, let us note the importance of not over-emphasizing it. Art as such does not imply the distinction between planning and execution. But (*a*) this is a merely negative characteristic, not a positive one. We must not erect the absence of plan into a positive force and call it inspiration, or the unconscious, or the like. (*b*) It is a permissible characteristic of art, not a compulsory one. If unplanned works of art are possible, it does not follow that no planned work is a work of art. That is the logical fallacy[1] that underlies one, or some, of the various things called romanticism. It may very well be true that the only works of art which can be made altogether without a plan are trifling ones, and that the greatest and most serious ones always contain an element of planning and therefore an element of craft. But that would not justify the technical theory of art.

(3) If neither means and end nor planning and execution can be distinguished in art proper, there obviously can be no reversal of order as between means and end, in planning and execution respectively.

(4) We next come to the distinction between raw material and finished product. Does this exist in art proper? If so, a poem is made out of certain raw material. What is the raw material out of which Ben Jonson made *Queene and Huntresse, chaste, and faire?* Words, perhaps. Well, what words? A smith makes a horseshoe not out of all the iron there is, but out of a certain piece of iron, cut off a certain bar that he keeps in the corner of the smithy. If Ben Jonson did anything at all like that, he said: "I want to make a nice little hymn to open Act v, Scene vi of *Cynthia's Revels*. Here is the English language, or as much of it as I know; I will use *thy* five times, *to* four times, *and, bright, excellently*, and *goddesse* three times each, and so on." He did nothing like this. The words which occur in the poem were never before his mind as a whole in an order different from that of the poem, out of which he shuffled them till the poem, as we have it, appeared. I do not deny that by sorting out the words, or the vowel sounds, or the consonant sounds, in a poem like this, we can make interesting and (I believe) important discoveries about the way in which Ben Jonson's mind worked when he made the poem; and I am willing to allow that the technical theory of art is doing good service if it leads people to explore these matters; but if it can only express what it is trying to do by calling these words or sounds the materials out of which the poem is made, it is talking nonsense.

But perhaps there is a raw material of another kind: a feeling or emotion, for example, which is present to the poet's mind at the commencement of his labour, and which that labour converts into the poem. "Aus meinem grossen Schmerzen mach' ich die kleinen Lieder," said Heine; and he was doubtless right; the poet's labour can be justly described as converting emotions into poems. But this conversion is a very different kind of thing from the conversion of iron into horseshoes. If the two kinds of conversion were the same, a blacksmith could make horseshoes out of his desire to pay the

---

[1]It is an example of what I have elsewhere called the fallacy of precarious margins. Because art and craft overlap, the essence of art is sought not in the positive characteristics of all art, but in the characteristics of those works of art which are not works of craft. Thus the only things which are allowed to be works of art are those marginal examples which lie outside the overlap of art and craft. This is a precarious margin because further study may at any moment reveal the characteristics of craft in some of these examples. See *Essay on Philosophical Method*.

rent. The something more, over and above that desire, which he must have in order to make horseshoes out of it, is the iron which is their raw material. In the poet's case that something more does not exist.

(5) In every work of art there is something which, in some sense of the word, may be called form. There is, to be rather more precise, something in the nature of rhythm, pattern, organization, design, or structure. But it does not follow that there is a distinction between form and matter. Where that distinction does exist, namely, in artifacts, the matter was there in the shape of raw material before the form was imposed upon it, and the form was there in the shape of a preconceived plan before being imposed upon the matter; and as the two coexist in the finished product we can see how the matter might have accepted a different form, or the form have been imposed upon a different matter. None of these statements applies to a work of art. Something was no doubt there before a poem came into being; there was, for example, a confused excitement in the poet's mind; but, as we have seen, this was not the raw material of the poem. There was also, no doubt, the impulse to write; but this impulse was not the form of the unwritten poem. And when the poem is written, there is nothing in it of which we can say, "this is a matter which might have taken on a different form," or "this is a form which might have been realized in a different matter."

When people have spoken of matter and form in connexion with art, or of that strange hybrid distinction, form and content, they have in fact been doing one of two things, or both confusedly at once. Either they have been assimilating a work of art to an artifact, and the artist's work to the craftsman's; or else they have been using these terms in a vaguely metaphorical way as means of referring to distinctions which really do exist in art, but are of a different kind. There is always in art a distinction between what is expressed and that which expresses it; there is a distinction between the initial impulse to write or paint or compose and the finished poem or picture or music; there is a distinction between an emotional element in the artist's experience and what may be called an intellectual element. All these deserve investigation; but none of them is a case of the distinction between form and matter.

(6) Finally, there is in art nothing which resembles the hierarchy of crafts, each dictating ends to the one below it, and providing either means or raw materials or parts to the one above. When a poet writes verses for a musician to set, these verses are not means to the musician's end, for they are incorporated in the song which is the musician's finished product, and it is characteristic of means, as we saw, to be left behind. But neither are they raw materials. The musician does not transform them into music; he sets them to music; and if the music which he writes for them had a raw material (which it has not), that raw material could not consist of verses. What happens is rather that the poet and musician collaborate to produce a work of art which

owes something to each of them; and this is true even if in the poet's case there was no intention of collaborating. . . .

Technique

As soon as we take the notion of craft seriously, it is perfectly obvious that art proper cannot be any kind of craft. Most people who write about art today seem to think that it is some kind of craft; and this is the main error against which a modern aesthetic theory must fight. Even those who do not openly embrace the error itself, embrace doctrines implying it. One such doctrine is that of artistic technique.

The doctrine may be stated as follows. The artist must have a certain specialized form of skill, which is called technique. He acquires his skill just as a craftsman does, partly through personal experience and partly through sharing in the experience of others who thus become his teachers. The technical skill which he thus acquires does not by itself make him an artist; for a technician is made, but an artist is born. Great artistic powers may produce fine works of art even though technique is defective; and even the most finished technique will not produce the finest sort of work in their absence; but all the same, no work of art whatever can be produced without some degree of technical skill, and, other things being equal, the better the technique the better will be the work of art. The greatest artistic powers, for their due and proper display, demand a technique as good in its kind as they are in their own. . . .

The theory of poetic technique implies that in the first place a poet has certain experiences which demand expression; then he conceives the possibility of a poem in which they might be expressed; then this poem, as an unachieved end, demands for its realization the exercise of certain powers or forms of skill, and these constitute the poet's technique. There is an element of truth in this. It is true that the making of a poem begins in the poet's having an experience which demands expression in the form of a poem. But the description of the unwritten poem as an end to which his technique is means is false; it implies that before he has written his poem he knows, and could state, the specification of it in the kind of way in which a joiner knows the specification of a table he is about to make. This is always true of a craftsman; it is therefore true of an artist in those cases where the work of art is also a work of craft. But it is wholly untrue of the artist in those cases where the work of art is not a work of craft; the poet extemporizing his verses, the sculptor playing with his clay, and so forth. In these cases (which after all are cases of art, even though possibly of art at a relatively humble level) the artist has no idea what the experience is which demands expression until he has expressed it. What he wants to say is not present to him as an end towards which means have to be devised; it becomes clear to him only as the poem takes shape in his mind, or the clay in his fingers. . . .

Art as a Psychological Stimulus

. . . [According to this theory of art,] the entire work of art is conceived as an artifact, designed (when a sufficient degree of skill is present to justify the word) as means to the realization of an end beyond it, namely, a state of mind in the artist's audience. In order to affect his audience in a certain way, the artist addresses them in a certain manner, by placing before them a certain work of art. In so far as he is a competent artist, one condition at least is fulfilled: the work of art does affect them as he intends it should. There is a second condition which may be fulfilled: the state of mind thus aroused in them may be in one way or another a valuable state of mind; one that enriches their lives, and thus gives him a claim not only on their admiration but also on their gratitude.

The first thing to notice about this stimulus-and-reaction theory of art is that it is not new. It is the theory of the tenth book of Plato's *Republic*, of Aristotle's *Poetics*, and of Horace's *Ars Poetica*. . . .

There are numerous cases in which somebody claiming the title of artist deliberately sets himself to arouse certain states of mind in his audience. The funny man who lays himself out to get a laugh has at his command a number of well-tried methods for getting it; the purveyor of sob-stuff is in a similar case; the political or religious orator has a definite end before him and adopts definite means for achieving it, and so on. We might even attempt a rough classification of these ends. First, the "artist's" purpose may be to arouse a certain kind of emotion. The emotion may be of almost any kind; a more important distinction emerges according as it is aroused simply for its own sake, as an enjoyable experience, or for the sake of its value in the affairs of practical life. The funny man and the sob-stuff monger fall on one side in this division, the political and religious orator on the other. Secondly, the purpose may be to stimulate certain intellectual activities. These again may be of very various kinds, but they may be stimulated with either of two motives: either because the objects upon which they are directed are thought of as worth understanding, or because the activities themselves are thought of as worth pursuing, even though they lead to nothing in the way of knowledge that is of importance. Thirdly, the purpose may be to stimulate a certain kind of action; here again with two kinds of motive: either because the action is conceived as expedient, or because it is conceived as right.

Here are six kinds of art falsely so called; called by that name because they are kinds of craft in which the practitioner can by the use of his skill evoke a desired psychological reaction in his audience, and hence they come under the obsolete, but not yet dead and buried, conception of poet-craft, painter-craft, and so forth; falsely so called, because the distinction of means and end, upon which every one of them rests, does not belong to art proper.

Let us give the six their right names. Where an emotion is aroused for its own sake, as an enjoyable experience, the craft of arousing it is amusement; where for the sake of its practical value, magic. . . . Where intellectual faculties are stimulated for the mere sake of their exercise, the work designed to stimulate them is a puzzle; where for the sake of knowing this or that thing, it is instruction. Where a certain practical activity is stimulated as expedient, that which stimulates it is advertisement or (in the current modern sense, not the old sense) propaganda; where it is stimulated as right, exhortation.

These six between them, singly or in combination, pretty well exhaust the function of whatever in the modern world wrongfully usurps the name of art. None of them has anything to do with art proper. This is not because (as Oscar Wilde said, with his curious talent for just missing a truth and then giving himself a prize for hitting it) "all art is quite useless," for it is not; a work of art may very well amuse, instruct, puzzle, exhort, and so forth, without ceasing to be art, and in these ways it may be very useful indeed. It is because, as Oscar Wilde perhaps meant to say, what makes it art is not the same as what makes it useful. Deciding what psychological reaction a so-called work of art produces (for example, asking yourself how a certain poem "makes you feel") has nothing whatever to do with deciding whether it is a real work of art or not. Equally irrelevant is the question what psychological reaction it is meant to produce. . . .

. . . These various kinds of pseudo-art are in reality various kinds of use to which art may be put. In order that any of these purposes may be realized, there must first be art, and then a subordination of art to some utilitarian end. Unless a man can write, he cannot write propaganda. Unless he can draw, he cannot become a comic draughtsman or an advertisement artist. These activities have in every case developed through a process having two phases. First, there is writing or drawing or whatever it may be, pursued as an art for its own sake, going its own way and developing its own proper nature, caring for none of these things. Then this independent and self-sufficient art is broken, as it were, to the plough, forced aside from its own original nature and enslaved to the service of an end not its own. Here lies the peculiar tragedy of the artist's position in the modern world. He is heir to a tradition from which he has learnt what art should be; or at least, what it cannot be. He has heard its call and devoted himself to its service. And then, when the time comes for him to demand of society that it should support him in return for his devotion to a purpose which, after all, is not his private purpose but one among the purposes of modern civilization, he finds that his living is guaranteed only on condition that he renounces his calling and uses the art which he has acquired in a way which negates its fundamental nature, by turning journalist or advertisement artist or the like; a degradation far more frightful than the prostitution or enslavement of the mere body.

Even in this denatured condition the arts are never mere means to the ends imposed upon them. For means rightly so called are devised in relation to the end aimed at; but here, there must first be literature, drawing, and so forth, before they can be turned to the purposes described. Hence it is a fundamental and fatal error to conceive art itself as a means to any of these ends, even when it is broken to their service.

Mimesis and Catharsis

ARISTOTLE

Our subject being Poetry, I propose to speak not only of the art in general but also of its species and their respective capacities; of the structure of plot required for a good poem; of the number and nature of the constituent parts of a poem; and likewise of any other matters in the same line of inquiry. Let us follow the natural order and begin with the primary facts.

Epic poetry and Tragedy, as also Comedy, Dithyrambic poetry, and most flute-playing and lyre-playing, are all, viewed as a whole, modes of imitation. But at the same time they differ from one another in three ways, either by a difference of kind in their means, or by differences in the objects, or in the manner of their imitations.

Just as colour and form are used as means by some, who (whether by art or constant practice) imitate and portray many things by their aid, and the voice is used by others; so also in the above-mentioned group of arts, the means with them as a whole are rhythm, language, and harmony—used, however, either singly or in certain combinations. A combination of harmony and rhythm alone is the means in flute-playing and lyre-playing, and any other arts there may be of the same description, e.g. imitative piping. Rhythm alone, without harmony, is the means in the dancer's imitations; for even he, by the rhythms of his attitudes, may represent men's characters, as well as what they do and suffer. There is further an art which imitates by language alone, without harmony, in prose or in verse, and if in verse, either in some one or in a plurality of metres. This form of imitation is to this day without a name. . . .

The objects the imitator represents are actions, with agents who are necessarily either good men or bad—the diversities of human character being nearly always derivative from this primary distinction, since the line between

From *The Oxford Translation of Aristotle* ed. by W.D. Ross, vol. II (1925). Reprinted by permission of Oxford University Press.

virtue and vice is one dividing the whole of mankind. It follows, therefore, that the agents represented must be either above our own level of goodness, or beneath it, or just such as we are. . . .

. . . This difference it is that distinguishes Tragedy and Comedy also; the one would make its personages worse, and the other better, than the men of the present day.

A third difference in these arts is in the manner in which each kind of object is represented. Given both the same means and the same kind of object for imitation, one may either (1) speak at one moment in narrative and at another in an assumed character, as Homer does; or (2) one may remain the same throughout, without any such change; or (3) the imitators may represent the whole story dramatically, as though they were actually doing the things described.

As we said at the beginning, therefore, the differences in the imitation of these arts come under three heads, their means, their objects, and their manner. . . .

It is clear that the general origin of poetry was due to two causes, each of them part of human nature. Imitation is natural to man from childhood, one of his advantages over the lower animals being this, that he is the most imitative creature in the world, and learns at first by imitation. And it is also natural for all to delight in works of imitation. The truth of this second point is shown by experience: though the objects themselves may be painful to see, we delight to view the most realistic representations of them in art, the forms for example of the lowest animals and of dead bodies. The explanation is to be found in a further fact: to be learning something is the greatest of pleasures not only to the philosopher but also to the rest of mankind, however small their capacity for it; the reason of the delight in seeing the picture is that one is at the same time learning—gathering the meaning of things, e.g. that the man there is so-and-so; for if one has not seen the thing before, one's pleasure will not be in the picture as an imitation of it, but will be due to the execution or colouring or some similar cause. Imitation, then, being natural to us—as also the sense of harmony and rhythm, the metres being obviously species of rhythms—it was through their original aptitude, and by a series of improvements for the most part gradual on their first efforts, that they created poetry out of their improvisations.

Poetry, however, soon broke up into two kinds according to the differences of character in the individual poets; for the graver among them would represent noble actions, and those of noble personages; and the meaner sort the actions of the ignoble. . . .

. . . Epic poetry, then, has been seen to agree with Tragedy to this extent, that of being an imitation of serious subjects in a grand kind of verse. It differs from it, however, (1) in that it is in one kind of verse and in narrative form; and (2) in its length—which is due to its action having no fixed limit of time, whereas Tragedy endeavours to keep as far as possible within a single circuit of the sun, or something near that. This, I say, is another point of difference between them, though at first the practice in this respect was just the same in tragedies as in epic poems. They differ also (3) in their constituents, some being common to both and others peculiar to Tragedy—hence a judge of good and bad in Tragedy is a judge of that in epic poetry also. All the parts of an epic are included in Tragedy; but those of Tragedy are not all of them to be found in the Epic.

Reserving hexameter poetry and Comedy for consideration hereafter, let us proceed now to the discussion of Tragedy; before doing so, however, we must gather up the definition resulting from what has been said. A tragedy then, is the imitation of an action that is serious and also, as having magnitude, complete in itself; in language with pleasurable accessories, each kind brought in separately in the parts of the work; in a dramatic, not in a narrative form; with incidents arousing pity and fear, wherewith to accomplish its catharsis of such emotions. Here by "language with pleasurable accessories" I mean that with rhythm and harmony or song superadded; and by "the kinds separately" I mean that some portions are worked out with verse only, and others in turn with song.

As they act the stories, it follows that in the first place the Spectacle (or stage-appearance of the actors) must be some part of the whole; and in the second Melody and Diction, these two being the means of their imitation. Here by "Diction" I mean merely this, the composition of the verses; and by "Melody," what is too completely understood to require explanation. But further: the subject represented also is an action; and the action involves agents, who must necessarily have their distinctive qualities both of character and thought, since it is from these that we ascribe certain qualities to their actions. There are in the natural order of things, therefore, two causes, Thought and Character, of their actions, and consequently of their success or failure in their lives. Now the action (that which was done) is represented in the play by the Fable or Plot. The Fable, in our present sense of the term, is simply this, the combination of the incidents, or things done in the story; whereas Character is what makes us ascribe certain moral qualities to the agents; and Thought is shown in all they say when proving a particular point or, it may be, enunciating a general truth. There are six parts consequently of every tragedy, as a whole (that is) of such or such quality, viz. a Fable or Plot, Characters, Diction, Thought, Spectacle, and Melody; two of them arising from the means, one from the manner, and three from the objects of the dramatic imitation; and there is nothing else besides these six. Of these, its formative elements, then, not a few of the dramatists have made due use, as every play, one may say, admits of Spectacle, Character, Fable, Diction, Melody and Thought.

The most important part of the six is the combination of the incidents of the story. Tragedy is essentially an imitation not of persons but of action and life, of happiness and misery. All human happiness or misery takes the form of action; the end for which we live is a certain kind of activity, not a quality. Character gives us qualities, but it is in our actions—what we do—that we are happy or the reverse. In a play accordingly they do not act in order to portray the Characters; they include the Characters for the sake of the action. So that it is the action in it, i.e. its Fable or Plot, that is the end and purpose of the tragedy; and the end is everywhere the chief thing. Besides this, a tragedy is impossible without action, but there may be one without Character. The tragedies of most of the moderns are characterless—a defect common among poets of all kinds, and with its counterpart in painting in Zeuxis as compared with Polygnotus; for whereas the latter is strong in character, the work of Zeuxis is devoid of it. And again: one may string together a series of characteristic speeches of the utmost finish as regards Diction and Thought, and yet fail to produce the true tragic effect; but one will have much better success with a tragedy which, however inferior in these respects, has a Plot, a combination of incidents, in it. And again: the most powerful elements of attraction in Tragedy, the Peripeties and Discoveries, are parts of the Plot. A further proof is in the fact that beginners succeed earlier with the Diction and Characters than with the construction of a story; and the same may be said of nearly all the early dramatists. We maintain, therefore, that the first essential, the life and soul, so to speak, of Tragedy is the Plot; and that the Characters come second—compare the parallel in painting, where the most beautiful colours laid on without order will not give one the same pleasure as a simple black-and-white sketch of a portrait. We maintain that Tragedy is primarily an imitation of action, and that it is mainly for the sake of the action that it imitates the personal agents. Third comes the element of Thought, i.e. the power of saying whatever can be said, or what is appropriate to the occasion. This is what, in the speeches in Tragedy, falls under the arts of Politics and Rhetoric; for the older poets make their personages discourse like statesmen, and the modern like rhetoricians. One must not confuse it with Character. Character in a play is that which reveals the moral purpose of the agents, i.e. the sort of thing they seek or avoid, where that is not obvious—hence there is no room for Character in a speech on a purely indifferent subject. Thought, on the other hand, is shown in all they say when proving or disproving some particular point, or enunciating some universal proposition. Fourth among the literary elements is the Diction of the personages, i.e., as before explained, the expression of their thoughts in words, which is practically the same thing with verse as with prose. As for the two remaining parts, the Melody is the greatest of the pleasurable accessories of Tragedy. The Spectacle, though an attraction, is the least artistic of all the parts, and has least to do with the art of poetry. The tragic effect is quite possible without a public performance and actors; and besides, the getting-up of the Spectacle is more a matter for the costumier than the poet.

Having thus distinguished the parts, let us now consider the proper construction of the Fable or Plot, as that is at once the first and the most important thing in Tragedy. We have laid it down that a tragedy is an imitation of an action that is complete in itself, as a whole of some magnitude; for a whole may be of no magnitude to speak of. Now a whole is that which has beginning, middle, and end. A beginning is that which is not itself necessarily after anything else, and which has naturally something else after it; an end is that which is naturally after something itself, either as its necessary or usual consequent, and with nothing else after it; and a middle, that which is by nature after one thing and has also another after it. A well-constructed Plot, therefore, cannot either begin or end at any point one likes; beginning and end in it must be of the forms just described. . . .

The Unity of a Plot does not consist, as some suppose, in its having one man as its subject. An infinity of things befall that one man, some of which it is impossible to reduce to unity; and in like manner there are many actions of one man which cannot be made to form one action. One sees, therefore, the mistake of all the poets who have written a *Heracleid,* a *Theseid,* or similar poems; they suppose that, because Heracles was one man, the story also of Heracles must be one story. Homer, however, evidently understood this point quite well, whether by art or instinct, just in the same way as he excels the rest in every other respect. In writing an *Odyssey*, he did not make the poem cover all that ever befell his hero—it befell him, for instance, to get wounded on Parnassus and also to feign madness at the time of the call to arms, but the two incidents had no necessary or probable connection with one another—instead of doing that, he took as the subject of the *Odyssey*, as also of the *Iliad*, an action with a Unity of the kind we are describing. The truth is that, just as in the other imitative arts one imitation is always of one thing, so in poetry the story, as an imitation of action, must represent one action, a complete whole, with its several incidents so closely connected that the transposal or withdrawal of any one of them will disjoin and dislocate the whole. For that which makes no perceptible difference by its presence or absence is no real part of the whole.

From what we have said it will be seen that the poet's function is to describe, not the thing that has happened, but a kind of thing that might happen, i.e. what is possible as being probable or necessary. The distinction between historian and poet is not in the one writing prose and the other verse—you might put the work of Herodotus into verse, and it would still be a species of history; it consists really in this, that the one describes the thing that has been, and the other a kind of thing that might be. Hence poetry is something more philosophic and of graver import than history, since its statements are of the nature rather of universals, whereas those of history are singulars. By a universal statement I mean one as to what such or such a kind of man will probably or necessarily say or do—which is the aim of poetry, though it affixes proper names to the characters; by a singular statement, one as to what, say, Alcibiades did or had done to him. In Comedy this has become clear by this time; it is only when their plot is already made up of probable incidents that they give it a basis of proper names, choosing for the purpose any names that may occur to them, instead of writing like the old iambic poets about particular persons. In Tragedy, however, they still adhere to the historic names; and for this reason: what convinces is the possible; now whereas we are not yet sure as to the possibility of that which has not happened, that which has happened is manifestly possible, else it would not have come to pass. . . .

It is evident from the above that the poet must be more the poet of his stories or Plots than of his verses, inasmuch as he is a poet by virtue of the imitative element in his work, and it is actions that he imitates. And if he should come to take a subject from actual history, he is none the less a poet for that; since some historic occurrences may very well be in the probable and possible order of things; and it is in that aspect of them that he is their poet.

Of simple Plots and actions the episodic are the worst. I call a Plot episodic when there is neither probability nor necessity in the sequence of its episodes. Actions of this sort bad poets construct through their own fault, and good ones on account of the players. His work being for public performance, a good poet often stretches out a Plot beyond its capabilities, and is thus obliged to twist the sequence of incident.

Tragedy, however, is an imitation not only of a complete action, but also of incidents arousing pity and fear. Such incidents have the very greatest effect on the mind when they occur unexpectedly and at the same time in consequence of one another; there is more of the marvellous in them then than if they happened of themselves or by mere chance. Even matters of chance seem most marvellous if there is an appearance of design as it were in them; as for instance the statue of Mitys at Argos killed the author of Mitys' death by falling down on him when a looker-on at a public spectacle; for incidents like that we think to be not without a meaning. A Plot therefore, of this sort is necessarily finer than others. . . .

The parts of Tragedy to be treated as formative elements in the whole were mentioned in a previous Chapter. From the point of view, however, of its quantity, i.e. the separate sections into which it is divided, a tragedy has the following parts: Prologue, Episode, Exode, and a choral portion, distinguished into Parode and Stasimon; these two are common to all tragedies, whereas songs from the stage and *Commoe* are only found in some. The Prologue is all that precedes the Parode of the chorus; an Episode all that comes in between two whole choral songs; the Exode all that follows after the last choral song. In the choral portion the Parode is the whole first statement of the chorus; a Stasimon, a song of the chorus without anapaests or trochees; a *Commos*, a lamentation sung by chorus and actor in concert. The parts of Tragedy to be used as formative elements in the whole we have already mentioned; the above are its parts from the point of view of its quantity, or the separate sections into which it is divided.

The next points after what we have said above will be these: (1) What is the poet to aim at, and what is he to avoid, in constructing his Plots? and (2) What are the conditions on which the tragic effect depends?

We assume that, for the finest form of Tragedy, the Plot must be not simple but complex; and further, that it must imitate actions arousing fear and pity, since that is the distinctive function of this kind of imitation. It follows, therefore, that there are three forms of Plot to be avoided. (1) A good man must not be seen passing from happiness to misery, or (2) a bad man from misery to happiness. The first situation is not fear-inspiring or piteous, but simply odious to us. The second is the most untragic that can be; it has no one of the requisites of Tragedy; it does not appeal either to the human feeling in us, or to our pity, or to our fears. Nor, on the other hand, should (3) an extremely bad man be seen falling from happiness into misery. Such a story may arouse the human feeling in us, but it will not move us to either pity or fear; pity is occasioned by undeserved misfortune, and fear by that of one like ourselves; so that there will be nothing either piteous or fear-inspiring in the situation. There remains, then, the intermediate kind of personage, a man not pre-eminently virtuous and just, whose misfortune, however, is brought upon him not by vice and depravity but by some error of judgement, of the number of those in the enjoyment of great reputation and prosperity; e.g. Oedipus, Thyestes, and the men of note of similar families. The perfect Plot, accordingly, must have a single, and not (as some tell us) a double issue; the change in the hero's fortunes must be not from misery to happiness, but on the contrary from happiness to misery; and the cause of it must lie not in any depravity, but in some great error on his part; the man himself being either such as we have described, or better, not worse, than that. Fact also confirms our theory. Though the poets began by accepting any tragic story that came to hand, in these days the finest tragedies are always on the story of some few houses, on that of Alcmeon, Oedipus, Orestes, Meleager, Thyestes, Telephus, or any others that may have been involved, as either agents or sufferers, in some deed of horror. The theoretically best tragedy, then, has a Plot of this description. The critics, therefore, are wrong who blame Euripides for taking this line in his tragedies, and giving many of them an unhappy ending. It is, as we have said, the right line to take. The best proof is this: on the stage, and in the public performances, such plays, properly worked out, are seen to be the most truly tragic; and Euripides, even if his execution be faulty in every other point, is seen to be nevertheless the most tragic certainly of the dramatists. After this comes the construction of Plot with some rank first, one with a double story (like the *Odyssey*) and an opposite issue for the good and the bad personages. It is ranked as first only through the weakness of the audiences; the poets merely follow their public, writing as its wishes dictate. But the pleasure here is not that of Tragedy. It belongs rather to Comedy, where the bitterest enemies in the piece (e.g. Orestes and Aegisthus) walk off good friends at the end, with no slaying of any one by any one.

The tragic fear and pity may be aroused by the Spectacle; but they may also be aroused by the very structure and incidents of the play—which is the better way and shows the better poet. The Plot in fact should be so framed that, even without seeing the things take place, he who simply hears the account of them shall be filled with horror and pity at the incidents; which is just the effect that the mere recital of the story in *Oedipus* would have on one. To produce this same effect by means of the Spectacle is less artistic, and requires extraneous aid. Those, however, who make use of the Spectacle to put before us that which is merely monstrous and not productive of fear, are wholly out of touch with Tragedy; not every kind of pleasure should be required of a tragedy, but only its own proper pleasure.

The tragic pleasure is that of pity and fear, and the poet has to produce it by a work of imitation; it is clear, therefore, that the causes should be included in the incidents of his story. Let us see, then, what kinds of incident strike one as horrible, or rather as piteous. In a deed of this description the parties most necessarily be either friends, or enemies, or indifferent to one another. Now when enemy does it on enemy, there is nothing to move us to pity either in his doing or in his meditating the deed, except so far as the actual pain of the sufferer is concerned; and the same is true when the parties are indifferent to one another. Whenever the tragic deed, however, is done within the family—when murder or the like is done or mediated by brother on brother, by son on father, by mother on son, or son on mother—these are the situations the poet should seek after. The traditional stories, accordingly, must be kept as they are, e.g. the murder of Clytaemnestra by Orestes and of Eriphyle by Alcmeon. At the same time even with these there is something left to the poet himself; it is for him to devise the right way of treating them. Let us explain more clearly what we mean by "the right way." The deed of horror may be done by the doer knowingly and consciously, as in the old poets, and in Medea's murder of her children in Euripides. Or he may do it, but in ignorance of his relationship, and discover that afterwards, as does the Oedipus in Sophocles. Here the deed is outside the play; but it may be within it, like the act of the Alcmeon in Astydamas, or that of the Telegonus in *Ulysses Wounded*. A third possibility is for one meditating some deadly injury to another, in ignorance of his relationship, to make the discovery in time to draw back. These exhaust the possibilities, since the deed must necessarily be either done or not done, and either knowingly or unknowingly.

The worst situation is when the personage is with full knowledge on the point of doing the deed, and leaves it undone. It is odious and also (through the absence of suffering) untragic; hence it is that no one is made to act thus except in some few instances, e.g. Haemon and Creon in *Antigone*. Next after this comes the actual perpetration of the deed mediated. A better situation than that, however, is for the deed to be done in ignorance, and the relationship discovered afterwards, since there is nothing odious in it, and the Discovery will serve to astound us. But the best of all is the last; what we have in *Cresphontes*, for example, where Merope, on the point of slaying her son, recognizes him in time; in *Iphigenia*, where sister and brother are in a like position; and in *Helle*, where the son recognizes his mother, when on the point of giving her up to her enemy.

This will explain why our tragedies are restricted (as we said just now) to such a small number of families. It was accident rather than art that led the poets in quest of subjects to embody this kind of incident in their Plots. They are still obliged, accordingly, to have recourse to the families in which such horrors have occurred.

On the construction of the Plot, and the kind of Plot required for Tragedy, enough has now been said. . . .

The question may be raised whether the epic or the tragic is the higher form of imitation. It may be argued that, if the less vulgar is the higher, and the less vulgar is always that which addresses the better public, an art addressing any and every one is of a very vulgar order. It is a belief that their public cannot see the meaning, unless they add something themselves, that causes the perpetual movements of the performers—bad fluteplayers, for instance, rolling about, if quoit-throwing is to be represented, and pulling at the conductor, if Scylla is the subject of the piece: Tragedy, then, is said to be an art of this order—to be in fact just what the later actors were in the eyes of their predecessors; foy Mynniscus used to call Callippides "the ape," because he thought he so overacted his parts; and a similar view was taken of Pindarus also. All Tragedy, however, is said to stand to the Epic as the newer to the older school of actors. The one, accordingly, is said to address a cultivated audience, which does not need the accompaniment of gesture; the other, an uncultivated one. If, therefore, Tragedy is a vulgar art, it must clearly be lower than the Epic.

The answer to this is twofold. In the first place, one may urge (1) that the censure does not touch the art of the dramatic poet, but only that of his interpreter; for it is quite possible to overdo the gesturing even in an epic recital, as did Sosistratus, and in a singing contest, as did Mnasitheus of Opus. (2) That one should not condemn all movement, unless one means to condemn even the dance, but only that of ignoble people—which is the point of the criticism passed on Callippides and in the present day on others, that their women are not like gentlewomen. (3) That Tragedy may produce its effect even without movement or action in just the same way as Epic poetry; for from the mere reading of a play its quality may be seen. So that, if it be superior in all other respects, this element of inferiority is no necessary part of it.

In the second place, one must remember (1) that Tragedy has everything that the Epic has (even the epic metre being admissible), together with a not inconsiderable addition in the shape of the Music (a very real factor in the pleasure of the drama) and the Spectacle. (2) That its reality of presentation is felt in the play as read, as well as in the play as acted. (3) That the tragic

imitation requires less space for the attainment of its end; which is a great
advantage, since the more concentrated effect is more pleasurable than one
with a large admixture of time to dilute it—consider the *Oedipus* of Sophocles,
for instance, and the effect of expanding it into the number of lines of the
Iliad. (4) That there is less unity in the imitation of the epic poets, as is proved
by the fact that any one work of theirs supplies matter for several tragedies;
the result being that, if they take what is really a single story, it seems curt
when briefly told, and thin and waterish when on the scale of length usual
with their verse. In saying that there is less unity in an epic, I mean an epic
made up of a plurality of actions, in the same way as the *Iliad* and *Odyssey*
have many such parts, each one of them in itself of some magnitude; yet the
structure of the two Homeric poems is as perfect as can be,and the action in
them is as nearly as possible one action. If, then, Tragedy is superior in these
respects, and also, besides these, in its poetic effect (since the two forms of
poetry should give us, not any or every pleasure, but the very special kind
we have mentioned), it is clear that, as attaining the poetic effect better than
the Epic, it will be the higher form of art.

So much for Tragedy and Epic poetry—for these two arts in general
and their species; the number and nature of their constituent parts; the causes
of success and failure in them; the Objections of the critics, and the Solutions
in answer to them.

Truth and the Stereotype

E. H. GOMBRICH

The schematism by which our understanding deals with the phenomenal world . . . is
a skill so deeply hidden in the human soul that we shall hardly guess the secret trick
that Nature here employs.

IMMANUEL KANT, *Kritik der reinen Vernunft*

In his charming autobiography, the German illustrator Ludwig Richter
relates how he and his friends, all young art students in Rome in the 1820's,
visited the famous beauty spot of Tivoli and sat down to draw. They looked
with surprise, but hardly with approval, at a group of French artists who
approached the place with enormous baggage, carrying large quantities of
paint which they applied to the canvas with big, coarse brushes. The Germans,

perhaps roused by this self-confident artiness, were determined on the opposite approach. They selected the hardest, best-pointed pencils, which could
render the motif firmly and minutely to its finest detail, and each bent down
over his small piece of paper, trying to transcribe what he saw with the utmost
fidelity. "We fell in love with every blade of grass, every tiny twig, and refused
to let anything escape us. Everyone tried to render the motif as objectively
as possible."

Nevertheless, when they then compared the fruits of their efforts in the
evening, their transcripts differed to a surprising extent. The mood, the color,
even the outline of the motif had undergone a subtle transformation in each
of them. Richter goes on to describe how these different versions reflected
the different dispositions of the four friends, for instance, how the melancholy
painter had straightened the exuberant contours and emphasized the blue
tinges. We might say he gives an illustration of the famous definition by Emile
Zola, who called a work of art "a corner of nature seen through a temperament."

It is precisely because we are interested in this definition that we must
probe it a little further. The "temperament" or "personality" of the artist,
his selective preferences, may be one of the reasons for the transformation
which the motif undergoes under the artist's hands, but there must be others—
everything, in fact, which we bundle together into the word "style," the style
of the period and the style of the artist. When this transformation is very
noticeable we say the motif has been greatly "stylized," and the corollary to
this observation is that those who happen to be interested in the motif, for
one reason or another, must learn to discount the style. This is part of that
natural adjustment, the change in what I call "mental set," which we all
perform quite automatically when looking at old illustrations. We can "read"
the Bayeux tapestry without reflecting on its countless "deviations from reality." We are not tempted for a moment to think the trees at Hastings in 1066
looked like palmettes and the ground at that time consisted of scrolls. It is
an extreme example, but it brings out the all-important fact that the word
"stylized" somehow tends to beg the question. It implies there was a special
activity by which the artist transformed the trees, much as the Victorian
designer was taught to study the forms of flowers before he turned them into
patterns. It was a practice which chimed in well with ideas of Victorian
architecture, when railways and factories were built first and then adorned
with the marks of a style. It was not the practice of earlier times.

The very point of Richter's story, after all, is that style rules even where
the artist wishes to reproduce nature faithfully, and trying to analyze these
limits to objectivity may help us get nearer to the riddle of style. One of these
limits . . . is indicated in Richter's story by the contrast between coarse brush
and fine pencil. The artist, clearly, can render only what his tool and his
medium are capable of rendering. His technique restricts his freedom of
choice. The features and relationships the pencil picks out will differ from

those the brush can indicate. Sitting in front of his motif, pencil in hand, the artist will, therefore, look out for those aspects which can be rendered in lines—as we say in a pardonable abbreviation, he will tend to see his motif in terms of lines, while, brush in hand, he sees it in terms of masses.

The question of why style should impose similar limitations is less easily answered, least of all when we do not know whether the artist's intentions were the same as those of Richter and his friends.

. . . Take the image on the artist's retina. It sounds scientific enough, but actually there never was *one* such image which we could single out for comparison with either photograph or painting. What there was was an endless succession of innumerable images as the painter scanned the landscape in front of him, and these images sent a complex pattern of impulses through the opic nerves to his brain. Even the artist knew nothing of these events, and we know even less. How far the picture that formed in his mind corresponded to or deviated from the photograph it is even less profitable to ask. What we do know is that these artists went out into nature to look for material for a picture and their artistic wisdom led them to organize the elements of the landscape into works of art of marvelous complexity that bear as much relationship to a surveyor's record as a poem bears to a police report.

Does this mean, then, that we are altogether on a useless quest? That artistic truth differs so much from prosaic truth that the question of objectivity must never be asked? I do not think so. We must only be a little more circumspect in our formulation of the question. . . .

. . . Logicians tell us—and they are not people to be easily gainsaid—that the terms "true" and "false" can only be applied to statements, propositions. And whatever may be the usage of critical parlance, a picture is never a statement in that sense of the term. It can no more be true or false than a statement can be blue or green. Much confusion has been caused in aesthetics

Hastings. From the Bayeux Tapestry, c. 1080, lithograph

by disregarding this simple fact. It is an understandable confusion because in our culture pictures are usually labeled, and labels, or captions, can be understood as abbreviated statements. When it is said "the camera cannot lie," this confusion is apparent. Propaganda in wartime often made use of photographs falsely labeled to accuse or exculpate one of the warring parties. Even in scientific illustrations it is the caption which determines the truth of the picture. In a *cause célèbre* of the last century, the embryo of a pig, labeled as a human embryo to prove a theory of evolution, brought about the downfall of a great reputation. Without much reflection, we can all expand into statements the laconic captions we find in museums and books. When we read the name "Ludwig Richter" under a landscape painting, we know we are thus informed that he painted it and can begin arguing whether this information is true or false. When we read "Tivoli," we infer the picture is to be taken as a view of that spot, and we can again agree or disagree with the label. How and when we agree, in such a case, will largely depend on what we want to know about the object represented. The Bayeux tapestry, for instance, tells us there was a battle at Hastings. It does not tell us what Hastings "looked like."

Now the historian knows that the information pictures were expected to provide differed widely in different periods. Not only were images scarce in the past, but so were the public's opportunities to check their captions. How many people ever saw their ruler in the flesh at sufficiently close quarters to recognize his likeness? How many traveled widely enough to tell one city from another? It is hardly surprising, therefore, that pictures of people and places changed their captions with sovereign disregard for truth. The print sold on the market as a portrait of a king would be altered to represent his successor or enemy.

WOLGEMUT: *Woodcuts from the "Nuremberg Chronicle,"* 1493

There is a famous example of this indifference to truthful captions in one of the most ambitious publishing projects of the early printing press, Hartmann Schedel's so-called "Nuremberg Chronicle" with woodcuts by Dürer's teacher Wolgemut. What an opportunity such a volume should give the historian to see what the world was like at the time of Columbus! But as we turn the pages of this big folio, we find the same woodcut of a medieval city recurring with different captions as Damascus, Ferrara, Milan, and Mantua. Unless we are prepared to believe these cities were as indistinguishable from one another as their suburbs may be today, we must conclude that neither the publisher nor the public minded whether the captions told the truth. All they were expected to do was to bring home to the reader that these names stood for cities.

These varying standards of illustration and documentation are of interest to the historian of representation precisely because he can soberly test the information supplied by picture and caption without becoming entangled too soon in problems of aesthetics. Where it is a question of information imparted by the image, the comparison with the correctly labeled photograph should be of obvious value. Three topographical prints representing various approaches to the perfect picture post card should suffice to exemplify the results of such an analysis.

The first shows a view of Rome from a German sixteenth-century newssheet reporting a catastrophic flood when the Tiber burst its banks. Where in Rome could the artist have seen such a timber structure, a castle with black-and-white walls, and a steep roof such as might be found in Nuremberg? Is this also a view of a German town with a misleading caption? Strangely enough, it is not. The artist, whoever he was, must have made some effort to portray the scene, for this curious building turns out to be the Castel Sant' Angelo in Rome, which guards the bridge across the Tiber. A comparison with a photograph shows that it does embody quite a number of features which belong or belonged to the castle: the angel on the roof that gives it its name, the main round bulk, founded on Hadrian's mausoleum, and the outworks with the bastions that we know were there.

I am fond of this coarse woodcut because its very crudeness allows us to study the mechanism of portrayal as in a slow-motion picture. There is no question here of the artist's having deviated from the motif in order to express his mood or his aesthetic preferences. It is doubtful, in fact, whether the designer of the woodcut ever saw Rome. He probably adapted a view of the city in order to illustrate the sensational news. He knew the Castel Sant' Angelo to be a castle, and so he selected from the drawer of his mental stereotypes the appropriate cliché for a castle—a German *Burg* with its timber structure and high-pitched roof. But he did not simply repeat his stereotype— he adapted it to its particular function by embodying certain distinctive features which he knew belonged to that particular building in Rome. He supplies

1   Anonymous: 1557, woodcut

Castel Sant' Angelo, Rome

2   Anonymous: c. 1540, pen and ink   3   Modern photograph

some information over and above the fact that there is a castle by a bridge. . . .

I do not want to be misunderstood here. I do not want to prove by these examples that all representation must be inaccurate or that all visual documents before the advent of photography must be misleading. Clearly, if we had pointed out to the artist his mistake, he could have further modified his scheme and rounded the windows. My point is rather that such matching will always be a step-by-step process—how long it takes and how hard it is will depend on the choice of the initial schema to be adapted to the task of serving as a portrait. I believe that in this respect these humble documents do indeed tell us a lot about the procedure of any artist who wants to make a truthful record of an individual form. He begins not with his visual impression but with his idea or concept: the German artist with his concept of a castle that he applies as well as he can to that individual castle. . . . The individual visual information, those distinctive features I have mentioned, are entered, as it were, upon a pre-existing blank or formulary. And, as often happens with blanks, if they have no provisions for certain kinds of information we consider essential, it is just too bad for the information.

The comparison, by the way, between the formularies of administration and the artist's stereotypes is not my invention. In medieval parlance there was one word for both, a *simile*, or pattern, that is applied to individual incidents in law no less than in pictorial art.

And just as the lawyer or the statistician could plead that he could never get hold of the individual case without some sort of framework provided by his forms or blanks, so the artist could argue that it makes no sense to look at a motif unless one has learned how to classify and catch it within the network of a schematic form. This, at least, is the conclusion to which psychologists have come who knew nothing of our historical series but who set out to investigate the procedure anyone adopts when copying what is called a "nonsense figure," an inkblot, let us say, or an irregular patch. By and large, it appears, the procedure is always the same. The draftsman tries first to classify the blot and fit it into some sort of familiar schema—he will say, for instance, that it is triangular or that it looks like a fish. Having selected such a schema to fit the form approximately, he will proceed to adjust it, noticing for instance that the triangle is rounded at the top, or that the fish ends in a pigtail. Copying, we learn from these experiments, proceeds through the rhythms of schema and correction. The schema is not the product of a process of "abstraction," of a tendency to "simplify"; it represents the first approximate, loose category which is gradually tightened to fit the form it is to reproduce. . . .

Not only must we surprise the artist when he is confronted with an unfamiliar task that he cannot easily adjust to his means; we must also know that his aim was in fact portrayal. Given these conditions, we may do without the actual comparison between photograph and representation that was our starting point. For, after all, nature is sufficiently uniform to allow us to judge the information value of a picture even when we have never seen the specimen portrayed. The beginnings of illustrated reportage, therefore, provide another test case where we need have no doubt about the will and can, consequently, concentrate on the skill. . . .

A . . . famous example comes from the period when medieval art was at its height, from the volume of plans and drawings by the Gothic master builder, Villard de Honnecourt, which tells us so much about the practice and outlook of the men who created the French cathedrals. Among the many architectural, religious, and symbolic drawings of striking skill and beauty to be found in this volume, there is a curiously stiff picture of a lion, seen *en face*. To us, it looks like an ornamental or heraldic image, but Villard's caption tells us that he regarded it in a different light: "*Et sacies bien,*" he says, "*qu'il fu contrefais*

VILLARD DE HONNECOURT: *Lion and Porcupine.* c. 1235, pen and ink

al vif." "Know well that it is drawn from life." These words obviously had a very different meaning for Villard than they have for us. He can have meant only that he had drawn his schema in the presence of a real lion. How much of his visual observation he allowed to enter into the formula is a different matter.

. . . The fate of exotic creatures in the illustrated books of the last few centuries before the advent of photography is as instructive as it is amusing. When Dürer published his famous woodcut of a rhinoceros, he had to rely on secondhand evidence which he filled in from his own imagination, colored, no doubt, by what he had learned of the most famous of exotic beasts, the dragon with its armored body. Yet it has been shown that this half-invented creature served as a model for all renderings of the rhinoceros, even in natural-history books, up to the eighteenth century. When, in 1790, James Bruce published a drawing of the beast in his *Travels to Discover the Source of the Nile*, he proudly showed that he was aware of this fact:

"The animal represented in this drawing is a native of Tcherkin, near Ras el Feel . . . and this is the first drawing of the rhinoceros with a double horn that has ever yet been presented to the public. The first figure of the Asiatic rhinoceros, the species having but one horn, was painted by Albert Dürer, from the life. . . . It was wonderfully ill-executed in all its parts, and was the origin of all the monstrous forms under which that animal has been painted, ever since. . . . Several modern philosophers have made amends for this in our days; Mr. Parsons, Mr. Edwards, and the Count de Buffon, have given good figures of it from life; they have indeed some faults, owing chiefly to preconceived prejudices and inattention. . . . This . . . is the first that has been published with two horns, it is designed from the life, and is an African."

If proof were needed that the difference between the medieval draftsman and his eighteenth-century descendant is only one of degree, it could be found here. For the illustration, presented with such flourishes of trumpets, is surely

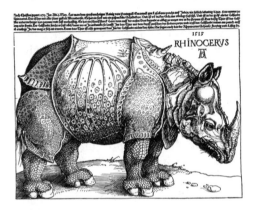

DÜRER: *Rhinoceros.* 1515, woodcut

HEATH: *Rhinoceros of Africa.* 1789, engraving

African rhinoceros

not free from "preconceived prejudices" and the all-pervading memory of Dürer's woodcut. We do not know exactly what species of rhinoceros the artist saw at Ras el Feel, and the comparison of his picture with a photograph taken in Africa may not, therefore, be quite fair. But I am told that none of the species known to zoologists corresponds to the engraving claimed to be drawn *al vif*!

The story repeats itself whenever a rare specimen is introduced into Europe. Even the elephants that populate the paintings of the sixteenth and seventeenth centuries have been shown to stem from a very few archetypes and to embody all their curious features, despite the fact that information about elephants was not particularly hard to come by.

These examples demonstrate, in somewhat grotesque magnification, a tendency which the student of art has learned to reckon with. The familiar will always remain the likely starting point for the rendering of the unfamiliar; an existing representation will always exert its spell over the artist even while he strives to record the truth. Thus it was remarked by ancient critics that several famous artists of antiquity had made a strange mistake in the portrayal of horses: they had represented them with eyelashes on the lower lid, a feature which belongs to the human eye but not to that of the horse. A German ophthalmologist who studied the eyes of Dürer's portraits, which to the layman appear to be such triumphs of painstaking accuracy, reports somewhat similar mistakes. Apparently not even Dürer knew what eyes "really look like."

This should not give us cause for surprise, for the greatest of all the visual explorers, Leonardo himself, has been shown to have made mistakes in his anatomical drawings. Apparently he drew features of the human heart which Galen made him expect but which he cannot have seen.

The study of pathology is meant to increase our understanding of health. The sway of schemata did not prevent the emergence of an art of scientific illustration that sometimes succeeds in packing more correct visual information into the image than even a photograph contains. But the diagrammatic maps of muscles in our illustrated anatomies are not "transcripts" of things seen but the work of trained observers who build up the picture of a specimen that has been revealed to them in years of patient study.

Now in this sphere of scientific illustration it obviously makes sense to say that . . . Villard himself could not have done what the modern illustrator can do. They lacked the relevant schemata, their starting point was too far removed from their motif, and their style was too rigid to allow a sufficiently supple adjustment. For so much certainly emerges from a study of portrayal in art: you cannot create a faithful image out of nothing. You must have learned the trick if only from other pictures you have seen.

In our culture, where pictures exist in such profusion, it is difficult to demonstrate this basic fact. There are freshmen in art schools who have facility in the objective rendering of motifs that would appear to belie this assumption.

But those who have given art classes in other cultural settings tell a different story. James Cheng, who taught painting to a group of Chinese trained in different conventions, once told me of a sketching expedition he made with his students to a famous beauty spot, one of Peking's old city gates. The task baffled them. In the end, one of the students asked to be given at least a picture post card of the building so that they would have something to copy. It is stories such as these, stories of breakdowns, that explain why art has a history and artists need a style adapted to a task.

I cannot illustrate this revealing incident. But luck allows us to study the next stage, as it were—the adjustment of the traditional vocabulary of Chinese art to the unfamiliar task of topographical portrayal in the Western sense. For some decades Chiang Yee, a Chinese writer and painter of great gifts and charm, has delighted us with contemplative records of the Silent Traveller, books in which he tells of his encounters with scenes and people of the English and Irish countryside and elsewhere. I take an illustration from the volume on the English Lakeland.

It is a view of Derwentwater. Here we have crossed the line that separates documentation from art. Mr. Chiang Yee certainly enjoys the adaptation of the Chinese idiom to a new purpose; he wants us to see the English scenery for once "through Chinese eyes." But it is precisely for this reason that it is so instructive to compare his view with a typical "picturesque" rendering from the Romantic period. We see how the relatively rigid vocabulary of the Chinese tradition acts as a selective screen which admits only the features for which schemata exist. The artist will be attracted by motifs which can be rendered in his idiom. As he scans the landscape, the sights which can be matched successfully with the schemata he has learned to handle will leap forward as centers of attention. The style, like the medium, creates a mental set which makes the artist look for certain aspects in the scene around him that he can render. Painting is an activity, and the artist will therefore tend to see what he paints rather than to paint what he sees.

It is this interaction between style and preference which Nietzsche summed up in his mordant comment on the claims of realism:

> "All Nature faithfully"—But by what feint
> Can Nature be subdued to art's constraint?
> Her smallest fragment is still infinite!
> And so he paints but what he likes in it.
> What does he like? He likes, what he can paint!

There is more in this observation than just a cool reminder of the limitations of artistic means. We catch a glimpse of the reasons why these limitations will never obtrude themselves within the domain of art itself. Art presupposes mastery, and the greater the artist the more surely will he instinctively avoid a task where his mastery would fail to serve him. The layman may wonder whether Giotto could have painted a view of Fiesole in sunshine, but the historian will suspect that, lacking the means, he would not have

CHIANG YEE: *Cows in Derwentwater.* 1936, brush and ink

wanted to, or rather that he could not have wanted to. We like to assume, somehow, that where there is a will there is also a way, but in matters of art the maxim should read that only where there is a way is there also a will. The individual can enrich the ways and means that his culture offers him; he can hardly wish for something that he has never known is possible.

The fact that artists tend to look for motifs for which their style and training equip them explains why the problem of representational skill looks different to the historian of art and to the historian of visual information. The one is concerned with success, the other must also observe the failures. But these failures suggest that sometimes we assume a little rashly that the ability of art to portray the visible world developed, as it were, along a uniform front. We know of specialists in art—of Claude Lorrain, the master of landscape whose figure paintings were poor, of Frans Hals who concentrated almost exclusively on portraits. May not skill as much as will have dictated this type of preference? Is not all naturalism in the art of the past selective?

A somewhat Philistine experiment would suggest that it is. Take the next magazine containing snapshots of crowds and street scenes and walk with it through any art gallery to see how many gestures and types that occur in life can be matched from old paintings. Even Dutch genre paintings that appear to mirror life in all its bustle and variety will turn out to be created from a limited number of types and gestures, much as the apparent realism of the picaresque novel or of Restoration comedy still applies and modifies

ANONYMOUS: *Derwentwater, looking toward Borrowdale.* 1826, lithograph

stock figures which can be traced back for centuries. There is no neutral naturalism. The artist, no less than the writer, needs a vocabulary before he can embark on a "copy" of reality.

Everything points to the conclusion that the phrase the "language of art" is more than a loose metaphor, that even to describe the visible world in images we need a developed system of schemata. This conclusion rather clashes with the traditional distinction, often discussed in the eighteenth century, between spoken words which are conventional signs and painting which uses "natural" signs to "imitate" reality. It is a plausible distinction, but it has led to certain difficulties. If we assume, with this tradition, that natural signs can simply be copied from nature, the history of art represents a complete puzzle. It has become increasingly clear since the late nineteenth century that primitive art and child art use a language of symbols rather than "natural signs." To account for this fact it was postulated that there must be a special kind of art grounded not on seeing but rather on knowledge, an art which operates with "conceptual images." The child—it is argued—does not look at trees; he is satisfied with the "conceptual" schema of a tree that fails to correspond to any reality since it does not embody the characteristics of, say, birch or beech, let alone of individual trees. This reliance on construction rather than on imitation was attributed to the peculiar mentality of children and primitives who live in a world of their own.

But we have come to realize that this distinction is unreal. Gustaf Britsch and Rudolf Arnheim have stressed that there is no opposition between the crude map of the world made by a child and the richer map presented in naturalistic images. All art originates in the human mind, in our reactions to the world rather than in the visible world itself, and it is precisely because all art is "conceptual" that all representations are recognizable by their style.

Without some starting point, some initial schema, we could never get hold of the flux of experience. Without categories, we could not sort our impressions. Paradoxically, it has turned out that it matters relatively little what these first categories are. We can always adjust them according to need. Indeed, if the schema remains loose and flexible, such initial vagueness may prove not a hindrance but a help. An entirely fluid system would no longer serve its purpose; it could not register facts because it would lack pigeonholes. But how we arrange the first filing system is not very relevant.

The progress of learning, of adjustment through trial and error, can be compared to the game of "Twenty Questions," where we identify an object through inclusion or exclusion along any network of classes. The traditional initial scheme of "animal, vegetable, or mineral" is certainly neither scientific nor very suitable, but it usually serves us well enough to narrow down our concepts by submitting them to the corrective test of "yes" or "no." The example of this parlor game has become popular of late as an illustration of that process of articulation through which we learn to adjust ourselves to the infinite complexity of this world. It indicates, however crudely, the way in which not only organisms but even machines may be said to "learn" by trial and error. Engineers at their thrilling work on what they call "servo mechanisms," that is, self-adjusting machines, have recognized the importance of some kind of "initiative" on the part of the machine. The first move such a machine may make will be, and indeed must be, a random movement, a shot in the dark. Provided a report of success or failure, hit or miss, can be fed back into the machine, it will increasingly avoid the wrong moves and repeat the correct ones. One of the pioneers in this field has recently described this machine rhythm of schema and correction in a striking verbal formula: he calls all learning "an arboriform stratification of guesses about the world." Arboriform, we may take it, here describes the progressive creation of classes and subclasses such as might be described in a diagrammatic account of "Twenty Questions."

We seem to have drifted far from the discussion of portrayal. But it is certainly possible to look at a portrait as a schema of a head modified by the distinctive features about which we wish to convey information. The American police sometimes employ draftsmen to aid witnesses in the identification of criminals. They may draw any vague face, a random schema, and let witnesses guide their modifications of selected features simply by saying "yes" or "no" to various suggested standard alterations until the face is sufficiently individualized for a search in the files to be profitable. This account of portrait drawing by remote control may well be over-tidy, but as a parable it may serve its purpose. It reminds us that the starting point of a visual record is not knowledge but a guess conditioned by habit and tradition.

Need we infer from this fact that there is no such thing as an objective likeness? That it makes no sense to ask, for instance, whether Chiang Yee's view of Derwentwater is more or less correct than the nineteenth- century lithograph in which the formulas of classical landscapes were applied to the same task? It is a tempting conclusion and one which recommends itself to the teacher of art appreciation because it brings home to the layman how much of what we call "seeing" is conditioned by habits and expectations. It is all the more important to clarify how far this relativism will take us. I believe it rests on the confusion between pictures, words, and statements which we saw arising the moment truth was ascribed to paintings rather than to captions.

If all art is conceptual, the issue is rather simple. For concepts, like pictures, cannot be true or false. They can only be more or less useful for the formation of descriptions. The words of a language, like pictorial formulas, pick out from the flux of events a few signposts which allow us to give direction to our fellow speakers in that game of "Twenty Questions" in which we are engaged. Where the needs of users are similar, the signposts will tend to correspond. We can mostly find equivalent terms in English, French, German, and Latin, and hence the idea has taken root that concepts exist independently of language as the constituents of "reality." But the English language erects a signpost on the roadfork between "clock" and "watch" where the German has only "Uhr." The sentence from the German primer, "*Meine Tante hat eine Uhr,*" leaves us in doubt whether the aunt has a clock or a watch. Either of the two translations may be wrong as a description of a fact. In Swedish, by the way, there is an additional roadfork to distinguish between aunts who are "father's sisters," those who are "mother's sisters," and those who are just ordinary aunts. If we were to play our game in Swedish we would need additional questions to get at the truth about the timepiece.

This simple example brings out the fact, recently emphasized by Benjamin Lee Whorf, that language does not give name to pre-existing things or concepts so much as it articulates the world of our experience. The images of art, we suspect, do the same. But this difference in styles or languages need not stand in the way of correct answers and descriptions. The world may be approached from a different angle and the information given may yet be the same.

From the point of view of information there is surely no difficulty in discussing portrayal. To say of a drawing that it is a correct view of Tivoli does not mean, of course, that Tivoli is bounded by wiry lines. It means that those who understand the notation will derive *no false information* from the drawing—whether it gives the contour in a few lines or picks out "every blade of grass" as Richter's friends wanted to do. The complete portrayal might be the one which gives as much correct information about the spot as we would obtain if we looked at it from the very spot where the artist stood.

Styles, like languages, differ in the sequence of articulation and in the number of questions they allow the artist to ask; and so complex is the information that reaches us from the visible world that no picture will ever embody it all. This is not due to the subjectivity of vision but to its richness. Where the artist has to copy a human product he can, of course, produce a facsimile which is indistinguishable from the original. The forger of banknotes succeeds only too well in effacing his personality and the limitations of a period style.

But what matters to us is that the correct portrait, like the useful map, is an end product on a long road through schema and correction. It is not a faithful record of a visual experience but the fruitful construction of a relational model.

Neither the subjectivity of vision nor the sway of conventions need lead us to deny that such a model can be constructed to any required degree of accuracy. What is decisive here is clearly the word "required." The form of representation cannot be divorced from its purpose and the requirements of the society in which the given visual language gains currency.

Reality Remade

NELSON GOODMAN

Art is not a copy of the real world. One of the damn things is enough.[1]

Denotation

Whether a picture ought to be a representation or not is a question much less crucial than might appear from current bitter battles among artists, critics,

Nelson Goodman, "Reality Remade," from *Languages of Art.* Reprinted by permission of Nelson Goodman and Hackett Publishing Company, Inc., Indianapolis, Indiana.

---

[1]Reported as occurring in an essay on Virginia Woolf. I have been unable to locate the source.

and propagandists. Nevertheless, the nature of representation wants early study in any philosophical examination of the ways symbols function in and out of the arts. That representation is frequent in some arts, such as painting, and unfrequent in others, such as music, threatens trouble for a unified aesthetics; and confusion over how pictorial representation as a mode of signification is allied to and distinguished from verbal description on the one hand and, say, facial expression on the other is fatal to any general theory of symbols.

The most naive view of representation might perhaps be put somewhat like this: "*A* represents *B* if and only if *A* appreciably resembles *B*," or "*A* represents *B* to the extent that *A* resembles *B*." Vestiges of this view, with assorted refinements, persist in most writing on representation. Yet more error could hardly be compressed into so short a formula.

Some of the faults are obvious enough. An object resembles itself to the maximum degree but rarely represents itself; resemblance, unlike representation, is reflexive. Again, unlike representation, resemblance is symmetric: *B* is as much like *A* as *A* is like *B*, but while a painting may represent the Duke of Wellington, the Duke doesn't represent the painting. Furthermore, in many cases neither one of a pair of very like objects represents the other: none of the automobiles off an assembly line is a picture of any of the rest; and a man is not normally a representation of another man, even his twin brother. Plainly, resemblance in any degree is no sufficient condition for representation.

Just what correction to make in the formula is not so obvious. We may attempt less, and prefix the condition "If *A* is a picture, . . . " Of course, if we then construe "picture" as "representation," we resign a large part of the question: namely, what constitutes a representation. But even if we construe "picture" broadly enough to cover all paintings, the formula is wide of the mark in other ways. A Constable painting of Marlborough Castle is more like any other picture than it is like the Castle, yet it represents the Castle and not another picture—not even the closest copy. To add the requirement that *B* must not be a picture would be desperate and futile; for a picture may represent another, and indeed each of the once popular paintings of art galleries represents many others.

The plain fact is that a picture, to represent an object, must be a symbol for it, stand for it, refer to it; and that no degree of resemblance is sufficient to establish the requisite relationship of reference. Nor is resemblance *necessary* for reference; almost anything may stand for almost anything else. A picture that represents—like a passage that describes—an object refers to and, more particularly, *denotes* it. Denotation is the core of representation and is independent of resemblance.

If the relation between a picture and what it represents is thus assimilated to the relation between a predicate and what it applies to, we must examine the characteristics of representation as a special kind of denotation. What does pictorial denotation have in common with, and how does it differ from, verbal or diagrammatic denotation? One not implausible answer is that resemblance, while no sufficient condition for representation, is just the feature that distinguishes representation from denotation of other kinds. Is it perhaps the case that if *A* denotes *B*, then *A* represents *B* just to the extent that *A* resembles *B*? I think even this watered-down and innocuous-looking version of our initial formula betrays a grave misconception of the nature of representation.

Imitation

"To make a faithful picture, come as close as possible to copying the object just as it is." This simple-minded injunction baffles me; for the object before me is a man, a swarm of atoms, a complex of cells, a fiddler, a friend, a fool, and much more. If none of these constitute the object as it is, what else might? If all are ways the object is, then none is *the* way the object is. I cannot copy all these at once; and the more nearly I succeeded, the less would the result be a realistic picture.

What I am to copy then, it seems, is one such aspect, one of the ways the object is or looks. But not, of course, any one of these at random—not, for example, the Duke of Wellington as he looks to a drunk through a raindrop. Rather, we may suppose, the way the object looks to the normal eye, at proper range, from a favorable angle, in good light, without instrumentation, unprejudiced by affections or animosities or interests, and unembellished by thought or interpretation. In short, the object is to be copied as seen under aseptic conditions by the free and innocent eye.

The catch here, as Ernest Gombrich insists, is that there is no innocent eye.[2] The eye comes always ancient to its work, obsessed by its own past and by old and new insinuations of the ear, nose, tongue, fingers, heart, and brain. It functions not as an instrument self-powered and alone, but as a dutiful member of a complex and capricious organism. Not only how but what it sees is regulated by need and prejudice. It selects, rejects, organizes, discriminates, associates, classifies, analyzes, constructs. It does not so much mirror as take and make; and what it takes and makes it sees not bare, as items without attributes, but as things, as food, as people, as enemies, as stars, as weapons. Nothing is seen nakedly or naked.

The myths of the innocent eye and of the absolute given are unholy accomplices. Both derive from and foster the idea of knowing as a processing of raw material received from the senses, and of this raw material as being discoverable either through purification rites or by methodical disinterpretation. But reception and interpretation are not separable operations; they

---

[2]In *Art and Illusion* (New York, Pantheon Books, 1960), pp. 297–298 and elsewhere.

are thoroughly interdependent. The Kantian dictum echoes here: the innocent eye is blind and the virgin mind empty. Moreover, what has been received and what has been done to it cannot be distinguished within the finished product. Content cannot be extracted by peeling off layers of comment.

All the same, an artist may often do well to strive for innocence of eye. The effort sometimes rescues him from the tired patterns of everyday seeing, and results in fresh insight. The opposite effort, to give fullest rein to a personal reading, can be equally tonic—and for the same reason. But the most neutral eye and the most biased are merely sophisticated in different ways. The most ascetic vision and the most prodigal, like the sober portrait and the vitriolic caricature, differ not in how *much* but only in *how* they interpret.

The copy theory of representation, then, is stopped at the start by inability to specify what is to be copied. Not an object the way it is, nor all the ways it is, nor the way it looks to the mindless eye. Moreover, something is wrong with the very notion of copying any of the ways an object is, any aspect of it. For an aspect is not just the object-from-a-given-distance-and-angle-and-in-a-given-light; it is the object as we look upon or conceive it, a version or construal of the object. In representing an object, we do not copy such a construal or interpretation—we *achieve* it.

In other words, nothing is ever represented either shorn of or in the fullness of its properties. A picture never merely represents *x*, but rather represents *x as* a man or represents *x to be* a mountain, or represents *the fact that x is* a melon. What could be meant by copying a fact would be hard to grasp even if there were any such things as facts; to ask me to copy *x* as a soandso is a little like asking me to sell something as a gift; and to speak of copying something to be a man is sheer nonsense. We shall presently have to look further into all this; but we hardly need to look further to see how little is representation a matter of imitation.

The case for the relativity of vision and of representation has been so conclusively stated elsewhere that I am relieved of the need to argue it at any length here. Gombrich, in particular, has amassed overwhelming evidence to show how the way we see and depict depends upon and varies with experience, practice, interests, and attitudes. But on one matter Gombrich and others sometimes seem to me to take a position at odds with such relativity; and I must therefore discuss briefly the question of the conventionality of perspective.

Perspective

An artist may choose his means of rendering motion, intensity of light, quality of atmosphere, vibrancy of color, but if he wants to represent space correctly, he must—almost anyone will tell him—obey the laws of perspective. The adoption of perspective during the Renaissance is widely accepted as a long stride forward in realistic depiction. The laws of perspective are supposed to provide absolute standards of fidelity that override differences in style of seeing and picturing. Gombrich derides "the idea that perspective is merely a convention and does not represent the world as it looks," and he declares "One cannot insist enough that the art of perspective aims at a correct equation: It wants the image to appear like the object and the object like the image."[3] . . .

Obviously the laws of the behavior of light are no more conventional than any other scientific laws. Now suppose we have a motionless, monochromatic object, reflecting light of medium intensity only. The argument runs:— A picture drawn in correct perspective will, under specified conditions, deliver to the eye a bundle of light rays matching that delivered by the object itself. This matching is a purely objective matter, measurable by instruments. And such matching constitutes fidelity of representation; for since light rays are all that the eye can receive from either picture or object, identity in pattern of light rays must constitute identity of appearance. Of course, the rays yielded by the picture under the specified conditions match not only those yielded by the object in question from a given distance and angle but also those yielded by any of a multitude of other objects from other distances and angles.[4] Identity in pattern of light rays, like resemblance of other kinds, is clearly no sufficient condition for representation: The claim is rather that such identity is a criterion of fidelity, of correct pictorial representation, where denotation is otherwise established.

If at first glance the argument as stated seems simple and persuasive, it becomes less so when we consider the conditions of observation that are prescribed. The picture must be viewed through a peephole, face on, from a certain distance, with one eye closed and the other motionless. The object also must be observed through a peephole, from a given (but not usually the same) angle and distance, and with a single unmoving eye. Otherwise, the light rays will not match.

Under these remarkable conditions, do we not have ultimately faithful representation? Hardly. Under these conditions, what we are looking at tends to disappear rather promptly. Experiment has shown that the eye cannot see normally without moving relative to what it sees; apparently, scanning is necessary for normal vision. The fixed eye is almost as blind as the innocent one. What can the matching of light rays delivered under conditions that make normal vision impossible have to do with fidelity of representation? To measure fidelity in terms of rays directed at a closed eye would be no more absurd. But this objection need not be stressed; perhaps enough eye motion could be allowed for scanning but not for seeing around the object. The basic trouble is that the specified conditions of observation are grossly abnormal.

---

[3]*Art and Illusion*, pp. 254 and 257.
[4]Cf. Gombrich's discussion of "gates" in *Art and Illusion*, pp. 250–251.

What can be the grounds of taking the matching of light rays delivered under such extraordinary conditions as a measure of fidelity? Under no more artificial conditions, such as the interposition of suitably contrived lenses, a picture far out of perspective could also be made to yield the same pattern of light rays as the object. That with clever enough stage-managing we can wring out of a picture drawn in perspective light rays that match those we can wring out of the object represented is an odd and futile argument for the fidelity of perspective.

Furthermore, the conditions of observation in question are in most cases not the same for picture and object. Both are to be viewed through a peephole with one transfixed eye; but the picture is to be viewed face on at a distance of six feet while the cathedral represented has to be looked at from, say, an angle of 45° to its façade and at a distance of two hundred feet. Now not only the light rays received but also the attendant conditions determine what and how we see; as psychologists are fond of saying, there is more to vision than meets the eye. Just as a red light says "stop" on the highway and "port" at sea, so the same stimulus gives rise to different visual experience under different circumstances. Even where both the light rays and the momentary external conditions are the same, the preceding train of visual experience, together with information gathered from all sources, can make a vast difference in what is seen. If not even the former conditions are the same, duplication of light rays is no more likely to result in identical perception than is duplication of the conditions if the light rays differ.

Pictures are normally viewed framed against a background by a person free to walk about and to move his eyes. To paint a picture that will under these conditions deliver the same light rays as the object, viewed under any conditions, would be pointless even if it were possible. Rather, the artist's task in representing an object before him is to decide what light rays, under gallery conditions, will succeed in rendering what he sees. This is not a matter of copying but of conveying. It is more a matter of "catching a likeness" than of duplicating—in the sense that a likeness lost in a photograph may be caught in a caricature. Translation of a sort, compensating for differences in circumstances, is involved. How this is best carried out depends upon countless and variable factors, not least among them the particular habits of seeing and representing that are ingrained in the viewers. Pictures in perspective, like any others, have to be read; and the ability to read has to be acquired. The eye accustomed solely to Oriental painting does not immediately understand a picture in perspective. Yet with practice one can accommodate smoothly to distorting spectacles or to pictures drawn in warped or even reversed perspective. And even we who are most inured to perspective rendering do not always accept it as faithful representation: the photograph of a man with his feet thrust forward looks distorted, and Pike's Peak dwindles dismally in a snapshot. As the saying goes, there is nothing like a camera to make a molehill out of a mountain.

So far, I have been playing along with the idea that pictorial perspective obeys laws of geometrical optics, and that a picture drawn according to the standard pictorial rules will, under the very abnormal conditions outlined above, deliver a bundle of light rays matching that delivered by the scene portrayed. Only this assumption gives any plausibility at all to the argument from perspective; but the assumption is plainly false. By the pictorial rules, railroad tracks running outward from the eye are drawn converging, but telephone poles (or the edges of a façade) running upward from the eye are drawn parallel. By the "laws of geometry" the poles should also be drawn converging. But so drawn, they look as wrong as railroad tracks drawn parallel. Thus we have cameras with tilting backs and elevating lens-boards to "correct distortion"—that is, to make vertical parallels come out parallel in our photographs; we do not likewise try to make the railroad tracks come out parallel. The rules of pictorial perspective no more follow from the laws of optics than would rules calling for drawing the tracks parallel and the poles converging. . . . The artist who wants to produce a spatial representation that the present-day Western eye will accept as faithful must defy the "laws of geometry." . . .

Sculpture

The troubles with the copy theory are sometimes attributed solely to the impossibility of depicting reality-in-the-round on a flat surface. But imitation is no better gauge of realism in sculpture than in painting. What is to be portrayed in a bronze bust is a mobile, many-faceted, and fluctuating person, encountered in ever changing light and against miscellaneous backgrounds. Duplicating the form of the head at a given instant is unlikely to yield a notably faithful representation. The very fixation of such a momentary phase embalms the person much as a photograph taken at too short an exposure freezes a fountain or stops a racehorse. To portray faithfully is to convey a person known and distilled from a variety of experiences. This elusive conceit is nothing that one can meaningfully try to duplicate or imitate in a static bronze on a pedestal in a museum. The sculptor undertakes, rather, a subtle and intricate problem of translation.

Even where the object represented is something simpler and more stable than a person, duplication seldom coincides with realistic representation. If in a tympanum over a tall Gothic portal, Eve's apple were the same size as a Winesap, it would not look big enough to tempt Adam. The distant or colossal sculpture has also to be *shaped* very differently from what it depicts in order to be realistic, in order to "look right." And the ways of making it "look right" are not reducible to fixed and universal rules; for how an object looks depends not only upon its orientation, distance, and lighting, but upon all we know of it and upon our training, habits, and concerns.

One need hardly go further to see that the basic case against imitation as a test of realism is conclusive for sculpture as well as for painting.

Fictions

So far, I have been considering only the representation of a particular person or group or thing or scene; but a picture, like a predicate, may denote severally the members of a given class. A picture accompanying a definition in a dictionary is often such a representation, not denoting uniquely some one eagle, say, or collectively the class of eagles, but distributively eagles in general.

Other representations have neither unique nor multiple denotation. What, for example, do pictures of Pickwick or of a unicorn represent? They do not represent anything; they are representations with null denotation. Yet how can we say that a picture represents Pickwick, or a unicorn, and also say that it does not represent anything? Since there is no Pickwick and no unicorn, what a picture of Pickwick and a picture of a unicorn represent is the same. Yet surely to be a picture of Pickwick and to be a picture of a unicorn are not at all the same.

The simple fact is that much as most pieces of furniture are readily sorted out as desks, chairs, tables, etc., so most pictures are readily sorted out as pictures of Pickwick, of Pegasus, of a unicorn, etc., without reference to anything represented. What tends to mislead us is that such locutions as "picture of" and "represents" have the appearance of mannerly two-place predicates and can sometimes be so interpreted. But "picture of Pickwick" and "represents a unicorn" are better considered unbreakable one-place predicates, or class-terms, like "desk" and "table." We cannot reach inside any of these and quantify over parts of them. From the fact that P is a picture of or represents a unicorn we cannot infer that there is something that P is a picture of or represents. Furthermore, a picture of Pickwick is a picture of a man, even though there is no man it represents. Saying that a picture represents a soandso is thus highly ambiguous as between saying what the picture denotes and saying what kind of picture it is. Some confusion can be avoided if in the latter case we speak rather of a "Pickwick-representing-picture" or a "unicorn-representing-picture" or a "man-representing-picture" or, for short, of a "Pickwick-picture" or "unicorn-picture" or "man-picture." Obviously a picture cannot, barring equivocation, both represent Pickwick and represent nothing. But a picture may be of a certain kind—be a Pickwick-picture or a man-picture—without representing anything.[5]

---

[5]The substance of this and the following two paragraphs is contained in my paper, "On Likeness of Meaning," *Analysis,* vol. 1 (1949), pp. 1-7, and discussed further in the sequel, "On Some Differences about Meaning," *Analysis,* vol. 13 (1953), pp. 90–96.

The difference between a man-picture and a picture of a man has a close parallel in the difference between a man-description (or man-term) and a description of (or term for) a man. "Pickwick," "the Duke of Wellington," "the man who conquered Napoleon," "a man," "a fat man," "the man with three heads," are all man-descriptions, but not all describe a man. Some denote a particular man, some denote each of many men, and some denote nothing.[6] And although "Pickwick" and "the three-headed man" and "Pegasus" all have the same null extension, the second differs from the first in being, for example, a many-headed-man-description, while the last differs from the other two in being a winged-horse-description.

The way pictures and descriptions are thus classified into kinds, like most habitual ways of classifying, is far from sharp or stable, and resists codification. Borderlines shift and blur, new categories are always coming into prominence, and the canons of the classification are less clear than the practice. But this is only to say that we may have some trouble in telling whether certain pictures (in common parlance) "represent a unicorn," or in setting forth rules for deciding in every case whether a picture is a man-picture. Exact and general conditions under which something is a soandso-picture or a soandso-description would indeed be hard to formulate. We can cite examples: Van Gogh's *Postman* is a man-picture; and in English, "a man" is a man-description. And we may note, for instance, that to be a soandso-picture is to be a soandso-picture as a whole, so that a picture containing or contained in a man-picture need not itself be a man-picture. But to attempt much more is to become engulfed in a notorious philosophical morass; and the frustrating, if fascinating, problems involved are no part of our present task. All that directly matters here, I repeat, is that pictures are indeed sorted with varying degrees of ease into man-pictures, unicorn-pictures, Pickwick-pictures, winged-horse-pictures, etc., just as pieces of furniture are sorted into desks, tables, chairs, etc. And this fact is unaffected by the difficulty, in either case, of framing definitions for the several classes or eliciting a general principle of classification.

The possible objection that we must first understand what a man or a unicorn is in order to know how to apply "man-picture" or "unicorn-picture" seems to me quite perverted. We can learn to apply "corncob pipe" or "staghorn" without first understanding, or knowing how to apply, "corn" or "cob" or "corncob" or "pipe" or "stag" or "horn" as separate terms. And we can learn, on the basis of samples, to apply "unicorn-picture" not only without ever having seen any unicorns but without ever having seen or heard the word "unicorn" before. Indeed, largely by learning what are unicorn-pictures and unicorn-descriptions do we come to understand the word "unicorn"; and our ability to recognize a staghorn may help us to recognize a stag when we

---

[6] Strictly, we should speak here of utterances and inscriptions; for different instances of the same term may differ in denotation.

see one. We may begin to understand a term by learning how to apply either the term itself or some larger term containing it. Acquiring any of these skills may aid in acquiring, but does not imply possessing, any of the others. Understanding a term is not a precondition, and may often be a result, of learning how to apply the term and its compounds.

Earlier I said that denotation is a necessary condition for representation, and then encountered representations without denotation. But the explanation is now clear. A picture must denote a man to represent him, but need not denote anything to be a man-representation. Incidentally, the copy theory of representation takes a further beating here; for where a representation does not represent anything there can be no question of resemblance to what it represents.

Use of such examples as Pickwick-pictures and unicorn-pictures may suggest that representations with null denotation are comparatively rare. Quite the contrary; the world of pictures teems with anonymous fictional persons, places, and things. The man in Rembrandt's *Landscape with a Huntsman* is presumably no actual person; he is just the man in Rembrandt's etching. In other words, the etching represents no man but is simply a man-picture, and more particularly a the-man-in-Rembrandt's-*Landscape-with-a-Huntsman*-picture. And even if an actual man be depicted here, his identity matters as little as the artist's blood-type. Furthermore, the information needed to determine what if anything is denoted by a picture is not always accessible. We may, for example, be unable to tell whether a given representation is multiple, like an eagle-picture in the dictionary, or fictive, like a Pickwick-picture. But where we cannot determine whether a picture denotes anything or not, we can only proceed as if it did not—that is, confine ourselves to considering what kind of picture it is. Thus cases of indeterminate denotation are treated in the same way as cases of null denotation.

But not only where the denotation is null or indeterminate does the classification of a picture need to be considered. For the denotation of a picture no more determines its kind than the kind of picture determines the denotation. Not every man-picture represents a man, and conversely not every picture that represents a man is a man-picture. And in the difference between being and not being a man-picture lies the difference, among pictures that denote a man, between those that do and those that do not represent him as a man. . . .

Realism

This leaves unanswered the minor question what constitutes realism of representation. Surely not, in view of the foregoing, any sort of resemblance to reality. Yet we do in fact compare representations with respect to their realism or naturalism or fidelity. If resemblance is not the criterion, what is?

One popular answer is that the test of fidelity is deception, that a picture is realistic just to the extent that it is a successful illusion, leading the viewer to suppose that it is, or has the characteristics of, what it represents. The proposed measure of realism, in other words, is the probability of confusing the representation with the represented. This is some improvement over the copy theory; for what counts here is not how closely the picture duplicates an object but how far the picture and object, under conditions of observation appropriate to each, give rise to the same responses and expectations. Furthermore, the theory is not immediately confounded by the fact that fictive representations differ in degree of realism; for even though there are no centaurs, a realistic picture might deceive me into taking it for a centaur.

Yet there are difficulties. What deceives depends upon what is observed, and what is observed varies with interests and habits. If the probability of confusion is 1, we no longer have representation—we have identity. Moreover, the probability seldom rises noticeably above zero for even the most guileful *trompe-l'œil* painting seen under ordinary gallery conditions. For seeing a picture as a picture precludes mistaking it for anything else; and the appropriate conditions of observation (e.g., framed, against a uniform background, etc.) are calculated to defeat deception. Deception enlists such mischief as a suggestive setting, or a peephole that occludes frame and background. And deception under such nonstandard conditions is no test of realism; for with enough staging, even the most unrealistic picture can deceive. Deception counts less as a measure of realism than as evidence of magicianship, and is a highly atypical mishap. In looking at the most realistic picture, I seldom suppose that I can literally reach into the distance, slice the tomato, or beat the drum. Rather, I recognize the images as signs for the objects and characteristics represented—signs that work instantly and unequivocally without being confused with what they denote. Of course, sometimes where deception does occur—say by a painted window in a mural—we may indeed call the picture realistic; but such cases provide no basis for the usual ordering of pictures in general as more or less realistic.

Thoughts along these lines have led to the suggestion that the most realistic picture is the one that provides the greatest amount of pertinent information. But this hypothesis can be quickly and completely refuted. Consider a realistic picture, painted in ordinary perspective and normal color, and a second picture just like the first except that the perspective is reversed and each color is replaced by its complementary. The second picture, appropriately interpreted, yields exactly the same information as the first. And any number of other drastic but information-preserving transformations are possible. Obviously, realistic and unrealistic pictures may be equally informative; informational yield is no test of realism.

So far, we have not needed to distinguish between fidelity and realism. The criteria considered earlier have been as unsatisfactory for the one as for the other. But we can no longer equate them. The two pictures just described are equally correct, equally faithful to what they represent, provide the same and hence equally true information; yet they are not equally realistic or literal. For a picture to be faithful is simply for the object represented to have the properties that the picture in effect ascribes to it. But such fidelity or correctness or truth is not a sufficient condition for literalism or realism.

The alert absolutist will argue that for the second picture but not the first we need a key. Rather, the difference is that for the first the key is ready at hand. For proper reading of the second picture, we have to discover rules of interpretation and apply them deliberately. Reading of the first is by virtually automatic habit; practice has rendered the symbols so transparent that we are not aware of any effort, of any alternatives, or of making any interpretation at all. Just here, I think, lies the touchstone of realism: not in quantity of information but in how easily it issues. And this depends upon how stereotyped the mode of representation is, upon how commonplace the labels and their uses have become.

Realism is relative, determined by the system of representation standard for a given culture or person at a given time. Newer or older or alien systems are accounted artificial or unskilled. For a Fifth-Dynasty Egyptian the straightforward way of representing something is not the same as for an eighteenth-century Japanese; and neither way is the same as for an early twentieth-century Englishman. Each would to some extent have to learn how to read a picture in either of the other styles. This relativity is obscured by our tendency to omit specifying a frame of reference when it is our own. "Realism" thus often comes to be used as the name for a particular style or system of representation. Just as on this planet we usually think of objects as fixed if they are at a constant position in relation to the earth, so in this period and place we usually think of paintings as literal or realistic if they are in a traditional European style of representation. But such egocentric ellipsis must not tempt us to infer that these objects (or any others) are absolutely fixed, or that such pictures (or any others) are absolutely realistic.

Shifts in standard can occur rather rapidly. The very effectiveness that may attend judicious departure from a traditional system of representation sometimes inclines us at least temporarily to install the newer mode as standard. We then speak of an artist's having achieved a new degree of realism, or having found new means for the realistic rendering of (say) light or motion. What happens here is something like the "discovery" that not the earth but the sun is "really fixed." Advantages of a new frame of reference, partly because of their novelty, encourage its enthronement on some occasions in place of the customary frame. Nevertheless, whether an object is "really fixed" or a picture is realistic depends at any time entirely upon what frame or mode is then standard. Realism is a matter not of any constant or absolute relationship between a picture and its object but of a relationship between the system of representation employed in the picture and the standard system. Most of the time, of course, the traditional system is taken as standard; and the literal or realistic or naturalistic system of representation is simply the customary one.

Realistic representation, in brief, depends not upon imitation or illusion or information but upon inculcation. Almost any picture may represent almost anything; that is, given picture and object there is usually a system of representation, a plan of correlation, under which the picture represents the object. How correct the picture is under that system depends upon how accurate is the information about the object that is obtained by reading the picture according to that system. But how literal or realistic the picture is depends upon how standard the system is. If representation is a matter of choice and correctness a matter of information, realism is a matter of habit. . . .

MIMESIS IN THE ARTS

An Essay on Criticism

ALEXANDER POPE

Part I

> 'Tis hard to say, if greater want of skill
> Appear in writing or in judging ill;
> But of the two less dangerous is the offense
> To tire our patience than mislead our sense.
> Some few in that, but numbers err in this,
> Ten censure wrong for one who writes amiss;
> A fool might once himself alone expose,
> Now one in verse makes many more in prose.
> 'Tis with our judgments as our watches, none
> Go just alike, yet each believes his own.
> In poets as true genius is but rare,

Alexander Pope, *An Essay on Criticism*, Part I.

True taste as seldom is the critic's share;
Both must alike from Heaven derive their light,
These born to judge, as well as those to write.
Let such teach others who themselves excel,
And censure freely who have written well.
Authors are partial to their wit, 'tis true,
But are not critics to their judgment too?
    Yet if we look more closely, we shall find
Most have the seeds of judgment in their mind:
Nature affords at least a glimmering light;
The lines, though touched but faintly, are drawn right.
But as the slightest sketch, if justly traced,
Is by ill coloring but the more disgraced,
So by false learning is good sense defaced;
Some are bewildered in the maze of schools,
And some made coxcombs Nature meant but fools.
In search of wit these lose their common sense,
And then turn critics in their own defense:
Each burns alike, who can, or cannot write,
Or with a rival's or an eunuch's spite.
All fools have still an itching to deride,
And fain would be upon the laughing side.
If Maevius scribble in Apollo's spite,
There are who judge still worse than he can write.
    Some have at first for wits, then poets passed,
Turned critics next, and proved plain fools at last.
Some neither can for wits nor critics pass,
As heavy mules are neither horse nor ass.
Those half-learn'd witlings, numerous in our isle,
As half-formed insects on the banks of Nile;
Unfinished things, one knows not what to call,
Their generation's so equivocal:
To tell them would a hundred tongues require,
Or one vain wit's, that might a hundred tire.
    But you who seek to give and merit fame,
And justly bear a critic's noble name,
Be sure yourself and your own reach to know,
How far your genius, taste, and learning go;
Launch not beyond your depth, but be discreet,
And mark that point where sense and dullness meet.
    Nature to all things fixed the limits fit,
And wisely curbed proud man's pretending wit.
As on the land while here the ocean gains,
In other parts it leaves wide sandy plains;
Thus in the soul while memory prevails,
The solid power of understanding fails;

Where beams of warm imagination play,
The memory's soft figures melt away.
One science only will one genius fit,
So vast is art, so narrow human wit.
Not only bounded to peculiar arts,
But oft in those confined to single parts.
Like kings we lose the conquests gained before,
By vain ambition still to make them more;
Each might his several province well command,
Would all but stoop to what they understand.
  First follow Nature, and your judgment frame
By her just standard, which is still the same;
Unerring Nature, still divinely bright,
One clear, unchanged, and universal light,
Life, force, and beauty must to all impart,
At once the source, and end, and test of art.
Art from that fund each just supply provides,
Works without show, and without pomp presides.
In some fair body thus the informing soul
With spirits feeds, with vigor fills the whole,
Each motion guides, and every nerve sustains;
Itself unseen, but in the effects remains.
Some, to whom Heaven in wit has been profuse,
Want as much more to turn it to its use;
For wit and judgment often are at strife,
Though meant each other's aid, like man and wife.
'Tis more to guide than spur the Muse's steed,
Restrain his fury than provoke his speed;
The wingéd courser, like a generous horse,
Shows most true mettle when you check his course.
  Those rules of old discovered, not devised,
Are Nature still, but Nature methodized;
Nature, like liberty, is but restrained
By the same laws which first herself ordained.
  Hear how learn'd Greece her useful rules indites,
When to repress and when indulge our flights:
High on Parnassus' top her sons she showed,
And pointed out those arduous paths they trod;
Held from afar, aloft, the immortal prize,
And urged the rest by equal steps to rise.
Just precepts thus from great examples given,
She drew from them what they derived from Heaven.
The generous critic fanned the poet's fire,
And taught the world with reason to admire.
Then criticism the Muse's handmaid proved,
To dress her charms, and make her more beloved:
But following wits from that intention strayed,
Who could not win the mistress, wooed the maid;

Against the poets their own arms they turned,
Sure to hate most the men from whom they learned.
So modern 'pothecaries, taught the art
By doctors' bills to play the doctor's part,
Bold in the practice of mistaken rules,
Prescribe, apply, and call their masters fools.
Some on the leaves of ancient authors prey,
Nor time nor moths e'er spoiled so much as they.
Some dryly plain, without invention's aid,
Write dull receipts how poems may be made.
These leave the sense their learning to display,
And those explain the meaning quite away.
　　　You then whose judgment the right course would steer,
Know well each ancient's proper character;
His fable, subject, scope in every page;
Religion, country, genius of his age:
Without all these at once before your eyes,
Cavil you may, but never criticize.
Be Homer's works your study and delight,
Read them by day, and meditate by night;
Thence form your judgment, thence your maxims bring,
And trace the Muses upward to their spring.
Still with itself compared, his text peruse;
And let your comment be the Mantuan Muse.
　　　When first young Maro in his boundless mind
A work to outlast immortal Rome designed,
Perhaps he seemed above the critic's law,
And but from Nature's fountains scorned to draw;
But when to examine every part he came,
Nature and Homer were, he found, the same.
Convinced, amazed, he checks the bold design,
And rules as strict his labored work confine
As if the Stagirite o'erlooked each line.
Learn hence for ancient rules a just esteem;
To copy Nature is to copy them.
　　　Some beauties yet no precepts can declare,
For there's a happiness as well as care.
Music resembles poetry, in each
Are nameless graces which no methods teach,
And which a master hand alone can reach.
If, where the rules not far enough extend
(Since rules were made but to promote their end)
Some lucky license answer to the full
The intent proposed, that license is a rule.
Thus Pegasus, a nearer way to take,
May boldly deviate from the common track.
From vulgar bounds with brave disorder part,
And snatch a grace beyond the reach of art,

Which without passing through the judgment, gains
The heart, and all its end at once attains.
In prospects thus, some objects please our eyes,
Which out of Nature's common order rise,
The shapeless rock, or hanging precipice.
Great wits sometimes may gloriously offend,
And rise to faults true critics dare not mend;
But though the ancients thus their rules invade
(As kings dispense with laws themselves have made)
Moderns, beware! or if you must offend
Against the precept, ne'er transgress its end;
Let it be seldom, and compelled by need;
And have at least their precedent to plead.
The critic else proceeds without remorse,
Seizes your fame, and puts his laws in force.

      I know there are, to whose presumptuous thoughts
Those freer beauties, even in them, seem faults.
Some figures monstrous and misshaped appear,
Considered singly, or beheld too near,
Which, but proportioned to their light or place,
Due distance reconciles to form and grace.
A prudent chief not always must display
His powers in equal ranks and fair array,
But with the occasion and the place comply,
Conceal his force, nay seem sometimes to fly.
Those oft are stratagems which errors seem,
Nor is it Homer nods, but we that dream.

      Still green with bays each ancient altar stands
Above the reach of sacrilegious hands,
Secure from flames, from envy's fiercer rage,
Destructive war, and all-involving age.
See, from each clime the learn'd their incense bring!
Here in all tongues consenting paeans ring!
In praise so just let every voice be joined,
And fill the general chorus of mankind.
Hail, bards triumphant! born in happier days,
Immortal heirs of universal praise!
Whose honors with increase of ages grow,
As streams roll down, enlarging as they flow;
Nations unborn your mighty names shall sound,
And worlds applaud that must not yet be found!
Oh, may some spark of your celestial fire,
The last, the meanest of your sons inspire
(That on weak wings, from far, pursues your flights,
Glows while he reads, but trembles as he writes)
To teach vain wits a science little known,
To admire superior sense, and doubt their own!

Discourses on Art

SIR JOSHUA REYNOLDS

Discourse 3 (December 14, 1770)

GENTLEMEN,

It is not easy to speak with propriety to so many students of different ages and different degrees of advancement. The mind requires nourishment adapted to its growth; and what may have promoted our earlier efforts, might retard us in our nearer approaches to perfection.

The first endeavours of a young painter, as I have remarked in a former discourse, must be employed in the attainment of mechanical dexterity, and confined to the mere imitation of the object before him. Those who have advanced beyond the rudiments, may, perhaps, find advantage in reflecting on the advice which I have likewise given them, when I recommended the diligent study of the works of our great predecessors; but I at the same time endeavoured to guard them against an implicit submission to the authority of any one master however excellent; or by a strict imitation of his manner, precluding themselves from the abundance and variety of nature. I will now add that nature herself is not to be too closely copied. There are excellencies in the art of painting beyond what is commonly called the imitation of nature: and these excellencies I wish to point out. The students who, having passed through the initiatory exercises, are more advanced in the art, and who, sure of their hand, have leisure to exert their understanding, must now be told, that a mere copier of nature can never produce any thing great; can never raise and enlarge the conceptions, warm the heart of the spectator.

The wish of the genuine painter must be more extensive: instead of endeavouring to amuse mankind with the minute neatness of his imitations, he must endeavour to improve them by the grandeur of his ideas; instead of seeking praise, by deceiving the superficial sense of the spectator, he must strive for fame, by captivating the imagination.

The principle now laid down, that the perfection of this art does not consist in mere imitation, is far from being new or singular. It is, indeed, supported by the general opinion of the enlightened part of mankind. The poets, orators, and rhetoricians of antiquity, are continually enforcing this position; that all the arts receive their perfection from an ideal beauty, superior to what is to be found in individual nature. They are ever referring to

Sir Joshua Reynolds, *Discourses on Art* (1797; rpt. Indianapolis: Bobbs-Merrill Publishing Co., 1965), selections from Discourses 3, 4, and 6.

the practice of the painters and sculptors of their times, particularly Phidias, (the favourite artist of antiquity,) to illustrate their assertions. As if they could not sufficiently express their admiration of his genius by what they knew, they have recourse to poetical enthusiasm. They call it inspiration; a gift from heaven. The artist is supposed to have ascended the celestial regions, to furnish his mind with this perfect idea of beauty. "He," says Proclus, "who takes for his model such forms as nature produces, and confines himself to an exact imitation of them, will never attain to what is perfectly beautiful. For the works of nature are full of disproportion, and fall very short of the true standard of beauty. So that Phidias, when he formed his Jupiter, did not copy any object ever presented to his sight; but contemplated only that image which he had conceived in his mind from Homer's description." And thus Cicero, speaking of the same Phidias: "Neither did this artist," says he, "when he carved the image of Jupiter or Minerva, set before him any one human figure, as a pattern, which he was to copy; but having a more perfect idea of beauty fixed in his mind, this he steadily contemplated, and to the imitation of this all his skill and labour were directed." . . .

It is not easy to define in what this great style consists; nor to describe, by words, the proper means of acquiring it, if the mind of the student should be at all capable of such an acquisition. Could we teach taste or genius by rules, they would be no longer taste and genius. But though there neither are, nor can be, any precise invariable rules for the exercise, or the acquisition, of these great qualities, yet we may truly say that they always operate in proportion to our attention in observing the works of nature, to our skill in selecting, and to our care in digesting, methodizing, and comparing our observations. There are many beauties in our art, that seem, at first, to lie without the reach of precept, and yet may easily be reduced to practical principles. Experience is all in all; but it is not every one who profits by experience; and most people err, not so much from want of capacity to find their object, as from not knowing what object to pursue. This great ideal perfection and beauty are not to be sought in the heavens, but upon earth. They are about us, and upon every side of us. But the power of discovering what is deformed in nature, or in other words, what is particular and uncommon, can be acquired only by experience; and the whole beauty and grandeur of the art consists, in my opinion, in being able to get above all singular forms, local customs, particularities, and details of every kind.

All the objects which are exhibited to our view by nature, upon close examination will be found to have their blemishes and defects. The most beautiful forms have something about them like weakness, minuteness, or imperfection. But it is not every eye that perceives these blemishes. It must be an eye long used to the contemplation and comparison of these forms; and which, by a long habit of observing what any set of objects of the same kind have in common, has acquired the power of discerning what each wants in particular. This long laborious comparison should be the first study of the painter, who aims at the greatest style. By this means, he acquires a just idea of beautiful forms; he corrects nature by herself, her imperfect state by her more perfect. His eye being enabled to distinguish the accidental deficiencies, excrescences, and deformities of things, from their general figures, he makes out an abstract idea of their forms more perfect than any one original; and what may seem a paradox, he learns to design naturally by drawing his figures unlike to any one object. This idea of the perfect state of nature, which the artist calls the ideal beauty, is the great leading principle, by which works of genius are conducted. By this Phidias acquired his fame. He wrought upon a sober principle, what has so much excited the enthusiasm of the world; and by this method you, who have courage to tread the same path, may acquire equal reputation.

This is the idea which has acquired, and which seems to have a right to the epithet of *divine*; as it may be said to preside, like a supreme judge, over all the productions of nature; appearing to be possessed of the will and intention of the Creator, as far as they regard the external form of living beings. When a man once possesses this idea in its perfection, there is no danger, but that he will be sufficiently warmed by it himself, and be able to warm and ravish every one else.

Thus it is from a reiterated experience, and a close comparison of the objects in nature, that an artist becomes possessed of the idea of that central form, if I may so express it, from which every deviation is deformity. But the investigation of this form, I grant, is painful, and I know but of one method of shortening the road; this is, by a careful study of the works of the ancient sculptors; who, being indefatigable in the school of nature, have left models of that perfect form behind them, which an artist would prefer as supremely beautiful, who had spent his whole life in that single contemplation. But if industry carried them thus far, may not you also hope for the same reward from the same labour? We have the same school opened to us, that was opened to them; for nature denies her instructions to none, who desire to become her pupils. . . .

Discourse 4

. . . Invention in painting does not imply the invention of the subject; for that is commonly supplied by the poet or historian. With respect to the choice, no subject can be proper that is not generally interesting. It ought to be either some eminent instance of heroick action, or heroick suffering. There must be something either in the action, or in the object, in which men are universally concerned, and which powerfully strikes upon the publick sympathy.

Strictly speaking, indeed, no subject can be of universal, hardly can it be of general, concern; but there are events and characters so popularly known in those countries where our art is in request, that they may be considered as sufficiently general for all our purposes. Such are the great events of Greek and Roman fable and history, which early education, and the usual course of reading, have made familiar and interesting to all Europe, without being degraded by the vulgarism of ordinary life in any country. Such too are the capital subjects of scripture history, which, besides their general notoriety, become venerable by their connection with our religion.

As it is required that the subject selected should be a general one, it is no less necessary that it should be kept unembarrassed with whatever may any way serve to divide the attention of the spectator. Whenever a story is related, every man forms a picture in his mind of the action and expression of the persons employed. The power of representing this mental picture on canvass is what we call invention in a painter. And as in the conception of this ideal picture, the mind does not enter into the minute peculiarities of the dress, furniture, or scene of action; so when the painter comes to represent it, he contrives those little necessary concomitant circumstances in such a manner, that they shall strike the spectator no more than they did himself in his first conception of the story.

I am very ready to allow that some circumstances of minuteness and particularity frequently tend to give an air of truth to a piece, and to interest the spectator in an extraordinary manner. Such circumstances therefore cannot wholly be rejected: but if there be any thing in the art which requires peculiar nicety of discernment, it is the disposition of these minute circumstantial parts; which, according to the judgment employed in the choice, become so useful to truth, or so injurious to grandeur.

However, the usual and most dangerous error is on the side of minuteness; and therefore I think caution most necessary where most have failed. The general idea constitutes real excellence. All smaller things, however perfect in their way, are to be sacrificed without mercy to the greater. The painter will not enquire what things may be admitted without much censure: he will not think it enough to shew that they may be there; he will shew that they must be there; that their absence would render his picture maimed and defective.

Thus, though to the principal group a second or third be added, and a second and third mass of light, care must be yet taken that these subordinate actions and lights, neither each in particular, nor all together, come into any degree of competition with the principal; they should merely make a part of that whole which would be imperfect without them. To every kind of painting this rule may be applied. Even in portraits, the grace, and, we may add, the likeness, consists more in taking the general air, than in observing the exact similitude of every feature. . . . there is not a fault, but what may take shelter under the most venerable authorities; yet that style only is perfect, in which the noblest principles are uniformly pursued; and those masters only are entitled to the first rank in our estimation, who have enlarged the boundaries of their art, and have raised it to its highest dignity, by exhibiting the general ideas of nature.

On the whole, it seems to me that there is but one presiding principle which regulates, and gives stability to every art. The works, whether of poets, painters, moralists, or historians, which are built upon general nature, live for ever; while those which depend for their existence on particular customs and habits, a partial view of nature, or the fluctuation of fashion, can only be coeval with that which first raised them from obscurity. Present time and future may be considered as rivals, and he who solicits the one must expect to be discountenanced by the other. . . .

Discourse 6

. . . But to bring us entirely to reason and sobriety, let it be observed, that a painter must not only be of necessity an imitator of the works of nature, which alone is sufficient to dispel this phantom of inspiration, but he must be as necessarily an imitator of the works of other painters: this appears more humiliating, but is equally true; and no man can be an artist, whatever he may suppose, upon any other terms.

However, those who appear more moderate and reasonable, allow, that our study is to begin by imitation; but maintain that we should no longer use the thoughts of our predecessors, when we are become able to think for ourselves. They hold that imitation is as hurtful to the more advanced student, as it was advantageous to the beginner.

For my own part, I confess, I am not only very much disposed to maintain the absolute necessity of imiation in the first stages of the art; but am of opinion, that the study of other masters, which I here call imitation, may be extended throughout our whole lives, without any danger of the inconveniences with which it is charged, of enfeebling the mind, or preventing us from giving that original air which every work undoubtedly ought always to have.

I am on the contrary persuaded, that by imitation only, variety, and even originality of invention, is produced. I will go further; even genius, at least what generally is so called, is the child of imitation. But as this appears to be contrary to the general opinion, I must explain my position before I enforce it.

Genius is supposed to be a power of producing excellencies, which are out of the reach of the rules of art; a power which no precepts can teach, and which no industry can acquire.

This opinion of the impossibility of acquiring those beauties, which stamp the work with the character of genius, supposes, that it is something more fixed than in reality it is; and that we always do, and ever did agree in opinion, with respect to what should be considered as the characteristick of genius. But the truth is, that the *degree* of excellence which proclaims *genius* is different, in different times and different places; and what shews it to be so is, that mankind have often changed their opinion upon this matter.

When the arts were in their infancy, the power of merely drawing the likeness of any object, was considered as one of its greatest efforts. The common people, ignorant of the principles of art, talk the same language, even to this day. But when it was found that every man could be taught to do this, and a great deal more, merely by the observance of certain precepts; the name of genius then shifted its application, and was given only to him who added the peculiar character of the object he represented; to him who had invention, expression, grace, or dignity; in short, those qualities, or excellencies, the power of producing which, could not *then* be taught by any known and promulgated rules.

We are very sure that the beauty of form, the expression of the passions, the art of composition, even the power of giving a general air of grandeur to a work, is at present very much under the dominion of rules. These excellencies were, heretofore, considered merely as the effects of genius; and justly, if genius is not taken for inspiration, but as the effect of close observation and experience. . . .

What we now call genius, begins, not where rules, abstractedly taken, end; but where known vulgar and trite rules have no longer any place. It must of necessity be, that even works of genius, like every other effect, as they must have their cause, must likewise have their rules; it cannot be by chance, that excellencies are produced with any constancy or any certainty, for this is not the nature of chance; but the rules by which men of extraordinary parts, and such as are called men of genius work, are either such as they discover by their own peculiar observations, or of such a nice texture as not easily to admit being expressed in words; especially as artists are not very frequently skilful in that mode of communicating ideas. Unsubstantial, however, as these rules may seem, and difficult as it may be to convey them in writing, they are still seen and felt in the mind of the artist; and he works from them with as much certainty, as if they were embodied, as I may say, upon paper. It is true, these refined principles cannot be always made palpable, like the more gross rules of art; yet it does not follow, but that the mind may be put in such a train, that it shall perceive, by a kind of scientifick sense, that propriety, which words, particularly words of unpractised writers, such as we are, can but very feebly suggest.

Invention is one of the great marks of genius; but if we consult experience, we shall find, that it is by being conversant with the inventions of others, that we learn to invent; as by reading the thoughts of others we learn to think. . . .

Constructionism and Mimesis

CHARLES BIEDERMAN

Less than three-quarters of a century after the appearance of the first successful Photograph, artists discovered how to invent their own art contents, independent of copying in any degree the macroscopic forms of nature. After 2,000 years of direct effort to do so, man is now able to use "invention" in his art, no longer frustrated by the Mimetic factor. *He no longer competes with nature at all*, but as we shall see, he *continues to employ nature*, in a more effective manner, to gain his desired objective of "invention."

. . . We discussed the early stages of the development of Sculpture, we remarked that the Inventive and Mimetic factors are never found isolated from each other throughout man's entire history of art; the problem always was a matter of *degrees* and *kinds* of Mimetic and Inventive behavior. This is still true as regards Constructionist art; the Constructionist, to mention only this one aspect, does not invent the notion of three-dimensional colored forms; he finds the source of this notion in the phenomena of nature. What he does invent is the *particular organization* of three-dimensional color-forms! In the past the artist "imitated" the *results* of nature-art; today the new artist only "imitates" the *method* of nature-art! This is the crux of the matter. As we have made clear in the chapter on the term "abstract," an artist, in order to avoid the Mimetic factor in any degree would have to exclude *all* the characteristics found in nature—an impossibility. . . .

Therefore, the prevalent notion is false that the Constructionist is concerned with the denial of nature: the Constructionist is striving to do what all the great innovators in art have always done, *to continue the evolution of the artist's ability to abstract from the objective world around him for purposes of achieving a legitimate contemporary art.*

We have noted that the new reality level from which the artist can now abstract is the Structural Process level, the *building method of nature*, and no longer the macro-level, the form-results of nature. We have also noted that many of the Painting artists were unconsciously struggling under various handicaps to abstract from the Structural Process level rather than from the results of that level.

Naturally the first move in the direction of abstracting from the Structural Process level would be to acquire the *reality characteristics* of this level. *To accomplish this objective it was necessary to employ a medium or mediums whose structure CORRESPONDED to the structure of reality.* Here lies the

Charles Biederman, *Art as the Evolution of Visual Knowledge* (Redwing, Minnesota: Charles Biederman, 1948), selections from Chapters 18 and 25, pp. 390, 552–568.

solution of one of the main difficulties which faced the Two-Dimensionalists and others—"the problem of reality." By making this change in medium the new art direction of invention acquired one of the characteristics of *reality* which was lacking in the linear medium, i.e., *actual* three-dimensionality in *actual* space. Thus a correction was made from the dead-end medium of the Two-Dimensionalists to the actual space-form art of the Constructionists. It was in that change that the Constructionists achieved an adequate reality for the new art. Now a man-invented form, for example, a man-made sphere, an actual three-dimensional sphere, was just as real as an apple, but there was no need for it to be the form of an apple: and since no Painting of a sphere was made, no illusion of it was made. Here was the solution for those who *painted* two- and three-dimensional illusions of invented forms. By giving the invented contents actual three dimensions in space, the Constructionists achieved a *structure for their new art contents which was SIMILAR (NON-IDENTITY) IN STRUCTURE TO THE STRUCTURE OF ACTUAL REALITY.* As in nature—the criterion of reality—the *art of man* now possesses the three-dimensional characteristics of REALITY.

. . . We are *not* dealing with a question of whether we are to be satisfied merely with depicting the "basic elements," or whether we will "add" the forms of nature. No one can paint or construct the "skeletal" or "basic elements" or what have you, which supposedly exist in past art or in nature, *without producing some kind of a nature recording.* There is simply no such thing as structure or "basic elements" or "composition" alone; there is only structure in a CONTEXT, the structure OF *something* in relation to something, of one part of something to another part of something, in one KIND of ORDER or another. There are only similarities and dissimilarities between man's art structures or form-results and unaided nature structures or form-results. All we can produce in our art are particular kinds of structural results, the kind being determined by the kind of abstracting from nature that is involved. . . .

Nature teaches us the methods and structural conditions by which to solve problems; but to copy the *results* of those methods is futile, unless the objective is to make a record. Today, therefore, the artist either uses a Camera, if he wishes to record nature's art, or else invents his art contents if he wishes to create. He cannot abstract from nature's art and presume that he is "creating" a man-art. Nature's art, however, has been the means by which man has arrived at the notion of man-art, just as the bird suggested the airplane. And as with the airplane, man must invent his own art by studying the Structural Process of nature and not by copying its results. By abstracting from the structural level of reality, man opens up for himself all the possibilities of that level as evidenced in the phenomena of nature all about us. Nature is no longer to be regarded as something to compete with, but as something which can be *extended according to natural laws in directions useful to man's evolving deeds.* Without man's great capacity to invent, human culture would be utterly impossible. The legitimate artists and scientists of today are simply continuing, i.e., extending, this process, a process of human evolution, the evolution of nature. . . .

Men once thought that ghosts and spirits inhabited animate and inanimate objects alike. Such beliefs determined the kind of interpretations men made of reality. For the greater part of man's existence his major concern has been with the macroscopic level of reality, just as the artist's major concern has been to record and abstract from that level of reality. Today, however, we live in a world of science, not magic or religion or philosophy, and men have found that hidden beneath the macroscopics of nature are not ghosts, and the like, but different levels of reality, the micro- and submicroscopic levels. Today artists and scientists alike are striving to penetrate the macroscopic level of nature towards a more adequate comprehension and exploitation of the world reality process in which we live. We know that the macrolevel is only one aspect or level of reality. Our problems today deal with *various levels of reality.* As man evolves so does his comprehension of the world in which he lives. It is our responsibility to recognize this, to recognize the particular stage of that development in our own times and to proceed accordingly.

Yet many of us still live on a cultural level comparable to that of the men who warned Columbus that he would drop over the edge of the world if he ventured too far out to sea or of those men who thought the whole universe revolved around the earth. Such men became hysterical, then violent when a few scientifically minded individuals discovered their error, just as their counterparts do today when advanced scientists and artists state the goals towards which they are directing their researches. It is just as absurd to allocate the problems of "art" and "reality" in a past context today as it is to expect the past to have faced the problems peculiar to the present. In short, we must historically allocate the problems of art. Then we shall find interests and opportunities unheard of in the past which today await the more adventuresome.

ILLUSTRATION 1
Vénus de Milo, reproduced by permission of
the Musée du Louvre.

ILLUSTRATION 2

SIR JOSHUA REYNOLDS, *Lady Elizabeth
Delmé and Her Children* (95), National Gal-
lery of Art, Washington, Andrew W. Mellon
Collection.

ILLUSTRATION 3

JOHN CONSTABLE, *Wivenhoe Park, Essex* (606), National Gallery of Art, Washington, Widener Collection.

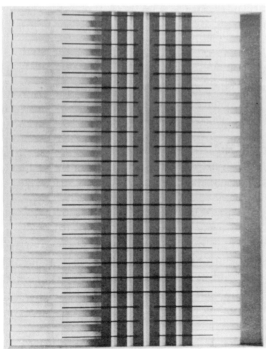

ILLUSTRATION 4

CHARLES BIEDERMAN, *Construction 10/39 (9)*, 1939. Reproduced with the permission of the artist.

2
Didacticism

The readings in the preceding chapter were concerned with what art is, and what works of art can or should *be*. The readings in this chapter concern what art can or should *do*. These theories, often called didactic theories, do not conceive of art as autonomous; rather, they examine the purposes of art. Some focus on the significance of the embodiment of values or truth in art and how these are communicated to an audience. Other views claim that because art is created by individuals and, because what is created is a perceivable phenomenon, art cannot be divorced from the purpose of the artist nor from its impact on viewers. And, if art is a unique cultural phenomenon, its purposes are unique to that phenomenon.

In a very famous passage, Sir Phillip Sidney stated:

> Poesy therefore is the art of imitation, for so Aristotle termeth it in his word *mimesis*, that is to say, a representing, counterfeiting, or figuring forth-to speak metaphorically, a speaking picture-with this end, to teach and delight. . . .

This statement illustrates a traditional Classical view that art is mimetic, and that art should be amusing, pleasant, even delightful, in order to function in a more important way: to teach its audience through proper representation.

Many philosophers argue that quality in art is not to be equated with amusement. Just because a work of art is entertaining is not necessarily a sign that it has aesthetic quality, and alternately, not all serious works of art are good. But Sidney had in mind something more profound in his statement. To delight, according to Sidney, is a means to interest the audience in what is being represented, thereby arousing their attention to what is being taught. Sidney was suggesting that art functions in such a way as to represent or correspond to an objective truth which can be communicated to an audience. Sidney's own work, *Thou Blind Man's Mark* (Illustration 5), illustrates these mimetic and functional roles of art.

Sidney's view emphasizes the didactic as well as the mimetic function of art. A didactic theory claims that art directly affects or should affect its audience and that this utilitarian function is essential to art. Art may function in one or all of the following ways: it may arouse emotions or attitudes among its viewers; it may perform an important social, moral, or religious function; or it may delight its audience or teach them something. In each case what the artwork *does*—that is, whether it teaches, delights, evaluates, or moralizes—is more important than what it *is*, for example, a presentation, a representation, or an expression. Aristotle's notion that art should communicate to its audience by arousing or evoking emotions is an early statement of didacticism in art theory.

Leo Tolstoy, the nineteenth-century Russian novelist and philosopher, developed another form of a didactic or communicative theory of art. Tolstoy argues that art is not mimetic, or representational, as Sidney claimed. Rather, art is a means through which an artist expresses his or her feelings and emotions. But what is expressed in art, Tolstoy claims, is automatically communicated to the audience through the perceived work and felt by the viewer. Because artworks are public, this communication takes place whether or not this is the deliberate intention of the artist. Thus all art "affects," or as Tolstoy suggests, "infects," its audiences. Tolstoy argues further that because all art communicates, the most valuable art should communicate the deepest and most profound human emotions. More specifically, Tolstoy claims that true art or universal art should communicate moral and, even more importantly, religious feelings. This leads Tolstoy to the conclusion that Christian art is the most universal of these, because, according to Tolstoy, it most sincerely and profoundly expresses man's feelings of brotherhood and spirituality in a way understood by everyone.

The difficulties with theories such as Sidney's or Tolstoy's are at least two-fold. First, if art should function to teach, delight, arouse, or communicate emotions to its audience, what of the many works which fail to do so? Second, some nonart phenomena communicate to audiences very well: amusement parks, sermons, moral treatises, and even philosophy may perform these didactic functions better than comparable works of art. Thus to identify art with some sort of value function does not necessarily focus on what is unique to art, and such a view may neglect mention of what works of art do best. On the other hand, Picasso's *Guernica* (Illustration 6) demonstrates how great works of art can express deep human truths which may or may not have a didactic effect.

The Purposes of Poetry

SIR PHILIP SIDNEY

Nature never set forth the earth in so rich tapestry as divers poets have done; neither with pleasant rivers, fruitful trees, sweet-smelling flowers, nor whatsoever else may make the too much loved earth more lovely. Her world is brazen, the poets only deliver a golden.

But let those things alone, and go to man—for whom as the other things are, so it seemeth in him her uttermost cunning is employed—and know whether she have brought forth so true a lover as Theagenes, so constant a friend as Pylades, so valiant a man as Orlando, so right a prince as Xenophon's Cyrus, so excellent a man every way as Virgil's Aeneas. Neither let this be jestingly conceived, because the works of the one be essential, the other in imitation or fiction; for any understanding knoweth the skill of the artificer standeth in that *Idea* or fore-conceit of the work, and not in the work itself. And that the poet hath that *Idea* is manifest, by delivering them forth in such excellency as he hath imagined them. Which delivering forth also is not wholly imaginative, as we are wont to say by them that build castles in the air; but so far substantially it worketh, not only to make a Cyrus, which had been but a particular excellency as Nature might have done, but to bestow a Cyrus upon the world to make many Cyruses, if they will learn aright why and how that maker made him.

Neither let it be deemed too saucy a comparison to balance the highest point of man's wit with the efficacy of Nature; but rather give right honour to the heavenly Maker of that maker, who having made man to His own likeness, set him beyond and over all the works of that second nature: which in nothing he showeth so much as in Poetry, when with the force of a divine breath he bringeth things forth far surpassing her doings, with no small argument to the incredulous of that first accursed fall of Adam: since our erected wit maketh us know what perfection is, and yet our infected will keepeth us from reaching unto it. But these arguments will by few be understood, and by fewer granted. Thus much (I hope) will be given me, that the Greeks with some probability of reason gave him the name above all names of learning.

Now let us go to a more ordinary opening of him, that the truth may be more palpable: and so I hope, though we get not so unmatched a praise as the etymology of his names will grant, yet his very description, which no man will deny, shall not justly be barred from a principal commendation.

Poesy therefore is an art of imitation, for so Aristotle termeth it in his word *mimesis,* that is to say, representing, counterfeiting, or figuring forth—

Sir Philip Sidney, *An Apology for Poetry*, ed. Geoffrey Shepherd (London; 1595; rpt. 1965).

to speak metaphorically, a speaking picture—with this end, to teach and delight.

Of this have been three several kinds. The chief, both in antiquity and excellency, were they that did imitate the inconceivable excellencies of God. Such were David in his Psalms; Solomon in his Song of Songs, in his Ecclesiastes, and Proverbs; Moses and Deborah in their Hymns; and the writer of Job: which, beside other, the learned Emanuel Tremellius and Franciscus Junius do entitle the poetical part of the Scripture. Against these none will speak that hath the Holy Ghost in due holy reverence. In this kind, though in a full wrong divinity, were Orpheus, Amphion, Homer in his Hymns, and many other, both Greeks and Romans. And this poesy must be used by whosoever will follow St. James's counsel in singing psalms when they are merry, and I know is used with the fruit of comfort by some, when, in sorrowful pangs of their death-bringing sins, they find the consolation of the never-leaving goodness.

The second kind is of them that deal with matters philosophical: either moral, as Tyrtaeus, Phocylides, and Cato; or natural, as Lucretius and Virgil's Georgics; or astronomical, as Manilius and Pontanus; or historical, as Lucan: which who mislike, the fault is in their judgements quite out of taste, and not in the sweet food of sweetly uttered knowledge.

But because this second sort is wrapped within the fold of the proposed subject, and takes not the course of his own invention, whether they properly be poets or no let grammarians dispute, and go to the third, indeed right poets, of whom chiefly this question ariseth. Betwixt whom and these second is such a kind of difference as betwixt the meaner sort of painters, who counterfeit only such faces as are set before them, and the more excellent, who having no law but wit, bestow that in colours upon you which is fittest for the eye to see: as the constant though lamenting look of Lucretia, when she punished in herself another's fault; wherein he painteth not Lucretia whom he never saw, but painteth the outward beauty of such a virtue. For these third be they which most properly do imitate to teach and delight, and to imitate borrow nothing of what is, hath been, or shall be; but range, only reined with learned discretion, into the divine consideration of what may be and should be. These be they that, as the first and most noble sort may justly be termed *vates,* so these are waited on in the excellentest languages and best understandings, with the foredescribed name of poets; for these indeed do merely make to imitate, and imitate both to delight and teach: and delight to move men to take that goodness in hand, which without delight they would fly as from a stranger, and teach, to make them know that goodness whereunto they are moved: which being the noblest scope to which ever any learning was directed, yet want there not idle tongues to bark at them. . . .

Now therein of all sciences (I speak still of human, and according to the human conceits) is our poet the monarch. For he doth not only show the way, but giveth so sweet a prospect into the way, as will entice any man to enter into it. Nay, he doth, as if your journey should lie through a fair vineyard, at the first give you a cluster of grapes, that full of that taste, you may long to pass further. He beginneth not with obscure definitions, which must blur the margent with interpretations, and load the memory with doubtfulness; but he cometh to you with words set in delightful proportion, either accompanied with, or prepared for, the well enchanting skill of music; and with a tale forsooth he cometh unto you, with a tale which holdeth children from play, and old men from the chimney corner. And, pretending no more, doth intend the winning of the mind from wickedness to virtue: even as the child is often brought to take most wholesome things by hiding them in such other as have a pleasant taste: which, if one should begin to tell them the nature of aloes or rhubarb they should receive, would sooner take their physic at their ears than at their mouth. So is it in men (most of which are childish in the best things, till they be cradled in their graves): glad they will be to hear the tales of Hercules, Achilles, Cyrus, and Aeneas; and, hearing them, must needs hear the right description of wisdom, valour, and justice; which, if they had been barely, that is to say philosophically, set out, they would swear they be brought to school again.

That imitation whereof Poetry is, hath the most conveniency to Nature of all other, insomuch that, as Aristotle saith, those things which in themselves are horrible, as cruel battles, unnatural monsters, are made in poetical imitation delightful. Truly, I have known men, that even with reading *Amadis de Gaule* (which God knoweth wanteth much of a perfect poesy) have found their hearts moved to the exercise of courtesy, liberality, and especially courage. Who readeth Aeneas carrying old Anchises on his back, that wisheth not it were his fortune to perform so excellent an act? Whom do not the words of Turnus move, the tale of Turnus having planted his image in the imagination?

> *Fugientem haec terra videbit?*
> *Usque adeone mori miserum est?*

Where the philosophers, as they scorn to delight, so must they be content little to move—saving wrangling whether virtue be the chief or the only good, whether the contemplative or the active life do excel—which Plato and Boethius well knew, and therefore made mistress Philosophy very often borrow the masking raiment of Poesy. For even those hard-hearted evil men who think virtue a school name, and know no other good but *indulgere genio,* and therefore despise the austere admonitions of the philosopher, and feel not the inward reason they stand upon, yet will be content to be delighted— which is all the good-fellow poet seemeth to promise—and so steal to see the form of goodness (which seen they cannot but love) ere themselves be aware, as if they took a medicine of cherries.

Infinite proofs of the strange effects of this poetical invention might be alleged; only two shall serve, which are so often remembered as I think all men know them. The one of Menenius Agrippa, who, when the whole people of Rome had resolutely divided themselves from the senate, with apparent show of utter ruin, though he were (for that time) an excellent orator, came not among them upon trust of figurative speeches or cunning insinuations, and much less with farfetched maxims of Philosophy, which (especially if they were Platonic) they must have learned geometry before they could well have conceived; but forsooth he behaves himself like a homely and familiar poet. He telleth them a tale, that there was a time when all the parts of the body made a mutinous conspiracy against the belly, which they thought devoured the fruits of each other's labour: they concluded they would let so unprofitable a spender starve. In the end, to be short (for the tale is notorious, and as notorious that it was a tale), with punishing the belly they plagued themselves. This applied by him wrought such effect in the people, as I never read that ever words brought forth but then so sudden and so good an alteration; for upon reasonable conditions a perfect reconcilement ensued. The other is of Nathan the prophet, who, when the holy David had so far forsaken God as to confirm adultery with murder, when he was to do the tenderest office of a friend, in laying his own shame before his eyes, sent by God to call again so chosen a servant, how doth he it but by telling of a man whose beloved lamb was ungratefully taken from his bosom?—the application most divinely true, but the discourse itself feigned; which made David (I speak of the second and instrumental cause) as in a glass to see his own filthiness, as that heavenly psalm of mercy well testifieth.

By these, therefore, examples and reasons, I think it may be manifest that the poet, with that same hand of delight, doth draw the mind more effectually than any other art doth. And so a conclusion not unfitly ensueth: that, as virtue is the most excellent resting place for all worldly learning to make his end of, so Poetry, being the most familiar to teach it, and most princely to move towards it, in the most excellent work is the most excellent workman.

So that since the ever-praiseworthy Poesy is full of virtue-breeding delightfulness, and void of no gift that ought to be in the noble name of learning; since the blames laid against it are either false or feeble; since the cause why it is not esteemed in England is the fault of poet-apes, not poets; since, lastly, our tongue is most fit to honour Poesy, and to be honoured by Poesy; I conjure you all that have had the evil luck to read this ink-wasting toy of mine, even in the name of the Nine Muses, no more to scorn the sacred mysteries of Poesy, no more to laugh at the name of poets, as though they were next inheritors to fools, no more to jest at the reverent title of a rhymer; but to believe, with Aristotle, that they were the ancient treasurers of the Grecians' divinity; to believe, with Bembus, that they were first bringers-in of all civility; to believe, with Scaliger, that no philosopher's precepts can sooner make you an honest man than the reading of Virgil; to believe, with Clauserus, the translator of Cornutus, that it pleased the heavenly Deity, by

Hesiod and Homer, under the veil of fables, to give us all knowledge, Logic, Rhetoric, Philosophy natural and moral, and *quid non?*; to believe, with me, that there are many mysteries contained in Poetry, which of purpose were written darkly, lest by profane wits it should be abused; to believe, with Landino, that they are so beloved of the gods that whatsoever they write proceeds of a divine fury; lastly, to believe themselves, when they tell you they will make you immortal by their verses.

Thus doing, your name shall flourish in the printers' shops; thus doing, you shall be of kin to many a poetical preface; thus doing, you shall be most fair, most rich, most wise, most all; you shall dwell upon superlatives. Thus doing, though you be *libertino patre natus,* you shall suddenly grow *Herculea proles,*

Si quid mea carmina possunt.

Thus doing, your soul shall be placed with Dante's Beatrix, or Virgil's Anchises. But if (fie of such a but) you be born so near the dull-making cataract of Nilus that you cannot hear the planet-like music of Poetry, if you have so earth-creeping a mind that it cannot lift itself up to look to the sky of Poetry, or rather, by a certain rustical disdain, will become such a mome as to be a Momus of Poetry; then, though I will not wish unto you the ass's ears of Midas, nor to be driven by a poet's verses (as Bubonax was) to hang himself, nor to be rhymed to death, as is said to be done in Ireland; yet thus much curse I must send you, in the behalf of all poets, that while you live, you live in love, and never get favour for lacking skill of a sonnet, and, when you die, your memory die from the earth for want of an epitaph.

The Moral and the Spiritual in Art

LEO TOLSTOY

In order correctly to define art, it is necessary, first of all, to cease to consider it as a means to pleasure and to consider it as one of the conditions of human life. Viewing it in this way we cannot fail to observe that art is one of the means of intercourse between man and man.

Every work of art causes the receiver to enter into a certain kind of relationship both with him who produced, or is producing, the art, and with all those who, simultaneously, previously, or subsequently, receive the same artistic impression.

Speech, transmitting the thoughts and experiences of men, serves as a means of union among them, and art acts in a similar manner. The peculiarity of this latter means of intercourse, distinguishing it from intercourse by means of words, consists in this, that whereas by words a man transmits his thoughts to another, by means of art he transmits his feelings.

The activity of art is based on the fact that a man, receiving through his sense of hearing or sight another man's expression of feeling, is capable of experiencing the emotion which moved the man who expressed it. To take the simplest example: one man laughs, and another who hears becomes merry; or a man weeps, and another who hears feels sorrow. A man is excited or irritated, and another man seeing him comes to a similar state of mind. By his movements or by the sounds of his voice, a man expresses courage and determination or sadness and calmness, and this state of mind passes on to others. A man suffers, expressing his sufferings by groans and spasms, and this suffering transmits itself to other people; a man expresses his feeling of admiration, devotion, fear, respect, or love to certain objects, persons, or phenomena, and others are infected by the same feelings of admiration, devotion, fear, respect, or love to the same objects, persons, and phenomena.

And it is upon this capacity of man to receive another man's expression of feeling and experience those feelings himself, that the activity of art is based.

If a man infects another or others directly, immediately, by his appearance or by the sounds he gives vent to at the very time he experiences the feeling; if he causes another man to yawn when he himself cannot help yawning, or to laugh or cry when he himself is obliged to laugh or cry, or to suffer when he himself is suffering—that does not amount to art.

Art begins when one person, with the object of joining another or others to himself in one and the same feeling, expresses that feeling by certain external indications. To take the simplest example: a boy, having experienced, let us say, fear on encountering a wolf, relates that encounter; and, in order to evoke in others the feeling he has experienced, describes himself, his condition before the encounter, the surroundings, the wood, his own light-heartedness, and then the wolf's appearance, its movements, the distance between himself and the wolf, etc. All this, if only the boy, when telling the story, again experiences the feelings he had lived through and infects the hearers and compels them to feel what the narrator had experienced, is art. If even the boy had not seen a wolf but had frequently been afraid of one, and if, wishing to evoke in others the fear he had felt, he invented an encounter with a wolf and recounted it so as to make his hearers share the feelings he experienced when he feared the wolf, that also would be art. And just in the same way it is art if a man, having experienced either the fear of suffering or the attraction of enjoyment (whether in reality or in imagination), expresses these feelings on canvas or in marble so that others are infected by them. And it is also art if a man feels or imagines to himself feelings of delight, gladness, sorrow, despair, courage, or despondency and the transition from one to another of these feelings, and expresses these feelings by sounds so that the hearers are infected by them and experience them as they were experienced by the composer.

The feelings with which the artist infects others may be most various— very strong or very weak, very important or very insignificant, very bad or very good: feelings of love for one's own country, self-devotion and submission to fate or to God expressed in a drama, raptures of lovers described in a novel, feelings of voluptuousness expressed in a picture, courage expressed in a triumphal march, merriment evoked by a dance, humor evoked by a funny story, the feeling of quietness transmitted by an evening landscape or by a lullaby, or the feeling of admiration evoked by a beautiful arabesque— it is all art.

If only the spectators or auditors are infected by the feelings which the author has felt, it is art.

To evoke in oneself a feeling one has once experienced, and having evoked it in oneself, then, by means of movements, lines, colors, sounds, or forms expressed in words, so to transmit that feeling that others may experience the same feeling—this is the activity of art.

Art is a human activity consisting in this, that one man consciously, by means of certain external signs, hands on to others feelings he has lived through, and that other people are infected by these feelings and also experience them.

Art is not, as the metaphysicians say, the manifestation of some mysterious Idea of beauty or God; it is not, as the aesthetical physiologists say, a game in which man lets off his excess of stored-up energy; it is not the expression of man's emotions by external signs; it is not the production of pleasing objects; and, above all, it is not pleasure; but is a means of union among men, joining them together in the same feelings, and indispensable for the life and progress toward well-being of individuals and of humanity.

As, thanks to man's capacity to express thoughts by words, every man may know all that has been done for him in the realms of thought by all humanity before his day, and can in the present, thanks to this capacity to understand the thoughts of others, become a sharer in their activity and can himself hand on to his contemporaries and descendants the thoughts he has assimilated from others, as well as those which have arisen within himself; so, thanks to man's capacity to be infected with the feelings of others by means of art, all that is being lived through by his contemporaries is accessible to him, as well as the feelings experienced by men thousands of years ago, and he has also the possibility of transmitting his own feelings to others. . . .

Art, in our society, has been so perverted that not only has bad art come to be considered good, but even the very perception of what art really is has been lost. In order to be able to speak about the art of our society, it is, therefore, first of all necessary to distinguish art from counterfeit art.

There is one indubitable indication distinguishing real art from its counterfeit, namely, the infectiousness of art. If a man, without exercising effort and without altering his standpoint on reading, hearing, or seeing another man's work, experiences a mental condition which unites him with that man and with other people who also partake of that work of art, then the object evoking that condition is a work of art. And however poetical, realistic, effectful, or interesting a work may be, it is not a work of art if it does not evoke that feeling (quite distinct from all other feelings) of joy and of spiritual union with another (the author) and with others (those who are also infected by it).

It is true that this indication is an *internal* one, and that there are people who have forgotten what the action of real art is, who expect something else from art (in our society the great majority are in this state), and that therefore such people may mistake for this aesthetic feeling the feeling of diversion and a certain excitement which they receive from counterfeits of art. But though it is impossible to undeceive these people, just as it is impossible to convince a man suffering from "Daltonism" that green is not red, yet, for all that, this indication remains perfectly definite to those whose feeling for art is neither perverted nor atrophied, and it clearly distinguishes the feeling produced by art from all other feelings.

The chief peculiarity of this feeling is that the receiver of a true artistic impression is so united to the artist that he feels as if the work were his own and not someone else's—as if what it expresses were just what he had long been wishing to express. A real work of art destroys, in the consciousness of the receiver, the separation between himself and the artist—not that alone, but also between himself and all whose minds receive this work of art. In this freeing of our personality from its separation and isolation, in this uniting of it with others, lies the chief characteristic and the great attractive force of art.

If a man is infected by the author's condition of soul, if he feels this emotion and this union with others, then the object which has effected this is art; but if there be no such infection, if there be not this union with the author and with others who are moved by the same work—then it is not art. And not only is infection a sure sign of art, but the degree of infectiousness is also the sole measure of excellence in art.

The stronger the infection, the better is the art as art, speaking now apart from its subject matter, i.e., not considering the quality of the feelings it transmits.

And the degree of the infectiousness of art depends on three conditions:

1. On the greater or lesser individuality of the feeling transmitted;

2. On the greater or lesser clearness with which the feeling is transmitted;

3. On the sincerity of the artist, i.e., on the greater or lesser force with which the artist himself feels the emotion he transmits.

The more individual the feeling transmitted the more strongly does it act on the receiver; the more individual the state of soul into which he is transferred, the more pleasure does the receiver obtain, and therefore the more readily and strongly does he join in it.

The clearness of expression assists infection because the receiver, who mingles in consciousness with the author, is the better satisfied the more clearly the feeling is transmitted, which, as it seems to him, he has long known and felt, and for which he has only now found expression.

But most of all is the degree of infectiousness of art increased by the degree of sincerity in the artist. As soon as the spectator, hearer, or reader feels that the artist is infected by his own production, and writes, sings, or plays for himself, and not merely to act on others, this mental condition of the artist infects the receiver; and contrariwise, as soon as the spectator, reader, or hearer feels that the author is not writing, singing, or playing for his own satisfaction—does not himself feel what he wishes to express—but is doing it for him, the receiver, a resistance immediately springs up, and the most individual and the newest feelings and the cleverest technique not only fail to produce any infection but actually repel.

I have mentioned three conditions of contagiousness in art, but they may be all summed up into one, the last, sincerity, i.e., that the artist should be impelled by an inner need to express his feeling. That condition includes the first; for if the artist is sincere he will express the feeling as he experienced it. And as each man is different from everyone else, his feeling will be individual for everyone else; and the more individual it is—the more the artist has drawn it from the depths of his nature—the more sympathetic and sincere will it be. And this same sincerity will impel the artist to find a clear expression of the feeling which he wishes to transmit.

Therefore this third condition—sincerity—is the most important of the three. It is always complied with in peasant art, and this explains why such art always acts so powerfully; but it is a condition almost entirely absent from our upper-class art, which is continually produced by artists actuated by personal aims of covetousness or vanity.

Such are the three conditions which divide art from its counterfeits, and which also decide the quality of every work of art apart from its subject matter.

The absence of any one of these conditions excludes a work from the category of art and relegates it to that of art's counterfeits. If the work does not transmit the artist's peculiarity of feeling and is therefore not individual, if it is unintelligibly expressed, or if it has not proceeded from the author's inner need for expression—it is not a work of art. If all these conditions are present, even in the smallest degree, then the work, even if a weak one, is yet a work of art.

The presence in various degrees of these three conditions—individuality, clearness, and sincerity—decides the merit of a work of art as art, apart from subject matter. All works of art take rank of merit according to the degree in which they fulfil the first, the second, and the third of these conditions. In one the individuality of the feeling transmitted may predominate; in another, clearness of expression; in a third, sincerity; while a fourth may have sincerity and individuality but be deficient in clearness; a fifth, individuality and clearness but less sincerity; and so forth, in all possible degrees and combinations.

Thus is art divided from that which is not art, and thus is the quality of art as art decided, independently of its subject matter, i.e., apart from whether the feelings it transmits are good or bad.

But how are we to define good and bad art with reference to its subject matter? . . .

Art, like speech, is a means of communication, and therefore of progress, i.e., of the movement of humanity forward toward perfection. Speech renders accessible to men of the latest generations all the knowledge discovered by the experience and reflection, both of preceding generations and of the best and foremost men of their own times; art renders accessible to men of the latest generations all the feelings experienced by their predecessors, and those also which are being felt by their best and foremost contemporaries. And as the evolution of knowledge proceeds by truer and more necessary knowledge, dislodging and replacing what is mistaken and unnecessary, so the evolution of feeling proceeds through art—feelings less kind and less needful for the well-being of mankind are replaced by others kinder and more needful for that end. That is the purpose of art. And, speaking now of its subject matter, the more art fulfills that purpose the better the art, and the less it fulfils it, the worse the art.

And the appraisement of feelings (i.e., the acknowledgment of these or those feelings as being more or less good, more or less necessary for the well-being of mankind) is made by the religious perception of the age.

In every period of history, and in every human society, there exists an understanding of the meaning of life which represents the highest level to which men of that society have attained, an understanding defining the highest good at which that society aims. And this understanding is the religious perception of the given time and society. And this religious perception is always clearly expressed by some advanced men, and more or less vividly perceived by all the members of the society. Such a religious perception and its corresponding expression exists always in every society. If it appears to us that in our society there is no religious perception, this is not because there really is none, but only because we do not want to see it. And we often wish not to see it because it exposes the fact that our life is inconsistent with that religious perception.

Religious perception in a society is like the direction of a flowing river. If the river flows at all, it must have a direction. If a society lives, there must be a religious perception indicating the direction in which, more or less consciously, all its members tend.

And so there always has been, and there is, a religious perception in every society. And it is by the standard of this religious perception that the feelings transmitted by art have always been estimated. Only on the basis of this religious perception of their age have men always chosen from the endlessly varied spheres of art that art which transmitted feelings making religious perception operative in actual life. And such art has always been highly valued and encouraged, while art transmitting feelings already outlived, flowing from the antiquated religious perceptions of a former age, has always been condemned and despised. All the rest of art, transmitting those most diverse feelings by means of which people commune together, was not condemned, and was tolerated, if only it did not transmit feelings contrary to religious perception. Thus, for instance, among the Greeks art transmitting the feeling of beauty, strength, and courage (Hesiod, Homer, Phidias) was chosen, approved, and encouraged, while art transmitting feelings of rude sensuality, despondency, and effeminacy was condemned and despised. Among the Jews, art transmitting feelings of devotion and submission to the God of the Hebrews and to His will (the epic of Genesis, the prophets, the Psalms) was chosen and encouraged, while art transmitting feelings of idolatry (the golden calf) was condemned and despised. All the rest of art—stories, songs, dances, ornamentation of houses, of utensils, and of clothes—which was not contrary to religious perception was neither distinguished nor discussed. Thus, in regard to its subject matter, has art been appraised always and everywhere, and thus it should be appraised; for this attitude toward art proceeds from the fundamental characteristics of human nature, and those characteristics do not change.

I know that according to an opinion current in our times religion is a superstition which humanity has outgrown, and that it is therefore assumed that no such thing exists as a religious perception, common to us all, by which art, in our time, can be evaluated. I know that this is the opinion current in the pseudo-cultured circles of today. People who do not acknowledge Christianity in its true meaning because it undermines all their social privileges, and who, therefore, invent all kinds of philosophic and aesthetic theories to hide from themselves the meaninglessness and wrongness of their lives, cannot think otherwise. These people intentionally, or sometimes unintentionally, confusing the conception of a religious cult with the conception of religious perception think that by denying the cult they get rid of religious perception. But even the very attacks on religion and the attempts to establish a life-conception contrary to the religious perception of our times most clearly demonstrate the existence of a religious perception condemning the lives that are not in harmony with it.

If humanity progresses, i.e., moves forward, there must inevitably be a guide to the direction of that movement. And religions have always furnished that guide. All history shows that the progress of humanity is accomplished not otherwise than under the guidance of religion. But if the race cannot progress without the guidance of religion—and progress is always going on, and consequently also in our own times—then there must be a religion of our times. So that, whether it pleases or displeases the so-called cultured people of today, they must admit the existence of religion—not of a religious cult, Catholic, Protestant, or another, but of religious perception—which, even in our times, is the guide always present where there is any progress. And if a religious perception exists among us, then our art should be appraised on the basis of that religious perception; and, as has always and everywhere been the case, art transmitting feelings flowing from the religious perception of our time should be chosen from all the indifferent art, should be acknowledged, highly esteemed, and encouraged, while art running counter to that perception should be condemned and despised, and all the remaining indifferent art should neither be distinguished nor encouraged. . . .

Whatever the work may be and however it may have been extolled, we have first to ask whether this work is one of real art or a counterfeit. Having acknowledged, on the basis of the indication of its infectiousness even to a small class of people, that a certain production belongs to the realm of art, it is necessary, on the basis of the indication of its accessibility, to decide the next question, Does this work belong to the category of bad, exclusive art, opposed to religious perception, or to Christian art uniting people? And having acknowledged an article to belong to real Christian art, we must then, according to whether it transmits the feelings flowing from love to God and man, or merely the simple feelings uniting all men, assign it a place in the ranks of religious art or in those of universal art.

Only on the basis of such verification shall we find it possible to select from the whole mass of what in our society claims to be art those works which form real, important, necessary spiritual food, and to separate them from all the harmful and useless art and from the counterfeits of art which surround us. Only on the basis of such verification shall we be able to rid ourselves of the pernicious results of harmful art and to avail ourselves of that beneficent action which is the purpose of true and good art and which is indispensable for the spiritual life of man and of humanity.

ILLUSTRATION 5

Thou Blind Man's Mark

SIR PHILIP SIDNEY

Thou blind man's mark, thou fool's self-chosen snare,
Fond fancy's scum, and dregs of scattered thought;
Band of all evils, cradle of causeless care;

Thou web of will, whose end is never wrought;
Desire, desire! I have too dearly bought,
With price of mangled mind, thy worthless ware;
Too long, too long, asleep thou has me brought,
Who should my mind to higher things prepare.
But yet in vain thou has my ruin sought;
In vain thou madest me to vain things aspire;
In vain thou kindlest all thy smoky fire;
For virtue hath this better lesson taught—
Within my self to seek my only hire,
Desiring naught but how to kill desire.

ILLUSTRATION 6

PABLO PICASSO, *Guernica*. (1937, May-early June) Oil on canvas, 11′5¹/₂″ × 25′5³/₄″. Museo del Prado, Madrid, Spain.

3

Formalism

In reaction to traditional mimetic and didactic theories of art, a group of thinkers in the early twentieth century developed a more formal approach to defining art, an approach which led to what is now called the "art for art's sake" movement in aesthetics. These aestheticians thought that to equate art with mimesis entailed relating the work of art to a subject matter which was external to the work. To emphasize the didactic elements of art was to relate an artwork to some sort of value-laden purpose—something meaningful to an audience but apart from the art object itself.

The formalists argue that works of art should be considered for their own sake. A work of art is an independent phenomenon. It exists apart from, and sometimes in spite of, its creator, the artist, and its audience or viewer. Works of art, then, should be considered as autonomous phenomena and examined accordingly. In an aesthetic examination one should look at the work itself to find out its meaning and value. The critic should divorce the work from the external subject matter to which it might refer, the life and intentions of the artist, and its possible impact on an audience. One should ignore the tradition in which the work might be a part or the historical situation which might have been an impetus for this creation. This ideal has seldom been realized even by the severest formalists, but the movement has been very influential in drawing attention to the work of art itself as the subject matter for aesthetic analysis and philosophical discussion.

Although the movement has roots in Kant and Coleridge, its first and foremost proponent was an early twentieth-century thinker Clive Bell. Bell was among a handful of theorists who argued that one needs to define art in terms of a common, exhibited, or inherent characteristic to distinguish works of art from other phenomena. This characteristic is an essential and unique feature of art; phenomena that do not exhibit this feature are not defined as art. And, according to Bell, if one cannot make such a definition, aesthetic theory is "gibber." The characteristic distinguishing works of art, according to Bell, is what he calls "significant form." In art significant form is the presentation of a peculiarly aesthetic emotion through the medium and the form of the work. In painting, for example, the visual form of the painting exhibits this character if the painting is a work of art.

Bell tries, with his concept of significant form, to single out what is unique to art. At the same time Bell is trying to explain why it is that some works of art evoke what he thinks is a peculiarly aesthetic experience. So Bell introduces the notion of aesthetic emotion, an idea which is similar to what James Joyce calls aesthetic pleasure (see Part III). Bell is considered a formalist because he argues that art can be appreciated for its own sake merely be experiencing significant form without any other knowledge or insight into art traditions, the intentions of the artist, or the subject of the work. And at the same time Bell is arguing that one's experiences of artworks are unique as well. *Sunday Afternoon on the Island of La Grande Jatte* (Illustration 20) might exemplify what Bell would consider a good work of art.

The art for art's sake movement has been particularly influential in literary criticism. One of the most famous proponents of this movement, called "new criticism," is the British-American poet T. S. Eliot. In "Tradition and the Individual Talent" reproduced in this chapter, Eliot points out that art arises out of tradition, and no artist can be a good artist who lacks training in, or disrespects, artistic traditions. All works of art, then, according to Eliot, are part of a continuum of aesthetic history. But the relation of a work of art to the artist is different. While artists cannot separate themselves from their traditional roots—which serve as creative catalysts—in producing great works of art, artists separate their personalities from what they create. Art is not autobiography—the personal expression of emotion. Rather, art, Eliot claims, is the impersonal expression of emotion. The greater the artist, the more perfectly she separates her creations from her personal feelings. This Impersonal Theory of Art, as Eliot terms his view, accounts for artistic autonomy in great art.

Formalism is often interpreted to mean that an artwork's most important features are its formal characteristics, e.g., the arrangement of the painting, the form of the sculpture. In painting, formalism is often identified with abstract art. Kline's *White Forms* (Illustration 21) and Biederman's works would be ideal examples of this interpretation of formalism. In architecture formalism is often identified with so-called "modern" buildings—cold geometric forms, functional perfection, and well-executed technical design. Formalism is then criticized for placing undue stress on empty abstract forms at the expense of critically and aesthetically important elements such as subject matter, content, and expression of emotions.

This interpretation of formalism may be an exaggeration of what more sophisticated formalists mean to say. These theorists argue that one must

examine the whole work of art as a finished independent unit to find out what the work is about. For example, one must read *Ulysses* rather than examine Joyce's personal life to find out about this novel. But in the examination of the artwork one looks at the subject matter *and* what is expressed in the work as well as its formal structure. All of these elements are equally important. The point is that each needs to be examined as it appears in the context of the work rather than as it relates to nature, to tradition, to the artist, or to a possible audience.

Formalism is sometimes called "absolutism," because of the formalist argument that the meaning of a work lies within the work itself, and any reference to external subject matter is meaningless in the interpretation of the art work. Music is often considered to be a prime example for the formalist view, and a formalist-absolutist theory of music is basic to the writings of Leonard B. Meyer, the author of a selection included in this chapter. Meyer argues that the meaning of music lies within the musical process itself. Specifically, emotion in music is embodied in the work, and the enjoyment of music lies in the listener's expectations generated within the work. Any extramusical reference or significance of an emotion expressed in music has nothing to do with its aesthetic value as music, nor does it affect the aesthetic appreciation of the work.

Meyer's thesis is brought into question by the contemporary philosopher, Donald Sherburne. What Sherburne calls his "Art for Life's Sake" view should be examined carefully as a strong criticism of the formalist position.

One of the strongest countermovements to formalism is the postmodernist movement that has come to fruition in the 1970s. This new movement is widespread in all the arts, but it is most clearly articulated in architecture. The architect and aesthetician Robert Stern summarizes the philosophy of postmodernism as it has developed in the last five years. Although Stern concentrates on architecture as an example, his remarks aptly apply to what is occurring throughout the postmodern aesthetic movement.

Postmodernism is a reaction to what is called "modernism." Modernism is difficult to define, but it clearly includes a focus on the present and the future at the expense of history and tradition, a pursuit of new art styles, an emphasis on the development of new sorts of formal structures to embody this style, and an emphasis on originality as the most important element in art. Thus modernism is a form of formalism.

In response to modernism, postmodernists have adopted at least two positions. At one end of the spectrum, postmodernism is held to be merely a continuation of the historical tradition of humanism begun in the Renaissance and temporarily abandoned by the modernists. Traditional postmodern art is an attempt to revitalize Sidney's and Tolstoy's notion that art is communicative and that artists have public responsibilities. To achieve this, postmodernists try to break up formalism in design, reduce abstractness in painting, and reintroduce affective and communicative elements in theatre. Traditional postmodern architecture seeks to integrate human and cultural concerns in its buildings. Philip Johnson's design of the A.T.&T. building is an early example of this trend.

At the other extreme, some postmodernists see themselves as breaking with all valued traditions—even the tradition of art itself. Schismatic postmodernism seeks to do something radical, contradictory, even nihilistic in art, even if this means destroying an art form. The music of John Cage (Illustration 8) is a fine example of schismatic postmodern art. Cage's work culminates in his piece *4'33"*,

> a piece for piano "performed" in utter silence as the pianist sits immobile before the keyboard for . . . four minutes and thirty-three seconds . . . marking the divisions of the three sections by closing and opening the fall-board of the piano at the prescribed moments.[1]

Whether art and art theory in the 1980's and 1990s will adopt traditional or schismatic postmodernism on a widespread scale remains to be seen.

Significant Form

CLIVE BELL

The starting-point for all systems of aesthetics must be the personal experience of a peculiar emotion. The objects that provoke this emotion we call works of art. All sensitive people agree that there is a peculiar emotion provoked by works of art. I do not mean, of course, that all works provoke the same emotion. On the contrary, every work produces a different emotion. But all these emotions are recognisably the same in kind; so far, at any rate, the best opinion is on my side. That there is a particular kind of emotion provoked by works of visual art, and that this emotion is provoked by every kind of visual art, by pictures, sculptures, buildings, pots, carvings, textiles, &c., &c., is not disputed, I think, by anyone capable of feeling it. This emotion is called the aesthetic emotion; and if we can discover some quality common and peculiar to all the objects that provoke it, we shall have solved what I take to be the central problem of aesthetics. We shall have discovered the essential

Clive Bell, *Art*. Reprinted by permission of G.P. Putnam's Sons, Chatto & Windus, and the author's Literary Estate.

---

[1]Peter S. Hansen, *An Introduction to Twentieth Century Music* (Boston, 1967), p. 393.

quality in a work of art, the quality that distinguishes works of art from all other classes of objects.

For either all works of visual art have some common quality, or when we speak of "works of art" we gibber. Everyone speaks of "art," making a mental classification by which he distinguishes the class "works of art" from all other classes. What is the justification of this classification? What is the quality common and peculiar to all members of this class? Whatever it be, no doubt it is often found in company with other qualities; but they are adventitious—it is essential. There must be some one quality without which a work of art cannot exist; possessing which, in the least degree, no work is altogether worthless. What is this quality? What quality is shared by all objects that provoke our aesthetic emotions? What quality is common to Sta. Sophia and the windows at Chartres, Mexican sculpture, a Persian bowl, Chinese carpets, Giotto's frescoes at Padua, and the masterpieces of Poussin, Piero della Francesca, and Cézanne? Only one answer seems possible—significant form. In each, lines and colours combined in a particular way, certain forms and relations of forms, stir our aesthetic emotions. These relations and combinations of lines and colours, these aesthetically moving forms, I call "Significant Form"; and "Significant Form" is the one quality common to all works of visual art.

At this point it may be objected that I am making aesthetics a purely subjective business, since my only data are personal experiences of a particular emotion. It will be said that the objects that provoke this emotion vary with each individual, and that therefore a system of aesthetics can have no objective validity. It must be replied that any system of aesthetics which pretends to be based on some objective truth is so palpably ridiculous as not to be worth discussing. We have no other means of recognising a work of art than our feeling for it. The objects that provoke aesthetic emotion vary with each individual. Aesthetic judgments are, as the saying goes, matters of taste; and about tastes, as everyone is proud to admit, there is no disputing. A good critic may be able to make me see in a picture that had left me cold things that I had overlooked, till at last, receiving the aesthetic emotion, I recognise it as a work of art. To be continually pointing out those parts, the sum, or rather the combination, of which unite to produce significant form, is the function of criticism. But it is useless for a critic to tell me that something is a work of art; he must make me feel it for myself. This he can do only by making me see; he must get at my emotions through my eyes. Unless he can make me see something that moves me, he cannot force my emotions. I have no right to consider anything a work of art to which I cannot react emotionally; and I have no right to look for the essential quality in anything that I have not *felt* to be a work of art. The critic can affect my aesthetic theories only by affecting my aesthetic experience. All systems of aesthetics must be based on personal experience—that is to say, they must be subjective.

Yet, though all aesthetic theories must be based on aesthetic judgments,

de gustibus

and ultimately all aesthetic judgments must be matters of personal taste, it would be rash to assert that no theory of aesthetics can have general validity. For, though A, B, C, D are the works that move me, and A, D, E, F the works that move you, it may well be that x is the only quality believed by either of us to be common to all the works in his list. We may all agree about aesthetics, and yet differ about particular works of art. We may differ as to the presence or absence of the quality x. My immediate object will be to show that significant form is the only quality common and peculiar to all the works of visual art that move me; and I will ask those whose aesthetic experience does not tally with mine to see whether this quality is not also, in their judgment, common to all works that move them, and whether they can discover any other quality of which the same can be said. . . .

Let no one imagine that representation is bad in itself; a realistic form may be as significant, in its place as part of the design, as an abstract. But if a representative form has value, it is as form, not as representation. The representative element in a work of art may or may not be harmful; always it is irrelevant. For, to appreciate a work of art we need bring with us nothing from life, no knowledge of its ideas and affairs, no familiarity with its emotions. Art transports us from the world of man's activity to a world of aesthetic exaltation. For a moment we are shut off from human interests; our anticipations and memories are arrested; we are lifted above the stream of life. The pure mathematician rapt in his studies knows a state of mind which I take to be similar, if not identical. He feels an emotion for his speculations which arises from no perceived relation between them and the lives of men, but springs, inhuman or super-human, from the heart of an abstract science. I wonder, sometimes, whether the appreciators of art and of mathematical solutions are not even more closely allied. Before we feel an aesthetic emotion for a combination of forms, do we not perceive intellectually the rightness and necessity of the combination? If we do, it would explain the fact that passing rapidly through a room we recognise a picture to be good, although we cannot say that it has provoked much emotion. We seem to have recognised intellectually the rightness of its forms without staying to fix our attention, and collect, as it were, their emotional significance. If this were so, it would be permissible to inquire whether it was the forms themselves or our perception of their rightness and necessity that caused aesthetic emotion. But I do not think I need linger to discuss the matter here. I have been inquiring why certain combinations of forms move us; I should not have travelled by other roads had I enquired, instead, why certain combinations are perceived to be right and necessary, and why our perception of their rightness and necessity is moving. What I have to say is this: the rapt philosopher, and he who contemplates a work of art, inhabit a world with an intense and peculiar significance of its own; that significance is unrelated to the significance of life. In this world the emotions of life find no place. It is a world with emotions of its own.

To appreciate a work of art we need bring with us nothing but a sense of form and colour and a knowledge of three-dimensional space. That bit of knowledge, I admit, is essential to the appreciation of many great works, since many of the most moving forms ever created are in three dimensions. To see a cube or a rhomboid as a flat pattern is to lower its significance, and a sense of three-dimensional space is essential to the full appreciation of most architectural forms. Pictures which would be insignificant if we saw them as flat patterns are profoundly moving because, in fact, we see them as related planes. If the representation of three-dimensional space is to be called "representation," then I agree that there is one kind of representation which is not irrelevant. Also, I agree that along with our feeling for line and colour we must bring with us our knowledge of space if we are to make the most of every kind of form. Nevertheless, there are magnificent designs to an appreciation of which this knowledge is not necessary: so, though it is not irrelevant to the appreciation of some works of art it is not essential to the appreciation of all. What we must say is that the representation of three-dimensional space is neither irrelevant nor essential to all art, and that every other sort of representation is irrelevant. . . .

. . . It is the mark of great art that its appeal is universal and eternal.[1] Significant form stands charged with the power to provoke aesthetic emotion in anyone capable of feeling it. The ideas of men go buzz and die like gnats; men change their institutions and their customs as they change their coats; the intellectual triumphs of one age are the follies of another; only great art remains stable and unobscure. Great art remains stable and unobscure because the feelings that it awakens are independent of time and place, because its kingdom is not of this world. To those who have and hold a sense of the significance of form what does it matter whether the forms that move them were created in Paris the day before yesterday or in Babylon fifty centuries ago? The forms of art are inexhaustible; but all lead by the same road of aesthetic emotion to the same world of aesthetic ecstasy.

---

[1]Mr. Roger Fry permits me to make use of an interesting story that will illustrate my view. When Mr. Okakura, the Government editor of *The Temple Treasures of Japan*, first came to Europe, he found no difficulty in appreciating the pictures of those who from want of will or want of skill did not create illusions but concentrated their energies on the creation of form. He understood immediately the Byzantine masters and the French and Italian Primitives. In the Renaissance painters, on the other hand, with their descriptive pre-occupations, their literary and anecdotic interests, he could see nothing but vulgarity and muddle. The universal and essential quality of art, significant form, was missing, or rather had dwindled to a shallow stream, overlaid and hidden beneath weeds, so the universal response, aesthetic emotion, was not evoked. It was not till he came on to Henri-Matisse that he again found himself in the familiar world of pure art. Similarly, sensitive Europeans who respond immediately to the significant forms of great Oriental art, are left cold by the trivial pieces of anecdote and social criticism so lovingly cherished by Chinese dilettanti. It would be easy to multiply instances did not decency forbid the labouring of so obvious a truth.

The Irrefutability of
Bell's Aesthetic Theory

BERYL LAKE STEELE

Clive Bell's Theory About Works of Art

Clive Bell is his own best brief expositor:

> The starting point for all systems of aesthetics must be the personal experience of a peculiar emotion. The objects which provoke this emotion we call works of art.
>
> This emotion is called the aesthetic emotion; and if we can discover some quality peculiar to all the objects that provoke it, we shall have solved what I take to be the eternal problem of aesthetics. We shall have discovered the essential quality in a work of art. . . .

This essential quality of works of art, Bell decides, is "significant form." Certain relations between forms, forms themselves, lines and colours are what stir our aesthetic emotions. If we ask which relations, etc., do this, the answer is, the significant ones. And if we ask, "Significant of what?" the answer is given by Bell's "metaphysical hypothesis," that they are significant ultimately of the reality of things, of "that which gives to all things their individual significance, the thing in itself, the ultimate reality."

The claim is first made that there exist aesthetic emotions which are only aroused by works of art. Then it is claimed that what is common to all works of art, or objects which arouse aesthetic emotions, is "significant form."

The assertion that sensitive people have aesthetic emotions is surely empirical. We should confirm or falsify this by asking those who are acknowledged to be sensitive people whether they experience an emotion which is unique to situations in which they are appraising works of art. We are not concerned here with the truth of this claim, but simply with its semantic type, *i.e.* its empirical or *a priori* character. And it certainly seems to be empirical. Many people would be prepared to admit that there is an aesthetic emotion, although some may wish to say that natural objects as well as works of art arouse it. We can believe that if Clive Bell had been confronted with constant denials of the existence of the aesthetic emotion he could still sincerely claim

Beryl Lake (Steele), "The Irrefutability of Two Aesthetic Theories," from *Aesthetics and Language*, ed. William Elton (New York: Philosophical Library, 1954). Reprinted by permission of Philosophical Library.

that he frequently experienced it. His experience at least would back his claim that such experiences do exist, and as a matter of fact many others admit having emotions of this sort. Yet we believe that Bell would say that if he had never had such an experience, his aesthetic theory would not have arisen; he insists that this personal emotion is the starting point. Bell's theory, then, seems to have what we might call empirical feet on the ground. But from there it soars into what we might call metaphysical heights, . . .

What is common to all the works of art, or objects which arouse the aesthetic emotion, is significant form. Bell never explains clearly what significant form is; the "metaphysical hypothesis" suggests that it is not merely a certain (unspecified) combination of lines and colours. (Bell concerns himself, as is evident, primarily with painting.) Roger Fry, who shared Bell's view, commented that significant form is more than pleasing patterns and so on, but that an attempt at full explanation would land him "in the depths of mysticism": "On the edge of that gulf I stop." As Wittgenstein's famous comment advises, "Whereof one cannot speak, thereof one must be silent."

Whatever significant form is, the questions here are "What are we to make of the view that it is the common denominator of works of art?" "In what position would a person be if he denied it?"

This is a way of asking if the view is empirical. How could someone convince Clive Bell that works of art (supposing, for the sake of argument, they have a common feature) do not have significant form as an essential feature, or never have significant form at all. Someone might say that Frith's "Paddington Station" is a work of art which, because it is purely descriptive of reality, has no significant form, and therefore Bell's view is false. But we know what Bell's answer would be; he gives it himself. "Paddington Station" is *not* a work of art precisely because it does not have significant form, precisely because it is merely descriptive painting. His critical judgments and his aesthetic theory seem to be in line. Apropos of the frequent praise he bestows on Cézanne in his critical works, he writes:

> Cézanne carried me off my feet before I ever noticed that his strongest characteristic was an insistence on the supremacy of significant form. When I noticed this, my admiration for Cézanne and some of his followers confirmed me in my aesthetic theories.

Bell is impressed with the formal qualities of paintings. He says:

> The pure mathematician rapt in his studies knows a state of mind which I take to be similar, if not identical . . . [with the aesthetic emotion aroused by significant form].

Any painting, then, which someone might try to point out as an example of art which does not have significant form, would be denied to be a work of art for this very reason. No instance could possibly be produced of a work of art which did not have significant form, for anything which did not have significant form would not be counted as a work of art. "Paddington Station" has not significant form; therefore, in spite of popular belief to the contrary, "Paddington Station" is not a work of art. Likewise, since "Paddington Station," Bell judges, is not worthy of the title "work of art," it cannot have significant form. The upshot of the theory is that nothing can count as a work of art unless it has significant form. It begins to look as if "Works of art have significant form" is like "Squares have four sides." "Is a work of art" and "has significant form" seem to mean the same, so that the latter does not say what anything must answer to in order to count as a work of art, except that it must be a work of art.

Certainly someone who wishes to deny that all works of art have significant form would not be able to produce any evidence to convince Bell. He might point to a Hogarth and say that it lacked significant form but was a work of art, but Bell would reply that either it has significant form or it is not a work of art. He might point to a Ben Nicholson and say that it had significant form but was not a work of art, or, for that matter, to a tree. But Bell is committed to the view that if something has significant form it is a work of art, and if something is a work of art, it has significant form. No exceptions are theoretically possible once his view is adopted. This is not the characteristic of an empirical view.

We can imagine water running uphill, but we cannot begin to imagine, according to Bell, a work of art which has no significant form. Adopting his view clearly amounts to deciding not to call anything which we do not also call "significant form," "work of art." We are reminded of the way in which we refuse to call anything "square" which we do not also call "four-sided." It looks as if "only those paintings, etc., are works of art which have significant form" is irrefutable, therefore non-empirical, and therefore in some sense *a priori*.

Of course, such sentences as "Works of art have significant form" do not in ordinary language express *a priori* propositions. But then the expression "significant form" is not an ordinary expression. There is reason for supposing that aestheticians have, in one sense, a special language adapted to the purposes of their own theories. Bell, for example, coined this phrase to establish his point that there is something which is very important to him about works of art. But he goes on to make it impossible to give an instance of even a purely imaginary thing which is both a work of art and lacks significant form.

. . . Clive Bell is impressed by the value of formal relationships of line and colour in certain kinds of painting, Cézanne's, for example. He is so impressed by this aspect of a certain kind of art that he declares that "Art is Significant Form." This statement, too, arising from an aesthetic fact (namely, that in some works it is the formal designs that arouse aesthetic emotion) transcends the other facts about other sorts of art which go against it. Descriptive painting, for example, he declares to be "not Art." Although Bell claims to have isolated what is a common characteristic of all works of art, as someone might isolate alcohol as the common characteristic of all cocktails, what he has really done is to restrict the use of the word "Art" to a certain sort of painting which seems to him very important and exciting. And of course it is impossible to refute someone who decides to restrict the meaning of a word. All we can do is sympathize with or regret his usage.

I conclude that very probably many conclusions in aesthetics are fabricated *a priori* statements, which originally arise from a desire to emphasize one fact about aesthetic objects and experience to the firm exclusion of the rest. A trivial example of the sort of statement I believe aesthetic statements to be like would be "The only Universities in England are Oxford and Cambridge," made by a person who was so impressed by the virtues (and by none of the drawbacks) of the ancient universities that he is utterly unconvinced by having pointed out to him the facts which show that London, Liverpool, Manchester, etc., also have Universities. He has made "The only Universities in England are Oxford and Cambridge" *a priori* true in so far as he refuses to say of any other educational institution in England that it is a "University," refuses to admit any possible counter-instance. He has restricted the use of the phrase "English University." Such a person has said nothing interesting, valuable, or exciting, of course, but the parallel with the aesthetician who says that "Art is such and such" is one of linguistic mechanism.

If what I believe about the nature of some aesthetic theories is correct, it is inappropriate to ask whether such theories are true or false, since they cannot be refuted empirically. It is inappropriate to point out counter-facts, since the theories are so stated that any such facts are impotent. It is only appropriate to sympathize with, or to feel opposed to, aesthetic theories, and to understand the artistic prejudices which have caused them.

Tradition and the Individual Talent

T. S. ELIOT

In English writing we seldom speak of tradition, though we occasionally apply its name in deploring its absence. We cannot refer to "the tradition" or to "a tradition"; at most, we employ the adjective in saying that the poetry of So-and-so is "traditional" or even "too traditional." Seldom, perhaps, does the word appear except in a phrase of censure. If otherwise, it is vaguely approbative, with the implication, as to the work approved, of some pleasing archaeological reconstruction. You can hardly make the word agreeable to English ears without this comfortable reference to the reassuring science of archaeology.

Certainly the word is not likely to appear in our appreciations of living or dead writers. Every nation, every race, has not only its own creative, but its own critical turn of mind; and is even more oblivious of the shortcomings and limitations of its critical habits than of those of its creative genius. We know, or think we know, from the enormous mass of critical writing that has appeared in the French language the critical method or habit of the French; we only conclude (we are such unconscious people) that the French are "more critical" than we, and sometimes even plume ourselves a little with the fact, as if the French were the less spontaneous. Perhaps they are; but we might remind ourselves that criticism is as inevitable as breathing, and that we should be none the worse for articulating what passes in our minds when we read a book and feel an emotion about it, for criticizing our own minds in their work of criticism. One of the facts that might come to light in this process is our tendency to insist, when we praise a poet, upon those aspects of his work in which he least resembles anyone else. In these aspects or parts of his work we pretend to find what is individual, what is the peculiar essence of the man. We dwell with satisfaction upon the poet's difference from his predecessors, especially his immediate predecessors; we endeavour to find something that can be isolated in order to be enjoyed. Whereas if we approach a poet without this prejudice we shall often find that not only the best, but the most individual parts of his work may be those in which the dead poets, his ancestors, assert their immortality most vigorously. And I do not mean the impressionable period of adolescence, but the period of full maturity.

Yet if the only form of tradition, of handing down, consisted in following the ways of the immediate generation before us in a blind or timid adherence to its successes, "tradition" should positively be discouraged. We have seen many such simple currents soon lost in the sand; and novelty is better than repetition. Tradition is a matter of much wider significance. It cannot be inherited, and if you want it you must obtain it by great labour. It involves, in the first place, the historical sense, which we may call nearly indispensable to anyone who would continue to be a poet beyond his twenty-fifth year; and the historical sense involves a perception, not only of the pastness of the past, but of its presence; the historical sense compels a man to write not merely with his own generation in his bones, but with a feeling that the whole of the literature of Europe from Homer and within it the whole of the literature of his own country has a simultaneous existence and composes a simultaneous order. This historical sense, which is a sense of the timeless as well as of the temporal and of the timeless and of the temporal together, is what makes a writer traditional. And it is at the same time what makes a writer most acutely conscious of his place in time, of his contemporaneity.

No poet, no artist of any art, has his complete meaning alone. His significance, his appreciation is the appreciation of his relation to the dead poets and artists. You cannot value him alone; you must set him, for contrast and comparison, among the dead. I mean this as a principle of aesthetic, not merely historical, criticism. The necessity that he shall conform, that he shall cohere, is not one-sided; what happens when a new work of art is created is something that happens simultaneously to all the works of art which preceded it. The existing monuments form an ideal order among themselves, which is modified by the introduction of the new (the really new) work of art among them. The existing order is complete before the new work arrives; for order to persist after the supervention of novelty, the *whole* existing order must be, if ever so slightly, altered; and so the relations, proportions, values of each work of art toward the whole are readjusted; and this is conformity between the old and the new. Whoever has approved this idea of order, of the form of European, of English literature, will not find it preposterous that the past should be altered by the present as much as the present is directed by the past. And the poet who is aware of this will be aware of great difficulties and responsibilities.

In a peculiar sense he will be aware also that he must inevitably be judged by the standards of the past. I say judged, not amputated, by them; not judged to be as good as, or worse or better than, the dead; and certainly not judged by the canons of dead critics. It is a judgment, a comparison, in which two things are measured by each other. To conform merely would be for the new work not really to conform at all; it would not be new, and would therefore not be a work of art. And we do not quite say that the new is more valuable because it fits in; but its fitting in is a test of its value—a test, it is true, which can only be slowly and cautiously applied, for we are none of us infallible judges of conformity. We say: it appears to conform, and is perhaps individual, or it appears individual, and may conform; but we are hardly likely to find that it is one and not the other.

To proceed to a more intelligible exposition of the relation of the poet to the past: he can neither take the past as a lump, an indiscriminate bolus, nor can he form himself wholly on one or two private admirations, nor can he form himself wholly upon one preferred period. The first course is inadmissible, the second is an important experience of youth, and the third is a pleasant and highly desirable supplement. The poet must be very conscious of the main current, which does not at all flow invariably through the most distinguished reputations. He must be quite aware of the obvious fact that art never improves, but that the material of art is never quite the same. He must be aware that the mind of Europe—the mind of his own country—a mind which he learns in time to be much more important than his own private mind—is a mind which changes, and that this change is a development which abandons nothing *en route*, which does not superannuate either Shakespeare, or Homer, or the rock drawing of the Magdalenian draughtsmen. That this development, refinement perhaps, complication certainly, is not, from the point of view of the artist, any improvement. Perhaps not even an improvement from the point of view of the psychologists or not to the extent which we imagine, perhaps only in the end based upon a complication in economics and machinery. But the difference between the present and the past is that the conscious present is an awareness of the past in a way and to an extent which the past's awareness of itself cannot show.

Some one said: "The dead writers are remote from us because we *know* so much more than they did." Precisely, and they are that which we know.

I am alive to a usual objection to what is clearly part of my programme for the *métier* of poetry. The objection is that the doctrine requires a ridiculous amount of erudition (pedantry), a claim which can be rejected by appeal to the lives of poets in any pantheon. It will even be affirmed that much learning deadens or perverts poetic sensibility. While, however, we persist in believing that a poet ought to know as much as will not encroach upon his necessary receptivity and necessary laziness, it is not desirable to confine knowledge to whatever can be put into a useful shape for examinations, drawing-rooms, or the still more pretentious modes of publicity. Some can absorb knowledge, the more tardy must sweat for it. Shakespeare acquired more essential history from Plutarch than most men could from the whole British Museum. What is to be insisted upon is that the poet must develop or procure the consciousness of the past and that he should continue to develop this consciousness throughout his career.

What happens is a continual surrender of himself as he is at the moment to something which is more valuable. The progress of an artist is a continual self-sacrifice, a continual extinction of personality.

There remains to define this process of depersonalization and its relation to the sense of tradition. It is in this depersonalization that art may be said to approach the condition of science. I shall, therefore, invite you to consider, as a suggestive analogy, the action which takes place when a bit of finely filiated platinum is introduced into a chamber containing oxygen and sulphur dioxide.

Honest criticism and sensitive appreciation are directed not upon the poet but upon the poetry. If we attend to the confused cries of the newspaper critics and the *susurrus* of popular repetition that follows, we shall hear the names of poets in great numbers; if we seek not Bluebook knowledge but the enjoyment of poetry, and ask for a poem, we shall seldom find it. In the last article I tried to point out the importance of the relation of the poem to other poems by other authors, and suggested the conception of poetry as a living whole of all the poetry that has ever been written. The other aspect of this Impersonal theory of poetry is the relation of the poem to its author. And I hinted, by an analogy, that the mind of the mature poet differs from that of the immature one not precisely in any valuation of "personality," not by being necessarily more interesting, or having "more to say," but rather by being a more finely perfected medium in which special, or very varied, feelings are at liberty to enter into new combinations.

The analogy was that of the catalyst. When the two gases previously mentioned are mixed in the presence of a filament of platinum, they form sulphurous acid. This combination takes place only if the platinum is present; nevertheless the newly formed acid contains no trace of platinum, and the platinum itself is apparently unaffected; has remained inert, neutral, and unchanged. The mind of the poet is the shred of platinum. It may partly or exclusively operate upon the experience of the man himself; but, the more perfect the artist, the more completely separate in him will be the man who suffers and the mind which creates; the more perfectly will the mind digest and transmute the passions which are its material.

The experience, you will notice, the elements which enter the presence of the transforming catalyst, are of two kinds: emotions and feelings. The effect of a work of art upon the person who enjoys it is an experience different in kind from any experience not of art. It may be formed out of one emotion, or may be a combination of several; and various feelings, inhering for the writer in particular words or phrases or images, may be added to compose the final result. Or great poetry may be made without the direct use of any emotion whatever: composed out of feelings solely. Canto XV of the *Inferno* (Brunetto Latini) is a working up of the emotion evident in the situation; but the effect, though single as that of any work of art, is obtained by considerable complexity of detail. The last quatrain gives an image, a feeling attaching to an image, which "came," which did not develop simply out of what precedes, but which was probably in suspension in the poet's mind until the proper combination arrived for it to add itself to. The poet's mind is in fact a receptacle for seizing and storing up numberless feelings, phrases, images, which remain there until all the particles which can unite to form a new compound are present together.

If you compare several representative passages of the greatest poetry you see how great is the variety of types of combination, and also how completely any semi-ethical criterion of "sublimity" misses the mark. For it is not the "greatness," the intensity, of the emotions, the components, but the intensity of the artistic process, the pressure, so to speak, under which the fusion takes place, that counts. The episode of Paolo and Francesca employs a definite emotion, but the intensity of the poetry is something quite different from whatever intensity in the supposed experience it may give the impression of. It is no more intense, furthermore, than Canto XXVI, the

voyage of Ulysses, which has not the direct dependence upon an emotion.
Great variety is possible in the process of transmution of emotion: the
murder of Agamemnon, or the agony of Othello, gives an artistic effect
apparently closer to a possible original than the scenes from Dante. In the
Agamemnon, the artistic emotion approximates to the emotion of an actual
spectator; in *Othello* to the emotion of the protagonist himself. But the difference between art and the event is always absolute; the combination which
is the murder of Agamemnon is probably as complex as that which is the
voyage of Ulysses. In either case there has been a fusion of elements. The
ode of Keats contains a number of feelings which have nothing particular
to do with the nightingale, but which the nightingale, partly, perhaps, because of its attractive name, and partly because of its reputation, served to
bring together.

The point of view which I am struggling to attack is perhaps related to
the metaphysical theory of the substantial unity of the soul: for my meaning
is, that the poet has, not a "personality" to express, but a particular medium,
which is only a medium and not a personality, in which impressions and
experiences combine in peculiar and unexpected ways. Impressions and experiences which are important for the man may take no place in the poetry,
and those which become important in the poetry may play quite a negligible
part in the man, the personality.

I will quote a passage which is unfamiliar enough to be regarded with
fresh attention in the light—or darkness—of these observations:

> And now methinks I could e'en chide myself
> For doating on her beauty, though her death
> Shall be revenged after no common action.
> Does the silkworm expend her yellow labours
> For thee? For thee does she undo herself?
> Are lordships sold to maintain ladyships
> For the poor benefit of a bewildering minute?
> Why does yon fellow falsify highways,
> And put his life between the judge's lips,
> To refine such a thing—keeps horse and men
> To beat their valours for her?, . . .

In this passage (as is evident if it is taken in its context) there is a combination
of positive and negative emotions: an intensely strong attraction toward beauty
and an equally intense fascination by the ugliness which is contrasted with it
and which destroys it. This balance of contrasted emotion is in the dramatic
situation to which the speech is pertinent, but that situation alone is inadequate to it. This is, so to speak, the structural emotion, provided by the
drama. But the whole effect, the dominant tone, is due to the fact that a

number of floating feelings, having an affinity to this emotion by no means superficially evident, have combined with it to give us a new art emotion.

It is not in his personal emotions, the emotions provoked by particular events in his life, that the poet is in any way remarkable or interesting. His particular emotions may be simple, or crude, or flat. The emotion in his poetry will be a very complex thing, but not with the complexity of the emotions of people who have very complex or unusual emotions in life. One error, in fact, of eccentricity in poetry is to seek for new human emotions to express; and in this search for novelty in the wrong place it discovers the perverse. The business of the poet is not to find new emotions, but to use the ordinary ones and, in working them up into poetry, to express feelings which are not in actual emotions at all. And emotions which he has never experienced will serve his turn as well as those familiar to him. Consequently, we must believe that "emotion recollected in tranquillity" is an inexact formula. For it is neither emotion, nor recollection, nor, without distortion of meaning, tranquillity. It is a concentration, and a new thing resulting from the concentration, of a very great number of experiences which to the practical and active person would not seem to be experiences at all; it is a concentration which does not happen consciously or of deliberation. These experiences are not "recollected," and they finally unite in an atmosphere which is "tranquil" only in that it is a passive attending upon the event. Of course this is not quite the whole story. There is a great deal, in the writing of poetry, which must be conscious and deliberate. In fact, the bad poet is usually unconscious where he ought to be conscious, and conscious where he ought to be unconscious. Both errors tend to make him "personal." Poetry is not a turning loose of emotion, but an escape from emotion; it is not the expression of personality, but an escape from personality. But, of course, only those who have personality and emotions know what it means to want to escape from these things.

This essay proposes to halt at the frontier of metaphysics or mysticism, and confine itself to such practical conclusions as can be applied by the responsible person interested in poetry. To divert interest from the poet to the poetry is a laudable aim: for it would conduce to a juster estimation of actual poetry, good and bad. There are many people who appreciate the expression of sincere emotion in verse, and there is a smaller number of people who can appreciate technical excellence. But very few know when there is expression of *significant* emotion, emotion which has its life in the poem and not in the history of the poet. The emotion of art is impersonal. And the poet cannot reach this impersonality without surrendering himself wholly to the work to be done. And he is not likely to know what is to be done unless he lives in what is not merely the present, but the present moment of the past, unless he is conscious, not of what is dead, but of what is already living.

FORMALISM IN THE ARTS

The Doubles of Post-Modern

ROBERT A. M. STERN

What has been called Modern architecture for the past 50 years is in disarray: though such leading architects as Paul Rudolph, I. M. Pei, and Kevin Roche continue to produce major new work, the forms as well as the theories on which that work is based are systematically being questioned by a growing number of younger architects who perceive the waning of modernism and who are questioning the prevailing philosophic basis for architecture and its form language. This questioning sensibility has come to be described, alternately and rather imprecisely, as "Post-Modern" or "Post-Modernist. . . ."[1]

The terms "modernism" and "post-modernism" have been used in other disciplines besides architecture, including political history and literary and art criticism. In each of these disciplines, they suggest two different conditions resulting in related sets of what I would describe as "doubles"—the doubles of modernism and of post-modernism. Both grow out of the same two distinct but interrelated sensibilities or conditions, and both fall within the Modern— that is Western Humanist/Post-Renaissance—period.

These conditions affect both modernism and post-modernism. Borrowing the term from Frank Kermode, I would label the first of these conditions "schismatic." The schismatic condition argues for a clean break with Western Humanism. I would label the second condition "traditional," borrowing the term from Stephen Spender. It argues for a recognition of the continuity of the Western Humanist tradition. Traditional modernism can be "conceived of as a return, at once spontaneous, willed to eternal values long forgotten or buried but which a reborn or renewed historical memory makes once again present"; schismatic modernism can be seen as a sensibility in which "the new and the modern [are] seen in terms of a birth rather than a rebirth, not

Robert A. M. Stern, "The Doubles of Post-Modern," *The Harvard Architecture Review* 1 (1980). Reprinted by permission of The MIT Press, Cambridge, Massachusetts. Copyright © 1980.

---

[1]Portions of this text are based on material introduced by me on previous occasions: See "Postscript at the Edge of Modernism," in my *New Directions in American Architecture*, 2nd edition, revised (New York: Braziller, 1977) 117–136; "Five Houses," G A *Houses*, 1 (1976) 36–41; *Architectural Design*, 47, #4 (May 1977): "Something Borrowed, Something New," *Horizon*, 20, #4 (December 1977) 50–57.

a restoration but . . . a construction of the present and future not on the foundations of the past but on the ruins of time."[2]

The two modernisms can be distinguished by their attitudes toward the past: "traditional" modernism, typified by the writings of Proust or Eliot or the paintings of Picasso, views the past as a source of order; "schismatic" modernism, typified by the work of Duchamp or Mondrian, views the past as a burden. Although the two kinds of modernism are distinct, they are linked by an apocalyptic view of the future and by a recognition of Western Humanism as an on-going condition.

It is important to reiterate that the Modern period as a whole encompasses a continuing tradition of humanistic thought and action though some of its stylistic movements—for example Dada and Surrealism—regard humanism as a yoke.

Like the two modernisms, the two post-modernisms can be distinguished by their attitudes toward the past. While the schismatic Post-Modern condition posits a break with both modernism and the Modern period itself, the traditional Post-Modern condition proposes to free new production from the rigid constraints of modernism, especially from its most radical and nihilistic aspects (as exemplified by Dada and Surrealism) while simultaneously reintegrating itself with other strains of Western Humanism, especially those which characterize its last pre-modernist phase, that of the Romanticism which flourished between 1750 and 1850. Thus, schismatic post-modernism is a sensibility that considers itself not only beyond modernism but also outside the Modern period, one which seeks to establish the mode of thought and artistic production that is as free from the 500-year tradition of Western Humanism as that mode was, in its turn, free from the previous Gothic era.

Thus the doubles of the Post-Modern: two distinct but interrelated Post-Modern sensibilities: a schismatic condition that argues for a *clean break* with the 400 year old tradition of Western Humanism and a "traditional" condition that argues for a return to, or a recognition of, the *continuity* of the cultural tradition of Western Humanism of which it holds modernism to be a part.

In order to clarify what is meant by the term "Modern" in the phrase "Post-Modern," it is necessary to establish clear definitions for the related terms "Modern" and "modernism." Such a seemingly pedantic exercise is necessary because the distinctions between the older terms have become blurred by daily use, and they have become ineffective for discourse.

What can be called the "Modern period" begins in the 15th century with the birth of Humanism. The renaissance of classicism in architecture is

---

[2]Renato Poggioli, *The Theory of the Avant Garde* (Cambridge, MA: Harvard, 1968) translated by Gerald Fitzgerald, 217; see also Daniel Bell, *The Cultural Contradictions of Capitalism* (New York: Basic Books, 1976) 34; Frank Kermode. *Continuities* (London: Routledge and Egon, Paul, 1968) 8.

the first of the Modern stylistic phases: the Baroque and the Roccoco are subsequent Modern styles. The International Style of ca. 1920–60 is also a Modern style, often thought to be *the* Modern Style in which the meaning of the word "Modern" is transformed and limited so as to represent only those values more properly described as "modernist," a term which describes the urge to produce new artistic work that eschews all known form-language and, ideally, all grammar, in favor of a new self-referential (i.e., in architecture, functionally and technologically determined) language of form whose principal cultural responsibility is toward its moment in time. Modernism sees art as a manifestation of the *zeitgeist*; it strives to reflect the moment of its conception. Modernism, in the most oversimplified terms, represents a moralistic application of a superior value to that which is not only new but also independent of all previous production.

Modernism views the present as a state of continuing crisis; it sees history only as a record of experiences, a body of myth, but not as objective truth, and it is apocalyptic in its relationship to the future. A person who believes in the sensibility of "modernism" is a "modernist" as well as a "Modern," the latter term being the more general one and simply referring to someone who has lived in the "Modern" period and has contended with or at least recognized the issue of "modernity" but who has not necessarily adopted a modernist stance.[3]

Modernism is not a style in and of itself in the sense that the Renaissance and Baroque were styles with unifying principles. It can be regarded as a succession of attempts to redefine the syntax and the grammar of artistic composition (the poems of Mallarmé, the stream of consciousness of Joyce and Woolf; the buildings of Mies van der Rohe and Le Corbusier). As a result, and rather perversely, to the extent that it has deliberately been made difficult and inaccessible, artistic production has also shown itself to be modernist. In some cases, there has been an effort to go beyond the issues of syntax and grammar and to seek to establish new form languages which, because they are not culturally based (that is, familiar), are by necessity personal or self-referential.[4]

Modernism does not accept the appearance of things as they are in nature and in the man-made world; it seeks always to take them apart in order to discover their hidden and presumably essential character. Modernism seeks to close and ultimately to eliminate the distance between the object perceived and the person perceiving the object. It seeks to do this in two

---

[3] See Kermode, op cit, 8, 13; Kermode observes that "the fact that defining the modern is a task that now imposes itself on many distinguished scholars may be a sign that the modern period is over," p. 28. See also, Bell, op cit, 40–52.

[4] See Clement Greenberg, "Modernist Painting" in Gregory Battcock, editor, *The New Art* (New York: Dutton, 1973, revised edition) 100–110.

William Jordy, "The Symbolic Essence of Modern European Architecture of the Twenties and its Continuing Influence," *JSAH*, XXII, #3 (October 1973) 117.

ways: by insisting that all experience and thereby all art exists in the present . . . and by insisting that each work of art and each act of artistic production is a personal act. This presentism and the self-referential aspect of
artistic production are fundamental to any examination of the nature of modernism in relationship to the issue of an on-going culture which we call the
Western Humanist tradition. . . .

Post-modernism should not be seen as a reaction against modernism; it
seeks to develop modernism's themes by attempting to examine them in
relationship to the wider framework of the Modern period as a whole.

The divided nature of modernism complicates our understanding of the
Post-Modern devolution. At the beginning of this essay, I defined two kinds
of Post-Modern sensibilities which can now be seen as related to modernism:
a traditional one and a schismatic one. But the complex nature of modernism
itself, with its two distinct conditions or types united by an apocalyptic view
of history—not to mention the claims that are sometimes made for modernism
as a sensibility completely independent of Western Humanism—complicate
the situation with regard to post-modernism. As a result, it can be argued
that there are not one but two sets of Post-Modern doubles: that there are
two types of traditional post-modernism and *two types of schismatic post-
modernism.*

The first type of traditional post-modernism—and the one which I would
argue is the more viable of the two—argues for a break with modernism
(where modernism is itself seen as a *break with* Western Humanism) and a
reintegration with a view of Western Humanism which includes modernism
among its many and sometimes conflicting conditions. The second type sees
itself as a continuation of modernism (in which modernism is itself seen as a
successor *sensibility* and *style* to the Baroque and Roccoco, a sensibility and
style that is contradictorily and inexplicably, in its present-ism, a contradiction
of the very notion of style.

This second type of traditional post-modernism is somewhat dubious:
at the very least it fails to account for the stylistic complexity of the Romantic
era, and it leads us to a question of whether such a post-modernism is really
different from modernism itself. For if traditional modernism is a condition
in which all art is seen as being in the present, though not breaking with the
values and symbols of Western Humanism, then where can this second type
of post-modernism stand in time? Is there a place beyond the present?

The first type of schismatic post-modernism—and the one which I would
argue is the more viable of the two—is the one which argues for a *continuity
with* modernism (in which modernism is itself seen as a *break with* Western'
Humanism). This kind of schismatic post-modernism, like the second type of
traditional post-modernism, is a continuing modernism, but the use of the
prefix "post" has meaning because it permits the designation of a condition
which is distinct from modernism because it breaks with the Western Humanist
tradition. Schismatic post-modernism of this type marks the full flowering of

a sensibility which has its origins in modernism's aspirations toward a clean break with the Western Humanist tradition.

The second type of schismatic post-modernism is itself seen as a *continuing* tradition. This is the so-called "post-modern breakthrough to post-modernity," in which a totally new state of consciousness is achieved that insists on the obsolescence of modernism as well as the entire Western Humanist tradition. Attractive though such an image seems to those who view the current situation as unnecessarily confusing, it is difficult to make clear just exactly how this new condition will emerge. . . .

Thus, though there are four conditions of post-modernism, it would seem that in the case of two, questions of considerable complexity remain unanswered at the present moment, thereby limiting the effectiveness of these conditions for artistic production if not for discourse. The difficulties raised by the second type of traditional post-modernism—that is, the notion of a continuing modernism—simultaneously claiming a position within Humanism and apart from history, seems hopelessly contradictory. It seems to be a condition which, despite the Post-Modern label that might be applied to it, is no more or no less than that of the traditional modernism of Marcel Proust, of the James Joyce of *Ulysses*, of Picasso, and of Le Corbusier.

The difficulties of the second type of schismatic post-modernism—the post-modernist breakthrough—have already been discussed. It takes as its point of departure the work of such writers as James Joyce but, as yet, it has not found a truly convincing voice. . . .

Thus it becomes clear that the second type of schismatic post-modernism is not just a shift of emphasis within modernism; its relationship to modernism is not comparable to that which post-impressionism had to impressionism; schismatic post-modernism is radical in the extreme.

The two conditions of the Post-Modern that are at this moment important, and the ones I should like to consider in some detail in the remaining pages of this essay, are: (1) the schismatic post-modernism that argues for a clean break with Western Humanism and a continuity with modernism and (2) the traditional post-modernism that argues for a break with modernism and a reintegration with the broader condition of Western Humanism, especially with the Romantic tradition. These seem the only possible categories because they are the only ones that contain in them the "double" sensibilities of continuity and change which are necessary to sustain generative cycles of creation.

The emergence of the Post-Modern sensibility can be seen as a logical result of the opposition between the Romantic and Modernist sensibilities, the former reveling in diversity, the latter struggling to find a universal cultural voice. Post-modernism is not revolutionary in either the political or artistic sense; in fact, it reinforces the effect of the technocratic and bureaucratic society in which we live—traditional post-modernism by accepting conditions and trying to modify them, schismatic post-modernism by proposing a condition *outside* Western Humanism, thereby permitting Western Humanist license to proceed uninterrupted although not necessarily unaffected. . . .

Schismatic post-modernism separates itself from traditionalist post-modernism by suggesting that it is not simply the crises of mid-century life that have irreparably changed the relationship of men to each other and to their ideas, but that these events have rendered untenable that relationship between men, objects, nature, and the sense of the ideal (the deity) which has been accepted since the Renaissance. Schismatic post-modernism sees the relationship between men and objects as a competitive one, and God as dead or, at least, removed from the fray. . . .

It may well be that the extreme position which Eisenman represents in architecture, Cage in music, and Gass in literature, marks an end part in a cycle, and that a viable post-modernism must be one that opens up possibilities for new production rather than describes a situation that can be seen as ultimately futile and nihilistic.

Traditional post-modernism is simultaneously inside contemporary society and critically detached from it; it uses art to comment on everyday life; it is at once "satiric" and accepting in its view of culture; in this sense it seeks to make telling interpretations of everyday life. Such a post-modernism begins to "restore that state of balance between unchecked fabulation and objective social realism" necessary to prevent artistic production from degenerating into trivial self-indulgence.

In painting and in architecture, traditional post-modernism relies increasingly on representational as opposed to abstract or conceptual modes. Nonetheless, traditional post-modernism does not advocate stylistic revival, though it does support the concept of emulation. Traditional post-modernism looks back to history to see how things were done and to remind itself that many good ways of doing things which were cast aside for ideological reasons can be usefully rediscovered. Thus, for example, inclusive post-modernism can employ recognizable imagery in an abstract way—it can be at once pre-modernist and modernist.

Architecture, of course, is by definition a public art. Yet in its modernist phase, it often spoke the private language of painting.

. . . It is an aspect of social and cultural responsibility—not in the narrowly simplistic sense of architectural do-goodism but in a broader and more profound sense of a genuine and unsentimental humanism—that characterized traditional post-modernism's distinction from the abstract, self-referential schismatic post-modernism which we have already discussed.

Traditional post-modernism rejects the anti-historical biases of modernism; influences from history are no longer seen as constraints on either personal growth or artistic excellence. History, no longer viewed as the dead hand of the past, now seems at the very least a standard of excellence in a continuing struggle to deal effectively with the present. Modernism looked toward the future as an escape from the past; traditional post-modernism struggles with the legacy of that attitude, a world filled with objects whose principle artistic impetus often came from a belief that in order to be "Modern" they must look and function as little as possible like anything that had been seen in the world before. The traditional post-modernist struggle then, is not to free itself from the past, but to relax what has been characterized as "the stubborn grip of the values created by the rebellion against the past." . . .

Traditional post-modernism recognizes that the public has lost confidence in architects (though it still believes in the symbolic power of architecture). Modernist architecture offered very little in the way of joy or visual pleasure, its conceptual basis was limited and disconcertingly materialistic. By once again recognizing the common assumptions a culture inherits from its past, traditional post-modernism is not only an announcement that Modern architecture has emerged from its puritan revolution, its catharsis at last behind it, but it is also an avowal of self-confidence in contemporary architecture's ability and willingness to re-establish itself on a basis which cannot only deal with the past but also match it, value for value, building for building.

Traditional post-modernism seeks to look backward in order to go forward. It should not be regarded as a jettisoning of Modern architecture itself, but as an attempt to pick up the threads of theory and style which were cut by the pioneers of the Modern Movement, especially the concerns for architectural history and for visually comprehensible relationships between old and new buildings. In its inclusiveness, traditional post-modernism does not propose an independent style; it is a sensibility dependent on forms and strategies drawn from the modernist and the pre-modernist work that preceded it, though it declares the obsolescence of both. It is *a* Modern style but not *the* Modern style. In its recognition of the transience and multiplicity of styles within the historical epoch we call Modern, it rejects the emphasis on unity of expression that was so central to modernism itself. Traditional post-modernism recognizes both the discursive and expressive meaning of formal language. It recognizes the language of form as communicating sign as well as infra-referential symbol: that is to say, it deals with both physical and associational experience, with the work of art as an act of "presentation" and "representation." It rejects the idea of a single style in favor of a view that acknowledges the existence of many styles (and the likely emergence of even more) each with its own meanings, sometimes permanently established, but more often shifting in relation to other events in the culture. . . .

The fundamental nature of this shift to post-modernism has to do with the reawakening of artists in every field to the public responsibilities of art. Once again art is being regarded as an act of communication as opposed to one of production or revelation (of the artist's ego and/or of his intentions for the building or his process of design). Though art is based on personal invention it requires public acceptance to achieve real value—to communicate meaning. An artist may choose to speak a private language, but a viewer must be willing and able to "read" the work, whether it be a book, a painting, or a building, for the work to have any kind of public life at all. To the extent that contemporary artists care about the public life of art, they are post-modernists (modernist artists make things for only themselves and/or for the gods); to the extent that an artist believes in the communicative role of form but is not willing to accept that such a role necessarily carries with it cultural meanings, that are not inherent to the form, his is a schismatic post-modernism.

Modernism in architecture was premised on a dialectic between things as they are and things as they ought to be; post-modernism seeks a resolution between—or at least a recognition of—things as they were and as they are. Modernism imagined architecture to be the product of purely rational and scientific process; post-modernism sees it as a resolution of social and technological processes with cultural concerns.

Post-modernism seeks to regain the public role that modernism denied architecture. The Post-Modern struggle is the struggle for cultural coherence, a coherence that is not falsely monolithic, as was attempted in the International Style in architecture or National Socialism in the politics of the 1920s and 30s, but one whose coherence is based on the heterogeneous substance and nature of modern society: post-modernism takes as its basis things as they are, *and* things as they were. Architecture is no longer an image of the world as architects wish it to be or as it will be, but as it is.

Emotion and Meaning in Music

LEONARD MEYER

The Problem of Meaning in Music

The meaning of music has of late been the subject of much confused argument and controversy. The controversy has stemmed largely from disagreements as to what music communicates, while the confusion has resulted for the most part from a lack of clarity as to the nature and definition of meaning itself.

The debates as to what music communicates have centered around the question of whether music can designate, depict, or otherwise communicate referential concepts, images, experiences, and emotional states. This is the old argument between the absolutists and the referentialists. . . .

Because it has not appeared problematical to them, the referentialists have not as a rule explicitly considered the problem of musical meaning. Musical meaning according to the referentialists lies in the relationship between a musical symbol or sign and the extramusical thing which it designates.

Since our concern in this study is not primarily with the referential meaning of music, suffice it to say that the disagreement between the referentialists and the absolutists is, as was pointed out at the beginning of this chapter, the result of a tendency toward philosophical monism rather than the result of any logical incompatibility. Both designative and non-designative meanings arise out of musical experience, just as they do in other types of aesthetic experience.

The absolutists have contended that the meaning of music lies specifically, and some would assert exclusively, in the musical processes themselves. For them musical meaning is non-designative. But in what sense these processes are meaningful, in what sense a succession or sequence of non-referential musical stimuli can be said to give rise to meaning, they have been unable to state with either clarity or precision. They have also failed to relate musical meaning to other kinds of meaning—to meaning in general. This failure has led some critics to assert that musical meaning is a thing apart, different in some unexplained way from all other kinds of meaning. This is simply an evasion of the real issue. For it is obvious that if the term "meaning" is to have any signification at all as applied to music, then it must have the same signification as when applied to other kinds of experience.

Without reviewing all the untenable positions to which writers have tenaciously adhered, it seems fair to say that much of the confusion and uncertainty as to the nature of non-referential musical meaning has resulted from two fallacies. On the one hand, there has been a tendency to locate meaning exclusively in one aspect of the communicative process; on the other hand, there has been a propensity to regard all meanings arising in human communication as designative, as involving symbolism of some sort.

Since these difficulties can be best resolved in the light of a general definition of meaning, let us begin with such a definition: ". . . anything acquires meaning if it is connected with, or indicates, or refers to, something beyond itself, so that its full nature points to and is revealed in that connection."[1]

Meaning is thus not a property of things. It cannot be located in the stimulus alone. The same stimulus may have many different meanings. To a geologist a large rock may indicate that at one time a glacier began to recede at a given spot; to a farmer the same rock may point to the necessity of having the field cleared for plowing; and to the sculptor the rock may indicate the

---

[1]Morris R. Cohen, *A Preface to Logic* (New York: Holt, Rinehart and Winston, 1944), p. 47.

possibility of artistic creation. A rock, a word, or motion in and of itself, merely as a stimulus, is meaningless.

Thus it is pointless to ask what the intrinsic meaning of a single tone or a series of tones is. Purely as physical existences they are meaningless. They become meaningful only in so far as they point to, indicate, or imply something beyond themselves.

Nor can meaning be located exclusively in the objects, events, or experiences which the stimulus indicates, refers to, or implies. The meaning of the rock is the product of the relationship between the stimulus and the thing it points to or indicates.

Though the perception of a relationship can only arise as the result of some individual's mental behavior, the relationship itself is not to be located in the mind of the perceiver. The meanings observed are not subjective. Thus the relationships existing between the tones themselves or those existing between the tones and the things they designate or connote, though a product of cultural experience, are real connections existing objectively in culture. They are not arbitrary connections imposed by the capricious mind of the particular listener.

Meaning, then, is not in either the stimulus, or of what it points to, or the observer. Rather it arises out of what both Cohen and Mead have called the "triadic" relationship between (1) an object or stimulus; (2) that to which the stimulus points—that which is its consequent; and (3) the conscious observer.

Discussions of the meaning of music have also been muddled by the failure to state explicitly what musical stimuli indicate or point to. A stimulus may indicate events or consequences which are different from itself in kind, as when a word designates or points to an object or action which is not itself a word. Or a stimulus may indicate or imply events or consequences which are of the same kind as the stimulus itself, as when a dim light on the eastern horizon heralds the coming of day. Here both the antecedent stimulus and the consequent event are natural phenomena. The former type of meaning may be called designative, the latter embodied.

Because most of the meanings which arise in human communication are of the designative type, employing linguistic signs or the iconic signs of the plastic arts, numerous critics have failed to realize that this is not necessarily or exclusively the case. This mistake has led even avowed absolutists to allow designation to slip in through the secret door of semantic chicanery.

But even more important than designative meaning is what we have called embodied meaning. From this point of view what a musical stimulus or a series of stimuli indicate and point to are not extramusical concepts and objects but other musical events which are about to happen. That is, one musical event (be it a tone, a phrase, or a whole section) has meaning because it points to and makes us expect another musical event. This is what music means from the viewpoint of the absolutist.

Embodied musical meaning is, in short, a product of expectation. If, on the basis of past experience, a present stimulus leads us to expect a more or less definite consequent musical event, then that stimulus has meaning.

From this it follows that a stimulus or gesture which does not point to or arouse expectations of a subsequent musical event or consequent is meaningless. Because expectation is largely a product of stylistic experience, music in a style with which we are totally unfamiliar is meaningless.

However, once the aesthetic attitude has been brought into play, very few gestures actually appear to be meaningless so long as the listener has some experience with the style of the work in question. For so long as a stimulus is possible within any known style, the listener will do his best to relate it to the style, to understand its meaning.

In and of themselves, for example, the opening chords of Beethoven's Third Symphony have no particular musical stylistic tendency. They establish no pattern of motion, arouse no tensions toward a particular fulfilment. Yet as part of the total aesthetic cultural act of attention they are meaningful. For since they are the first chords of a piece, we not only expect more music but our expectations are circumscribed by the limitations of the style which we believe the piece to be in and by the psychological demand for a more palpable pattern. . . .

Thus the phrase "past experience," used in the definition of meaning given above, must be understood in a broad sense. It includes the immediate past of the particular stimulus or gesture; that which has already taken place in this particular work to condition the listener's opinion of the stimulus and hence his expectations as to the impending, consequent event. In the example given above, the past was silence. But this fact of the past is just as potent in conditioning expectation as a whole section of past events. The phrase "past experience" also refers to the more remote, but ever present, past experience of similar musical stimuli and similar musical situations in other works. That is it refers to those past experiences which constitute our sense and knowledge of style. The phrase also comprehends the dispositions and beliefs which the listener brings to the musical experience . . . as well as the laws of mental behavior which govern his organization of stimuli into patterns and the expectations aroused on the basis of those patterns. . . .

The words "consequent musical event" must be understood to include: (1) those consequents which are envisaged or expected; (2) the events which do, in fact, follow the stimulus, whether they were the ones envisaged or not; and (3) the more distant ramifications or events which, because the total series of gestures is presumed to be causally connected, are considered as being the later consequences of the stimulus in question. Seen in this light, the meaning of the stimulus is not confined to or limited by the initial triadic relationship out of which it arises. As the later stages of the musical process establish new relationships with the stimulus, new meanings arise. These later meanings coexist in memory with the earlier ones and, combining with them, constitute the meaning of the work as a total experience.

In this development three stages of meaning may be distinguished.

"Hypothetical meanings" are those which arise during the act of expectation. Since what is envisaged is a product of the probability relationships which exist as part of style, . . . and since these probability relationships always involve the possibility of alternative consequences, a given stimulus invariably gives rise to several alternative hypothetical meanings. One consequent may, of course, be so much more probable than any other that the listener, though aware of the possibility of less likely consequences, is really set and ready only for the most probable. In such a case hypothetical meaning is without ambiguity. In other cases several consequents may be almost equally probable, and, since the listener is in doubt as to which alternative will actually materialize, meaning is ambiguous, though not necessarily less forceful and marked. . . .

Though the consequent which is actually forthcoming must be possible within the style, it may or may not be of those which was most probable. Or it may arrive only after a delay or a deceptive diversion through alternative consequences. But whether our expectations are confirmed or not, a new stage of meaning is reached when the consequent becomes actualized as a concrete musical event.

"Evident meanings" are those which are attributed to the antecedent gesture when the consequent becomes a physico-psychic fact and when the relationship between the antecedent and consequent is perceived. Since the consequent of a stimulus itself becomes a stimulus with consequences, evident meaning also includes the later stages of musical development which are presumed to be the products of a chain of causality. Thus in the following sequence, where a stimulus (S) leads to a consequent (C), which is also a stimulus that indicates and is actualized in further consequents,

$$S_2 \ldots \ldots C_1 S_2 \ldots \ldots C_2 S_3 \ldots \ldots \text{etc.,}$$

evident meaning arises not only out of the relationship between S_1 and C_1 but also out of the relationships between S_1 and all subsequent consequences, in so far as these are considered to issue from S_1. It is also important to realize that the motion $S_1 \ldots \ldots C_2$ may itself become a gesture that gives rise to envisaged and actual consequents and hence becomes a term or gesture on another level of triadic relationships. In other words, both evident and hypothetical meanings come into being and exist on several architectonic levels.

Evident meaning is colored and conditioned by hypothetical meaning. For the actual relationship between the gesture and its consequent is always considered in the light of the expected relationship. In a sense the listener even revises his opinion of the hypothetical meaning when the stimulus does not move to the expected consequent.

"Determinate meanings" are those meanings which arise out of the relationships existing between hypothetical meaning, evident meaning, and the later stages of the musical development. In other words, determinate meaning arises only after the experience of the work is timeless in memory, only when all the meanings which the stimulus has had in the particular experience are realized and their relationships to one another comprehended as fully as possible.

A distinction must be drawn between the understanding of musical meaning which involves the awareness of the tendencies, resistances, tensions, and fulfilments embodied in a work and the self-conscious objectification of that meaning in the mind of the individual listener. The former may be said to involve a meaningful experience, the latter involves knowing what that meaning is, considering it as an objective thing in consciousness.

The operation of intelligence in listening to music need never become self-conscious. We are continually behaving in an intelligent way, comprehending meanings and acting upon our perceptions, cognitions, and evaluations without ever making the meanings themselves the objects of our scrutiny—without ever becoming self-conscious about what experience means. What Bertrand Russell says about understanding language also applies to the understanding of music: "Understanding language is . . . like understanding cricket: it is a matter of habits acquired in oneself and rightly presumed in others."[2]

Meanings become objectified only under conditions of self-consciousness and when reflection takes place. "One attains self-consciousness only as he takes, or finds himself stimulated to take, the attitude of the other."[3] Though training may make for a generally self-conscious attitude, one is stimulated to take the attitude of the other when the normal habits of response are disturbed in some way; when one is driven to ask one's self: What does this mean, what is the intention of this passage? Reflection is likewise brought into play where some tendency is delayed, some pattern of habitual behavior disturbed. So long as behavior is automatic and habitual there is no urge for it to become self-conscious, though it may become so. If meaning is to become objectified at all, it will as a rule become so when difficulties are encountered that make normal, automatic behavior impossible. In other words, given a mind disposed toward objectification, meaning will become the focus of attention, an object of conscious consideration, when a tendency or habit reaction is delayed or inhibited.

It thus appears that the same processes which were said to give rise to affect are now said to give rise to the objectification of embodied meaning.

---

[2]Bertrand Russell, *Selected Papers* (New York: Random House [Modern Library]), p. 358.
[3]George H. Mead, *Mind, Self, and Society* (Chicago: University of Chicago Press, 1934), p. 194.

But this is a dilemma only so long as the traditional dichotomy between reason and emotion and the parent polarity between mind and body are adopted. Once it is recognized that affective experience is just as dependent upon intelligent cognition as conscious intellection, that both involve perception, taking account of, envisaging, and so forth, then thinking and feeling need not be viewed as polar opposites but as different manifestations of a single psychological process.

There is no diametric opposition, no inseparable gulf, between the affective and the intellectual responses made to music. Though they are psychologically differentiated as responses, both depend upon the same perceptive processes, the same stylistic habits, the same modes of mental organization; and the same musical processes give rise to and shape both types of experience. Seen in this light, the formalist's conception of musical experience and the expressionist's conception of it appear as complementary rather than contradictory positions. They are considering not different processes but different ways of experiencing the same process.

Whether a piece of music gives rise to affective experience or to intellectual experience depends upon the disposition and training of the listener. To some minds the disembodied feeling of affective experience is uncanny and unpleasant and a process of rationalization is undertaken in which the musical processes are objectified as conscious meaning. Belief also probably plays an important role in determining the character of the response. Those who have been taught to believe that musical experience is primarily emotional and who are therefore disposed to respond affectively will probably do so. Those listeners who have learned to understand music in technical terms will tend to make musical processes an object of conscious consideration. This probably accounts for the fact that most trained critics and aestheticians favor the formalist position. Thus while the trained musician consciously waits for the expected resolution of a dominant seventh chord the untrained, but practiced, listener feels the delay as affect.

Meanings and affects may, however, arise without communication taking place. Individual A observes another individual B wink and interprets the wink as a friendly gesture. It has meaning for A who observes it. But if the wink was not intentional—if, for instance, B simply has a nervous tic—then no communication has taken place, for to B the act had no meaning. Communication, as Mead has pointed out, takes place only where the gesture made has the same meaning for the individual who makes it that it has for the individual who responds to it.

It is this internalization of gestures, what Mead calls "taking the attitude of the other"[4] (the audience), which enables the creative artist, the composer, to communicate with listeners. It is because the composer is also a listener that he is able to control his inspiration with reference to the listener. For

---

[4]Ibid., p. 47.

instance, the composer knows how the listener will respond to a deceptive cadence and controls the later stages of the composition with reference to that supposed response. The performer too is continually "taking the attitude of the other"—of the listener. As Leopold Mozart puts it, the performer "must play everything in such a way that he will himself be moved by it."[5]

It is precisely because he is continually taking the attitude of the listener that the composer becomes aware and conscious of his own self, his ego, in the process of creation. In this process of differentiation between himself as composer and himself as audience, the composer becomes self-conscious and objective.

But though the listener participates in the musical process, assuming the role which the composer envisaged for him, and though he must, in some sense, create his own experience, yet he need not take the attitude of the composer in order to do so. He need not ask: How will someone else respond to this stimulus? Nor is he obliged to objectify his own responses, to ask, How am I responding? Unlike the composer, the listener may and frequently does "lose himself in the music"; and, in following and responding to the sound gestures made by the composer, the listener may become oblivious of his own ego, which has literally become one with that of the music.

We must, then, be wary of easy and high-sounding statements to the effect that "we cannot understand a work of art without, to a certain degree, repeating and reconstructing the creative process by which it has come into being."[6] Certainly the listener must respond to the work of art as the artist intended, and the listener's experience of the work must be similar to that which the composer envisaged for him. But this is a different thing from experiencing the "creative process which brought it into being."

However, the listener may take the attitude of the composer. He may be self-conscious in the act of listening. Those trained in music, and perhaps those trained in the other arts as well, tend, because of the critical attitudes which they have developed in connection with their own artistic efforts, to become self-conscious and objective in all their aesthetic experiences. And it is no doubt partly for this reason that, as noted above, trained musicians tend to objectify meaning, to consider it as an object of conscious cognition. . . .

Finally, and perhaps most important of all, this analysis of communication emphasizes the absolute necessity of a common universe of discourse in art. For without a set of gestures common to the social group, and without common habit responses to those gestures, no communication whatsoever would be possible. Communication depends upon, presupposes, and arises out of the universe of discourse which in the aesthetics of music is called style.

---

[5]Leopold Mozart, *Versuch einer gründlichen Violinschule*, quoted in *Source Readings in Music History*, ed., Oliver Strunk (New York: W. W. Norton Co., Inc., 1950), p. 602.

[6]Ernst Cassirer, *An Essay on Man: An Introduction to a Philosophy of Human Culture* (New York: Doubleday & Co., Inc., 1953), p. 191.

Meaning and Music

DONALD SHERBURNE

This paper defends the view that music has meaning and that this meaning is a referential meaning referring to the extramusical world of emotional states. Part I examines and then rejects the widely read, frequently discussed views of Leonard B. Meyer, who defends in a modern, fascinating way the position of the Absolutist that any meaning which music may have lies within the context of the work itself and in the perception of the relationships set forth in the work, and that any emotion which may arise in response to music exists quite apart from the realm of extramusical emotions. Part II is the constructive section of the paper; it accepts in general outline the position of Susanne Langer but quickly goes beyond her analysis to new suggestions derived from the author's work in Whitehead's metaphysics. Part III suggests the larger implications for aesthetic theory of these proposals.

I

"Expectation" is the key notion in Meyer's theory, as that theory is developed in his book, *Emotion and Meaning in Music*.[1] Musical meaning is a product of expectation. A series of musical stimuli refer beyond themselves, not to extramusical events or concepts, but to other musical events which are about to happen and which are more or less expected as a result of what has gone before. Musical meaning is possible, on this theory, because of style; a given composition falls within a stylistic tradition which supports a musical syntax, a syntax which leads one to expect given sorts of kinetic development in given sorts of situations. If a musical phrase thwarts expectation and works itself out in a novel, unexpected way, then its musical significance is considerable. If a musical phrase perfectly confirms predictions and expectations, then it is trivial.

   This theory of meaning in Meyer gets its full impact when joined to his theory of musical emotion. Arguing away from John Dewey's conflict-theory of emotions, which holds that emotion in any area of experience is evoked when a tendency to respond is inhibited, Meyer holds that when expectation is generated and then frustrated by unexpected progressions and resolutions, emotion, as well as musical interest and significance, is generated. The secret of powerfully moving, significant, and meaningful music is thus before us: it is music (1) within a style, (2) which therefore generates expectations, (3)

Donald Sherburne, "Meaning and Music," *Journal of Aesthetics and Art Criticism*, 24 (1966), reprinted with permission.

---

[1](Chicago, 1956).

which expectations are, however, baffled and thwarted by unanticipated novelties of development and resolution, which simultaneously generate emotion and create musical interest and significance.

This is an ingenious, imaginative, plausible theory. Yet upon reflection I find Meyer's theory wanting, and I turn now to some criticisms of his position, which I have so hastily adumbrated. The first and most damaging criticism is that certain inferences about musical experience which the theory forces us to draw are totally at odds with our actual experience. If the theory were correct, the first hearing of a work should reek with meaning and send emotional tingles to the tips of the toes; but with subsequent hearings the significance and emotional impact of a work ought to decline rapidly as the unexpected becomes the expected, as expectation becomes replaced by recollection and anticipation. In fact, the far more common experience is that works tend to become more compelling as one gets inside them and obtains a growing familiarity with them. In short, Meyer's theory seems to be incompatible with the ordinary conviction that fine music can be reheard and re-enjoyed many, many times, frequently with heightened appreciation.

As Meyer himself has noted, when this objection to his theory has been raised in the past,[2] it is difficult to determine whether the theory conforms to the facts of musical life precisely because it is not easy to establish just what these facts are. Ultimately each person must be judge in these matters for himself. But it strikes me that even granting Meyer's counter-arguments—for example, that memory is fallible and that it takes repeated hearings in order to grasp the implications of a musical event—still, it is just at the point where memory has mastered its material that musical experience emerges as most intense, and this is not what Meyer's theory leads one to predict. Also, Meyer considers it a virtue of his theory that it explains why the performer tends to change his interpretation of works he knows well, namely, to revitalize them for himself; and, also, Meyer feels that his theory explains the proliferation on the market of recordings of a given composition: namely, to meet the demand of listeners for new interpretations of familiar works. To start with the last point first, I think the proliferation of recordings of a given composition can be explained in economic terms, and several of the most sophisticated listeners whom I know are great partisans of particular recordings of particular works; so that if it is Conductor X's reading of a given work to which they are partial, then they have no use for Conductor Y's reading or Conductor Z's reading. Meyer's theory would not lead us to predict this. On the first point, the point that the performer tends to change his interpretation of works he knows well, here I plead ignorance of the facts; but I am not convinced that performers do "tend," across the board, to modify interpretations once they have one that by general acclaim is exciting, brilliant, and so forth. And even if performers *do* modify interpretations, there is still

---

[2] *J. of the American Musicological Society,* XIV, 2 (1961), 257–267.

the question of their *motives* for so doing—perhaps it is more accurate to say that a sense of dissatisfaction with the *quality* of their performances motivates them to introduce modifications into subsequent performances. Here, again, it is not obvious to me that Meyer's theory predicts what we in fact find to be the case.

So much for my first objection to Meyer's theory, the objection centering upon rehearing music. But there is a second: Meyer is forced to reject as meaningless and trivial the music that results from recent experiments to produce non-teleological music, music avowedly without tendency or direction. Such music, sometimes complete with built-in randomizers, is written with the purpose of destroying purpose, destroying syntax, and eliminating expectation, so that the listener will concentrate not on relations, but on the immediate sense surface of the sound. Such music can be reheard indefinitely, Meyer admits, without any change in emotional value and meaningfulness at all—but this is, he holds, because of, and proof of, its total lack of musical value. Now it is a virtue in Meyer's theory that it possesses a clean-cut, direct honesty—it leads him to conclude that works like those of Stockhausen and Cage are without value as music. But this kind of virtue is a dangerous one. Though many may feel like giving three cheers for a theory with this particular implication, one is sobered by the recollection that history has a way of incorporating principles from fringe movements into the mainstream of aesthetic development. One has only to think of painting and the phenomenal rise of abstract impressionism to begin to feel uneasy about a theory which out of hand rejects the non-telic approach.

II

In this controversy over meaning in music, the Absolutists who hold that music illuminates nothing whatever are most certainly wrong, but so are the extremists at the opposite pole who, like Wagner, insist that music illuminates everything in heaven and on earth. I agree with J. W. N. Sullivan when he says that ". . . no class of people is to be more avoided than those who look for, and find, a 'story' in every musical composition."[3] It has been reported that Strauss, at the height of his programmatic frenzy, asserted that the day would come when a composer could compose the silverware on the table so that the listener could distinguish the knives from the forks. This is obvious nonsense, and I want to make it clear that I repudiate this lunatic fringe just as Meyer, it might be added, repudiates those Absolutists who deny that music has any meaning at all.

But what do I assert? As a beginning I accept certain points from Hanslick and Langer, and depart from a point made in Hanslick's *The Beautiful*

---

[3] J. W. N. Sullivan, *Beethoven: His Spiritual Development* (New York, Vintage Books), p. 9.

in Music. In one interesting passage, to be quoted directly, Hanslick is arguing that music can represent neither the object of a feeling nor the feeling itself. He is right, but, nevertheless, this passage, which Hanslick advances to crush the referentialists, really contains the foundation for limited, viable referentialism. Hanslick writes:

> What part of the feelings, then, can music represent, if not the subject involved in them? Only their dynamic properties. It may reproduce the motion accompanying psychical action according to its momentum: speed, slowness, strength, weakness, increasing and decreasing intensity. But motion is only one of the concomitants of feeling, not the feeling itself. It is a popular fallacy to suppose that the descriptive power of music is sufficiently qualified by saying that, although incapable of representing the subject of a feeling, it may represent the feeling itself—not the object of love, but the feeling of love. In reality, however, music can do neither. It cannot reproduce the feeling of love but only the element of motion. . . . This is the element which music has in common with our emotions and which, with creative power, it contrives to exhibit in an endless variety of forms and contrasts.[4]

In this passage Hanslick has granted a certain analogy between music and emotions, an analogy of dynamic structure. Morris Weitz has correctly argued that even this small admission makes Hanslick a heteronomist in a very limited sense.[5] Susanne Langer pushes this insight of Hanslick's even further in creating her limited referentialist position. She argues that Hanslick's implicit semantic is far too narrow and primitive: "Because he considered nothing but conventional denotation as 'meaning,' he insisted that music could not mean anything."[6] She further argues that the analogy between music and emotions pointed out by Hanslick satisfies the basic requirement for a connotative relationship between music and subjective experience, namely a similarity of logical form, and with this to work on, she proceeds to argue that music is the kind of symbol which she calls *presentational*. Such a symbol is a dynamic instrument of discovery and clarification rather than a purveyor of static references; it is an unconsummated symbol which does not assert but rather articulates—it is not expres*sion*, it is expres*sive*.

Mrs. Langer's position is basically sound, but the meaning of her account can be expanded beyond her intent. In analyzing ordinary statements we distinguish a subject and a predicate. We could, if we wanted to be Whiteheadian about it, distinguish the logical subject of a proposition on the one hand and the predicative pattern of a proposition on the other. I should like to suggest that music is sheer predicative pattern. As Hanslick insisted, music cannot represent specific feelings, it cannot convey a subject, but it does

[4]Eduard Hanslick, *The Beautiful in Music* (New York, 1957), pp. 24–25.
[5]Ibid., p. xii.
[6]Susanne K. Langer, *Philosophy in a New Key* (New York, 1954), p. 194.

convey the dynamic properties of feelings, and this is what I mean by saying that music is sheer predicative pattern.

Three observations will, I think, clarify this proposal. First, it is a fact that people have said over and over again that music is the most abstract of the arts; for this reason it has been called the Queen of the Arts. In some sense this is true, but in what sense? Sound is as concrete a datum as any other—there is nothing abstract about it. How, then, can the character of music be abstract? It is abstract precisely in the sense that it is sheer predicative pattern. But in the aesthetic *experience* of music there is more than predicative pattern; there is a subject also. I contend that this subject is provided by the listener in response to the predicative pattern. The predicative pattern elicits the subject: It is in this way that I interpret Langer's assertion that the presentational symbol is an unconsummated symbol which discovers, clarifies, articulates. In itself the music is an abstract predicative pattern, but in musical *experience* it becomes the pattern *of* a subject-feeling provided by the listener.

Second, numerous writers have noted that there are myriads of emotions, only a few of which have been singled out and named. The emotional life is hopelessly complex and varied. Music leads us to a heightened awareness of our emotional existence by causing us to isolate segments of it as subjects for the predicative patterns it thrusts upon us.

Third, my proposal takes on clarity when compared to a point made by William James in the penultimate chapter of *The Varieties of Religious Experience*. James concludes that there are great revitalizing forces in the subconscious which, when released, refresh and strengthen the soul. But these powers do not automatically flow in upon the soul. They are released by the over-beliefs of a person's religion, over-beliefs being those non-empirical convictions at the heart of any religious tradition.

> . . . the spiritual excitement in which the gift appears a real one will often fail to be aroused in an individual until certain particular intellectual beliefs or ideas which, as we say, come home to him, are touched. These ideas will thus be essential to that individual's religion;—which is as much as to say that over-beliefs in various directions are absolutely indispensable . . .[7]

There is, I believe, a parallel situation in music. Music has great power but it requires something analogous to the over-beliefs of religion for that power to be released. I suggest that the clarifying, articulating, communicating dimension of music is released when the listener engages its predicative power by providing a subject for that predicative pattern.

This, then, is the sense of my referentialism. In one sense music is concrete, but in another it is abstract and points beyond itself, as do predicative patterns, which by themselves are abstract possibilities and point be-

---

[7]Mentor Edition, p. 388.

yond themselves to concrete actual entities for their logical subjects. Music as predicative pattern points beyond itself to the emotional dimension of human existence. As a result, in music more than in any other art the very nature of the art-object is a function of the contemplator, who shares in the creation of the aesthetic object by providing from his own experience the emotional subject which completes the pure predicative pattern. DeWitt Parker's distinction between aesthetic instrument and aesthetic object is relevant here. As he uses these terms, the aesthetic instrument is the physical object that scientists can measure, thieves steal, and so forth, while the aesthetic object is the total experience which combines an aesthetic instrument, a sensuous form, with the meanings which underlie the form and exist in the life of the imagination. According to this terminology it would follow that the aesthetic instrument in music is the sensuous sounds constituting the pure predicative pattern, while the aesthetic object in music is the total response of a listener using the aesthetic instrument (predicative pattern) as a vehicle for the imagination, which creates the aesthetic object from the interaction between the aesthetic instrument and its own nature, its own nature providing the emotional subject which completes, and releases the spiritual power of, the pure predicative pattern.

It should be noted that this theory does not succumb to either of the objections which have been raised against Meyer's theory. First, the present theory leads one to predict that a rehearing of a composition would intensify, not diminish, the emotional impact of that composition upon a listener; for the articulating, clarifying power of the "unconsummated symbol," as Langer calls music, would increasingly penetrate into the emotional life of the listener as familiarity led him to select, even if unconsciously, an increasingly precise and effective logical subject for that increasingly familiar predicative pattern. And, second, the present theory would lead one to suggest that the compositions of Cage and Stockhausen may be predicative patterns with some real power to articulate the vague, incoherent emotions associated with the *angst*, the dread, the meaninglessness, the absurdity which existentialism, for example, finds in the soul of modern man.

III

What larger implications for aesthetic theory now come to the fore? Aestheticians are divided into those who argue that Art is life-oriented, revelatory, pulsing with human significance and insight into reality, and those who argue that Art exists for Art's sake alone, that it is aloof, exclusive, autonomous, cut off from the world so that its practitioners and its customers need bring nothing with them from the world when they enter its Olympian domain. This latter group focuses on the immediate sense surface, the significant form; the former group speaks of expression, communication, revelation.

In the debate between partisans of these two rival positions, music is often used as the prime weapon of the autonomists, the purists, the formalists of the second camp. To the claim of a Croce or a Collingwood that Art expresses in the sense that it clarifies and articulates, the autonomists reply by smugly pointing to music as does John Hospers, for example, when he writes: ". . . I cannot say that the *Prelude and Fugue in G Minor* is expressive of anything. . . ."[8] The Croce-Collingwood theory operates very successfully in poetry, while the formalists here become a bit embarrassed; the "pure music" theory of poetry has never made much headway. But on the other hand the purists seem to be strong when they speak of music and modern art.

Is it the case that we are left with these two ultimate positions, each unassailable in those media it prefers to discuss? I mean this question to be rhetorical, for it has been the purpose of this paper to show that an Art for Life's sake view can meaningfully and plausibly extend to music. If it can, then the partisans of this view of Art have captured a hostage whom the purists desperately wish to defend and protect as their own.

The Future of Music: Credo

JOHN CAGE

I BELIEVE THAT THE USE OF NOISE

Wherever we are, what we hear is mostly noise. When we ignore it, it disturbs us. When we listen to it, we find it fascinating. The sound of a truck at fifty miles per hour. Static between the stations. Rain. We want to capture and control these sounds, to use them not as sound effects but as musical instruments. Every film studio has a library of "sound effects" recorded on film. With a film phonograph it is now possible to control the amplitude and frequency of any one of these sounds and to give to it rhythms within or beyond the reach of the imagination. Given four film phonographs,

John Cage, "The Future of Music: Credo," from *Silence*. Copyright © 1958 by John Cage, reprinted by permission of Wesleyan University Press. The text was delivered as a talk at a meeting of a Seattle arts society organized by Bonnie Bird in 1937. It was printed in the brochure accompanying George Avakian's recording of Cage's twenty-five-year retrospective concert at Town Hall, New York, in 1958.

[8]John Hospers, "The Concept of Artistic Expression," originally published in *Proceedings of the Aristotelian Society* (1954–55), pp. 313–344; reprinted in Morris Weitz, *Problems in Aesthetics* (New York, 1959), pp. 193–217, this statement appearing on p. 206.

we can compose and perform a quartet for explosive motor, wind, heartbeat, and landslide.

TO MAKE MUSIC

If this word "music" is sacred and reserved for eighteenth- and nineteenth-century instruments, we can substitute a more meaningful term: organization of sound.

WILL CONTINUE AND INCREASE UNTIL WE REACH A MUSIC PRODUCED THROUGH THE AID OF ELECTRICAL INSTRUMENTS

Most inventors of electrical musical instruments have attempted to imitate eighteenth- and nineteenth-century instruments, just as early automobile designers copied the carriage. The Novachord and the Solovox are examples of this desire to imitate the past rather than construct the future. When Theremin provided an instrument with genuinely new possibilities, Thereminists did their utmost to make the instrument sound like some old instrument, giving it a sickeningly sweet vibrato, and performing upon it, with difficulty, masterpieces from the past. Although the instrument is capable of a wide variety of sound qualities, obtained by the turning of a dial, Thereministes act as censors, giving the public those sounds they think the public will like. We are shielded from new sound experiences.

The special function of electrical instruments will be to provide complete control of the overtone structure of tones (as opposed to noises) and to make these tones available in any frequency, amplitude, and duration.

WHICH WILL MAKE AVAILABLE FOR MUSICAL PURPOSES ANY AND ALL SOUNDS THAT CAN BE HEARD. PHOTOELECTRIC, FILM, AND MECHANICAL MEDIUMS FOR THE SYNTHETIC PRODUCTION OF MUSIC

It is now possible for composers to make music directly, without the assistance of intermediary performers. Any design repeated often enough on a sound track is audible. Two hundred and eighty circles per second on a sound track will produce one sound, whereas a portrait of Beethoven repeated fifty times per second on a sound track will have not only a different pitch but a different sound quality.

WILL BE EXPLORED. WHEREAS, IN THE PAST, THE POINT OF DISAGREEMENT HAS BEEN BETWEEN DISSONANCE AND CONSONANCE, IT WILL BE, IN THE IMMEDIATE FUTURE, BETWEEN NOISE AND SO-CALLED MUSICAL SOUNDS.

THE PRESENT METHODS OF WRITING MUSIC, PRINCIPALLY THOSE WHICH EMPLOY HARMONY AND ITS REFERENCE TO PARTICULAR STEPS IN THE FIELD OF SOUND, WILL BE INADEQUATE FOR THE COMPOSER, WHO WILL BE FACED WITH THE ENTIRE FIELD OF SOUND.

The composer (organizer of sound) will be faced not only with the entire field of sound but also with the entire field of time. The "frame" or fraction of a second, following established film technique, will probably be the basic unit in the measurement of time. No rhythm will be beyond the composer's reach.

NEW METHODS WILL BE DISCOVERED, BEARING A DEFINITE RELATION TO SCHOEN-
BERGS TWELVE-TONE SYSTEM

Schoenberg's method assigns to each material, in a group of equal materials, its function with respect to the group. (Harmony assigned to each material, in a group of unequal materials, its function with respect to the fundamental or most important material in the group.) Schoenberg's method is analogous to a society in which the emphasis is on the group and the integration of the individual in the group.

AND PRESENT METHODS OF WRITING PERCUSSION MUSIC

Percussion music is a contemporary transition from keyboard-influenced music to the all-sound music of the future. Any sound is acceptable to the composer of percussion music; he explores the academically forbidden "non-musical" field of sound insofar as is manually possible.

Methods of writing percussion music have as their goal the rhythmic structure of a composition. As soon as these methods are crystallized into one or several widely accepted methods, the means will exist for group improvisations of unwritten but culturally important music. This has already taken place in Oriental cultures and in hot jazz.

AND ANY OTHER METHODS WHICH ARE FREE FROM THE CONCEPT OF A FUN-
DAMENTAL TONE.

THE PRINCIPLE OF FORM WILL
BE OUR ONLY CONSTANT CONNECTION WITH THE PAST. ALTHOUGH THE GREAT FORM
OF THE FUTURE WILL NOT BE AS IT WAS IN THE PAST, AT ONE TIME THE FUGUE
AND AT ANOTHER THE SONATA, IT WILL BE RELATED TO THESE AS THEY ARE TO
EACH OTHER:

Before this happens, centers of experimental music must be established. In these centers, the new materials, oscillators, turntables, generators, means for amplifying small sounds, film phonographs, etc., available for use. Composers at work using twentieth-century means for making music. Performances of results. Organization of sound for extra-musical purposes (theatre, dance, radio, film).

THROUGH THE
PRINCIPLE OF ORGANIZATION OR MAN'S COMMON ABILITY TO THINK.

ILLUSTRATION 7

PHILIP JOHNSON and JOHN
BURGEE, A. T. & T. Corporate
Headquarters, N.Y.

ILLUSTRATION 8

JOHN CAGE, *Solo for Piano (Concert for Piano and Orchestra)*. Copyright © 1960 by Henmar Press Inc. Reprinted by permission of C. F. Peters Corporation.

4

Marxist Aesthetics

Postmodernism is a new movement in art and in aesthetic theory. An earlier reaction to formalism, embodying both mimetic and didactic elements, were the Marxist theories of aesthetics (although Marxist aesthetics is still very much in the forefront of contemporary art theory). Marxist aestheticians trace the roots of their views to the nineteenth-century philosopher and political theorist Karl Marx. Although Marx himself said little about art in his writings, his ideas about the historical and social nature of people form the philosophical basis for a Marxist philosophy of art. This chapter begins with a brief selection from Marx's early work, the *Economic and Philosophic Manuscripts of 1844*. In this essay, in brief, Marx premises that human beings in their original states are merely natural animals. Persons differ from other animals only in that degree of intelligence which enables them to develop self-consciousness. In the first instance people lived in nature like other animals and, like other animals, were related to nature through their life-activities—our work. Unlike other animals, however, we have become conscious of our relationship to nature. Labor or work has become our "free conscious activity" by which we first define a relationship to nature, and then through which we transform nature into a human, socioeconomic world. This socioeconomic world we have created is now the antecedent condition of any individual's existence, because one is born into this prestructured environment, and one's consciousness develops from this starting point. This anthropomorphized social world is also historical. Reality is constantly changing and developing as "men themselves make their history"[1] by redefining their given historical situation for their own conscious ends.

From these views Marx argued that in a capitalist economy the life-

---

[1]Karl Marx, *The Eighteenth Brumaire of Louis Bonaparte* (1853; rpt. Moscow: Foreign Languages Publishing House [no date or translator available]), p. 15.

activity of human beings is misdirected. This is because the intrinsic worker-object relationship is diverted. The worker becomes alienated in a capitalistic economy because he is treated as an object, a means for production under the capitalist system, where the goal is not the activity of labor's relating a person to his or her work, but rather the production of surplus goods and capital. Most Marxists argue that in a capitalist society the situation of the artist is similar to that of the worker. Artists are alienated from society because their views may not accord with those of capitalist philosophy or because the worthiness of the artists' works are not always appreciated, since most works of art do not contribute to the increase of productivity or capital of the economy. And the work of a recognized artist often is treated like a commodity—a price-tagged object of certain monetary worth rather than as a work of conscious labor.

Included in this section is a selection from the writings of Adolfo Sánchez Vázquez, a contemporary Spanish thinker who uses Marx's theories of society, labor, and alienation to develop his view of art. According to Vázquez, the work of an artist develops out of his or her particular historical and cultural context. Because of this, any work of art reflects or speaks to this context. Art, then, has an inevitable sociological and ideological role in human history. But art is not merely ideology, according to Vázquez. Art is a form of knowledge or cognition because great works of art, although conditioned by particular historical and social circumstances, make universal statements about the human condition through artistic reflection on a particular human event. Like other Marxists, Vázquez argues that "all great art is realist art."[2] However Vázquez refuses to reduce realism to mimetic resemblance. He claims that almost any subject matter for art is "real" if that subject matter reflects a vision of the world. Even pure abstract art is a form of realism, according to Vázquez, because artists in this instance are transforming and reforming their perceptions of their personal insights into reality as each artist views it. And Vázquez emphasizes the creative element of art, because one of its essential features is its ability to embody ideological content into a new reality created by the artist. One major criticism of Marxist aesthetics is that Marxists sometimes place too much emphasis on the ideological function of art. But Vázquez suggests that this criticism may be an exaggerated view of at least some Marxist ideas about art.

Included in this section are comments from the famous Marxist playwright, Bertolt Brecht. Brecht claims that modern theatre is a means to present ideological content in an intelligent and aesthetic framework. The modern theatre, according to Brecht, is, or should be, what he calls the epic

---

[2]Georg Lukács, in an interview to Antonin Liehm for *La Nouvelle Critque,* 156–7 (June–July, 1964), quoted in Adolfo Sánchez Vázquez, *Art and Society* (New York: Monthly Review Press, 1973), p. 37.

theatre, a term which he contrasts with the traditional mimetic dramatic theatre. The purpose of epic theatre is to involve the spectator on a rational rather than on an emotional level. An epic piece presents a series of events which confront the audience in such a way that one is intellectually challenged rather than passively receptive of the situation depicted in the drama. Brecht's early play *The Measures Taken* (Illustration 9), illustrates Brecht's idea of the modern play. Whether or not the play is Marxist or anti-Marxist is left as Brecht's intellectual challenge to the judgment of the reader.

Brecht's views of theatre, while proposing substantial changes, places theatre within a historical and cultural tradition. A more radical approach to theatre is proposed by Antonin Artaud. Artaud was a twentieth-century activist in the French theatre who argued that the theatre should forget the past, obliterate traditional drama from its repertoire, and concentrate on involving, interesting, and arousing the audience with issues of contemporary importance. Theatre for Artaud should be a form of revolutionary confrontation, and quality in art should be measured only by its effect on the audience. Thus theatre, for example, should be cruel and violent in order to relate to the audience and to revitalize modern life. The short selection from the play, *For Colored Girls* (Illustration 28) illustrates in mild form what Artaud might have had in mind. Artaud suggests theses which are, at best, undeveloped and incomplete. However his views might give the reader a preview into the aesthetic theories of the future.

Creativity and Alienation

KARL MARX

First Manuscript: Alienated Labour

. . . [XXIV] We have now to infer a third characteristic of *alienated labour* from the two we have considered.

Man is a species-being not only in the sense that he makes the community (his own as well as those of other things) his object both practically and theoretically, but also (and this is simply another expression for the same thing) in the sense that he treats himself as the present, living species, as a *universal* and consequently free being.

Karl Marx, *Economic and Philosophic Manuscripts of 1844*, trans. T. B. Bottomore, reprinted by permission of Pitman Books Ltd., London.

Species-life, for man as for animals, has its physical basis in the fact that man (like animals) lives from inorganic nature, and since man is more universal than an animal so the range of inorganic nature from which he lives is more universal. Plants, animals, minerals, air, light, etc. constitute, from the theoretical aspect, a part of human consciousness as objects of natural science and art; they are man's spiritual inorganic nature, his intellectual means of life, which he must first prepare for enjoyment and perpetuation. So also, from the practical aspect, they form a part of human life and activity. In practice man lives only from these natural products, whether in the form of food, heating, clothing, housing, etc. The universality of man appears in practice in the universality which makes the whole of nature into his inorganic body: (1) as a direct means of life; and equally (2) as the material object and instrument of his life activity. Nature is the inorganic body of man; that is to say nature, excluding the human body itself. To say that man *lives* from nature means that nature is his *body* with which he must remain in a continuous interchange in order not to die. The statement that the physical and mental life of man, and nature, are interdependent means simply that nature is interdependent with itself, for man is a part of nature.

Since alienated labour: (1) alienates nature from man; and (2) alienates man from himself, from his own active function, his life activity; so it alienates him from the species. It makes *species-life* into a means of individual life. In the first place it alienates species-life and individual life, and secondly, it turns the latter, as an abstraction, into the purpose of the former, also in its abstract and alienated form.

For labour, *life activity, productive life,* now appear to man only as *means* for the satisfaction of a need, the need to maintain his physical existence. Productive life is, however, species-life. It is life creating life. In the type of life activity resides the whole character of a species, its species-character; and free, conscious activity is the species-character of human beings. Life itself appears only as a *means of life*.

The animal is one with its life activity. It does not distinguish the activity from itself. It is *its activity*. But man makes his life activity itself an object of his will and consciousness. He has a conscious life activity. It is not a determination with which he is completely identified. Conscious life activity distinguishes man from the life activity of animals. Only for this reason is he a species-being. Or rather, he is only a self-conscious being, i.e. his own life is an object for him, because he is a species-being. Only for this reason is his activity free activity. Alienated labour reverses the relationship, in that man because he is a self-conscious being makes his life activity, his *being*, only a means for his *existence*.

The practical construction of an *objective world*, the *manipulation* of inorganic nature, is the confrontation of man as a conscious species-being, i.e., a being who treats the species as his own being or himself as a species-being. Of course, animals also produce. They construct nests, dwellings, as in the case of bees, beavers, ants, etc. But they only produce what is strictly necessary for themselves or their young. They produce only in a single direction, while man produces universally. They produce only under the compulsion of direct physical needs, while man produces when he is free from physical need and only truly produces in freedom from such need. Animals produce only themselves, while man reproduces the whole of nature. The products of animal production belong directly to their physical bodies, while man is free in face of his product. Animals construct only in accordance with the standards and needs of the species to which they belong, while man knows how to produce in accordance with the standards of every species and knows how to apply the appropriate standard to the object. Thus man constructs also in accordance with the laws of beauty.

It is just in his work upon the objective world that man really proves himself as a *species-being*. This production is his active species-life. By means of it nature appears as *his* work and his reality. The object of labour is, therefore, the *objectification of man's species-life*; for he no longer reproduces himself merely intellectually, as in consciousness, but actively and in a real sense, and he sees his own reflection in a world which he has constructed. While, therefore, alienated labour takes away the object of production from man, it also takes away his *species-life*, his real objectivity as a species-being, and changes his advantage over animals into a disadvantage in so far as his inorganic body, nature, is taken from him.

Just as alienated labour transforms free and self-directed activity into a means, so it transforms the species-life of man into a means of physical existence.

Consciousness, which man has from his species, is transformed through alienation so that species-life becomes only a means for him. (3) Thus alienated labour turns the *species-life of man*, and also nature as his mental species-property, into an *alien* being and into a *means* for his *individual existence*. It alienates from man his own body, external nature, his mental life and his *human* life. (4) A direct consequence of the alienation of man from the product of his labour, from his life activity and from his species-life, is that *man is alienated* from other *men*. When man confronts himself he also confronts *other* men. What is true of man's relationship to his work, to the product of his work and to himself, is also true of his relationship to other men, to their labour and to the objects of their labour.

In general, the statement that man is alienated from his species-life means that each man is alienated from others, and that each of the others is likewise alienated from human life.

Human alienation, and above all the relation of man to himself, is first realized and expressed in the relationship between each man and other men. Thus in the relationship of alienated labour every man regards other men according to the standards and relationships in which he finds himself placed as a worker. . . .

Third Manuscript: Private Property and Communism

. . . [VI] Social activity and social mind by no means exist *only* in the form of activity or mind which is directly communal. Nevertheless, communal activity and mind, i.e. activity and mind which express and confirm themselves directly in a *real association* with other men, occur everywhere where this direct expression of sociability arises from the content of the activity or corresponds to the nature of mind.

Even when I carry out *scientific* work, etc., an activity which I can seldom conduct in direct association with other men, I perform a *social*, because *human*, act. It is not only the material of my activity—such as the language itself which the thinker uses—which is given to me as a social product. My *own existence* is a social activity. For this reason, what I myself produce I produce for society, and with the consciousness of acting as a social being.

My universal consciousness is only the *theoretical* form of that whose *living* form is the real community, the social entity, although at the present day this universal consciousness is an abstraction from real life and is opposed to it as an enemy. That is why the *activity* of my universal consciousness as such is my *theoretical* existence as a social being.

It is above all necessary to avoid postulating "society" once again as an abstraction confronting the individual. The individual *is* the *social being*. The manifestation of his life—even when it does not appear directly in the form of a communal manifestation, accomplished in association with other men— is, therefore, a manifestation and affirmation of *social life*. Individual human life and species-life are not different things, even though the mode of existence of individual life is necessarily either a more *specific* or a more *general* mode of species-life, or that of species-life a *specific* or more *general* mode of individual life.

In his *species-consciousness* man confirms his real *social life*, and reproduces his real existence in thought; while conversely, species-life confirms itself in species-consciousness and exists for itself in its universality as a thinking being. Though man is a unique individual—and it is just his particularity which makes him an individual, a really *individual* communal being—he is equally the *whole*, the ideal whole, the subjective existence of society as thought and experienced. He exists in reality as the representation and the real mind of social existence, and as the sum of human manifestations of life.

Thought and being are indeed *distinct* but they also form a unity. *Death* seems to be a harsh victory of the species over the individual and to contradict their unity; but the particular individual is only a *determinate species-being* and as such he is mortal.

4. Just as *private property* is only the sensuous expression of the fact that man is at the same time an *objective* fact for himself and becomes an alien and non-human object for himself; just as his manifestation of life is also his alienation of and his self-realization a loss of reality, the emergence of an *alien* reality; so the positive supersession of private property, i.e. the *sensuous* appropriation of the human essence and of human life, of objective man and of human *creations*, by and for man, should not be taken only in the sense of *immediate*, exclusive *enjoyment*, or only in the sense of *possession* or *having*. Man appropriates his manifold being in an all-inclusive way, and thus as a whole man. All his *human* relations to the world—seeing, hearing, smelling, tasting, touching, thinking, observing, feeling, desiring, acting, loving—in short, all the organs of his individuality, like the organs which are directly communal in form, are in their objective action (their *action in relation to the object*) the appropriation of this object, the appropriation of human reality. The way in which they react to the object is the confirmation of *human reality*. It is human effectiveness and human *suffering*, for suffering humanly considered is an enjoyment of the self for man.

Private property has made us so stupid and partial that an object is only *ours* when we have it, when it exists for us as capital or when it is directly eaten, drunk, worn, inhabited, etc., in short, *utilized* in some way. But private property itself only conceives these various forms of possession as *means of life*, and the life for which they serve as means is the *life* of *private property*— labour and creation of capital.

Thus *all* the physical and intellectual senses have been replaced by the simple alienation of *all* these senses; the sense of *having*. The human being had to be reduced to this absolute poverty in order to be able to give birth to all his inner wealth.

The supersession of private property is, therefore, the complete *emancipation* of all the human qualities and senses. It is such an emancipation because these qualities and senses have become *human*, from the subjective as well as the objective point of view. The eye has become a *human* eye when its *object* has become a *human*, social object, created by man and destined for him. The senses have, therefore, become directly theoreticians in practice. They relate themselves to the thing for the sake of the thing, but the thing itself is an *objective human* relation to itself and to man, and vice versa. Need and enjoyment have thus lost their *egoistic* character and nature has lost its mere *utility* by the fact that its utilization has become *human* utilization.

Similarly, the senses and minds of other men have become my *own* appropriation. Thus besides these direct organs, *social* organs are constituted, in the form of society; for example, activity in direct association with others has become an organ for the manifestation of life and a mode of appropriation of *human* life.

It is evident that the human eye appreciates things in a different way from the crude, non-human eye, the human *ear* differently from the crude ear. As we have seen, it is only when the object becomes a *human* object, or objective *humanity*, that man does not become lost in it. This is only possible when man himself becomes a *social* object; when he himself becomes a social being and society becomes a being for him in this object.

On the one hand, it is only when objective reality everywhere becomes for man in society the reality of human faculties, human reality, and thus the reality of his own faculties, that all *objects* become for him the *objectification of himself*. The objects then confirm and realize his individuality, they are *his own* objects, i.e. man himself becomes the object. *The manner in which these objects* become his own depends upon the *nature of the object* and the nature of the corresponding faculty; for it is precisely the *determinate character* of this relation which constitutes the specific *real* mode of affirmation. The object is not the same for the *eye* as for the *ear*, for the ear as for the eye. The *distinctive character* of each faculty is precisely its *characteristic* essence and thus also the characteristic mode of its objectification, of its *objectively real*, living *being*. It is therefore not only in thought, but through *all* the senses that man is affirmed in the objective world.

Let us next consider the subjective aspect. Man's musical sense is only awakened by music. The most beautiful music has no meaning for the non-musical ear, is not an object for it, because my object can only be the confirmation of one of my own faculties. It can only be so for me in so far as my faculty exists for itself as a subjective capacity, because the meaning of an object for me extends only as far as the sense extends (only makes sense for an appropriate sense). For this reason, the *senses* of social man are *different* from those of non-social man. It is only through the objectively deployed wealth of the human being that the wealth of subjective *human* sensibility (a musical ear, an eye which is sensitive to the beauty of form, in short, senses which are capable of human satisfaction and which confirm themselves as human faculties) is cultivated or created. For it is not only the five senses, but also the so-called spiritual senses, the practical senses (desiring, loving, etc.), in brief, human sensibility and the human character of the senses, which can only come into being through the existence of *its* object, through humanized nature. The cultivation of the five senses is the work of all previous history. Sense which is subservient to crude needs has only a restricted meaning. For a starving man the human form of food does not exist, but only its abstract character as food. It could just as well exist in the most crude form, and it is impossible to say in what way this feeding-activity would differ from that of animals. The needy man, burdened with cares, has no appreciation of the most beautiful spectacle. The dealer in minerals sees only their commercial value, not their beauty or their particular characteristics; he has no mineralogical sense. Thus, the objectification of the human essence, both theoretically and practically, is necessary in order to *humanize* man's senses, and also to create the *human senses* corresponding to all the wealth of human and natural being.

Just as society at its beginnings finds, through the development of *private property* with its wealth and poverty (both intellectual and material), the materials necessary for this *cultural development*, so the fully constituted society produces man in all the plenitude of his being, the wealthy man endowed with all the senses, as an enduring reality. It is only in a social context that subjectivism and objectivism, spiritualism and materialism, activity and passivity, cease to be antinomies and thus cease to exist as such antinomies. The resolution of the *theoretical* contradictions is possible *only* through practical means, only through the *practical* energy of man. Their resolution is not by any means, therefore, only a problem of knowledge, but is a *real* problem of life which philosophy was unable to solve precisely because it saw there a purely theoretical problem.

Marxist Aesthetics

ADOLFO SÁNCHEZ VÁZQUEZ

Contemporary Marxism and Art

Several basic tendencies can be seen in the panorama of current Marxist research, all reflecting a return to the source of Marxism, but their principles differing in response to the enriching and invigorating contact with artistic practice. Art is a phenomenon that constantly defies vacuous and hasty generalizations that result from a one-dimensional point of view. Within the Marxist camp today we can see profound differences in the emphasis given a particular aspect or function of artistic creation. These emphases derive from a shared conception of humanity and society and should not be considered exclusive as long as no one of them walls itself in and closes its doors to a different basic approach to art. It is only when a relative truth elevates itself to the level of the absolute that what was valid invalidates by this transgression whatever contribution it might have made to our knowledge, and in this way ceases to be an open aesthetic conception and becomes rigid and closed. It is precisely this kind of open conception, which does not mutilate the richness, diversity, and dynamism of art in its historical development or in its current manifestations, that Marxist aestheticians are seeking through a variety of interpretations. Very well then, what are these different interpretations?

Adolfo Sánchez Vázquez, *Art and Society,* trans. Maro Riofrancos. Copyright © 1973 by Monthly Review Press. Reprinted by permission of Monthly Review Press.

Art as ideology

Let us look first at the concept of art that reduces it to a form of ideology. Of course, this view of art carries good credentials as Marxist thought; in fact, Marxism has all along emphatically insisted on the ideological nature of artistic creation. According to its cardinal thesis of the relationship between the economic base and the superstructure, art belongs to the superstructure and, in a society divided into classes, is linked to definite interests of particular social classes. But the expression of these interests takes on form: the artist's political, moral, or religious ideas are integrated in an artistic structure or totality that has its own set of laws. As a result of this process of integration or formation, the artistic work appears to be endowed with a certain internal coherence and relative autonomy which thwarts its reduction to a mere ideological phenomenon. The writings of Marx and Engels on the complex web in which artistic phenomena exist, on the endurability of Greek art across changing historical conditions, on the autonomy and dependence of spiritual creations, including art, and on the uneven development of art and society, proscribe the placement of an equal sign between art and ideology in the name of the ideological character of an artistic work. Nevertheless, until only a few years ago one of the most frequent temptations for Marxist aestheticians—and, above all, for literary and artistic critics confronted with specific works of art—has been to overestimate the role of the ideological factor and consequently to minimize the form, the internal coherence, and the specific laws of the work of art.

The Marxist thesis that the artist is socially and historically conditioned, and that his ideological positions play a particular role, in some cases bearing on the artistic fate of his work, does not in any way imply a need to reduce a work of art to its ideological components. And there is even less justification for equating the aesthetic value of a work with the value of its ideas. Even when a particular work clearly shows its class roots, it will continue to live, although those roots—already dry—may not bear new fruits. The work of art thus outgrows the socio-historical ground which give it birth. Because of its class origin, its ideological character, art is an expression of the social division or gash in humanity; but because of its ability to extend a bridge between people across time and social divisions, art manifests a vocation for universality, and in a certain way prefigures that universal human destiny which will only be effectively realized in a new society, with the abolition of the material and ideological particularisms of social classes. Just as Greek art survived the ideology of slavery, the art of our times will outlive its ideology.

To characterize art according to its ideological content ignores a key historical fact: class ideologies come and go, but true art persists. If the specific nature of art lies in its transcendence, because of its durability, of the ideological limits which made it possible; if it lives or survives by its vocation for universality, thanks to which people living in actual socialist societies can coexist with Greek, medieval, or Renaissance art, then its reduction to *ideology*—and to its particular elements, its *here* and *now*—is a betrayal of its very essence. But at the same time we should not forget that art is made by men who are historically conditioned, and that the universality that art achieves is not the abstract and timeless universality that idealist aestheticians speak of after creating an abyss between art and ideology, or between art and society, but the human universality that is manifested *in* and *through* the particular.

Thus we see that the relationship between art and ideology is extremely complex and contradictory, and in dealing with this relationship we must avoid—as two equally noxious extremes—either an identification or a radical opposition between art and ideology. The first is characteristic of ideologizing, subjectivist, or crudely sociological positions; and the second is found at times among those who carry their distinction between art and ideology to the point of denying the ideological character of art, thus placing themselves outside Marxism. . . .

Art as a Form of Cognition

Art . . . appears in the classics of Marxism-Leninism as a form of knowledge; and that is why the cognitive value of art is currently given an emphasis opposed to merely ideological interpretations, and instead informed by the writings of Marx, Engels, and Lenin on the great realist writers of their time. While according to the ideological conception the artist addresses himself to reality in order to express his vision of the world, as well as of his time and class, the conception of art as cognition emphasizes that the artist is approaching reality. The artist approaches reality to capture its essential features, to reflect it, but without dissociating his artistic reflection from his attitude to reality, that is, from the ideological content of the work. In that sense, art is a means of cognition.

The concept of reflection as applied to art does not infer, or at least should not infer, as we previously pointed out, a mechanical transformation of an epistemological category into an aesthetic one. Artistic truth is not determined by a full correspondence between art and ideology, but neither is it determined—and this differentiates it from scientific knowledge—by a complete congruence with an objective reality existing apart from and independently of man. In a painting or a poem about a tree, for example, what we have is not a tree in itself, or a tree as seen by a botanist, but rather a humanized tree, a tree that attests to a human presence. Consequently, when we speak of artistic truth or the reflection of reality in art we must go beyond a general philosophical level to aesthetics itself. Only in this way, by giving it a specific significance, can we speak of art as a form of knowledge. What does that humanized tree refer to? Purely and simply, the real tree that grows alone, untouched by human hand? Or man himself, humanizing the tree? These questions are enough to make us realize the need to proceed cautiously when speaking of art as a form or means of knowledge, until we can establish *what* it is that we know, definitively, in art, and *how* this knowledge comes to us. . . .

Man is the specific object of art even if he is not always the object of artistic representation. Nonhuman objects that are represented artistically are not simply represented objects, but are objects in a certain relationship to humankind; that is, they show us not what they are in themselves, but what they are for man—they are humanized. The represented object embodies a social significance, a human world. Therefore, in reflecting objective reality the artist involves us in human reality. In this way, art as knowledge of reality can show us a portion of reality—not in its objective essence, which is the specific task of science, but in its relationship to human nature. There is a science which deals with trees, classifying them, studying their morphological and functional characteristics; but where is the science that deals with *humanized* trees? These are precisely the objects art is concerned with.

But what happens when the object of artistic representation is man, not man revealed by things in relation to him, but man in a direct and immediate way? Here again, art does not duplicate the work of what are called the human or social sciences. Dostoevsky does not limit himself to repeating psychiatric truths, nor is Balzac's *Human Comedy* an explanation of the ideas about capitalist economic relations in Marx's *Capital*. Art does not look at human relationships in general, but rather in their individual manifestations. It presents concrete live human beings in the unity and richness of their determinations, where the general and the particular merge in a particular way. But the knowledge art can give us about people is gained by particular means which do not include the imitation or reproduction of concrete reality; art goes from what we will call an objective concreteness to an artistic concreteness. The artist sees before him the immediate, given, concrete reality, but he cannot remain on that level, limiting himself to reproducing it. Human reality reveals its secrets to the artist only to the extent that, starting from the immediate and individual, he rises to a universal level, to return again to the concrete. But this new individual or artistic concreteness is precisely the fruit of a process of creation, not of imitation.

Art can only be knowledge—specific knowledge of a specific reality: man as a unique, concrete, and living totality—which transforms external reality, departing from it to bring forth a new reality, a work of art. Artistic knowledge is the fruit of an activity: the artist makes art into a means of knowledge not by copying a reality, but by creating a new one. Art is knowledge only to the extent that it is creation. Only thus can it serve truth and discover the essential aspects of human reality.

Definitions of Realism

Art which thus serves truth as a specific means of knowledge both in its form and object is realism. We call realist art all art that, starting with the existence of an objective reality, constructs a new reality which gives us truths about concrete men who live in a given society, in historically and socially conditioned human relationships, within which they work, struggle, suffer, rejoice, or dream.

In the definition of realism we just formulated, we find the category of reality on three different levels: external reality, marginal to man; the new or humanized reality man engenders, transcending or humanizing external reality; and human reality, radiating through humanized external reality and enriching our knowledge of man. This definition enables us to distinguish between realism, which represents a reality that reflects the essence of human phenomena, and art, which cannot or does not want to have a cognitive function. The latter category includes primarily the false realism which, by trying to deal exclusively with either an external reality or an internal human reality, fails to enrich our knowledge of man, either because man ceases to be the specific object of artistic knowledge, or because the artistic methods it uses preclude a penetration into the essential aspects of human reality.

It is a false realism which, in the name of knowing reality—an expression used vaguely by some Marxists—makes the representation of things an end rather than a means at the service of truth. This type of realism is not a way of knowing reality, but simply a way of representing it; that is, it is an attempt to present it anew in the way a copy or an imitation presents the original. The boundaries of this supposed realism are rigid: they extend no further than the boundaries of the object. Sometimes the artist pretends to reproduce every detail, thus falling into naturalism, or a documentary, anecdotal, photographic realism; at other times the artist presents the object on a higher level, pretending to capture the essence of things, their secret rhythms or intimate structures, in a doomed attempt to compete with science or philosophy. It is a hopeless enterprise: things and their essential reality go on waiting for the scientist, while the artist—absorbed by things, by their objective essence—loses his grip on the human content they may bear.

Another type of false realism is that which has human reality as its object, but seeks in it not what it is but what it should be, and transforms things so that they reflect a prettified human reality, with the edges smoothed. This type of realism falls into the trap of artistic unrealism or idealism. For the most part, what was made to pass for socialist realism during the Stalinist period was nothing but its transformation into "socialist" idealism. Of course, not all the artistic and literary works of that time presented the new socialist reality through rose-colored glasses, and the novels of Sholokhov are but one example; those that did deserve to be called neither socialist nor realist. True socialist realism has no reason to mystify reality. Lies kill it; the truth it can reveal justifies and legitimizes its existence. Therefore, if art is a form of knowledge that captures human reality in its essential aspects and tears off the veil of its mystification, if art in the service of truth can serve humanity in its construction of a new human reality, then there is nothing—short of some new form of dogmatism—that can prevent a socialist realist conception of art that is neither sectarian nor exclusive.

The task of presenting a profoundly realistic vision of new social realities from the ideological perspective—Marxism-Leninism—that facilitates such a vision, far from being an enterprise without a future, still has a long way to go. A truly realist and socialist art has yet to say it's last word on the new social reality that is in the process of emerging—a reality with light and shadow, conflict, and a vital, constant, and at times dramatic struggle between the old and the new. . . .

Art as Creation

So let realism extend its boundaries without excluding or absorbing other artistic phenomena, and let us look for a more profound and primary stratum of art, one that does not identify art with a particular tendency—realist, symbolist, abstract, etc.—or rigidly restrict its development, and one that enables us to understand art in its totality as an essential human activity. Only in this way can we avoid, from a Marxist point of view, the limitations of a merely ideological, sociological, or cognitive conception of art.

Certainly, art has an ideological content, but only in the proportion that ideology loses its substantiveness by being integrated into the new reality of the work of art. That is, the ideological problems that the artist chooses to deal with have to be solved *artistically*. Art can have a cognitive function also, that of reflecting the essence of the real; but this function can only be fulfilled by *creating a new reality*, not by copying or imitating existing reality. In other words, the cognitive problems that the artist chooses to deal with have to be solved *artistically*. To forget this—that is, to reduce art to ideology or to a mere form of knowledge—is to forget that the work of art is, above all, creation, a manifestation of the creative power of man. In the failure to recognize this lie the limitations of the concept of art we examined previously. . . .

The idea of art as creation does not demand a unanimous attitude to reality (a fidelity to its shapes and figures, or a distancing from them); it underlines, above all, the relationship between art and the human essence. Man elevates and affirms himself in the process of transforming and humanizing reality, and art satisfies this need. That is why there is no such thing as "art for art's sake," nor can there be; there is only art by and for man. Since man is essentially a creative being, he creates works of art to feel his affirmation, his creativity, that is, his humanity.

This fertile idea, which is gaining ground in current Marxist aesthetics, has come about only by a reevaluation of Marx's idea that art and work are two essential spheres of human life. The idea of art as a particular form of creative work does not prevent us from recognizing its possible ideological or cognitive functions; but neither does it reduce art to its ideological content or its cognitive value. To reduce art to ideology is to lose sight of its essential dimension, the creative one; and to see art only as a form of reflecting reality is to fail to understand its fundamental character: the artistic product is a new reality that attests, above all else, to the presence of the human being as creator. . . .

The Ideas of Marx on the Source and Nature of the Aesthetic

. . . Alienation and Artistic Work

In capitalist society, a work of art is "productive" when it is market-oriented, when it submits itself to the exigencies of the market, the fluctuations of supply and demand. And since there is no objective measure by which to determine the value of his particular merchandise,[1] the artist is subject to the tastes, preferences, ideas, and aesthetic notions of those who influence the market. Inasmuch as he produces works of art destined for a market that absorbs them, the artist cannot fail to heed the exigencies of this market: they often affect the content as well as the form of a work of art, thus placing limitations on the artist, stifling his creative potential, his individuality.

A form of alienation is thus produced, denaturalizing the essence of artistic work. The artist does not fully recognize himself in his product, because anything produced in response to external necessity is alien to him. This alienation becomes total when the sense of artistic creation is inverted, and artistic activity becomes not an end but a means of subsistence. The material utility required of the products of human labor is a necessary condition, for these products are intended for satisfaction of material needs; and it is only within the framework of these needs that man can affirm, objectify, and recognize himself. But the predominance of material utility in the work of art contradicts the very essence of art; for unlike common merchandise its primary aim is not the satisfaction of determinate needs but the satisfaction of man's general need to express and affirm himself in the objective world.

In this manner, capitalist society deprives the artist of creative freedom. In a society where a work of art can sink to the level of merchandise, art

---

[1] ". . . that which determines the magnitude of the value of any article is the amount of labour socially necessary, or the labour-time socially necessary for its production." (Marx, *Capital*, p. 39) Because the work of art cannot be reduced to the socially necessary labor time invested in its creation, its exchange value can be established only according to a category as subjective and superficial as price, fixed in relation to the preferences of the bourgeois public.

becomes alienated or impoverished; it loses its essence. When Marx pointed out in the *Economic and Philosophic Manuscripts* that art under capitalism "falls under the general law of production," he was clearly alluding to this degradation of artistic creation; these early remarks formed the basis of his later theories on the contradiction between art and capitalism, between production for profit and creative freedom.

But even under capitalism the artist tries to escape alienation, for alienated art is the very negation of art. The artist does not resign himself to becoming a salaried worker. By seeking to satisfy his inner need as a social being, the artist tends to transcend the alienation that inverts the sense of artistic creation, and thus he tends to overcome the alienation of his own existence. He searches for ways of escaping alienation, refusing to submit his work to the fate of all merchandise, winning his freedom at the price of terrible privations. But the source of this alienation lies outside of art; it is fundamentally a socioeconomic alienation. Therefore, according to Marx, only a change in social relations can enable labor to reclaim its true human sense and art to be a means of satisying profound spiritual needs. That is why the salvation of art is not in art itself, but in the revolutionary transformation of the socioeconomic relations which permit the degradation of artistic work by placing it under the general law of capitalist commodity production.[2]

The Essence of the Aesthetic

We may sum up the fundamental aesthetic ideas of Marx's *Economic and Philosophic Manuscripts* in the following terms:

1. A particular relationship exists between subject and object (creation "in accordance to the laws of beauty" or "artistic assimilation of reality") in which the subject transforms the object by giving a determinate form to raw matter. The result is a new object, the aesthetic object, in which the human wealth of the subject is objectified or revealed.

2. This subject-object relationship, the aesthetic relationship, has a social character; it evolves on a socio-historical basis, in the process of humanizing nature by means of work, and of objectifying the human being.

3. The aesthetic assimilation of reality reaches its most developed stage in art as superior human labor which tends to satisfy the artist's inner need to objectify, express, and reveal his essential powers in a concrete-sensuous object. By freeing itself from the narrow material utility of the products of labor, art raises to a higher level the objectification and affirmation of the

---

[2]In the *Economic and Philosophic Manuscripts* Marx did not explicitly speak of artistic alienation, but by pointing out the transformation of the work of art into a commodity within the framework of capitalist social relations, he opened up the way for such an analysis. In our view, this analysis agrees with the later development of Marx's thought, especially with the theory of alienation as "commodity fetishism," in *Capital.*

human being which, within the framework of material utility, are realized to a limited extent in those products.

4. The aesthetic relationship between man and reality, inasmuch as it is a social relationship, creates not only the object but also the subject. The aesthetic object exists—in its human, aesthetic essence—only for social beings.

5. Art is alienated when it falls under the general law of capitalist production, that is, when the work of art is regarded as merchandise.

MARXIST PERSPECTIVES IN THE ARTS

The Modern Theatre

BERTOLT BRECHT

The Epic Theatre and Its Difficulties

Any theatre that makes a serious attempt to stage one of the new plays risks being radically transformed. What the audience sees in fact is a battle between theatre and play, an almost academic operation where, in so far as it takes any interest in the process of renovating the theatre, all it has to do is observe whether the theatre emerges as victor or vanquished from this murderous clash. (Roughly speaking, the theatre can only emerge victorious over the play if it manages to avoid the risk of the play's transforming it completely— as at present it nearly always succeeds in doing.) It is not the play's effect on the audience but its effect on the theatre that is decisive at this moment.

This situation will continue until our theatres have worked out the style of production that our plays need and encourage. It won't be an adequate answer if theatres invent some kind of special style for them, in the same way as the so-called Munich Shakespearean stage was invented, which could only be used for Shakespeare. It has to be a style that can lend new force to a whole section of the theatrical repertoire which is still capable of life today.

It is understood that the *radical transformation of the theatre* can't be the result of some artistic whim. It has simply to correspond to the whole radical transformation of the mentality of our time. The symptoms of this transformation are familiar enough, and so far they have been seen as symptoms of disease. There is some justification for this, for of course what one sees first of all are the signs of decline in whatever is *old*. But it would be wrong to see these phenomena, so-called *Amerikanismus* for instance, as anything but unhealthy changes stimulated by the operation of really new mental influences on our culture's aged body. And it would be wrong too to treat these new ideas as if they were not ideas and not *mental* phenomena at all, and to try to build up the theatre against them as a kind of bastion of the mind. On the contrary it is precisely theatre, art and literature which have to form the "ideological superstructure" for a solid, practical rearrangement of our age's way of life.

In its works the new school of play-writing lays down that the *epic theatre* is the theatrical style of our time. To expound the principles of the epic theatre in a few catch-phrases is not possible. They still mostly need to be worked out in detail, and include representation by the actor, stage technique, dramaturgy, stage music, use of the film, and so on. The essential point of the epic theatre is perhaps that it appeals less to the feelings than to the spectator's reason. Instead of sharing an experience the spectator must come to grips with things. At the same time it would be quite wrong to try and deny emotion to this kind of theatre. It would be much the same thing as trying to deny emotion to modern science.

. . . Opera had to be brought up to the technical level of the modern theatre. The modern theatre is the epic theatre. The following table shows certain changes of emphasis as between the dramatic and the epic theatre:

Dramatic Theatre	*Epic Theatre*
plot	narrative
implicates the spectator in a stage situation	turns the spectator into an observer, but
wears down his capacity for action	arouses his capacity for action
provides him with sensations	forces him to take decisions
experience	picture of the world
the spectator is involved in something	he is made to face something
suggestion	argument
instinctive feelings are preserved	brought to the point of recognition
the spectator is in the thick of it, shares the experience	the spectator stands outside, studies
the human being is taken for granted	the human being is the object of the inquiry

he is unalterable	he is alterable and able to alter
eyes on the finish	eyes on the course
one scene makes another	each scene for itself
growth	montage
linear development	in curves
evolutionary determinism	jumps
man as a fixed point	man as a process
thought determines being	social being determines thought
feeling	reason

When the epic theatre's methods begin to penetrate the opera the first result is a radical *separation of the elements*. The great struggle for supremacy between words, music and production—which always brings up the question "which is the pretext for what?": is the music the pretext for the events on the stage, or are these the pretext for the music? etc.—can simply be by-passed by radically separating the elements. So long as the expression "Gesamtkunstwerk" (or "integrated work of art") means that the integration is a muddle, so long as the arts are supposed to be "fused" together, the various elements will all be equally degraded, and each will act as a mere "feed" to the rest. The process of fusion extends to the spectator, who gets thrown into the melting pot too and becomes a passive (suffering) part of the total work of art. Witchcraft of this sort must of course be fought against. Whatever is intended to produce hypnosis, is likely to induce sordid intoxication, or creates fog, has got to be given up.

Words, music and setting must become more independent of one another.

a. Music
For the music, the change of emphasis proved to be as follows:

Dramatic Opera	*Epic Opera*
The music dishes up	The music communicates
music which heightens the text	music which sets forth the text
music which proclaims the text	music which takes the text for granted
music which illustrates	which takes up a position
music which paints the psychological situation	which gives the attitude

Music plays the chief part in our thesis.

b. Text

We had to make something straightforward and instructive of our fun, if it was not to be irrational and nothing more. The form employed was that of the moral tableau. The tableau is performed by the characters in the play. The text had to be neither moralizing nor sentimental, but to put morals and sentimentality on view. Equally important was the spoken word and the written word (of the titles). Reading seems to encourage the audience to adopt the most natural attitude towards the work.

c. Setting

Showing independent works of art as part of a theatrical performance is a new departure. Neher's projections adopt an attitude towards the events on the stage; as when the real glutton sits in front of the glutton whom Neher has drawn. In the same way the stage unreels the events that are fixed on the screen. These projections of Neher's are quite as much an independent component of the opera as are Weill's music and the text. They provide its visual aids.

Of course such innovations also demand a new attitude on the part of the audiences who frequent opera houses. . . .

Theatre for Pleasure or Theatre for Instruction

. . . The Epic Theatre

Many people imagine that the term "epic theatre" is self-contradictory, as the epic and dramatic ways of narrating a story are held, following Aristotle, to be basically distinct. The difference between the two forms was never thought simply to lie in the fact that the one is performed by living beings while the other operates via the written word; epic works such as those of Homer and the medieval singers were at the same time theatrical performances, while dramas like Goethe's *Faust* and Byron's *Manfred* are agreed to have been more effective as books. Thus even by Aristotle's definition the difference between the dramatic and epic forms was attributed to their different methods of construction, whose laws were dealt with by two different branches of aesthetics. The method of construction depended on the different way of presenting the work to the public, sometimes via the stage, sometimes through a book; and independently of that there was the "dramatic element" in epic works and the "epic element" in dramatic. The bourgeois novel in the last century developed much that was "dramatic," by which was meant the strong centralization of the story, a momentum that drew the separate parts into a common relationship. A particular passion of utterance, a certain emphasis on the clash of forces are hallmarks of the "dramatic." The epic writer Döblin provided an excellent criterion when he said that with an epic work, as opposed to a dramatic, one can as it were take a pair of scissors and cut it into individual pieces, which remain fully capable of life.

This is no place to explain how the opposition of epic and dramatic lost its rigidity after having long been held to be irreconcilable. Let us just point out that the technical advances alone were enough to permit the stage to incorporate an element of narrative in its dramatic productions. The possibility of projections, the greater adaptability of the stage due to mechanization, the film, all completed the theatre's equipment, and did so at a point where the most important transactions between people could no longer be shown simply by personifying the motive forces or subjecting the characters to invisible metaphysical powers.

To make these transactions intelligible the environment in which the people lived had to be brought to bear in a big and "significant" way.

This environment had of course been shown in existing drama, but only as seen from the central figure's point of view, and not as an independent element. It was defined by the hero's reactions to it. It was seen as a storm can be seen when one sees the ships on a sheet of water unfolding their sails, and the sails filling out. In the epic theatre it was to appear standing on its own.

The stage began to tell a story. The narrator was no longer missing, along with the fourth wall. Not only did the background adopt an attitude to the events on the stage—by big screens recalling other simultaneous events elsewhere, by projecting documents which confirmed or contradicted what the characters said, by concrete and intelligible figures to accompany abstract conversations, by figures and sentences to support mimed transactions whose sense was unclear—but the actors too refrained from going over wholly into their role, remaining detached from the character they were playing and clearly inviting criticism of him.

The spectator was no longer in any way allowed to submit to an experience uncritically (and without practical consequences) by means of simple empathy with the characters in a play. The production took the subject-matter and the incidents shown and put them through a process of alienation: the alienation that is necessary to all understanding. When something seems "the most obvious thing in the world" it means that any attempt to understand the world has been given up.

What is "natural" must have the force of what is startling. This is the only way to expose the laws of cause and effect. People's activity must simultaneously be so and be capable of being different.

It was all a great change.

The dramatic theatre's spectator says: Yes, I have felt like that too—Just like me—It's only natural—It'll never change—The sufferings of this man appal me, because they are inescapable—That's great art; it all seems the most obvious thing in the world—I weep when they weep, I laugh when they laugh.

The epic theatre's spectator says: I'd never have thought it—That's not the way—That's extraordinary, hardly believable—It's got to stop—The sufferings of this man appal me, because they are unnecessary—That's great art: nothing obvious in it—I laugh when they weep, I weep when they laugh.

The Instructive Theatre

The stage began to be instructive.

Oil, inflation, war, social struggles, the family, religion, wheat, the meat market, all became subjects for theatrical representation. Choruses enlightened the spectator about facts unknown to him. Films showed a montage of events from all over the world. Projections added statistical material. And as the "background" came to the front of the stage so people's activity was subjected to criticism. Right and wrong courses of action were shown. People were shown who knew what they were doing, and others who did not. The theatre became an affair for philosophers, but only for such philosophers as wished not just to explain the world but also to change it. So we had philosophy, and we had instruction. And where was the amusement in all that? Were they sending us back to school, teaching us to read and write? Were we supposed to pass exams, work for diplomas?

Generally there is felt to be a very sharp distinction between learning and amusing oneself. The first may be useful, but only the second is pleasant. So we have to defend the epic theatre against the suspicion that it is a highly disagreeable, humourless, indeed strenuous affair.

Well: all that can be said is that the contrast between learning and amusing oneself is not laid down by divine rule; it is not one that has always been and must continue to be.

Undoubtedly there is much that is tedious about the kind of learning familiar to us from school, from our professional training, etc. But it must be remembered under what conditions and to what end that takes place.

It is really a commercial transaction. Knowledge is just a commodity. It is acquired in order to be resold. All those who have grown out of going to school have to do their learning virtually in secret, for anyone who admits that he still has something to learn devalues himself as a man whose knowledge is inadequate. Moreover the usefulness of learning is very much limited by factors outside the learner's control. There is unemployment, for instance, against which no knowledge can protect one. There is the division of labour, which makes generalized knowledge unnecessary and impossible. Learning is often among the concerns of those whom no amount of concern will get any forwarder. There is not much knowledge that leads to power, but plenty of knowledge to which only power can lead.

Learning has a very different function for different social strata. There are strata who cannot imagine any improvement in conditions: they find the conditions good enough for them. Whatever happens to oil they will benefit from it. And: they feel the years beginning to tell. There can't be all that many years more. What is the point of learning a lot now? They have said their final word: a grunt. But there are also strata 'waiting their turn' who are discontented with conditions, have a vast interest in the practical side of learning, want at all costs to find out where they stand, and know that they are lost without learning; these are the best and keenest learners. Similar differences apply to countries and peoples. Thus the pleasure of learning depends on all sorts of things; but none the less there is such a thing as pleasurable learning, cheerful and militant learning.

If there were not such amusement to be had from learning the theatre's whole structure would unfit it for teaching.

Theatre remains theatre even when it is instructive theatre, and in so far as it is good theatre it will amuse.

Theatre and Knowledge

But what has knowledge got to do with art? We know that knowledge can be amusing, but not everything that is amusing belongs in the theatre.

I have often been told, when pointing out the invaluable services that modern knowledge and science, if properly applied, can perform for art and specially for the theatre, that art and knowledge are two estimable but wholly distinct fields of human activity. This is a fearful truism, of course, and it is as well to agree quickly that, like most truisms, it is perfectly true. Art and science work in quite different ways: agreed. But, bad as it may sound, I have to admit that I cannot get along as an artist without the use of one or two sciences. This may well arouse serious doubts as to my artistic capacities. People are used to seeing poets as unique and slightly unnatural beings who reveal with a truly godlike assurance things that other people can only recognize after much sweat and toil. It is naturally distasteful to have to admit that one does not belong to this select band. All the same, it must be admitted. It must at the same time be made clear that the scientific occupations just confessed to are not pardonable side interests, pursued on days off after a good week's work. We all know how Goethe was interested in natural history, Schiller in history; as a kind of hobby, it is charitable to assume. I have no wish promptly to accuse these two of having needed these sciences for their poetic activity; I am not trying to shelter behind them; but I must say that I do need the sciences. I have to admit, however, that I look askance at all sorts of people who I know do not operate on the level of scientific understanding: that is to say, who sing as the birds sing, or as people imagine the birds to sing. I don't mean by that that I would reject a charming poem about the taste of fried fish or the delights of a boating party just because the writer had not studied gastronomy or navigation. But in my view the great and complicated things that go on in the world cannot be adequately recognized by people who do not use every possible aid to understanding.

Let us suppose that great passions or great events have to be shown which influence the fate of nations. The lust for power is nowadays held to be such a passion. Given that a poet "feels" this lust and wants to have someone strive for power, how is he to show the exceedingly complicated machinery within which the struggle for power nowadays takes place? If his hero is a politician, how do politics work? If he is a business man, how does business work? And yet there are writers who find business and politics nothing like so passionately interesting as the individual's lust for power. How are they to acquire the necessary knowledge? They are scarcely likely to learn enough by going round and keeping their eyes open, though even then it is more than they would get by just rolling their eyes in an exalted frenzy. The foundation of a paper like the *Völkischer Beobachter* or a business like Standard Oil is a pretty complicated affair, and such things cannot be conveyed just like that. One important field for the playwright is psychology. It is taken for granted that a poet, if not an ordinary man, must be able without further instruction to discover the motives that lead a man to commit murder; he must be able to give a picture of a murderer's mental state "from within himself." It is taken for granted that one only has to look inside oneself in such a case; and then there's always one's imagination. . . . There are various reasons why I can no longer surrender to this agreeable hope of getting a result quite so simply. I can no longer find in myself all those motives which the press or scientific reports show to have been observed in people. Like the average judge when pronouncing sentence, I cannot without further ado conjure up an adequate picture of a murderer's mental state. Modern psychology, from psychoanalysis to behaviourism, acquaints me with facts that lead me to judge the case quite differently, especially if I bear in mind the findings of sociology and do not overlook economics and history. You will say: but that's getting complicated. I have to answer that it *is* complicated. Even if you let yourself be convinced, and agree with me that a large slice of literature is exceedingly primitive, you may still ask with profound concern: won't an evening in such a theatre be a most alarming affair? The answer to that is: no.

Whatever knowledge is embodied in a piece of poetic writing has to be wholly transmuted into poetry. Its utilization fulfils the very pleasure that the poetic element provokes. If it does not at the same time fulfil that which is fulfilled by the scientific element, none the less in an age of great discoveries and inventions one must have a certain inclination to penetrate deeper into things—a desire to make the world controllable—if one is to be sure of enjoying its poetry.

Is the Epic Theatre Some Kind of "Moral Institution?"

According to Friedrich Schiller the theatre is to supposed to be a moral institution. In making this demand it hardly occurred to Schiller that by moralizing from the stage he might drive the audience out of the theatre. Audiences had no objection to moralizing in his day. It was only later that

Friedrich Nietzsche attacked him for blowing a moral trumpet. To Nietzsche any concern with morality was a depressing affair; to Schiller it seemed thoroughly enjoyable. He knew of nothing that could give greater amusement and satisfaction than the propagation of ideas. The bourgeoisie was setting about forming the ideas of the nation.

Putting one's house in order, patting oneself on the back, submitting one's account, is something highly agreeable. But describing the collapse of one's house, having pains in the back, paying one's account, is indeed a depressing affair, and that was how Friedrich Nietzsche saw things a century later. He was poorly disposed towards morality, and thus towards the previous Friedrich too.

The epic theatre was likewise often objected to as moralizing too much. Yet in the epic theatre moral arguments only took second place. Its aim was less to moralize than to observe. That is to say it observed, and then the thick end of the wedge followed: the story's moral. Of course we cannot pretend that we started our observations out of a pure passion for observing and without any more practical motive, only to be completely staggered by their results. Undoubtedly there were some painful discrepancies in our environment, circumstances that were barely tolerable, and this not merely on account of moral considerations. It is not only moral considerations that make hunger, cold and oppression hard to bear. Similarly the object of our inquiries was not just to arouse moral objections to such circumstances (even though they could easily be felt—though not by all the audience alike; such objections were seldom for instance felt by those who profited by the circumstances in question) but to discover means for their elimination. We were not in fact speaking in the name of morality but in that of the victims. These truly are two distinct matters, for the victims are often told that they ought to be contented with their lot, for moral reasons. Moralists of this sort see man as existing for morality, not morality for man. At least it should be possible to gather from the above to what degree and in what sense the epic theatre is a moral institution.

Can Epic Theatre Be Played Anywhere?

Stylistically speaking, there is nothing all that new about the epic theatre. Its expository character and its emphasis on virtuosity bring it close to the old Asiatic theatre. Didactic tendencies are to be found in the medieval mystery plays and the classical Spanish theatre, and also in the theatre of the Jesuits.

These theatrical forms corresponded to particular trends of their time, and vanished with them. Similarly the modern epic theatre is linked with certain trends. It cannot by any means be practised universally. Most of the great nations today are not disposed to use the theatre for ventilating their problems. London, Paris, Tokyo and Rome maintain their theatres for quite different purposes. Up to now favourable circumstances for an epic and didactic theatre have only been found in a few places and for a short period of time. In Berlin Fascism put a very definite stop to the development of such a theatre.

It demands not only a certain technological level but a powerful movement in society which is interested to see vital questions freely aired with a view to their solution, and can defend this interest against every contrary trend.

The epic theatre is the broadest and most far-reaching attempt at large-scale modern theatre, and it has all those immense difficulties to overcome that always confront the vital forces in the sphere of politics, philosophy, science and art.

No More Masterpieces

ANTONIN ARTAUD

One of the reasons for the asphyxiating atmosphere in which we live without possible escape or remedy—and in which we all share, even the most revolutionary among us—is our respect for what has been written, formulated, or painted, what has been given form, as if all expression were not at last exhausted, were not at a point where things must break apart if they are to start anew and begin fresh.

We must have done with this idea of masterpieces reserved for a self-styled elite and not understood by the general public; the mind has no such restricted districts as those so often used for clandestine sexual encounters.

Masterpieces of the past are good for the past: they are not good for us. We have the right to say what has been said and even what has not been said in a way that belongs to us, a way that is immediate and direct, corresponding to present modes of feeling, and understandable to everyone.

It is idiotic to reproach the masses for having no sense of the sublime, when the sublime is confused with one or another of its formal manifestations, which are moreover always defunct manifestations. And if for example a contemporary public does not understand *Oedipus Rex*, I shall make bold to say that it is the fault of *Oedipus Rex* and not of the public.

In *Oedipus Rex* there is the theme of incest and the idea that nature

Antonin Artaud, *The Theatre and Its Double* (New York: Grove Press, 1958). Reprinted by permission of Grove Press.

mocks at morality and that there are certain unspecified powers at large which we would do well to beware of, call them *destiny* or anything you choose.

There is in addition the presence of a plague epidemic which is a physical incarnation of these powers. But the whole in a manner and language that have lost all touch with the rude and epileptic rhythm of our time. Sophocles speaks grandly perhaps, but in a style that is no longer timely. His language is too refined for this age, it is as if he were speaking beside the point.

However, a public that shudders at train wrecks, that is familiar with earthquakes, plagues, revolutions, wars; that is sensitive to the disordered anguish of love, can be affected by all these grand notions and asks only to become aware of them, but on condition that it is addressed in its own language, and that its knowledge of these things does not come to it through adulterated trappings and speech that belong to extinct eras which will never live again.

Today as yesterday, the public is greedy for mystery: it asks only to become aware of the laws according to which destiny manifests itself, and to divine perhaps the secret of its apparitions.

Let us leave textual criticism to graduate students, formal criticism to esthetes, and recognize that what has been said is not still to be said; that an expression does not have the same value twice, does not live two lives; that all words, once spoken, are dead and function only at the moment when they are uttered, that a form, once it has served, cannot be used again and asks only to be replaced by another, and that the theater is the only place in the world where a gesture, once made, can never be made the same way twice.

If the public does not frequent our literary masterpieces, it is because those masterpieces are literary, that is to say, fixed; and fixed in forms that no longer respond to the needs of the time.

Far from blaming the public, we ought to blame the formal screen we interpose between ourselves and the public, and this new form of idolatry, the idolatry of fixed masterpieces which is one of the aspects of bourgeois conformism.

This conformism makes us confuse sublimity, ideas, and things with the forms they have taken in time and in our minds—in our snobbish, precious, aesthetic mentalities which the public does not understand.

How pointless in such matters to accuse the public of bad taste because it relishes insanities, so long as the public is not shown a valid spectacle; and I defy anyone to show me *here* a spectacle valid—valid in the supreme sense of the theater—since the last great romantic melodramas, i.e., since a hundred years ago.

The public, which takes the false for the true, has the sense of the true and always responds to it when it is manifested. However it is not upon the stage that the true is to be sought nowadays, but in the street; and if the crowd in the street is offered an occasion to show its human dignity, it will always do so.

If people are out of the habit of going to the theater, if we have all finally come to think of theater as an inferior art, a means of popular distraction, and to use it as an outlet for our worst instincts, it is because we have learned too well what the theater has been, namely, falsehood and illusion. It is because we have been accustomed for four hundred years, that is since the Renaissance, to a purely descriptive and narrative theater—storytelling psychology; it is because every possible ingenuity has been exerted in bringing to life on the stage plausible but detached beings, with the spectacle on one side, the public on the other—and because the public is no longer shown anything but the mirror of itself.

Shakespeare himself is responsible for this aberration and decline, this disinterested idea of the theater which wishes a theatrical performance to leave the public intact, without setting off one image that will shake the organism to its foundations and leave an ineffaceable scar.

If, in Shakespeare, a man is sometimes preoccupied with what transcends him, it is always in order to determine the ultimate consequences of this preoccupation within him, i.e., psychology.

Psychology, which works relentlessly to reduce the unknown to the known, to the quotidian and the ordinary, is the cause of the theater's abasement and its fearful loss of energy, which seems to me to have reached its lowest point. And I think both the theater and we ourselves have had enough of psychology.

I believe furthermore that we can all agree on this matter sufficiently so that there is no need to descend to the repugnant level of the modern and French theater to condemn the theater of psychology.

Stories about money, worry over money, social careerism, the pangs of love unspoiled by altruism, sexuality sugar-coated with an eroticism that has lost its mystery have nothing to do with the theater, even if they do belong to psychology. These torments, seductions, and lusts before which we are nothing but Peeping Toms gratifying our cravings, tend to go bad, and their rot turns to revolution: we must take this into account.

But this is not our most serious concern.

If Shakespeare and his imitators have gradually insinuated the idea of art for art's sake, with art on one side and life on the other, we can rest on this feeble and lazy idea only as long as the life outside endures. But there are too many signs that everything that used to sustain our lives no longer does so, that we are all mad, desperate, and sick. And I call for *us* to react.

This idea of a detached art, of poetry as a charm which exists only to distract our leisure, is a decadent idea and an unmistakable symptom of our power to castrate.

. . . We must get rid of our superstitious valuation of texts and *written* poetry. Written poetry is worth reading once, and then should be destroyed. Let the dead poets make way for others. Then we might even come to see that it is our veneration for what has already been created, however beautiful and valid it may be, that petrifies us, deadens our responses, and prevents us from making contact with that underlying power, call it thought-energy, the life force, the determinism of change, lunar menses, or anything you like. Beneath the poetry of the texts, there is the actual poetry, without form and without text. And just as the efficacy of masks in the magic practices of certain tribes is exhausted—and these masks are no longer good for anything except museums—so the poetic efficacy of a text is exhausted; yet the poetry and the efficacy of the theater are exhausted least quickly of all, since they permit the *action* of what is gesticulated and pronounced, and which is never made the same way twice.

It is a question of knowing what we want. If we are prepared for war, plague, famine, and slaughter we do not even need to say so, we have only to continue as we are; continue behaving like snobs, rushing en masse to hear such and such a singer, to see such and such an admirable performance which never transcends the realm of art (and even the Russian ballet at the height of its splendor never transcended the realm of art), to marvel at such and such an exhibition of painting in which exciting shapes explode here and there but at random and without any genuine consciousness of the forces they could rouse.

This empiricism, randomness, individualism, and anarchy must cease.

Enough of personal poems, benefitting those who create them much more than those who read them.

Once and for all, enough of this closed, egoistic, and personal art.

Our spiritual anarchy and intellectual disorder is a function of the anarchy of everything else—or rather, everything else is a function of this anarchy.

I am not one of those who believe that civilization has to change in order for the theater to change; but I do believe that the theater, utilized in the highest and most difficult sense possible, has the power to influence the aspect and formation of things: and the encounter upon the stage of two passionate manifestations, two living centers, two nervous magnetisms is something as entire, true, even decisive, as, in life, the encounter of one epidermis with another in a timeless debauchery.

That is why I propose a theater of cruelty.—With this mania we all have for depreciating everything, as soon as I have said "cruelty," everybody will at once take it to mean "blood." But *"theater of cruelty"* means a theater difficult and cruel for myself first of all. And, on the level of performance, it is not the cruelty we can exercise upon each other by hacking at each other's bodies, carving up our personal anatomies, or, like Assyrian emperors, sending parcels of human ears, noses, or neatly detached nostrils through the mail, but the much more terrible and necessary cruelty which things can exercise against us. We are not free. And the sky can still fall on our heads. And the theater has been created to teach us that first of all.

Either we will be capable of returning by present-day means to this superior idea of poetry and poetry-through-theater which underlies the Myths told by the great ancient tragedians, capable once more of entertaining a religious idea of the theater (without meditation, useless contemplation, and vague dreams), capable of attaining awareness and a possession of certain dominant forces, of certain notions that control all others, and (since ideas, when they are effective, carry their energy with them) capable of recovering within ourselves those energies which ultimately create order and increase the value of life, or else we might as well abandon ourselves now, without protest, and recognize that we are no longer good for anything but disorder, famine, blood, war, and epidemics.

Either we restore all the arts to a central attitude and necessity, finding an analogy between a gesture made in painting or the theater, and a gesture made by lava in a volcanic explosion, or we must stop painting, babbling, writing, or doing whatever it is we do.

I propose to bring back into the theater this elementary magical idea, taken up by modern psychoanalysis, which consists in effecting a patient's cure by making him assume the apparent and exterior attitudes of the desired condition.

I propose to renounce our empiricism of imagery, in which the unconscious furnishes images at random, and which the poet arranges at random too, calling them poetic and hence hermetic images, as if the kind of trance that poetry provides did not have its reverberations throughout the whole sensibility, in every nerve, and as if poetry were some vague force whose movements were invariable.

I propose to return through the theater to an idea of the physical knowledge of images and the means of inducing trances, as in Chinese medicine which knows, over the entire extent of the human anatomy, at what points to puncture in order to regulate the subtlest functions.

Those who have forgotten the communicative power and magical mimesis of a gesture, the theater can reinstruct, because a gesture carries its energy with it, and there are still human beings in the theater to manifest the force of the gesture made.

To create art is to deprive a gesture of its reverberation in the organism, whereas this reverberation, if the gesture is made in the conditions and with the force required, incites the organism and, through it, the entire individuality, to take attitudes in harmony with the gesture.

The theater is the only place in the world, the last general means we still possess of directly affecting the organism and, in periods of neurosis and petty sensuality like the one in which we are immersed, of attacking this sensuality by physical means it cannot withstand.

If music affects snakes, it is not on account of the spiritual notions it offers them, but because snakes are long and coil their length upon the earth, because their bodies touch the earth at almost every point; and because the musical vibrations which are communicated to the earth affect them like a very subtle, very long massage; and I propose to treat the spectators like the snakecharmer's subjects and conduct them *by means of their organisms* to an apprehension of the subtlest notions.

At first by crude means, which will gradually be refined. These immediate crude means will hold their attention at the start.

That is why in the "theater of cruelty" the spectator is in the center and the spectacle surrounds him.

In this spectacle the sonorisation is constant: sounds, noises, cries are chosen first for their vibratory quality, then for what they represent.

Among these gradually refined means light is interposed in its turn. Light which is not created merely to add color or to brighten, and which brings its power, influence, suggestions with it. And the light of a green cavern does not sensually dispose the organism like the light of a windy day.

After sound and light there is action, and the dynamism of action: here the theater, far from copying life, puts itself whenever possible in communication with pure forces. And whether you accept or deny them, there is nevertheless a way of speaking which gives the name of "forces" to whatever brings to birth images of energy in the unconscious, and gratuitous crime on the surface.

A violent and concentrated action is a kind of lyricism: it summons up supernatural images, a bloodstream of images, a bleeding spurt of images in the poet's head and in the spectator's as well.

Whatever the conflicts that haunt the mind of a given period, I defy any spectator to whom such violent scenes will have transferred their blood, who will have felt in himself the transit of a superior action, who will have seen the extraordinary and essential movements of his thought illuminated in extraordinary deeds—the violence and blood having been placed at the service of the violence of the thought—I defy that spectator to give himself up, once outside the theater, to ideas of war, riot, and blatant murder.

So expressed, this idea seems dangerous and sophomoric. It will be claimed that example breeds example, that if the attitude of cure induces cure, the attitude of murder will induce murder. Everything depends upon the manner and the purity with which the thing is done. There is a risk. But let it not be forgotten that though a theatrical gesture is violent, it is disinterested; and that the theater teaches precisely the uselessness of the action which, once done, is not to be done, and the superior use of the state unused by the action and which, *restored*, produces a purification.

I propose then a theater in which violent physical images crush and hypnotize the sensibility of the spectator seized by the theater as by a whirlwind of higher forces.

A theater which, abandoning psychology, recounts the extraordinary, stages natural conflicts, natural and subtle forces, and presents itself first of all as an exceptional power of redirection. A theater that induces trance, as the dances of Dervishes induce trance, and that addresses itself to the organism by precise instruments, by the same means as those of certain music cures which we admire on records but are incapable of originating among ourselves.

There is a risk involved, but in the present circumstances I believe it is a risk worth running. I do not believe we have managed to revitalize the world we live in, and I do not believe it is worth the trouble of clinging to; but I do propose something to get us out of our marasmus, instead of continuing to complain about it, and about the boredom, inertia, and stupidity of everything.

ILLUSTRATION 9

The Measures Taken

BERTOLT BRECHT

CHARACTERS

Control Chorus	Two Coolies
Four Agitators	Two Textile Workers
Young Comrade	Trader
Leader	Policeman
Overseer	

CONTROL CHORUS: Step forward! Your work has been successful. In yet another country the ranks of the fighters are joined, and the revolution marches on. We agree to what you have done.

FOUR AGITATORS: Stop! We have something to say. We announce the death of a comrade.

CONTROL CHORUS: Who killed him?

FOUR AGITATORS: We killed him. We shot him and threw him into a lime pit.

CONTROL CHORUS: Demonstrate how it happened and why, and you will hear our verdict.

FOUR AGITATORS: We shall respect your verdict.

1
THE CLASSICAL WRITINGS

FOUR AGITATORS: We came from Moscow as agitators. We were to travel to the city of Mukden to make propaganda, and build up the Chinese Party in the factories. We were to announce ourselves at the last Party Headquarters from the frontier and demand a guide. In the anteroom a young comrade came to us, and we spoke of the nature of our assignment. We shall repeat what was said.

Three of them stand together. The other, presenting the YOUNG COMRADE, *stands by himself.*

YOUNG COMRADE: I am the secretary at the last Party Headquarters from the frontier. My heart beats for the revolution. The sight of injustice drove me into the ranks of the fighters. I am for freedom. I believe in humanity. And I am for the measures taken by the Communist Party which fights for the classless society against exploitation and ignorance.

THREE AGITATORS: We come from Moscow.

YOUNG COMRADE: We expected you.

THREE AGITATORS: Why?

YOUNG COMRADE: We're getting nowhere. There is scarcity and disorder, little bread and much struggle. Many are brave, but few can read. Few machines, and no one understands them. Our locomotives have broken down. Have you brought any locomotives with you?

THREE AGITATORS: No.

YOUNG COMRADE: Have you any tractors?

THREE AGITATORS: No.

YOUNG COMRADE: Our farmers are still straining their muscles at old wooden plows. And so we have no way of putting our fields in order. Have you brought any seed?

THREE AGITATORS: No.

YOUNG COMRADE: Have you got munitions at least and machine guns?

THREE AGITATORS: No.

YOUNG COMRADE: There are just two of us to defend the revolution here. Surely you've brought us a letter from the Central Committee telling us what to do?

THREE AGITATORS: No.

YOUNG COMRADE: Then you yourselves are going to help us?

THREE AGITATORS: No.

YOUNG COMRADE: Day and night we never get out of our clothes, in the struggle against hunger, decay, and counterrevolution. Yet you bring us nothing.

THREE AGITATORS: Exactly so: we bring you nothing. But over the frontier to Mukden we bring the Chinese workers the teachings of the classic writers and the propagandists, the ABC of communism; to the ignorant, instruction about their condition; to the oppressed, class consciousness; and to the class conscious, the experience of revolution. From you, however, we are to demand an automobile and a guide.. . .

YOUNG COMRADE: Then I was wrong to ask?

THREE AGITATORS: No, but a good question led to a better answer. We see that everything has already been asked of you. But even more will be asked of you: one of you two must guide us to Mukden.

YOUNG COMRADE: Then I'll leave my post, which was too hard for two, but which one alone must now learn to handle. I shall go with you. Marching forward, spreading the teaching of the communist classics: World Revolution.

CONTROL CHORUS:

Praise of the U.S.S.R.

Certainly our misery
Was something to talk about.
But seated at our sparse table
Was the Hope of all the oppressed
Who is satisfied with water.
And in a clear voice
Behind the broken-down door
Knowledge taught the guests.
When the doors are broken
We only become visible from a little further away
We whom frost does not kill, nor hunger
Untiringly conferring about
The world's destinies.

FOUR AGITATORS: In this way, the Young Comrade of the frontier station agreed to
the general character of our work and we came—four men and one woman—
before the leader at Party Headquarters.

2
THE BLOTTING OUT

FOUR AGITATORS: But the work in Mukden was illegal, so, before we crossed the
frontier, we had to blot out our faces. Our Young Comrade agreed to this. We
will repeat the incident.

One of the AGITATORS *presents the* LEADER *at Party Headquarters.*

LEADER: I am the Leader at the last headquarters. I have agreed that the comrade
from my station should go along as guide. But there is unrest in the Mukden
factories. At the present time the eyes of the world are on this city to see if one
of us won't be found leaving a Chinese worker's hut. And I hear that gunboats
stand ready on the rivers and armored trains in the sidings, ready to attack us
at once, if one of us is seen there. And so I am having the comrades cross the
frontier as Chinese. (*To the* AGITATORS:) You must not be seen.

TWO AGITATORS: We shall not be seen.

LEADER: If one of you is wounded, he must not be found.

TWO AGITATORS: He will not be found.

LEADER: Then you are ready to die and to hide the dead one?

TWO AGITATORS: Yes.

LEADER: Then you are yourselves no longer. You are not Karl Schmitt from Berlin,
you are not Anna Kjersk from Kazan, and you are not Peter Sawitch from
Moscow. One and all of you are nameless and motherless, blank pages on which
the revolution writes its instructions.

TWO AGITATORS: Yes.

LEADER (*gives them masks; they put them on*): Then, from this time on, you are no
one no longer. From this time on, and probably until you disappear, you are

unknown workers, fighters, Chinese, born of Chinese mothers, with yellow skin, speaking Chinese in fever and in sleep.

TWO AGITATORS: Yes.

LEADER: In the interests of communism, agreeing to the advance of the proletarian masses of all lands, saying Yes to the revolutionizing of the world.

TWO AGITATORS: Yes. And in the way the Young Comrade demonstrated his agreement to the blotting-out of his face.

CONTROL CHORUS: Who fights for communism must be able to fight and not to fight; to speak the truth and not to speak the truth; to perform services and not to perform services; to keep promises and not to keep promises; to go into danger and to keep out of danger; to be recognizable and not to be recognizable. Who fights for communism has only one of all the virtues: that he fights for communism.

FOUR AGITATORS: As Chinese, we went to Mukden, four men and one woman, to make propaganda and support the Chinese workers through the teachings of the classics and the propagandists, the ABC of communism: to bring to the ignorant instruction about their situation; to the oppressed, class-consciousness; and to the class-conscious, the experience of revolution.

CONTROL CHORUS:

Praise of Illegal Work

It is splendid
To take up the word as a weapon in the class war
To rouse the masses to the fight in a loud and ringing voice
To crush the oppressors
To free the oppressed.
Hard and useful is the small daily labor
The grim, persistent tying and spreading of the Party's net
For the capitalists' guns
To speak
But conceal the speaker
To win the victory
But conceal the victor
To die
But hide the death.
Who would not do much for fame
But who would do it for silence?
Yet the impoverished host invites Honor to supper
And out of the tiny and tumble-down hut steps irresistibly
Greatness
And Fame calls in vain
On the doers of the great deed.

FOUR AGITATORS: In the city of Mukden, we made propaganda among the workers. We had no bread for the hungry but only knowledge for the ignorant. Therefore we spoke of the root cause of poverty, did not abolish poverty, but spoke of the abolition of the root cause.

3
THE STONE

FOUR AGITATORS: First, we went down into the lower section of the city. Coolies were dragging a barge with a rope. But the ground on the bank was slippery. So when one of them slipped, and the overseer hit him, we said to the Young Comrade: "Go after them, make propaganda among them after work. But don't give way to pity!" And we asked: "Do you agree to it?" And he agreed to it and hurried away and at once gave way to pity. We will show you.

TWO AGITATORS *present* COOLIES, *fastening a rope to a hook, and then pulling the rope over their shoulders. One presents the* YOUNG COMRADE, *one the* OVERSEER.

TWO COOLIES: We are the coolies and we pull the rice barge up the river.
CONTROL CHORUS:

Song of the Rice Barge Coolies

In the city up the river
A mouthful of rice awaits us
But the barge is heavy that we must pull up the river
And the water flows down the river
We shall never get there
>   Pull faster
>   We want our dinner
>   Pull evenly
>   Don't jostle the next man
In the barge is rice
The farmer who grew it received a few cents
We get even less
An ox would cost more
Than we do
There are too many of us
>   Pull faster
>   We want our dinner
>   Pull evenly
>   Don't jostle the next man
Night will soon fall
A resting place smaller than a dog's shadow
Costs us a mouthful of rice
Because the river bank is slippery
We are making no headway
>   Pull faster
>   We want our dinner
>   Pull evenly
>   Don't jostle the next man

YOUNG COMRADE: It is repulsive to hear how the torture of these men's labor is masked by beauty!

OVERSEER: I am the Overseer. I must get the rice to the city by evening. Pull faster.

CONTROL CHORUS:

> Our fathers pulled the barge from the river mouth
> A little farther upstream
> Our children will reach the source
> We come between
>> Pull faster
>> We want our dinner
>> Pull evenly
>> Don't jostle the next man

ONE COOLIE (*slipping out of line*):   I can't keep going.

CONTROL CHORUS (*while the* COOLIES *stand and are whipped*):

> The rope that cuts into our shoulders
> Holds longer than we do
> The Overseer's whip has seen four generations
> We are not the last
>> Pull faster
>> We want our dinner
>> Pull evenly
>> Don't jostle the next man

YOUNG COMRADE: It is hard to see these men without pity. (*To the* OVERSEER:) Can't you see the ground is slippery?

OVERSEER: The ground is what?

YOUNG COMRADE: Slippery! (*To the* COOLIE:) I now take a stone and lay it in the mud. Now walk!

CONTROL CHORUS:

> When the rice arrives in the city
> And children ask who dragged the heavy barge
> The answer given is:
> The barge was dragged
>> Pull faster
>> We want our dinner
>> Pull evenly
>> Don't jostle the next man

OVERSEER: What? You claim this bank is so slippery it's impossible to pull a barge full of rice?

YOUNG COMRADE: I've only put a stone there for this man.

OVERSEER: Then you think we can't pull the barge without you? Or that the city of Mukden doesn't need rice?

YOUNG COMRADE: The men can't pull the barge if they fall down.

OVERSEER: Should I provide a stone for each of them to walk on—from here to the city of Mukden?

YOUNG COMRADE: I don't know what *you* should do, but

> I know what *they* should do.
> The food from down there
> Feeds people up here

Those who brought it up for them
Have not fed

COOLIE (*to* OVERSEER):   This fellow's a fool. They all laugh at him.
OVERSEER.   No, he's one of those that stir up the workers. Hello there! Hold that man!
FOUR AGITATORS: And they at once took hold of him. And they pursued him for two days till he met us. Then they pursued us and him together in the city of Mukden for a whole week. They wouldn't let us get near the central section of the city.

DISCUSSION

CONTROL CHORUS:
But is it not right to support the weak man
And help him wherever he confronts us?
To help the exploited man
In his daily hardships and oppressed as he is?

FOUR AGITATORS: He did not help him. But he did hinder us from making propaganda in our section of the city.
CONTROL CHORUS: We agree to that.
FOUR AGITATORS: The Young Comrade perceived that he had put his feelings above his understanding. But we comforted him and spoke to him the words of Comrade Lenin:
CONTROL CHORUS:
Intelligence is not to make no mistakes
But quickly to see how to make them good.

4
JUSTICE

FOUR AGITATORS: We founded the first Party cells in the factories and trained the first functionaries, established a Party school and taught them how to make the forbidden literature secretly available. Then we spread propaganda in the textile works, and each man had his assignment, and we said to the Young Comrade: "Place yourself at the factory door and hand out leaflets, but don't give yourself away." Then suspicion fell upon a man who stood near him and was seized in his stead. And he could not keep quiet. We will show it.
THREE AGITATORS: With the barge workers you failed.
YOUNG COMRADE: Yes.
THREE AGITATORS: Did that teach you something?
YOUNG COMRADE: Yes.
THREE AGITATORS: Will you handle yourself better with the textile workers?
YOUNG COMRADE: Yes.

Two agitators play Textile Workers.

Two Textile Workers: We are workers in the textile works.
Control Chorus:

The Song of the Textile Workers

Today once again
There was less money in the pay envelope
If we leave the looms
Others will take our places
We cannot leave.

Young Comrade: Strike! Your wages are too low. Leave your looms! Place yourselves at the gates and let no one get to your looms!
Control Chorus:

If we place ourselves in the gateways and
Let no one get to our looms
The soldiers will come and shoot at us
We cannot place ourselves in the gateways.

Young Comrade: Strike! Your wages are too low. Place yourselves in the gateways
and fight the soldiers!
Control Chorus:

Who will be first to go hungry? Who first
Will set his face against the guns? Who
Will begin? Who will be able
To eat his supper?

Young Comrade: Strike! Your wages are too low. All begin together. Every man
must be the first man!
Two Textile Workers: When the factory closes, we're going home. We are very
dissatisfied but we don't know what to do.
Young Comrade (*sticking a leaflet in front of one of them, the other stands inactive*):
Read it and pass it on. When you've read it, you'll know what to do.

First Textile Worker *takes it and walks on.*

One of the agitators plays a Policeman.

Policeman: I am a policeman and get my bread from the ruling class for combating
discontent. (*He takes the leaflet away from the* First Textile Worker.) Who
gave you that leaflet?
First Textile Worker: I don't know. Somebody just stuck it in my hand as I was
passing.
Policeman (*stepping up to the* Second Textile Worker).   *You* gave him the leaflet!
We have orders to hunt up the ones that give out the leaflets.
Second Textile Worker: I didn't give out any leaflet.
Young Comrade: Is it a crime to teach them they are ignorant of their situation?
Policeman: These teachings lead to God knows what. Teach a factory that sort of

stuff, and they don't know who the owner is any more. This little leaflet is more dangerous than ten cannon.

YOUNG COMRADE: What's in it?

POLICEMAN: How would I know? (*To the* SECOND TEXTILE WORKER:) What's in it?

SECOND TEXTILE WORKER: I don't know the leaflet. I didn't hand it out.

YOUNG COMRADE: I know he didn't.

POLICEMAN (*to* YOUNG COMRADE): Did *you* give him the leaflet?

YOUNG COMRADE: No.

POLICEMAN (*to* SECOND TEXTILE WORKER): Then *you* gave it to him.

YOUNG COMRADE (*to* FIRST TEXTILE WORKER): What'll happen to him?

FIRST TEXTILE WORKER: He could be shot.

YOUNG COMRADE: What do you want to shoot him for? Aren't you a proletarian, too, policeman?

POLICEMAN (*to* SECOND TEXTILE WORKER): Come with me. (*Strikes him on the head.*)

YOUNG COMRADE (*trying to stop him*): It wasn't him.

POLICEMAN: Then it *was* you!

SECOND TEXTILE WORKER: It wasn't him.

POLICEMAN: Then it was the both of you!

FIRST TEXTILE WORKER: Run, you fool, run, your pocket's full of leaflets!

POLICEMAN *cuts the* SECOND TEXTILE WORKER *down.*

YOUNG COMRADE (*pointing at* POLICEMAN. *To the* FIRST TEXTILE WORKER): He's killed an innocent man. You are a witness.

FIRST TEXTILE WORKER (*attacking the* POLICEMAN): Hireling!

POLICEMAN *draws his revolver.*

YOUNG COMRADE *grabs the* POLICEMAN *by the neck from behind. The* FIRST TEXTILE WORKER *twists his arm back slowly. The shot goes wild. The* POLICEMAN *is disarmed.*

YOUNG COMRADE (*yelling*): Help, Comrades! Help! They're shooting innocent bystanders!

FOUR AGITATORS: The workers at once came running out of the factories to demonstrate against police violence. That is how the textile workers' strike arose. But the coolie organization demanded the punishment of the policeman, and the policeman was punished. But the strike was discontinued for a long time, and the guards were reinforced in the factories. Everyone talked about the murder of the innocent man; but we were banished from the factories.

DISCUSSION

CONTROL CHORUS: But is it not right to act justly and always to combat injustice wherever it may be found?

FOUR AGITATORS: In order to uphold the great injustice the small justice was conceded. But the great strike was knocked out of our hands.

CONTROL CHORUS: We agree to that.

5
WHAT IS A HUMAN BEING ACTUALLY?

FOUR AGITATORS: Daily we fought those old associates: oppression and despair. We taught the workers to transform a struggle for higher wages into a struggle for power. Taught them the use of weapons and the art of street fighting. Then we heard there was conflict between the merchants and the British, who ruled the city, on account of tariffs. In order to exploit this rulers' quarrel for the benefit of the ruled, we sent the Young Comrade with a letter to the richest of merchants. It said: "Arm the coolies!" We said to the Young Comrade: "Win his confidence." But when the food came on the table, he didn't keep his mouth shut. We will show you.

THREE AGITATORS: In the spinning mills you failed.

YOUNG COMRADE: Yes.

THREE AGITATORS: Did you learn something by it?

YOUNG COMRADE: Yes.

THREE AGITATORS: Will you bring arms from the merchants?

YOUNG COMRADE: Yes.

An agitator as TRADER.

TRADER: I am the trader. I'm expecting a letter from the coolie organization about the possibility of our getting together against the British.

YOUNG COMRADE: Here is the letter from the coolie organization.

TRADER: Please come and dine with me.

YOUNG COMRADE: It's an honor for me to be permitted to dine with you.

TRADER: While dinner's being prepared, I'd like to give you my opinion of coolies. Please sit down over here.

YOUNG COMRADE: I'm very interested in your opinion.

TRADER: Why do I get everything cheaper than anyone else? And why would a coolie work for me almost without pay?

YOUNG COMRADE: I don't know.

TRADER: Because I'm bright. You're pretty bright yourselves or how would you squeeze union dues out of your coolies?

YOUNG COMRADE: That's true.—Incidentally, are you going to arm the coolies against the British?

TRADER: Maybe, maybe.—I know how to handle a coolie. You must give him enough rice to keep him from dying. Otherwise, you can't get any work out of him. Is that right?

YOUNG COMRADE: Yes. That is right.

TRADER: I say it is not right. If coolies are cheaper than rice, I can get me a new coolie. Isn't that nearer the truth?

YOUNG COMRADE: Yes, that's nearer the truth.—Incidentally, when will you start sending weapons into our section of the city?

TRADER: Soon, soon.—You couldn't help noticing that the coolies who load my leather eat my rice in the canteen?

YOUNG COMRADE: I couldn't help noticing.

TRADER: What do you think: do I pay a lot for the work?
YOUNG COMRADE: No, but your rice is expensive, and you insist on the work being well done, and your rice is bad rice.
TRADER: You people are bright.
YOUNG COMRADE: And when will you arm the coolies against the British?
TRADER: After dinner we can inspect the arsenal. Now I'm going to sing you my favorite song.

The Song of Supply and Demand

Down the river there is rice
In the provinces up the river people need rice:
If we leave the rice in the warehouses
The rice will cost them more
Those who pull the rice barge will then get less rice
And rice will be even cheaper for me
    What is rice actually?
    Do I know what rice is?
    God knows what rice is!
    I don't know what rice is!
    I only know its price

Winter comes, the people need clothing
One must buy up the cotton
And not let go of it
When the cold weather comes, clothing will cost more
The cotton-spinning mills pay too high wages
There's too much cotton around anyway
    What is cotton actually?
    Do I know what cotton is?
    God knows what cotton is!
    I don't know what cotton is
    I only know its price

Likewise men—they need too much food
And so men get to cost more
To make the food, men are needed
Cooks make the food cheaper
But those who eat it make it cost more
There aren't enough men around anyway.
    What is a man actually?
    Do I know what a man is?
    God knows what a man is!
    I don't know what a man is
    I only know his price

(To the YOUNG COMRADE:*)*

And now we're going to eat my good rice.

YOUNG COMRADE (*stands up*):   I can't eat with you.

FOUR AGITATORS: That's what he said. And neither threats nor laughter could bring him to eat with a man he despised. And the trader drove him out of the house, and the coolies were not armed.

DISCUSSION

CONTROL CHORUS: But isn't it right to put honor before everything else?

FOUR AGITATORS: No.

CONTROL CHORUS: We agree to that

Change the World, It Needs It

With whom would the right-minded man not sit
To help the right?
What medicine would taste too bad
To a dying man?
What baseness would you not commit
To root out baseness?
If, finally, you could change the world
What task would you be too good for?
Sink down in the filth
Embrace the butcher
But change the world: it needs it!
Who are you?
Stinking, be gone from
The room that has been cleaned! Would that
You were the last of the filth which
You had to remove!

FOUR AGITATORS: Yet in those days we managed to spread the net of the Party for the capitalists' guns.

6
REBELLION AGAINST THE TEACHING

FOUR AGITATORS: That week the persecutions sharply increased. All we had left was a secret room for the hectograph machine and the pamphlets. On the evening of the third day, reaching our retreat not without risk, we found the Young Comrade in the doorway. And there were bundles in front of the house in the rain. We shall repeat what was said.

THREE AGITATORS: What are these bundles?

YOUNG COMRADE: Our propaganda.

THREE AGITATORS: What are you going to do with it?

YOUNG COMRADE: I have something to tell you. The new leaders of the unemployed came here today and convinced me that we begin by taking action—right away.

We want to hand out the propaganda leaflets. We led off by calling for a general strike.

THREE AGITATORS: Now you have betrayed us four times over.

YOUNG COMRADE: Poverty is spreading, unrest is growing in the city.

THREE AGITATORS: The ignorant are beginning to recognize their situation.

YOUNG COMRADE: The unemployed have adopted our teaching.

THREE AGITATORS: The oppressed are learning class consciousness.

YOUNG COMRADE: They go out into the streets and want to demolish the spinning mills.

THREE AGITATORS: The roads to revolution show themselves. Our responsibility increases. And at this point you place the propaganda leaflets at the door so everyone can see them!

YOUNG COMRADE: The unemployed can wait no longer
Nor can I
Wait any longer
There are too many paupers.

THREE AGITATORS: But not enough fighters.

YOUNG COMRADE: Their sufferings are enormous.

THREE AGITATORS: It is not enough to suffer.

YOUNG COMRADE: Inside with us here are seven who came to us representing the unemployed. Behind them stand seven thousand and they know: Unhappiness doesn't grow on the chest like leprosy. Poverty won't fall off the roof like a loose tile, no: poverty and unhappiness are man's doing. Scarcity is all the meat in their oven, and their own wailing is all they have to eat! But they know all this.

THREE AGITATORS: Do they know how many regiments the government has?

YOUNG COMRADE: No.

THREE AGITATORS: Then they know too little. Where are your weapons?

YOUNG COMRADE (*showing his hands*):   We shall fight tooth and nail!

THREE AGITATORS: Tooth and nail won't suffice. Therefore hear this: on orders from the Party, we have spoken about the situation with the coolie organization which leads the working masses, and we have decided to postpone armed action till the delegates of the farmers' organizations have arrived in the city.

YOUNG COMRADE: Then hear what *I* say: I see with my two eyes that poverty cannot wait. I see how easily, if we do nothing, they run away and go home. I therefore set my face against your decision to wait.

THREE AGITATORS:

Do not see with your own eyes!
The individual has two eyes
The Party has a thousand eyes
The Party sees seven states
The individual sees one city
The individual has his hour
But the Party has many hours.
The individual can be wiped out
But the Party cannot be wiped out
For it rests on the teaching of the classic writers

Which is created from acquaintance with reality
And is destined to change it
For the teaching will take hold of the masses.

YOUNG COMRADE: Let me ask this: is it in line with the classic writers to let misery wait?

THREE AGITATORS: They speak, not of pity, but of the deed which does away with pity.

YOUNG COMRADE: Then the classic writers don't advocate helping every poor man at once and putting that before everything else?

THREE AGITATORS: No.

YOUNG COMRADE: Then the classic writers are dirt. I tear them up. For man, living man, cries out. His misery tears down the dikes of mere teaching. And that's why I'm going into action—right now, this minute! For *I* cry out too. *I* tear down the dikes of the teaching! (*He tears up the writings.*)

THREE AGITATORS:
Do not tear them!
We need every one of them.
Take a look at reality!
Your revolution is quickly made and lasts one day
And is strangled the morning after
But our revolution begins tomorrow
Conquers and changes the world.
Your revolution stops when you stop.
When you have stopped
Our revolution marches on.

CONTROL CHORUS:

Praise of the Party

The individual has two eyes
The Party has a thousand eyes
The Party sees seven states
The individual sees one city
The individual has his hour
But the Party cannot be wiped out
For it rests on the teaching of the classic writers
Which is created from acquaintance with reality
And is destined to change it
For the teaching will take hold of the masses.

YOUNG COMRADE: That's no good any more. Looking at the struggle as it is now, I throw away all that was good yesterday, I reject every agreement *with* everybody and do what alone is human. Here is action. I place myself at the head of it. My heart beats for the revolution, and the revolution is here!

THREE AGITATORS: Silence!

YOUNG COMRADE: The sight of injustice drove me into the ranks of the fighters. Here is injustice.

THREE AGITATORS: Silence!
YOUNG COMRADE: Here is oppression. I am for freedom!
THREE AGITATORS: Silence! You are betraying us.
YOUNG COMRADE:

> I have seen too much.
> I shall therefore go before them
> As what I am
> And state
> What is.

He takes off his mask and shouts.

> We have come to help you!
> We come from Moscow!

He tears up the mask.

FOUR AGITATORS:

> And we saw him and in the twilight saw
> His naked face, human, open, guileless.
> He had torn up his mask.
> And the exploited shouted from their houses:
> "Who disturbs the sleep of the poor?"
> And a window opened and a voice shouted:
> "Foreigners! Throw the troublemakers out!"
> We were now recognizable.
> And in that hour we heard of unrest in the lower section of the city
> And the ignorant waited in the meeting houses and
> The unarmed in the streets.
> And we struck him down
> And lifted him up and left the city in haste.

7
FINAL PURSUIT AND ANALYSIS

CONTROL CHORUS: They left the city!
> Unrest grows in the city
> But the leadership flees over the city line.
> What measures did you take?

FOUR AGITATORS: Wait a moment. When in the course of our flight we came near
the lime pits outside the city limits, we saw our pursuers behind us.
CONTROL CHORUS:
> They run like race horses.
> The factory councils come to the central office for consultation
> But the shelterless slept on the propaganda leaflets.
> What measures did you take?

FOUR AGITATORS: Wait a moment. Yes, even now we helped him. Helped him along
till we reached the lime pits.

CONTROL CHORUS:
>   The masses wait in the meeting houses
>   But the speakers are off at the mines.
>   What measures did you take?

FOUR AGITATORS: Wait a moment.
>   It is easy to know what is right
>   Far from the shooting
>   When you have months of time
>   But we
>   Had ten minutes' time and
>   Enemy guns to think of and
>   Had to see the face of the unhappy one
>   Our comrade.

CONTROL CHORUS: Your measure! Your measure!
FOUR AGITATORS: Wait a moment.
>   As even an animal
>   Will help an animal
>   We too wished to help
>   Him who fought for our cause at our side.

CONTROL CHORUS:
>   In time of extreme persecution and
>   The confusion of theory
>   The fighters depict the structure of the situation
>   And weigh the stakes and the possibilities.

FOUR AGITATORS: We did just that.

THE ANALYSIS

FIRST AGITATOR: The masses are in the streets, we said.
SECOND AGITATOR: But we must assemble them in meetings.
THIRD AGITATOR: Or they won't know what to do, and will disperse, before the delegates of the farmers' organizations have arrived in the city.
SECOND AGITATOR: Therefore we cannot get our comrade over the border.
THIRD AGITATOR: But if we hide him and he later reappears, what happens when he is recognized?
FIRST AGITATOR: There were gunboats on the rivers and armored trains in the railroad sidings, ready to attack whenever one of us was found. He must not be found.
FOUR AGITATORS:
>   If we are found, no matter where,
>   The cry goes up: "The rulers are in danger
>   Of annihilation!"
>   And the cannon fire.
>
>   Wherever the starving groan and hit back
>   Their tormentors shout

That we have bribed them
To groan and hit back.

CONTROL CHORUS:
    It is written on our foreheads
    That we are against exploitation.
    In the letter of information against us is written:
    "They are for the oppressed!"

    Who helps the despairing
    Passes for the scum of the earth
    We are the scum of the earth
    We must not be found.

8
THE INTERMENT

THREE AGITATORS:
    We decided:
    Then he must disappear, and totally.
    For we must return to our work
    And cannot take him with us and cannot leave him behind
    We must therefore shoot him and throw him in the lime pit
    For the lime will burn him.
    We will repeat our last conversation
    And demand your verdict.

FIRST AGITATOR: We are going to ask him if he agrees, for he was a brave fighter.
SECOND AGITATOR: But even if he does not agree, he must disappear, and totally.
FIRST AGITATOR (*to the* YOUNG COMRADE):   We must shoot you and throw you in the lime pit so the lime will burn you. And we ask you: do you agree to this?
YOUNG COMRADE: Yes.
THREE AGITATORS: He said Yes.
CONTROL CHORUS: His answer was in accord with reality. Did you find no way out, whereby the young fighter might be preserved to fight again?
FOUR AGITATORS:
    The time was short. We
    Found no way out.
    In sight of our pursuers
    We reflected for five minutes
    On a better possibility.
    You too, think now about
    A better possibility.

    Pause.

    Lamenting, we beat our heads with our fists
    Since they had only this fearful counsel to offer: forthwith

To cut off a foot from our own body for
IT IS A FEARSOME THING TO KILL.
But we will kill ourselves and not just others if necessary
Since only by force can this dying world be changed
As every living man knows.
It is not granted to us, we said,
Not to kill.
At one with the inflexible will to change the world
We formulated
The measures to be taken.

CONTROL CHORUS:
    Go on with the story
    You are assured of our sympathy
    It was not easy to do what was right.

THREE AGITATORS: Where shall we put you, we asked him.
YOUNG COMRADE: In the lime pit, he said.
THREE AGITATORS: We asked: Will you do it alone?
YOUNG COMRADE: Help me.
THREE AGITATORS:
    We said: lean your head on our arms
    Close your eyes
    We will carry you.

YOUNG COMRADE (*unseen*):
    He then said:
    "In the interests of communism
    Agreeing to the advance of the proletarian masses of all lands
    Saying Yes to the revolutionizing of the world."

THREE AGITATORS:
    Then we shot him
    And threw him down into the lime pit
    And when the lime had devoured him
    We returned to our work.

CONTROL CHORUS:
    And your work was successful
    You have spread
    The teachings of the classics
    The ABC of communism:
    To the ignorant, instruction about their situation
    To the oppressed, class consciousness
    And to the class conscious, the experience of revolution.
    In yet another country the revolution advances
    In another land the ranks of the fighters are joined
    We agree to what you have done.

PART II: THE CREATIVE PROCESS

5

Expressive Theories
of Art

The theories of art that Part I presents play down one important aspect of art: the creative process which goes into the making of artworks. Part II concentrates on theories which emphasize this creativity. Each reading within it explains the nature and extent of the artist's activities when he or she engages in producing an artwork. Theories which emphasize the creative element in art are often called *expressive* theories of art. Expressive theories focus on the artist almost to the exclusion of other elements in art. Subject matter, formal structure, and the relation of the artwork to an audience are secondary considerations. The expression of the emotions and imagination of the artist are the sources of creativity and originality in a work of art. Therefore these expressions are the most important features of art.

Expressive ideas about art have been implicit in philosophical thinking as early as Aristotle. He argued that one of the most important functions of great art is to evoke or arouse emotions in its audience. But there are at least three forms of expressive theories. (1) Art communicates or evokes emotions in its audience. Theories such as Tolstoy's in Part I are good examples of a Type I expressive theory. (2) Works of art are symbolic representations, but not necessarily personal expressions, of emotions. Susanne Langer's theory of art, included in Chapter 7, illustrates the representational theory of expression. (3) Art is the self-expression of the artist. The idea of art as self-expression emphasizes the imagination of the artist as the source of originality and creativity, and the essential characteristic of art is its personal, unique, and even idiosyncratic character engendered by the imaginative expressiveness of the artist. The writings included in this chapter formulate some of the general features of self-expressive theories of art.

The focus in this chapter is explicitly on the relationship between the artist and his/her artifact. Central to expressive theories of art is the idea that the important element in art is what is expressed rather than what is represented. What artists may be expressing are their feelings, emotions, thoughts or ideas, or they may be recreating in the work of art the processes of their imagination. But the role of the artist is that of an innovator. Artists do not copy nature. At the minimum they transform what they see through their feelings and imaginations. The essential characteristic of art becomes its expressiveness, and a good work of art is a unique expression of the artist's point of view.

Self-expressive theories of art assume that the creative mind is the source of aesthetic activity. One of the most influential thinkers on this view was the eighteenth-century German philosopher Immanuel Kant. Kant's importance to the philosophy of art derives in part from (1) his claim that the mind plays a constitutive role in its cognitive and creative experiences, (2) his notion that the self is not part of its experiences, (3) and his theory of imagination. In his chapter "The Imagination," a selection from *The Critique of Pure Reason* included in this chapter, Kant claims,

> There are three subjective sources of knowledge upon which rests the possibility of experience in general and of knowledge of its objects—*sense*, *imagination*, and *apperception*.

Sense, according to Kant, provides the data for our experiences. But while sensations provide the content of our experiences, what we call "experience" is not merely the sum of our sensations, nor of generalizations from a range of perceptions. Because individual sensations never repeat themselves, we cannot deal cognitively with the flux of sensations as each appears individually. Kant observes that while there is a constant flow of phenomenal data which makes up our experiences, what one calls experience is not merely this data because our experiences are structured, organized, and interconnected.

Kant argues further that the structure of our experience cannot come from perceptual data of sensations themselves. This is because one never has a *sensation* of space or of time, for example. One merely perceives phenomena related spacially and temporally. Because these organizing principles which structure our experiences (Kant calls them "categories" or "concepts of the understanding") accompany every perception yet are not perceived themselves, Kant argues that these categories originate in the mind of the perceiver as modes of constituting and structuring phenomena. Thus we experience perceptual data spatially, temporally, and in sequential and relational order through the organizing structures of our minds. Kant is NOT saying that the objects of our perception are confused sensations which we organize. He is saying that the nature of our experiences is such that we perceive sensations "organizedly" just as we see things "coloredly." We never perceive unstructured sensations just as we never experience the structure of these sensations without content. Experience is the inseparable unity of this structured data. It is only the philosopher, in analyzing the nature of experience, who understands that there are two components of experience: the phenomenal data, and the organizing processes of the mind.

Imagination, according to Kant, operates in the cognitive process of experiencing in at least two important ways. What Kant calls the reproductive imagination synthesizes and reproduces the nonreoccurring individual sensations in order to make perception and memory possible. The productive imagination (to which Kant sometimes refers as the *a priori* imagination) brings together one's perceptions with the categories of understanding in order to make experience and knowledge about experiences possible. The imagination simultaneously (1) links individual impressions and (2) affects their organization through the categories to produce experiences. Thus the reproductive and productive imaginations are essential linking elements in the cognitive process without which cognition could not function.

In *The Critique of Judgment*—selections of which also appear in this chapter—Kant introduces a third, more creative role for imagination which he sometimes calls "free play." Imagination as free play does not merely synthesize our experiences. Rather it can apprehend or present what Kant calls aesthetic ideas, ideas which are neither derived from nor refer to empirical intuitions, and which are thus free from the laws of association, the categories. Imagination as free play can intuit images or ideas "without purpose," that is, without a necessarily logical organization or a correspondence to an actual experience. Free play produces aesthetic ideas which Kant claims are "inexponible" or not needing of explanation. And genius for Kant is a fully developed faculty of imagination which creates aesthetic ideas. Genius is a quality found in artists, exhibited in works of art, and evident in critical judgments of taste about art.

Finally apperception, according to Kant, accompanies and unifies all experiences in one subject or self. This unity—of apperception or the self—is "transcendental" according to Kant because the subject of experiencing is not part of the experiences it holds together. The notion that the subject self is not part of its own experiences was adopted by nineteenth-century poets such as William Blake and William Butler Yeats who then claimed that the artist is a sort of mystic who develops the transcendental subject to comprehend phenomena beyond ordinary experiences, and to see into the deeper mysteries of the universe. In reading the works of these artists—such as Yeat's poem *The Second Coming* (Illustration 17)—readers can decide for themselves whether this is the case.

Kant's concept of the aesthetic imagination as free play is not clearly defined in *The Critique of Judgment*. However the nineteenth-century English poet Samuel Taylor Coleridge elaborated on Kant's theories of imagination and apperception in his own famous theory of art. Coleridge was primarily a poet; his philosophical writings are often obtuse, and much of what he says is extraordinarily fragmented. Nevertheless Coleridge is well known for two important contributions to aesthetic theory: (1) his theory of imagination, which he derives from Kant; and (2) his concept of organic form, which translated into the important twentieth-century notion of organic unity.

Coleridge distinguishes three imaginative processes, which he assumes are distinct from sensibility and from cognition: (1) fancy, (2) the primary imagination, and (3) the secondary imagination—each of which is similar to, but not identical with, Kant's concepts of the reproductive, productive, and aesthetic imaginations. Fancy, according to Coleridge, operates somewhat like both reproductive and productive imagination in that it organizes perceptions, memories, and ideas. But fancy works mimetically: it receives its materials from experience, it is the source of representation, but it does not create aesthetic ideas. The primary imagination, on the other hand, would appear to be the self, the subject from whom creativity (or its lack) generates. The secondary imagination appears to operate like Kant's notion of free play, yet for Coleridge it is different in some important respects. The secondary imagination depends on the primary imagination for the source and vitality of its creative energy. Moreover the secondary imagination is itself a vital organic process according to Coleridge. It can reshape and even create its own images so that it is more innovative than Kant's free play. And the secondary imagination does not merely use the experiences and ideas of the mind; it also "brings the whole soul of man into activity," which includes man's emotions and feelings as well. The artist for Coleridge is the person who uses fancy and develops his or her secondary imagination through the power of the primary imagination, then expresses the emotions and ideas generated by the power of this creativity in a work of art.

One of the most important aesthetic developments to emerge from the nineteenth century is the concept of organic unity. This notion originated in Coleridge's second theory: the concept of organic form. A great work of art, according to Coleridge,

> Evolve like a plant by an inner principle, according not to rules but to the laws of its own growth, until it achieves an organic unity—a living interdependence of parts and wholes, in which . . . "each part is at once end and means."

Four statements outline the important aspects of organic forms:

1. A work of art is a synthesis and transformation of natural perceptual experiences through the subjective imagination of the artist, into an objective artifact.

2. A work of art is an autonomous, independent phenomenon in which its elements of form, content, and subject matter are carefully integrated.

3. A work of art has its own "personality" such that one cannot separate out the original components from which it was formed without destroying the character of the work.

4. As an organism, a great work of art has its own life, growth, and development such that it, like other organisms, evolves. Coleridge does not mean that a work of art such as his poem "Kubla Khan" (Illustration 10), for example, literally accretes words and lines on its own. What he does mean is that a good work of art can never be completely explicated. This is because, as an independent organic unit, this work always says or reveals something new on each viewing or reading.

The idea of organic unity embraces much of the self-expressive aesthetic: the idea of the active imagination, and the importance of expressiveness in art. Simultaneously this theory introduces a major twentieth-century idea: that a work of art is an independent autonomous phenomenon, distinct in its own right from its creator, from the experiences out of which it was created, and from the audience who experiences it.

Many twentieth-century formalists have adopted organic unity as a criterion for great art, and this chapter includes writings by several modern authors sharing this perspective: an essay by the contemporary British aesthetician, Harold Osborne, "Organic Unity"; and a selection from Nathaniel West's *The Day of the Locust* (Illustration 13), a work of art that exemplifies this concept in literature.

The aesthetic theory of R. G. Collingwood is one of the best examples of a modern expressive theory of art. Collingwood, a well-known British philsopher who died in 1943, focuses on the role of emotion in the unique expressiveness of art. From Coleridge's idea that the expressions of the artist are not derived merely from perceptions, Collingwood argues that the expression of imagination and emotion is what accounts for originality and uniqueness in art. If art is distinct from craft and the artist is more than a craftsman, then art is not representation and the artist is not a mimic, according to Collingwood. Craft and mimesis require great skill but not great originality of feeling. What distinguishes art is that it expresses the individual emotions and imaginative experiences of a particular person. A work of art is an outward manifestation of personal expression. Art which is not craft is created for its own sake, and great art has no other reason for being created. Because Collingwood locates originality and uniqueness in art in the expressive activities of the artist, he also claims that the true work of art *is* this expressive activity. What we perceive (e.g., a painting) is merely a by-product of this activity, and the real work of art resides within the mind of the artist. One can see that Collingwood's theory raises a number of questions. Is all art expressive? Are all expressions of emotion works of art? If the real work of art is merely an imaginative or expressive experience, are we not all artists? And how can one make aesthetic judgements about works which one can never view? Nevertheless, Collingwood's theory that art is the expression of the artists' emotions and imagination illustrates the modern aesthetic preoccupation with emotional expression and originality in art—which originated in nineteenth-century art theory.

Also included in Part II is a selection from a book by modern artist Wassily Kandinsky, *Concerning the Spiritual in Art*. Kandinsky, like Collingwood, argues that the expression of emotion is the distinguishing feature of art, and that the artist's inner emotions determine the character of the art work. But Kandinsky also insists that works of art have three important elements: the emotions of the artist, the actual work of art in which these feelings are embodied, and the emotions the work arouses in its audience. And, according to Kandinsky, a work of art is a physical bridge between the immaterial emotions of the observer-audience. The reader should examine closely Kandinsky's painting *Large Study* (Illustration 11) to see how it exemplifies Kandinsky's view about art.

The Imagination

IMMANUEL KANT

The Synthesis of Reproduction in Imagination

It is a merely empirical law, that representations which have often followed or accompanied one another finally become associated, and so are set in a relation whereby, even in the absence of the object, one of these representations can, in accordance with a fixed rule, bring about a transition of the mind to the other. But this law of reproduction presupposes that appearances are themselves actually subject to such a rule, and that in the manifold of these representations a coexistence or sequence takes place in conformity with certain rules. Otherwise our empirical imagination would never find opportunity for exercise appropriate to its powers, and so would remain concealed within the mind as a dead and to us unknown faculty. If cinnabar were sometimes red, sometimes black, sometimes light, sometimes heavy, if a man changed sometimes into this and sometimes into that animal form, if the country on the longest day were sometimes covered with fruit, sometimes with ice and snow, my empirical imagination would never find opportunity when representing red colour to bring to mind heavy cinnabar. Nor could there be an empirical synthesis of reproduction, if a certain name were some-

From Immanuel Kant, *Critique of Pure Reason*, Norman Kemp Smith, translator. © 1929 MacMillan & Co., Ltd. Reprinted by permission of St. Martin's Press, Inc.

times given to this, sometimes to that object, or were one and the same thing named sometimes in one way, sometimes in another, independently of any rule to which appearances are in themselves subject.

There must then be something which, as the *a priori* ground of a necessary synthetic unity of appearances, makes their reproduction possible. What that something is we soon discover, when we reflect that appearances are not things in themselves, but are the mere play of our representations, and in the end reduce to determinations of inner sense. For if we can show that even our purest *a priori* intuitions yield no knowledge, save in so far as they contain a combination of the manifold such as renders a thoroughgoing synthesis of reproduction possible, then this synthesis of imagination is likewise grounded, antecedently to all experience, upon *a priori* principles; and we must assume a pure transcendental synthesis of imagination as conditioning the very possibility of all experience. For experience as such necessarily presupposes the reproducibility of appearances. When I seek to draw a line in thought, or to think of the time from one noon to another, or even to represent to myself some particular number, obviously the various manifold representations that are involved must be apprehended by me in thought one after the other. But if I were always to drop out of thought the preceding representations (the first parts of the line, the antecedent parts of the time period, or the units in the order represented), and did not reproduce them while advancing to those that follow, a complete representation would never be obtained; none of the above-mentioned thoughts, not even the purest and most elementary representations of space and time, could arise.

The synthesis of apprehension is thus inseparably bound up with the synthesis of reproduction. And as the former constitutes the transcendental ground of the possibility of all modes of knowledge whatsoever—of those that are pure *a priori* no less than of those that are empirical—the reproductive synthesis of the imagination is to be counted among the transcendental acts of the mind. We shall therefore entitle this faculty the transcendental faculty of imagination.

. . .

What we have expounded separately and singly in the preceding section, we shall now present in systematic interconnection. There are three subjective sources of knowledge upon which rests the possibility of experience in general and knowledge of its objects—*sense, imagination,* and *apperception.* Each of these can be viewed as empirical, namely in its application to given appearances. But all of them are likewise *a priori* elements or foundations, which make this empirical employment itself possible. *Sense* represents appearances empirically in *perception, imagination* in *association* (and reproduction), *apperception* in the *empirical consciousness* of the identity of the reproduced representations with the appearances whereby they were given, that is, in recognition.

But all perceptions are grounded *a priori* in pure intuition (in time, the form of their inner intuition as representations), association in pure synthesis of imagination, and empirical consciousness in pure apperception, that is, in the thoroughgoing identity of the self in all possible representations.

If, now, we desire to follow up the inner ground of this connection of the representations to the point upon which they have all to converge in order that they may therein for the first time acquire the unity of knowledge necessary for a possible experience, we must begin with pure apperception. Intuitions are nothing to us, and do not in the least concern us if they cannot be taken up into consciousness, in which they may participate either directly or indirectly. In this way alone is any knowledge possible. We are conscious *a priori* of the complete identity of the self in respect of all representations which can ever belong to our knowledge, as being a necessary condition of the possibility of all representations. For in me they can represent something only in so far as they belong with all others to one consciousness, and therefore must be at least capable of being so connected. This principle holds *a priori*, and may be called the transcendental principle of the *unity* of all that is manifold in our representations, and consequently also in intuition. Since this unity of the manifold in one subject is synthetic, pure apperception supplies a principle of the synthetic unity of the manifold in all possible intuition.

This synthetic unity presupposes or includes a synthesis, and if the former is to be *a priori* necessary, the synthesis must also be *a priori*. The transcendental unity of apperception thus relates to the pure synthesis of imagination, as an *a priori* condition of the possibility of all combination of the manifold in one knowledge. But only the *productive* synthesis of the imagination can take place *a priori*; the reproductive rests upon empirical conditions. Thus the principle of the necessary unity of pure (productive) synthesis of imagination, prior to apperception, is the ground of the possibility of all knowlege, especially of experience.

We entitle the synthesis of the manifold in imagination transcendental, if without distinction of intuitions it is directed exclusively to the *a priori* combination of the manifold; and the unity of this synthesis is called transcendental, if it is represented as *a priori* necessary in relation to the original unity of apperception. Since this unity of apperception underlies the possibility of all knowledge, the transcendental unity of the synthesis of imagination is the pure form of all possible knowledge; and by means of it all objects of possible experience must be represented *a priori*.

The unity of apperception in relation to the synthesis of imagination is the *understanding*; and this same unity, with reference to the *transcendental synthesis* of the imagination, the *pure understanding*. In the understanding there are then pure *a priori* modes of knowledge which contain the necessary unity of the pure synthesis of imagination in respect of all possible appearances. These are the *categories*, that is, the pure concepts of understanding.

The empirical faculty of knowledge in man must therefore contain an understanding which relates to all objects of the senses, although only by means of intuition and of its synthesis through imagination. All appearances, as data for a possible experience, are subject to this understanding. This relation of appearances to possible experience is indeed necessary, for otherwise they would yield no knowledge and would not in any way concern us. We have, therefore, to recognise that pure understanding, by means of the categories, is a formal and synthetic principle of all experiences, and that appearances have *a necessary relation to the understanding.*

We will now, starting from below, namely, with the empirical, strive to make clear the necessary connection in which understanding, by means of the categories, stands to appearances. What is first given to us is appearance. When combined with consciousness, it is called perception. (Save through its relation to a consciousness that is at least possible, appearance could never be for us an object of knowledge, and so would be nothing to us; and since it has in itself no objective reality, but exists only in being known, it would be nothing at all.) Now, since every appearance contains a manifold, and since different perceptions therefore occur in the mind separately and singly, a combination of them, such as they cannot have in sense itself, is demanded. There must therefore exist in us an active faculty for the synthesis of this manifold. To this faculty I give the title, imagination. Its action, when immediately directed upon perceptions, I entitle apprehension.[1] Since imagination has to bring the manifold of intuition into the form of an image, it must previously have taken the impressions up into its activity, that is, have apprehended them.

But it is clear that even this apprehension of the manifold would not by itself produce an image and a connection of the impressions, were it not that there exists a subjective ground which leads the mind to reinstate a preceding perception alongside the subsequent perception to which it has passed, and so to form whole series of perceptions. This is the reproductive faculty of imagination, which is merely empirical.

If, however, representations reproduced one another in any order, just as they happened to come together, which would not lead to any determinate connection of them, but only to accidental collocations; and so would not give rise to any knowledge. Their reproduction must, therefore, conform to a rule, in accordance with which a representation connects in the imagination with some one representation in preference to another. This subjective and

---

[1]Psychologists have hitherto failed to realise that imagination is a necessary ingredient of perception itself. This is due partly to the fact that that faculty has been limited to reproduction, partly to the belief that the senses not only supply impressions but also combine them so as to generate images of objects. For that purpose something more than the mere receptivity of impressions is undoubtedly required, namely, a function for the synthesis of them.

empirical ground of reproduction according to rules is what is called the *association* of representations.

Now if this unity of association had not also an objective ground which makes it impossible that appearances should be apprehended by the imagination otherwise than under the condition of a possible synthetic unity of this apprehension, it would be entirely accidental that appearances should fit into a connected whole of human knowledge. For even though we should have the power of associating perceptions, it would remain entirely undetermined and accidental whether they would themselves be associable; and should they not be associable, there might exist a multitude of perceptions, and indeed an entire sensibility, in which much empirical consciousness would arise in my mind, but in a state of separation, and without belonging to a consciousness of myself. This, however, is impossible. For it is only because I ascribe all perceptions to one consciousness (original apperception) that I can say of all perceptions that I am conscious of them. There must, therefore, be an objective ground (that is, one that can be comprehended *a priori*, antecedently to all empirical laws of the imagination) upon which rests the possibility, nay, the necessity, of a law that extends to all appearances—a ground, namely, which constrains us to regard all appearances as data of the sense that must be associable in themselves and subject to universal rules of a thoroughgoing connection in their reproduction. This objective ground of all association of appearances I entitle their *affinity*. It is nowhere to be found save in the principle of the unity of apperception, in respect of all knowledge which is to belong to me. According to this principle all appearances, without exception, must so enter the mind or be apprehended, that they conform to the unity of apperception. Without synthetic unity in their connection, this would be impossible; and such synthetic unity is itself, therefore, objectively necessary.

The objective unity of all empirical consciousness in one consciousness, that of original apperception, is thus the necessary condition of all possible perception; and [this being recognised we can prove that] the affinity of all appearances, near or remote, is a necessary consequence of a synthesis in imagination which is grounded *a priori* on rules.

Since the imagination is itself a faculty of *a priori* synthesis, we assign to it the title, productive imagination. In so far as it aims at nothing but necessary unity in the synthesis of what is manifold in appearance, it may be entitled the transcendental function of imagination. That the affinity of appearances, and with it their association, and through this, in turn their reproduction according to laws, and so [as involving these various factors] experience itself, should only be possible by means of this transcendental function of imagination, is indeed strange, but is none the less an obvious consequence of the preceding argument. For without this transcendental function no concepts of objects would together make up a unitary experience.

The abiding and unchanging 'I' (pure apperception) forms the correlate of all our representations in so far as it is to be at all possible that we should become conscious of them. All consciousness as truly belongs to an all-comprehensive pure apperception, as all sensible intuition, as representation, does to a pure inner intuition, namely, to time. It is this apperception which must be added to pure imagination, in order to render its function intellectual. For since the synthesis of imagination connects the manifold only as it *appears* in intuition, as, for instance, in the shape of a triangle, it is, though exercised *a priori*, always in itself sensible. And while concepts, which belong to the understanding, are brought into play through relation of the manifold to the unity of apperception, it is only by means of the imagination that they can be brought into relation to sensible intuition.

A pure imagination, which conditions all *a priori* knowledge, is thus one of the fundamental faculties of the human soul. By its means we bring the manifold of intuition on the one side, into connection with the condition of the necessary unity of pure apperception on the other. The two extremes, namely sensibility and understanding, must stand in necessary connection with each other though the mediation of this transcendental function of imagination, because otherwise the former, though indeed yielding appearances, would supply no objects of empirical knowledge, and consequently no experience. Actual experience, which is constituted by apprehension, association (reproduction), and finally recognition of appearances, contains in recognition, the last and highest of these merely empirical elements of experience, certain concepts which render possible the formal unity of experience, and therewith all objective validity (truth) of empirical knowledge. These grounds of the recognition of the manifold, so far as they concern *solely the form of an experience in general*, are the *categories*. Upon them is based not only all formal unity in the [transcendental] synthesis of imagination, but also, thanks to that synthesis, all its empirical employment (in recognition, reproduction, association, apprehension) in connection with the appearances. For only by means of these fundamental concepts can appearances belong to knowledge or even to our consciousness, and so to ourselves.

Thus the order and regularity in the appearances, which we entitle *nature*, we ourselves introduce. We could never find them in appearances, had not we ourselves, or the nature of our mind, originally set them there. For this unity of nature has to be a necessary one, that is, has to be an *a priori* certain unity of the connection of appearances; and such synthetic unity could not be established *a priori* if there were not subjective grounds of such unity contained *a priori* in the original cognitive powers of our mind, and if these subjective conditions, inasmuch as they are the grounds of the possibility of knowing any object whatsoever in experience, were not at the same time objectively valid. . . .

The Application of the Categories to Objects of the Senses in General

The pure concepts of understanding relate, through the mere understanding, to objects of intuition in general, whether that intuition be our own or any other, provided only it be sensible. The concepts are, however, for this very reason, mere *forms of thought*, through which alone no determinate object is known. The synthesis or combination of the manifold in them relates only to the unity of apperception, and is thereby the ground of the possibility of *a priori* knowledge, so far as such knowledge rests on the understanding. This synthesis, therefore, is at once transcendental and also purely intellectual. But since there lies in us a certain form of *a priori* sensible intuition, which depends on the receptivity of the faculty of representation (sensibility), the understanding, as spontaneity, is able to determine inner sense through the manifold of given representations, in accordance with the synthetic unity of apperception, and so to think synthetic unity of the apperception of the manifold of *a priori sensible intuition*—that being the condition under which all objects of our human intuition must necessarily stand. In this way the categories, in themselves mere forms of thought, obtain objective reality, that is, application to objects which can be given us in intuition. These objects, however, are only appearances, for it is solely of appearances that we can have *a priori* intuition.

This synthesis of the manifold of sensible intuition, which is possible and necessary *a priori*, may be entitled *figurative* synthesis (*synthesis speciosa*), to distinguish it from the synthesis which is thought in the mere category in respect of the manifold of an intuition in general, and which is entitled combination through the understanding (*synthesis intellectualis*). Both are *transcendental*, not merely as taking place *a priori*, but also as conditioning the possibility of other *a priori* knowledge.

But the figurative synthesis, if it be directed merely to the original synthetic unity of apperception, that is, to the transcendental unity which is thought in the categories, must, in order to be distinguished from the merely intellectual combination, be called the *transcendental synthesis of imagination*. *Imagination* is the faculty of representing in intuition an object that is *not itself present*. Now since all our intuition is sensible, the imagination, owing to the subjective condition under which alone it can give to the concepts of understanding a corresponding intuition, belongs to *sensibility*. But inasmuch as its synthesis is an expression of spontaneity, which is determinative and not, like sense, determinable merely, and which is therefore able to determine sense *a priori* in respect of its form in accordance with the unity of apperception, imagination is to that extent a faculty which determines the sensibility *a priori*; and its synthesis of intuitions, conforming as it does to the *categories*, must be the transcendental synthesis of *imagination*. This synthesis is an action of the understanding on the sensibility; and is its first application—and thereby the ground of all its other applications—to the objects of our possible intuition. As figurative, it is distinguished from the intellectual synthesis, which is carried out by the understanding alone, without the aid of the imagination. In so far as imagination is spontaneity, I sometimes also entitle it the *productive* imagination, to distinguish it from the *reproductive* imagination, whose synthesis is entirely subject to empirical laws, the laws, namely, of association, and which therefore contributes nothing to the explanation of the possibility of *a priori* knowledge. The reproductive synthesis falls within the domain, not of transcendental philosophy, but of psychology.

Of Art in General[1]

(1) Art is distinguished from nature as doing (*facere*) is distinguished from acting or working generally (*agere*), and as the product or result of the former is distinguished as work (*opus*) from the working (*effectus*) of the latter.

By right we ought only to describe as art, production through freedom, i.e. through a will that places reason at the basis of its actions. For although we like to call the product of bees (regularly built cells of wax) a work of art, this is only by way of analogy; as soon as we feel that this work of theirs is based on no proper rational deliberation, we say that it is a product of nature (of instinct), and as art only ascribe it to their Creator.

If, as sometimes happens, in searching through a bog we come upon a bit of shaped wood, we do not say, this is a product of nature, but of art. Its producing cause has conceived a purpose to which the plank owes its form. Elsewhere too we should see art in everything which is made, so that a representation of it in its cause must have preceded its actual existence (as even in the case of the bees), though without the effect of it even being capable of being *thought*. But if we call anything absolutely a work of art, in order to distinguish it from a natural effect, we always understand by that a work of man.

(2) Art regarded as human skill differs from science (as *can* from *know*) as a practical faculty does from a theoretical, as technique does from theory (as mensuration from geometry). And so what we *can* do, as soon as we merely *know* what ought to be done and therefore are sufficiently cognizant of the desired effect, is not called art. Only that which a man, even if he knows it completely, may not therefore have the skill to accomplish belongs to art. . . .

(3) Art also differs from handicraft; the first is called "free," the other may be called "mercenary." We regard the first as if it could only prove purposive as play, i.e. as occupation that is pleasant in itself. But the second is regarded as if it could only be compulsorily imposed upon one as work,

---

[1]From Immanuel Kant, *The Critique of Judgment,* trans. J. H. Bernard (New York: Hafner Publishing Company, 1951).

i.e. as occupation which is unpleasant (a trouble) in itself and which is only attractive on account of its effect (e.g. the wage). Whether or not in the grade of the professions we ought to count watchmakers as artists, but smiths only as handicraftsmen, would require another point of view from which to judge than that which we are here taking up, viz. [we should have to consider] the proportion of talents which must be assumed requisite in these several occupations. Whether or not, again, under the so-called seven free arts, some may be included which ought to be classed as sciences and many that are akin rather to handicraft I shall not here discuss. But it is not inexpedient to recall that, in all free arts, there is yet requisite something compulsory or as it is called, mechanism, without which the spirit, which must be free in art and which alone inspires the work, would have no body and would evaporate altogether; e.g. in poetry there must be an accuracy and wealth of language, and also prosody and measure. . . .

Beautiful Art Is the Art of Genius

Genius is the talent (or natural gift) which gives the rule to art. Since talent, as the innate productive faculty of the artist, belongs itself to nature, we may express the matter thus: Genius is the innate mental disposition (*ingenium*) *through which* nature gives the rule to art.

Whatever may be thought of this definition, whether it is merely arbitrary or whether it is adequate to the concept that we are accustomed to combine with the word *genius* (which is to be examined in the following paragraphs), we can prove already beforehand that, according to the signification of the word here adopted, beautiful arts must necessarily be considered as arts of *genius.*

For every art presupposes rules by means of which in the first instance a product, if it is to be called artistic, is represented as possible. But the concept of beautiful art does not permit the judgment upon the beauty of a product to be derived from any rule which has a *concept* as its determining ground, and therefore has at its basis a concept of the way in which the product is possible. Therefore beautiful art cannot itself devise the rule according to which it can bring about its product. But since at the same time a product can never be called art without some precedent rule, nature in the subject must (by the harmony of its faculties) give the rule to art; i.e. beautiful art is only possible as a product of genius.

We thus see (1) that genius is a *talent* for producing that for which no definite rule can be given; it is not a mere aptitude for what can be learned by a rule. Hence *originality* must be its first property. (2) But since it also can produce original nonsense, its products must be models, i.e. *exemplary,* and they consequently ought not to spring from imitation, but must serve as a standard or rule of judgment for others. (3) It cannot describe or indicate scientifically how it brings about its products, but it gives the rule just as nature does. Hence the author of a product for which he is indebted to his genius does not know himself how he has come by his ideas; and he has not the power to devise the like at pleasure or in accordance with a plan, and to communicate it to others in percepts that will enable them to produce similar products. (Hence it is probable that the word "genius" is derived from *genius*, that peculiar guiding and guardian spirit given to a man at his birth, from whose suggestion these original ideas proceed.) (4) Nature, by the medium of genius, does not prescribe rules to science but to art, and to it only in so far as it is to be beautiful art. . . .

Of the Faculties of the Mind that Constitute Genius

We say of certain products of which we expect that they should at least in part appear as beautiful art, they are without *spirit*, although we find nothing to blame in them on the score of taste. A poem may be very neat and elegant, but without spirit. A history may be exact and well arranged, but without spirit. A festal discourse may be solid and at the same time elaborate, but without spirit. Conversation is often not devoid of entertainment, but it is without spirit; even of a woman we say that she is pretty, an agreeable talker, and courteous, but without spirit. What then do we mean by spirit?

Spirit, in an aesthetical sense, is the name given to the animating principle of the mind. But that by means of which this principle animates the soul, the material which it applies to that [purpose], is what puts the mental powers purposively into swing, i.e. into such a play as maintains itself and strengthens the mental powers in their exercise.

Now I maintain that this principle is no other than the faculty of presenting *aesthetical ideas*. And by an aesthetical idea I understand that representation of the imagination which occasions much thought, without however any definite thought, i.e. any *concept*, being capable of being adequate to it; it consequently cannot be completely compassed and made intelligible by language. We easily see that it is the counterpart (pendant) of a *rational idea*, which conversely is a concept to which no *intuition* (or representation of the imagination) can be adequate.

The imagination (as a productive faculty of cognition) is very powerful in creating another nature, as it were, out of the material that actual nature gives it. We entertain ourselves with it when experience becomes too commonplace, and by it we remold experience, always indeed in accordance with analogical laws, but yet also in accordance with principles which occupy a higher place in reason (laws, too, which are just as natural to us as those by which understanding comprehends empirical nature). Thus we feel our freedom from the law of association (which attaches to the empirical employment of imagination); so that the material supplied to us by nature in accordance with this law can be worked up into something different which surpasses nature.

Such representations of the imagination we may call *ideas*, partly because they at least strive after something which lies beyond the bounds of experience and so seek to approximate to a presentation of concepts of reason (intellectual ideas), thus giving to the latter the appearance of objective reality, but especially because no concept can be fully adequate to them as internal intuitions. The poet ventures to realize to sense, rational ideas of invisible beings, the kingdom of the blessed, hell, eternity, creation, etc.; or even if he deals with things of which there are examples in experience—e.g. death, envy and all vices, also love, fame, and the like—he tries, by means of imagination, which emulates the play of reason in its quest after a maximum, to go beyond the limits of experience and to present them to sense with a completeness of which there is no example in nature. This is properly speaking the art of the poet, in which the faculty of aesthetical ideas can manifest itself in its entire strength. But this faculty, considered in itself, is properly only a talent (of the imagination).

If now we place under a concept a representation of the imagination belonging to its presentation, but which occasions in itself more thought than can ever be comprehended in a definite concept and which consequently aesthetically enlarges the concept itself in an unbounded fashion, the imagination is here creative, and it brings the faculty of intellectual ideas (the reason) into movement; i.e. by a representation more thought (which indeed belongs to the concept of the object) is occasioned than can in it be grasped or made clear.

Those forms which do not constitute the presentation of a given concept itself but only, as approximate representations of the imagination express the consequences bound up with it and its relationship to other concepts, are called (aesthetical) *attributes* of an object whose concept as a rational idea cannot be adequately presented. Thus Jupiter's eagle with the lightning in its claws is an attribute of the mighty king of heaven, as the peacock is of his magnificent queen. They do not, like *logical attributes*, represent what lies in our concepts of the sublimity and majesty of creation, but something different, which gives occasion to the imagination to spread itself over a number of kindred representations that arouse more thought than can be expressed in a concept determined by words. They furnish an *aesthetical idea*, which for that rational idea takes the place of logical presentation; and thus, as their proper office, they enliven the mind by opening out to it the prospect into an illimitable field of kindred representations. But beautiful art does this not only in the case of painting or sculpture (in which the term "attribute" is commonly employed); poetry and rhetoric also get the spirit that animates their works simply from the aesthetical attributes of the object, which accompany the logical and stimulate the imagination, so that it thinks more by their aid, although in an undeveloped way, than could be comprehended in a concept and therefore in a definite form of words. . . .

. . . On the other hand, an intellectual concept may serve conversely as an attribute for a representation of sense, and so can quicken this latter by means of the idea of the supersensible, but only by the aesthetical [element], that subjectively attaches to the concept of the latter, being here employed. . . .

In a word, the aesthetical idea is a representation of the imagination associated with a given concept, which is bound up with such a multiplicity of partial representations in its free employment that for it no expression marking a definite concept can be found; and such a representation, therefore, adds to a concept much ineffable thought, the feeling of which quickens the cognitive faculties, and with language, which is the mere letter, binds up spirit also.

The mental powers, therefore, whose union (in a certain relation) constitutes genius are imagination and understanding. In the employment of the imagination for cognition, it submits to the constraint of the understanding and is subject to the limitation of being conformable to the concept of the latter. On the contrary, in an aesthetical point of view it is free to furnish unsought, over and above that agreement with a concept, abundance of undeveloped material for the understanding, to which the understanding paid no regard in its concept but which it applies, though not objectively for cognition, yet subjectively to quicken the cognitive powers and therefore also indirectly to cognitions. Thus genius properly consists in the happy relation [between these faculties], which no science can teach and no industry can learn, by which ideas are found for a given concept; and, on the other hand, we thus find for these ideas the expression by means of which the subjective state of mind brought about by them, as an accompaniment of the concept, can be communicated to others. The latter talent is, properly speaking, what is called spirit; for to express the ineffable element in the state of mind implied by a certain representation and to make it universally communicable—whether the expression be in speech or painting or statuary—this requires a faculty of seizing the quickly passing play of imagination and of unifying it in a concept (which is even on that account original and discloses a new rule that could not have been inferred from any preceding principles or examples) that can be communicated without any constraint [of rules].

If, after this analysis, we look back to the explanation given above of what is called *genius*, we find: first, that it is a talent for art, not for science, in which clearly known rules must go beforehand and determine the procedure. Secondly, as an artistic talent it presupposes a definite concept of the product as the purpose, and therefore understanding; but it also presupposes a representation (although an indeterminate one) of the material, i.e. of the intuition, for the presentment of this concept, and therefore a relation between the imagination and the understanding. Thirdly, it shows itself, not so much in the accomplishment of the proposed purpose in a presentment of a definite concept, as in the enunciation or expression of aesthetical ideas which contain abundant material for that very design; and consequently it represents the imagination as free from all guidance of rules and yet as purposive in reference to the presentment of the given concept. Finally, in the fourth place, the unsought undesigned subjective purposiveness in the free accordance of the imagination with the legality of the understanding presupposes such a proportion and disposition of these faculties as no following of rules, whether of science or of mechanical imitation, can bring about, but which only the nature of the subject can produce.

In accordance with these suppositions, genius is the exemplary originality of the natural gifts of a subject in the *free* employment of his cognitive faculties. In this way the product of a genius (as regards what is to be ascribed to genius and not to possible learning or schooling) is an example, not to be imitated (for then that which in it is genius and constitutes the spirit of the work would be lost), but to be followed by another genius, whom it awakens to a feeling of his own originality and whom it stirs so to exercise his art in freedom from the constraint of rules, that thereby a new rule is gained for art; and thus his talent shows itself to be exemplary. . . .

Remark I

As we so often find occasion in transcendental philosophy for distinguishing ideas from concepts of the understanding, it may be of use to introduce technical terms to correspond to this distinction. I believe that no one will object if I propose some. In the most universal signification of the word, ideas are representations referred to an object, according to a certain (subjective or objective) principle, but so that they can never become a cognition of it. They are either referred to an intuition, according to a merely subjective principle of the mutual harmony of the cognitive powers (the imagination and the understanding), and they are then called *aesthetical*; or they are referred to a concept according to an objective principle, although they can never furnish a cognition of the object, and are called *rational ideas*. In the latter case the concept is a *transcendent* one, which is different from a concept of the understanding, to which an adequately corresponding experience can always be supplied and which therefore is called *immanent*.

An *aesthetical idea* cannot become a cognition because it is an *intuition* (of the imagination) for which an adequate concept can never be found. A *rational idea* can never become a cognition because it involves a concept (of the supersensible) corresponding to which an intuition can never be given.

Now I believe we might call the aesthetical idea an *inexponible* representation of the imagination, and a rational idea an *indemonstrable* concept of reason. It is assumed of both that they are not generated without grounds, but (according to the above explanation of an idea in general) in conformity with certain principles of the cognitive faculties to which they belong (subjective principles in the one case, objective in the other).

Concepts of the understanding must, as such, always be demonstrable [if by demonstration we understand, as in anatomy, merely *presentation*], i.e. the object corresponding to them must always be capable of being given in intuition (pure or empirical), for thus alone could they become cognitions. The concept of *magnitude* can be given *a priori* in the intuition of space, e.g. of a right line, etc.; the concept of *cause* in impenetrability, in the collision of bodies, etc. Consequently both can be authenticated by means of an empirical intuition, i.e. the thought of them can be proved (demonstrated, verified) by an example; and this must be possible, for otherwise we should not be certain that the concept was not empty, i.e. devoid of any object.

In logic we ordinarily use the expressions "demonstrable" or "indemonstrable" only in respect of *propositions*, but these might be better designated by the titles respectively of *mediately and immediately certain* propositions; for pure philosophy has also propositions of both kinds, i.e. true propositions, some of which are susceptible of proof and others not. It can, as philosophy, prove them on *a priori* grounds, but it cannot demonstrate them, unless we wish to depart entirely from the proper meaning of this word, according to which *to demonstrate* (*ostendere, exhibere*) is equivalent to presenting a concept in intuition (whether in proof or merely in definition). If the intuition is *a priori* this is called construction; but if it is empirical, then the object is displayed by means of which objective reality is assured to the concept. Thus we say of an anatomist that he demonstrates the human eye if, by a dissection of this organ, he makes intuitively evident the concept which he has previously treated discursively.

It hence follows that the rational concept of the supersensible substrate of all phenomena in general, or even of that which must be placed at the basis of our arbitrary will in respect of the moral law, viz. of transcendental freedom, is already, in kind, an indemonstrable concept and a rational idea, while virtue is so in degree. For there can be given in experience, as regards its quality, absolutely nothing corresponding to the former, whereas in the latter case no empirical product attains to the degree of that causality which the rational idea prescribes as the rule.

As in a rational idea the *imagination* with its intuitions does not attain to the given concept, so in an aesthetical idea the *understanding* by its concepts never attains completely to that internal intuition which the imagination binds up with a given representation. Since, now, to reduce a representation of the imagination to concepts is the same thing as to *expound* it, the aesthetical idea may be called an *inexponible* representation of the imagination (in its free play). I shall have occasion in the sequel to say something more of ideas of this kind; now I only note that both kinds of ideas, rational and aesthetical, must have their principles and must have them in reason—the one in the objective, the other in the subjective principles of its employment.

We can consequently explain *genius* as the faculty of aesthetical ideas, by which at the same time is shown the reason why in the products of genius it is the nature (of the subject), and not a premeditated purpose, that gives the rule to the art (of the production of the beautiful). For since the beautiful must not be judged by concepts, but by the purposive attuning of the imagination to agreement with the faculty of concepts in general, it cannot be rule and precept which can serve as the subjective standard of that aesthetical but unconditioned purposiveness in beautiful art that can rightly claim to please everyone. It can only be that in the subject which is nature and cannot be brought under rules of concepts, i.e. the supersensible substrate of all his faculties (to which no concept of the understanding extends), and consequently that with respect to which it is the final purpose given by the intelligible [part] of our nature to harmonize all our cognitive faculties. Thus alone is it possible that there should be *a priori* at the basis of this purposiveness, for which we can prescribe no objective principle, a principle subjective and yet of universal validity.

Fancy and Imagination

SAMUEL TAYLOR COLERIDGE

"On the Imagination, or Esemplastic[1] Power"

The IMAGINATION, then, I consider either as primary, or secondary. The primary IMAGINATION I hold to be the living power and prime agent of all human perception, and as a repetition in the finite mind of the eternal act of creation

From Samuel Taylor Coleridge, *Biographia Literaria* (London: (1907) selections from Chapters 13 and 14, and "Lectures on Shakespeare," from *Essays and Lectures on Shakespeare* (London: 1907) rpt. from *The Norton Anthology of English Literature*, ed. M. H. Abrams, et.al. (New York: W. W. Norton, 1962).

[1]Coleridge coined this word and used it to mean "molding into unity."

in the infinite I AM. The secondary I consider as an echo of the former, coexisting with the conscious will, yet still as identical with the primary in the *kind* of its agency, and differing only in *degree*, and in the *mode* of its operation. It dissolves, diffuses, dissipates, in order to recreate; or where this process is rendered impossible, yet still, at all events, it struggles to idealize and to unify. It is essentially *vital*, even as all objects (*as* objects) are essentially fixed and dead.

FANCY, on the contrary, has no other counters to play with but fixities and definites. The fancy is indeed no other than a mode of memory emancipated from the order of time and space; and blended with, and modified by that empirical phenomenon of the will which we express by the word CHOICE. But equally with the ordinary memory it must receive all its materials ready made from the law of association.[2]

. . . My own conclusions on the nature of poetry, in the strictest use of the word, have been in part anticipated in the preceding disquisition on the fancy and imagination. What is poetry? is so nearly the same question with, what is a poet? that the answer to the one is involved in the solution of the other. For it is a distinction resulting from the Poetic genius itself, which sustains and modifies the images, thoughts, and emotions of the poet's own mind. The poet, described in *ideal* perfection, brings the whole soul of man into activity, with the subordination of its faculties to each other, according to their relative worth and dignity. He diffuses a tone and spirit of unity that blends and (as it were) *fuses*, each into each, by that synthetic and magical power to which we have exclusively appropriated the name of imagination. This power, first put in action by the will and understanding and retained under their irremissive, though gentle and unnoticed control . . . reveals itself in the balance or reconciliation of opposite or discordant qualities: of sameness, with difference; of the general, with the concrete; the idea, with the image; the individual, with the representative; the sense of novelty and freshness, with old and familiar objects; a more than usual state of emotion, with more than usual order; judgment ever awake and steady self-possession, with enthusiasm and feeling profound or vehement; and while it blends and harmonizes the natural and the artificial, still subordinates art to nature; the manner to the matter; and our admiration of the poet to our sympathy with the poetry. "Doubtless," as Sir John Davies observes of the soul (and his words may with slight alteration be applied, and even more appropriately, to the poetic IMAGINATION):

---

[2]Coleridge conceives God's creation to be a continuous process, which has an analogy in the creative perception ("primary imagination") of all human minds. The creative process is repeated, or "echoed," on still a third level, by the "secondary imagination" of the poet, which dissolves the products of primary perception in order to shape them into a new and unified creation—the imaginative passage or poem. The "fancy," on the other hand, can only manipulate "fixities and definites" which, linked by association, come to it ready-made from perception. Its products, therefore, are not re-creations (echoes of God's original creative process), but mosaic-like reassemblies of existing bits and pieces.

Doubtless this could not be, but that she turns
Bodies to spirit by sublimation strange,
As fire converts to fire the things it burns,
As we our food into our nature change.

From their gross matter she abstracts their forms,
And draws a kind of quintessence from things;
Which to her proper nature she transforms
To bear them light on her celestial wings.

Thus does she, when from individual states
She doth abstract the universal kinds;
Which then reclothed in divers names and fates
Steal access through our senses to our minds.[3]

Finally, GOOD SENSE is the BODY of poetic genius, FANCY its DRAPERY MOTION its LIFE, and IMAGINATION the SOUL that is everwhere, and in each; and forms all into one graceful and intelligent whole.

From "Lectures on Shakespeare"[4]

In the preceding lecture we have examined with what armor clothed and with what titles authorized Shakespeare came forward as a poet to demand the throne of fame as the dramatic poet of England; we have now to observe and retrace the excellencies which compelled even his contemporaries to seat him on that throne, although there were giants in those days contending for the same honor. Hereafter we shall endeavor to make out the title of the English drama, as created by and existing in Shakespeare, and its right to the supremacy of dramatic excellence in general. I have endeavored to prove that he had shown himself a *poet*, previously to his appearance [as] a dramatic poet—and that had no *Lear*, no *Othello*, no *Henry the Fourth*, no *Twelfth Night* appeared, we must have admitted that Shakespeare possessed the chief if not all the requisites of a poet—namely, deep feeling and exquisite sense of beauty, both as exhibited to the eye in combinations of form, and to the ear in sweet and appropriate melody (with the exception of Spenser he is [the sweetest of English poets]); that these feelings were under the command of *his own will*—that in his very first productions he projected his mind out of his own particular being, and felt and made others feel, on subjects [in] no way connected with himself, except by force of contemplation, and that sub-

---

[3]Adapted from John Davies's *Nosce Tiepsum* ("Know Thyself"), a philosophical poem (1599).

[4]Although Coleridge's series of public lectures on Shakespeare and other poets contained much of his best criticism, he published none of this material, leaving only fragmentary remains of his lectures in notebooks, scraps of manuscript, and notes written in the margins of books. The following selections, which develop some of the basic ideas presented in *Biographia Literaria*, are taken from T. M. Raysor's edition, based on Coleridge's manuscripts and on contemporary reports of *Coleridge's Shakespearean Criticism* (1930).

lime faculty, by which a great mind becomes that which it meditates on. To this we are to add the affectionate love of nature and natural objects, without which no man could have observed so steadily, or painted so truly and passionately the very minutest beauties of the external world. Next, we have shown that he possessed fancy, considered as the faculty of bringing together images dissimilar in the main by some one point or more of likeness distinguished.[5]

> Full gently now she takes him by the hand,
> A lily prisoned in a jail of snow,
> Or ivory in an alabaster band—
> So white a friend engirts so white a foe.

Still mounting, we find undoubted proof in his mind of imagination, or the power by which one image or feeling is made to modify many others and by a sort of *fusion to force many into one*—that which after showed itself in such might and energy in *Lear*, where the deep anguish of a father spreads the feeling of ingratitude and cruelty over the very elements of heaven. Various are the workings of this greatest faculty of the human mind—both passionate and tranquil. In its tranquil and purely pleasurable operation, it acts chiefly by producing out of many things, as they would have appeared in the description of an ordinary mind, described slowly and in unimpassioned succession, a oneness, even as nature, the greatest of poets, acts upon us when we open our eyes upon an extended prospect. Thus the flight of Adonis from the enamored goddess in the dusk of evening—

> Look how a bright star shooteth from the sky—
> So glides he in the night from Venus' eye.[6]

How many images and feelings are here brought together without effort and without discord—the beauty of Adonis—the rapidity of his flight—the yearning yet hopelessness of the enamored gazer—and a shadowy ideal character thrown over the whole.[7]— Or it acts by impressing the stamp of humanity, of human feeling, over inanimate objects . . .

---

[5]Coleridge here applies the distinction between fancy and imagination presented in *Biographia Literaria*, Chapter XIII. This passage from the narrative poem *Venus and Adonis* (lines 361-64) is an instance of fancy because the elements brought together remain an assemblage of recognizable and independent "fixities and definites," despite the isolated points of likeness which form the grounds of the comparison.

[6]*Venus and Adonis*, lines 815–16.

[7]An instance of imagination, Coleridge claims, because the component parts—the shooting star and the flight of Adonis, together with the feelings with which both are perceived—dissolve into a new and seamless unity, different in character from the sum of its parts. In the following instance (lines 853–58), the imagination is said to fuse the neutral and inanimate objects with the human nature and feelings of the observer.

> Lo, here the gentle lark, weary of rest,
> From his moist cabinet mounts up on high
> And wakes the morning, from whose silver breast
> The sun riseth in his majesty;
> Who doth the world so gloriously behold
> That cedar tops and hills seem burnished gold.

And lastly, which belongs only to a great poet, the power of so carrying on the eye of the reader as to make him almost lose the consciousness of word—to make him *see* everything—and this without exciting any painful or laborious attention, without any *anatomy* of description (a fault not uncommon in descriptive poetry) but with the sweetness and easy movement of nature.

Lastly, he previously to his dramas, gave proof of a most profound, energetic, and philosophical mind, without which he might have been a very delightful poet, but not the great dramatic poet. . . . But chance and his powerful instinct combined to lead him to his proper province—in the conquest of which we are to consider both the difficulties that opposed him, and the advantages.

Organic Form

SAMUEL TAYLOR COLERIDGE

[Mechanic vs. Organic Form][1]

The subject of the present lecture is no less than a question submitted to your understandings, emancipated from national prejudice: Are the plays of Shakespeare works of rude uncultivated genius, in which the splendor of the parts

From Samuel Taylor Coleridge, *Essays and Lectures on Shakespeare* (London: 1907), rpt. from *The Norton Anthology of English Literature*, ed. M. H. Abrams, et. al. (New York: W. W. Norton, 1962).

---

[1]Coleridge is opposing the earlier view that, because he violates the critical "rules" based on classical drama, Shakespeare is a highly irregular dramatist whose occasional successes are the result of innate and untutored genius, operating without artistry or judgment. Coleridge's refutation is based on his distinction between the "mechanical form" conceived by neoclassical criticism, and "organic form." Mechanical form results from imposing a pattern of pre-existing rules on the literary material. Shakespeare's organic form, on the other hand, evolves like a plant by an inner principle, according not to rules but to the laws of its own growth, until it achieves an organic unity—a living interdependence of parts and whole in which, as Coleridge says, "each part is at once end and means." The concept of "organic form," in one or another interpretation, has become a cardinal principle in much modern criticism.

compensates, if aught can compensate, for the barbarous shapelessness and irregularity of the whole? To which not only the French critics, but even his own English admirers, say [yes]. Or is the form equally admirable with the matter, the judgment of the great poet not less deserving of our wonder than his genius? Or to repeat the question in other words, is Shakespeare a great dramatic poet on account only of these beauties and excellencies which he possesses in common with the ancients, but with diminished claims to our love and honor to the full extent of his difference from them? Or are these very differences additional proofs of poetic wisdom, at once results and symbols of living power as contrasted with lifeless mechanism, of free and rival originality as contradistinguished from servile imitation, or more accurately, [from] a blind copying of effects instead of a true imitation of the essential principles? Imagine not I am about to oppose genius to rules. No! the comparative value of these rules is the very cause to be tried. The spirit of poetry, like all other living powers, must of necessity circumscribe itself by rules, were it only to unite power with beauty. It must embody in order to reveal itself; but a living body is of necessity an organized one—and what is organization but the connection of parts to a whole, so that each part is at once end and means! This is no discovery of criticism; it is a necessity of the human mind—and all nations have felt and obeyed it, in the invention of meter and measured sounds as the vehicle and involucrum of poetry, itself a fellow growth from the same life, even as the bark is to the tree.

No work of true genius dare want its appropriate form; neither indeed is there any danger of this. As it must not, so neither can it, be lawless! For it is even this that constitutes its genius—the power of acting creatively under laws of its own origination. How then comes it that not only single Zoili, but whole nations have combined in unhesitating condemnation of our great dramatist, as a sort of African nature, fertile in beautiful monsters, as a wild heath where islands of fertility look greener from the surrounding waste, where the loveliest plants now shine out among unsightly weeds and now are choked by their parasitic growth, so intertwined that we cannot disentangle the weed without snapping the flower. In this statement I have had no reference to the vulgar abuse of Voltaire,[2] save as far as his charges are coincident with the decisions of his commentators and (so they tell you) his almost idolatrous admirers. The true ground of the mistake, as has been well remarked by a continental critic, lies in the confounding mechanical regularity with organic form. The form is mechanic when on any given material we impress a predetermined form, not necessarily arising out of the properties of the material, as when to a mass of wet clay we give whatever shape we

---

[2]Voltaire (1694–1778) wrote critiques treating Shakespeare as a barbarous, irregular, and sometimes indecent natural genius.

August Wilhelm Schlegel, German critic and literary historian, whose *Lectures on Dramatic Art and Literature* (1808–9) present many of the ideas Coleridge develops in this lecture.

wish it to retain when hardened. The organic form, on the other hand, is innate; it shapes as it develops itself from within, and the fulness of its development is one and the same with the perfection of its outward form. Such is the life, such the form. Nature, the prime genial artist, inexhaustible in diverse powers, is equally inexhaustible in forms. Each exterior is the physiognomy of the being within, its true image reflected and thrown out from the concave mirror. And even such is the appropriate excellence of her chosen poet, of our own Shakespeare, himself a nature humanized, a genial understanding directing self-consciously a power and an implicit wisdom deeper than consciousness.[3]

Organic Unity

HAROLD OSBORNE

The concept of "organic unity," or more loosely "unity in variety," is commonly traced back to classical antiquity, though there is in fact little about it in the surviving literature. The not entirely happy metaphor which compares the unity of a work of art with the functional unity of a living organism goes back to a casual remark in Plato's *Phaedrus* (264c), which may not warrant the burden of significance which has in later ages been read into it. In discussing the art of rhetoric he makes Socrates say: "Any discourse ought to be constructed like a living creature, with its own body, as it were; it must not lack either head or feet; it must have a middle and extremities so composed as to suit each other and the whole work." Plato himself in the dialogue draws from this no more recondite conclusions than that a good speech must have a beginning, a middle, and an end and that these should fit together coherently. The concept is further developed by Aristotle.

In the *Metaphysics* (1024a) Aristotle distinguishes between a "whole" and an "aggregate." Collections "to which the position of the parts in relation to each other makes no difference are 'aggregates,' those to which it does make a difference are 'wholes.' " Aristotle further adds that a genuine part of a "whole" cannot retain its own character except in the whole of which it

---

[3]I.e., the organic process of the imagination is in part unconscious.

is a part. He also says that removal of a part is apt to make the whole mutilated and any transposition of the parts will damage or even destroy its unity. The last statement is both important and obscure. It is, of course, the case, as McTaggart showed, that any change in any of the parts of an *aggregate* changes the whole aggregate. What Aristotle appears to mean when he advances this as a point of difference between an aggregate and a unified whole is that in the case of the whole but not in the case of the aggregate any change in any part produces changes in the nature and relations of all the remaining parts as parts of that whole. This idea is very important to the modern notion of an organic unity as applied to works of art.

In the *Poetics* Aristotle applies his concept of unity to drama (chs. 7 and 8). The plot, he says, must represent an action which is "whole and complete and of a certain magnitutde." A whole is "that which has a beginning, middle, and end." In discussing magnitude he assumes the very important principle that a beautiful thing must be a thing which can be apprehended in a single act of "synoptic" perception, *seen* as a single thing or unity, and not seen as an aggregate of parts which are connected by theoretical reason, discursively.

In Chapter xii of the First Treatise in his *Inquiry* Hutcheson showed himself also aware of this difference.

> Let every one here consider how different we must suppose the perception to be with which a Poet is transported upon the prospect of any of those objects of natural beauty which ravish us even in his description, from that cold lifeless Conception which we imagine in a dull Critick or one of the Virtuosi without what we call a fine Taste. This latter class of men may have greater perfection in that knowledge which is derived from external sensation; they can tell all the specifick differences of trees, herbs, minerals, metals; they know the form of every leaf, stalk, root, flower and seed of all the species, about which the Poet is often very ignorant. And yet the Poet shall have a vastly more delightful perception of the whole; and not only the Poet, but any man of fine taste. Our external sense may by measuring teach us all the proportions or architecture to the tenth of an inch, and the situation of every muscle in the human body; and a good memory may retain these. And yet there is still something further necessary not only to make a man a compleat master in architecture, painting or statuary, but even a tolerable judge of these works or capable of receiving the highest pleasure in contemplating them.

Hutcheson accepted the "passive" notion of perception common to the psychology of his time. Therefore, since the external senses receive particular sense impressions, he had to postulate an "internal sense" to receive the impressions of the whole as a combination of unity and variety. Baumgarten, however, inherited the active notion of perception which was current in the Leibnizian tradition and he was therefore able to define beauty as the expansion and perfection or ordinary perception. "The object of aesthetics," he says, "is the perfection of sensory cognition as such. And this is beauty." The emergence to importance in modern times of the concept of organic perceptual wholes owed something to Gestalt psychology, when toward the end of last century it revived the idea of perceptual configurations with configurational properties which cannot be reduced to or built up from more simple "atomic" elements of sensation combined according to external relations which leave them internally unaffected.

The modern conception of an artistic unity combines the old Aristotelian concept of a whole with the *gestalt* idea of a perceptual unity displaying emergent or "field" qualities which belong to the whole but not to the parts. In aesthetic appreciation the art object is isolated from its environment and framed apart in attention as a single individual, apprehended as a single complex impression and not as an aggregate. For when we apprehend something as an aggregate we apprehend it discursively; we are aware of a manifold of interrelated parts, and we recognize each part for what it is independently of the whole to which it belongs. We do not become directly aware of any properties of the whole which are not constructed from our prior knowledge of the parts. But in aesthetic appreciation we become aware of the object in its internal complexity by a direct act of synoptic perception; we do not "construct" it in thought by discursive reason, though of course the final appreciative awareness may often be *prepared* by much preliminary study. Ideally, in aesthetic contemplation, we become aware of a total presentation manifesting qualities which are not built up from, or fully analyzable into, the properties and relations of the constitutent parts. The whole in apprehension is more than the sum of the parts. Although the contained parts may be attended to separately in the perhaps lengthy process of becoming acquainted with the total work of art, they become fully articulate only when they are perceived as parts of the particular whole in which they occur, in the completed act of appreciation. We cannot know the parts as they are without knowing the whole. Although the whole is composed of its parts, the qualities of the whole permeate and determine the parts and the parts are what they are only in the context of the whole in which they are apprehended. It is, in the words of Coleridge, "a whole that is presupposed by all its parts."

A major problem has been to pinpoint the difference between aesthetic objects and other sorts of configurations. It has been pointed out that what has been said about organic wholes in general could also be said about non-aesthetic wholes, such as human faces. We recognize a face by a certain overall configurational character which makes it unique, not by adding together an assemblage of remembered features. We can also recognize a likeness in profile though turning it from full face to side view causes every feature to change beyond recognition in terms of abstract form. Faces also display "expressive" properties which are also configurational but are not identical with the configurational characters by which we recognize them. We can recognize the face of a friend whether it is angry or sad, calm or convulsed. Contrariwise we can "read" the expression on a face whether it is the face of a friend or of an unknown person. These gestalt properties have nothing directly to do with aesthetic enjoyment: we perceive them whether the face is beautiful or plain and our perception of them does not provide a basis for an aesthetic judgment. These are practical everyday acts of perception not perception in the aesthetic mode. When on the contrary we contemplate a work of art (or for that matter a face for its beauty) we do not simply recognize it by some overall configuration or "read" its expressive features as a piece of information about it: we dwell upon it, hold attention deeply with it and concentrate our energies on actualizing it in perception. One can take up an aesthetic attitude of "disinterested" attention to anything at all, fixing it in awareness not for the sake of recognition or any other practical purpose. But some objects—and these we call aesthetic objects—favor disinterested contemplation, while others repel it and are too jejune to sustain it. Not all organic wholes in perception are meet for aesthetic contemplation. Aesthetic objects are organic wholes which in suitably conditioned persons are able to attract and sustain intense, prolonged or repeated, and fruitful perceptive attention in the nonpractical aesthetic mode. It has not been easy to explain the qualities of "organic unity" which successful works of art and other things of beauty possess and which nonaesthetic configurational wholes do not possess. Aesthetic unity would have to be understood in such a way that it could serve as a criterion of excellence in judging artworks yet without favoring some art styles above others. It should not, for example, lead to the ascription of superior excellence to works manifesting formal classical proportion over those which have greater Romanic freedom and asymmetry or demand a preference for the Neoplasticism of Mondrian rather than the apparent randomness of Action Painting. For to do so would conflict with accepted critical verdicts. In practice it has proved so difficult to render the notion of aesthetic unity concrete while keeping it free from stylistic bias that some philosophers have despaired of using it profitably. . . . On the other hand it has been suggested that works of art tend to differ from other perceptual configurations in that the qualities of artistic wholes are not only "emergent" from the parts in the way which has been described but are to some extent reflected back upon the parts so that the parts of an artistic whole themselves display something of the distinctive aesthetic character of the whole. This is why, for example, a torso or even an isolated limb reflects something of the beauty of the whole statue from which it came. It is not certain, however, whether this feature applies generally to all art objects and much work remains still to be done on the elucidation of the concept of organic unity in relation to aesthetic objects.

Emotion and Imagination

R. G. COLLINGWOOD

Expressing Emotion and Arousing Emotion

Our first question is this. Since the artist proper has something to do with emotion, and what he does with it is not to arouse it, what is it that he does? It will be remembered that the kind of answer we expect to this question is an answer derived from what we all know and all habitually say; nothing original or recondite, but something entirely commonplace.

Nothing could be more entirely commonplace than to say he expresses them. The idea is familiar to every artist, and to every one else who has any acquaintance with the arts. To state it is not to state a philosophical theory or definition of art; it is to state a fact or supposed fact about which, when we have sufficiently identified it, we shall have later to theorize philosophically. For the present it does not matter whether the fact that is alleged, when it is said that the artist expresses emotion, is really a fact or only supposed to be one. Whichever it is, we have to identify it, that is, to decide what it is that people are saying when they use the phrase. Later on, we shall have to see whether it will fit into a coherent theory.

They are referring to a situation, real or supposed, of a definite kind. When a man is said to express emotion, what is being said about him comes to this. At first, he is conscious of having an emotion, but not conscious of what this emotion is. All he is conscious of is a perturbation or excitement, which he feels going on within him, but of whose nature he is ignorant. While in this state, all he can say about his emotion is: "I feel . . . I don't know what I feel." From this helpless and oppressed condition he extricates himself by doing something which we call expressing himself. This is an activity which has something to do with the thing we call language: he expresses himself by speaking. It has also something to do with consciousness: the emotion expressed is an emotion of whose nature the person who feels it is no longer unconscious. It has also somthing to do with the way in which he feels the emotion. As unexpressed, he feels it in what we have called a helpless and oppressed way; as expressed, he feels it in a way from which this sense of oppression has vanished. His mind is somehow lightened and eased.

This lightening of emotions which is somehow connected with the expression of them has a certain resemblance to the "catharsis" by which emotions are earthed through being discharged into a make-believe situation; but the

Excerpts from R. G. Collingwood, *Principles of Art* (London: Oxford University Press, 1938).

two things are not the same. Suppose the emotion is one of anger. If it is effectively earthed, for example by fancying oneself kicking some one down stairs, it is thereafter no longer present in the mind as anger at all: we have worked it off and are rid of it. If it is expressed, for example by putting it into hot and bitter words, it does not disappear from the mind; we remain angry; but instead of the sense of oppression which accompanies an emotion of anger not yet recognized as such, we have that sense of alleviation which comes when we are conscious of our own emotion as anger, instead of being conscious of it only as an unidentified perturbation. This is what we refer to when we say that it "does us good" to express our emotions.

The expression of an emotion by speech may be addressed to some one; but if so it is not done with the intention of arousing a like emotion in him. If there is any effect which we wish to produce in the hearer, it is only the effect which we call making him understand how we feel. But, as we have already seen, this is just the effect which expressing our emotions has on ourselves. It makes us, as well as the people to whom we talk, understand how we feel. A person arousing emotion sets out to affect his audience in a way in which he himself is not necessarily affected. He and his audience stand in quite different relations to the act, very much as physician and patient stand in quite different relations towards a drug administered by the one and taken by the other. A person expressing emotion, on the contrary, is treating himself and his audience in the same kind of way; he is making his emotions clear to his audience, and that is what he is doing to himself.

It follows from this that the expression of emotion, simply as expression, is not addressed to any particular audience. It is addressed primarily to the speaker himself, and secondarily to any one who can understand. Here again, the speaker's attitude towards his audience is quite unlike that of a person desiring to arouse in his audience a certain emotion. If that is what he wishes to do, he must know the audience he is addressing. He must know what type of stimulus will produce the desired kind of reaction in people of that particular sort; and he must adapt his language to his audience in the sense of making sure that it contains stimuli appropriate to their peculiarities. If what he wishes to do is to express his emotions intelligibly, he has to express them in such a way as to be intelligible to himself; his audience is then in the position of persons who overhear him doing this. Thus the stimulus-and-reaction terminology has no applicability to the situation.

The means-and-end, or technique, terminology too is inapplicable. Until a man has expressed his emotion, he does not yet know what emotion it is. The act of expressing it is therefore an exploration of his own emotions. He is trying to find out what these emotions are. There is certainly here a directed process: an effort, that is, directed upon a certain end; but the end is not something foreseen and preconceived, to which appropriate means can be thought out in the light of our knowledge of its special character. Expression is an activity of which there can be no technique.

Expression and Individualization

Expressing an emotion is not the same thing as describing it. To say "I am angry" is to describe one's emotion, not to express it. The words in which it is expressed need not contain any reference to anger as such at all. Indeed, so far as they simply and solely express it, they cannot contain any such reference. The curse of Ernulphus, as invoked by Dr. Slop on the unknown person who tied certain knots, is a classical and supreme expression of anger; but it does not contain a single word descriptive of the emotion it expresses.

This is why, as literary critics well know, the use of epithets in poetry, or even in prose where expressiveness is aimed at, is a danger. If you want to express the terror which something causes, you must not give it an epithet like "dreadful." For that describes the emotion instead of expressing it, and your language becomes frigid, that is inexpressive, at once. A genuine poet, in his moments of genuine poetry, never mentions by name the emotions he is expressing.

Some people have thought that a poet who wishes to express a great variety of subtly differentiated emotions might be hampered by the lack of a vocabulary rich in words referring to the distinctions between them; and that psychology, by working out such a vocabulary, might render a valuable service to poetry. This is the opposite of the truth. The poet needs no such words at all; the existence or nonexistence of a scientific terminology describing the emotions he wishes to express is to him a matter of perfect indifference. If such a terminology, where it exists, is allowed to affect his own use of language, it affects it for the worse.

The reason why description, so far from helping expression, actually damages it, is that description generalizes. To describe a thing is to call it a thing of such and such a kind: to bring it under a conception, to classify it. Expression, on the contrary, individualizes. The anger which I feel here and now, with a certain person, for a certain cause, is no doubt an instance of anger, and in describing it as anger one is telling truth about it; but it is much more than mere anger: it is a peculiar anger, not quite like any anger that I ever felt before, and probably not quite like any anger I shall ever feel again. To become fully conscious of it means becoming conscious of it not merely as an instance of anger, but as this quite peculiar anger. Expressing it, we saw, has something to do with becoming conscious of it; therefore, if being fully conscious of it means being conscious of all its peculiarities, fully expressing it means expressing all its peculiarities. The poet, therefore, in proportion as he understands his business, gets as far away as possible from merely labelling his emotions as instances of this or that general kind, and takes enormous pains to individualize them by expressing them in terms which reveal their difference from any other emotion of the same sort.

This is a point in which art proper, as the expression of emotion, differs sharply and obviously from any craft whose aim it is to arouse emotion. The end which a craft sets out to realize is always conceived in general terms, never individualized. However accurately defined it may be, it is always defined as the production of a thing having characteristics that could be shared by other things. A joiner, making a table out of these pieces of wood and no others, makes it to measurements and specifications which, even if actually shared by no other table, might in principle be shared by other tables. A physician treating a patient for a certain complaint is trying to produce in him a condition which might be, and probably has been, often produced in others, namely, the condition of recovering from that complaint. So an "artist" setting out to produce a certain emotion in his audience is setting out to produce not an individual emotion, but an emotion of a certain kind. It follows that the means appropriate to its production will be not individual means but means of a certain kind: that is to say, means which are always in principle replaceable by other similar means. As every good craftsman insists, there is always a "right way" of performing any operation. A "way" of acting is a general pattern to which various individual actions may conform. In order that the "work of art" should produce its intended psychological effect, therefore, whether this effect be magical or merely amusing, what is necessary is that it should satisfy certain conditions, possess certain characteristics: in other words be, not this work and no other, but a work of this kind and of no other. . . .

The Artist and the Ordinary Man

I have been speaking of "the artist," in the present chapter, as if artists were persons of a special kind, differing somehow either in mental endowment or at least in the way they use their endowment from the ordinary persons who make up their audience. But this segregation of artists from ordinary human beings belongs to the conception of art as craft; it cannot be reconciled with the conception of art as expression. If art were a kind of craft, it would follow as a matter of course. Any craft is a specialized form of skill, and those who possess it are thereby marked out from the rest of mankind. If art is the skill to amuse people, or in general to arouse emotions in them, the amusers and the amused form two different classes, differing in their respectively active and passive relation to the craft of exciting determinate emotions; and this difference will be due, according to whether the artist is "born" or "made," either to a specific mental endowment in the artist, which in theories of this type has gone by the name of "genius," or to a specific training.

If art is not a kind of craft, but the expression of emotion, this distinction of kind between artist and audience disappears. For the artist has an audience only in so far as people hear him expressing himself, and understand what they hear him saying. Now, if one person says something by way of expressing what is in his mind, and another hears and understands him, the hearer who understands him has that same thing in his mind. The question whether he would have had it if the first had not spoken need not here be raised; however it is answered, what has just been said is equally true. If some one says "Twice two is four" in the hearing of some one incapable of carrying out the simplest arithmetical operation, he will be understood by himself, but not by his hearer. The hearer can understand only if he can add two and two in his own mind. Whether he could do it before he heard the speaker say those words makes no difference. What is here said of expressing thoughts is equally true of expressing emotions. If a poet expresses, for example, a certain kind of fear, the only hearers who can understand him are those who are capable of experiencing that kind of fear themselves. Hence, when some one reads and understands a poem, he is not merely understanding the poet's expression of his, the poet's, emotions, he is expressing emotions of his own in the poet's words, which have thus become his own words. As Coleridge put it, we know a man for a poet by the fact that he makes us poets. We know that he is expressing his emotions by the fact that he is enabling us to express ours.

Thus, if art is the activity of expressing emotions, the reader is an artist as well as the writer. There is no distinction of kind between artist and audience. This does not mean that there is no distinction at all. When Pope wrote that the poet's business was to say "what all have felt but none so well express'd," we may interpret his words as meaning (whether or no Pope himself consciously meant this when he wrote them) that the poet's difference from his audience lies in the fact that, though both do exactly the same thing, namely express this particular emotion in these particular words, the poet is a man who can solve for himself the problem of expressing it, whereas the audience can express it only when the poet has shown them how. The poet is not singular either in his having that emotion or in his power of expressing it; he is singular in his ability to take the initiative in expressing what all feel, and all can express. . . .

In the light of this discussion let us recapitulate and summarize our attempt to answer the question, what is a work of art? What, for example, is a piece of music?

(1) In the pseudo-aesthetic sense for which art is a kind of craft, a piece of music is a series of audible noises. The psychological and "realistic" aestheticians, as we can now see, have not got beyond this pseudo-aesthetic conception.

(2) If "work of art" means work of art proper, a piece of music is not something audible, but something which may exist solely in the musician's head.

(3) To some extent it must exist solely in the musician's head (including, of course, the audience as well as the composer under that name), for his imagination is always supplementing, correcting, and expurgating what he actually hears.

(4) The music which he actually enjoys as a work of art is thus never sensuously or "actually" heard at all. It is something imagined.

(5) But it is not imagined sound (in the case of painting, it is not imagined colour-patterns, &c.). It is an imagined experience of total activity.

(6) Thus a work of art proper is a total activity which the person enjoying it apprehends, or is conscious of, by the use of his imagination. . . .

. . . By creating for ourselves an imaginary experience or activity, we express our emotions; and this is what we call art.

6

Contemporary Theories of the Imagination

Kant's and Coleridge's theories of the imagination have been widely influential in many modern schools of thought. Contemporary philosophers, who call themselves phenomenologists, in particular have developed the notion of imagination. Many phenomenologists agree with Kant that the mind is not merely a receptacle of experiences. Rather, we select, structure, individualize, and even discard elements of what we experience through what the phenomenologist calls "intentional modalities." And basic to any phenomenological theory is the concept of *intention*. Briefly stated, intentionality describes the way in which we experience. According to this view every experience has two aspects: the attitude or mode of experience, and the object or event experienced. All experience is an experience *of* something through some form of experience or intention. How an object or an event is experienced depends on the kind of intention through which it is experienced. Thus the *way* in which one experiences an event is as important to that experience and one's knowledge of that experience as the object or the event itself. For example, a deaf person's experience of a film is different from a blind person's because of the differences in the ways each perceives the object. An imagined film is different from a perceived film both because of different forms of intentionality (i.e., imagining and perceiving) and because of different objects of intention (i.e., image and film).

Using this sort of theory the late French philosopher Jean-Paul Sartre tried to discern how imagining is a special function of the experiencing consciousness. In imagining, one's consciousness frees itself from the perceptual world. Images are special objects for consciousness which have their own peculiar existence. Specifically, images are not identical to objects or events in the perceptual world. And Sartre argues that imagination *is* consciousness as it disengages itself and becomes totally free from the world. Thus imagining, according to Sartre, is a source of human freedom and the occasion for creativity and novelty in art.

In contrast to Sartre, the contemporary British philosopher Gilbert Ryle claims there is no special aesthetic faculty of imagination. Instead, Ryle holds that this is a misuse of the term "imagination," which actually refers to a form of make-believe or pretending. Likewise, so-called "images," the objects of the faculty of imagination, do not exist as "pictures in the mind's eye" but rather describe one's ability to remember, recognize, and recreate what one has seen.

If Ryle is correct, his position severely damages any expressive view of art. To answer Ryle, the contemporary American philosopher Edward Casey develops further Sartre's notion of imagination to demonstrate the existence and function of this aesthetic activity. Casey suggests that imagining is the conscious projection of pure possibilities for their own sake, possibilities whose existence or nonexistence is not a concern for the imagination. The French phenomenologist Maurice Merleau-Ponty's analysis of the film is an ideal illustration of the phenomenological as well as the gestalt view of perception.

Included in this chapter is an article by the aesthetician Monroe Beardsley. Beardsley is a strong critic of Collingwood's theory of artistic creativity and questions the emphasis of the all-important role of imagination. Using the example of Paul Valery's "Le Cimetière Marin" (Illustration 12), Beardsley suggests that the creative process, whatever it is, is triggered by what he calls an "incept"—some event or experience or idea which triggers the artistic activity of the artist. While the creative activity of the artist needs an impetus (an incept), this source need not be the artist's inner emotions and imagination. The incept might be an inspiration from the imagination, but it is just as likely to be something external. It might be a traumatic event in the life of the artist—such as Picasso's experiences in the Spanish Civil War, which partly inspired *Guernica*—or it might be something as mundane as a stomach ache. The location of all creativity in imagination and self-expression, then, according to Beardsley, is grossly exaggerated.

The Psychology of Imagination

JEAN-PAUL SARTRE

Consciousness and Imagination

We are now in a position to raise the metaphysical question which has been gradually shaping itself by these studies of phenomenological psychology. We may formulate it as follows: What are the characteristics that can be attributed

Jean-Paul Sartre, *The Psychology of Imagination*, trans. Hazel Barnes (New York: Philosophical Library, 1948) reprinted with permission.

to consciousness from the fact that it is a consciousness capable of *imagining*. This question can be taken in the sense of a critical analysis under the form: what must be the nature of consciousness in general in order that the construction of an image should always be possible? And, no doubt, it is under this form that our minds, accustomed to raising philosophical questions in the Kantian perspective, will best understand it. But, as a matter of fact, the problem in its deepest meaning can only be grasped from a phenomenological point of view. . . .

. . . We shall begin with the question: what must a consciousness be in order for it to possess the power to imagine, which we shall try to develop by the usual procedures of critical analysis, that is, by a regressive method. Next we shall compare the results we obtain with those the Cartesian intuition gives us of the consciousness realized by the cogito and we shall see whether the necessary conditions for realizing an imaginative consciousness are *the same* or *different* from the conditions of possibility of a consciousness in general.

In truth, the problem stated thus may appear to be completely new and even trifling to French psychologists. And, in fact, as long as we are the victims of the illusion of immanence, there is no general problem of imagination. Images are in fact supplied in these theories by a type of existence strictly like that of things. They are reborn sensations which may differ in degree, in cohesion, in meaning from primary sensations but which belong, as do sensations, to *intra-mundane* existence. The image is as real as any other existence. The only question concerning the image is the problem of its relationship to other existences but whatever this relationship may be the existence of the image remains intact. This is like saying that whether the portrait of King Charles VI is or is not a true likeness, whether the king is dead or alive or even whether he ever existed, the portrait is nevertheless something that exists in the world. There is therefore no existential problem of the image.

But if the image is looked upon as we have viewed it in this work, the existential problem of the image can no longer be sidetracked. In fact, to the existence of an object for consciousness there corresponds noetically a hypothesis or position of existence. Now, the hypothesis of the imaginative consciousness is radically different from the hypothesis of a consciousness of the real. This means that the type of existence of the object of the image *as long as it is imagined* differs in nature from the type of existence of the object grasped as real. And surely, if I now form an image of Peter, my imaginative consciousness includes a certain position of the existence of Peter, insofar as he is now at this very moment in Berlin or London. But while he *appears to me as an image*, this Peter who is in London *appears to me absent*. This absence in actuality, this essential nothingness of the imagined object is enough to distinguish it from the object of perception. What then must be the nature of a consciousness in order that it be able to successively posit *real* objects and *imagined* objects?

We must at once make an important observation, which the reader could have made himself if he had studied with us the problem of the relationships between perception and imagery. For an object or any element of an object there is very much of a difference between *being envisioned as nothing* and *being given-as-absent*. In a perception of whatever sort many empty intentions are directed, from the elements of the object now given, towards other aspects and other elements of the object which no longer reveal themselves to our intuition. For instance, the arabesques of the rug I am viewing are both in part given to my intuition. The legs of the armchair which stands before the window conceal certain curves, certain designs. But I nevertheless seize these hidden arabesques as *existing now*, as hidden but not at all as absent. And I grasp them not for themselves in trying to present them by means of an analogoue but in the very way in which I grasp what has been given me of their continuation. I *perceive* the beginnings and the endings of the hidden arabesques (which appear to me in front and in back of the leg of the chair) as *continuing* under the legs of the chair. It is therefore *in the way in which I grasp the data* that I posit that which is not given as being real. Real by the same right as the data, as that which gives it its meaning and its very nature. Likewise the successive tones of a melody are grasped by appropriate retentions as that which makes of the tone now heard exactly what it is. In this sense, to perceive this or that real datum is to perceive it on the foundation of total reality *as a whole*. This reality does not make the object of any special act of my attention but it is co-present as an essential condition of the existence of the reality actually perceived. Here we see that the imaginative act is the reverse of the act of reality. If I want to imagine the hidden arabesques, I direct my attention upon them and I isolate them, just as I isolate on a foundation of an undifferentiated universe the thing I now see. I cease to grasp them in a vacuum as constituting the sense of the perceived reality, *I present them to myself*, in themselves, but precisely as I cease to envision them from the beginning of a present, in order to grasp them by themselves, I grasp them as *absent*, they appear to me as empty data. Of course they really exist yonder under the chair and it is yonder that I envision them but precisely as I envision them where they are not given to me I grasp them as nothing for me. Thus the imaginative act is at once *constituting, isolating* and *annihilating*. . . .

We now can see what the essential requisite is in order that a consciousness may be able to imagine; it must have the possibility of positing an hypothesis of unreality. But we must clarify this requisite. It does not mean that consciousness must cease being consciousness *of* something. It is of the very nature of consciousness to be intentional and a consciousness that would cease to be consciousness of something would for that very reason cease to exist. But consciousness should be able to form and posit objects possessing a certain trait of nothingness in relation to the whole of reality. In fact, we recall that the imaginary object can be posited as non-existent or as absent or as existing elsewhere or not posited as existing. . . . We know, besides, that the totality of the real, so long as it is grasped by consciousness as a synthetic *situation* for that consciousness, is the world. There is then a two-fold requisite if consciousness is to imagine: it must be able to posit the world in its synthetic totality, and, it must be able to posit the imagined object as being out of reach of this synthetic totality, that is, posit the world as a nothingness in relation to the image. From this it follows clearly that all creation of the imaginary would be completely impossible to a consciousness whose nature it would be precisely to be "in-the-midst-of-the-world." If we assume a consciousness placed in the very bosom of the world as one existence among others, we must conceive it hypothetically as completely subjected to the action of a variety of realities—without its being able to avoid the detail of these realities by an intuition which would embrace their totality. This consciousness could therefore contain only real modifications aroused by real actions and all imagination would be prohibited to it, exactly in the degree to which it would be engulfed in the real. This conception of an imagination enmired in the world is not unknown to us since it is precisely that of psy-chological determinism. We can affirm fearlessly that if consciousness is a succession of determined psychical facts it is entirely impossible for it ever to produce anything but the real. For a consciousness to be able to imagine it must be able to escape from the world by its very nature, it must be able by its own efforts to withdraw from the world. In a word it must be free. Thus the thesis of unreality has yielded us the possibility of negation as its condition. Now, the latter is possible only by the "negation" of the world as a whole, and this negation has revealed itself to us as being the reverse of the very freedom of consciousness. . . .

. . . To be able to imagine, it is enough that consciousness be able to surpass the real in constituting it as a world, since the negating of the real is always implied by its constitution in the world. But this surpassing cannot be brought about by any means whatever, and the freedom of consciousness must not be confused with the arbitrary. For an image is not purely and simply the *world-negated*, it is always *the world negated from a certain point of view*, namely, the one that permits the positing of the absence or the non-existence of the object presented "as an image." The arbitrary position of the real as a world will not of itself cause the appearance of the centaur as an unreal object. For the centaur to emerge as unreal the world must be grasped as a world-where-the-centaur-is-not, and this can only happen if consciousness is led by different motivations to grasp the world as being exactly the sort in which the centaur has no place. Likewise, if my friend Peter is to be given me as absent I must be led to grasp the world as that sort of a whole in which Peter cannot *actually exist* and *be present to me*. (He can actually be present for others—in Berlin, for instance.) What motivates the appearance of the unreal is not necessarily nor most often the *representative* intuition of the world from some point of view. Consciousness as a fact has many other ways of *surpassing the real in order to make a world of it*; the surpassing can and should happen at first by affectivity or by action. The appearance of a dead friend as unreal, for instance, is built on the foundation of affective expectation of the real as an *empty world* from this point of view.

. . . We may therefore conclude that imagination is not an empirical and superadded power of consciousness, it is the whole of consciousness as it realizes its freedom; every concrete and real situation of consciousness in the world is big with imagination in as much as it always presents itself as a withdrawing from the real. It does not follow that all perception of the real must reverse itself in imagination, but as consciousness is always "in a situation" because it is always free, it always and at each moment has the concrete possibility of producing the unreal. These are the various motivations which decide at each moment whether consciousness will only be realized or whether it will imagine. The unreal is produced outside of the world by a consciousness which *stays in the world* and it is because he is transcendentally free that man can imagine. . . .

Now we are at the point of understanding the meaning and the value of the imaginary. The imaginary appears "on the foundation of the world," but reciprocally all apprehension of the real as world implies a hidden surpassing towards the imaginary. All imaginative consciousness uses the world as the negated foundation of the imaginary and reciprocally all consciousness of the world calls and motivates an imaginative consciousness as grasped from the particular *meaning* of the situation. The apprehension of nothingness could not occur by an immediate unveiling, it develops in and by the free succession of acts of consciousness, the nothingness is the material of the surpassing of the world towards the imaginary. It is as such that it is *lived*, without ever being posited for itself. There could be no developing consciousness without an imaginative consciousness, and vice versa. So imagination, far from appearing as an *actual* characteristic of consciousness turns out to be an essential and transcendental condition of consciousness. It is as absurd to conceive of a consciousness which would not imagine as it would be to conceive of a consciousness which could not realize the cognito. . . .

Imagination

GILBERT RYLE

I have mentioned the terminological fact that "mental" is occasionally used as synonym of "imaginary." A hypochondriac's symptoms are sometimes

Gilbert Ryle, "Imagination," from *The Concept of Mind* (New York: Harper & Row, 1949), reprinted by permission of Harper and Row and Hutchison Publishing Group.

discounted as "purely mental." But much more important than this linguistic oddity is the fact that there exists a quite general tendency among theorists and laymen alike to ascribe some sort of an other-worldly reality to the imaginary and then to treat minds as the clandestine habitats of such fleshless beings. Operations of imagining are, of course, exercises of mental powers. But I attempt in this chapter to show that to try to answer the question, "Where do the things and happenings exist which people imagine existing?" is to try to answer a spurious question. They do not exist anywhere, though they are imagned as existing, say, in this room, or in Juan Fernandez.

The crucial problem is that of describing what is "seen in the mind's eye" and what is "heard in one's head." What are spoken of as "visual images," "mental pictures," "auditory images" and, in one use, "ideas" are commonly taken to be entities which are genuinely found existing and found existing elsewhere than in the external world. So minds are nominated for their theatres. But, as I shall try to show, the familiar truth that people are constantly seeing things in their minds' eyes and hearing things in their heads is no proof that there exist things which they see and hear, or that the people are seeing or hearing. Much as stage-murders do not have victims and are not murders, so seeing things in one's mind's eye does not involve either the existence of things seen or the occurrence of acts of seeing them. So no asylum is required for them to exist or occur in. . . .

Picturing and Seeing

To see is one thing; to picture or visualise is another. A person can see things, only when his eyes are open, and when his surroundings are illuminated; but he can have pictures in his mind's eyes, when his eyes are shut and when the world is dark. Similarly, he can hear music only in situations in which other people could also hear it; but a tune can run in his head, when his neighbour can hear no music at all. Moreover, he can see only what is there to be seen and hear only what is there to be heard, and often he cannot help seeing and hearing what is there to be seen and heard; but on some occasions he can choose what pictures shall be before his mind's eye and what verses or tunes he shall go over in his head.

One way in which people tend to express this difference is by writing that, whereas they see trees and hear music, they only "see," in inverted commas, and "hear" the objects of recollection and imagination. The victim of *delirium tremens* is described by others not as seeing snakes, but as "seeing" snakes. This difference of idiom is reinforced by another. A person who says that he "sees" the home of his childhood is often prepared to describe his vision as "vivid," "faithful" or "lifelike," adjectives which he would never apply to his sight of what is in front of his nose. For while a doll can be called "lifelike," a child cannot; or while a portrait of a face may be faithful, the face cannot be any such thing. In other words, when a person says that he "sees" something which he is not seeing, he knows what he is doing is something which is totally different in kind from seeing, just because the verb is inside inverted commas and the vision can be described as more or less faithful or vivid. He may say "I might be there now," but the word "might" is suitable just because it declares that he is not there now. The fact that in certain conditions he fails to realise that he is not seeing, but only "seeing," as in dreams, delirium, extreme thirst, hypnosis and conjuring-shows, does not in any degree tend to obliterate the distinction between the concept of seeing and that of "seeing," any more than the fact that it is often difficult to tell an authentic from a forged signature tends to obliterate the distinction between the concept of a person signing his own name and that of someone else forging it. The forgery can be described as a good or bad imitation of the real thing; an authentic signature could not be characterised as an imitation at all, since it is the real thing without which the forger would have nothing to imitate.

As visual observation has pre-eminence over observation by the other sense, so with most people visual imagination is stronger than auditory, tactual, kinaesthetic, olfactory and gustatory imagination, and consequently the language in which we discuss these matters is largely drawn from the language of seeing. People speak, for example, of "picturing" or "visualising" things, but they have no corresponding generic verbs for imagery of the other sorts.

An unfortunate result ensues. Among the common objects of visual observation there exist both visible things and visible simulacra of them, both faces and portraits, both signatures and forged signatures, both mountains and snapshots of mountains, both babies and dolls; and this makes it natural to construe the language in which we describe imaginations in an analogous way.

If a person says that he is picturing his nursery, we are tempted to construe his remark to mean that he is somehow contemplating, not his nursery, but another visible object, namely a picture of his nursery, only not a photograph or an oil-painting, but some counterpart of a photograph, one made of a different sort of stuff. Moreover, this paperless picture, which we suppose him to be contemplating, it not one of which we too can have a view, for it is not in a frame on the wall in front of all of our noses, but somewhere else in a gallery which only he can visit. And then we are inclined to say that the picture of his nursery which he contemplates must be in his mind; and that the "eyes" with which he contemplates it are not his bodily eyes, which perhaps we see to be shut, but his mind's eyes. So we inadvertently subscribe to the theory that "seeing" is seeing after all, and what is "seen" by him is as genuine a likeness and as genuinely seen as is the oil-painting which is seen by everyone. True, it is a short-lived picture, but so are cinematograph-pictures. True, too, it is reserved for the one spectator to whom it and its gallery belong; but monopolies are not uncommon.

I want to show that the concept of picturing, visualising or "seeing" is a proper and useful concept, but that its use does not entail the existence of pictures which we contemplate or the existence of a gallery in which such pictures are ephemerally suspended. Roughly, imaging occurs, but images are not seen. I do have tunes running in my head, but no tunes are being heard, when I have them running there. True, a person picturing his nursery is, in a certain way, like that person seeing his nursery, but the similarity does not consist in his really looking at a real likeness of his nursery, but in his really seeming to see his nursery itself, when he is not really seeing it. He is not being a spectator of a resemblance of his nursery, but he is resembling a spectator of his nursery.

The Theory of Special Status Pictures

Let us first consider some implications of the other doctrine, that in visualising I am, in a nearly ordinary sense of the verb, seeing a picture with a special status. It is part of this doctrine that the picture that I see is not, as snapshots are, in front of my face; on the contrary, it has to be not in physical space, but in a space of another kind. The child, then, who imagines her wax-doll smiling is seeing a picture of a smile. But the picture of the smile is not where the doll's lips are, since they are in front of the child's face. So the imagined smile is not on the doll's lips at all. Yet this is absurd. No one can imagine an unattached smile, and no doll-owner would be satisfied with an unsmiling doll plus a separate and impossible simulacrum of a smile suspended somewhere else. In fact she does not really see a Cheshire smile elsewhere than on the doll's lips; she fancies she sees a smile on the doll's lips in front of her face, though she does not see one there and would be greatly frightened if she did. Similarly the conjuror makes us "see" (not see) rabbits coming out of the hat in his hand on the stage in front of our noses; he does not induce us to see (not "see") shadow-rabbits coming out of a second spectral hat, which is not in his hand, but in a space of another kind.

The pictured smile is not, then, a physical phenomenon, i.e. a real contortion of the doll's face; nor yet is it a non-physical phenomenon observed by the child taking place in a field quite detached from her perambulator and her nursery. There is not a smile at all, and there is not an effigy of a smile either. There is only a child fancying that she sees her doll smiling. So, though she is really picturing her doll smiling, she is not looking at a picture of a smile; and though I am fancying that I see rabbits coming out of the hat, I am not seeing real phantasms of rabbits coming out of real phantasms of hats. There is not a real life outside, shadowily mimicked by some bloodless likenesses inside; there are just things and events, people witnessing some of these things and events, and people fancying themselves witnessing things and events that they are not witnessing.

Take another case. I start to write down a long and unfamiliar word and after a syllable or two, I find that I am not sure how the word should go on. I then, perhaps, imagine myself consulting a dictionary and in some cases I can then "see" how the last three syllables are printed. In this sort of case it is tempting to say that I am really seeing a picture of a printed word, only the picture is "in my head," or "in my mind," since reading off the letters of the word that I "see" feels rather like reading off the letters from a dictionary-item, or a photograph of such an item, which I really do see. But in another case, I start writing the word and I "see" the next syllable or two on the page on which I am writing and in the place where I am to write them. I feel rather as if I were merely inking in a word-shadow lying across the page. Yet here it is impossible to say that I am having a peep at a picture or ghost of a word in a queer space other than physical space, for what I "see" is on my page just to the right of my nib. Again we must say that though I picture the word in a certain place, printed in a certain type, or written in a certain handwriting, and though I can read off the spelling of the word from the way I picture it as printed or written, yet there exists no picture, shadow or ghost of the word and I see no picture, shadow or ghost of it. I seem to see the word on the page itself, and the more vividly and sustainedly I seem to see it, the more easily can I transcribe what I seem to see onto my paper with my pen. . . .

Similarly, there are not two species of murderers, those who murder people, and those who act the parts of murderers on the stage; for these last are not murderers at all. They do not commit murders which have the elusive attribute of being shams; they pretend to commit ordinary murders, and pretending to murder entails, not murdering, but seeming to murder. As mock-murders are not murders, so imagined sights and sounds are not sights or sounds. They are not, therefore, dim sights, or faint sounds. And they are not private sights or sounds either. There is no answer to the spurious question, "Where have you deposited the victim of your mock murder?" since there was no victim. There is no answer to the spurious question, "Where do the objects reside that we fancy we see?" since there are no such objects.

It will be asked, "How can a person seem to hear a tune running in his head, unless there is a tune to hear?" Part of the answer is easy, namely that he would not be seeming to hear, or fancying that he heard, a tune, if he were really hearing one, any more than the actor would be simulating murder, if he were really murdering someone. But there is more to be said than this. The question, "How can a person seem to hear a tune, when there is no tune to be heard?" has the form of a "wires and pulleys" question. It suggests that there exists a mechanical or para-mechanical problem (like those that are properly asked about conjuring-tricks and automatic telephones), and that we need to have described to us the hidden workings that constitute what a person does, when he fancies himself listening to a tune. But to understand what is meant by saying that someone is fancying that he hears a tune does not require information about any ulterior processes which may be going on when he does so. We already know, and have known since childhood, in what situations to describe people as imagining that they see or hear or do things. The problem, so far as it is one, is to construe these descriptions without falling back into the idioms in which we talk of seeing horse-races, hearing concerts and committing murders. It is into these idioms that we fall back the moment we say that to fancy one sees a dragon is to see a real dragon-phantasm, or that to pretend to commit a murder is to commit a real mock-murder, or that to seem to hear a tune is to hear a real mental tune. To adopt such linguistic practices is to try to convert into species-concepts concepts which are designed, anyhow partly, to act as factual disclaimers. To say that an action is a mock-murder is to say, not that a certain sort of mild or faint murder has been committed, but that no sort of murder has been committed; and to say that someone pictures a dragon is to say, not that he dimly sees a dragon of a peculiar kind, or something else very like a dragon, but that he does not see a dragon, or anything dragon-like at all. Similarly a person who "sees Helvellyn in his mind's eye" is not seeing either the mountain, or a likeness of the mountain; there is neither a mountain in front of the eyes in his face, nor a mock-mountain in front of any other non-facial eyes. But it is still true that he "might be seeing Helvellyn now" and even that he may fail to realise that he is not doing so. . . .

There are usually ocular ways of distinguishing between things and snap-shots or effigies of them; a picture is flat, has edges and perhaps a frame; it can be turned round and turned upside down, crumpled and torn. Even an echo, or a recording, or a voice can be distinguished, if not audibly, at least by certain mechanical criteria from the voice itself. But no such discriminations can be made between a smell and a copy of a smell, a taste and a likeness of a taste, a tickle and a dummy-tickle; indeed, it makes no sense to apply words like "copy," "likeness" and "dummy" to smells, tastes and feelings. Consequently we have no temptation to say that a person who "smells" the smithy is really smelling a facsimile or likeness of anything. He seems to smell, or he fancies he smells, something, but there is no way of talking as if there existed an internal smell replica, or smell facsimile, or smell echo. In this case, therefore, it is clear that to "smell" entails not smelling and therefore that imaging is not perceiving a likeness, since it is not perceiving at all. . . .

Imagining

It will probably be asked, "What then is it for a person to fancy that he sees or smells something? How can he seem to hear a tune that he does not really hear? And, in particular, how can a person fail to be aware that he is only seeming to hear or see, as the dipsomaniac certainly fails? In what precise respects is 'seeing' so like seeing that the victim often cannot, with the best will and the best wits, tell which he is doing?" Now if we divest these questions of associations with any "wires and pulleys" questions, we can see that they are simply questions about the concept of imagining or make-believe, a concept of which I have so far said nothing positive. I have said nothing about it so far, because it seemed necessary to begin by vaccinating ourselves against the theory, often tacitly assumed, that imagining is to be described as the seeing of pictures with a special status.

But I hope I have now shown that what people commonly describe as "having a mental picture of Helvellyn" or "having Helvellyn before the mind's eye" is actually a special case of imagining, namely imagining that we see Helvellyn in front of our noses, and that having a tune running in one's head is imagining that one has the tune being played in one's hearing, maybe in a concert-hall. If successful, then I have also shown that the notion that a mind is a "place," where mental pictures are seen and reproductions of voices and tunes are heard, is also wrong.

There are hosts of widely divergent sorts of behaviour in the conduct of which we should ordinarily and correctly be described as imaginative. The mendacious witness in the witness-box, the inventor thinking out a new machine, the constructor of a romance, the child playing bears, and Henry Irving are all exercising their imaginations; but so, too, are the judge listening to the lies of the witness, the colleague giving his opinion on the new invention, the novel reader, the nurse who refrains from admonishing the "bears" for their subhuman noises, the dramatic critic and the theatre-goers. Nor do we say that they are all exercising their imaginations because we think that, embedded in a variety of often widely different operations, there is one common nuclear operation which all alike are performing, any more than we think that what makes two men both farmers is some nuclear operation which both do in exactly the same way. Just as ploughing is one farming job and tree-spraying is another farming job, so inventing a new machine is one way of being imaginative and playing bears is another. No one thinks that there exists a nuclear farming operation by the execution of which alone a man is entitled to be called "a farmer"; but the concepts wielded in theories of knowledge are apt to be less generously treated. It is often assumed that there does exist one nuclear operation in which imagination proper consists; it is assumed, that is, that the judge following the witness's mendacities, and the child playing bears, are both exercising their imaginations only if they are both executing some specifically identical ingredient operation. This supposed nuclear operation is often supposed to be that of seeing things in the mind's eye, hearing things in one's head and so on, i.e. some piece of fancied perceiving. Of course, it is not denied that the child is doing lots of other things as well; he roars, he pads around the floor, he gnashes his teeth and he pretends to sleep in what he pretends is a cave. But, according to this view, only if he sees pictures in his mind's eye of his furry paws, his snowbound den and so on, is he imagining anything. His noises and antics may be a help to his picturing, or they may be special effects of it, but it is not in making these noises, or performing these antics, that he is exercising his imagination, but only in his "seeing," "hearing," "smelling," "tasting" and "feeling" things which are not there to be perceived. And the corresponding things will be true of the attentive, if sceptical, judge.

Put as bluntly as this, the doctrine is patently absurd. Most of the things for which we ordinarily describe children as imaginative are ruled out in favour of a limited number of operations the occurrence and qualities of which it is difficult to ascertain, especially from relatively inarticulate children. We see and hear them play, but we do not see or hear them "seeing" or "hearing" things. We read what Conan Doyle wrote, but we do not get a view of what he saw in his mind's eye. So, on this theory, we cannot easily tell whether children, actors or novelists are imaginative or not, though the word "imagination" came to be wielded in theories of knowledge just because we all know how to wield it in our everyday descriptions of children, actors and novelists.

There is no special Faculty of Imagination, occupying itself single-mindedly in fancied viewings and hearings. On the contrary, "seeing" things is one exercise of imagination, growling somewhat like a bear is another; smelling things in the mind's nose is an uncommon act of fancy, malingering is a very common one, and so forth. Perhaps the chief motive from which many theorists have limited the exercises of imagination to the special class of fancied perceptions is that they have supposed that, since the mind is officially tri-partitioned into the Three Estates of Cognition, Volition and Emotion, and since imagination was born into the first, it must therefore be excluded from the others. Cognitive malpractices are notoriously due to the pranks of undisciplined Imagination, and some cognitive successes are in debt to its primmer activities. So, being an (erratic) Squire of Reason, it cannot serve the other masters. But we need not pause to discuss this feudal allegory. Indeed, if we are asked whether imagining is a cognitive or a non-cognitive activity, our proper policy is to ignore the question. "Cognitive" belongs to the vocabulary of examination papers. . . .

Pretending, Fancying and Imaging

There is not much difference between a child playing at being a pirate, and one fancying that he is a pirate. So far as there is a difference, it seems to come to this, that we use words like "play," "pretend" and "act the part," when we think of spectators finding the performance more or less convincing, whereas we use words like "fancy" and "imagine" when we are thinking of the actor himself being half-convinced; and we use words like "play" and "pretend" for deliberate, concerted and rehearsed performances, whereas we are more ready to use words like "fancy" and "imagine" for those activites of make-believe into which people casually and even involuntarily drift. Underlying these two differences there is, perhaps, this more radical difference, that we apply the words "pretend" and "act the part," where an overt and muscular representation is given of whatever deed or condition is being put on, while we tend, with plenty of exceptions, to reserve "imagine" and "fancy" for some things that people do inaudibly and invisibly because "in their heads," i.e. for their fancied perceptions and not for their mock-actions.

It is with this special brand of make-believe that we are here chiefly concerned, namely what we call "imaging," "visualising," "seeing in the mind's eye" and "going through in one's head." Even people who might allow that sparring consists in going through some of the motions of fighting in a hypothetical manner will not readily allow that the same sort of account holds good of seeing Helvellyn in one's mind's eye. What motions are there here to go through in a hypothetical manner? Even though in describing how the dipsomaniac "sees" snakes we use inverted commas, as we do in describing how the child "scalps" his nurse, or how the boxer "punishes" his sparring partner, it will be urged that the force of these commas is not the same in the two sorts of cases. Picturing is not sham-seeing in the way that sparring is sham-fighting.

We have, I hope, got rid of the idea that picturing Helvellyn is seeing a picture of Helvellyn, or that having "Lillibullero" running in one's head is listening to a private reproduction, or internal echo, of that tune. It is necessary now to get rid of a more subtle superstition. Epistemologists have long encouraged us to suppose that a mental picture, or a visual image, stands to a visual sensation in something like the relation of an echo to a noise, a bruise to a blow or a reflection in a mirror to the face reflected. To make this point more specific, it has been supposed that what is taking place, when I "see," or "hear," or "smell," corresponds to that element in perceiving which is purely sensuous; and not to that element which constitutes recognising or making out; i.e. that imaging is a piece of near-sentience and not of a function of intelligence, since it consists in having, not indeed a proper sensation, but a shadow-sensation.

But this opinion is completely false. Whereas an unknown tune may be played in a person's hearing, so that he hears the tune without knowing how it goes, we cannot say of a person in whose head a tune is running that he does not know how it goes. Having a tune running in one's head is one familiar way in which knowledge of how that tune goes is utilised. So having a tune running in one's head is not to be likened to the mere having of auditory sensations; it is to be likened rather to the process of following a familiar tune, and following a heard tune is not a function of sentience.

Similarly, if I peer through a hole in a hedge on a misty day, I may not be able to identify what I see as a watercourse flowing in spate down a mountainside. But it would be absurd for someone to say "I vividly see something in my mind's eyes, but I cannot make out even what sort of a thing it is." True, I can see a face in my mind's eye and fail to put a name to its owner, just as I can have a tune in my head, the name of which I have forgotten. But I know how the tune goes and I know what sort of a face I am picturing. Seeing the face in my mind's eye is one of the things which my knowledge of the face enables me to do; describing it in words is another and a rare ability; recognising it at sight in the flesh is the commonest of all.

. . . Perceiving entails both having sensations and something else which can be called, in a strained sense, "thinking." We can now say that to picture, image or fancy one sees or hears also entails thinking, in this strained sense. Indeed, this should be obvious, if we consider that our picturing of something must be characterisable as more or less vivid, clear, faithful and accurate, adjectives which connote not merely the possession but the use of the knowledge of how the object pictured does or would really look. It would be absurd for me to say that the smell of burning peat comes vividly back to me, but that I should not recognise the smell, if the peat were smoking in my presence. Imaging, therefore, is not a function of pure sentience; and a creature which had sensations, but could not learn, could not "see," or picture things any more than it could spell.

A person with a tune running in his head is using his knowledge of how the tune goes; he is in a certain way realising what he would be hearing, if he were listening to the tune being played. Somewhat as the boxer, when sparring, is hitting and parrying in a hypothetical manner, so the person with a tune running in his head may be described as following the tune in a hypothetical manner. Further, just as the actor is not really murdering anyone, so the person picturing Helvellyn is not really seeing Helvellyn. Indeed, as we know, he may have his eyes shut, while he pictures the mountain. Picturing Helvellyn, so far from having, or being akin to having, visual sensations, is compatible with having no such sensations and nothing akin to them. There is nothing akin to sensations. Realising, in this way, how Helvellyn would look is doing something which stands in the same relation to seeing Helvellyn as sophisticated performances stand to those more naive performances, whose mention is obliquely contained in the description of the higher order performances.

But there remains, or appears to remain, a crucial difference, which may be brought out thus. A sailor, asked to demonstrate how a certain knot is tied, finds that he has no cord with which to demonstrate. However, he does nearly as well by merely going through the motions of knotting a cord empty-handed. His spectators see how he would tie the knot by seeing how he maneuvres his hands and fingers without any cord in them. Now although he is, so to speak, hypothetically knotting cord, still he is really moving his hands and fingers. But a person picturing Helvellyn with his eyes shut, while he is certainly enjoying, so to speak, only a hypothetical view of the mountain, does not seem to be really doing anything. Perhaps his non-existent visual sensations correspond to the movements of his hands and fingers? The sailor does show the spectators how the knot would be tied; but the person visualising Helvellyn does not thereby show to his companion its contours or its colouring. Does he even show them to himself?

This difference between the two varieties of make-believe is, however, nothing but a consequence of the difference between perceiving something and bringing something about. This difference is not a difference between bringing something about privily and bringing something about overtly, for perceiving is not bringing anything about. It is getting something, or sometimes, keeping something; but it is not effecting anything. Seeing and hearing are neither witnessed nor unwitnessed doings, for they are not doings. It makes no sense to say "I saw you seeing the sunset," or "I failed to watch myself hearing the music." And if it makes no sense to speak of my witnessing, or failing to witness, a piece of hearing or seeing, *a fortiori* it makes no sense to speak of my witnessing, or failing to witness, a piece of fancied hearing or fancied seeing. No hearing or seeing is taking place.

In the concert-hall a man's neighbour can, perhaps, see him beating time to the music and even overhear him half-whistling or half-humming to himself the tune the band is playing. But not only do we not say that his neighbour sees, or overhears, him hearing the music, as he sees or overhears him accompanying it, but we do not say, either, that his neighbour fails to witness him hearing the music. "Secretly" and "openly" do not attach to "hearing," as they can attach to "cursing" and "plotting." *A fortiori*, while his neighbour in the train may detect him beating time to a tune that is running in his head, he does not claim either to detect, or to fail to detect, his "hearing" of the imagined tune.

Next . . . following a known tune involves not only hearing the notes, but also much more than that. It involves, so to speak, having the proper niche ready for each note as it comes. Each note comes as and when it was expected to come; what is heard is what was listened for. This listening for the due notes entails having learned and not forgotten the tune and is therefore a product of training and is not a mere function of aural sensitiveness. A deafish man may follow a tune better than one who hears it better. . . .

The application of this account to visual and other imagery is not difficult. Seeing Helvellyn in one's mind's eye does not entail, what seeing Helvellyn and seeing snapshots of Helvellyn entail, the having of visual sensations. It does involve the thought of having a view of Helvellyn and it is therefore a more sophisticated operation than that of having a view of Helvellyn. It is one utilisation among others of the knowledge of how Helvellyn should look, or, in one sense of the verb, it is thinking how it should look. The expectations which are fulfilled in the recognition at sight of Helvellyn are not indeed fulfilled in picturing it, but the picturing of it is something like a rehearsal of getting them fulfilled. So far from picturing involving the having of faint sensations, or wraiths of sensations, it involves missing just what one would be due to get, if one were seeing the mountain.

Certainly not all imaging is the picturing of real faces and mountains, or the "hearing" of familiar tunes and known voices. We can fancy ourselves looking at fabulous mountains. Composers, presumably, can fancy themselves listening to tunes that have never yet been played. It may be supposed, accordingly, that in such cases there is no question of the imaginary scene being pictured right, or of the tune still under composition being "heard" to go otherwise than as it really goes; any more than Hans Andersen could be either accused of misreporting the careers of his characters, or praised for the factual fidelity of his narratives.

Consider the parallels of pretending and quoting. An actor on one day plays the part of a Frenchman; on the next day he has to play the part of a visitor from Mars. We know how the former representation might be convincing or unconvincing; but how could the latter? Or I might start by quoting what you have said and go on by giving utterance to what you would or could have said. We know what it is for a quotation to be accurate, but a pretence quotation cannot be either accurate or inaccurate; it can only be, in some remoter sense, in character or out of character, by being, or failing to be, the sort of thing that you would or could have said. None the less, the actor is pretending to give a convincing representation of the man from Mars, and I am pretending that I am quoting your very words. It is just a piece of double representation. A boy mimicking a boxer sparring is in a similar case, for he is not fighting and he is not rehearsing fighting; he is staging some of the moves of a person rehearsing fighting. He is mock-mock-fighting. As the predicates by which we comment on fighting do not attach to sparring, so the predicates by which we comment on sparring do not attach to mimicries of sparring. Correspondingly, not only do the predicates by which we comment on our view of Helvellyn not attach to the manner in which we picture Helvellyn, but also the predicates by which we comment on our visualisations of Helvellyn do not attach to our visualisations of Atlantis or Jack's Beanstalk. None the less, we pretend that this is how Atlantis and the Beanstalk would have looked. We are doing a piece of double imagining.

Imagination: Imaging and the Image

EDWARD CASEY

I

. . . Even if most contemporary philosophers would agree with Gilbert Ryle that "there is no special Faculty of Imagination," we need not give equal assent to his claim that there is also no "nuclear operation" of imagining.[1] Of course, under the term "imagining" we may include quite disparate phenomena—anything from perceptual illusion to pretending. But the fact that we do not ordinarily consider such things to be examples of imagining in the fullest sense indicates that there is a more typical kind of imagining which manifests an operation or function common to all acts of imagining proper. This more typical case is that of "merely imagining" in the sense of revery, daydreaming, and certain more controlled acts (such as we find in artistic creation). What then is the central operation of imagining in this sense?

I conceive the basic, invariant function of imagining proper to be *the conscious projection and contemplation of objects posited as pure possibilities*. Thus baldly stated, this cursory definition may seem vacuous or at best trivial. It might be asked, what else do we project mentally *but* possibilities? Is this same activity not found as well in the act of understanding? It is evident that the first thing we must clarify is the vexing notion of possibility itself.

One important, if obvious, distinction is that between hypothetical and pure possibility. A hypothetical possibility is the sort of possibility that is contemplated with a view to its realizability in experience. Thus, by "hypothetical" I refer not so much to the pure "as if" character of a possibility as to the related notion of "as if it were *real*." Construed in this sense, hypothetical possibilities are essential to certain acts of imagining which are employed as aids in coming to know or understand something. In these auxiliary acts, we project possibilities as hypotheses, ideas, or options through which we can gain a more certain inroad into empirical reality—the spatiotemporal world of everyday experience—in any of its past, present, or future forms. The crucial point is that hypothetical possibilities are not projected or entertained for their own sake, but only with a certain aim in mind (whether the aim is implicit or explicit does not alter the essential character of the act). This aim is, in most cases of understanding, a clearer and more encompassing grasp

Edward Casey. "Imagination: Imaging and the Image," *Philosophy and Phenomenological Research* 31 (1971). Reprinted with permission

---

[1] Gilbert Ryle, *The Concept of Mind* (New York: Harper and Row, 1949), p. 257. (See also selection from this book included in this volume. ed.)

of our perceptual experience, historical situation, or existential condition. Hypothetical possibilities are projected as means to this improved comprehension.

Imagining proper is an act differing significantly from the kind of imagining that may be involved in coming to know or understand something. The reason for this is that in imagining proper we project or entertain possibilities for *their own sake*. More exactly, we posit objects as possibilities *simpliciter*, not as possibilities that might be confirmed or discredited by experience. In a paradigmatic imagining act (e.g., in daydreaming or an artist's inspirational state) there is no attempt made to treat possibilities as hypothetical constructs or as explanations of experience. Rather, possibilities are contemplated as what we could call "mere" or "pure" possibilities. This does not mean that such possibilities have no reference at all to experiential reality; but such references as they do have involves no direct effort to comprehend, and much less to manipulate, this reality. As contrasted with hypothetical possibilities, these possibilities are not grasped as primarily applicable to experience by way of explaining, copying, or anticipating it. They are not schematic statements of what we have experienced, or even of what we do or will experience. It is in this largely negative sense that they are "pure"—pure, that is, of a certain application or use, namely that by which we come to know and control empirical reality more completely.

But it is not enough to characterize imagining proper negatively and by way of contrast alone with other less central kinds of imagining. For imagining proper has its own sort of object and its own positing or "thetic" character. Without being wholly redundant, we can say that the object of an act of imagining proper is an "imaginary" object or state of affairs; this means that in being imagined it is posited as merely possible. But this object or state of affairs may be in itself either (a) empirically real or (b) wholly unreal. Let us consider the former case first—that in which the object is real. We can very well imagine a real person, place, or event; any of these real entities or occasions can be "visualized" in what Leonardo da Vinci called "the darkness of the mind's eye."[2] This envisioning of real objects does not, however, entail the additional assertion of Leonardo's that the imagined "object does not come from without."[3] It is clearly the case that, in many instances of imagining, the whole object imagined is also a possible object of our perceptual experience, although the real object as imagined is felt to be absent from our *present* perceptions. This is true even in the case of imagining an object derived from memory, because memory is in turn founded upon perception of the empirically real. Thus, it would be mistaken to claim that all imagined objects are themselves imaginary in the sense of empirically unreal.

But it remains true that even when we imagine real objects that are absent from perception, we imagine them in a special way; we posit them as

---

[2] In the *Trattato della Pittura*.
[3] *Ibid.*

purely possible. As Collingwood has seen, this act of positing cannot be reduced to ascribing unreality to such objects: "to imagine an object is not to commit oneself in thought to its unreality; it is to be wholly indifferent to its reality."[4] Yet this view, like Sartre's similar notion of "neutralization," does not go far enough in positively characterizing the thetic aspect of imagining proper. For, beyond "indifference" and "neutrality," there is a special thetic modification involved in all prototypical imagining. This concerns the positing of the imagined object as "merely possible" in the sense discussed above. The imagined object thus possesses an existential status of its own: that of pure possibility, which cannot be explicated in terms of reality or unreality or a mixture of the two together. In imagining proper, we posit an object merely *as possible*, and nothing more; we do not posit it as either real or unreal, nor are we entirely neutral or indifferent toward it.

Entering now upon the second of the two cases mentioned above, we are nevertheless forced to observe that the object thus posited as merely possible may be in fact unreal. We can and do imagine unreal objects—that is, objects that we do not expect to, and indeed cannot, find in our ordinary experiential world. In imagining, we do not posit such objects *as* unreal, but upon analysis they may be revealed to be so. Thus, in the fervor of imagining the poet may speak of, and even "describe," a hippogriff; in this act, the poet is not concerned with whether such a mythical monster is real or unreal; he only assumes that it is an imaginative possibility—a possibility perhaps called for by the context of the poem he is writing. Upon reflection or investigation, he may discover that there never has been—and most likely, never will be—such a creature and that it is therefore eminently "unreal." This is not to deny that some or even all of the *parts* of the imagined hippogriff are drawn from what the poet has perceived—that is, from some segment of his personal experience. They may also be drawn from what the poet remembers of accounts he has read concerning certain real animals—accounts which in turn are based on direct observation and perception.

I have chosen the hippogriff because it is a classic example of what we would call a "complex unreal object." Such an example seems to provide ammunition for the traditional veiw of imagining as an act of associating images. In this view, the particular images we associate would each be directly traceable to a specific sensation (sometimes through the intermediary of memory). Thus, what Kant called "reproductive" imagination in its empirical employment involves the mere combination of what is already presented in the sensible manifold; and Coleridge spoke similarly of "fancy" as the mechanical association of "fixities and definites."[5] Before these two thinkers, there was general agreement, at least in the empiricist tradition, that the act

---

[4]R. G. Collingwood, *Essays in the Philosophy of Art,* ed. Alan Donagan (Bloomington: University of Indiana Press, 1964), p. 54. (See also selection from Collingwood in this volume. ed.)

[5]See I. Kant, *Critique of Pure Reason,* B. 152, 181; and S. T. Coleridge, *Biographia Literaria* (Oxford: Oxford University Press, 1907), I, 202. (See these selections in this volume also. ed.)

of imagining was merely the construction of "complex ideas" on the basis of associating "simple ideas," and these latter turned out to be copies of impressions or sensations. From this restricted standpoint, the image (or more exactly, the imagined object) could only be a conjunction of simple ideas, each of which must arise from a determinate impression. "Imagining" consisted in the mere arrangement or rearrangement of these ideas.

One aspect of the philosophical revolution initiated by Kant and continued by Coleridge is that they refused to accept the thesis that the objects we imagine are complex in the sense of merely associational. It was Kant's notion of "synthesis," applied to the special case of imagining, that allowed a new vision of the imagined object to emerge. Without denying the role of a reproductive imagination—indeed, even admitting its essentiality—Kant discerned another function of imagining; the "productive." The productive imagination is what is primarily responsible for the synthetic character of imagined objects—that is, the sense in which they cannot be analyzed exhaustively in terms of the mere association of simple ideas. For association clearly does not exhaust synthesis understood as productive.[6] Each imagined object—real or unreal—represents a synthetic totality defying an analysis that would reduce the synthesis to a mere collocation of constituent elements. Such elements and their ultimate rooting in perception are not denied a function in the creation of the total imagined object; but their merely associative combination is no longer regarded as a sufficient explanation of the emergent synthetic quality of this object. Coleridge termed this new and irreducible quality "esemplastic" or unified in an organic way. Kant was much more elaborate in his analysis of the various modes of possible combination by which synthetic unities could arise. But both men grasped a dimension of imagining that had been overlooked by the empiricist tradition: the distinctly synthetic, wholistic character of imagined objects.

. . . Kant would not restrict his thesis to complex unreal objects of imagination. In his view, every full act of imagining is productively synthetic; hence even simple imagined objects, real or unreal, are not fully comprehensible as simulacra or faded copies of impressions. The epistemological and ontological continuity between impression and idea is broken by a basic difference in type; accordingly, sensations and images are fundamentally different *kinds* of things. This means that, while constituents or parts of images may be correlated with or even traceable to certain specific sensations, the image as a whole (whether simple or complex) cannot be adequately accounted for in terms of the mere combination of such sensations or the direct transcription of such a combination at a higher level of awareness.

This bifurcation of type becomes more difficult to maintain when one attends to the *objects* of images. Our identifying references are often strikingly similar in the case of the objects of both imagination and perception. I can refer to my friend "Robert" with the same proper name whether I perceive

---

[6]*Critique*, B. 152. Strictly speaking, association belongs to reproductive imagination alone.

or "image" him. Moreover, the identifiable object of an image often presents itself as being the same general kind of thing that we perceive; it seems to be perceivable "in principle." The combination of these two factors makes it difficult to deny at first the seemingly plausible claim that "the imagination appears to have the same *sort* of objects as perception."[7] But the emphasis in this sentence should really be on "appears" and not on "sort." For the only meaning that "sort" has in this context is an extremely tenuous one; it points to a very diffuse genus that includes objects with similar identifying references but in fact sharing only a quite weak "theoretical" perceivability. Of course, some imagined objects—namely, those that are in themselves empirically real—are perceivable in a stronger sense in subsequent acts of apprehension, that is, once they are "disimagined" by being taken out of the imaginary sphere altogether. But unreal imagined objects are perceivable only in the weak sense that they are the sort of thing that *might* be perceived if the nature of the world or our co-ordinate conceptual framework were somehow altered. They are not perceivable, as we say, "in the normal course of events." Only if this course of events were radically altered would they become perceivable—for instance, if the hippogriff's mythical world were magically substituted for the present experiential world. Yet this move, in the present world-order, can be effected by imagination alone; it is not anything that the perceptual world itself suggests or elicits.

Therefore to talk about unreal imagined objects as "in principle" or "theoretically" perceivable is to make a largely insubstantial claim. The hippogriff belongs essentially—given our present perceptual apparatus—to an imaginary realm; this is the only kind of domain in which it could be perceived, and to claim that it is perceivable in principle is to limit oneself to the odd and attenuated sense in which hippogriffs are somehow "perceived" or rather quasi-perceived in imaginary space. To claim this is to fall prey to a false analogy between imagining and perceiving, as if there could be an act of paraperceiving which is neither wholly perceptual nor wholly imaginational in character. To make hippogriffs perceivable, even in an imaginary world, is already to change our concept of a hippogriff: it is to include the rider that a hippogriff is "unperceivable except in imaginary space." But perception in an imaginary world would be itself a form of imagination; thus the hippogriff, however much we may qualify its concept, remains unperceivable in fact *and* in theory (in any strong sense of this latter term).

II

In turning from the act of imagining to the image, I want to consider first a claim that is frequently made or at least implied: viz., that a mental image is

---

[7] Robert R. Ehman, "Imagination, Dream, and the World of Perception," in *The Journal of Existentialism* (Summer, 1965), p. 390. The italics are Ehman's.

in some sense perceivable as a whole, or that the unreal object of such an image is perceivable. We have already touched on the second part of this claim, though we shall return to it below. For the moment, I want to examine the first part of the claim, that concerning the perceivability of the mental image.

It might be thought that such a claim is absurd *ab initio* on the ground that there are no such things as mental images to start with. Such seems to be the position of Ryle, who simply denies the existence of mental images.[8] But imagining as an intentional act requires an image to complete its intentional structure. It will not do to substitute "mental picture" for "image,"[9] for this tends to restrict images to representational ones. If mental images always contain imagined objects, these objects (real or unreal) are not necessarily *depicted* by the image. In fact, the image plays a more basic role, which we shall examine shortly. I want now only to indicate that a rejection of mental images altogether is simply misguided.

My argument in brief is that there are features of the imagining experience that cannot be attributed either to the act itself or to the real or unreal objects we imagine—hence the need for a third element, the image. To take J. M. Shorter's example: how do we account for the experience of having a "blurred image" of someone's face? Is it merely that our *act* of imagining is itself vague (as Sartre would suggest)? This seems insufficient as an explanation, for the act may be distracted or fragmentary, but hardly *blurred* in itself. Is it then the object of the act that is vague? This seems more plausible— at least until we examine the phenomenon more closely. What we find is that the imagined object often presents itself as *indeterminate* in a special sense: incomplete and yet not completable by further inspection or examination. No amount of extra scrutiny will help to determine more accurately the nature of the object *as imagined*. Thus the object is not so much blurred or vague as simply undeterminable. This leaves the *image itself* as the blurred item. It is in fact the image that is vague because, as we shall see, the image is really nothing but the mode in which the imagined object is presented to consciousness. This interpretation fits with our common-sense tendency to say that it is the *way* the object is presented in imagination that is vague, not the object itself. Thus, we can agree with Shorter that "the blur does not represent anything in the face visualized. It is, so to speak, a feature of the image in its own right." But it is dangerous to interpret the image as a quasi-picture or depiction, as Shorter proceeds to do. For this view takes us perilously close to the traditional error which Ryle has correctly exposed: the notion that we somehow "see" images in a private theater of the mind. . . .

In an effort to combat the view that mental images are thing-like it is

---

[8]Ryle, *op. cit.*, p. 246 f.

[9]J. M. Shorter, "Imagination," in D. F. Gustafson, *Essays in Philosophical Psychology* (Anchor, 1954), p. 264 f.

perhaps natural to go to the other extreme and claim that mental images are simply acts of consciousness. This is what Sartre does when he proclaims that "the image is an act, not some thing."[10] But such a move flies in the face of language and exact description, for the act of imagination is what we call "imagining," not the "image." A more adequate interpretation of the image is found in regarding it as *the presentation of an imagined object to consciousness*. "Presentation" here has the force of *a* presentation—something possessing direct givenness—and not an *act* of presenting. The image (henceforth shorthand for "mental image") is the mode or pattern in which an imagined object is apprehended by our consciousness. This mode assumes the form of a *field* in which the imagined object (real or unreal, simple or complex) appears as the focal point of our attention. This field forms the ground for the imagined object as the explicit figure or theme. The image, then, is a field phenomenon—and it occurs necessarily in acts of imagining proper. The imagined object is given *with* and *in* the field formed by the image as a whole; it also appears *through* it in that the image as field is what makes the appearances of the object manifest to consciousness.

In any event, it is certain that the image does not necessarily refer directly to something sensuously perceivable. In many instances, an image will be primarily self-referential; any connection we may trace between it and empirical reality is secondary and often related to a concern for proving a causal-genetic analysis of the image. This does not mean, however, that Wittgenstein is justified in claiming that "Images tell us nothing, either right or wrong, about the external world."[11] This is correct only if it is meant that they tell us nothing *directly* about the world, for there are a significant number of indirect links between images and empirical experience. For one thing, they often utilize or presuppose knowledge that is founded upon this experience; that is to say, they often involve such cognitive factors as recognition, identification, or time-sense. These factors may be employed in the act of imagining itself. Nevertheless, this act does not inform us in any immediate way about the experiential world. At the most, images present to us certain cognitive possibilities; but these possibilities, as we have seen, are not related to this world (or to the self, for that matter) in any necessarily descriptive, explanatory, or even hypothetical way. This does not mean that they may not *lead* to eventual knowledge concerning the empirically real—and perhaps also to metaphysical insight. But in themselves, pure possibilities are not empirically falsifiable; only subsequent interpretation and application in the light of memory, perception, or theory bring them into a corrigible relation to reality. But precisely at this later point, they cease to be pure possibilities. They become images deflected from their inner nisus: the transcendence of

---

[10]Jean-Paul Sartre, *Imagination*, p. 146. (See selection in this volume also. ed.)

[11]*Zettel*, ed. G. E. M. Anscombe and G. H. von Wright (Berkeley: University of California Press, 1967), par. 621.

the real toward the purely possible. The illumination which, as pure possibles, they may cast on the experiential world it not direct, but inferred. The independence of images from reality—more generally, of imagination from perception—may be precarious and even relative, but it is nonetheless essential.

As nonfalsifiable, imagined objects and images themselves might seem to be wholly subjective and idiosyncratic items. Yet they do possess an objectivity that goes beyond even their intrinsic meaning or structure. Or rather, we should say that the objectivity of this meaning or structure is somehow reinforced when imagined objects or images are described and made comprehensible to others. The objectivity I have in mind here is not reducible to the way in which an imagined real object may refer to its "noematic correlate,"[12] for centaurs and hippogriffs, which lack noematic correlates, can also become publicly accessible. How is this so, when it is the case that something unreal by nature cannot be conveyed *directly* by perceptual means to someone else? Such an object seems to remain an object of what Shakespeare called "the soul's imaginary sight," and as such only an object of an individual imagining consciousness. Yet poets—as well as painters and occasionally even philosophers—do succeed in expressing to *others* the pure possibilities they posit or envision. How is this to be accounted for?

The phenomenon is to be explained, I believe, in terms of a distinction between the image itself (including the object presented in it) and its physical "bearer" or "support." While the image is not itself perceivable—since it is not composed of anything empirically real in the form of sense-data, secondary qualities, or any other psychophysical constituents—what bears and presents it to perception *is* physically, spatiotemporally real. It is this material support that we can in fact perceive: the canvas and oil paint in the case of the painter, the printed or spoken word in the case of the philosopher and poet. Such inherently perceivable bearers are what makes expression of otherwise private mental images possible in a social universe like our own. The bearers make manifest and public what is otherwise doomed to lie latent in the relatively supine and isolated imagining consciousness; and this public character of mental images is not a new trait they gain, but a potentiality they realize when embodied and revealed in various material supports.

The reason why this phenomenon is often overlooked is that our thematic attention in imagining is focused on the imagined object; only marginally are we aware of the image as its presentational field. This means that the bearer is typically neglected, and often assumes the character of "hiddenness." This is most evident in art, where the medium or support may be spontaneously transcended toward the objects borne and "meant" by this support. But the artist more frequently calls attention to his medium than does the philosopher, who tends to demand the immediate surpassing of the printed

---

[12]In Husserl's sense of the term in *Ideen*, sect. 128–133.

page or spoken word toward a carefully cultivated realm of concepts. But both artist and philosopher, poet and prose-writer, typically direct us to something beyond the range of the perceivable. In this paper, those metaperceivable entities called concepts have been purposely neglected in order to concentrate on another decisive class of metaperceivable items: imagined objects and the images in which they appear. These objects, posited as purely possible, and the images that present them are the intentional correlates of the act of imagining treated in Part I. Together, they compose the total phenomenon of imagination in its most essential form.

On the Creation of Art

MONROE BEARDSLEY

From the times of Homer and Hesiod, creative artists have wondered about the source of their power to summon into existence things hitherto unseen and even unthought. In our day, it has begun to seem feasible to solve this problem with something like conclusiveness. Yet much of its mystery remains.

A number of distinct questions are involved here, only one of which I shall take up. For example, I shall not inquire why the artist creates in the first place—what obscure impulses compel him to make shapes or melodies, to dance or tell stories. This question has been given two sorts of answer. The first is in terms of conscious motives (the artist wants fame, money, love, power, etc.)—and here it seems pretty evident that there must be a vast variety of true answers, depending on the artist, the work at hand, and even the time of day or night. The second is in terms of unconscious needs and drives—and this I am not competent to pursue. Again, I shall not inquire how the creative process begins—what evokes the first stroke of the brush, the first words of the poem. In the creation of every work, no doubt something does come first, perhaps a single little fragment, perhaps a rush of ideas. This initial element of what later becomes the work has been referred to by various metaphors, some of them misleading, as we shall see—*germ, cell, seed, nucleus*; I will call it the *inceptive element*, or for short, *incept*. The incept of the work may simply pop into the artist's mind—like Mozart's melodies or Housman's verses—or it may come from extrenal sources, accidentally, like the notes struck by a cat on the keyboard or the pattern made by mud in the gutter. When it does come from within, it no doubt has preconscious causal conditions, though to trace them would surely be a difficult undertaking.

Monroe Beardsley, "On the Creation of Art," *Journal of Aesthetics and Art Criticism*, 23 (1965); reprinted by permission.

What I mean by the creative process is that stretch of mental and physical activity between the incept and the final touch—between the thought "I may be on to something here" and the thought "It is finished." My problem is about what goes on in this interval—how the work of art itself comes into existence and takes on its character through the stages or phases of this process.

Many students of art have assumed, or expected to find, that there is such a thing as *the* process of art creation—that is, a pattern universally or characteristically discoverable whenever substantial works of art are produced. They would allow, of course, for many differences between one creative process and another, depending on the artist's habits and temperament, the medium in which he moves, and the demands of the particular work in progress. But they argue that beneath these differences there is what we might call the *normal creative pattern*, and that to understand this pattern would contribute much to our understanding of the finished product.

Nor is it unreasonable to suppose that there is such a creative pattern to be isolated and described. First, it might be said, the common character of works of art in all media—whatever it is that enables us to class them together—presents a prima-facie case for a creative pattern. For things that are alike may well have been produced in a similar way. Second, there is the analogy with aesthetic experience. For if there is a pattern of appreciation common to the arts, then why should there not be a pattern of creation, which would, in a sense, be its inverse? Third, there is the analogy with other kinds of creative activity. Dewey's classic description of the process of inquiry, or problem-solving, remains the standard one, though it has been refined and extended since its first appearance in *How We Think*. Practical and scientific problems differ considerably among themselves, just as works of art do, and if there is a common pattern of thought provoked by the former, there may be a common pattern of activity required for the latter.

It is true that the theory of a common character of the arts and the theory of a special aesthetic experience have been questioned in recent years.[1] I appreciate the force of the objections, which I won't go into here, but, like many others, I am not ready to abandon either of the theories. In any case, of course, the three arguments I have mentioned above are not conclusive; they are but suggestive analogies. If there is a common creative pattern, then it can be discovered only by direct study of creative processes. And we might expect to find three main sources of evidence: the artist, the psychologist, and the philosopher.

Our first inclination, of course, is to turn to the creative artist himself,

---

[1]The former by Paul Ziff and Morris Weitz, whose views I have discussed in "Art and the Definitions of the Arts," *JAAC,* 20 (1961), 175–87; the latter by George Dickie, in "Is Psychology Relevant to Aesthetics?" *Philosophical Review,* 71 (1962), 285–302, "The Myth of the Aesthetic Attitude," *American Philosophical Quarterly* 1 (January, 1964), 56–65, and "Beardsley's Phantom Aesthetic Experience," *Journal of Philosophy,* 62 (1965), 129–36.

for he ought to know, if anyone does, what is going on in his mind during that mysterious interval between the first pin-fall or brick-fall of an idea and the final laying down of pen or brush. And it is true that much of our best and most useful information about creative processes does come from artists. The trouble is that, for reasons of their own, they are often inclined to the most whimsical and bizarre statements, and seem to enjoy being deliberately misleading. For example, Christian Zervos tells us that Picasso once said to him:

> I take a walk in the forest of Fontainbleau. There I get an indigestion of green-ness. I must empty this sensation into a picture. Green dominates it. The painter paints as if in urgent need to discharge himself of his sensations and his visions.[2]

But this is a most curious description of the creative process. If the painter suffers from a surfeit of green, does he avoid looking at green any more for a while? No, he goes to his studio, squeezes out the green pigment, and proceeds to cover a canvas with it. This is like drinking grapefruit juice to cure an acid stomach. To make the indigestion theory of artistic creation plausible, the green-surfeited painter would surely go off to paint a *red* painting—red being the chromatic analogue of sodium bicarbonate. . . .

As for the psychologists, despite the considerable effort (or at least speculation) that has gone into the study of the artist's unconscious, not much is available by way of well-established conclusions about the way the poet's or painter's mind is actually working when he is on the job. Some of the most interesting contributions have been made by gestalt psychologists, for example, Rudolf Arnheim, in his psychological study of some materials in the Buffalo collection, and in his recent study of *Guernica*.[3] . . .

Philosophic reflection on the available empirical data has given us two widely-held accounts of the creative process. When we consider any artistic work of major proportions, whose creation we know something about, we are often struck by the gap between the final achievement and its humble incept. Clearly, the process between can be said to have moved in a desirable direction. Now in the usual case, although lucky accidents may make an important contribution, this process appears to be at least partly controlled. The problem for the aesthetician is, then: What is the nature of this control?

The earliest people who raised this question—Homer, Hesiod, and Pindar—were inclined to give it a supernatural answer, attributing their own feats to the intervention of the Muses. And the theory of divine inspiration, often in a pantheistic version, remains with us. But if we insist upon a naturalistic theory of artistic creation, we find two main ones. And these are distinguished in a way familiar to other branches of philosophy.

---

[2]Brewster Ghiselin, ed., *The Creative Process: A Sympsoium* (U. of California, 1952), p. 51.

[3]*Poets at Work* (New York, 1948), by various authors, and *Picasso's Guernica: The Genesis of a Painting* (U. of California, 1962).

According to what I shall call the Propulsive Theory, the controlling agent is something that exists prior to the creative process, and presides over it throughout. According to the Finalistic Theory, the controlling agent is the final goal toward which the process aims. No doubt the two theories run into each other in the minds of some philosophers, and perhaps we need not strain to keep them wholly distinct. But even if there are not two theories, there are at least two errors—and this is what I am most concerned to note.

The theory of art as expression is probably the most popular form of the Propulsive Theory of the creative process. And I shall take R. G. Collingwood as representative of expressionism at its best.

> When a man is said to express emotion, what is being said about him comes to this. At first, he is conscious of having an emotion, but not conscious of what this emotion is. All he is conscious of is a perturbation or excitement, which he feels going on within him, but of whose nature he is ignorant.[4]

Before the emotion is expressed, the artist is oppressed by it; he works so his mind will become "lightened and eased." His aim is to make his emotion clear to himself—indeed, to discover what the emotion is. Thus Collingwood postulates a single emotion that preserves its identity throughout the process of creation—if the work is to be genuine—and determines the main course of that process.

The first difficulty with this theory is that no principle of identity can be provided for this emotion.

> If artists only find out what their emotions are in the course of finding out how to express them, they cannot begin the work of expression by deciding what emotion to express [Collingwood, p. 117].

Well said. But, on the other hand, after the artist has expressed his emotion, and come to experience it clearly, how does he know it is the same emotion he started with? He cannot compare them, since the other was unknown to him. How does he know that the emotion he feels now is not a new and different emotion—an emotion that is perhaps felt as the *effect* of the finished work, rather than its cause? As far as I can see, Collingwood has no answer to this. And, moreover, in order to preserve this theory he has to say some rather surprising things. For example,

> No artist, therefore, so far as he is an artist proper, can set out to write a comedy, a tragedy, an elegy, or the like. So far as he is an artist proper, he is just as likely to write any one of these as any other [Collingwood, p. 116].

I am sure that statement would have startled Sophocles or Shakespeare—not to mention Racine and Molière. According to Collingwood, the genuine artist

---

[4]R. G. Collingwood, *The Principles of Art* (Oxford, 1983), p. 109. See also Alan Donagan, *The Later Philosophy of R. G. Collingwood* (Oxford, 1962), Ch. 5, Sect. 3.

says, "I feel an emotion coming on; no telling what it is until I write something (or paint it, or compose it); how will I know what I've felt until I see what I've done?" If he insists from the start on writing a tragedy, he will be forcing his emotion into some channel, and the result cannot be art.

The whole concept of *clarifying* an emotion is itself very obscure. I have a suspicion that when Bruckner finished one of his enormous symphonies, his emotions were no more clear to him than they were at the start. At least, they are no more clear to me. They are big emotions; anyone can see that. But clarity is hardly the word for them. On the other hand, nothing could be more clear than the special quality of the opening of Mozart's *G Minor Symphony*; but what reason do we have for thinking that Mozart's composition of this symphony began with some obscure or indescribable emotion, rather than with the subject of the first four bars? And what about artists who have spent years on a single work—are we to say that the very same emotion was there throughout, striving to clarify itself?

An interesting and well-worked-out version of the Finalistic or goal-directed theory of art creation has recently been presented by David Ecker.[5] He describes the creative process as "qualitative problem-solving," borrowing the concept from John Dewey. The stages of the process, he says, consist of a series of problems and solutions: if I use this cool green here I can get this plane to recede; "this jagged shape contrasts sharply with those open volumes" ([Ecker], p. 285), etc. Now he makes it clear that the problems posed are within the work itself: "Artistic problem solving takes place in the artist's medium" (p. 285). The problem need not be verbally formulated (p. 286), and various logical terms that might be applied to the process (such as "verification" and "hypothesis") are "grossly misleading" (p. 288). But the process is to be analyzed in terms of the categories of means and end; the choices involved, and the general direction, are controlled by the previsioned goal. (It is plain that Ecker's account would be strongly repudiated by Collingwood; according to Ecker the poet *must* begin by intending to write a tragedy, or comedy, or something—for otherwise he has no problem to solve.) . . .

The trouble appears when this is called a *problem*. What is the problem? It might be: "How can I make a good drawing using these lines I've already drawn?" Or "How can I make a good sculpture of a reclining figure?" Or "How can I make a good sculpture out of this block of marble?" But these are queer things to call *problems*: they are really *tasks*, the terms of which are voluntarily accepted by the artist. The main question involved in each of them is simply: "What do I do next?" A problem arises out of a conflict of some kind—a goad that the sculptor does not require. And it calls for a specific and determinate solution or set of solutions—which is not what the sculptor achieves. . . .

The error here is a subtle one, but a very crucial one in talking about

5"The Artistic Process as Qualitative Problem Solving," *JAAC*, 21 (1963), 283–290.

art. It consists in jumping from the fact that regional qualities depend upon their perceptual conditions to the conclusion that the former are therefore always ends-in-view and the latter means, in the process of creation. Perhaps no great harm would usually be done, but this way of speaking leads to an impasse, which is fully exhibited in a sentence quoted from John Dewey by Ecker:

> The doing or making is artistic when the perceived result is of such a nature that *its* qualities *as perceived* have controlled the question of production.[6]

Take the finished painting; note its quality. Now suppose we have photographs of various stages of the work, taken at daily or hourly intervals, let us say, while the painter was working. None of these, of course, has the *specific* quality of the finished painting. But Dewey says this quality was all along controlling the artist's work. Since the quality did not exist until the painting was finished, it could only have been in the artist's mind. Does that mean that from the earliest stages of a painting, from the incept onward, the painter has definitely in mind some regional quality that he is trying to bring into existence on the canvas? It is conceivable that this is sometimes the case, but most of the experience of artists goes against it: it would be remarkable if the exact regional quality of the final painting were that plain to the painter from the start.

Now, Dewey's statement can be interpreted in a somewhat more plausible way, if we introduce the notion of degrees of intensity for these regional qualities. The final painting, let us say, is characterized by a firm semi-geometrical solidity and rigidity, with decisive lines and interlocking forms. We look at the first tentative strokes put down by the painter, in the earliest photograph, and we seen that somehow, dimly but unmistakably, this final quality is foreshadowed in the early draft—a touch of it is already there, though nothing like the way it is there at the end. So the process of creation lying between these stages could be described, at least in part, as one in which a regional quality hit upon early in the game is gradually intensified with the complication of new lines and colors. So in this sense, it could be that the final quality has been at work throughout—not as a foreseen goal to which the process is heading teleologically, but as a present quality whose immediately perceivable value suggests to the painter that it would be even more valuable if there were, so to speak, more of it.

There is no doubt that something like this does often happen. Sometimes we can see in the earliest stages of a great work that the quality we value so highly in the finished product has begun to emerge. But this is not always the case, by any means. Sometimes the quality that appears most definitely at the start turns out not to be fruitful; the artist's attempt to intensify it leads

---

[6]*Art as Experience* (New York, 1934), p. 48.

to radical formal rearrangements that end by destroying the original quality and substituting a very different one. The melody that was first tried out as a quick rondo theme becomes the subject of a slow movement—almost unrecognizably altered. The poem that started out as a few ironic lines about a current political issue transforms itself, almost against the poet's will, into a moving meditation on the human condition. Nor is such a process—contrary to what Dewey implies—any the less artistic because not the same, but different, qualities have been active in generating the process at different stages. . . .

The real nature of the artist's control over the creative process will elude anyone who looks for a single guiding factor, whether a need or an end. It is internal to the process itself. I do not plan to argue for a single creative pattern, but to show how, in the absence of any such general pattern, each individual process that eventuates in a work of art *generates* its own direction and momentum. For the crucial controlling power at every point is the particular stage or condition of the unfinished work itself, the possibilities it presents, and the developments it permits. There are three things to discuss here, and I will say something about each—the incept, the development, and the completion of the work.

The first control over the artistic process is set up by the incept itself. And I want to emphasize, as I have said before, that the incept may be any sort of thing: the first sentence of a story or the last, a simple plot situation, a character, theme, scene, figure of speech, or tone or style. Paul Valéry has told us, instructively:

My poem *Le Cimetière marin* began in me by a rhythm, that of a French line . . . of ten syllables, divided into four and six. I had as yet no idea with which to fill out this form. Gradually a few hovering words settled in it, little by little determining the subject, and my labor (a very long labor) was before me.[7]

Elsewhere, Valéry adds that his playing around with possiblities of this rhythm led to a certain kind of stanza, then—

Between the stanzas, contrasts or correspondences would be set up. This last condition soon required the potential poem to be a monologue of "self," in which the simplest and most enduring themes of my affective and intellectual life, as they had imposed themselves upon my adolescence, associated with the sea and the light of a particular spot on the Mediterranean coast, were called up, woven together, opposed . . . All this led to the theme of death and suggested the theme of pure thought.[8]

---

[7]"Poetry and Abstract Thought," *The Art of Poetry*, trans. Denise Folliot (New York, 1961), p. 80.

[8]"Concerning '*Le Cimetière marin*,' " ibid, p. 148.

This is exactly opposite to the usual idea that the poet must begin with his theme, or thesis, and that he characteristically then devises a suitable subject or set of images, and finally settles on the appropriate stanzaic form and meter. Now, I'll have to confess at this point that I am wide open to one kind of skeptical criticism. Considering that this particular poem is one of the most obscure poems in the French language, it might be said, we can draw no general conclusions from Valéry's method of composing it—what can you expect from a poet who begins with rhythms and ends with themes? Still, Valéry's account shows there is no one, privileged, order in which a poem has to get written. And even in the composition of more conventional poems, many different items (including metrical patterns) actually come first. . . .

One of the most important questions about the role of the incept in the creative process is this: Does it exercise a pervasive influence throughout? If the Propulsive Theory is correct, one would expect to find the incept dominating the whole process, for whatever appears first would presumably be closely related to the original emotion. On second thought, I am not sure this really follows; it is hard to say what can be predicted from Collingwood's unknown and unknowable emotion. Again, if the Finalist Theory is correct, one would also expect the incept to dominate, for it would presumably embody the original problem or goal which directs the process to the end.

Now, one thing is evident: once an element is chosen, it sets up demands and suggestions as to what may come next, and also places limits upon it. Draw a single line on a piece of paper. If you do not think what you have there is worth much attention, the question is what you can do next to improve upon it. You can balance it, cross or oppose it by other lines, thicken and emphasize it, transform it into a more complex line or shape, etc. Or, of course, you can erase it—but then you are rejecting it as an incept, and putting an end to that particular creative process. That every stage of the process powerfully affects the succeeding stage is plain; but our present question is whether the first stage is somehow dominant over all. Artists have spoken rather differently about this. For instance, Picasso once said that "Basically a picture doesn't change, that the first 'vision' remains almost intact, in spite of appearances."[9] But he also said that a picture cannot be thought out ahead of time, and "changes as one's thoughts change." The sketches for *Guernica* do have a notable continuity despite all the changes. The bull and the horse were there in the first sketch, and a woman appeared in one of the later sketches done the same day. . . .

Once the work is underway, with a tentative commitment to some incept, the creative process is kept going by tensions between what has been done and what might have been done. At each stage there must be a perception of deficiencies in what now exists, plus the sense of unrealized possibilities of improvement. The motivating force, as Tomas says, is a negative critical

---

[9]Arnheim, op. cit., p. 30.

judgment. And this same point has been made by Valéry. To understand poetry, he remarks, we must study

> word combinations, not so much through the conformity of the meanings of these groups to an idea or thought that one thinks should be *expressed*, as, on the contrary through their effects once they are formed, from which one chooses.[10]

In other words, as the poet moves from stage to stage, it is not that he is looking to see whether he is saying what he already meant, but that he is looking to see whether he wants to mean what he is saying. Thus, according to Valéry, "Every true poet is necessarily a first rate critic"—not necessarily of others' work, but of his own.[11]

Each time the artist—whether poet, or painter, or composer—takes a step, he adds something to what is already there (A), and makes another and different object (B). If he judges B worse than A, he must go back. If B is better than A, the question is whether it is good enough to stand alone as a work of art. If not, the question is whether B can be transformed into still another and better object C. If this is impossible, if every attempt to improve it only makes it worse, then the whole project is left unfinished, for it is unfinishable.

One of the most puzzling questions about the creative process is how the artist knows when to stop. If the Propulsion Theory is correct, the answer is that he stops when his original impulse has exhausted itself. If the Finalistic Theory is correct, then the artist compares his work at every stage with the intact memory of his original vision of his goal, and when they match the work is done. But without these theories, it becomes more difficult to explain what it means to come to an end of a creative process.

There are really two questions here: how the artist knows when *he* is finished, and how he knows when the *work* is finished. The first question is no doubt the easier. The artist comes to a point when he can no longer think of any way to improve his work. This becomes more and more difficult as the work progresses. In the early stages, lines and colors, stanzas and melodic fragments, can be added quite freely to see whether they can be assimilated. But in the later stages, as the work becomes more complex, the effect of every addition or alteration is more serious; a wrong line or color, a wrong word or melodic figure, can throw the whole thing badly off. Of course, the artist can never be certain he has done all he can. . . . Many a painter has been notorious for a never-say-die determination to hang on to his paintings in the hope that he will think of a way of bettering them—unless extreme poverty or a wily dealer induces him to part with them. (Valéry, by the way, says he wouldn't

---

[10]"A Poet's Notebook," op. cit., p. 178.

[11]"Poetry and Abstract Thought," ibid., p. 76. This is echoed by Richard Wilbur in *The Nature of Creative Thinking*, p. 59, and by Ben Shahn, in *The Shape of Content* (see selection on Tomas, op. cit., p. 20).

have published "*Le Cimetière marin*" when he did, had it not been snatched from him. "Nothing is more decisive than the mind of an editor of a review," he remarks—though perhaps he could have put up more of a fight.)

The artist generally knows, then, pretty well whether *he* is finished—but that is not the same as saying that the *work* is finished. For when the artist has done all he can, the question remains whether the work has enough to it, whether it is worthy of standing by itself, as an object of aesthetic enjoyment. If he judges so, the artist says it is done. If he judges not, the artist says it is unfinished. And of course the threshold of contentment varies enormously from artist to artist. . . .

In one respect, the foregoing account diverges from a remark by Rudolf Arnheim in his study of Picasso's *Guernica*. Arnheim speaks of the creative process as being "goal-directed throughout"[12]—a view I challenged earlier. And summing up the whole process, he says,

> A germinal idea, precise in its general tenor but unsettled in its aspects, acquired its final character by being tested against a variety of possible visual realizations. When at the end, the artist was willing to rest his case on what his eyes and hands had arrived at, he had become able to see what he meant.[13]

I would not put such stress upon the words, if these two sentences had not been so exact and eloquent up to the final clause. But the words "become able to see what he meant" seem to imply that what Picasso ended with was an expression, an explication, an embodiment, a realization, or whatever of what was already in his mind at the start. Better, I think, to say that he had become able to mean something much better than he was able to mean a few months before, and that what he now was able to mean—that is, to make—was enough.

To draw together these remarks and examples, perhaps we can decide how far to generalize. Though there are no universal *stages* of the creative process, there are two clearly marked *phases*, which constantly alternate throughout. They involve an interplay between conscious and preconcious activities. There is the *inventive* phase, traditionally called *inspiration*, in which new ideas are formed in the preconscious and appear in consciousness. And there is the *selective* phase, which is nothing more than criticism, in which the conscious chooses or rejects the new idea after perceiving its relationships to what has already tentatively been adopted.

The problem of what goes on in the preconscious is apparently still unsolved. We would like to know how it is that a composer, having sung two bars to himself, suddenly thinks of a way to continue it—or that a painter, having outlined a figure, thinks of certain colors that might be added—or that a poet may look at a line he has just written and think of possible substitute

---

[12]Arnheim, op. cit., p. 134.
[13]Arnheim, op. cit., p. 135.

words. To take a few examples from R. P. Blackmur,[14] suppose the poet has written "breathless tiptoeing," and it occurs to him that "flowering tiptoeing" might be better; or suppose he has written "chance deepening to choice" and substitutes "chance flowering to choice." Whether the new words are better than the old is the question to be decided by his conscious mind; but why one set of words rather than another comes to consciousness is the more mysterious question.

The psychological dispute seems to be formulable this way: to what extent are the preconscious processes associative; to what extent do they involve closure or strengthening of gestalts? As far as I can make out both of these processes seem necessary to account for what the preconscious presents to the conscious. If, for example, "flowering" replaces "deepening" because of some meaningful connection of this figure with other images earlier in the poem, then we can say that the unconscious has found some degree of closure. On the other hand, the substitution may have only a very remote relationship to other words already set down, but it may serve to break down an existing gestalt, to introduce a more unstable cluster of meanings, which may lead to a more inclusive synthesis later. In this case, the word *flowering* would be described as due to free—or at least freer—association. It seems evident, in any case, that unless the preconscious can produce both kinds of ideas—those that close a gestalt and those that break one—poems could not get composed, nor could paintings or musical works.

EXPRESSION AND IMAGINATION IN THE ARTS

Concerning the Spiritual in Art

WASSILY KANDINSKY

The Two Elements of an Artwork

A work of art consists of two elements, the inner and the outer.

The inner is the emotion in the soul of the artist; this emotion has the capacity to evoke a similar emotion in the observer.

Being connected with the body, the soul is affected through the medium

Excerpts from Wassily Kandinsky, *Concerning the Spiritual in Art,* trans. Michael Sadlier, pp. 33–35, 53–57. Reprinted by permission of Constable & Co.

---

[14]*Poets at Work*, p. 48.

of the senses—the felt. Emotions are aroused and stirred by what is sensed. Thus the sensed is the bridge, i.e., the physical relation, between the immaterial (which is the artist's emotion) and the material, which results in the production of a work of art. And again, what is sensed is the bridge from the material (the artist and his work) to the immaterial (the emotion in the soul of the observer).

The sequence is: emotion (in the artist) → the sensed → the art-work → the sensed → emotion (in the observer).

The two emotions will be like and equivalent to the extent that the work of art is successful. In this respect painting is in no way different from a song: each is a communication. The successful singer arouses in listeners his emotions; the successful painter should do no less.

The inner element, i.e., emotion, must exist; otherwise the work of art is a sham. The inner element determines the form of the work of art.

In order that the inner element, which at first exists only as an emotion, may develop into a work of art, the second element, i.e., the outer, is used as an embodiment. Emotion is always seeking means of expression, a material form, a form that is able to stir the sense. The determining and vital element is the inner one, which controls the outer form, just as an idea in the mind determines the words we use, and not *vice versa*. The determination of the form of a work of art is therefore determined by the irresistible inner force: this is the only unchanging law in art. A beautiful work is the consequence of an harmonious cooperation of the inner and the outer; i.e., a painting is an intellecutal organism which, like every other material organism, consists of many parts.[1] . . .

. . . Inner necessity originates from three elements: (1) Every artist, as a creator, has something in him which demands expression (this is the element of personality). (2) Every artist, as the child of his time, is impelled to express the spirit of his age (this is the element of style)—dictated by the period and particular country to which the artist belongs (it is doubtful how long the latter distinction will continue). (3) Every artist, as a servant of art, has to help the cause of art (this is the quintessence of art, which is constant in all ages and among all nationalities).

A full understanding of the first two elements is necessary for a realization of the third. But he who realizes this will recognize that a rudely carved Indian column is an expression of the spirit that actuates any advance-guard work.

There has been in the past, and there is now, much talk of "personality" in art. Talk of the coming "style" is more frequent each day. But in spite of their importance now, these questions will lose their edge under the perspective of time.

---

[1] . . . This explanation by Kandinsky of the relation between internal and external, or inner and outer, is a slightly revised version of a translation by Arthur Jerome Eddy of part of an article by Kandinsky which appeared in *Der Sturm*, Berlin, 1913; cf. *Cubists and Post-Impressionists*, A. C. McClurg, Chicago, 1914, pp. 119–20.

Only the third element—that of quintessential art—will remain forever. Time, far from diminishing its importance, increases it. An Egyptian carving moves us more deeply today than it did its contemporaries; for they judged it with the restrictive knowledge of period and personality. But we can judge it as an expression of an eternal art.

Similarly, the greater the part played in a modern work of art by the elements of style and personality, the better will it be appreciated by people today; but a modern work of art which is full of the third element will fail to reach the contemporary soul. Sometimes centuries have to pass before the third element is understood. But the artist in whose work this third element predominates is the great artist.

These three mystical necessities are the constituent elements of a work of art, which interpenetrate and constitute unity of the work. Nevertheless, the first two elements include what belongs to time and space, while in the pure and eternal artistry, which is beyond time and space, this forms a relatively non-transparent shell. The process in the development in art consists of the separation of its quintessence from the style of the time and the element of personality. Thus, these two elements are not only a cooperative but also a hindering force. The personality and the style of the time create in every epoch many precise forms, which in spite of apparent major differences are so organically related that they can be designated as one single form: their inner sound is finally but one major chord. These two elements are of a subjective nature. The entire epoch desires to reflect itself, to express artistically its life. Likewise, the artist wishes to express himself and chooses only forms which are sympathetic to his inner self. Thus, gradually is formed the style of an epoch, i.e., a certain external and subjective form. The pure and eternal art is, however, the objective element which becomes comprehensible with the help of the subjective.

The inevitable desire for expression of the *objective* is the impulse here defined as "internal necessity." This impulse is the lever or spring driving the artist forward. Because the spirit progresses, today's internal laws of harmony are tomorrow's external laws, which in their further application live only through this necessity which has become external. It is clear, therefore, that the inner spirit of art uses the external form of any particular period as a stepping-stone to further development.

In short, the effect of internal necessity and the development of art is an ever advancing expression of the eternal and objective in terms of the historical and subjective.

Because the objective is forever exchanging the subjective expression of today for that of the morrow, each new extension of liberty in the use of external form is hailed as final and supreme. At present we say that an artist may use any form, so long as he draws on forms that exist in nature. But this limitation, like all its predecessors, is temporary. From the point of view of inner need, no limitation can be made. The artist may use any form which his expression demands; his inner impulse must find suitable external form.

Thus one sees finally (and this is of utmost importance for today or any time) that to seek for personality and "style," for nationality, to achieve this deliberately, is not only impossible but comparatively unimportant. The general relationship of those works of art which through the centuries are not weakened but always more and more strengthened, does not lie in the "external" but in the deep roots of mystical inner content. Therefore, the following of schools, the searching for the "mode," the desire for principles in a work and the insistence upon certain media of expression of a period can only be misleading and must bring misunderstanding, obscurity and silence.

The artist must ignore distinctions between "recognized" or "unrecognized" conventions of form, the transitory knowledge and demands of his particular age. He must watch his own inner life and hearken to the demands of internal necessity. Then he may safely employ means sanctioned or forbidden by his contemporaries. This is the only way to express the mystical necessity. All means are sacred which are called for by internal necessity. All means are sinful which are not drawn from inner necessity.

It is impossible to theorize about this idea. In real art, theory does not precede practice but follows it. Everything is at first a matter of feelings. Even though the general structure may be formulated theoretically, there is still an additional something which constitutes the soul of creation. Any theoretical scheme will be lacking in the essential of creation—the internal desire for expression—which cannot be formulated. Despite the most accurate weights and balances to be had, a purely deductive weighing can never suffice. True proportions cannot be calculated, nor true scales be found ready-made. Proportions and scales are not outside the artist but within him; they are what we may call a feeling for boundaries, artistic tact—qualities which are innate and which may be raised by enthusiasm to genius. In this sense we may understand the possibility of a general base to painting, as envisaged by Goethe. Such a grammar of painting is at present a matter of conjecture, and should it ever be achieved, it will be not so much according to physical laws (which have often been tried and which the cubists try today), as according to the laws of internal necessity, which is of the soul. . . .

Artist and Work of Art

A work of art is born of the artist in a mysterious and secret way. Detached from him it acquires autonomous life, becomes an entity. Nor is its existence casual and inconsequent; it has a definite and purposeful strength, alike in its material and spiritual life. It exists and has power to create spiritual atmosphere; and from this internal standpoint alone can one judge whether it is a good work of art or bad. If its form is "poor," it is too weak to call forth spiritual vibration.[2] Likewise a picture is not necessarily "well painted" if it possesses the "values" of which the French so constantly speak. It is only well painted if its spiritual value is completed and satisfying. "Good drawing" is drawing that cannot be altered without destruction of this inner value, quite irrespective of its correctness as anatomy, botany or any other science. This is not a question of a violation of natural form, but of the need of the artist for such a form. Similarly, colors are not used because they are true to nature but because they are necessary to the particular picture. The artist is not only justified in using, but is under a moral obligation to use, only those forms which fulfill his *own need*. Absolute freedom from anatomy or anything else of the kind must be given to the artist in his choice of means. Such spiritual freedom is as necessary in art as it is in life.[3]

But blind following of scientific precept is less blameworthy than its blind and purposeless rejection. At least the former produces an imitation of material objects which may have some use.[4] The latter is an artistic fraud, bringing confusion in its train. The former leaves the spiritual atmosphere empty; the latter poisons it.

Painting is an art; and art is not vague production, transitory and isolated, but a power which must be directed to the development and refinement of the human soul, to raising the triangle of the spirit.

If art rejects this work, a pit remains unbridged; no other power can take the place of art in this activity. And sometimes when the human soul is gaining greater strength, art also grows in power, for the two are inextricably connected and complementary. Conversely, at those times when the soul tends to be choked by materialist lack of belief, art becomes purposeless, and it is said that art exists for art's sake alone.[5] The relation between art and the soul is, as it were, doped into unconsciousness. The artist and the public drift apart, until at last the public turns its back, or regards the artist as a juggler whose skill and dexterity alone are worthy of applause. It is important for the artist to gauge his position correctly, to realize that he has a duty to his art and to himself, that he is not a king but a servant of a noble end. He must search his soul deeply, develop it and guard it, so

---

[2] So-called "immoral" pictures either are not capable of causing vibrations of the soul (in which case they are not art), or are capable. In the latter case they are not to be spurned, even though they produce purely aphrodisiac vibrations.

[3] This absolute liberty must be based on internal necessity, which might be called honesty. The principle holds good in life and in art. It is the most effective weapon against Philistines.

[4] Plainly, an imitation of nature, if made by the hand of a true artist, is not a mere reproduction. The voice of the soul will in some degree make itself heard. As a contrast one may cite a landscape by Canaletto, and those sadly famous heads by Denner (in the Alte Pinakothek, Munich).

[5] This phrase "art for art's sake" is really the best ideal such an age can attain. It is an unconscious protest against materialism, against the demand that everything should have a use and practical value. It is proof of the indestructibility of art and the human soul, which can never be killed, but only temporarily dazed.

that his art may have something on which to rest and does not remain flesh without bones.

The artist must have something to communicate, since mastery over form is not the end but, instead, the adapting of form to internal significance.[6]

The artist's life is not one of pleasure. He must not live irresponsibly; he has a difficult work to perform, one which often proves a crown of thorns. He must realize that his acts, feelings and thoughts are the imponderable but sound material from which his work is to rise; he is free in art, but not in life.

Compared with non-artists the artist has a triple responsibility: (1) he must return the talent which he has; (2) his actions, feelings and thoughts, like those of every man, create a spiritual atmosphere which is either pure or infected; (3) his actions and thoughts are the material for his creations, which in turn influence the spiritual atmosphere. The artist is a king, as Peladan says, not only because he has great powers, but also because he has great obligations.

If the artist be guardian of beauty, beauty can be measured only by the yardstick of internal greatness and necessity.

That is beautiful which is produced by internal necessity, which springs from the soul.[7]

Maeterlinck, one of the first modern artists of the soul, says: "There is nothing so curious of beauty or so absorbent of it as a soul. For that reason few mortal souls are able to withstand the leadership of a soul that gives itself to beauty."

This property of the soul facilitates the slow, scarcely visible, but irresistible movement of the spiritual triangle, upwards and forwards.

. . . [The] constructional tendencies in painting . . . fall into two divisions:

(1) Simple composition, which is regulated according to an obvious and simple form. This kind of composition I call *melodic*.

(2) Complex composition, consisting of various forms subjected more

---

[6]This does not mean that the artist is to instill forcibly and deliberately into his work a meaning. The generation of a work of art is a mystery. If artistry exists, there is no need of theory or logic to direct the painter's activity. The inner voice tells him what forms he needs, whether inside or outside nature. Every artist who works with feeling knows how suddenly the right form comes. Böcklin said that a true work of art must be a grand improvisation; that is, meditation and composition should be steps to a goal which the artist will glimpse unawares. In this sense may the coming counterpoint be understood.

[7]By this "beauty" we do not mean the contemporary external or even inner morality, but that quality which, itself imponderable, enriches and refines the soul. In painting any color is intrinsically beautiful, for each color causes a spiritual vibration. Each vibration, in turn, enriches the soul. Thus any outward ugliness contains potential beauty.

or less completely to a principal form. The principal form may be hard to detect, and by the same token it increases inner resonance. This kind of composition I call *symphonic*.

Between the two lie various transitional forms in which the melodic principle definitely exists. The history of the development is closely parallel to that of music.

If, in considering an example of melodic composition, one forgets the material appearance and probes the artistic reason of the whole, one finds primitive geometrical forms or an arrangement of simple lines which help a general motion. This general motion is repeated in various sections and may be varied by a single line or form. Such isolated variations serve different purposes. For instance, they may act as a sudden check or, to use a musical term, a "fermata." Each form that makes up the composition has a simple spiritual value, which has in its turn a melody. For this reason I call the composition melodic. Through Cézanne and, later, Hodler, this kind of composition won a new life and earned the name "rhythmic." This was the beginning of a compositional renascence. The limitations of the term "rhythmic" are obvious. In music and nature everything has a rhythm of its own, as in painting. In nature this rhythm is often unclear, because its purpose is not clear. We then speak of it as "unrhythmic." The terms "rhythmic" and "unrhythmic" are conventional, as are "harmony" and "discord," which have no actuality.

Complex rhymical composition, with a strong symphonic cast, is to be seen in many paintings, woodcuts, miniatures, and so on, of the past. One might mention the work of the old German masters, of the Persians, of the Japanese, Russian ikons, broadsides, etc.

In nearly all these works the symphonic composition is strongly allied to the melodic. By disregarding the concrete we discover a composition built from a feeling of rest, quiet repetition and even distribution.[8] We think at once of old choral compositions, of Mozart and Beethoven. These works are more or less germane to the majesty of a Gothic cathedral: poise and systematic arrangement of parts is the criterion of such constructions. They are transitional, in a sense.

. . . New symphonic composition[s] in which the melodic element plays an infrequent and subordinate part . . . represent three different sources of inspiration:

---

[8]Tradition plays a large part, especially in popular art. Such works occur mainly during the flowering of a culture. In times of stress there are too many struggling and clogging elements for an art work to grow serenely. In the final analysis, of course, every serious work is tranquil. But this tranquility is not easily discovered by contemporaries. Every serious work resembles in poise the quiet phrase: "I am here." Like or dislike for the work evaporates; but the sound of that phrase is eternal.

(1) A direct impression of nature, expressed in purely pictorial form. This I call an "Impression."

(2) A largely unconscious, spontaneous expression of inner character, nonmaterial nature. This I call an "Improvisation."

(3) An expression of a slowly formed inner feeling, tested and worked over repeatedly and almost pedantically. This I call a "Composition." Reason, consciousness, purpose, play an overwhelming part. But of calculation nothing appears: only feeling. What type of construction—conscious or unconscious—really underlies my work, the reader will readily understand.

I should like to remark finally that, in my opinion, we are fast approaching a time of reasoned and conscious composition, in which the painter will be proud to declare his work constructional—this in contrast to the claim of the impressionists that they could explain nothing, that their art came by inspiration. We have before us an age of conscious creation, and this new spirit in painting is going hand in hand with thought towards an *epoch of great spirituality*.

The Film and the New Psychology[1]

MAURICE MERLEAU-PONTY

Classical psychology considers our visual field to be a sum or mosaic of sensations, each of which is strictly dependent on the local retinal stimulus which corresponds to it. The new psychology reveals, first of all, that such a parallelism between sensations and the nervous phenomenon conditioning them is unacceptable, even for our simplest and most immediate sensations. Our retina is far from homogeneous: certain parts, for example, are blind to blue or red, yet I do not see any discolored areas when looking at a blue or red surface. This is because, starting at the level of simply seeing colors, my perception is not limited to registering what the retinal stimuli prescribe but reorganizes these stimuli so as to re-establish the field's homogeneity. Broadly speaking, we should think of it not as a mosaic but as a system of configurations. Groups rather than juxtaposed elements are principal and primary in our perception. We group the stars into the same constellations as the

Maurice Merleau-Ponty, "The Film and the New Psychology," from *Sense and Non-Sense*, trans. Hubert and Patricia Dreyfus (Evanston: Northwestern University Press, 1974), reprinted with permission of Northwestern and Les Editions Nagel.

[1]Lecture delivered March 13, 1945, at l'Institut des Hautes Études Cinématographiques.

ancients, yet it is *a priori* possible to draw the heavenly map many other ways. Given the series:

$$ab \quad cd \quad ef \quad gh \quad ij$$

we will always pair the data according to the formula a-b, c-d, e-f, etc., although the grouping b-c, d-e, f-g, etc. is equally probable in principle. A sick person contemplating the wallpaper in his room will suddenly see it transformed if the pattern and figure become the ground while what is usually seen as ground becomes the figure. The idea we have of the world would be overturned if we could succeed in seeing the intervals between things (for example, the space between the trees on the boulevard) as *objects* and, inversely, if we saw the things themselves—the trees—as the ground. This is what happens in puzzles: we cannot see the rabbit or the hunter because the elements of these figures are dislocated and are integrated into other forms: for example, what is to be the rabbit's ear is still just the empty interval between two trees in the forest. The rabbit and the hunter become apparent through a new partition of the field, a new organization of the whole. Camouflage is the art of masking a form by blending its principal defining lines into other, more commanding forms.

The same type of analysis can be applied to hearing: it will simply be a matter of temporal forms rather than spatial ones. A melody, for example, is a figure of sound and does not mingle with the background noises (such as the siren one hears in the distance during a concert) which may accompany it. The melody is not a sum of notes, since each note only counts by virtue of the function it serves in the whole, which is why the melody does not perceptibly change when transposed, that is, when all its notes are changed while their interrelationships and the structure of the whole remain the same. On the other hand, just one single change in these interrelationships will be enough to modify the entire make-up of the melody. Such a perception of the whole is more natural and more primary than the perception of isolated elements; it has been seen from conditioned-reflex experiments, where, through the frequent association of a piece of meat with a light or a sound, dogs are trained to respond to that light or sound by salivating, that the training acquired in response to a certain series of notes is simultaneously acquired for any melody with the same structure. Therefore analytical perception, through which we arrive at absolute value of the separate elements, is a belated and rare attitude—that of the scientist who observes or of the philosopher who reflects. The perception of forms, understood very broadly as structure, grouping, or configuration should be considered our spontaneous way of seeing.

There is still another point on which modern psychology overthrows the prejudices of classical physiology and psychology. It is a commonplace to say that we have five senses, and it would seem, at first glance, that each of them is like a world out of touch with the others. The light or colors which act upon the eye do not affect the ears or the sense of touch. Nevertheless it has been known for a long time that certain blind people manage to represent the colors they cannot see by means of the sounds which they hear: for example, a blind man said that red ought to be something like a trumpet peal. For a long time it was thought that such phenomena were exceptional, whereas they are, in fact, general. For people under mescaline, sounds are regularly accompanied by spots of color whose hue, form, and vividness vary with the tonal quality, intensity, and pitch of the sounds. Even normal subjects speak of hot, cold, shrill, or hard colors, of sounds that are clear, sharp, brilliant, rough, or mellow, of soft noises and of penetrating fragrances. Cézanne said that one could see the velvetiness, the hardness, the softness, and even the odor of objects. My perception is therefore not a sum of visual, tactile, and audible givens: I perceive in a total way with my whole being; I grasp a unique structure of the thing, a unique way of being, which speaks to all my senses at once.

Naturally, classical psychology was well aware that relationships exist between the different parts of my visual field just as between the data of my different senses—but it held this unity to be a construction and referred it to intelligence and memory. In a famous passage from the *Méditations* Descartes wrote: I say that I see men going by in the street, but what exactly do I really see? All I see are hats and coats which might equally well be covering dolls that only move by springs, and if I say that I see men, it is because I apprehend "through an inspection of the mind what I thought I beheld with my eyes." I am convinced that objects continue to exist when I no longer see them (behind my back, for example). But it is obvious that, for classical thought, these invisible objects subsist for me only because my judgment keeps them present. Even the objects right in front of me are not truly seen but merely thought. Thus I cannot see a cube, that is, a solid with six surfaces and twelve edges; all I ever see is a perspective figure of which the lateral surfaces are distorted and the back surface completely hidden. If I am able to speak of cubes, it is because my mind sets these appearances to rights and restores the hidden surface. I cannot see a cube as its geometrical definition presents it: I can only think it. The perception of movement shows even more clearly the extent to which intelligence intervenes in what claims to be vision. When my train starts, after it has been standing in the station, I often "see" the train next to mine begin to move. Sensory data are therefore neutral in themselves and can be differently interpreted according to the hypothesis on which my mind comes to rest. Broadly speaking, classical psychology made perception a real deciphering of sense data by the intelligence, a beginning of science, as it were. I am given certain signs from which I must dig out the meaning; I am presented with a text which I must read or interpret. Even when it takes the unity of the perceptual field into account, classical psychology remains loyal to the notion of sensation which was the starting point of the analysis. Its original conception of visual data as a mosaic of sensations forces it to base the unity of the perceptual field on an operation of the intelligence. What does *gestalt* theory tell us on this point? By resolutely rejecting the notion of sensation it teaches us to stop distinguishing between signs and their significance, between what is sensed and what is judged. How could we define the exact color of an object without mentioning the substance of which it is made, without saying, of this blue rug, for example, that it is a "woolly blue"? Cézanne asked how one is to distinguish the color of things from their shape. It is impossible to understand perception as the imputation of a certain significance to certain sensible signs, since the most immediate sensible texture of these signs cannot be described without referring to the object they signify.

Our ability to recognize an object defined by certain constant properties despite changes of lighting stems, not from some process by which our intellect takes the nature of the incident light into account and deduces the object's real color from it, but from the fact that the light which dominates the environment acts as *lighting* and immediately assigns the object its true color. If we look at two plates under unequal lighting, they will appear equally white and unequally lighted as long as the beam of light from the window figures in our visual field. On the other hand, if we observe the same plates through a hole in a screen, one will immediately appear gray and the other white; and even if we *know* that it is nothing but an effect of the lighting, no intellectual analysis of the way they appear will make us see the true color of the plates. When we turn on the lights at dusk, the electric light seems yellow at first but a moment later tends to lose all definite color; correlatively, the objects, whose color was at first perceptibly modified, resume an appearance comparable to the one they have during the day. Objects and lighting form a system which tends toward a certain constancy and a certain level of stability—not through the operation of intelligence but through the very configuration of the field. I do not think the world in the act of perception: it organizes itself in front of me. When I perceive a cube, it is not because my reason sets the perspectival appearances straight and thinks the geometrical definition of a cube with respect to them. I do not even notice the distortions of perspective, much less correct them; I am at the cube itself in its manifestness through what I see. The objects behind my back are likewise not represented to me by some operation of memory or judgment; they are present, they *count* for me, just as the ground which I do not see continues nonetheless to be present beneath the figure which partially hides it. Even the perception of movement, which at first seems to depend directly on the point of reference chosen by the intellect is in turn only one element in the global organization of the field. For, although it is true that, when either my train or the one next to it starts, first one, then the other may appear to be moving, one should note that the illusion is not arbitrary and that I cannot willfully induce it by the completely intellectual choice of a point of reference. If I am playing cards in my compartment, the other train will start moving; if, on the other hand, I am looking for someone in the adjacent train, then mine will begin to roll. In each instance the one which seems stationary is the one we have chosen as our abode and which, for the time being, is our environment. Movement and rest distribute themselves in our surroundings not according to the hypotheses which our intelligence is pleased to construct but according to the way we settle ourselves in the world and the position our bodies assume in it. Sometimes I see the steeple motionless against the sky with clouds floating above it, and sometimes the clouds appear still and the steeple falls through space. But here again the choice of the fixed point is not made by the intelligence: the looked-at object in which I anchor myself will always seem fixed, and I cannot take this meaning away from it except by looking elsewhere. Nor do I give it this meaning through thought. Perception is not a sort of beginning science, an elementary exercise of the intelligence; we must rediscover a commerce with the world and a presence to the world which is older than intelligence.

Finally, the new psychology also brings a new concept of the perception of others. Classical psychology unquestioningly accepted the distinction between inner observation, or introspection, and outer observation. "Psychic facts"—anger or fear, for example—could be directly known only from the inside and by the person experiencing them. It was thought to be self-evident that I can grasp only the corporal *signs* of anger or fear from the outside and that I have to resort to the anger or fear I know in myself through introspection in order to interpret these signs. Today's psychologists have made us notice that in reality introspection gives me almost nothing. If I try to study love or hate purely from inner observation, I will find very little to describe: a few pangs, a few heart-throbs—in short, trite agitations which do not reveal the essence of love or hate. Each time I find something worth saying, it is because I have succeeded in studying it as a way of behaving, as a modification of my relations with others and with the world, because I have managed to think about it as I would think about the behavior of another person whom I happened to witness. In fact, young children understand gestures and facial expressions long before they can reproduce them on their own; the meaning must, so to speak, adhere to the behavior. We must reject that prejudice which makes "inner realities" out of love, hate or anger, leaving them accessible to one single witness: the person who feels them. Anger, shame, hate, and love are not psychic facts hidden at the bottom of another's consciousness: they are types of behavior or styles of conduct which are visible from the outside. They exist *on* this face or *in* those gestures, not hidden behind them. Psychology did not begin to develop until the day it gave up the distinction between mind and body, when it abandoned the two correlative methods of interior observation and physiological psychology. We learned nothing about emotion as long as we limited ourselves to measuring the rate of respiration or heartbeat in an angry person, and we didn't learn anything more when we tried to express the qualitative and inexpressible nuances of lived anger. To create a psychology of anger is to try to ascertain the *meaning* of anger, to ask oneself how it functions in human life and what purpose it serves. So we find that emotion is, as Janet said, a disorganizing reaction which comes into play whenever we are stuck. On a deeper level, as Sartre has shown, we find that anger is a magical way of acting by which we afford ourselves a completely symbolic satisfaction in the imagination after re-nouncing effective action in the world, just as, in a conversation, a person who cannot convince his partner will start hurling insults at him which prove nothing or as a man who does not dare strike his opponent will shake his fist at him from a distance. Since emotion is not a psychic, internal fact but rather a variation in our relations with others and the world which is expressed in our bodily attitude, we cannot say that only the signs of love or anger are given to the outside observer and that we understand others indirectly by interpreting these signs: we have to say that others are directly manifest to us as behavior. Our behavioral science goes much farther than we think. When unbiased subjects are confronted with photographs of several faces, copies of several kinds of handwriting, and recordings of several voices and are asked to put together a face, a silhouette, a voice, and a handwriting, it has been shown that the elements are usually put together correctly or that, in any event, the correct matchings greatly outnumber the incorrect ones. Michelangelo's handwriting is attributed to Raphael in 36 cases, but in 221 instances it is correctly identified, which means that we recognize a certain common structure in each person's voice, face, gestures and bearing and that each person is nothing more nor less to us than this structure or way of being in the world. One can see how these remarks might be applied to the psy-chology of language: just as a man's body and "soul" are but two aspects of his way of being in the world, so the word and the thought it indicates should not be considered two externally related terms: the word bears its meaning in the same way that the body incarnates a manner of behavior.

The new psychology has, generally speaking, revealed man to us not as an understanding which constructs the world but as a being thrown into the world and attached to it by a natural bond. As a result it re-educates us in how to see this world which we touch at every point of our being, whereas classical psychology abandoned the lived world for the one which scientific intelligence succeeded in constructing.

If we now consider the film as a perceptual object, we can apply what we have just said about perception in general to the perception of a film. We will see that this point of view illuminates the nature and significance of the movies and that the new psychology leads us straight to the best observations of the aestheticians of the cinema.

Let us say right off that a film is not a sum total of images but a temporal *gestalt.* This is the moment to recall Pudovkin's famous experiment which clearly shows the melodic unity of films. One day Pudovkin took a close-up of Mosjoukin with a completely impassive expression and projected it after showing: first, a bowl of soup, then, a young woman lying dead in her coffin, and, last, a child playing with a teddy-bear. The first thing noticed was that Mosjoukin seemed to be looking at the bowl, the young woman, and the child, and next one noted that he was looking pensively at the dish, that he wore an expression of sorrow when looking at the woman, and that he had a glowing smile for the child. The audience was amazed at his variety of expression although the same shot had actually been used all three times and was, if anything, remarkably inexpressive. The meaning of a shot therefore depends on what precedes it in the movie, and this succession of scenes creates a new reality which is not merely the sum of its parts. In an excellent article in *Esprit*, R. Leenhardt added that one still has to bring in the time-factor for each shot: a short duration is suitable for an amused smile, one of intermediate length for an indifferent face, and an extended one for a sorrowful expression.[2] Leenhardt drew from this the following definition of cinematographic rhythm: "A certain order of shots and a certain duration for each of these shots or views, so that taken together they produce the desired impression with maximum effectiveness." There really is, then, a cinematographic system of measurements with very precise and very imperious requirements. "When you see a movie, try to guess the moment when a shot has given its all and must move on, and be replaced either by changing the angle, the distance, or the field. You will get to know that constriction of the chest produced by an overlong shot which brakes the movement and that deliciously intimate acquiescence when a shot fades at the right moment." Since a film consists not only of montage (the selection of shots or views, their order and length) but also of cutting (the selection of scenes or sequences, and their order and length), it seems to be an extremely complex form inside of which a very great number of actions and reactions are taking place at every moment. The laws of this form, moreover, are yet to be discovered, having until now only been sensed by the flair or tact of the director, who handles cinematographic language as a man manipulates syntax: without explicitly thinking about it and without always being in a position to formulate the rules which he spontaneously obeys.

What we have just said about visual films also applies to sound movies, which are not a sum total of words or noises but are likewise a *gestalt.* A rhythm exists for sounds just as for images. There is a montage of noises and sounds, as Leenhardt's example of the old sound movie *Broadway Melody* shows. "Two actors are on stage. We are in the balcony listening to them

---

[2] *Esprit*, 1936.

speak their parts. Then immediately there is a close-up whispering, and we are aware of something they are saying to each other under their breath. . . .'' The expressive force of this montage lies in its ability to make us sense the coexistence, the simultaneity of lives in the same world, the actors as they are for us and for themselves, just as, previously, we saw Pudovkin's visual montage linking the man and his gaze to the sights which surround him. Just as a film is not merely a play photographed in motion and the choice and grouping of the shots constitutes an original means of expression for the motion picture, so, equally, the soundtrack is not a simple phonographic reproduction of noises and words but requires a certain internal organization which the film's creator must invent. The real ancestor of the movie sound-track is not the phonograph but the radio play.

Nor is that all. We have been considering sight and sound by turns, but in reality the way they are put together makes another new whole, which cannot be reduced to its component parts. A sound movie is not a silent film embellished with words and sounds whose only function is to complete the cinematographic illusion. The bond between sound and image is much closer, and the image is transformed by the proximity of sound. This is readily apparent in the case of dubbed films, where thin people are made to speak with the voices of fat people, the young have the voices of the old, and tall people the voices of tiny ones—all of which is absurd if what we have said is true—namely, that voice, profile, and character form an indivisible unit. And the union of sound and image occurs not only in each character but in the film as a whole. It is not by accident that characters are silent at one moment and speak at another. The alternation of words and silence is manipulated to create the most effective image. There are three sorts of dialogue, as Malraux said in *Verve* (1940). First may be noted expository dialogue, whose purpose is to make the circumstances of the dramatic action known. The novel and the film both avoid this sort of dialogue. Then there is *tonal* dialogue, which gives us each character's particular accent and which dominates, for example, in Proust where the characters are very hard to visualize but are admirably recognizable as soon as they start to talk. The extravagant or sparing use of words, their richness or emptiness, their precision or affectation reveal the essence of a character more surely than many descriptions. Tonal dialogue rarely occurs in movies, since the visible presence of the actor with his own particular manner of behaving rarely lends itself to it. Finally we have dramatic dialogue which presents the discussion and confrontation of the characters and which is the movies' principal form of dialogue. But it is far from continuous. One speaks ceaselessly in the theatre but not in the film. "Directors of recent movies," said Malraux, "*break into* dialogue after long stretches of silence, just as a novelist breaks into dialogue after long narrative passages." Thus the distribution of silences and dialogue constitutes a metrics above and beyond the metrics of vision and sound, and the pattern of words and silence, more complex than the other two, superimposes its requirements upon them. To complete the analysis one would still have to study the role of music in this ensemble: let us only say that music should be incorporated into it, not juxtaposed to it. Music should not be used as a stopgap for sonic holes or as a completely exterior commentary on the sentiments or the scenes as so often happens in movies: the storm of wrath unleashes the storm of brass, or the music laboriously imitates a footstep or the sound of a coin falling to the ground. It should intervene to mark a change in a film's style: for example, the passage from an action scene to the "inside" of the character, to the recollection of earlier scenes, or to the description of a landscape. Generally speaking, it should accompany and help bring about a "rupture in the sensory balance," as Jaubert said.[3] Lastly, it must not be another means of expression juxtaposed to the visual expression. "By the use of strictly musical means (rhythm, form, instrumentation) and by a mysterious alchemy of correspondences which ought to be the very foundation of the film composer's profession, it should recreate a sonorous substance beneath the plastic substance of the image, should, finally, make the internal rhythm of the scene physically palpable without thereby striving to translate its sentimental, dramatic, or poetic content" (Jaubert). It is not the job of words in a movie to add ideas to the images, nor is it the job of music to add sentiments. The ensemble tells us something very precise which is neither a thought nor a reminder of sentiments we have felt in our own lives.

What, then, does the film *signify*: what does it mean? Each film tells a *story*: that is, it relates a certain number of events which involve certain characters and which could, it seems, also be told in prose, as, in effect, they are in the scenario on which the film is based. The talking film, frequently overwhelmed by dialogue, completes this illusion. Therefore motion pictures are often conceived as the visual and sonic representation, the closest possible reproduction of a drama which literature could evoke only in words and which the movie is lucky enough to be able to photograph. What supports this ambiguity is the fact that movies do have a basic realism: the actors should be natural, the set should be as realistic as possible; for "the power of reality released on the screen is such that the least stylization will cause it to go flat" (Leenhardt). That does not mean, however, that the movies are fated to let us see and hear what we would see and hear if we were present at the events being related; nor should films suggest some general view of life in the manner of an edifying tale. Aesthetics has already encountered this problem in connection with the novel or with poetry. A novel always has an idea that can be summed up in a few words, a scenario which a few lines can express. A

---

[3]Ibid.

poem always refers to things or ideas. And yet the function of the pure novel or pure poetry is not simply to tell us these facts. If it were, the poem could be exactly transposed into prose and the novel would lose nothing in summary. Ideas and facts are just the raw materials of art: the art of the novel lies in the choice of what one says and what one does not say, in the choice of perspectives (this chapter will be written from the point of view of this character, that chapter from another's point of view), in the varying tempo of the narrative; the essence of the art of poetry is not the didactic description of things or the exposition of ideas but the creation of a machine of language which almost without fail puts the reader in a certain poetic state. Movies, likewise, always have a story and often an idea (for example, in *l'Etrange sursis* the idea that death is terrible only for the man who has not consented to it), but the function of the film is not to make these facts or ideas known to us. Kant's remark that, in knowledge imagination serves the understanding, whereas in art the understanding serves the imagination, is a profound one. In other words, ideas or prosaic facts are only there to give the creator an opportunity to seek out their palpable symbols and to trace their visible and sonorous monogram. The meaning of a film is incorporated into its rhythm just as the meaning of a gesture may immediately be read in that gesture: the film does not mean anything but itself. The idea is presented in a nascent state and emerges from the temporal structure of the film as it does from the coexistence of the parts of a painting. The joy of art lies in its showing how something takes on meaning—not by referring to already established and acquired ideas but by the temporal or spatial arrangement of elements. As we saw above, a movie has meaning in the same way that a thing does: neither of them speaks to an isolated understanding; rather, both appeal to our power tacitly to decipher the world or men and to coexist with them. It is true that in our ordinary lives we lose sight of this aesthetic value of the tiniest perceived thing. It is also true that the perceived form is never perfect in real life, that it always has blurs, smudges, and superfluous matter, as it were. Cinematographic drama is, so to speak, finer-grained than real-life dramas: it takes place in a world that is more exact than the real world. But in the last analysis perception permits us to understand the meaning of the cinema. A movie is not thought; it is perceived.

This is why the movies can be so gripping in their presentation of man: they do not give us his *thoughts* as novels have done for so long, but his conduct or behavior. They directly present to us that special way of being in the world, of dealing with things and other people, which we can see in the sign language of gesture and gaze and which clearly defines each person we know. If a movie wants to show us someone who is dizzy, it should not attempt to portray the interior landscape of dizziness, as Daquin in *Premier de cordée* and Maltraux in *Sierra de Terruel* wished to do. We will get a much better

sense of dizziness if we see it from the outside, if we contemplate that unbalanced body contorted on a rock or that unsteady step trying to adapt itself
to who knows what upheaval of space. For the movies as for modern psychology dizziness, pleasure, grief, love, and hate are ways of behaving.

This psychology shares with contemporary philosophies the common
feautre of presenting consciousness thrown into the world, subject to the gaze
of others and learning from them what it is: it does not, in the manner of the
classical philosophies, present mind *and* world, each particular consciousness
and the others. Phenomenological or existential philosophy is largely an
expression of surprise at this inherence of the self in the world and in others,
a description of this paradox and permeation, and an attempt to make us *see*
the bond between subject and world, between subject and others, rather than
to *explain* it as the classical philosophies did by resorting to absolute spirit.
Well, the movies are peculiarly suited to make manifest the union of mind
and body, mind and world, and the expression of one in the other. That is
why it is not surprising that a critic should evoke philosophy in connection
with a film. Astruc in his review of *Défunt récalcitrant* uses Sartrian terms to
recount the film, in which a dead man lives after his body and is obliged to
inhabit another. The man remains the same for *himself* but is different *for
others*, and he cannot rest until through love a girl recognizes him despite his
new exterior and the harmony between the *for itself* and the *for others* is re-
established. The editors of *Le Canard enchaîné* are annoyed at this and would
like to send Astruc back to his philosophical investigations. But the truth is
that both parties are right: one because art is not meant to be a showcase for
ideas, and the other because contemporary philosophy consists not in stringing
concepts together but in describing the mingling of consciousness with the
world, its involvement in a body, and its coexistence with others; and because
this is movie material *par excellence*.

Finally, if we ask ourselves why it is precisely in the film era that this
philosophy has developed, we obviously should not say that the movies grew
out of the philosophy. Motion pictures are first and foremost a technical
invention in which philosophy counts for nothing. But neither do we have
the right to say that this philosophy has grown out of the cinema which it
transposes to the level of ideas, for one can make bad movies; after the
technical instrument has been invented, it must be taken up by an artistic will
and, as it were, re-invented before one can succeed in making real films.
Therefore, if philsophy is in harmony with the cinema, if thought and technical
effort are heading in the same direction, it is because the philosopher and
the moviemaker share a certain way of being, a certain view of the world
which belongs to a generation. It offers us yet another chance to confirm that
modes of thought correspond to technical methods and that, to use Goethe's
phrase, "What is inside is also outside."

Illustration 10

Kubla Khan

SAMUEL TAYLOR COLERIDGE, c. 1797–98.

In Xanadu did Kubla Khan
A stately pleasure dome decree:
Where Alph, the sacred river, ran
Through caverns measureless to man
Down to a sunless sea.
So twice five miles of fertile ground
With walls and towers were girdled round:
And there were gardens bright with sinuous rills,
Where blossomed many an incense-bearing tree;
And here were forests ancient as the hills,
Enfolding sunny spots of greenery.

But oh! that deep romantic chasm which slanted
Down the green hill athwart a cedarn cover!
A savage place! as holy and enchanted
As e'er beneath a waning moon was haunted
By woman wailing for her demon lover!
And from this chasm, with ceaseless turmoil seething,
As if this earth in fast thick pants were breathing,
A mighty fountain momently was forced:
Amid whose swift half-intermitted burst
Huge fragments vaulted like rebounding hail,
or Chaffy grain beneath the thresher's flail:
And 'mid these dancing rocks at once and ever
It flung up momently the sacred river.
Five miles meandering with a mazy motion
Through wood and dale the sacred river ran,
Then reached the caverns measureless to man,
And sank in tumult to a lifeless ocean:
And 'mid this tumult Kubla heard from far
Ancestral voices prophesying war!
The shadow of the dome of pleasure
Floated midway on the waves;
Where was heard the mingled measure
From the fountain and the caves.
It was a miracle of rare device,
A sunny pleasure dome with caves of ice!

A damsel with a dulcimer
In a vision once I saw:
It was an Abyssinian maid,
And on her dulcimer she played,
Singing of Mount Abora.
Could I revive within me
Her symphony and song,
To such a deep delight 'twould win me,
That with music loud and long,
I would build that dome in air,
That sunny dome? those caves of ice?
And all who heard should see them there,
And all should cry, Beware! Beware!
His flashing eyes, his floating hair!
Weave a circle round him thrice,
And close your eyes with holy dread,
For he on honeydew hath fed,
And drunk the milk of Paradise.

ILLUSTRATION 11

WASSILY KANDINSKY, *Large Study,*
1914, reproduced with the permission of the Museum Boymansvan
Beuningen.

ILLUSTRATION 12

Le Cimetière marin
(The Graveyard by the Sea)

PAUL VALERY

1 This peaceful roof where doves are walking
  Pulses between the tombs, between the pines;
  Noonday the just composes out of fires
  The sea, the sea, for ever recommencing!
  After a thought, O then what recompense
  A long gaze at the gods' serenity!

2 How finely worked the flashing that consumes
  Many a diamond of invisible foam,
  How true the peace that seems to be conceived!
  A sun reposes over the abyss
  And, pure creations of an eternal cause,
  Time scintillates and Dreaming is to know.

3 Minerva's temple unadorned, sure treasure,
  Mass of calm and visible reserve,
  Haughty and pensive water, Eye concealing
  So much of sleep under a veil of flame,
  My silence! . . . Mansion in the soul, and Roof!
  Yes, golden summit of ten thousand tiles!

4 Temple of Time, in a single sigh resumed,
  To this pure pitch ascending, I attune
  Myself, surrounded by my gazing sea;
  As a supreme offering to the gods,
  This tranquil scintillation sows upon
  The altitude a sovereign disdain.

5 And as a fruit into enjoyment melts,
  Its form dissolving, dying in the mouth,
  Changing its absence into sweetness, here

Paul Valery, *Le Cimetière marin,* trans. Graham Dunstan Martin (Edinburgh: University of Edinburgh Press, 1971).

I breathe the elusive smoke I shall become,
And to my incandescent soul the sky
Sings alteration in the restless shores.

6 Look on me, sky of truth and beauty, me
   The changeable! For after all my pride,
   My singular but potent idleness,
   Now to this brilliant space I abdicate,
   Across the houses of the dead my shadow
   Passes, subduing me to its frail motion.

7 My soul exposed to the torches of the solstice,
   O admirable justice of the light,
   I yet sustain your pitiless attack,
   Render you, pure, to your primordial place:
   Look on yourself! . . . But to reflect the light
   Supposes a dark half always in shadow.

8 For me alone, to me, within myself,
   Close to the heart and at the poem's spring,
   Between abeyance and the pure event,
   I await the echo of my secret depths,
   A salt, sombre, sonorous well resounding
   An always future hollow in the soul.

9 And you, feigned captive of the leaves, and gulf
   Devouring these thin railings, do you know
   The mysteries that dazzle my closed eyes,
   What body drags me to its lazy end,
   What mind attracts it to this bone-dry earth?
   A spark within recalls my absent dead.

10 Closed, sacred, full of immaterial fire,
   Fragment of earth wide open to the light,
   This place appeals, commanded by its torches,
   A composition of dark trees, of stone
   And gold, with marble tremulous on shadow,
   And sleeping on my tombs the faithful sea.

11 Resplendent watchdog, keep your guard against
   The idolater! When I, a solitary,
   A smiling shepherd, pasture long my sheep,
   The white mysterious flock of peaceful tombs,
   Hold off the overprudent doves, the empty
   Dreams, the quaint and prying seraphim.

12 Once here, the future is pure idleness.
   The brittle insect scrapes at the dry grit,
   All is consumed, destroyed, evaporated
   Into the air, into who knows what stern
   Essence. And life is vast, heady with absence,
   And bitterness is sweet and the mind clear.

13 The dead lie blanketed and easy here,
   Warmed by the earth, their mystery parched away,
   While, up above, Noonday the motionless
   Suffices to itself and thinks itself . . .
   Complete diadem, capital of perfection,
   In you I follow, am, the hidden change.

14 There is no other to contain your fears!
   It is my doubts, repentances, constraints
   That are the flaw in your great diamond.
   But underneath their stifling night of marble
   A shadow folk among the cypress roots'
   Are on your way already lingering.

15 They have dissolved into a dense absence,
   Their human whiteness drunk by the red clay,
   The gift of life has passed on to the flowers.
   Where are the dead's familiar turns of speech,
   Personal talents, individual souls?
   The larva threads where tears used to form.

16 The shrill cries of girls teased and tickled,
   The shining eyes and teeth, moist eyelids,
   The charming breast playing with fire, the blood
   Glowing at their surrendering lips, the last
   Favours, the hands defending them, it all
   Goes under earth and back into the game.

17 And you, fine soul, are you in hopes to see
   A dream without the illusive colouring
   This gold and water have for mortal eyes?
   Tell me: when thou art vapour, wilt thou sing?
   Come, come! The world is fugitive, my presence
   Porous, even divine impatience dies!

18 Gaunt immortality in black and gold,
   Consoler grimly wreathed in laurel, making
   Believe that death's a warm maternal breast,

Sublime falsehood, consecrated fraud!
Who does not recognize them and reject
That empty skull, that everlasting grin!

19 Profound forefathers, empty-headed ghosts,
Who under the weight of so much shovelled earth
Are mingled with it and confound our steps,
The real, the irrefutable gnawing worm
Is not for you, asleep beneath the table,
He lives on life, he never gives me rest!

20 Self-love, maybe, or hatred of myself?
His secret hunger biting in so close
That any name would suit him equally.
No matter! For he sees, wills, thinks and touches,
I am his meat and even on my couch
I live through my belonging to his life.

21 Zeno! Cruel Zeno! Zeno of Elea!
And have you pinned me down with your barbed arrow
Vibrating, flying and which cannot fly!
The sound engenders me, the arrow kills!
Ah! the sun . . . For the soul a tortoise-shadow,
Achilles at full stride and motionless!

22 No, no! . . . Stand up! Into successive time!
Breathe, my lungs, the birth of the wind! Shatter,
My body, this reflective attitude!
A freshness, exhalation of the sea,
Restores to me my soul . . . Salt potency!
Let's run to the waves and be flung back alive!

23 Yes! Immense sea, dowered with ecstasy,
Rippling skin of panther, ruffled chlamys
Holed with a myriad idols of the sun,
Intoxicated with your own blue flesh,
O Hydra free and absolute, who bite
Your sparkling tail in tumult like a silence,

24 The wind rises! . . . Life calls to be attempted!
The boundless air opens and shuts my book,
Bravely the waves in powder from the rocks
Burst! Take to your wings, dazzled pages!
Break, waves! Break with delighted water
This peaceful roof where sails were pecking!

ILLUSTRATION 13

The Movie Set

NATHANAEL WEST

Faye moved out of the San Berdoo the day after the funeral. Ted didn't know where she had gone and was getting up the courage to call Mrs. Jenning when he saw her from the window of his office. She was dressed in the costume of a Napoleonic vivandière. By the time he got the window open, she had almost turned the corner of the building. He shouted for her to wait. She waved, but when he got downstairs she was gone.

From her dress, he was sure that she was working in the picture called "Waterloo." He asked a studio policeman where the company was shooting and was told on the back lot. He started toward it at once. A platoon of cuirassiers, big men mounted on gigantic horses, went by. He knew that they must be headed for the same set and followed them. They broke into a gallop and he was soon outdistanced.

The sun was very hot. His eyes and throat were choked with the dust thrown up by the horses' hooves and his head throbbed. The only bit of shade he could find was under an ocean liner made of painted canvas with real life boats hanging from its davits. He stood in its narrow shadow for a while, then went on toward a great forty-foot papier màché sphinx that loomed up in the distance. He had to cross a desert to reach it, a desert that was continually being made larger by a fleet of trucks dumping white sand. He had gone only a few feet when a man with a megaphone ordered him off.

He skirted the desert, making a wide turn to the right, and came to a Western street with a plank sidewalk. On the porch of the "Last Chance Saloon" was a rocking chair. He sat down on it and lit a cigarette.

From there he could see a jungle compound with a water buffalo tethered to the side of a conical grass hut. Every few seconds the animal groaned musically. Suddenly an Arab charged by on a white stallion. He shouted at the man, but got no answer. A little while later he saw a truck with a load of snow and several malamute dogs. He shouted again. The driver shouted something back, but didn't stop.

Throwing away his cigarette, he went through the swinging doors of the saloon. There was no back to the building and he found himself in a Paris street. He followed it to its end, coming out in a Romanesque courtyard. He

Nathanael West, *The Day of the Locust*, Chapter 18 (New York: New Directions Publishing Corporation, 1939). Reprinted by permission of New Directions Publishing and Laurence Pollinger Limited.

heard voices a short distance away and went toward them. On a lawn of fiber, a group of men and women in riding costume were picnicking. They were eating cardboard food in front of a cellophane waterfall. He started toward them to ask his way but was stopped by a man who scowled and held up a sign—"Quiet, Please, We're Shooting." When Tod took another step forward, the man shook his fist threateningly.

Next he came to a small pond with large celluloid swans floating on it. Across one end was a bridge with a sign that read, "To Kamp Komfit." He crossed the bridge and followed a little path that ended at a Greek temple dedicated to Eros. The god himself lay face downward in a pile of old newspapers and bottles.

From the steps of the temple, he could see in the distance a road lined with Lombardy poplars. It was the one on which he had lost the cuirassiers. He pushed his way through a tangle of briars, old flats, and iron junk, skirting the skeleton of a Zeppelin, a bamboo stockade, an adobe fort, the wooden horse of Troy, a flight of baroque palace stairs that started in a bed of weeds and ended against the branches of an oak, part of the Fourteenth Street elevated station, a Dutch windmill, the bones of a dinosaur, the upper half of the Merrimac, a corner of a Mayan temple, until he finally reached the road.

He was out of breath. He sat down under one of the poplars on a rock made of brown plaster and took off his jacket. There was a cool breeze blowing and he soon felt more comfortable.

He had lately begun to think not only of Goya and Daumier but also of certain Italian artists of the seventeenth and eighteenth centuries, of Salvator Rosa, Francesco Guardi and Monsu Desiderio, the painters of Decay and Mystery. Looking down hill now, he could see compositions that might have actually been arranged from the Calabrian work of Rosa. There were partially demolished buildings and broken monuments, half hidden by great, tortured trees, whose exposed roots writhed dramatically in the arid ground, and by shrubs that carried, not flowers or berries, but armories of spikes, hooks and swords.

For Guardi and Desiderio there were bridges which bridged nothing, sculpture in trees, palaces that seemed of marble until a whole stone portico began to flap in the light breeze. And there were figures as well. A hundred yards from where Tod was sitting a man in a derby hat leaned drowsily against the gilded poop of a Venetian barque and peeled an apple. Still farther on, a charwoman on a stepladder was scrubbing with soap and water the face of a Buddha thirty feet high.

He left the road and climbed across the spine of the hill to look down on the other side. From there he could see a ten-acre field of cockleburs spotted with clumps of sunflowers and wild gum. In the center of the field was a gigantic pile of sets, flats and props. While he watched, a ten-ton truck added another load to it. This was the final dumping ground. He thought of Janvier's "Sargasso Sea." Just as that imaginary body of water was a history of civilization in the form of a marine junkyard, the studio lot was one in the form of a dream dump. A Sargasso of the imagination! And the dump grew continually, for there wasn't a dream afloat somewhere which wouldn't sooner or later turn up on it, having first been made photographic by plaster, canvas, lath and paint. Many boats sink and never reach the Sargasso, but no dream ever entirely disappears. Somewhere it troubles some unfortunate person and some day, when that person has been sufficiently troubled, it will be reproduced on the lot.

When he saw a red glare in the sky and heard the rumble of cannon, he knew it must be Waterloo. From around a bend in the road trotted several cavalry regiments. They wore casques and chest armor of black cardboard and carried long horse pistols in their saddle holsters. They were Victor Hugo's soldiers. He had worked on some of the drawings for their uniforms himself, following carefully the descriptions in "Les Miserables."

He went in the direction they took. Before long he was passed by the men of Lefebvre-Desnouttes, followed by a regiment of gendarmes d'élite, several companies of chasseurs of the guard and a flying detachment of Rimbaud's lancers.

They must be moving up for the disastrous attack on La Haite Santée. He hadn't read the scenario and wondered if it had rained yesterday. Would Grouchy or Blucher arrive? Grotenstein, the producer, might have changed it.

The sound of cannon was becoming louder all the time and the red fan in the sky more intense. He could smell the sweet, pungent odor of blank powder. It might be over before he could get there. He started to run. When he topped a rise after a sharp bend in the road, he found a great plain below him covered with early nineteenth-century troops, wearing all the gay and elaborate uniforms that used to please him so much when he was a child and spent long hours looking at the soldiers in an old dictionary. At the far end of the field, he could see an enormous hump around which the English and their allies were gathered. It was Mont St. Jean and they were getting ready to defend it gallantly. It wasn't quite finished, however, and swarmed with grips, property men, set dressers, carpenters and painters.

Tod stood near a eucalyptus tree to watch, concealing himself behind a sign that read, " 'Waterloo'—A Charles H. Grotenstein Production." Nearby a youth in a carefully torn horse guard's uniform was being rehearsed in his lines by one of the assistant directors.

"Vive l'Empereur!" the young man shouted, then clutched his breast and fell forward dead. The assistant director was a hard man to please and made him do it over and over again.

In the center of the plain, the battle was going ahead briskly. Things looked tough for the British and their allies. The Prince of Orange commanding the center, Hill the right and Picton the left wing, were being pressed hard by the veteran French. The desperate and intrepid Prince was in an especially bad spot. Tod heard him cry hoarsely above the din of battle, shouting to the Hollande-Belgians, "Nassau! Brunswick! Never retreat!" Nevertheless, the retreat began. Hill, too, fell back. The French killed General Picton with a ball through the head and he returned to his dressing room. Alten was put to the sword and also retired. The colors of the Lunenberg battalion, borne by a prince of the family of Deux-Ponts, were captured by a famous child star in the uniform of a Parisian drummer boy. The Scotch Grays were destroyed and went to change into another uniform. Ponsonby's heavy dragoons were also cut to ribbons, Mr. Grotenstein would have a large bill to pay at the Western Costume Company.

Neither Napoleon nor Wellington was to be seen. In Wellington's absence, one of the assistant directors, a Mr. Crane, was in command of the allies. He reinforced his center with one of Chasse's brigades and one of Wincke's. He supported these with infantry from Brunswick, Welsh foot, Devon yeomanry and Hanoverian light horse with oblong leather caps and flowing plumes of horsehair.

For the French, a man in a checked cap ordered Milhaud's cuirassiers to carry Mont St. Jean. With their sabers in their teeth and their pistols in their hands, they charged. It was a fearful sight.

The man in the checked cap was making a fatal error. Mont St. Jean was unfinished. The paint was not yet dry and all the struts were not in place. Because of the thickness of the cannon smoke, he had failed to see that the hill was still being worked on by property men, grips and carpenters.

It was the classic mistake, Tod realized, the same one Napoleon had made. Then it had been wrong for a different reason. The Emperor had ordered the cuirassiers to charge Mont St. Jean not knowing that a deep ditch was hidden at its foot to trap his heavy cavalry. The result had been disaster for the French; the beginning of the end.

This time the same mistake had a different outcome. Waterloo instead of being the end of the Grand Army, resulted in a draw. Neither side won, and it would have to be fought over again the next day. Big losses, however, were sustained by the insurance company in workmen's compensation. The man in the checked cap was sent to the dog house by Mr. Grotenstein just as Napoleon was sent to St. Helena.

When the front rank of Milhaud's heavy division started up the slope of Mont St. Jean, the hill collapsed. The noise was terrific. Nails screamed with agony as they pulled out of joists. The sound of ripping canvas was like that of little children whimpering. Lath and scantling snapped as though they were brittle bones. The whole hill folded like an enormous umbrella and covered Napoleon's army with painted cloth.

It turned into a rout. The victors of Bersina, Leipsic, Austerlitz, fled like schoolboys who had broken a pane of glass. "Sauve qui peut!" they cried, or, rather, "Scram!"

The armies of England and her allies were too deep in scenery to flee. They had to wait for the carpenters and ambulances to come up. The men of the gallant Seventy-Fifth Highlanders were lifted out of the wreck with block and tackle. They were carted off by the stretcher-bearers, still clinging bravely to their claymores.

7

Expression
and Symbolism

The writings of two modern philosophers, Rudolf Arnheim and Susanne Langer—appear in this chapter. Both these thinkers are important in aesthetics, but their works are difficult to classify. Their interest is the psychology and philosophy of art, and Arnheim's views of art, in particular, are derived partly from a Gestalt theory of perception. According to this theory, one does not perceive discrete sensations and piece them together to form perceptual experiences. Nor is it the case that the mind is constitutive of the forms of our experiences as Kant suggests. Rather, each of our individual perceptions is a picture, or a "gestalt," of a total experiential view. For example, when one perceives a room, one experiences a presentational totality of three-dimensional colored objects interrelated with each other in a space-time continuum. Moreover, one never merely perceives a room and then superimposes one's feelings on the perception according to Arnheim. Nor are the feelings and emotions which one experiences simply one's personal intentional projections upon a perception. Rather—meanings, emotions, and symbols are embodied in the presentation of the perception. The perceived room is experienced as "mine," "strange," "fearful," and so on. In other words, one perceives emotionally and symbolically just as one perceives spatially and temporally, and the entire pattern of feelings and meanings is embodied in the perception or gestalt of the room. Arnheim calls this pattern "expressiveness," and he claims that expressiveness—like color, sound, shape, and space—is part of the structure of every perceived or experienced phenomenon.

Artists, according to Arnheim, are highly sensitive to the expressive qualities of experience, and try to capture this expressiveness in a work of art, to communicate it through an artwork's complex patterns and structure. The work of art, then, symbolizes expressiveness (which is part of every experience). The symbolism is not achieved, according to Arnheim, through the use of contrived conventional symbols, but rather because expressiveness is embodied in the subject matter, the form, the content, and the whole structure of the work of art. And great works of art—such as Michelangelo's *Creation of Man* (Illustration 14)—achieve this expressive symbolism in the most direct and integrated manner.

Susanne Langer focuses on art's unique ability to capture and symbolize nonverbal human feelings. Subjective inner emotions and feelings, according to Langer, have structure just as perceptions. But the structure of subjective feelings is difficult if not impossible to describe. Thus Langer distinguishes two kinds of symbolism. Discursive symbols are those present in language and discourse. Presentational symbols are nonverbal representations of what is itself inarticulate or nonverbal: the emotions and feelings which accompany every perceptual and inner subjective experience. A work of art, according to Langer, is a presentational symbol or an expressive form, because art represents symbolically but nondiscursively the form of human feelings and emotions.

Langer distinguishes the presentational symbol, which *is* the work of art, from the devisive *use* of symbols in art. This difference is clearly seen in Herbert Read's analysis of the symbolism in Hieronymus Bosch's *The Garden of Earthly Delights* (Illustration 15), the concluding reading in this chapter.

Whether the theories of Arnheim or Langer can be classified as mimetic, as expressive, or as unique ways to analyze art phenomena is left to the judgment of the reader. But the important contributions of these theorists to the philosophy and psychology of art cannot be overlooked.

Art and Visual Perception

RUDOLF ARNHEIM

All perceptual qualities have generality. We see redness, roundness, smallness, remoteness, swiftness, embodied in individual examples, but conveying a *kind* of experience, rather than a uniquely particular one. This is equally true for dynamics. We see compactness, striving, twisting, expanding, yielding—generalities again, but in this case not limited to what the eye sees. Dynamic qualities are structural; they are experienced in sound, in touch, in muscular sensations, as well as in vision. What is more, they also describe the nature and behavior of the human mind, and they do so quite compellingly. The aggressiveness of lightning comes with the swift zigzag of its descent, and sneakiness comes with the locomotions of a snake whenever these motions are seen as more than geometrically definable curves. Colors serve to symbolize human temperaments, as they have done in many cultures, only when

Rudolph Arnheim, *Art and Visual Perception* (Berkeley: University of California Press, 1974); selections from Chapter 10. Reprinted by permission.

these colors are perceived as dynamic. And the dynamic differences between Romanesque and Gothic architecture translate themselves automatically into states of mind characterizing the corresponding cultural periods.

Thus, *we define expression as modes of organic or inorganic behavior displayed in the dynamic appearance of perceptual objects or events.* The structural properties of these modes are not limited to what is grasped by the external senses; they are conspicuously active in the behavior of the human mind, and they are used metaphorically to characterize an infinity of non-sensory phenomena: low morale or the high cost of living, the spiraling of prices, the lucidity of argument, the compactness of resistance. . . .

I shall mention in passing that the theory of empathy has afflicted generations of aestheticians with a host of pseudoproblems. One asked: Are the feelings expressed in sights and sounds those of the artist who created them or those of the recipient? Does one have to be in a melancholy mood in order to produce, perform, or apprehend a melancholy composition? Can "emotions" be expressed in a Bach fugue or a painting by Mondrian? These and other similar questions become incomprehensible once one has understood that expression resides in perceptual qualities of the stimulus pattern.

Expression Embedded in Structure

William James was less certain that body and mind have nothing intrinsically in common. "I cannot help remarking that the disparity between motions and feelings, on which these authors lay so much stress, is somewhat less absolute than at first sight it seems. Not only temporal succession, but such attributes as intensity, volume, simplicity or complication, smooth or impeded change, rest or agitation, are habitually predicated of both physical facts and mental facts." Evidently James reasoned that although body and mind are different media—the one being material, the other not—they might still resemble each other in certain structural properties.

This point was insisted upon by gestalt psychologists. Max Wertheimer in particular asserted that the perception of expression is much too immediate and compelling to be explainable merely as a product of learning. When we watch a dancer, the sadness or happiness of the mood seems to be directly inherent in the movements themselves. Wertheimer concluded that this was true because formal factors in the dance reproduced identical factors in the mood. What he meant may be illustrated by reference to an experiment by Jane Binney. Members of a college dance group were asked individually to give improvisations of such subjects as sadness, strength, or night. The dancers' performances showed much agreement. For example, in the representation of sadness the movement was slow and confined to a narrow range. It was mostly curved in shape and showed little tension. The direction was indefinite, changing, wavering; and the body seemed to yield passively to the force of gravity rather than being propelled by its own initiative. It will be admitted that the psychical mood of sadness has a similar pattern. In a depressed person the mental processes are slow and rarely go beyond matters closely related to immediate experiences and momentary interests. All his thinking and striving displays softness and lack of energy. He shows little determination, and activity is often controlled by outside forces.

To be sure, there is a traditional way of representing sadness in a dance, and the performances of the students may have been influenced by it. What counts, however, is that the movements, whether spontaneously invented or copied from other dancers, exhibited a formal structure so strikingly similar to that of the intended mood. And since such visual qualities as speed, shape, or direction are immediately accessible, it seems legitimate to assume that they are the carriers of an expression directly comprehensible to the eye. . . .

We are beginning to see that perceptual expression does not necessarily relate to a mind "behind it." This is true even for responses to human behavior. Köhler has pointed out that people normally respond to external behavior in itself, rather than thinking of it explicitly as a mere reflection of mental attitudes. People perceive the slow, listless, "droopy" movements of one person as contrasted to the brisk, straight, vigorous movements of another, but do not necessarily go beyond the appearance to think of psychic weariness or alertness behind it. Weariness and alertness are contained in the physical behavior itself; they are not distinguished in any essential way from the weariness of slowly floating tar or the energetic ring of the telephone bell. It is true, of course, that during a crucial conversation one person may be greatly concerned with trying to read the other's thoughts and feelings through what can be seen in his face and gestures. "What is he up to? How is he taking it?" But in such circumstances one clearly goes beyond what is apparent in the perception of expression itself.

From here it takes only one small further step to acknowledge that visual expression resides in any articulately shaped object or event. A steep rock, a willow tree, the colors of a sunset, the cracks in a wall, a tumbling leaf, a flowing fountain, and in fact a mere line or color, or the dance of an abstract shape on the movie screen have as much expression as the human body, and may serve the artist equally well. In some ways they serve him even better, for the human body is a particularly complex pattern, not easily reduced to the simplicity of shape and motion that transmits compelling expression. In addition, it is overloaded with non-visual associations. . . .

If one thinks of expression as something reserved for human behavior, one can account for the expression perceived in nature only as the result of the "pathetic fallacy"—a notion apparently introduced by John Ruskin and intended to describe, say, the sadness of weeping willows as a figment of empathy, anthropomorphism, primitive animism. However, if expression is an inherent characteristic of perceptual patterns, its manifestations in the human figure are but a special case of a more general phenomenon. The comparison of an object's expression with a human state of mind is a secondary process. The willow is not "sad" because it looks like a sad person. Rather, because the shape, direction, and flexibility of the branches convey passive hanging, a comparison with the structurally similar state of mind and body that we call sadness imposes itself secondarily. . . .

The Priority of Expression

Let me emphasize once more that in our particular civilization we have come to think of perception as the recording of shapes, distances, hues, motions. The awareness of these measurable characteristics is actually a fairly late accomplishment of the human mind. Even in twentieth-century Western man, it presupposes special conditions. It is the attitude of the scientist and the engineer, or of the salesman who estimates the size of a customer's waist, the shade of a lipstick, the weight of a suitcase. But when I sit in front of a fireplace and watch the flames, I do not normally register certain shades of red, various degrees of brightness, geometrically defined shapes moving at such and such a speed. I see the graceful play of aggressive tongues, flexible striving, lively color. The face of a person is more readily perceived and remembered as being alert, tense, and concentrated than it is as being tri-angularly shaped, having slanted eyebrows, straight lips, and so on. This priority of expression, although somewhat modified in adults by a scientifically oriented education, is striking in children and primitives, as has been shown by Werner and Köhler. The profile of a mountain is soft or threateningly harsh; a blanket thrown over a chair is twisted, sad, tired.

The priority of physiognomic properties should not come as a surprise. Our senses are not self-contained recording devices operating for their own sake. They have been developed by the organism as an aid in reacting to the environment, and the organism is primarily interested in the forces active around it—their place, strength, direction. Hostility and friendliness are at-tributes of forces. And the perceived impact of forces makes for what we call expression.

If expression is the primary content of vision in daily life, the same should be all the more true of the way the artist looks at the world. The expressive qualities are his means of communication. They capture his atten-tion, they enable him to understand and interpret his experiences, and they determine the form patterns he creates. Therefore the training of art students should be expected to consist basically in sharpening their sense of these qualities, and in teaching them to look to expression as the guiding criterion for every stroke of the pencil, brush, or chisel. In fact many good art teachers do precisely this. But in other cases the student's spontaneous sensitivity to expression not only is not developed further, it is even impaired and sup-pressed. There is, for example, an old-fashioned but not extinct way of teaching students to draw from the model by asking them to establish the exact length and direction of contour lines, the relative position of points, the shape of masses. In other words, students are to concentrate on the geometric-technical qualities of what they see. In its modern version this method consists in urging the young artist to think of the model or of a freely invented design as a configuration of masses, planes, direction. Again interest is focused on geometric technical qualities. . . .

It will be evident that what is advocated here is not so-called "self-expression." The method of self-expression plays down, or even annihilates, the theme to be represented. It recommends a passive, "projective" pouring-out of what is felt inside. On the contrary, the method discussed here requires active, disciplined concentration of all organizing powers upon the expression found in one's vision of the world. . . .

Symbolism in Art

All perceptual qualities have generality. I mentioned this earlier, and I intended the statement to mean that to some extent we see redness in every red spot or speed in every fast movement. The same is true for expression. When Picasso conveys to us in a painting the gentle ways in which a mother guides the first steps of her unsteadily walking child, we see gentleness as a general quality exemplified in a particular case. In this sense it is valid to say that Picasso's picture symbolizes gentleness. In fact, for our purpose, the terms expression and symbolization can be used interchangeably. The example also suggests that the task of expressing or symbolizing a universal content through a particular image is carried out not only by the formal pattern, but by the subject matter as well, if there is one. . . .

In great works of art the deepest significance is transmitted to the eye with powerful directness by the perceptual characteristics of the compositional pattern. The "story" of Michelangelo's *Creation of Man,* on the ceiling of the Sistine Chapel in Rome (Figure 1), is understood by every reader of the book of Genesis. But even the story is modified in a way that makes it more comprehensible and impressive to the eye. The Creator, instead of breathing a living soul into the body of clay—a motif not easily translatable into an expressive pattern—reaches out toward the arm of Adam as though an animating spark, leaping from fingertip to fingertip, were transmitted from the maker to the creature. The bridge of the arm visually connects two separate worlds: the self-contained compactness of the mantle that encloses God and is given forward motion by the diagonal of his body; and the incomplete, flat slice of the earth, whose passivity is expressed in the backward slant of its contour. There is passivity also in the concave curve over which the body of Adam is molded. It is lying on the ground and enabled partly to rise by the attractive power of the approaching creator. The desire and potential capacity to get up and walk are indicated as a subordinate theme in the left leg, which also serves as a support of Adam's arm, unable to maintain itself freely like the energy-charged arm of God.

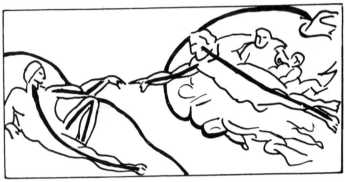

Figure 1.

Our analysis shows that the ultimate theme of the image, the idea of creation, is conveyed by what strikes the eye first and continues to organize the composition as we examine its details. The structural skeleton reveals the dynamic theme of the story. And since the pattern of transmitted, life-giving energy is not simply recorded by the sense of vision but presumably arouses in the mind a corresponding configuration of forces, the observer's reaction is more than a mere taking cognizance of an external object. The forces that characterize the meaning of the story come alive in the observer and produce the kind of stirring participation that distinguishes artistic experience from the detached acceptance of information.

What matters most is that the image does not just elucidate the meaning of the individual story presented in the work. The dynamic theme revealed by the compositional pattern is not limited to the biblical episode at hand, but is valid for any number of situations that may occur in the psychical and physical world. Not only is the perceptual pattern a means of understanding the story of the creation of man, but the story becomes a means of illustrating a kind of event that is universal and therefore abstract and therefore in need of being clad with flesh and blood so that the eye may see it.

Consequently, the visual form of a work of art is neither arbitrary nor a mere play of shapes and colors. It is indispensable as a precise interpreter of the idea the work is meant to express. Similarly, the subject matter is neither arbitrary nor unimportant. It is exactly correlated with the formal pattern to supply a concrete embodiment of an abstract theme. The kind of connoisseur who looks only for the pattern does as little justice to the work as the kind of layman who looks only for the subject matter. When Whistler called the portrait of his mother *Arrangement in Gray and Black,* he treated his picture as one-sidedly as someone who sees nothing in it but a dignified lady sitting in a chair. Neither the formal pattern nor the subject matter is the final content of the work of art. Both are instruments of artistic form. They serve to give body to an invisible universal.

Viewed in this fashion, traditional representational art leads without a break to the nonmimetic, "abstract" art of our century. Anyone who has grasped the abstraction in representational art will see the continuity, even though art ceases to depict objects of nature. In its own way, nonmimetic art does what art has always done. Each successful work presents a skeleton of forces whose meaning can be read as directly as that inherent in Michelangelo's story of the first man. Such "abstract" art is not "pure form," because we have discovered that even the simplest line expresses visible meaning and is therefore symbolic. It does not offer intellectual abstractions, because there is nothing more concrete than color, shape, and motion. It does not limit itself to the inner life of man, or to the unconscious, because for art the distinctions between the outer and the inner world and the conscious and the unconscious mind are artificial. The human mind receives, shapes, and interprets its image of the outer world with all its conscious and unconscious powers, and the realm of the unconscious could never enter our experience without the reflection of perceivable things. There is no way of presenting the one without the other. But the nature of the outer and inner worlds can be reduced to a play of forces, and this "musical" approach is attempted by the misnamed abstract artists.

We do not know what the art of the future will look like. No one particular style is art's final climax. Every style is but one valid way of looking at style is art's final climax. Every style is but one valid way of looking at the world, one view of the holy mountain, which offers a different image from every place but can be seen as the same everywhere.

The Art Symbol
and the Symbol in Art

SUSANNE LANGER

The problems of semantics and logic seem to fit into one frame, those of feeling into another. But somewhere, of course, mentality has arisen from more primitive vital processes. Somehow they belong into one and the same scientific frame. I am scouting the possibility that *rationality arises as an elaboration of feeling.*

Such a hypothesis leads one, of course, to the possible forms of feeling, and raises the problem of how they can be conceived and abstractly handled. Every theoretical construction requires a model. Especially if you want to get into elaborate structures you have to have a model—not an instance, but a symbolic form that can be manipulated, to convey, or perhaps to hold, your conceptions.

Language is the symbolic form of rational thought. It is more than that, but at least it can be fairly well pared down to abstract the elements of such thought and cognition. The structure of discourse expresses the forms of rational cogitation; that is why we call such thinking "discursive."

But discursive symbols offer no apt model of primitive forms of feeling. There has been a radical change—a special organization—in the making of rationality, perhaps under the influence of very specialized perception, perhaps under some other controlling condition. To express the forms of what might be called "unlogicized" mental life (a term we owe to Professor Henry M. Sheffer of Harvard), or what is usually called the "life of feeling," requires a different symbolic form.

This form, I think, is characteristic of art and is, indeed, the essence and measure of art. If this be so, then a work of art is a symbolic form in another way than the one (or ones) usually conceded to it. We commonly think of a work of art as representing something, and of its symbolic function, therefore, as representation. But this is not what I mean; not even secret or disguised representation. Many works represent nothing whatever. A building, a pot, a tune is usually beautiful without intentionally representing anything; and its unintentional representation may be found in bad and ugly pieces too. But if it is beautiful it is expressive; what it expresses is not an idea of some other thing, but an idea of a feeling. Representational works, if they are good art, are so for the same reason as non-representational ones. They have more than one symbolic function—representation, perhaps after two kinds, and also artistic expression, which is presentation of ideas of feeling.

There are many difficulties connected with the thesis that a work of art is primarily an expression of feeling—an "expression" in the logical sense, presenting the fabric of sensibility, emotion, and the strains of more concerted cerebration, for our impersonal cognition—that is, *in abstracto*. This sort of symbolization is the prime office of works of art, by virtue of which I call a work of art an *expressive form*. . . .

As a work of art is an expressive form somewhat like a symbol, and has import which is something like meaning, so it makes a logical abstraction, but not in the familiar way of genuine symbols—perhaps, indeed, a pseudo-abstraction. The best way to understand all these pseudo-semantics is to consider what a work of art is and does, and then compare it with language, and its doings with what language (or any genuine symbolism) does.

The expressive form, or art symbol, is, as I said before, the work of art itself, as it meets the eye (let us, for simplicity's sake, stay in the realm of pictorial art). It is the visible form, the apparition created out of paint deployed on a ground. The paint and the ground themselves disappear. One does not see a picture as a piece of spotted canvas, any more than one sees a screen with shadows on it in a movie. Whether there be things and persons in the picture or not, it presents volumes in a purely created space. These volumes define and organize the pictorial space which they are, in fact, creating; the purely visual space seems to be alive with their balanced or strained interactions. The lines that divide them (which may be physically drawn, or implied) create a rhythmic unity, for what they divide they also relate, to the point of complete integration. If a picture is successful it presents us with something quite properly, even though metaphorically, called "living form." . . .

A work of art is such an individual form given directly to perception. But it is a special kind of form, since it seems to be more than a visual phenomenon—seems, indeed, to have a sort of life, or be imbued with feeling, or somehow, without being a genuine practical object, yet present the beholder with more than an arrangement of sense data. It carries with it something that people have sometimes called a quality (Clive Bell called "significant form" a quality), sometimes an emotional content, or the emotional tone of the work, or simply its life. This is what I mean by *artistic import*. It is not one of the qualities to be distinguished in the work, though our perception of it has the immediacy of qualitative experience; artistic import is *expressed*, somewhat as meaning is expressed in a genuine symbol, yet not exactly so. The analogy is strong enough to make it legitimate, even though easily misleading, to call the work of art the art symbol.

The difference, however, between an art symbol and a genuine symbol is of great interest and importance, for they illuminate the relations that obtain between many kinds of symbols, or things that have been so called, and show up the many levels on which symbolic and pseudo-symbolic functions may lie. I think a study of artistic expressiveness shows up a need of a more adaptable, that is to say more general, definition of "symbol" than the one accepted in current semantics and analytical philosophy. But we had better defer this problem to a later point. Let us, for the time being, call a *genuine symbol* whatever meets the strictest definition. Here is a definition offered by Ernest Nagel, in an article called "Symbolism and Science": "By a symbol I understand any occurrence (or type of occurrence), usually linguistic in status, which is taken to signify something else by way of tacit or explicit conventions or rules of language."

A word, say a familiar common noun, is a symbol of this sort. I would say that it conveys a concept, and refers to, or denotes, whatever exemplifies that concept. The word "man" conveys what we call the concept of "man," and denotes any being that exemplifies the concept—i.e., any man.

Now, words—our most familiar and useful symbols—are habitually used not in isolation, but in complex concepts of states of affairs, rather than isolated things, and refer to facts or possibilities or even impossibilities: those bigger units are descriptions and statements and other forms of *discourse*.

In discourse, another function of symbols comes into play, that is present but not very evident in the use of words simply to name things. This further function is the expression of ideas *about* things. A thing cannot be asserted by a name, only mentioned. As soon as you make an assertion you are symbolizing some sort of relation between concepts of things, or maybe things and properties, such as: "The grapes are sour." "All men are born equal." "I hate logic." Assertions, of course, need not be true—that is, they need not refer us to facts.

That brings us to the second great office of symbols, which is not to refer to things and communicate facts, but to express ideas; and this, in turn, involves a deeper psychological process, the formulation of ideas, or conception itself. Conception—giving form and connection, clarity and proportion to our impressions, memories, and objects of judgment—is the beginning of all rationality. Conception itself contains the elementary principles of knowledge: that an object of thought keeps its identity (as Aristotle put it, "A = A"), that it may stand in many relations to other things, that alternative possibilities exclude each other, and one decision entails another. Conception is the first requirement for thought.

This basic intellectual process of conceiving things in connection belongs, I think, to the same deep level of the mind as symbolization itself. That is the level where imagination is born. Animal intelligence or response to signs, of course, goes further back than that. The process of symbolic presentation is the beginning of human mentality, "mind" in a strict sense. Perhaps that beginning occurs at the stage of neural development where speech originates, and with speech the supreme talent of *envisagement*.

Response to stimuli, adaptation to conditions may occur without any envisagement of anything. Thought arises only where ideas have taken shape, and actual or possible conditions imagined. The word "imagined" contains the key to a new world: the image. I think the popular notion of an image as a replica of a sense impression has made epistemologists generally miss the most important character of images, which is that they are symbolic. That is why, in point of sensuous character, they may be almost indescribably vague, fleeting, fragmentary, or distorted; they may be sensuously altogether unlike what they represent. We think of mathematical relations in images that are just arbitrarily posited symbols; but these symbols are our mathematical images. They may be visual or auditory or what not, but functionally they are images, that articulate the logical relations we contemplate by means of them.

The great importance of reference and communication by means of symbols has led semanticists to regard these uses as the defining properties of symbols—that is, to think of a symbol as essentially a sign which stands for something else and is used to represent that thing in discourse. This preoccupation has led them to neglect, or even miss entirely, the more primitive function of symbols, which is to formulate experience as something imaginable in the first place—to fix entities, and formulate facts and the fact-like elements of thought called "fantasies." This function is *articulation*. Symbols articulate ideas. Even such arbitrarily assigned symbols as mere names serve this purpose, for whatever is named becomes an entity in thought. Its unitary symbol automatically carves it out as a unit in the world pattern.

Now let us return to the Art Symbol. I said before that it is a symbol in a somewhat special sense, because it performs some symbolic functions, but not all; especially, it does not stand for something else, nor refer to anything that exists apart from it. According to the usual definition of "symbol," a work of art should not be classed as a symbol at all. But that usual definition overlooks the greatest intellectual value and, I think, the prime office of symbols—their power of formulating experience, and presenting it objectively for contemplation, logical intuition, recognition, understanding. That is articulation, or logical expression. And this function every good work of art does perform. It formulates the appearance of feeling, of subjective experience, the character of so-called "inner life," which discourse—the normal use of words—is peculiarly unable to articulate, and which therefore we can only refer to in a general and quite superficial way. The actual felt process of life, the tensions interwoven and shifting from moment to moment, the flowing and slowing, the drive and directedness of desires, and above all the rhythmic continuity of our selfhood, defies the expressive power of discursive symbolism. The myriad forms of subjectivity, the infinitely complex sense of life, cannot be rendered linguistically, that is, stated. But they are precisely what comes to light in a good work of art (not necessarily a "masterpiece"; there are thousands of works that are good art without being exalted achievements). A work of art is an expressive form, and vitality, in all its manifestations from sheer sensibility to the most elaborate phases of awareness and emotion, is what it may express.

But what is meant by saying it does not connote a concept or denote its instances? What I mean is that a genuine symbol, such as a word, is only a sign; in appreciating its meaning our interest reaches beyond it to the concept. The word is just an instrument. Its meaning lies elsewhere, and once we have grasped its connotation or identified something as its denotation we do not need the word any more. But a work of art does not point us to a meaning beyond its own presence. What is expressed cannot be grasped apart from the sensuous or poetic form that expresses it. In a work of art we have the direct presentation of a feeling, not a sign that points to it. That is why "significant form" is a misleading and confusing term: an Art Symbol does not signify, but only articulate and present its emotive content; hence the peculiar impression one always gets that feeling is in a beautiful and integral form. The work seems to be imbued with the emotion or mood or other vital experience that it expresses. That is why I call it an "expressive form," and call that which it formulates for us not its meaning, but its *import*. The import of art is perceived as something in the work, articulated by it but not further abstracted; as the import of a myth or a true metaphor does not exist apart from its imaginative expression.

The work as a whole is the image of feeling, which may be called the Art Symbol. It is a single organic composition, which means that its elements are not independent constituents, expressive, in their own right, of various emotional ingredients, as words are constituents of discourse, and have meanings in their own right, which go to compose the total meaning of the discourse. Language is a *symbolism*, a system of symbols with definable though fairly elastic meanings, and rules of combination whereby larger units—phrases, sentences, whole speeches—may be compounded, expressing similarly built-up ideas. Art, contrariwise, is not a symbolism. The elements in a work are always newly created with the total image, and although it is possible to analyze what they contribute to the image, it is not possible to assign them any of its import apart from the whole. That is characteristic of organic form. The import of a work of art is its "life," which, like actual life, is an indivisible phenomenon. Who could say how much of a natural organism's life is in the lungs, how much in the legs, or how much more life would be added to us if we were given a lively tail to wave? The Art Symbol is a single symbol, and its import is not compounded of partial symbolic values. It is, I think, what Cecil Day Lewis means by "the poetic image," and what some painters, valiantly battling against popular misconceptions, call "the absolute image." It is the objective form of life-feeling in terms of space, or musical passage, or other fictive and plastic medium.

At last we come to the issue proposed in the title of this lecture. If the Art Symbol is a single, indivisible symbol, and its import is never compounded of contributive cargoes of import, what shall we make of the fact that many artists incorporate symbols in their works? Is it a mistake to interpret certain elements in poems or pictures, novels or dances, as symbols? Are the symbolists, imagists, surrealists, and the countless religious painters and poets before them all mistaken—everybody out of step except Johnnie?

Symbols certainly do occur in art, and in many, if not most, cases contribute notably to the work that incorporates them. Some artists work with a veritable riot of symbols; from the familiar halo of sacrosanct personages to the terrible figures of the *Guernica*, from the obvious rose of womanhood or the lily of chastity to the personal symbols of T.S. Eliot, sometimes concentric as a nest of tables, painters and poets have used symbols. . . .

All such elements, however, are genuine symbols; they have meanings, and the meanings may be stated. Symbols in art connote holiness, or sin, or rebirth, womanhood, love, tyranny, and so forth. These meanings enter into the work of art as elements, creating and articulating its organic form, just as its subject-matter—fruit in a platter, horses on a beach, a slaughtered ox, or a weeping Magdalen—enter into its construction. Symbols used in art lie on a different semantic level from the work that contains them. Their meanings are not part of its import, but elements in the form that has import, the expressive form. The meanings of incorporated symbols may lend richness, intensity, repetition or reflection or a transcendent unrealism, perhaps an entirely new balance to the work itself. But they function in the normal manner of symbols: they mean something beyond what they present in themselves. . . .

The use of symbols in art is, in fine, a principle or construction—a device, in the most general sense of that word, "device." But there is a difference, often missed by theorists, between principles of construction and principles of art. The principles of art are few: the creation of what might be termed "an apparition" (this term would bear much discussion, but we have no time for it, and I think any one conversant with the arts knows what I mean), the achievement of organic unity or "livingness," the articulation of feeling. These principles of art are wholly exemplified in every work that merits the name of "art" at all, even though it be not great or in the current sense "original" (the anonymous works of ancient potters, for instance, were rarely original designs). Principles of construction, on the other hand, are very many; the most important have furnished our basic devices, and given rise to the Great Traditions of art. Representation in painting, diatonic harmony in music, metrical versification in poetry are examples of such major devices of composition. They are exemplified in thousands of works; yet they are not indispensable. Painting can eschew representation, music can be atonal, poetry can be poetry without any metrical scaffold. . . .

In summary, then, it may be said that the difference between the Art Symbol and the symbol used in art is a difference not only of function but of kind. Symbols occuring in art are symbols in the usual sense, though of all degrees of complexity, from simplest directness to extreme indirectness, from singleness to deep interpenetration, from perfect lucidity to the densest overdetermination. They have meanings, in the full sense that any semanticist would accept. And those meanings, as well as the images that convey them, enter into the work of art as elements in its composition. They serve to create the work, the expressive form.

The art symbol, on the other hand, *is* the expressive form. It is not a symbol in the full familiar sense, for it does not convey something beyond itself. Therefore it cannot strictly be said to have a meaning; what it does have is import. It is a symbol in a special and derivative sense, because it does not fulfill all the functions of a true symbol: it formulates and objectifies experience for direct intellectual perception, or intuition, but it does not abstract a concept for discursive thought. Its import is seen in it; not, like the meaning of a genuine symbol, by means of it but separable from the sign. The symbol in art is a metaphor, an image with overt or covert literal signification; the art symbol is the absolute image—the image of what otherwise would be irrational, as it is literally ineffable: direct awareness, emotion, vitality, personal identity—life lived and felt, the matrix of mentality.

Animadversions on Imitation and Expression

ELISEO VIVAS

Before considering the two functions of literature that go under the rubric, "the theory of imitation" and "the theory of expression," it is desirable to lay down what I take to be a satisfactory solution of the problem of the function of literature. We want to know what is the function of poetry—for I shall use the term "poetry" to refer to imaginative literature in general, whether in prose or verse. But we do not wish to know the many uses to which it has been put, but its intrinsic use. And we shall know that we have found it, when we come upon a function which poetry alone and no other human product can perform. I cannot argue this assumption—it would be the subject of several essays. Let me only say that the assumption means that the arts are a basic mode of human activity for which there can be no substitute.

It was Plato, in Western philosophy, who started what he referred to as "the ancient feud between philosophy and poetry." He challenged the poet to show reasons why he should not be kept out of the ideal republic. Arraigned before this stern judge, the poet was lost before his defense began. Plato gave a higher primacy to the truth than most philosophers do, and his distrust of poets sprang from the fact that their products were lies twice removed from the truth. For the poet was an imitator of imitations. The crime was compounded by the fact that Homer and his fellow poets were what today we might think of as writers of *Olympus Confidentials*, the spreaders of scurrilous tales about the Gods.

This is a well-known story. I remind you of it in order to call to your attention the fact that it was Plato who defined the terms of all future philosophizing about the arts. It would not be altogether false, nor would it take great ingenuity, were we to interpret the history of Western aesthetics as an effort to justify or to expose the error of Plato's indictment of poetry. And

Eliseo Vivas, "Animadversions on Imitation and Expression," *Journal of Aesthetics and Art Criticism* 19 (1961), pp. 425–432.

the first man to make the effort was Aristotle, a man quite different in temperament from his teacher, but at least in terms of influence, just as great.

Aristotle did not address himself explicitly to Plato's indictment. But in the eighth book of the *Politics* and in the *Poetics* he met Plato's criticism of poetry. In the *Politics* he asserted that music—and we should remember that his use of the term was wider than ours—should be part of the education of the young, because of three benefits: the first is that it forms character; the second is that it purges the emotions; and the third, that it gives pleasure. On this account, it would seem as if Aristotle was not interested in showing that poetry can give us knowledge. But by defining poetry in terms of imitation, his followers were forced to face the problem of truth. For of an imitation it is always meaningful to ask: How far does it depart from the thing it imitates? The word "truth" need not appear in the question, of course; but the question is clearly about the truth of the imitation.

One objection to the theory of imitation is so obvious and has been made so often that it does not deserve extended treatment. Interpret it in any way you like, it denies the creativity of the poet. This objection gains in force when we remember Aristotle's epistemology, which makes no room, as Kant's does, for the constitutive action of the mind in the act of perception and of knowledge. And it gains even more force when we remember how, in *De Anima*, Aristotle defined "imagination" as weakened sensation. What John Dewey used to call "the mirror theory of mind," makes Aristotle's theory radically realistic and forces him by implication to deny the creative factor that the poet brings to the act of making. But the denial of creativity is not only a serious defect in itself, it also confines the functions of poetry to the formation of character, to purgation and to pleasure—objectives for which means can easily be found that are superior to poetry.

The problem of truth comes into the *Poetics* by another route. I refer to the well known passage in Chapter IX, in which Aristotle contrasts poetry with history. In the following quotation I use Gerald Else's translation, to be found in his admirable commentary, *Aristotle's Poetics: The Argument*. The passage is the following:

> . . . In fact . . . the writing of poetry is a more philosophical activity, and one to be taken more seriously, than the writing of history; for poetry tells us rather the universals, history the particulars. "Universal" means what kinds of things a certain kind of person will say or do in accordance to probability or necessity, which is what poetic composition aims at, tacking on names afterwards; while "particular" is what Alcibiades did or had done to him.

. . . Important as is the passage from the *Poetics* regarding the relation of poetry to history, because it reveals Aristotle's defective conception of the nature of poetry, it is even more important because it shows that while he disagrees with Plato, his theory makes truth a component of poetry. On Aristotle's view it is not proper to ask, Did the action really happen? But it is proper to ask, Could it have happened? And it is here, let me say diffidently but unambiguously, that Aristotle gained a strangle-hold on poetic theory until almost our day, a hold from which not all astheticians and critics have managed to free themselves.

Let us see why the strangle-hold is fatal. Consider, first, that the object imitated and the imitating work of art are two distinct things, and each therefore is capable of being perceived separately from the other. I can look at the person *and* at the portrait, but on the theory of imitation I do not need the latter to see the former. But how does one decide the probability or necessity of a poem's action? The question suggests a difficulty which can be stated in several ways. The following is a clear enough formulation of it: How does the aesthetician and the critic define the probable and the necessary, in order to approve or disapprove of what the poet presents? Commenting on Chapter XXIV, Professor Else tells us that Aristotle meant by these terms "that which is physically possible under the ordinary laws of reality." And this indeed is what Aristotle seems to mean when we consider the central thrust, so to speak, of the *Poetics*, and reflect on what the term "imitation" seems to mean in the context.

But Aristotle gets into a serious difficulty when he recognizes that the poet does better if he presents us with a likely impossibility than with an unconvincing possibility. Let us see why. What is a likely impossibility? The criterion of such a strange creature cannot be the ordinary laws of reality; it is defined by what the reader or spectator will accept. And what he accepts in a work of art, if he is interested in art and not in something else, is what is contextually coherent. The reader will take anything as valid, within the work, during his reading or witnessing of it, if he reads with rapt attention, and if the whole, as it develops before his mind's eye, excludes external experience, because of its internal coherence. This is to say that in recognizing the fact that a likely impossibility is preferable to an unconvincing possibility, Aristotle has abandoned the principle of imitation and has fallen back on another—one I call "the intransitivity of experience," which is made possible by the coherence of the work. And the question is not whether under some other doctrine than that of the *Poetics*, the two could be made to go together, but whether in the *Poetics* as we have it, the two are compatible. It is of course true that Aristotle insists on the organic nature of the work of art. And that recognizing its organic nature, he makes room for an intransitive experience. But the point of my observation is that an object which is viewed intransitively, is not one that is viewed in terms of possibility, for the latter calls for a comparison between the object and something else—the ordinary laws of reality. . . .

It is, I conclude, as simple as this: In order to make the theory of imitation flexible enough to account for the complex data, Aristotle introduces the notion of likely improbability. But this notion can only be accounted for in terms of a principle of intransitive attention whose consistency with the principles that govern the *Poetics* he does not show and that seems unlikely to be consistent with them. The principle of imitation is clearly and firmly enough grounded. The notion of likely improbability is incompatible with the rest of the theory.

The reader may be wondering why I spend so much energy beating a dead horse. The answer is that the horse is anything but dead. In practical criticism the theory of imitation reigns untroubled, as if aestheticians had never uttered a word of criticism against it. . . .

. . . In Anglo-American philsophy, at least, one does not find many writers expounding imitation theories. But many expression theories are but disguised theories of imitation. Let me give you an example. In all that Mrs. Langer has written on art since her *Philosophy in a New Key,* she has put forth the theory that the aim of art is to express our feelings and emotions or, in a variant formulation, "the dynamics of the affective life." Offered initially as a solution of the difficult problem of meaning in music, Mrs. Langer has generalized her theory and applied it to all the arts. In *Philosophy in a New Key* we read: "there are certain aspects of the so-called 'inner life'— physical or mental—which have formal patterns similar to those of music— patterns of motion and rest, of tension and release, of agreement and disagreement, preparation, fulfillment, excitation, sudden change, etc." This is the heart of her theory, and later formulations, either in *Feeling and Form* or in the essays collected in *Problems of Art,* have not brought about a discernible change. When we examine this theory it is not difficult to see that what Mrs. Langer means by "expression" is really "imitation."

What art in general does is imitate "the dynamics of subjective experience," because our affective life is similar in pattern to the patterns of art. That I have not employed a popular technique of scholarly exegesis and extrapolated far beyond the data can be seen from the fact that in an essay entitled "Imitation and Transformation in the Arts," we are told, among other things, that "the primitive art impulse is to *imitate* natural forms which the artist finds expressive." In this sentence it is Mrs. Langer who underlines the word "imitate." It is implied that the forms imitated are inherently expressive. But what does it mean to say that these natural forms are expressive—expressive prior to objectification in and through the object or art? And if they are inherently expressive, what account shall we give of the intense drive felt by the artist to embody them again in his medium? These are questions on which at least one of her readers would welcome some light. . . .

. . . There is, however, an important difference between Mrs. Langer's theory and that of her sources or predecessors. She holds fast to an important distinction that neither Aristotle nor Eliot made: that between arousal of the emotion in the reader by the object of art and the expression of the emotion by it. This distinction was not discovered by Mrs. Langer, but she is quite clear about it, and it is indispensable.

In order to hold her theory, Mrs. Langer is forced to assert that "subjective" or "affective" experience is not in itself formless, is not a mere disturbance of the organism, but has a structure of its own. The theory stands or falls with the validity of this assertion. But is it valid? The full demonstration of its worthlessness would take us too far afield. I shall have to confine my remarks to a number of statements that I hope will not seem over-dogmatic. The first is that feeling *qua* feeling, emotion *qua* emotion, have no other structure than that given them by the body processes that accompany them, such as respiration and the circulation of the blood. Consider emotion or feeling in abstraction from the stimulus that gives it rise and but for the primitive somatic rhythms it gains, it is inchoate and formless; it is, so to speak, mere biology barely identifiable in consciousness. This is equally true of what psychologists used to call floating moods. When, however, we consider emotions or feelings in relation to the stimulus (which always comes involved in a complex situation), they gain discreteness and achieve identity by means of the stimulus in the situation that gives rise to them.

But perhaps I am doing our aesthetician a great injustice; perhaps her emotions and feelings are indeed as complex and subtle in structure as a Bach fugue; perhaps joy gurgles out of her soul without external stimulus to structure it and is of such informed complexity that it can be said to be imitated by the last movement of Beethoven's *Ninth Symphony*. I ought not to speak for her and ought to concede that what I have said about a stimulus in a situation structuring emotion and feeling is a mere empirical generalization and not an *a priori* statement, and therefore it is susceptible of such exceptions as we actually encounter. We shall have to accept Mrs. Langer's word when she writes that the affective life posesses intrinsic structure of such complexity that it can be imitated by a movement of a symphony. She may have gathered the fact by introspection. But I have a right to speak for myself and the ordinary man whom I so adequately represent: for me it would be a gratuitous and fatuous self-flattery to say that my affective life possesses intrinsically a structure that can be imitated by the subtleties of a sonata or a cantata or a fugue.

It is true that after commenting on a statement by Richard Wagner in *Philosophy in a New Key,* Mrs. Langer writes that "music is not self-expression, but *formulation* and *representation* of emotions, moods, mental tensions and resolutions" which no one need have felt. (Italics in text.) But the criticism stands, for such occurrences could not have been felt by anyone until the music gave them form. There is a radical difference between representing the formal structure of the inner life and informing its matter, matter that prior to the act of information had only a rudimentary kind of structure at best.

I do not put into question, however, that it is quite proper to characterize music and the other arts in terms we use to speak of emotions and feelings: we say of a composition that it is gay or sad. Of the world of *King Lear* we would have to use a more complex characterization, but the central reference in it would be to a quality or qualities properly referred to by the language of the emotions—its terror, its cruelty, its pathos, the tenderness of its last scene. This fact suggests that there is some sort of relation between art and our affective life. But the problem remains: exactly what is that relation? And my contention is that the relation is not one of imitation, for the reason I have somewhat dogmatically advanced. Nor is it, if I may say it in passing, a problem that can be elucidated linguistically, as Professor Bowsma attempted to do some time ago. What we have before us is a substantive problem involving questions of psychology and of aesthetic values and traits, and to suppose that we can settle the puzzle by analysis of language exclusively is to give evidence either of a feeble grasp of the nature of the problem or of a capacity to float on the surface of complex issues and indulge in what is nothing but persiflage.

Mrs. Langer's theory is open to another criticism and one which I must bring up in sorrow, for after all she was a student of the logician, Sheffer, and started out herself as a logician. But it must be pointed out that her theory is an explanation of the obscure by the more obscure. The structure of a work of art is something that can be inspected more or less easily—in the case of a poem in verse, we can point to the rhyme scheme, the meter, and other objective features as regards which a modicum of agreement is possible. But "the structure of our affective life," by whatever words we may choose to refer to it, is an essentially obscure notion, and calls for elucidation which would have to be grounded on a mind-body theory to be at all convincing. If the structure of our affective life is independent of somatic processes, one would like to have a detailed account of the theory of mind which would enable a thinker to put forth such a claim. If it is not independent, my criticism is relevant—the structure of our affective life, considered in abstraction from a stimulus in a situation, has the primitive and coarse form it gains from elementary body processes.

It is as a result of considerations of this nature—for I would go into the problem more fully did space allow it—that in spite of the prestige, the popularity, and the antiquity of the theory of imitation, I decided long ago that it is fundamentally wrong, if one takes the term to mean what the dictionary says it means. That some products of human skill can best be interpreted as objects that imitate probable or necessary actions I do not question. That there are similarities between objects of fine art and natural objects I do not question either. No doubt all of Cézanne's "Mont Saint-Victoires" resemble Mont Saint-Victoire in some respects and no doubt we could have recognized Whistler's mother from her picture. But to speak of art as imitative is to overlook what makes it art: to overlook the creative component, that element which but for the artist's talent the object would lack. . . .

Let me now turn to the expression theory. And let me begin by saying that to speak of the theory of expression, in the singular, is as inaccurate as it is to speak of the theory of imitation: there are as many theories of expression or of imitation as there are writers on the subject—or very nearly. When elaborated by philosophers of the power of a Samuel Alexander, a Collingwood, or a Dewey, the expression theory is considerably more adequate to the phenomena that it seeks to elucidate than the theory of imitation. But in spite of this relative superiority, expression theories suffer from a generic defect that, to me, makes them inadmissible.

In order to expose their flaw let us ask defenders of theories of expression what function does expression perform that cannot be performed by any other means? The answer we are given is that it is by means of expression that our affective life achieves clarification, and, in Collingwood's metaphor, it is through expression that emotion is grounded. Expression, objectification, and clarification of our affective life are but "moments," at most, of a single act, are ends in themselves, self-evidently desirable for their own sake, when contrasted with the condition they supplant. Collingwood points out correctly that prior to the act of expression, so far from our emotions and feelings having a structure of their own, they are in a massive, chaotic, utterly inchoate condition, which is disruptive and which is the reason we seek to "ground them," which is to say, to objectify them and, by giving them form, to be relieved from the oppressiveness they cause prior to expression. Aristotle, wrong as he was, had a point when he spoke of catharsis, although there is still the question as to how the metaphor should be interpreted.

Those of us, the majority, who have a very limited creative power, find in ritualistic behavior of a rudimentary nature, the relief from the formlessness of our affective life. When we hear an unexpected piece of good news, if our up-bringing has not been utterly inhibited, we want to skip, to shout, to do something that will enable our joy to pour out. In the pouring of it through these stereotyped means, we give it structure and we "ground" it. After a successful operation by the VIII Army, General MacArthur writes General Eichelberger a note of congratulation, closing with a pat on the back. Had Eichelberger been present and had both generals been Venezuelans and not Americans, MacArthur would have given his successful general a warm embrace. We are all acquainted with, to us, the odious photograph of Hitler dancing a jig in front of his generals on the occasion of the capitulation of the French.

So far as it goes, then, the theory of expression seems to be faultless. The difference between ritualistic behavior of a stereotyped nature through which non-creative persons seek to "ground" their emotions and the work of the artist is one of degree—degree of complexity, depth, and novelty. The crying, the sobbing, the wringing of hands, the desolation expressed through tender thoughts of a lost friend is shallow and inadequate compared to the expression of the complex attitude achieved by Milton when he wrote *Lycidas*. But that art, and for our purposes poetry, is the only means of expressing our affective life is hardly acceptable. I knew a woman who expressed her anger by washing the kitchen floor. If it should be replied that washing the kitchen floor is an art, I would retort that emotion can be expressed by non-artistic means. Consider what happens to the analysand when undergoing psychoanalytic treatment. We are told that the treatment consists essentially of bringing to the light of rational awareness the components of an essentially affective nature that have been repressed and find expression through neurotic symptoms. If psychoanalytic doctrine is true—and it is too late in the century of Freud to put it in doubt—expression by means of art suffers from several defects as compared to the expressing that takes place in psychic therapy.

The first of these is that the affective material expressed is expressed symbolically. The writing of *Hamlet*—if we allow the instance for the sake of the argument and confine ourselves to the incestual component, a factor which is there, although Doctor Jones exaggerated it, in my opinion—could not have done for its author what a treatment by an analyst could have done. The second defect that must be noted is that even though poetry may have a cathartic effect, the catharsis achieved is not permanent as, ideally at least, the effect of therapy is. A third defect is that the theory is built on a metaphor. Collingwood uses a metaphor from electricity: the act of expression "grounds" the emotion. But a metaphor is not an explanation—although frequently we have to be content with the former in the absence of the latter. But in my view, the most serious criticism is that if the function of art is expression, art is something for which at least one substitute—psychic therapy—can be found. This therefore cannot be the intrinsic or resident function of art, although there is no doubt that it is a non-residential one.

What then is the resident function of art for which there is no substitute? It is, to put it in a succinct formula, to organize the primary data of experience by means of the creation of *constitutive symbols*. Philosophers have no difficulty understanding the formula. For all it expresses is what Cassire referred to under the term, "symbolic form." . . .

SYMBOLISM IN THE ARTS

Hieronymus Bosch: Symbolic Integration

HERBERT READ

If, as I have already proposed, we accept the distinction which Coleridge and other philosophers of the Romantic Period made between the imagination

Reprinted from *Art and Alienation* by Herbert Read. Copyright © 1967 by permission of the publisher, Horizon Press, New York.

and fancy, then in the art of painting there is no better representative of the second faculty than Hieronymus Bosch. He indeed practised "a mode of memory emancipated from the order of time and space"; he had "no other counters to play with, but fixities and definites," and "equally with the ordinary memory" his fancy received all its materials "ready made from the law of association." But having made this distinction, it is still necessary to define the manner in which Bosch elaborated his fancy.

Though Bosch lived at the dawn of the Renaissance, he is essentially a late medieval or Gothic artist. He was a religious mystic, not yet touched by any desire to assert his own individuality. Any meaning we may discover in his paintings is transcendental, not humorous or whimsical. The human beings he depicts are not so much "personalities" as types. We recognize his work, not by its style, but by its exceptional content. He is an image-maker, a symbolist, and our main task, as critics, is to interpret his message.

The traditional approach to the work of Bosch has been to treat him as a "faizeur de diables," a man who allowed his fancy free and undisciplined range, an artist whose only aim was to amuse us, to shock us, even to terrify us. In reaction to this superficial treatment there have been, in recent years, two methods of investigation which we might call the psychological and the iconographical. The first, at its crudest and least aesthetic, seeks to interpret Bosch's symbols by the techniques of psycho-analysis; at its most subtle and perceptive, as in the monograph by Charles de Tolnay, it analyses Bosch's art in order to reveal his spiritual aspirations. The second or iconographical method of investigation, represented by Wilhelm Fränger, attempts to relate Bosch's paintings to specific documents and religious beliefs. There seems to be no reason why both methods should not be combined: if the images correspond to specific ideas, then we can determine to what extent Bosch's illustration of them was idiosyncratic. . . .

Bosch is characterized above all by his systematic symbolism—systematic in the sense that the same symbols, with obviously identical significance, appear in more than one work. But there are degrees of complexity in the meaning of these symbols; and discretion in the use of them. . . .

What I have called the major symbolic works are four in number, *The Hay Wain* formerly in the Escorial now in the Prado Museum, *The Temptation of St. Anthony* in the National Museum of Lisbon, *The Last Judgement* in the Academy of Fine Arts, Vienna, and the *Garden of Delights* triptych also now in the Prado. To analyse these four masterpieces in detail would exceed my present purpose, but it is evident that the same intelligence, using the same symbolic vocabulary, is expressing itself in all these paintings. *The Garden of Delights*, the object of Fränger's analysis, is the most complex of these works, and since it is important to discuss his hypothesis, I will concentrate on this work.

We must begin with some general observations on Bosch's vision of the world, a philosophy which was basically Christian but at the same time critical of the institutions of the Church, above all the monasteries. Bosch undoubtedly belonged to that reformist movement which was presently to be represented by the great figures of Erasmus and Luther. We know that he belonged to the Confraternity of Our Lady, in whose registers his name is recorded from 1480 onwards (his death is recorded in the same registers in 1516). The records also tell us that Bosch supplied designs for a crucifix and windows in the chapel of the Confraternity in the cathedral at 's Hertogenbosch. But the membership of this Confraternity, though a mark of devotion, would not in itself account for Bosch's "mode of visual thought" nor for the complex symbolism which is displayed in the great triptychs. It has therefore been suggested by Wilhelm Fränger that Bosch belonged to another and more secret organization, the Brothers and Sisters of the Free Spirit, and that his symbolism is a coherent representation of the beliefs of this heretical sect. . . .

The Brotherhood of the Free Spirit seems to have derived its main doctrine from the twelfth-century Christian mystic, Joachim of Floris, and it is just possible that Bosch was inspired by the same source. Joachim divides the history of humanity into three periods—the age of the Law, or of the Father, the age of the Gospel, or of the Son, and the age of the Spirit, which will bring the ages to an end. Before each of these ages there is a period of incubation, or initiation; the first age begins with Abraham, but the period of initiation with the first man Adam. The initiation period of the third age begins with St. Benedict, while the actual age of the Spirit is not to begin until 1260, the Church—*mulier amicta sole* (Rev. XII, I)—remaining hidden in the wilderness for 1260 days. This conception of history (I take this summary from the eleventh edition of the Encyclopaedia Britannica) is richly elaborated in the voluminous writings of Joachim, and his ideas, never formally condemned by the Church, persisted certainly to the sixteenth century, and were propagated by various orders, the Segarellists, the Dolcimists, and above all by the "Spirituals," Franciscans who proclaimed the coming of Joachim's third age. . . .

Fränger's interpretation of the *Garden of Delights* triptych must be read in all its detail—one hundred and fifty pages of close analysis. He succeeds in demonstrating that "what was previously regarded as only the uncontrolled ravings of a mind that was a prey to the medieval obsession with the Devil . . . now turns out to be a system of sexual–ethical teachings, in which the pictorial motifs were didactic symbols, and above all clear reflections of Renaissance natural philosophy, and hence patterns of a modern intellectual kind, pointing towards the future." Let us take one example of the method which Fränger uses to substantiate this bold claim—the strange Monster that dominates the Hell of the right wing of the triptych and is probably the most haunting image in all Bosch's work.

Fränger rightly observes that up to the present the significance of this monster has never been explained. "Like so many of Bosch's unexplained symbols, it has been regarded only as the grotesque product of a demonomanic obsession." According to Fränger, the monster represents the Tree of Knowledge, "gaunt and racked, standing in the centre of Hell, a counterpart of the Tree of Life in the centre of the Garden of Eden" (seen in the left wing of the triptych). The Tree of Life is turned into a Tree of Death. The fact that it has no roots in earth, but forms the mast of a ship, indicates that it is "the uncertain ship of time, the transient vessel drifting in the ocean of the eternal element." All other details, the scene on the disc which the monster bears on his head (the world–disc), the bagpipe (a symbol of vanity), the procession round the disc, the tavern–scene in the broken egg–shell of a body (tree–male principle, egg–female principle), the monster's backward glance (striving Lucifer-like for knowledge), all are contributory symbols to the one symbolic form, which represents the Ego, the corrupted nature of sensual man.

It is an ordered world of "signatures," and what Fränger emphasized is that Bosch, in these great masterpeices, has learnt not only to *see* and *know*, but has gained beyond these "the *vision* and *understanding* that come from a deeper perception, one that combines an infallible eye for the characteristic detail of an object with a feeling for its inner nature." Tolnay, in his great essay on Bosch, which for the first time established a credible chronological corpus of his work, comes to a conclusion no less positive. This painter, he says, not only reveals the vanity and disquieting beauty of the world as we know it; his revelation leads to a new range of consciousness, no longer entirely linked to religious teachings, but announcing an independence of spirit that will prevail over future generations. Even the cautious Baldass ends by claiming that the outstanding feature of Bosch's achievement as a whole, which is unique in the history of art and has for so long been misunderstood, "is the coherence and lucidity of his conception of the world, manifest in every painting he produced. Such qualities are only to be found in the true spiritual leaders of humanity."

It may be objected that an art that remains so esoteric and mysterious cannot justify such sweeping claims. But we have learnt in our time, which was a common assumption in Bosch's time and not subject to a sceptical intelligence, that the power of the symbol is most effective when received uncritically. Bosch's eschatological visions are not part of our enlightened cosmology: Hell and eternal torment no less than the serene joys of Paradise are therefore no longer significant symbols for modern man. Such is our complacent assumption, but why then are we fascinated by Bosch's paintings? Because, I suggest, they correspond so closely to our dreams. They are not representations of dreams, though we may suppose Bosch derived many of his images from his dreams. As Jung pointed out in his autobiography (*Memories, Dreams, Reflections*, 1963) "day after day we live far beyond the bounds of our consciousness; without our knowledge, the life of the unconscious is also going on within us. The more the critical reason dominates, the more impoverished life becomes; but the more of the unconscious, and the more of myths we are capable of making conscious, the more of life we integrate."

Bosch is a painter, the supreme of his kind, who by his wealth of symbols, compels us, even to this day, to integrate "more of life."

Integration, or individuation as Jung prefers to call it, is first and foremost a process of *differentiation,* the process of forming and specializing the individual nature of a personality. But "since the individual is not a single, separate being, but by his very existence also presupposes a collective relationship, the process of individuation must clearly lead to a more intensive and universal collective solidarity." In other words, the individual at the same time that he completes his selfhood, loses his sense of isolation and develops a natural appreciation of the kind of collective life that is necessary for the social solidarity of the group. His personality is no longer either submerged by the unconscious norms of collectivity nor does it react blindly against such norms. The individual is at peace with himself and with his environment.

Bosch may have found such a balanced relationship within such a community as the Brothers and Sisters of the Free Spirit; his rich and complete symbolism is a visual representation of the primal unity and innocence which the members of such a community wished to establish within the limits of their secret society. His *Millennium* is the complex but coherent representation of this ideal of human solidarity and happiness. It celebrates the end of alienation.

ILLUSTRATION 14

MICHELANGELO, *The Creation of Man,* Sistene Chapel, 1509–1512, reprinted with permission of the Vatican Museums.

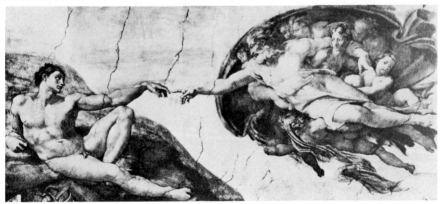

ILLUSTRATION 15

HIERONYMUS BOSCH, *The Garden of Earthly Delights,* detail, 1500. Reprinted with the permission of the Museo del Prado, Madrid, Spain. All rights reserved.

8

Art As a Psychological Phenomenon

This chapter analyzes, in diverse ways, the role of psychological phenomena in artistic creativity and in art criticism. Earlier Rudolf Arnheim and Susanne Langer introduced the reader to the possible relationship between psychological theories and art. This relationship is explored in this section by two thinkers, Friedrich Nietzsche and Sigmund Freud.

Friedrich Nietzsche was a nineteenth-century German thinker who is considered one of the first existentialist philosophers. In aesthetics he is well known for his analysis of the Apollinian and Dionysian elements in art. Nietzsche suggests that these two principles have influenced the creation and development of art. These principles, which are evident in all art phenomena, are psychological tendencies through which human beings interpret and transform the world. And it is only through introducing these elements into one's experiences, according to Nietzsche, that human life is interesting, bearable, and possible. Apollinian—a word taken from the Greek god Apollo, the god of dreams—describes the tendency of our rational nature to interpret reality in such a way as to make the world intelligible, rational, and perfect. Apollinian art is formal, orderly, and moral because it presents reality as it should be. *The Venus de Milo* is an example of Apollinian art. Dionysian—a term taken from the god of wine and fertility—on the other hand, describes that which springs from the human imagination. It is the emotional tendency of human beings to feel the agonies and the joys of life and to transform reality into emotional experiences. Dionysian art, exemplified in music, is emotional and intoxicating. *The Garden of Earthly Delights* is a good example of Dionysian art. These two tendencies—Apollinian and Dionysian—are obviously opposite. But Nietzsche suggests that sometimes they come together in great works of art such as tragedies. *Hamlet* would be an example of such a unity, according to Nietzsche. Nietzsche is concerned with the creative inspiration of the artist which he traces to psychological elements. But it is not clear in reading Nietzsche whether or not the Apollinian and Dionysian are conscious or unconscious sources of inspiration. The role of the unconscious in artistic creation hinted at by Nietzsche is later developed by the psychologist Sigmund Freud.

Freud, a Viennese psychologist, is probably the most famous and influential psychologist in the history of that discipline. Freud is credited with the theory that the human psyche is made up of three elements: the conscious ego, the unconscious id which is the source of instincts and desires, and the unconscious super-ego which exhibits itself as human conscience and is the source of value judgments. Evidence for the unconscious elements in the psyche comes from inexplicable neurotic human behavior, slips of the tongue, and most importantly, from dreams. When one is sleeping, according to Freud, one's conscious ego relaxes and unconscious elements exert themselves in dreams. In the selection included in this section, Freud is particularly interested in dream phenomena as evidence for the unconscious influence on artistic creativity. Using a specific example, the myth of Oedipus, Freud argues that the story developed out of primitive dream material in which a male child's unconscious wish to marry his mother and kill his father was depicted. And the continued audience fascination in the Oedipus plot springs from every man's unconscious wish to have sexual relations with his mother and to do away with his father, a phenomenon aptly called the Oedipus complex. Freud argues further that the Oedipus complex is exemplified in William Shakespeare's characterization of Hamlet. This complex explains Hamlet's inexplicable hesitation to kill his stepfather, as illustrated in the selection from the play (Illustration 16), a murder which according to rational thinking is justified. Freud suggests that this inability is due to Hamlet's unconscious sexual attachment to his mother which makes him incapable of killing the man who is living out Hamlet's repressed desire. Although this interpretation of *Hamlet* is controversial, it illustrates the role of psychological theory in creativity and in the interpretation of art.

Evidence of the possible influence of the unconscious in art is nicely illustrated in William Butler Yeat's mystical poem, *The Second Coming* (Illustration 17). What is the symbol of the Sphinx? How does Yeats view the role of the unconscious in history and in historical revelation? The pictorial rendition of the poem by Richard Saliaris (Illustration 18) lets the reader explore some of these ideas through images.

The role of psychological theory in the analysis of artistic creativity and in art criticism is of continuing interest and controversy. The positions of Nietzsche, Freud, and to a lesser extent Arnheim and Langer illustrate such analyses. Whether or not psychology can contribute significantly to aesthetic theory and literary criticism is still much in question.

Apollo and Dionysus

FRIEDRICH NIETZSCHE

We shall have gained much for the science of aesthetics, once we perceive not merely by logical inference, but with the immediate certainty of vision, that the continuous development of art is bound up with the *Apollinian* and *Dionysian* duality—just as procreation depends on the duality of the sexes, involving perpetual strife with only periodically intervening reconciliations. The terms Dionysian and Apollinian we borrow from the Greeks, who disclose to the discerning mind the profound mysteries of their view of art, not, to be sure, in concepts, but in the intensely clear figures of their gods. Through Apollo and Dionysus, the two art deities of the Greeks, we come to recognize that in the Greek world there existed a tremendous opposition, in origin and aims, between the Apollinian art of sculpture, and the nonimagistic, Dionysian art of music. These two different tendencies run parallel to each other, for the most part openly at variance; and they continually incite each other to new and more powerful births, which perpetuate an antagonism, only superficially reconciled by the common term "art"; till eventually, by a metaphysical miracle of the Hellenic "will," they appear coupled with each other, and through this coupling ultimately generate an equally Dionysian and Apollinian form of art—Attic tragedy.

In order to grasp these two tendencies, let us first conceive of them as the separate art worlds of *dreams* and *intoxication*. These physiological phenomena present a contrast analogous to that existing between the Apollinian and the Dionysian. It was in dreams, says Lucretius, that the glorious divine figures first appeared to the souls of men; in dreams the great shaper beheld the splendid bodies of superhuman beings; and the Hellenic poet, if questioned about the mysteries of poetic inspiration, would likewise have suggested dreams and he might have given an explanation like that of Hans Sachs in the *Meistersinger:*

> The poet's task is this, my friend,
> to read his dreams and comprehend.
> The truest human fancy seems
> to be revealed to us in dreams:
> all poems and versification
> are but true dreams' interpretation.[1]

From Friedrich Nietzsche, *The Birth of Tragedy,* trans. Walter Kaufmann (New York: Random House, 1966).

---

[1]Wagner's original text reads:
Mein Freund, das grad' ist Dichters Werk,

The beautiful illusion[2] of the dream worlds, in the creation of which every man is truly an artist, is the prerequisite of all plastic art, and, as we shall see, of an important part of poetry also. In our dreams we delight in the immediate understanding of figures; all forms speak to us; there is nothing unimportant or superfluous. But even when this dream reality is most intense, we still have, glimmering through it, the sensation that it is *mere appearance:* at least this is my experience, and for its frequency—indeed, normality—I could adduce many proofs, including the sayings of the poets.

Philosophical men even have a presentiment that the reality in which we live and have our being is also mere appearance, and that another, quite different reality lies beneath it. Schopenhauer actually indicates as the criterion of philosophical ability the occasional ability to view men and things as mere phantoms or dream images. Thus the aesthetically sensitive man stands in the same relation to the reality of dreams as the philosopher does to the reality of existence; he is a close and willing observer, for these images afford him an interpretation of life, and by reflecting on these processes he trains himself for life.

It is not only the agreeable and friendly images that he experiences as something universally intelligible: the serious, the troubled, the sad, the gloomy, the sudden restraints, the tricks of accident, anxious expectations, in short, the whole divine comedy of life, including the inferno, also pass before him, not like mere shadows on a wall—for he lives and suffers with these scenes— and yet not without that fleeting sensation of illusion. And perhaps many will, like myself, recall how amid the dangers and terrors of dreams they have occasionally said to themselves in self-encouragement, and not without success: "It is a dream! I will dream on!" I have likewise heard of people who were able to continue one and the same dream for three and even more successive nights— facts which indicate clearly how our innermost being, our common ground, experiences dreams with profound delight and a joyous necessity.

This joyous necessity of the dream experience has been embodied by the Greeks in their Apollo: Apollo, the god of all plastic energies, is at the same time the soothsaying god. He, who (as the etymology of the name indicates) is the "shining one," the deity of light, is also ruler over the beautiful illusion of the inner world of fantasy. The higher truth, the perfection of these states in contrast to the incompletely intelligible everyday world, this deep consciousness of nature, healing and helping in sleep and dreams, is at the same time the symbolical analogue of the soothsaying faculty and of the

---

dass er sein Träumen deut' und merk'.
Glaubt mir, des Menschen wahrster Wahn
wird ihm im Traume aufgethan:
all' Dichtkunst und Poëterei
ist nichts als Wahrtraum-Deuterei.

[2]*Schein* has been rendered in these pages sometimes as "illusion" and sometimes as "mere appearance."

arts generally, which make life possible and worth living. But we must also include in our image of Apollo that delicate boundary which the dream image must not overstep lest it have a pathological effect (in which case mere appearance would deceive us as if it were crude reality). We must keep in mind that measured restraint, that freedom from the wilder emotions, that calm of the sculptor god. His eye must be "sunlike," as befits his origin; even when it is angry and distempered it is still hallowed by beautiful illusion. And so, in one sense, we might apply to Apollo the words of Schopenhauer when he speaks of the man wrapped in the veil of *māyā* (*Welt als Wille und Vorstellung*, I, p. 416[3]): "Just as in a stormy sea that, unbounded in all directions, raises and drops mountainous waves, howling, a sailor sits in a boat and trusts in his frail bark: so in the midst of a world of torments the individual human being sits quietly, supported by and trusting in the *principium individuationis*."[4] In fact, we might say of Apollo that in him the unshaken faith in this *principium* and the calm repose of the man wrapped up in it receive their most sublime expression; and we might call Apollo himself the glorious divine image of the *principium individuationis*, through whose gestures and eyes all the joy and wisdom of "illusion," together with its beauty, speak to us.

In the same work Schopenhauer has depicted for us the tremendous *terror* which seizes man when he is suddenly dumfounded by the cognitive form of phenomena because the principle of sufficient reason, in some one of its manifestations, seems to suffer an exception. If we add to this terror the blissful ecstasy that wells from the innermost depths of man, indeed of nature, at this collapse of the *principium individuationis*, we steal a glimpse into the nature of the *Dionysian*, which is brought home to us most intimately by the analogy of intoxication.

Under the charm of the Dionysian not only is the union between man and man reaffirmed, but nature which has become alienated, hostile, or subjugated, celebrates once more her reconciliation with her lost son,[5] man. Freely, earth proffers her gifts, and peacefully the beasts of prey of the rocks and desert approach. The chariot of Dionysus is covered with flowers and garlands; panthers and tigers walk under its yoke. Transform Beethoven's "Hymn to Joy" into a painting; let your imagination conceive the multitudes bowing to the dust, awestruck—then you will approach the Dionysian. Now the slave is a free man; now all the rigid, hostile barriers that necessity, caprice, or "impudent convention"[6] have fixed between man and man are broken. Now, with the gospel of universal harmony, each one feels himself not only

---

[3]This reference, like subsequent references to the same work, is Nietzsche's own and refers to the edition of 1873 edited by Julius Frauenstädt—still one of the standard editions of Schopenhauer's works.

[4]Principle of individuation.

[5]In German, "the prodigal son" is *der verlorene Sohn* (the lost son).

[6]An allusion to Friedrich Schiller's hymn *An die Freude* (to joy), used by Beethoven in the final movement of his Ninth Symphony.

united, reconciled, and fused with his neighbor, but as one with him, as if the veil of *māyā* had been torn aside and were now merely fluttering in tatters before the mysterious primordial unity.

In song and in dance man expresses himself as a member of a higher community; he has forgotten how to walk and speak and is on the way toward flying into the air, dancing. His very gestures express enchantment. Just as the animals now talk, and the earth yields milk and honey, supernatural sounds emanate from him, too: he feels himself a god, he himself now walks about enchanted, in ecstasy, like the gods he saw walking in his dreams. He is no longer an artist, he has become a work of art: in these paroxysms of intoxication the artistic power of all nature reveals itself to the highest gratification of the primordial unity. The noblest clay, the most costly marble, man, is here kneaded and cut, and to the sound of the chisel strokes of the Dionysian world-artist rings out the cry of the Eleusinian mysteries: "Do you prostrate yourselves, millions? Do you sense your Maker, world?"[7]

Thus far we have considered the Apollinian and its opposite, the Dionysian, as artistic energies which burst forth from nature herself, *without the mediation of the human artist*—energies in which nature's art impulses are satisfied in the most immediate and direct way—first in the image world of dreams, whose completeness is not dependent upon the intellectual attitude or the artistic culture of any single being; and then as intoxicated reality, which likewise does not heed the single unit, but even seeks to destroy the individual and redeem him by a mystic feeling of oneness. With reference to these immediate art-states of nature, every artist is an "imitator," that is to say, either an Apollinian artist in dreams, or a Dionysian artist in ecstasies, or finally—as for example in Greek tragedy—at once artist in both dreams and ecstasies; so we may perhaps picture him sinking down in his Dionysian intoxication and mystical self-abnegation, alone and apart from the singing revelers, and we may imagine how, through Apollinian dream-inspiration, his own state, i.e., his oneness with the inmost ground of the world, is revealed to him in a *symbolical dream image*. . . .

Now the dream analogy may throw some light on the naïve artist. Let us imagine the dreamer: in the midst of the illusion of the dream world and without disturbing it, he calls out to himself: "It is a dream, I will dream on." What must we infer? That he experiences a deep inner joy in dream contemplation; on the other hand, to be at all able to dream with this inner joy in contemplation, he must have completely lost sight of the waking reality and its ominous obtrusiveness. Guided by the dream-reading Apollo, we may interpret all these phenomena in roughly this way.

---

[7]Quotation from Schiller's hymn.

Though it is certain that of the two halves of our existence, the waking and the dreaming states, the former appeals to us as infinitely preferable, more important, excellent, and worthy of being lived, indeed, as that which alone is lived—yet in relation to that mysterious ground of our being of which we are the phenomena, I should, paradoxical as it may seem, maintain the very opposite estimate of the value of dreams. For the more clearly I perceive in nature those omnipotent art impulses, and in them an ardent longing for illusion, for redemption through illusion, the more I feel myself impelled to the metaphysical assumption that the truly existent primal unity, eternally suffering and contradictory, also needs the rapturous vision, the pleasurable illusion, for its continuous redemption. And we, completely wrapped up in this illusion and composed of it, are compelled to consider this illusion as the truly nonexistent—i.e., as a perpetual becoming in time, space, and causality—in other words, as empirical reality. If, for the moment, we do not consider the question of our own "reality," if we conceive of our empirical existence, and of that of the world in general, as a continuously manifested representation of the primal unity, we shall then have to look upon the dream as a *mere appearance of mere appearance*, hence as a still higher appeasement of the primordial desire for mere appearance. And that is why the innermost heart of nature feels that ineffable joy in the naïve artist and the naïve work of art, which is likewise only "mere appearance of mere appearance." . . .

. . . For to our humiliation *and* exaltation, one thing above all must be clear to us. The entire comedy of art is neither performed for our betterment or education nor are we the true authors of this art world. On the contrary, we may assume that we are merely images and artistic projections for the true author, and that we have our highest dignity in our significance as works of art—for it is only as an *aesthetic phenomenon* that existence and the world are eternally *justified*—while of course our consciouness of our own significance hardly differs from that which the soldiers painted on canvas have of the battle represented on it. Thus all our knowledge of art is basically quite illusory, because as knowing beings we are not one and identical with that being which, as the sole author and spectator of this comedy of art, prepares a perpetual entertainment for itself. Only insofar as the genius in the act of artistic creation coalesces with this primordial artist of the world, does he know anything of the eternal essence of art; for in this state he is, in a marvelous manner, like the weird image of the fairy tale which can turn its eyes at will and behold itself; he is at once subject and object, at once poet, actor, and spectator. . . .

We must now avail ourselves of all the principles of art considered so far, in order to find our way through the labyrinth, as we must call it, of *the origin of Greek tragedy*: I do not think I am unreasonable in saying that the problem of this origin has as yet not even been seriously posed, to say nothing of solved, however often the ragged tatters of ancient tradition have been sewn together in various combinations and torn apart again. This tradition tells us quite unequivocally *that tragedy arose from the tragic chorus*, and was originally only chorus and nothing but chorus. Hence we consider it our duty to look into the heart of this tragic chorus as the real proto-drama, without resting satisfied with such arty clichés as that the chorus is the "ideal spectator" or that it represents the people in contrast to the aristocratic region of the scene. This latter explanation has a sublime sound to many a politician—as if the immutable moral law had been embodied by the democratic Athenians in the popular chorus, which always won out over the passionate excesses and extravagances of kings. This theory may be ever so forcibly suggested by one of Aristotle's observations; still, it has no influence on the original formation of tragedy, inasmuch as the whole opposition of prince and people—indeed the whole politico-social sphere—was excluded from the purely religious origins of tragedy. But even regarding the classical form of the chorus in Aeschylus and Sophocles, which is known to us, we should deem it blasphemy to speak here of intimations of "constitutional popular representation." From this blasphemy, however, others have not shrunk. Ancient constitutions knew of no constitutional representation of the people in *praxi*, and it is to be hoped that they did not even "have intimations" of it in tragedy.

. . . With this chorus the profound Hellene, uniquely susceptible to the tenderest and deepest suffering, comforts himself, having looked boldly right into the terrible destructiveness of so-called world history as well as the cruelty of nature, and being in danger of longing for a Buddhistic negation of the will. Art saves him, and through art—life.

For the rapture of the Dionysian state with its annihilation of the ordinary bounds and limits of existence contains, while it lasts, a *lethargic* element in which all personal experiences of the past become immersed. This chasm of oblivion separates the worlds of everyday reality and of Dionysian reality. But as soon as this everyday reality re-enters consciousness, it is experienced as such, with nausea: an ascetic, will-negating mood is the fruit of these states.

In this sense the Dionysian man resembles Hamlet: both have once looked truly into the essence of things, they have *gained knowledge*, and nausea inhibits action; for their action could not change anything in the eternal nature of things; they feel it to be ridiculous or humiliating that they should be asked to set right a world that is out of joint. Knowledge kills action; action requires the veils of illusion: that is the doctrine of Hamlet, not that cheap wisdom of Jack the Dreamer who reflects too much and, as it were, from an excess of possibilities does not get around to action. Not reflection, no—true knowledge, an insight into the horrible truth, outweighs any motive for action, both in Hamlet and in the Dionysian man.

Now no comfort avails any more; longing transcends a world after death, even the gods; existence is negated along with its glittering reflection in the gods or in an immortal beyond. Conscious of the truth he has once seen, man now sees everywhere only the horror or absurdity of existence; now he understands what is symbolic in Ophelia's fate; now he understands the wisdom of the sylvan god, Silenus: he is nauseated.

Here, when the danger to his will is greatest, *art* approaches as a saving sorceress, expert at healing. She alone knows how to turn these nauseous thoughts about the horror or absurdity of existence into notions with which one can live: these are the *sublime* as the artistic taming of the horrible, and the *comic* as the artistic discharge of the nausea of absurdity. The satyr chorus of the dithyramb is the saving deed of Greek art; faced with the intermediary world of these Dionysian companions, the feelings described here exhausted themselves. . . .

Among the peculiar art effects of musical tragedy we had to emphasize an Apollinian *illusion* by means of which we were supposed to be saved from the immediate unity with Dionysian music, while our musical excitement could discharge itself in an Apollinian field and in relation to a visible intermediary world that had been interposed. At the same time we thought that we had observed how precisely through this discharge the intermediary world of the action on the state, and the drama in general, had been made visible and intelligible from the inside to a degree that in all other Apollinian art remains unattained. Where the Apollinian receives wings from the spirit of music and soars, we thus found the highest intensification of its powers, and in this fraternal union of Apollo and Dionysus we had to recognize the apex of the Apollinian as well as the Dionysian aims of art.

To be sure, the Apollinian projection that is thus illuminated from inside by music does not achieve the peculiar effect of the weaker degrees of Apollinian art. What the epic or the animated stone can do, compelling the contemplative eye to find calm delight in the world of individuation, that could not be attained here, in spite of a higher animation and clarity. We looked at the drama and with penetrating eye reached its inner world of motives—and yet we felt as if only a parable passed us by, whose most profound meaning we almost thought we could guess and that we wished to draw away like a curtain in order to behold the primordial image behind it. The brightest clarity of the image did not suffice us, for this seemed to wish just as much to reveal something as to conceal something. Its revelation, being like a parable, seemed to summon us to tear the veil and to uncover the mysterious background; but at the same time this all-illuminated total visibility cast a spell over the eyes and prevented them from penetrating deeper.

Those who have never had the experience of having to see at the same time that they also longed to transcend all seeing will scarcely be able to imagine how definitely and clearly these two processes coexist and are felt at the same time, as one contemplates the tragic myth. But all truly aesthetic spectators will confirm that among the peculiar effects of tragedy this coexistence is the most remarkable. Now transfer this phenomenon of the aesthetic spectator into an analogous process in the tragic artist, and you will have understood the genesis of the *tragic myth*. With the Apollinian art sphere he shares the complete pleasure in mere appearance and in seeing, yet at the same time he negates this pleasure and finds a still higher satisfaction in the destruction of the visible world of mere appearance.

The content of the tragic myth is, first of all, an epic event and the glorification of the fighting hero. But what is the origin of this enigmatic trait that the suffering and the fate of the hero, the most painful triumphs, the most agonizing oppositions of motives, in short, the exemplification of this wisdom of Silenus, or, to put it aesthetically, that which is ugly and disharmonic, is represented ever anew in such countless forms and with such a distinct preference—and precisely in the most fruitful and youthful period of a people? Surely a higher pleasure must be perceived in all this.

That life is really so tragic would least of all explain the origin of an art form—assuming that art is not merely imitation of the reality of nature but rather a metaphysical supplement of the reality of nature, placed beside it for its overcoming. The tragic myth, too, insofar as it belongs to art at all, participates fully in this metaphysical intention of art to transfigure. But what does it transfigure when it presents the world of appearance in the image of the suffering hero? Least of all the "reality" of this world of appearance, for it says to us: "Look there! Look closely! This is your life, this is the hand on the clock of your existence."

And the myth should show us this life in order to thus transfigure it for us? But if not, in what then lies the aesthetic pleasure with which we let these images, too, pass before us? I ask about the aesthetic pleasure, though I know full well that many of these images also produce at times a moral delight, for example, under the form of pity or moral triumph. But those who would derive the effect of the tragic solely from these moral sources—which, to be sure, has been the custom in aesthetics all too long—should least of all believe that they have thus accomplished something for art, which above all must demand purity in its sphere. If you would explain the tragic myth, the first requirement is to seek the pleasure that is peculiar to it in the purely aesthetic sphere, without transgressing into the region of pity, fear, or the morally sublime. How can the ugly and the disharmonic, the content of the tragic myth, stimulate aesthetic pleasure?

Here it becomes necessary to take a bold running start and leap into a metaphysics of art, by repeating the sentence written above, that existence and the world seem justified only as an aesthetic phenomenon. In this sense, it is precisely the tragic myth that has to convince us that even the ugly and disharmonic are part of an artistic game that the will in the eternal amplitude of its pleasure plays with itself. But this primordial phenomenon of Dionysian art is difficult to grasp, and there is only one direct way to make it intelligible and grasp it immediately: through the wonderful significance of *musical dissonance*. Quite generally, only music, placed beside the world, can give us an idea of what is meant by the justification of the world as an aesthetic phenomenon. The joy aroused by the tragic myth has the same origin as the joyous sensation of dissonance in music. The Dionysian, with its primordial joy experienced even in pain, is the common source of music and tragic myth.

Is it not possible that by calling to our aid the musical relation of dissonance we may meanwhile have made the difficult problem of the tragic effect much easier? For we now understand what it means to wish to see tragedy and at the same time to long to get beyond all seeing: referring to the artistically employed dissonances, we should have to characterize the corresponding state by saying that we desire to hear and at the same time long to get beyond all hearing. That striving for the infinite, the wing-beat of longing that accompanies the highest delight in clearly perceived reality, reminds us that in both states we must recognize a Dionysian phenomenon: again and again it reveals to us the playful construction and destruction of the individual world as the overflow of a primordial delight. Thus the dark Heraclitus compares the world-building force to a playing child that places stones here and there and builds sand hills only to overthrow them again.

Music and tragic myth are equally expressions of the Dionysian capacity of a people, and they are inseparable. Both derive from a sphere of art that lies beyond the Apollinian; both transfigure a region in whose joyous chords dissonance as well as the terrible image of the world fade away charmingly; both play with the sting of displeasure, trusting in their exceedingly powerful magic arts; and by means of this play both justify the existence of even the "worst world." Thus the Dionysian is seen to be, compared to the Apollinian, the eternal and original artistic power that first calls the whole world of phenomena into existence—and it is only in the midst of this world that a new transfiguring illusion[8] becomes necessary in order to keep the animated world of individuation alive.

If we could imagine dissonance become man—and what else is man?— this dissonance, to be able to live, would need a splendid illusion that would cover dissonance with a veil of beauty. This is the true artistic aim of Apollo in whose name we comprehend all those countless illusions of the beauty of mere appearance that at every moment make life worth living at all and prompt the desire to live on in order to experience the next moment.

Of this foundation of all existence—the Dionysian basic ground of the world—not one whit more may enter the consciousness of the human individual than can be overcome again by this Apollinian power of transfiguration. Thus these two art drives must unfold their powers in a strict proportion, according to the law of eternal justice. Where the Dionysian powers rise up as impetuously as we experience them now, Apollo, too, must already have

---

[8]*Verklärungsschein* could also mean a transfiguring halo.

descended among us, wrapped in a cloud; and the next generation will probably behold his most ample beautiful effects.

That this effect should be necessary, everybody should be able to feel most assuredly by means of intuition, provided he has ever felt, if only in a dream, that he was carried back into an ancient Greek existence. Walking under lofty Ionic colonnades, looking up toward a horizon that was cut off by pure and noble lines, finding reflections of his transfigured shape in the shining marble at his side, and all around him solemnly striding or delicately moving human beings, speaking with harmonious voices and in a rhythmic language of gestures—in view of this continual influx of beauty, would he not have to exclaim, raising his hand to Apollo: "Blessed people of Hellas! How great must Dionysus be among you if the god of Delos considers such magic necessary to heal your dithyrambic madness!"

To a man in such a mood, however, an old Athenian, looking up at him with the sublime eyes of Aeschylus, might reply: "But say this, too, curious stranger: how much did this people have to suffer to be able to become so beautiful! But now follow me to witness a tragedy, and sacrifice with me in the temple of both deities!"

Oedipus and Hamlet

SIGMUND FREUD

According to my already extensive experience, parents play a leading part in the infantile psychology of all persons who subsequently become psychoneurotics. Falling in love with one parent and hating the other forms part of the permanent stock of the psychic impulses which arise in early childhood, and are of such importance as the material of the subsequent neurosis. But I do not believe that psychoneurotics are to be sharply distinguished in this respect from other persons who remain normal—that is, I do not believe that they are capable of creating something absolutely new and peculiar to themselves. It is far more probable—and this is confirmed by incidental observations of normal children—that in their amorous or hostile attitude toward their parents, psychoneurotics do no more than reveal to us, by magnification, something that occurs less markedly and intensively in the minds of the majority of children. Antiquity has furnished us with legendary matter which corrob-

Sigmund Freud, *The Interpretation of Dreams*, from the *Basic Writings of Sigmund Freud*, trans. and edited by Dr. A. A. Brill (New York: The Modern Library, 1938). Reprinted by permission of Gloria Bernheim and Edmund Brill © copyright 1965.

orates this belief, and the profound and universal validity of the old legends is explicable only by an equally universal validity of the above-mentioned hypothesis of infantile psychology.

I am referring to the legend of King Oedipus and the *Oedipus Rex* of Sophocles. Oedipus, the son of Laius, king of Thebes, and Jocasta, is exposed as a suckling, because an oracle had informed the father that his son, who was still unborn, would be his murderer. He is rescued, and grows up as a king's son at a foreign court, until, being uncertain of his origin, he, too, consults the oracle, and is warned to avoid his native place, for he is destined to become the murderer of his father and the husband of his mother. On the road leading away from his supposed home he meets King Laius, and in a sudden quarrel strikes him dead. He comes to Thebes, where he solves the riddle of the Sphinx, who is barring the way to the city, whereupon he is elected king by the grateful Thebans, and is rewarded with the hand of Jocasta. He reigns for many years in peace and honour, and begets two sons and two daughters upon his unknown mother, until at last a plague breaks out—which causes the Thebans to consult the oracle anew. Here Sophocles' tragedy begins. The messengers bring the reply that the plague will stop as soon as the murderer of Laius is driven from the country. But where is he?

> "Where shall be found,
> Faint, and hard to be known, the trace of the ancient guilt?"

The action of the play consists simply in the disclosure, approached step by step and artistically delayed (and comparable to the work of a psycho-analysis) that Oedipus himself is the murderer of Laius, and that he is the son of the murdered man and Jocasta. Shocked by the abominable crime which he has unwittingly committed, Oedipus blinds himself, and departs from his native city. The prophecy of the oracle has been fulfilled.

The *Oedipus Rex* is a tragedy of fate; its tragic effect depends on the conflict between the all-powerful will of the gods and the vain efforts of human beings threatened with disaster; resignation to the divine will, and the perception of one's own impotence is the lesson which the deeply moved spectator is supposed to learn from the tragedy. Modern authors have therefore sought to achieve a similar tragic effect by expressing the same conflict in stories of their own invention. But the playgoers have looked on unmoved at the unavailing efforts of guiltless men to avert the fulfilment of curse or oracle; the modern tragedies of destiny have failed of their effect.

If the *Oedipus Rex* is capable of moving a modern reader or playgoer no less powerfully than it moved the contemporary Greeks, the only possible explanation is that the effect of the Greek tragedy does not depend upon the conflict between fate and human will, but upon the peculiar nature of the material by which this conflict is revealed. There must be a voice within us which is prepared to acknowledge the compelling power of fate in the *Oedipus*, while we are able to condemn the situations occurring in *Die Ahnfrau* or other tragedies of fate as arbitrary inventions. And there actually is a motive in the story of King Oedipus which explains the verdict of this inner voice. His fate moves us only because it might have been our own, because the oracle laid upon us before our birth the very curse which rested upon him. It may be that we were all destined to direct our first sexual impulses toward our mothers, and our first impulses of hatred and violence toward our fathers; our dreams convince us that we were. King Oedipus, who slew his father Laius and wedded his mother Jocasta, is nothing more or less than a wish-fulfilment—the fulfilment of the wish of our childhood. But we, more fortunate than he, in so far as we have not become psychoneurotics, have since our childhood succeeded in withdrawing our sexual impulses from our mothers, and in forgetting our jealousy of our fathers. We recoil from the person for whom this primitive wish of our childhood has been fulfilled with all the force of the repression which these wishes have undergone in our minds since childhood. As the poet brings the guilt of Oedipus to light by his investigation, he forces us to become aware of our own inner selves, in which the same impulses are still extant, even though they are suppressed. The antithesis with which the chorus departs:—

> ". . . Behold, this is Oedipus,
> Who unravelled the great riddle, and was first in power,
> Whose fortune all the townsmen praised and envied;
> See in what dread adversity he sank!"

—this admonition touches us and our own pride, us who since the years of our childhood have grown so wise and so powerful in our own estimation. Like Oedipus, we live in ignorance of the desires that offend morality, the desires that nature has forced upon us and after their unveiling we may well prefer to avert our gaze from the scenes of our childhood.

In the very text of Sophocles' tragedy there is an unmistakable reference to the fact that the Oedipus legend had its source in dream-material of immemorial antiquity, the content of which was the painful disturbance of the child's relations to its parents caused by the first impulses of sexuality. Jocasta comforts Oedipus—who is not yet enlightened, but is troubled by the recollection of the oracle—by an allusion to a dream which is often dreamed, though it cannot, in her opinion, mean anything:—

> "For many a man hath seen himself in dreams
> His mother's mate, but he who gives no heed
> To suchlike matters bears the easier life."

The dream of having sexual intercourse with one's mother was as common then as it is to-day with many people, who tell it with indignation and astonishment. As may well be imagined, it is the key to the tragedy and the complement to the dream of the death of the father. The Oedipus fable is the reaction of fantasy to these two typical dreams, and just as such a dream, when occurring to an adult, is experienced with feelings of aversion, so the content of the fable must include terror and self-chastisement. The form which it subsequently assumed was the result of an uncomprehending secondary elaboration of the material, which sought to make it serve a theological intention. The attempt to reconcile divine omnipotence with human responsibility must, of course, fail with this material as with any other.

Another of the great poetic tragedies, Shakespeare's *Hamlet*, is rooted in the same soil as *Oedipus Rex*. But the whole difference in the psychic life of the two widely separated periods of civilization, and the progress, during the course of time, of repression in the emotional life of humanity, is manifested in the differing treatment of the same material. In *Oedipus Rex* the basic wish-phantasy of the child is brought to light and realized as it is in dreams; in *Hamlet* it remains repressed, and we learn of its existence—as we discover the relevant facts in a neurosis—only through the inhibitory effects which proceed from it. In the more modern drama, the curious fact that it is possible to remain in complete uncertainty as to the character of the hero has proved to be quite consistent with the overpowering effect of the tragedy. The play is based upon Hamlet's hesitation in accomplishing the task of revenge assigned to him; the text does not give the cause or the motive of this hesitation, nor have the manifold attempts at interpretation succeeded in doing so. According to the still prevailing conception, a conception for which Goethe was first responsible, Hamlet represents the type of man whose active energy is paralysed by excessive intellectual activity: "Sicklied o'er with the pale cast of thought." According to another conception, the poet has endeavoured to portray a morbid, irresolute character, on the verge of neurasthenia. The plot of the drama, however, shows us that Hamlet is by no means intended to appear as a character wholly incapable of action. On two separate occasions we see him assert himself: once in a sudden outburst of rage, when he stabs the eavesdropper behind the arras, and on the other occasion when he deliberately, and even craftily, with the complete unscrupulousness of a prince of the Renaissance, sends the two courtiers to the death which was intended for himself. What is it, then, that inhibits him in accomplishing the task which his father's ghost has laid upon him? Here the explanation offers itself that it is the peculiar nature of this task. Hamlet is able to do anything but take vengeance upon the man who did away with his father and has taken his father's place with his mother—the man who shows him in realization the repressed desires of his own childhood. The loathing which should have driven him to revenge is thus replaced by self-reproach, by conscientious scruples, which tell him that he himself is no better than the murderer whom he is required to punish. I have here translated into consciousness what had to remain unconscious in the mind of the hero; if anyone wishes to call Hamlet an hysterical subject I cannot but admit that this is the deduction to be drawn from my interpretation. The sexual aversion which Hamlet expresses in conversation with Ophelia is perfectly consistent with this deduction—the same sexual aversion which during the next few years was increasingly to take possession of the poet's soul, until it found its supreme utterance in *Timon of Athens*. It can, of course, be only the poet's own psychology with which we are confronted in *Hamlet*; and in a work on Shakespeare by Georg Brandes (1896) I find the statement that the drama was composed immediately after the death of Shakespeare's father (1601)—that is to say, when he was still mourning his loss, and during a revival, as we may fairly assume, of his own childish feelings in respect of his father. It is known, too, that Shakespeare's son, who died in childhood, bore the name of Hamnet (identical with Hamlet). Just as *Hamlet* treats of the relation of the son to his parents, so *Macbeth*, which was written about the same period, is based upon the theme of childlessness. Just as all neurotic symptoms, like dreams themselves, are capable of hyper-interpretation, and even require such hyper-interpretation before they become perfectly intelligible, so every genuine poetical creation must have proceeded from more than one motive, more than one impulse in the mind of the poet, and must admit of more than one interpretation. I have here attempted to interpret only the deepest stratum of impulses in the mind of the creative poet.

ILLUSTRATION 16

Hamlet

WILLIAM SHAKESPEARE

ACT I. SCENE 2

Hamlet.   O, that this too too solid flesh would melt,
        Thaw, and resolve itself into a dew!
        Or that the Everlasting had not fix'd
        His canon 'gainst self-slaughter! O God! God!
        How weary, stale, flat, and unprofitable,
        Seem to me all the uses of this world!
        Fie on't! Ah, fie! 'tis an unweeded garden,
        That grows to seed; things rank and gross in nature
        Possess it merely. That it should come to this!
        But two months dead! Nay, not so much, not two.

So excellent a king that was to this
Hyperion to a satyr; so loving to my mother,
That he might not beteem the winds of heaven
Visit her face too roughly. Heaven and earth!
Must I remember? Why, she would hang on him
As if increase of appetite had grown
By what it fed on; and yet, within a month—
Let me not think on't. Frailty, thy name is woman!—
A little month, or ere those shoes were old
With which she followed my poor father's body,
Like Niobe, all tears—why she, even she—
O God! a beast that wants discourse of reason
Would have mourn'd longer—married with my uncle,
My father's brother; but no more like my father
Than I to Hercules. Within a month,
Ere yet the salt of most unrighteous tears
Had left the flushing in her galled eyes,
She married. O, most wicked speed, to post
With such dexterity to incestuous sheets!
It is not, nor it cannot come to good.
But break, my heart, for I must hold my tongue.

ACT III. SCENE 4

The Queen's *closet*

Enter Queen *and* Polonius

POLONIUS. 'A will come straight. Look you lay home to him;
Tell him his pranks have been too broad to bear with,
And that your Grace hath screen'd and stood between
Much heat and him. I'll silence me even here.
Pray you be round with him.
HAMLET. [*Within*] Mother, mother, mother!
QUEEN. I'll warrant you. Fear me not.
Withdraw, I hear him coming.

[Polonius *goes behind the arras*]

Enter Hamlet

HAMLET. Now, mother, what's the matter?
QUEEN. Hamlet, thou hast thy father much offended.
HAMLET. Mother, you have my father much offended.
QUEEN. Come, come, you answer with an idle tongue.
HAMLET. Go, go, you question with a wicked tongue.

QUEEN.   Why, how now, Hamlet!

HAMLET.   What's the matter now?

QUEEN.   Have you forgot me?

HAMLET.   No, by the rood, not so:

> You are the Queen, your husband's brother's wife;
> And—would it were not so!—you are my mother.

QUEEN.   Nay then, I'll set those to you that can speak.

HAMLET.   Come, come, and sit you down; you shall not budge.

> You go not till I set you up a glass
> Where you may see the inmost part of you.

QUEEN.   What wilt thou do? Thou wilt not murder me?

> Help, help, ho!

POLONIUS.   [*Behind*] What, ho! help, help, help!

HAMLET.   [*Draws*] How now! a rat?

> Dead, for a ducat, dead!
>> [*Kills* Polonius *with a pass through the arras*]

POLONIUS.   [*Behind*] O, I am slain!

QUEEN.   O me, what hast thou done?

HAMLET.   Nay, I know not:

> Is it the King?

QUEEN.   O, what a rash and bloody deed is this!

HAMLET.   A bloody deed!—almost as bad, good mother,

> As kill a king and marry with his brother.

QUEEN.   As kill a king!

HAMLET.   Ay, lady, it was my word.   [*Parting the arras*]

> Thou wretched, rash, intruding fool, farewell!
> I took thee for thy better. Take thy fortune;
> Thou find'st to be too busy is some danger.
> Leave wringing of your hands. Peace; sit you down,
> And let me wring your heart; for so I shall,
> If it be made of penetrable stuff;
> If damned custom have not braz'd it so
> That it be proof and bulwark against sense.

QUEEN.   What have I done that thou dar'st wag thy tongue

> In noise so rude against me?

HAMLET.   Such an act

> That blurs the grace and blush of modesty;
> Calls virtue hypocrite; takes off the rose
> From the fair forehead of an innocent love,
> And sets a blister there; makes marriage-vows
> As false as dicers' oaths. O, such a deed
> As from the body of contraction plucks
> The very soul, and sweet religion makes
> A rhapsody of words. Heaven's face does glow
> O'er this solidity and compound mass
> With heated visage, as against the doom—
> Is thought-sick at the act.

QUEEN.   Ay me, what act,
> That roars so loud and thunders in the index?
HAMLET.   Look here upon this picture and on this,
> The counterfeit presentment of two brothers.
> See what a grace was seated on this brow;
> Hyperion's curls; the front of Jove himself;
> An eye like Mars, to threaten and command;
> A station like the herald Mercury
> New lighted on a heaven-kissing hill—
> A combination and a form indeed
> Where every god did seem to set his seal,
> To give the world assurance of a man.
> This was your husband. Look you now what follows:
> Here is your husband, like a mildew'd ear
> Blasting his wholesome brother. Have you eyes?
> Could you on this fair mountain leave to feed,
> And batten on this moor? Ha! have you eyes?
> You cannot call it love; for at your age
> The heyday in the blood is tame, it's humble,
> And waits upon the judgment; and what judgment
> Would step from this to this? Sense, sure, you have,
> Else could you not have motion; but sure that sense
> Is apoplex'd; for madness would not err,
> Nor sense to ecstasy was ne'er so thrall'd
> But it reserv'd some quantity of choice
> To serve in such a difference. What devil was't
> That thus hath cozen'd you at hoodman-blind?
> Eyes without feeling, feeling without sight,
> Ears without hands or eyes, smelling sans all,
> Or but a sickly part of one true sense
> Could not so mope. O shame! where is thy blush?
> Rebellious hell,
> If thou canst mutine in a matron's bones,
> To flaming youth let virtue be as wax
> And melt in her own fire; proclaim no shame
> When the compulsive ardour gives the charge,
> Since frost itself as actively doth burn,
> And reason panders will.
QUEEN.   O Hamlet, speak no more!
> Thou turn'st my eyes into my very soul;
> And there I see such black and grained spots
> As will not leave their tinct.
HAMLET.   Nay, but to live
> In the rank sweat of an enseamed bed,
> Stew'd in corruption, honeying and making love
> Over the nasty sty!
QUEEN.   O, speak to me no more!

These words like daggers enter in my ears;
      No more, sweet Hamlet.
HAMLET.   A murderer and a villain!
      A slave that is not twentieth part the tithe
      Of your precedent lord; a vice of kings;
      A cutpurse of the empire and the rule,
      That from a shelf the precious diadem stole
      And put it in his pocket!
QUEEN.   No more!

      Enter Ghost

HAMLET.   A king of shreds and patches—
      Save me, and hover o'er me with your wings,
      You heavenly guards! What would your gracious figure?
QUEEN.   Alas, he's mad!
HAMLET.   Do you not come your tardy son to chide,
      That, laps'd in time and passion, lets go by
      Th' important acting of your dread command?
      O, say!
GHOST.   Do not forget; this visitation
      Is but to whet thy almost blunted purpose.
      But look, amazement on thy mother sits.
      O, step between her and her fighting soul!
      Conceit in weakest bodies strongest works.
      Speak to her, Hamlet.
HAMLET.   How is it with you, lady?
QUEEN.   Alas, how is't with you,
      That you do bend your eye on vacancy,
      And with th' incorporal air do hold discourse?
      Forth at your eyes your spirits wildly peep;
      And, as the sleeping soldiers in th' alarm,
      Your bedded hairs like life in excrements
      Start up and stand an end. O gentle son,
      Upon the heat and flame of thy distemper
      Sprinkle cool patience! Whereon do you look?
HAMLET.   On him, on him! Look you how pale he glares.
      His form and cause conjoin'd, preaching to stones,
      Would make them capable.—Do not look upon me,
      Lest with this piteous action you convert
      My stern effects; then what I have to do
      Will want true colour—tears perchance for blood.
QUEEN.   To whom do you speak this?
HAMLET.   Do you see nothing there?
QUEEN.   Nothing at all; yet all that is I see.
HAMLET.   Nor did you nothing hear?
QUEEN.   No, nothing but ourselves.
HAMLET.   Why, look you there. Look how it steals away.

My father, in his habit as he liv'd!
Look where he goes even now out at the portal.

Exit Ghost

QUEEN.   This is the very coinage of your brain.
     This bodiless creation ecstasy
     Is very cunning in.
HAMLET.   Ecstasy!
     My pulse as yours doth temperately keep time,
     And makes as healthful music. It is not madness
     That I have utt'red. Bring me to the test,
     And I the matter will re-word which madness
     Would gambol from. Mother, for love of grace,
     Lay not that flattering unction to your soul,
     That not your trespass but my madness speaks:
     It will but skin and film the ulcerous place,
     Whiles rank corruption, mining all within,
     Infects unseen. Confess yourself to heaven;
     Repent what's past; avoid what is to come;
     And do not spread the compost on the weeds,
     To make them ranker. Forgive me this my virtue;
     For in the fatness of these pursy times
     Virtue itself of vice must pardon beg,
     Yea, curb and woo for leave to do him good.
QUEEN.   O Hamlet, thou hast cleft my heart in twain.
HAMLET.   O, throw away the worser part of it,
     And live the purer with the other half.
     Good night—but go not to my uncle's bed;
     Assume a virtue, if you have it not.
     That monster custom, who all sense doth eat,
     Of habits devil, is angel yet in this,
     That to the use of actions fair and good
     He likewise gives a frock or livery
     That aptly is put on. Refrain to-night;
     And that shall lend a kind of easiness
     To the next abstinence; the next more easy;
     For use almost can change the stamp of nature,
     And either curb the devil, or throw him out,
     With wondrous potency. Once more, good night;
     And when you are desirous to be blest,
     I'll blessing beg of you. For this same lord
     I do repent; but Heaven hath pleas'd it so,
     To punish me with this, and this with me,
     That I must be their scourge and minister.
     I will bestow him, and will answer well
     The death I gave him. So, again, good night.
     I must be cruel only to be kind;

Thus bad begins and worse remains behind.
One word more, good lady.
QUEEN.   What shall I do?
HAMLET.   Not this, by no means, that I bid you do:
Let the bloat King tempt you again to bed;
Pinch wanton on your cheek; call you his mouse;
And let him, for a pair of reechy kisses,
Or paddling in your neck with his damn'd fingers,
Make you to ravel all this matter out,
That I essentially am not in madness,
But mad in craft. 'Twere good you let him know;
For who that's but a queen, fair, sober, wise,
Would from a paddock, from a bat, a gib,
Such dear concernings hide? Who would do so?
No, in despite of sense and secrecy,
Unpeg the basket on the house's top,
Let the birds fly, and, like the famous ape,
To try conclusions, in the basket creep
And break your own neck down.
QUEEN.   Be thou assur'd, if words be made of breath
And breath of life, I have no life to breathe
What thou hast said to me.
HAMLET.   I must to England; you know that?
QUEEN.   Alack,
I had forgot. 'Tis so concluded on.
HAMLET.   There's letters seal'd; and my two school-fellows,
Whom I will trust as I will adders fang'd—
They bear the mandate; they must sweep my way
And marshal me to knavery. Let it work;
For 'tis the sport to have the engineer
Hoist with his own petar; and't shall go hard
But I will delve one yard below their mines
And blow them at the moon. O, 'tis most sweet
When in one line two crafts directly meet.
This man shall set me packing.
I'll lug the guts into the neighbour room.
Mother, good night. Indeed, this counsellor
Is now most still, most secret, and most grave,
Who was in life a foolish prating knave.
Come, sir, to draw toward an end with you.
Good night, mother.

Exeunt severally; Hamlet *tugging in* Polonius

ILLUSTRATION 17

The Second Coming

WILLIAM BUTLER YEATS

Turning and turning in the widening gyre
The falcon cannot hear the falconer;
Things fall apart; the center cannot hold;
Mere anarchy is loosed upon the world,
The blood-dimmed tide is loosed, and everywhere
The ceremony of innocence is drowned;
The best lack all conviction, while the worst
Are full of passionate intensity.

Surely some revelation is at hand;
Sure the Second Coming is at hand.
The Second Coming! Hardly are those words out
When a vast image out of *Spiritus Mundi*
Troubles my sight: somewhere in sands of the desert
A shape with lion body and the head of a man,
A gaze blank and pitiless as the sun,
Is moving its slow thighs, while all about it
Reel shadows of the indignant desert birds.
The darkness drops again; but now I know
That twenty centuries of stony sleep
Were vexed to nightmare by a rocking cradle,
And what rough beast, its hour come round at last,
Slouches towards Bethlehem to be born?

ILLUSTRATION 18

RICHARD SALIARIS, *The Second Coming,* reproduced by permission of the artist.

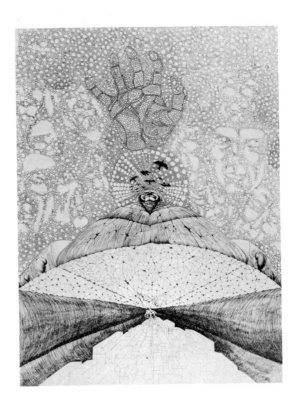

9

Historical Perspectives

Walter Pater, in an essay included in Part III, remarks,

> "To define beauty . . . is the aim of the true student of aesthetics."   ♭)

In contrast, R. G. Collingwood said that,

> "Aesthetic theory is a theory not of beauty but of art."[1]   ß

These two quotations sum up conflicting positions on the role of the idea of beauty in art and in aesthetics. The readings in Part III analyze these conflicting positions and clarify the historical and contemporary evolution of the various meanings of the notion of beauty, related ideas of taste, and the concept of the aesthetic. Historically beauty was defined as an objective quality of an object, and it was thought that one of the most important characteristics of a work of art was its aesthetic quality of beauty. Philosophy of art, the idea of beauty, and the theory of aesthetics were synonymous terms. Later, the idea of the beautiful came to be defined subjectively in terms of a response to an object rather than as an objective quality in an artwork, and the term "aesthetic" was applied to the sources of one's responses: one's taste. This led to theories of the aesthetic which dealt primarily with the ideas of beauty and taste, and these theories became distinct from philosophy of art which, in principle, analyzes works of art and the role of the artist. In contemporary philosophy the term "aesthetic" sometimes defines a particular set of concepts differentiating aesthetic from nonaesthetic qualities. Sometimes it refers to a particular kind of perception or response. And the word "aesthetic" is also used as an equivalent to "philosophy of art." But in none of these modern uses is the word "aesthetic" synonymous with the idea of beauty or identified with art. To sort out the evolution of the concept of the aesthetic, this chapter presents readings from historical analyses

---

[1]R. G. Collingwood, *Principles of Art* (London: Oxford University Press, 1938), p. 41.

341

of the concepts of beauty, taste, and the aesthetic. Chapter 10 discusses modern views on these ideas.

One of the earliest important statements of a theory of beauty was suggested by the neo-Platonic philosopher, Plotinus, who lived and wrote in the third century A.D. Plotinus's theory of beauty is based on Plato's theory of Forms, a thesis discussed in Part I. Plotinus argues, in brief, that in the intelligible world of Forms, there is a hierarchy of Forms of which Beauty is the highest. This is because Beauty is the source of perfection and the standard by which one judges the relative beauty of all objects and other Forms. Plotinus claims that art is not simply mimetic nor does the artist merely imitate nature. Rather an artist, according to Plotinus, first intellectually comprehends the Form of Beauty. Then the artist transmits this Form through his materials to compose a work of art. Thus the mind of the artist is active in creating a work of art by intellectually seeking and recreating a Form rather than merely copying nature or appearances. In contrast to Plato Plotinus claims that art reflects the Form of Beauty more closely than phenomena of nature or works of craftsmen because the artist is able to manipulate nature and manipulate materials with the Form of Beauty in mind. Plotinus is claiming, then, that beauty is an independent objective quality in art which participates in the Form of Beauty, that one can make true or false aesthetic statements about this quality, and that because of the artist's ability to comprehend and to recreate the Form of Beauty, beauty is an essential characteristic of works of art.

A difficulty with a position such as Plotinus's is that beauty, unlike qualities such as redness or symmetry, is not easily isolated and there is, in general, little agreement as to what counts as a true claim about beauty. Moreover, even if one agrees on what beauty is, beauty is not a unique feature of art since it is found in other phenomena as well. Because of these difficulties it is often argued that the ideal of the beautiful is objectively evoked by certain kinds of qualities. The aesthetic element in art lies not in any qualities in the work but rather in the relationship between certain qualities and one's response to those qualities.

One of the clearest statements of this position comes from the medieval philosopher and theologian Saint Thomas Aquinas. The idea of beauty, according to a Thomistic point of view (represented in this section by James Joyce as well as St. Thomas), originates in a series of perceptions evoked by an object, but these perceptions are unified in the mind to form an idea of beauty as a cognitive delight. The qualities in an object which evoke such a response are sensuous qualities, formal elements, and the integrity or proportion of the work as a whole. The response is an intellectual reaction to the totality of these elements which affect our perception and imagination, according to Aquinas's theory. Moreover the response is not related to any desire for, or use of, the contemplated object. Thus Aquinas introduces the modern notion that the characteristic of an aesthetic response is a purely contemplative or "disinterested" appreciation of qualities. St. Thomas's theory assumes that the idea of beauty has both objective elements, qualities in an object which trigger a response, and subjective elements, the aesthetic response. And both Plotinus and the Thomists emphasize the contemplative and intellectual character of the aesthetic.

In contrast, a purely subjective theory of beauty argues that the idea of the beautiful develops merely from personal responses to phenomena which please, interest, or stimulate emotional reactions. George Santayana, an American philosopher, claims, for example, that beauty is found merely in one's personal sensual reactions to objects which please. The claim that beauty is a quality in an object does not arise because one experiences any such objective features of beauty. Rather, it stems from what Santayana calls the objectification of our pleasurable responses. When one reacts pleasurably to something one tends to objectify that subjective pleasurable feeling by arguing that another's response to that object should also be pleasurable. Thus Santayana denies that beauty exists anywhere except in one's subjective emotional reactions. Note that when beauty is defined subjectively as a feeling, the idea of the aesthetic is identified with this subjective activity. And the relation of beauty to the aesthetic is described in terms of an aesthetic response rather than in relation to objective qualities. Beauty, then, according to philosophers such as Santayana is "in the eye of the beholder."[2]

The difficulties in defining beauty as an objective quality or a set of qualities led, in the eighteenth century, to the development of theories of taste where taste is the determining factor in aesthetic judgments. Taste was originally defined as an internal existing faculty of sense found universally in every person. Just as each of us has faculties of sense perception, so it was claimed we also have internal faculties, one of which is the sense of taste which detects beauty in objects just as eyes detect color. The faculty of taste accounts for one's selective responses to certain objective qualities wherein one makes an aesthetic judgment: "It is beautiful." The nature of the aesthetic response was thought to be a disinterested contemplative appreciation by some philosophers, and as a disinterested sense of pleasure by others. Moreover, philosophers of taste disagreed as to what sorts of features might evoke a sense of taste. Anthony Ashley Cooper (Lord Shaftesbury), an early eighteenth-century British philosopher of taste, argued in brief, that one's sense of taste was evoked by apprehending the Platonic Form of Beauty as it appears in perceived phenomena. According to Francis Hutcheson, another famous

---

[2]This quotation has been attributed to various philosophers including Saint Thomas Aquinas and David Hume. According to Bartlett, the source of this expression in this form is Margaret Wolf Hungerford in *Molly Bawn* (1878). See John Bartlett, *Bartlett's Familiar Quotations* (Boston: Little, Brown & Co., 1968), p. 831b.

English philosopher of that era, in a selection included in this section, "What we call Beautiful in Objects . . . seems to be in a compound Ratio of Unity and Variety." These formal qualities are perceived by an internal sense, according to Hutcheson, and they give rise to a disinterested sense of pleasure, a feeling shared universally by all those perceiving these qualities.

Theories of taste culminate in the aesthetic theory of Immanuel Kant whose writings were also included in Part II. In a selection from the *Critique of Judgment* included in this section Kant, claims that

> Taste is the faculty of judging an object or a mode of representing it by a wholly disinterested pleasure or displeasure. The object of such pleasure is called *beautiful*.

Taste, according to Kant, is a faculty of the imagination through which one responds qualitatively to art and to other phenomena. The response is "disinterested," since one responds to qualities in things rather than to the purposes for which a thing exists. The response is subjective, but the aesthetic judgment is universal (a) because it is triggered by universally perceived qualities; or (b) by universally known structures of experiences (the categories of the understanding); and (c) because the faculty of taste is also universally part of the constitution of every mind.

Few philosophers today claim that we have an internal sense of taste which is a faculty of the mind. But theories of taste are interesting because they distinguish philosophy of art, which deals with works of art, from a theory of beauty—the source of which is objective qualities in experienced phenomena. Philosophy of art and theories of beauty so defined are different from theories of the aesthetic in which the aesthetic is defined as the subjective response of taste, a response which is nevertheless the source for universal aesthetic judgments. Moreover theories of taste are important because these theories develop the notion of disinterest in aesthetic judgments: they try to answer the problem of whether or not beauty is merely subjective, and these theories are the source of the contemporary notion of the aesthetic attitude, an idea which is introduced later in this chapter. The selection from Joyce's *Portrait of an Artist* (Illustration 19) illustrates a modern version of Aquinas's aesthetic theory which takes into account some of the other views discussed in this section.

Chapter 9 concludes with a selection from Oscar Wilde's famous essay, "The Decay of Lying." Wilde, a well-known and infamous nineteenth-century British playwright and critic, deals a death blow to mimesis by arguing that Life imitates Art. And following the suggestion of his teacher Walter Pater, Wilde proposes that the aesthetic is a distinctive feature of true art. Art itself should personify the aesthetic, according to Wilde, and he states that "the proper aim of art" is purely aesthetic, the disinterested presentation of "beautiful untrue things." In the Preface to his novel, *The Picture of Dorian Gray*, Wilde reiterates his view that "life imitates art."

The Idea of the Beautiful

PLOTINUS

Beauty

Beauty addresses itself chiefly to sight; but there is a beauty for the hearing too, as in certain combinations of words and in all kinds of music, for melodies and cadences are beautiful; and minds that lift themselves above the realm of sense to a higher order are aware of beauty in the conduct of life, in actions, in character, in the pursuits of the intellect; and there is the beauty of the virtues. What loftier beauty there may be, yet, our argument will bring to light.

What, then, is it that gives comeliness to material forms and draws the ear to the sweetness perceived in sounds, and what is the secret of the beauty there is in all that derives from Soul?

Is there some One Principle from which all take their grace, or is there a beauty peculiar to the embodied and another for the bodiless? Finally, one or many, what would such a Principle be?

Consider that some things, material shapes for instance, are gracious not by anything inherent but by something communicated, while others are lovely of themselves, as, for example, Virtue.

The same bodies appear sometimes beautiful, sometimes not; so that there is a good deal between being body and being beautiful.

What, then, is this something that shows itself in certain material forms? This is the natural beginning of our inquiry.

What is it that attracts the eyes of those to whom a beautiful object is presented, and calls them, lures them, towards it, and fills them with joy at the sight? If we possess ourselves of this, we have at once a standpoint for the wider survey.

Almost everyone declares that the symmetry of parts towards each other and towards a whole, with, besides, a certain charm of colour, constitutes the beauty recognized by the eye, that in visible things, as indeed in all else, universally, the beautiful thing is essentially symmetrical, patterned.

But think what this means.

Only a compound can be beautiful, never anything devoid of parts; and only a whole; the several parts will have beauty, not in themselves, but only as working together to give a comely total. Yet beauty in an aggregate de-

From Plotinus, *The Enneads,* trans. Stephen MacKenna (London: Faber and Faber, 1930), Selections from Book I.

mands beauty in details: it cannot be constructed out of ugliness; its law must run throughout.

All the loveliness of colour and even the light of the sun, being devoid of parts and so not beautiful by symmetry, must be ruled out of the realm of beauty. And how comes gold to be a beautiful thing? And lightning by night, and the stars, why are these so fair?

In sounds also the simple must be proscribed, though often in a whole noble composition each several tone is delicious in itself.

Again since the one face, constant in symmetry, appears sometimes fair and sometimes not, can we doubt that beauty is something more than symmetry, that symmetry itself owes its beauty to a remoter principle?

Turn to what is attractive in methods of life or in the expression of thought; are we to call in symmetry here? What symmetry is to be found in noble conduct, or excellent laws, in any form of mental pursuit?

What symmetry can there be in points of abstract thought?

The symmetry of being accordant with each other? But there may be accordance or entire identity where there is nothing but ugliness: the proposition that honesty is merely a generous artlessness chimes in the most perfect harmony with the proposition that morality means weakness of will; the accordance is complete.

Then again, all the virtues are a beauty of the Soul, a beauty authentic beyond any of these others; but how does symmetry enter here? The Soul, it is true, is not a simple unity, but still its virtue cannot have the symmetry of size or of number: what standard of measurement could preside over the compromise or the coalescence of the Soul's faculties or purposes?

Finally, how by this theory would there be beauty in the Intellectual-Principle, essentially the solitary?

Let us, then, go back to the source, and indicate at once the Principle that bestows beauty on material things.

Undoubtedly this Principle exists; it is something that is perceived at the first glance, something which the Soul names as from an ancient knowledge and, recognizing, welcomes it, enters into unison with it.

But let the Soul fall in with the Ugly and at once it shrinks within itself, denies the thing, turns away from it, not accordant, resenting it.

Our interpretation is that the Soul—by the very truth of its nature, by its affiliation to the noblest Existents in the hierarchy of Being—when it sees anything of that kin, or any trace of that kinship, thrills with an immediate delight, takes its own to itself, and thus stirs anew to the sense of its nature and of all its affinity.

But, is there any such likeness between the loveliness of this world and the splendours in the Supreme? Such a likeness in the particulars would make the two orders alike: but what is there in common between beauty here and beauty There?

We hold that all the loveliness of this world comes by communion in Ideal-Form.

All shapelessness whose kind admits of pattern and form, as long as it remains outside of Reason and Idea, is ugly by that very isolation from the Divine Reason-Principle. And this is the Absolute Ugly: an ugly thing is something that has not been entirely mastered by pattern, that is by Reason, the Matter not yielding at all points and in all respects to Ideal-Form.

But where the Ideal-Form has entered, it has grouped and coordinated what from a diversity of parts was to become a unity: it has rallied confusion into cooperation: it has made the sum one harmonious coherence: for the Idea is a unity and what it moulds must come to unity as far as multiplicity may.

And on what has thus been compacted to unity, Beauty enthrones itself, giving itself to the parts as to the sum: when it lights on some natural unity, a thing of like parts, then it gives itself to that whole. Thus, for an illustration, there is the beauty, conferred by craftsmanship, of all a house with all its parts, and the beauty which some natural quality may give to a single stone.

This, then, is how the material thing becomes beautiful—by communicating in the Reason-Principle that flows from the Divine.

And the Soul includes a faculty peculiarly addressed to Beauty—one incomparably sure in the appreciation of its own, when Soul entire is enlisted to support its judgement.

Or perhaps the faculty acts immediately, affirming the Beautiful where it finds something accordant with the Ideal-Form within itself, using this Idea as a canon of accuracy in its decision.

But what accordance is there between the material and that which antedates all Matter?

On what principle does the architect, when he finds the house standing before him correspondent with his inner ideal of a house, pronounce it beautiful? Is it not that the house before him, the stones apart, is the inner idea stamped upon the mass of exterior matter, the indivisible exhibited in diversity?

So with the perceptive faculty: discerning in certain objects the Ideal-Form which has bound and controlled shapeless matter, opposed in nature to Idea, seeing further stamped upon the common shapes some shape excellent above the common, it gathers into unity what still remains fragmentary, catches it up and carries it within, no longer a thing of parts, and presents it to the inner Ideal-Principle as something concordant and congenial, a natural friend: the joy here is like that of a good man who discerns in a youth the early signs of a virtue consonant with the achieved perfection within his own soul.

The beauty of colour is also the outcome of a unification: it derives from shape, from the conquest of the darkness inherent in Matter by the pouring-in of light, the unembodied, which is a Rational-Principle and an Ideal-Form.

Hence it is that Fire itself is splendid beyond all material bodies, holding the rank of Ideal-Principle to the other elements, making ever upwards, the subtlest and sprightliest of all bodies, as very near to the unembodied; itself alone admitting no other, all the others penetrated by it: for they take warmth but this is never cold; it has colour primally; they receive the Form of colour from it: hence the splendour of its light, the splendour that belongs to the Idea. And all that has resisted and is but uncertainly held by its light remains outside of beauty, as not having absorbed the plentitude of the Form of colour.

And harmonies unheard in sound create the harmonies we hear and wake the Soul to the consciousness of beauty, showing it the one essence in another kind: for the measures of our sensible music are not arbitrary but are determined by the Principle whose labour is to dominate Matter and bring pattern into being.

Thus far of the beauties of the realm of sense, images and shadow-pictures, fugitives that have entered into Matter—to adorn, and to ravish, where they are seen. . . .

For, as the ancient teaching was, moral-discipline and courage and every virtue, not even excepting Wisdom itself, all is purification.

Hence the Mysteries with good reason adumbrate the immersion of the unpurified in filth, even in the Nether-World, since the unclean loves filth for its very filthiness, and swine foul of body find their joy in foulness.

What else is Sophrosyny, rightly so-called, but to take no part in the pleasures of the body, to break away from them as unclean and unworthy of the clean? So too, Courage is but being fearless of the death which is but the parting of the Soul from the body, an event which no one can dread whose delight is to be his unmingled self. And Magnanimity is but disregard for the lure of things here. And Wisdom is but the Act of the Intellectual-Principle withdrawn from the lower places and leading the Soul to the Above.

The Soul thus cleansed is all Idea and Reason, wholly free of body, intellective, entirely of that divine order from which the wellspring of Beauty rises and all the race of Beauty.

Hence the Soul heightened to the Intellectual-Principle is beautiful to all its power. For Intellection and all that proceeds from Intellection are the Soul's beauty, a graciousness native to it and not foreign, for only with these is it truly Soul. And it is just to say that in the Soul's becoming a good and beautiful thing is its becoming like to God, for from the Divine comes all the Beauty and all the Good in beings.

We may even say that Beauty *is* the Authentic-Existents and Ugliness is the Principle contrary to Existence: and the Ugly is also the primal evil; therefore its contrary is at once good and beautiful, or is Good and Beauty:

and hence the one method will discover to us the Beauty-Good and the Ugliness-Evil.

And Beauty, this Beauty which is also The Good, must be posed as The First: directly deriving from this First is the Intellectual-Principle which is pre-eminently the manifestation of Beauty; through the Intellectual-Principle Soul is beautiful. The beauty in things of a lower order—actions and pursuits for instance—comes by operation of the shaping Soul which is also the author of the beauty found in the world of sense. For the Soul, a divine thing, a fragment as it were of the Primal Beauty, makes beautiful to the fullness of their capacity all things whatsoever that it grasps and moulds. . . .

On the Intellectual Beauty

It is a principle with us that one who has attained to the vision of the Intellectual Cosmos and grasped the beauty of the Authentic Intellect will be able also to come to understand the Father and Transcendent of that Divine Being. It concerns us, then, to try to see and say, for ourselves and as far as such matters may be told, how the Beauty of the divine Intellect and of the Intellectual Cosmos may be revealed to contemplation.

Let us go to the realm of magnitudes:—suppose two blocks of stone lying side by side: one is unpatterned, quite untouched by art; the other has been minutely wrought by the craftsman's hands into some statue of god or man, a Grace or a Muse, or if a human being, not a portrait but a creation in which the sculptor's art has concentrated all loveliness.

Now it must be seen that the stone thus brought under the artist's hand to the beauty of form is beautiful not as stone—for so the crude block would be as pleasant—but in virtue of the Form or Idea introduced by the art. This form is not in the material; it is in the designer before ever it enters the stone; and the artificer holds it not by his equipment of eyes and hands but by his participation in his art. The beauty, therefore, exists in a far higher state in the art; for it does not come over integrally into the work; that original beauty is not transferred; what comes over is a derivative and a minor: and even that shows itself upon the statue not integrally and with entire realization of intention but only in so far as it has subdued the resistance of the material.

Art, then, creating in the image of its own nature and content, and working by the Idea or Reason-Principle of the beautiful object it is to produce, must itself be beautiful in a far higher and purer degree since it is the seat and source of that beauty, indwelling in the art, which must naturally be more complete than any comeliness of the external. In the degree in which the beauty is diffused by entering into matter, it is so much the weaker than that concentrated in unity; everything that reaches outwards is the less for it, strength less strong, heat less hot, every power less potent, and so beauty less beautiful.

Then again every prime cause must be, within itself, more powerful than its effect can be: the musical does not derive from an unmusical source but from music; and so the art exhibited in the material work derives from an art yet higher.

Still the arts are not to be slighted on the ground that they create by imitation of natural objects; for, to begin with, these natural objects are themselves imitations; then, we must recognize that they give no bare reproduction of the thing seen but go back to the Reason-Principles from which Nature itself derives, and, furthermore, that much of their work is all their own; they are holders of beauty and add where nature is lacking. Thus Pheidias wrought the Zeus upon no model among things of sense but by apprehending what form Zeus must take if he chose to become manifest to sight.

But let us leave the arts and consider those works produced by Nature and admitted to be naturally beautiful which the creations of art are charged with imitating, all reasoning life and unreasoning things alike, but especially the consummate among them, where the moulder and maker has subdued the material and given the form he desired. Now what is the beauty here? It has nothing to do with the blood or the menstrual process: either there is also a colour and form apart from all this or there is nothing unless sheer ugliness or (at best) a bare recipient, as it were the mere Matter of beauty.

Whence shone forth the beauty of Helen, battle-sought; or of all those women like in loveliness to Aphrodite; or of Aphrodite herself; or of any human being that has been perfect in beauty; or of any of these gods manifest to sight, or unseen but carrying what would be beauty if we saw?

In all these is it not the Form-Idea, something of that realm but communicated to the produced from within the producer, just as in works of art, we held, it is communicated from the arts to their creations? Now we can surely not believe that, while the made thing and the Reason-Principle thus impressed upon Matter are beautiful, yet the Principle not so alloyed but resting still with the creator—the Idea primal and immaterial—is not Beauty.

If material extension were in itself the ground of beauty, then the creating principle, being without extension, could not be beautiful: but beauty cannot be made to depend upon magnitude since, whether in a large object or a small, the one Idea equally moves and forms the mind by its inherent power. A further indication is that as long as the object remains outside us we know nothing of it; it affects us by entry; but only as an Ideal-Form can it enter through the eyes which are not of scope to take an extended mass: we are, no doubt, simultaneously possessed of the magnitude which, however, we take in not as mass but by an elaboration upon the presented form.

Then again the principle producing the beauty must be, itself, ugly, neutral, or beautiful: ugly, it could not produce the opposite; neutral, why should its product be the one rather than the other? The Nature, then, which creates things so lovely must be itself of a far earlier beauty; we, undisciplined

ARCHETYE
Jun 6

in discernment of the inward, knowing nothing of it, run after the outer, never understanding that it is the inner which stirs us; we are in the case of one who sees his own reflection but not realizing whence it comes goes in pursuit of it.

But that the thing we are pursuing is something different and that the beauty is not in the concrete object is manifest from the beauty there is in matters of study, in conduct and custom; briefly, in soul or mind. And it is precisely here that the greater beauty lies, perceived whenever you look to the wisdom in a man and delight in it, not wasting attention on the face, which may be hideous, but passing all appearance by and catching only at the inner comeliness, the truly personal; if you are still unmoved and cannot acknowledge beauty under such conditions, then looking to your own inner being you will find no beauty to delight you and it will be futile in that state to seek the greater vision, for you will be questing it through the ugly and impure.

This is why such matters are not spoken of to everyone; you, if you are conscious of beauty within, remember.

Thus there is in the Nature-Principle itself an Ideal archetype of the beauty that is found in material forms and, of that archetype again, the still more beautiful archetype in Soul, source of that in Nature. In the proficient soul this is brighter and of more advanced loveliness: adorning the soul and bringing to it a light from that greater light which is Beauty primally, its immediate presence sets the soul reflecting upon the quality of this prior, the archetype which has no such entries, and is present nowhere but remains in itself alone, and thus is not even to be called a Reason-Principle but is the creative source of the very first Reason-Principle which is the Beauty to which Soul serves as Matter.

This prior, then, is the Intellectual-Principle, the veritable, abiding and not fluctuant since not taking intellectual quality from outside itself. By what image, thus, can we represent it? We have nowhere to go but to what is less. Only from itself can we take an image of it; that is, there can be no representation of it, except in the sense that we represent gold by some portion of gold—purified, either actually or mentally, if it be impure—insisting at the same time that this is not the total thing gold, but merely the particular gold of a particular parcel. In the same way we learn in this matter from the purified Intellect in ourselves or, if you like, from the gods and the glory of the Intellect in them. . . .

All that comes to be, work of nature or of craft, some wisdom has made: everywhere a wisdom presides at a making.

No doubt the wisdom of the artist may be the guide of the work; it is sufficient explanation of the wisdom exhibited in the arts; but the artist himself goes back, after all, to that wisdom in Nature which is embodied in himself; and this is not a wisdom built up of theorems but one totality, not a wisdom consisting of manifold detail co-ordinated into a unity but rather a unity working out into detail.

Now, if we could think of this as the primal wisdom, we need look no further, since, at that, we have discovered a principle which is neither a derivative nor a "stranger in something strange to it." But if we are told that, while this Reason-Principle is in Nature, yet Nature itself is its source, we ask how Nature came to possess it; and, if Nature derived it from some other source, we ask what that other source may be; if, on the contrary, the principle is self-sprung, we need look no further: but if (as we assume) we are referred to the Intellectual-Principle we must make clear whether the Intellectual-Principle engendered the wisdom: if we learn that it did, we ask whence: if from itself, then inevitably it is itself Wisdom.

The true Wisdom, then (found to be identical with the Intellectual-Principle), is Real Being; and Real Being is Wisdom; it is wisdom that gives value to Real Being; and Being is Real in virtue of its origin in wisdom. It follows that all forms of existence not possessing wisdom are, indeed, Beings in right of the wisdom which went to their forming, but, as not in themselves possessing it, are not Real Beings.

We cannot, therefore, think that the divine Beings of that sphere, or the other supremely blessed There, need look to our apparatus of science: all of that realm (the very Beings themselves), all is noble image, such images as we may conceive to lie within the soul of the wise—but There not as inscription but as authentic existence. The ancients had this in mind when they declared the Ideas (Forms) to be Beings, Essentials. . . .

Beauty and Art

ST. THOMAS AQUINAS

First Part, Q. 5
Article 4. Whether Good Has the Aspect of a Final Cause?

We proceed thus to the Fourth Article: It seems that good has not the aspect of a final cause, but rather of the other causes.

Objection 1. For, as Dionysius says (*Div. Nom.* iv), "Goodness is praised

From St. Thomas Aquinas, *Summa Theologica*, trans. Fathers of the English Dominican Province (New York: Benzinger Brothers, Inc., 1948), short selections.

as beauty." But beauty has the aspect of a formal cause. Therefore goodness has the aspect of a formal cause.

Obj. 2. Further, goodness is self-giving, according to Dionysius who says (*loc. cit.*) that goodness is "that whereby all things subsist, and are." But to be self-giving implies the aspect of an efficient cause. Therefore goodness has the aspect of an efficient cause.

Obj. 3. Further, Augustine says that "we are, because God is good." But we are from God as from an efficient cause. Therefore goodness implies the aspect of an efficient cause.

On the contrary, The Philosopher says that "that is to be considered as the end and the good of other things for the sake of which something is." Therefore good has the aspect of a final cause.

I answer that, Since good is that which all things desire, and since this has the aspect of an end, it is clear that good implies the aspect of an end. Nevertheless the notion of good presupposes the notion of an efficient cause, and also of a formal cause. For we see that what is first in causing is last in the thing caused. Fire, for instance, heats first of all before bringing in the form of fire, though the heat in the fire follows from the substantial form. Now in causing, good and the end, which move the agent to act, come first; second, the action of the agent moving to the form; third, the form comes. Hence in that which is caused the converse ought to take place, so that there should be first, the form whereby it is a being; secondly, we consider in it its effecting power, whereby it is perfect in being, for a thing is perfect when it can reproduce its like, as the Philosopher says, thirdly, there follows the aspect of good which is the basic principle in a being of perfection.

Reply Obj. 1. Beauty and good in a subject are the same, for they are based upon the same thing, namely, the form; and consequently good is praised as beauty. But they differ logically, for good properly relates to the appetite (good being what all things desire), and therefore it has the aspect of an end (for the appetite is a kind of movement towards a thing). On the other hand, beauty relates to the knowing power, for beautiful things are those which please when seen. Hence beauty consists in due proportion, for the senses delight in things duly proportioned, as in what is after their own kind—because even sense is a sort of reason, just as is every knowing power. Now, since knowledge is by assimilation, and likeness relates to form, beauty properly belongs to the nature of a formal cause.

Reply Obj. 2. Good is described as self-giving in the sense that an end is said to move.

Reply Obj. 3. He who has a will is said to be good, so far as he has a good will, because it is by our will that we employ whatever powers we may have. Hence a man is said to be good, not by his good understanding, but by his good will. Now the will relates to the end as to its proper object. Thus the saying, "we are because God is good" has reference to the final cause.

First Part, Q. 39
Article 8. Whether the Essential Attributes Are Appropriated to the Persons in a Fitting Manner by the Holy Doctors?

We proceed thus to the Eighth Article: It would seem that the essential attributes are appropriated to the persons unfittingly by the holy doctors.

Objection 1. For Hilary says (*De Trin.* ii), "Eternity is in the Father, the species is in the Image; and use is in the Gift." In these words he designates three names proper to the persons: the name of the Father, the name Image proper to the Son (Q. XXXV, A. 2), and the name Bounty or Gift, which is proper to the Holy Ghost (Q. XXXVIII, A. 2). He also designates three appropriated terms. For he appropriates eternity to the Father, species to the Son, and use to the Holy Ghost. This he does apparently without reason. For eternity imports duration of being; species, the principle of being; and use belongs to the operation. But essence and operation are not found to be appropriated to any person. Therefore the above terms are not fittingly appropriated to the persons.

I answer that, Our intellect, which is led to the knowledge of God from creatures, must consider God according to the mode derived from creatures. In considering any creature four points present themselves to us in due order. First, the thing itself taken absolutely is considered as a being. Secondly, it is considered as one. Thirdly, its intrinsic power of operation and causality is considered. The fourth point of consideration embraces its relation to its effects. Hence this fourfold consideration comes to our mind in reference to God.

According to the first point of consideration, whereby we consider God absolutely in His being, the appropriation mentioned by Hilary applies, according to which eternity is appropriated to the Father, species to the Son, use to the Holy Ghost. For eternity in so far as it means a being without a principle, has a likeness to the property of the Father, Who is a principle without a principle. Species or beauty has a likeness to the property of the Son. For beauty includes three conditions: integrity or perfection, since those things which are impaired are by the very fact ugly; due proportion or harmony; and lastly, brightness, or clarity, whence things are called beautiful which have an elegant colour. . . .

We must now consider the cause of love, and under this head there are four points of inquiry: (1) Whether good is the only cause of love? (2) Whether knowledge is a cause of love? (3) Whether likeness is a cause of love? (4) Whether any other passion of the soul is the cause of love?

Part I of the Second Part, Q. 27
Article 1. Whether Good Is the Only Cause of Love?

We proceed thus to the First Article: It seems that good is not the only cause of love.

Objection 1. For good does not cause love, unless because it is loved. But it happens that evil also is loved, according to Ps. 10.6: *He that loveth iniquity, hateth his own soul;* otherwise every love would be good. Therefore good is not the only cause of love.

Obj. 2. Further, the Philosopher says that "we love those who acknowledge their evils." Therefore it seems that evil is the cause of love.

Obj. 3. Further, Dionysius says (*Div. Nom.* iv) that "not the good only but also the beautiful is beloved by all."

Reply Obj. 3. The beautiful is the same as the good, and they differ in aspect only. For since good is what all seek, that which calms the desire is implied in the notion of good, while that which calms the desire by being seen or known pertains to the notion of the beautiful. Consequently those senses especially have to do with the beautiful which are the best avenues of knowledge, namely, sight and hearing, as ministering to reason; for we speak of beautiful sights and beautiful sounds. But in reference to the other objects of the other senses, we do not use the expression beautiful, for we do not speak of beautiful tastes, or of beautiful odours. Thus it is evident that beauty adds to goodness a relation to the knowing power, so that good means that which pleases absolutely the appetite, while the beautiful is something pleasant to apprehend.

Part II of the Second Part, Q. 180
Article 2. Whether the Moral Virtues Pertain to the Contemplative Life?

We proceed thus to the Second Article: It seems that the moral virtues pertain to the contemplative life.

Obj. 3. Further, Gregory says (*Hom.* ii ix *Ezech.*) that "the contemplative life gives beauty to the soul," and so it is signified by Rachel, of whom it is said (Gen. 29.17) that she was *of a beautiful countenance.* Now the beauty of the soul consists in the moral virtues, especially temperance, as Ambrose says (De *Offic.* i, 43). Therefore it seems that the moral virtues pertain to the contemplative life.

On the contrary, The moral virtues are directed to external actions. Now Gregory says (*Hom.* ii *in Ezech.*) that it belongs to the contemplative life "to rest from external action." Therefore the moral virtues do not pertain to the contemplative life.

Reply Obj. 3. Beauty, as stated above (Q. CXLV, A. 2), consists in a certain clarity and due proportion. Now each of these has its roots in the reason, because both the light that makes beauty seen, and the establishing of due proportion among things belong to reason. Hence since the contemplative life consists in an act of the reason, there is beauty in it *per se* and essentially; therefore it is written (Wis. 8. 2) of the contemplation of wisdom: *I became a lover of her beauty.* On the other hand, beauty is in the moral virtues by participation, in so far that is as they share the order of reason; and above all is it in temperance, which restrains the concupiscences which especially darken the light of reason. Hence it is that the virtue of chastity most of all makes man apt for contemplation, since sexual pleasures most of all weigh the mind down to sensible objects, as Augustine says (*Soliloq.* i, 10).

The Universal Sense of Beauty

FRANCIS HUTCHESON

. . . The only Pleasure of Sense, which many Philosophers seem to consider, is that which accompanys the simple ideas of Sensation: But there are far greater Pleasures in those complex Ideas of Objects, which obtain the Names of *Beautiful, Regular, Harmonious.* . . . So in Musick, the Pleasure of *fine Composition* is incomparably greater than that of any one Note, how sweet, full, or swelling soever. . . .

I should rather choose to call our Power of perceiving these Ideas, an internal Sense. . . . Many Men have in the common Meaning, the Senses of Seeing and Hearing perfect enough; they perceive all the *simple Ideas* separately, and have their Pleasures; . . . And yet perhaps they shall find no Pleasure in Musical Compositions, in Painting, Architecture, natural Landskip; or but a very weak one in comparison of what others enjoy. . . .

This superior Power of Perception is justly called *a Sense,* because of its Affinity to the other Senses in this, that the Pleasure does not arise from

From Francis Hutcheson, *An Inquiry Into the Original of Our Ideas of Beauty and Virtue, Collected Works,* vol. 1 (Hildesheim, Germany: 1725; rpt. 1971).

any *Knowledge* of Principles, Proportions, Causes, or of the Usefulness of the Object; but strikes us at first with the Idea of Beauty. . . .

Beauty is either *Original* or *Comparative*; or if any like the Terms better, *Absolute*, or *Relative*: Only let it be observ'd, that by *Absolute* or *Original* Beauty, is not understood any Quality suppos'd to be in the Object, which should of itself be beautiful, without any Relation to any Mind which perceives it: For Beauty, like other Names of sensible Ideas, properly denotes the *Perception* of some Mind. . . . We therefore by *Absolute* Beauty understand only that Beauty, which we perceive in Objects without *comparison* to any thing external, of which the Object is suppos'd an imitation, or Picture; such as that Beauty perceiv'd from the *Works of Nature, artificial Forms, Figures, Theorems*. *Comparative* or *Relative* Beauty is that which we perceive in Objects, commonly considered as *Imitations* or *Resemblances* of something else. . . .

Of Original *or* Absolute Beauty

What we call Beautiful in Objects, to speak in the Mathematical Style, seems to be in a compound *Ratio* of *Uniformity* and *Variety*: so that where the *Uniformity* of Bodys is equal, the Beauty is as the *Variety*; and where the *Variety* is equal, the Beauty is as the *Uniformity*. . . .

As to that most powerful Beauty in *Countenances, Airs, Gestures, Motion*, we shall shew in the second Treatise, that it arises from some imagin'd *Indication* of morally good Dispositions of Mind. In motion there is also a natural Beauty, when at fixed periods like Gestures and Steps are regularly repeated. . . .

The *Beauty* arising from Mechanism, apparently adapted to the Necessitys and Advantages of any Animal; which pleases us, even tho there be no Advantage to our selves ensuing from it; will be consider'd under the Head of *Relative Beauty*, or *Design*. . . .

Under *Original Beauty* we may include *Harmony*, or *Beauty of Sound*, if that Expression can be allow'd, because *Harmony* is not usually conceiv'd as an Imitation of anything else. *Harmony* often raises Pleasure in those who know not what is the Occasion of it: and yet the Foundation of this Pleasure is known to be a sort of *Uniformity*. . . .

Of Relative *or* Comparative Beauty

This *Beauty* is founded on a *Conformity* or a kind of *Unity* between the Original and the Copy. . . . To obtain *comparative Beauty* alone, it is not necessary that there be any Beauty in the Original.

Everything in *Nature*, by our strange inclination to *Resemblance*, shall be brought to represent other things, even the most remote, especially the

Passions and Circumstances of human Nature in which we are more nearly concern'd.

Concerning our Reasoning about Design and Wisdom in the Cause, from the Beauty or Regularity of Effects

As there are an Infinity of *Forms* possible into which any System may be reduc'd, an Infinity of *Places* in which Animals may be situated, and an Infinity of *Relishes* or *Senses* in these Animals is suppos'd possible; that in the immense Spaces any one Animal should by chance be plac'd in a System agreeable to its Taste, must be improbable as *infinite* to one at least. . . . There is another kind of *Beauty* from which we conclude Wisdom in the Cause, as well as Design, *when we see many useful or beautiful Effects flowing from one general Cause.* . . . How incomparably more *beautiful* is this Structure, than if we suppos'd so many *distinct Volitions* in the DEITY, producing every particular Effect, and preventing some of the incidental Evils which casually flow from the *General Law*.

Of the Universality of the Sense of Beauty among Men

Since we know not how great a *Variety* of Senses there may be among Animals, there is no Form in *Nature* concerning which we can pronounce, "That it has no *Beauty*;" for it may still please some *perceiving Power*. But our *Inquiry* is confin'd to Men. . . . There is no Form which seems necessarily disagreeable of itself, when we dread no other Evil from it, and compare it with nothing better of the Kind. . . . No Composition of Objects which give not unpleasant simple Ideas seems positively unpleasant.

. . . Our *Sense of Beauty* seems design'd to give us positive Pleasure, but not positive Pain or Disgust, any further than what arises from disappointment. . . .

Of the Power of Custom, Education and Example, as to our Internal Senses

There is a *natural* Power of *Perception*, or *Sense of Beauty* in Objects, antecedent to all *Custom, Education,* or *Example*. . . .

Education and *Custom* may influence our *internal Senses*, where they are antecedently, by enlarging the Capacity of our Minds to retain and compare the Parts of complex Compositions: And then if the finest Objects are presented to us, we grow conscious of a Pleasure far superior to what common Performances excite. But all this presupposes our *Sense* of *Beauty* to be *natural*.

Of the Importance of the Internal Senses in Life, and the final Causes of them

Those Objects of Contemplation in which there is *Uniformity amidst Variety*, are more distinctly and easily comprehended and retain'd than *irregular Objects*. . . . Hence we see how suitable it is to the *sagacious Bounty* which we suppose in the DEITY, to constitute our *internal Senses* in the manner in which they are; by which Pleasure is join'd to the Contemplation of *those Objects* which a finite *Mind* can best imprint and retain the Ideas of with the least Distraction.

The Analytic of the Beautiful

IMMANUEL KANT

Of the Judgment of Taste,[1] According to Quality

The Judgment of Taste is Aesthetical

In order to distinguish whether anything is beautiful or not, we refer the representation, not by the understanding to the object for cognition, but by the imagination (perhaps in conjunction with the understanding) to the

From Immanuel Kant, *The Critique of Judgment*, trans. J. H. Bernard (New York: Hafner Publishing Co., 1951), printed by permission.

---

[1]The definition of "taste" which is laid down here is that it is the faculty of judging of the beautiful. But the analysis of judgments of taste must show what is required in order to call an object beautiful. The moments to which this judgment has regard in its reflection I have sought in accordance with the guidance of the logical functions of judgment (for in a judgment of taste a reference to the understanding is always involved). I have considered the moment of quality first because the aesthetical judgment upon the beautiful first pays attention to it.

subject and its feeling of pleasure or pain. The judgment of taste is therefore not a judgment of cognition, and is consequently not logical but aesthetical, by which we understand that whose determining ground can be *no other than subjective*. Every reference of representations, even that of sensations, may be objective (and then it signifies the real [element] of an empirical representation), save only the reference to the feeling of pleasure and pain, by which nothing in the object is signified, but through which there is a feeling in the subject as it is affected by the representation.

To apprehend a regular, purposive building by means of one's cognitive faculty (whether in a clear or a confused way of representation) is something quite different from being conscious of this representation as connected with the sensation of satisfaction. Here the representation is altogether referred to the subject and to its feeling of life, under the name of the feeling of pleasure or pain. This establishes a quite separate faculty of distinction and of judgment, adding nothing to cognition, but only comparing the given representation in the subject with the whole faculty of representations, of which the mind is conscious in the feeling of its state. Given representations in a judgment can be empirical (consequently, aesthetical); but the judgment which is formed by means of them is logical, provided they are referred in the judgment to the object. Conversely, if the given representations are rational, but are referred in a judgment simply to the subject (to its feeling), the judgment is so far always aesthetical. . . .

Comparison of the Three Specifically Different Kinds of Satisfaction

The pleasant and the good have both a reference to the faculty of desire, and they bring with them, the former a satisfaction pathologically conditioned (by impulses, *stimuli*), the latter a pure practical satisfaction which is determined not merely by the representation of the object but also by the represented connection of the subject with the existence of the object. [It is not merely the object that pleases, but also its existence.] On the other hand, the judgment of taste is merely *contemplative*; i.e., it is a judgment which, indifferent as regards the existence of an object, compares its character with the feeling of pleasure and pain. But this contemplation itself is not directed to concepts; for the judgment of taste is not a cognitive judgment (either theoretical or practical), and thus is not *based* on concepts, nor has it concepts as its *purpose*.

The pleasant, the beautiful, and the good designate then three different relations of representations to the feeling of pleasure and pain, in reference to which we distinguish from one another objects or methods of representing them. And the expressions corresponding to each, by which we mark our complacency in them, are not the same. That which *gratifies* a man is called *pleasant*; that which merely *pleases* him is *beautiful*; that which is *esteemed* [or *approved*] by him, i.e. that to which he accords an objective worth, is *good*. Pleasantness concerns irrational animals also, but beauty only concerns men, i.e. animal, but still rational, beings—not merely *quâ* rational (e.g. spirits), but *quâ* animal also—and the good concerns every rational being in general. This is a proposition which can only be completely established and explained in the sequel. We may say that, of all these three kinds of satisfaction, that of taste in the beautiful is alone a disinterested and *free* satisfaction; for no interest, either of sense or of reason, here forces our assent. Hence we may say of satisfaction that it is related in the three aforesaid cases to *inclination*, to *favor*, or to *respect*. Now *favor* is the only free satisfaction. An object of inclination and one that is proposed to our desire by a law of reason leave us no freedom in forming for ourselves anywhere an object of pleasure. All interest presupposes or generates a want, and, as the determining ground of assent, it leaves the judgment about the object no longer free. . . .

Explanation of the Beautiful Resulting from the First Moment: Taste is the faculty of judging an object or a method of representing it by an *entirely disinterested* satisfaction or dissatisfaction. The object of such satisfaction is called *beautiful*.

Of the Judgment of Taste, According to Quantity

The Beautiful Is that which Apart from Concepts Is Represented as the Object of a Universal Satisfaction

This explanation of the beautiful can be derived from the preceding explanation of it as the object of an entirely disinterested satisfaction. For the fact of which everyone is conscious, that the satisfaction is for him quite disinterested, implies in his judgment a ground of satisfaction for all men. For since it does not rest on any inclination of the subject (nor upon any other premeditated interest), but since the person who judges feels himself quite *free* as regards the satisfaction which he attaches to the object, he cannot find the ground of this satisfaction in any private conditions connected with his own subject, and hence it must be regarded as grounded on what he can presuppose in every other person. Consequently he must believe that he has reason for attributing a similar satisfaction to everyone. He will therefore speak of the beautiful as if beauty were a characteristic of the object and the judgment logical (constituting a cognition of the object by means of concepts of it), although it is only aesthetical and involves merely a reference of the representation of the object to the subject. For it has this similarity to a logical judgment that we can presuppose its validity for all men. But this universality cannot arise from concepts; for from concepts there is no transition to the feeling of pleasure or pain (except in pure practical laws, which bring an interest with them such as is not bound up with the pure judgment of taste). Consequently the judgment of taste, accompanied with the consciousness of separation from all interest, must claim validity for every man, without this universality depending on objects. That is, there must be bound up with it a title to subjective universality. . . .

The Universality of the Satisfaction Is Represented in a Judgment of Taste Only as Subjective

This particular determination of the universality of an aesthetical judgment, which is to be met with in a judgment of taste, is noteworthy, not indeed for the logician, but for the transcendental philosopher. It requires no small trouble to discover its origin, but we thus detect a property of our cognitive faculty which without this analysis would remain unknown.

First, we must be fully convinced of the fact that in a judgment of taste (about the beautiful) the satisfaction in the object is imputed to *everyone*, without being based on a concept (for then it would be the good). Further, this claim to universal validity so essentially belongs to a judgment by which we describe anything as *beautiful* that, if this were not thought in it, it would never come into our thoughts to use the expression at all, but everything which pleases without a concept would be counted as pleasant. In respect of the latter, everyone has his own opinion; and no one assumes in another agreement with his judgment of taste, which is always the case in a judgment of taste about beauty. I may call the first the taste of sense, the second the taste of reflection, so far as the first lays down mere private judgments and the second judgments supposed to be generally valid (public), but in both cases aesthetical (not practical) judgments about an object merely in respect of the relation of its representation to the feeling of pleasure and pain. Now here is something strange. As regards the taste of sense, not only does experience show that its judgment (of pleasure or pain connected with anything) is not valid universally, but everyone is content not to impute agreement with it to others (although actually there is often found a very extended concurrence in these judgments). On the other hand, the taste of reflection has its claim to the universal validity of its judgments (about the beautiful) rejected often enough, as experience teaches, although it may find it possible (as it actually does) to represent judgments which can demand this universal agreement. In fact it imputes this to everyone for each of its judgments of taste, without the persons that judge disputing as to the possibility of such a claim, although in particular cases they cannot agree as to the correct application of this faculty.

Here we must, in the first place, remark that a universality which does not rest on concepts of objects (not even on empirical ones) is not logical but aesthetical; i.e. it involves no objective quantity of the judgment, but only that which is subjective. For this I use the expression *general validity*, which signifies the validity of the reference of a representation, not to the cognitive faculty, but to the feeling of pleasure and pain for every subject. (We can avail ourselves also of the same expression for the logical quantity of the judgment, if only we prefix "objective" to "universal validity," to distinguish it from that which is merely subjective and aesthetical.)

A judgment with *objective universal validity* is also always valid subjectively; i.e. if the judgment holds for everything contained under a given concept, it holds also for everyone who represents an object by means of this concept. But from a *subjective universal validity*, i.e. aesthetical and resting on no concept, we cannot infer that which is logical because that kind of judgment does not extend to the object. But, therefore, the aesthetical universality which is ascribed to a judgment must be of a particular kind, because it does not unite the predicate of beauty with the concept of the object, considered in its whole logical sphere, and yet extends it to the whole sphere of judging persons. . . .

Explanation of the Beautiful Resulting from the Second Moment: The *beautiful* is that which pleases universally without [requiring] a concept.

Of Judgments of Taste, According to the Relation of the Purposes which are Brought into Consideration in Them

. . .

The Judgment of Taste Has Nothing at Its Basis but the Form of the Purposiveness of an Object (or of Its Mode of Representation)

Every purpose, if it be regarded as a ground of satisfaction, always carries with it an interest—as the determining ground of the judgment—about the object of pleasure. Therefore no subjective purpose can lie at the basis of the judgment of taste. But also the judgment of taste can be determined by no representation of an objective purpose, i.e. of the possibility of the object itself in accordance with principles of purposive combination, and consequently by no concept of the good, because it is an aesthetical and not a cognitive judgment. It therefore has to do with no *concept* of the character and internal or external possibility of the object by means of this or that cause, but merely with the relation of the representative powers to one another, so far as they are determined by a representation.

Now this relation in the determination of an object as beautiful is bound up with the feeling of pleasure, which is declared by the judgment of taste to be valid for everyone; hence a pleasantness [merely] accompanying the representation can as little contain the determining ground [of the judgment] as the representation of the perfection of the object and the concept of the good can. Therefore it can be nothing else than the subjective purposiveness in the representation of an object without any purpose (either objective or subjective), and thus it is the mere form of purposiveness in the representation by which an object is *given* to us, so far as we are conscious of it, which constitutes the satisfaction that we without a concept judge to be universally communicable; and, consequently, this is the determining ground of the judgment of taste. . . .

Of the Ideal of Beauty

. . . First, it is well to remark that the beauty for which an ideal is to be sought cannot be *vague* beauty, but is *fixed* by a concept of objective purposiveness; and thus it cannot appertain to the object of a quite pure judgment of taste, but to that of a judgment of taste which is in part intellectual. That is, in whatever grounds of judgment an ideal is to be found, an idea of reason in accordance with definite concepts must lie at its basis, which determines *a priori* the purpose on which the internal possibility of the object rests. An ideal of beautiful flowers, of a beautiful piece of furniture, of a beautiful view, is inconceivable. But neither can an ideal be represented of a beauty dependent on definite purposes, e.g. of a beautiful dwelling house, a beautiful tree, a beautiful garden, etc.; presumably because their purpose is not sufficiently determined and fixed by the concept, and thus the purposiveness is nearly as free as in the case of *vague* beauty. The only being which has the purpose of its existence in itself is *man,* who can determine his purposes by reason; or, where he must receive them from external perception, yet can compare them with essential and universal purposes and can judge this their accordance aesthetically. This *man* is, then, alone of all objects in the world, susceptible of an ideal of *beauty,* as it is only *humanity* in his person, as an intelligence, that is susceptible of the ideal of *perfection.*

But there are here two elements. *First,* there is the aesthetical *normal idea,* which is an individual intuition (of the imagination), representing the standard of our judgment [upon man] as a thing belonging to a particular animal species. *Secondly,* there is the *rational idea* which makes the purposes of humanity, so far as they cannot be sensibly represented the principle for judging of a figure through which, as their phenomenal effect, those purposes are revealed. The normal idea of the figure of an animal of a particular race must take its elements from experience. But the greatest purposiveness in the construction of the figure that would be available for the universal standard of aesthetical judgment upon each individual of this species—the image which is as it were designedly at the basis of nature's technique, to which only the whole race and not any isolated individual is adequate—this lies merely in the idea of the judging [subject]. And this, with its proportions as an aesthetical idea, can be completely presented *in concreto* in a model. . . .

We must yet distinguish the *normal idea* of the beautiful from the *ideal,* which latter, on grounds already alleged, we can only expect in the *human* figure. In this the ideal consists in the expression of the *moral,* without which the object would not please universally and thus positively (not merely negatively in an accurate presentation). The visible expression of moral ideas that rule men inwardly can indeed only be gotten from experience; but to make its connection with all which our reason unites with the morally good in the idea of the highest purposiveness—goodness of heart, purity, strength, peace, etc.—visible as it were in bodily manifestation (as the effect of that which is internal) requires a union of pure ideas of reason with great imaginative power even in him who wishes to judge of it, still more in him who wishes to present it. The correctness of such an ideal of beauty is shown by its permitting no sensible charm to mingle with the satisfaction in the object, and yet allowing us to take a great interest therein. This shows that a judgment in accordance with such a standard can never be purely aesthetical, and that a judgment in accordance with an ideal of beauty is not a mere judgment of taste.

Explanation of the Beautiful Derived from this Third Moment: Beauty is the form of the *purposiveness* of an object, so far as this is perceived in it *without any representation of a purpose.*[2]

---

[2]It might be objected to this explanation that there are things in which we see a purposive form without cognizing any purpose in them, like the stone implements often gotten from old sepulchral tumuli with a hole in them, as if for a handle. These, although they plainly indicate by their shape a purposiveness of which we do not know the purpose, are nevertheless not described as beautiful. But if we regard a thing as a work of art, that is enough to make us admit that its shape has reference to some design and definite purpose. And hence there is no immediate satisfaction in the contemplation of it. On the other hand a flower, e.g. a tulip, is regarded as beautiful, because in perceiving it we find a certain purposiveness which, in our judgment, is referred to no purpose at all.

Of the Judgment of Taste, According to the Modality of the Satisfaction in the Object

What the Modality in a Judgment of Taste Is

I can say of every representation that it is at least *possible* that (as a cognition) it should be bound up with a pleasure. Of a representation that I call *pleasant* I say that it *actually* excites pleasure in me. But the *beautiful* we think as having a *necessary* reference to satisfaction. Now this necessity is of a peculiar kind. It is not a theoretical objective necessity, in which case it would be cognized *a priori* that everyone *will feel* this satisfaction in the object called beautiful by me. It is not a practical necessity, in which case, by concepts of a pure rational will serving as a rule for freely acting beings, the satisfaction is the necessary result of an objective law and only indicates that we absolutely (without any further design) ought to act in a certain way. But the necessity which is thought in an aesthetical judgment can only be called exemplary, i.e. a necessity of the assent of *all* to a judgment which is regarded as the example of a universal rule that we cannot state. Since an aesthetical judgment is not an objective cognitive judgment, this necessity cannot be derived from definite concepts and is therefore not apodictic. Still less can it be inferred from the universality of experience (of a complete agreement of judgments as to the beauty of a certain object). For not only would experience hardly furnish sufficiently numerous vouchers for this, but also, on empirical judgments, we can base no concept of the necessity of these judgments.

The Subjective Necessity, which We Ascribe to the Judgment of Taste, Is Conditioned

The judgment of taste requires the agreement of everyone, and he who describes anything as beautiful claims that everyone *ought* to give his approval to the object in question and also describe it as beautiful. The *ought* in the aesthetical judgment is therefore pronounced in accordance with all the data which are required for judging, and yet is only conditioned. We ask for the agreement of everyone else, because we have for it a ground that is common to all; and we could count on this agreement, provided we were always sure that the case was correctly subsumed under that ground as rule of assent. . . .

Explanation of the Beautiful Resulting from the Fourth Moment: The *Beautiful* is that which without any concept is cognized as the object of a *necessary* satisfaction.

The Sense of Beauty

GEORGE SANTAYANA

The Differentia of Aesthetic Pleasure Not Its Disinterestedness

The distinction between pleasure and the sense of beauty has sometimes been said to consist in the unselfishness of aesthetic satisfaction. In other pleasures, it is said, we gratify our senses and passions; in the contemplation of beauty we are raised above ourselves, the passions are silenced and we are happy in the recognition of a good that we do not seek to possess. The painter does not look at a spring of water with the eyes of a thirsty man, nor at a beautiful woman with those of a satyr. The difference lies, it is urged, in the impersonality of the enjoyment. But this distinction is one of intensity and delicacy, not of nature, and it seems satisfactory only to the least aesthetic minds.

In the second place, the supposed disinterestedness of aesthetic delights is not very fundamental. Appreciation of a picture is not identical with the desire to buy it, but it is, or ought to be, closely related and preliminary to that desire. The beauties of nature and of the plastic arts are not consumed by being enjoyed; they retain all the efficacy to impress a second beholder. But this circumstance is accidental, and those aesthetic objects which depend upon change and are exhausted in time, as are all performances, are things the enjoyment of which is an object of rivalry and is coveted as much as any other pleasure. And even plastic beauties can often not be enjoyed except by a few, on account of the necessity of travel or other difficulties of access, and then this aesthetic enjoyment is as selfishly pursued as the rest.

The truth which the theory is trying to state seems rather to be that when we seek aesthetic pleasures we have no further pleasure in mind; that we do not mix up the satisfactions of vanity and proprietorship with the delight of contemplation. This is true, but it is true at bottom of all pursuits and enjoyments. Every real pleasure is in one sense disinterested. It is not sought with ulterior motives, and what fills the mind is no calculation, but the image of an object or event, suffused with emotion. A sophisticated consciousness may often take the idea of self as the touchstone of its inclinations; but this self, for the gratification and aggrandizement of which a man may live, is itself only a complex of aims and memories, which once had their direct objects, in which he had taken a spontaneous and unselfish interest. The

Excerpts from George Santayana, *The Sense of Beauty* (New York: Charles Scribner's Sons, 1896, rpt. 1955).

gratifications which, merged together, make the selfishness are each of them ingenuous, and no more selfish than the most altruistic, impersonal emotion. The content of selfishness is a mass of unselfishness. There is no reference to the nominal essence called oneself either in one's appetites or in one's natural affections; yet a man absorbed in his meat and drink, in his houses and lands, in his children and dogs, is called selfish because these interests, although natural and instinctive in him, are not shared by others. The unselfish man is he whose nature has a more universal direction, whose interests are more widely diffused.

But as impersonal thoughts are such only in their object, not in their subject or agent, since all thoughts are the thoughts of somebody: so also unselfish interests have to be somebody's interests. If we were not interested in beauty, if it were of no concern to our happiness whether things were beautiful or ugly, we should manifest not the maximum, but the total absence of aesthetic faculty. The disinterestedness of this pleasure is, therefore, that of all primitive and intuitive satisfactions, which are in no way conditioned by a reference to an artificial general concept, like that of the self, all the potency of which must itself be derived from the independent energy of its component elements. I care about myself because "myself" is a name for the things I have at heart. To set up the verbal figment of personality and make it an object of concern apart from the interests which were its content and substance, turns the moralist into a pedant, and ethics into a superstition. The self which is the object of *amour propre* is an idol of the tribe, and needs to be disintegrated into the primitive objective interests that underlie it before the cultus of it can be justified by reason.

The Differentia of Aesthetic Pleasure Not Its Universality

The supposed disinterestedness of our love of beauty passes into another characteristic of it often regarded as essential—its universality. The pleasures of the senses have, it is said, no dogmatism in them; that anything gives me pleasure involves no assertion about its capacity to give pleasure to another. But when I judge a thing to be beautiful, my judgment means that the thing is beautiful in itself, or (what is the same thing more critically expressed) that it should seem so to everybody. The claim to universality is, according to this doctrine, the essence of the aesthetic; what makes the perception of beauty a judgment rather than a sensation. All aesthetic precepts would be impossible, and all criticism arbitrary and subjective, unless we admit a paradoxical universality in our judgment, the philosophical implications of which we may then go on to develop. But we are fortunately not required to enter the labyrinth into which this method leads; there is a much simpler and clearer way of studying such questions, which is to challenge and analyze the assertion before us and seek its basis in human nature. Before this is done, we should run the risk of expanding a natural misconception or inaccuracy of thought into an inveterate and pernicious prejudice by making it the centre of an elaborate construction.

That the claim of universality is such a natural inaccuracy will not be hard to show. There is notoriously no great agreement upon aesthetic matters; and such agreement as there is, is based upon similarity of origin, nature, and circumstance among men, a similarity which, where it exists, tends to bring about identity in all judgments and feelings. It is unmeaning to say that what is beautiful to one man *ought* to be beautiful to another. If their senses are the same, their associations and dispositions similar, then the same thing will certainly be beautiful to both. If their natures are different, the form which to one will be entrancing will be to another even invisible, because his classifications and discriminations in perception will be different, and he may see a hideous detached fragment or a shapeless aggregate of things, in what to another is a perfect whole—so entirely are the unities of objects unities of function and use. It is absurd to say that what is invisible to a given being *ought* to seem beautiful to him. Evidently this obligation of recognizing the same qualities is conditioned by the possession of the same faculties. But no two men have exactly the same faculties, nor can things have for any two exactly the same values.

What is loosely expressed by saying that any one ought to see this or that beauty is that he would see it if his disposition, training, or attention were what our ideal demands for him; and our ideal of what any one should be has complex but discoverable sources. We take, for instance, a certain pleasure in having our own judgments supported by those of others; we are intolerant, if not of the existence of a nature different from our own, at least of its expression in words and judgments. We are confirmed or made happy in our doubtful opinions by seeing them accepted universally. We are unable to find the basis of our taste in our own experience and therefore refuse to look for it there. If we were sure of our ground, we should be willing to acquiesce in the naturally different feelings and ways of others, as a man who is conscious of speaking his language with the accent of the capital confesses its arbitrariness with gayety, and is pleased and interested in the variations of it he observes in provincials; but the provincial is always zealous to show that he has reason and ancient authority to justify his oddities. So people who have no sensations, and do not know why they judge, are always trying to show that they judge by universal reason.

Thus the frailty and superficiality of our own judgments cannot brook contradiction. We abhor another man's doubt when we cannot tell him why we ourselves believe. Our ideal of other men tends therefore to include the agreement of their judgments with our own; and although we might acknowledge the fatuity of this demand in regard to natures very different from the human, we may be unreasonable enough to require that all races should admire the same style of architecture, and all ages the same poets.

The great actual unity of human taste within the range of conventional history helps the pretension. But in principle it is untenable. Nothing has less to do with the real merit of a work of imagination than the capacity of all men to appreciate it; the true test is the degree and kind of satisfaction it can give to him who appreciates it most. The symphony would lose nothing if half mankind had always been deaf, as nine-tenths of them actually are to the intricacies of its harmonies; but it would have lost much if no Beethoven had existed. And more: incapacity to appreciate certain types of beauty may be the condition *sine qua non* for the appreciation of another kind; the greatest capacity both for enjoyment and creation is highly specialized and exclusive, and hence the greatest ages of art have often been strangely intolerant.

The invectives of one school against another, perverse as they are philosophically, are artistically often signs of health, because they indicate a vital appreciation of certain kinds of beauty, a love of them that has grown into a jealous passion. The architects that have pieced out the imperfections of ancient buildings with their own thoughts, like Charles V. when he raised his massive palace beside the Alhambra, may be condemned from a certain point of view. They marred much by their interference; but they showed a splendid confidence in their own intuitions, a proud assertion of their own taste, which is the greatest evidence of aesthetic sincerity. On the contrary, our own gropings, eclecticism, and archaeology are the symptoms of impotence. If we were less learned and less just, we might be more efficient. If our appreciation were less general, it might be more real, and if we trained our imagination into exclusiveness, it might attain to character.

The Differentia of Aesthetic Pleasure: Its Objectification

There is, however, something more in the claim to universality in aesthetic judgments than the desire to generalize our own opinions. There is the expression of a curious but well-known psychological phenomenon, viz., the transformation of an element of sensation into the quality of a thing. If we say that other men should see the beauties we see, it is because we think those beauties *are in the object*, like its colour, proportion, or size. Our judgment appears to us merely the perception and discovery of an external existence, of the real excellence that is without. But this notion is radically absurd and contradictory. Beauty, as we have seen, is a value; it cannot be conceived as an independent existence which affects our senses and which we consequently perceive. It exists in perception, and cannot exist otherwise. A beauty not perceived is a pleasure not felt, and a contradiction. But modern philosophy has taught us to say the same thing of every element of the perceived world; all are sensations; and their grouping into objects imagined to be permanent and external is the work of certain habits of our intelligence. We should be incapable of surveying or retaining the diffused experiences of life, unless we organized and classified them, and out of the chaos of impressions framed the world of conventional and recognizable objects.

How this is done is explained by the current theories of perception. External objects usually affect various senses at once, the impressions of which are thereby associated. Repeated experiences of one object are also associated on account of their similarity; hence a double tendency to merge and unify into a single percept, to which a name is attached, the group of those memories and reactions which in fact had one external thing for their cause. But this percept, once formed, is clearly different from those particular experiences out of which it grew. It is permanent, they are variable. They are but partial views and glimpses of it. The constituted notion therefore comes to be the reality, and the materials of it merely the appearance. The distinction between substance and quality, reality and appearance, matter and mind, has no other origin.

The objects thus conceived and distinguished from our ideas of them, are at first compacted of all the impressions, feelings, and memories, which offer themselves for association and fall within the vortex of the amalgamating imagination. Every sensation we get from a thing is originally treated as one of its qualities. Experiment, however, and the practical need of a simpler conception of the structure of objects lead us gradually to reduce the qualities of the object to a minimum, and to regard most perceptions as an effect of those few qualities upon us. These few primary qualities, like extension which we persist in treating as independently real and as the quality of a substance, are those which suffice to explain the order of our experiences. All the rest, like colour, are relegated to the subjective sphere, as merely effects upon our minds, and apparent or secondary qualities of the object.

But this distinction has only a practical justification. Convenience and economy of thought alone determine what combination of our sensations we shall continue to objectify and treat as the cause of the rest. The right and tendency to be objective is equal in all, since they are all prior to the artifice of thought by which we separate the concept from its materials, the thing from our experiences.

The qualities which we now conceive to belong to real objects are for the most part images of sight and touch. One of the first classes of effects to be treated as secondary were naturally pleasures and pains, since it could commonly conduce very little to intelligent and successful action to conceive our pleasures and pains as resident in objects. But emotions are essentially capable of objectification, as well as impressions of sense; and one may well believe that a primitive and inexperienced consciousness would rather people the world with ghosts of its own terrors and passions than with projections of those luminous and mathematical concepts which as yet it could hardly have formed.

This animistic and mythological habit of thought still holds its own at the confines of knowledge, where mechanical explanations are not found. In ourselves, where nearness makes observation difficult, in the intricate chaos of animal and human life, we still appeal to the efficacy of will and ideas, as also in the remote night of cosmic and religious problems. But in all the intermediate realm of vulgar day, where mechanical science has made progress, the inclusion of emotional or passionate elements in the concept of the reality would be now an extravagance. Here our idea of things is composed exclusively of perceptual elements, of the ideas of form and of motion.

The beauty of objects, however, forms an exception to this rule. Beauty is an emotional element, a pleasure of ours, which nevertheless we regard as a quality of things. But we are now prepared to understand the nature of this exception. It is the survival of a tendency originally universal to make every effect of a thing upon us a constituent of its conceived nature. The scientific idea of a thing is a great abstraction from the mass of perceptions and reactions which that thing produces; the aesthetic idea is less abstract, since it retains the emotional reaction, the pleasure of the perception, as an integral part of the conceived thing.

Nor is it hard to find the ground of this survival in the sense of beauty of an objectification of feeling elsewhere extinct. Most of the pleasures which objects cause are easily distinguished and separated from the perception of the object: the object has to be applied to a particular organ, like the palate, or swallowed like wine, or used and operated upon in some way before the pleasure arises. The cohesion is therefore slight between the pleasure and the other associated elements of sense; the pleasure is separated in time from the perception, or it is localized in a different organ, and consequently is at once recognized as an effect and not as a quality of the object. But when the process of perception itself is pleasant, as it may easily be, when the intellectual operation, by which the elements of sense are associated and projected, and the concept of the form and substance of the thing produced, is naturally delightful, then we have a pleasure intimately bound up in the thing, inseparable from its character and constitution, the seat of which in us is the same as the seat of the perception. We naturally fail, under these circumstances, to separate the pleasure from the other objectified feelings. It becomes, like them, a quality of the object, which we distinguish from pleasures not so incorporated in the perception of things, by giving it the name of beauty.

The Definition of Beauty

We have now reached our definition of beauty, which, in the terms of our successive analysis and narrowing of the conception, is value positive, intrinsic, and objectified. Or, in less technical language, Beauty is pleasure regarded as the quality of a thing.

This definition is intended to sum up a variety of distinctions and identifications which should perhaps be here more explicitly set down. Beauty is a value, that is, it is not a perception of a matter of fact or of a relation: it is an emotion, an affection of our volitional and appreciative nature. An object cannot be beautiful if it can give pleasure to nobody: a beauty to which all men were forever indifferent is a contradiction in terms.

In the second place, this value is positive, it is the sense of the presence of something good, or (in the case of ugliness) of its absence. It is never the perception of a positive evil, it is never a negative value. That we are endowed with the sense of beauty is a pure gain which brings no evil with it. When the ugly ceases to be amusing or merely uninteresting and becomes disgusting, it becomes indeed a positive evil: but a moral and practical, not an aesthetic one. In aesthetics that saying is true—often so disingenuous in ethics—that evil is nothing but the absence of good: for even the tedium and vulgarity of an existence without beauty is not itself ugly so much as lamentable and degrading. The absence of aesthetic goods is a moral evil: the aesthetic evil is merely relative, and means less of aesthetic good than was expected at the place and time. No form in itself gives pain, although some forms give pain by causing a shock of surprise even when they are really beautiful: as if a mother found a fine bull pup in her child's cradle, when her pain would not be aesthetic in its nature.

Further, this pleasure must not be in the consequence of the utility of the object or event, but in its immediate perception; in other words, beauty is an ultimate good, something that gives satisfaction to a natural function, to some fundamental need or capacity of our minds. Beauty is therefore a positive value that is intrinsic; it is a pleasure. These two circumstances sufficiently separate the sphere of aesthetics from that of ethics. Moral values are generally negative, and always remote. Morality has to do with the avoidance of evil and the pursuit of good: aesthetics only with enjoyment.

Finally, the pleasures of sense are distinguished from the perception of beauty, as sensation in general is distinguished from perception; by the objectification of the elements and their appearance as qualities rather of things than of consciousness. The passage from sensation to perception is gradual, and the path may be sometimes retraced: so it is with beauty and the pleasures of sensation. There is no sharp line between them, but it depends upon the degree of objectivity my feeling has attained at the moment whether I say "It pleases me," or "It is beautiful." If I am self-conscious and critical, I shall probably use one phrase; if I am impulsive and susceptible, the other. The more remote, interwoven, and inextricable the pleasure is, the more objective it will appear; and the union of two pleasures often makes one beauty. In Shakespeare's LIVth sonnet are these words:

O how much more doth beauty beauteous seem
By that sweet ornament which truth doth give!
The rose looks fair, but fairer we it deem
For that sweet odour which doth in it live.
The canker-blooms have full as deep a dye
As the perfumèd tincture of the roses,
Hang on such thorns, and play as wantonly
When summer's breath their maskèd buds discloses.
But, for their beauty only is their show,
They live unwooed and unrespected fade;
Die to themselves. Sweet roses do not so:
Of their sweet deaths are sweetest odours made.

One added ornament, we see, turns the deep dye, which was but show and mere sensation before, into an element of beauty and reality; and as truth is here the co-operation of perceptions, so beauty is the co-operation of pleasures. If colour, form, and motion are hardly beautiful without the sweetness of the odour, how much more necessary would they be for the sweetness itself to become a beauty! If we had the perfume in a flask, no one would think of calling it beautiful: it would give us too detached and controllable a sensation. There would be no object in which it could be easily incorporated. But let it float from the garden, and it will add another sensuous charm to objects simultaneously recognized, and help to make them beautiful. Thus beauty is constituted by the objectification of pleasure. It is pleasure objectified.

BEAUTY AND THE AESTHETIC IN THE ARTS

The Aesthetic

WALTER PATER

Many attempts have been made by writers on art and poetry to define beauty in the abstract, to express it in the most general terms, to find some universal

From Walter Pater, *The Renaissance* (1873; rpt. New York: Boni & Liveright 1959), selections from the Preface.

formula for it. The value of these attempts has most often been in the suggestive and penetrating things said by the way. Such discussions help us very little to enjoy what has been well done in art or poetry, to discriminate between what is more and what is less excellent in them, or to use words like beauty, excellence, art, poetry, with a more precise meaning than they would otherwise have. Beauty, like all other qualities presented to human experience, is relative; and the definition of it becomes unmeaning and useless in proportion to its abstractness. To define beauty, not in the most abstract but in the most concrete terms possible, to find not its universal formula, but the formula which expresses most adequately this or that special manifestation of it, is the aim of the true student of aesthetics.

"To see the object as in itself it really is," has been justly said to be the aim of all true criticism whatever; and in aesthetic criticism the first step towards seeing one's object as it really is, is to know one's own impression as it really is, to discriminate it, to realise it distinctly. The objects with which aesthetic criticism deals—music, poetry, artistic and accomplished forms of human life—are indeed receptacles of so many powers or forces: they possess, like the products of nature, so many virtues or qualities. What is this song or picture, this engaging personality presented in life or in a book, to *me?* What effect does it really produce on me? Does it give me pleasure? and if so, what sort or degree of pleasure? How is my nature modified by its presence, and under its influence? The answers to these questions are the original facts with which the aesthetic critic has to do; and, as in the study of light, of morals, of number, one must realise such primary data for one's self, or not at all. And he who experiences these impressions strongly, and drives directly at the discrimination and analysis of them, has no need to trouble himself with the abstract question what beauty is in itself, or what its exact relation to truth or experience—metaphysical questions, as unprofitable as metaphysical questions elsewhere. He may pass them all by as being, answerable or not, of no interest to him.

The aesthetic critic, then, regards all the objects with which he has to do, all works of art, and the fairer forms of nature and human life, as powers or forces producing pleasurable sensations, each of a more or less peculiar or unique kind. This influence he feels, and wishes to explain, by analysing and reducing it to its elements. To him, the picture, the landscape, the engaging personality in life or in a book, *La Gioconda,* the hills of Carrara, Pico of Mirandola, are valuable for their virtues, as we say, in speaking of a herb, a wine, a gem; for the property each has of affecting one with a special, a unique, impression of pleasure. Our education becomes complete in proportion as our susceptibility to these impressions increases in depth and variety. And the function of the aesthetic critic is to distinguish, to analyse, and separate from its adjuncts, the virtue by which a picture, a landscape, a fair personality in life or in a book, produces this special impression of beauty or pleasure, to indicate what the source of that impression is, and under what conditions it is experienced. His end is reached when he has disengaged that virtue, and noted it, as a chemist notes some natural element, for himself and others; and the rule for those who would reach this end is stated with great exactness in the words of a recent critic of Sainte-Beuve:—*De se borner à connâitre de près les belles choses, et à s'en nourrir en exquis amateurs, en humanistes accomplis.*

What is important, then, is not that the critic should possess a correct abstract definition of beauty for the intellect, but a certain kind of temperament, the power of being deeply moved by the presence of beautiful objects. He will remember always that beauty exists in many forms. To him all periods, types, schools of taste, are in themselves equal. In all ages there have been some excellent workmen, and some excellent work done. The question he asks is always:—In whom did the stir, the genius, the sentiment of the period find itself? where was the receptacle of its refinement, its elevation, its taste? "The ages are all equal," says William Blake, "but genius is always above its age."

The Decay of Lying

OSCAR WILDE

CYRIL[1] (*coming in through the open window from the terrace*):   My dear Vivian, don't coop yourself up all day in the library. It is a perfectly lovely afternoon. The air is exquisite. There is a mist upon the woods like the purple bloom upon a plum. Let us go and lie on the grass, and smoke cigarettes, and enjoy Nature.

VIVIAN: Enjoy Nature! I am glad to say that I have entirely lost that faculty. People tell us that Art makes us love Nature more than we loved her before; that it reveals her secrets to us; and that after a careful study of Corot and Constable[2] we see things in her that had escaped our observation. My own experience is that the more we study Art, the less we care for Nature. What Art really reveals

Oscar Wilde, "The Decay of Lying," *The Artist as Critic,* ed. Richard Ellmann (New York: Random House, 1891, rpt. 1969).

---

[1]Cyril and Vyvyan were the names of Wilde's sons.

[2]Jean Baptiste Camille Corot (1796–1875), French painter; John Constable (1776–1837), English painter.

to us is Nature's lack of design, her curious crudities, her extraordinary monotony, her absolutely unfinished condition. Nature has good intentions, of course, but, as Aristotle once said, she cannot carry them out. When I look at a landscape I cannot help seeing all its defects. It is fortunate for us, however, that Nature is so imperfect, as otherwise we should have had no art at all. Art is our spirited protest, our gallant attempt to teach Nature her proper place. As for the infinite variety of Nature, that is pure myth. It is not to be found in Nature herself. It resides in the imagination, or fancy, or cultivated blindness of the man who looks at her.

CYRIL: Well, you need not look at the landscape. You can lie on the grass and smoke and talk.

VIVIAN: But Nature is so uncomfortable. Grass is hard and lumpy and damp, and full of dreadful black insects. Why, even Morris's[3] poorest workman could make you a more comfortable seat than the whole of Nature can. Nature pales before the furniture of "the street which from Oxford has borrowed its name," as the poet you love so much once vilely phrased it. I don't complain. If Nature had been comfortable, mankind would never have invented architecture, and I prefer houses to the open air. . . .

CYRIL: . . . However, proceed with your article.

VIVIAN (*reading*): "Art begins with abstract decoration with purely imaginative and pleasurable work dealing with what is unreal and nonexistent. This is the first stage. Then Life becomes fascinated with this new wonder, and asks to be admitted into the charmed circle. Art takes life as part of her rough material, re-creates it, and refashions it in fresh forms, is absolutely indifferent to fact, invents, imagines, dreams, and keeps between herself and reality the impenetrable barrier of beautiful style, of decorative or ideal treatment. The third stage is when life gets the upper hand, and drives Art out into the wilderness. This is the true decadence, and it is from this that we are now suffering.

"Take the case of the English drama. At first in the hands of the monks Dramatic Art was abstract, decorative, and mythological. Then she enlisted Life in her service, and using some of life's external forms, she created an entirely new race of beings, whose sorrows were more terrible than any sorrow man has ever felt, whose joys were keener than lover's joys, who had the rage of the Titans and the calm of the gods, who had monstrous and marvelous sins, monstrous and marvelous virtues. To them she gave a language different from that of actual use, a language full of resonant music and sweet rhythm, made stately by solemn cadence, or made delicate by fanciful rhyme, jeweled with wonderful words, and enriched with lofty diction. She clothed her children in strange raiment and gave them masks, and at her bidding the antique world rose from its marble tomb. A new Caesar stalked through the streets of risen Rome, and with purple sail and flute-led oars another Cleopatra passed up the river to

---

[3]William Morris (1834–1896), English artist, artisan, poet, and socialist.

Antioch. Old myth and legend and dream took shape and substance. History was entirely rewritten, and there was hardly one of the dramatists who did not recognize that the object of Art is not simple truth but complex beauty. In this they were perfectly right. Art itself is really a form of exaggeration; and selection, which is the very spirit of art, is nothing more than an intensified mode of overemphasis.

"But Life soon shattered the perfection of the form. Even in Shakespeare we can see the beginning of the end. It shows itself by the gradual breaking up of the blank verse in the later plays, by the predominance given to prose, and by the over-importance assigned to characterization. The passages in Shakespeare—and they are many—where the language is uncouth, vulgar, exaggerated, fantastic, obscene even, are entirely due to Life calling for an echo of her own voice, and rejecting the intervention of beautiful style, through which alone should Life be suffered to find expression. Shakespeare is not by any means a flawless artist. He is too fond of going directly to life, and borrowing life's natural utterance. He forgets that when Art surrenders her imaginative medium she surrenders everything. Goethe says, somewhere—

In der Beschränkung zeigt sich erst der Meister

'It is in working within limits that the master reveals himself,' and the limitation, the very condition of any art is style. However, we need not linger any longer over Shakespeare's realism. *The Tempest* is the most perfect of palinodes. All that we desired to point out was, that the magnificent work of the Elizabethan and Jacobean artists contained within itself the seeds of its own dissolution, and that, if it drew some of its strength from using life as rough material, it drew all its weakness from using life as an artistic method. As the inevitable result of this substitution of an imitative for a creative medium, this surrender of an imaginative form, we have the modern English melodrama. The characters in these plays talk on the stage exactly as they would talk off it; they have neither aspirations nor aspirates; they are taken directly from life and reproduce its vulgarity down to the smallest detail; they present the gait, manner, costume, and accent of real people; they would pass unnoticed in a third-class railway carriage. And yet how wearisome the plays are! They do not succeed in producing even that impression of reality at which they aim, and which is their only reason for existing. As a method, realism is a complete failure. . . .

"Art finds her own perfection within, and not outside of, herself. She is not to be judged by any external standard of resemblance. She is a veil, rather than a mirror. She has flowers that no forests know of, birds that no woodland possesses. She makes and unmakes many worlds, and can draw the moon from heaven with a scarlet thread. Hers are the 'forms more real than living man,' and hers the great archetypes of which things that have existence are but unfinished copies. Nature has, in her eyes, no laws, no uniformity. . . ."

CYRIL: . . . I can quite understand your objection to art being treated as a mirror.

You think it would reduce genius to the position of a cracked looking-glass. But you don't mean to say that you seriously believe that Life imitates Art, that Life is in fact the mirror, and Art the reality?

VIVIAN: Certainly I do. Paradox though it may seem—and paradoxes are always dangerous things—it is none the less true that Life imitates Art far more than Art imitates Life. . . .

CYRIL: . . . But in order to avoid making any error I want you to tell me briefly the doctrines of the new aesthetics.

VIVIAN: Briefly, then, they are these. Art never expresses anything but itself. It has an independent life, just as Thought has, and develops purely on its own lines. It is not necessarily realistic in an age of realism, nor spiritual in an age of faith. So far from being the creation of its time, it is usually in direct opposition to it, and the only history that it preserves for us is the history of its own progress. Sometimes it returns upon its footseps, and revives some antique form, as happened in the archaistic movement of late Greek Art, and in the pre-Raphaelite movement of our own day. At other times it entirely anticipates its age, and produces in one century work that it takes another century to understand, to appreciate, and to enjoy. In no case does it reproduce its age. To pass from the art of a time to the time itself is the great mistake that all historians commit.

The second doctrine is this. All bad art comes from returning to Life and Nature, and elevating them into ideals. Life and Nature may sometimes be used as part of Art's rough material, but before they are of any real service to art they must be translated into artistic conventions. The moment Art surrenders its imaginative medium it surrenders everything. As a method Realism is a complete failure, and the two things that every artist should avoid are modernity of form and modernity of subject-matter. To us, who live in the nineteenth century, any century is a suitable subject for art except our own. The only beautiful things are the things that do not concern us. It is, to have the pleasure of quoting myself, exactly because Hecuba is nothing to us that her sorrows are so suitable a motive for a tragedy. Besides, it is only the modern that ever becomes old-fashioned. M. Zola sits down to give us a picture of the Second Empire. Who cares for the Second Empire now? It is out of date. Life goes faster than Realism, but Romanticism is always in front of Life.

The third doctrine is that Life imitates Art far more than Art imitates Life. This results not merely from Life's imitative instinct, but from the fact that the self-conscious aim of Life is to find expression, and that Art offers it certain beautiful forms through which it may realize that energy. It is a theory that has never been put forward before, but it is extremely fruitful, and throws an entirely new light upon the history of Art.

It follows, as a corollary from this, that external Nature also imitates Art. The only effects that she can show us are effects that we have already seen through poetry, or in paintings. This is the secret of Nature's charm, as well as the explanation of Nature's weakness.

The final revelation is that Lying, the telling of beautiful untrue things, is the proper aim of Art.

Preface from
The Picture of Dorian Gray

OSCAR WILDE

The artist is the creator of beautiful things.

To reveal art and conceal the artist is art's aim.

The critic is he who can translate into another manner or a new material his impression of beautiful things.

The highest, as the lowest, form of criticism is a mode of autobiography.

Those who find ugly meanings in beautiful things are corrupt without being charming. This is a fault.

Those who find beautiful meanings in beautiful things are the cultivated. For these there is hope.

They are the elect to whom beautiful things mean only Beauty.

There is no such thing as a moral or an immoral book. Books are well written or badly written. That is all.

The nineteenth-century dislike of Realism is the rage of Caliban seeing his own face in a glass.

The nineteenth-century dislike of Romanticism is the rage of Caliban not seeing his own face in a glass.

The moral and immoral life of man forms part of the subject matter of the artist, but the morality of art consists in the perfect use of an imperfect medium.

No artist desires to prove anything. Even things that are true can be proved.

No artist has ethical sympathies. An ethical sympathy in an artist is an unpardonable mannerism of style.

No artist is ever morbid. The artist can express everything.

Thought and language are to the artist instruments of an art.

Vice and virtue are to the artist materials for an art.

From the point of view of form, the type of all the arts is the art of the musician. From the point of view of feeling, the actor's craft is the type.

All art is at once surface and symbol.

Those who go beneath the surface do so at their peril.

Those who read the symbol do so at their peril.

It is the spectator, and not life, that art really mirrors.

Diversity of opinion about a work of art shows that the work is new, complex, and vital.

When critics disagree the artist is in accord with himself.

Oscar Wilde, The Preface from *The Picture of Dorian Gray* (New York: Charterhouse Press, 1904).

We can forgive a man for making a useful thing as long as he does not admire it. The only excuse for making a useless thing is that one admires it intensely.

All art is quite useless.

ILLUSTRATION 19

A Portrait of the Artist
As a Young Man

JAMES JOYCE

They lit their cigarettes and turned to the right. After a pause Stephen began:

—Aristotle has not defined pity and terror. I have. I say . . .

Lynch halted and said bluntly:

—Stop! I won't listen! I am sick. I was out last night on a yellow drunk with Horan and Goggins.

Stephen went on:

—Pity is the feeling which arrests the mind in the presence of whatsoever is grave and constant in human sufferings and unites it with the human sufferer. Terror is the feeling which arrests the mind in the presence of whatsoever is grave and constant in human sufferings and unites it with the secret cause.

—Repeat, said Lynch.

Stephen repeated the definitions slowly.

—A girl got into a hansom a few days ago, he went on, in London. She was on her way to meet her mother whom she had not seen for many years. At the corner of a street the shaft of a lorry shivered the window of the hansom in the shape of a star. A long fine needle of the shivered glass pierced her heart. She died on the instant. The reporter called it a tragic death. It is not. It is remote from terror and pity according to the terms of my definitions.

—The tragic emotion, in fact, is a face looking two ways, towards terror and towards pity, both of which are phases of it. You see I use the word *arrest.* I mean that the tragic emotion is static. Or rather the dramatic emotion is. The feelings excited by improper art are kinetic, desire or loathing. Desire urges us to possess, to go to something; loathing urges us to abandon, to go

James Joyce, *Portrait of the Artist As a Young Man* (New York: Viking Press, 1916), selections from Part 5.

from something. These are kinetic emotions. The arts which excite them, pornographical or didactic, are therefore improper arts. The esthetic emotion (I use the general term) is therefore static. The mind is arrested and raised above desire and loathing.

—You say that art must not excite desire, said Lynch. I told you that one day I wrote my name in pencil on the backside of the Venus of Praxiteles in the Museum. Was that not desire?

—I speak of normal natures, said Stephen. You also told me that when you were a boy in that charming carmelite school you ate pieces of dried cowdung.

Lynch broke again into a whinny of laughter and again rubbed both his hands over his groins but without taking them from his pockets.

—O I did! I did! he cried.

Stephen turned towards his companion and looked at him for a moment boldly in the eyes. Lynch, recovering from his laughter, answered his look from his humbled eyes. The long slender flattened skull beneath the long pointed cap brought before Stephen's mind the image of a hooded reptile. The eyes, too, were reptilelike in glint and gaze. Yet at that instant, humbled and alert in their look, they were lit by one tiny human point, the window of a shrivelled soul, poignant and selfembittered.

—As for that, Stephen said in polite parenthesis, we are all animals. I also am an animal.

—You are, said Lynch.

—But we are just now in a mental world, Stephen continued. The desire and loathing excited by improper esthetic means are really unesthetic emotions not only because they are kinetic in character but also because they are not more than physical. Our flesh shrinks from what it dreads and responds to the stimulus of what it desires by a purely reflex action of the nervous system. Our eyelid closes before we are aware that the fly is about to enter our eye.

—Not always, said Lynch critically.

—In the same way, said Stephen, your flesh responded to the stimulus of a naked statue but it was, I say, simply a reflex action of the nerves. Beauty expressed by the artist cannot awaken in us an emotion which is kinetic or a sensation which is purely physical. It awakens, or ought to awaken, or induces, or ought to induce, an esthetic stasis, an ideal pity or an ideal terror, a stasis called forth, prolonged and at last dissolved by what I call the rhythm of beauty.

—What is that exactly? asked Lynch.

—Rhythm, said Stephen, is the first formal esthetic relation of part to part in any esthetic whole or of an esthetic whole to its part or parts or of any part of the esthetic whole of which it is a part.

—If that is rhythm, said Lynch, let me hear what you call beauty: and, please remember, though I did eat a cake of cowdung once, that I admire only beauty.

Stephen raised his cap as if in greeting. Then, blushing slightly, he laid his hand on Lynch's thick tweed sleeve.

—We are right, he said, and the others are wrong. To speak of these things and to try to understand their nature and, having understood it, to try slowly and humbly and constantly to express, to press out again, from the gross earth or what it brings forth, from sound and shape and colour which are the prison gates of our soul, an image of the beauty we have come to understand—that is art.

They had reached the canal bridge and, turning from their course, went on by the trees. A crude grey light, mirrored in the sluggish water, and a smell of wet branches over their heads seemed to war against the course of Stephen's thought.

—But you have not answered my question, said Lynch. What is art? What is the beauty it expresses?

—That was the first definition I gave you, you sleepy-headed wretch, said Stephen, when I began to try to think out the matter for myself. Do you remember the night? Cranly lost his temper and began to talk about Wicklow bacon.

—I remember, said Lynch. He told us about them flaming fat devils of pigs.

—Art, said Stephen, is the human disposition of sensible or intelligible matter for an esthetic end. You remember the pigs and forget that. You are a distressing pair, you and Cranly.

Lynch made a grimace at the raw grey sky and said:

—If I am to listen to your esthetic philosophy give me at least another cigarette. I don't care about it. I don't even care about women. Damn you and damn everything. I want a job of five hundred a year. You can't get me one.

Stephen handed him the packet of cigarettes. Lynch took the last one that remained, saying simply:

—Proceed!

—Aquinas, said Stephen, says that is beautiful the apprehension of which pleases.

Lynch nodded.

—I remember that, he said. *Pulcra sunt quæ visa placent.*

—He uses the word *visa*, said Stephen, to cover esthetic apprehensions of all kinds, whether through sight or hearing or through any other avenue of apprehension. This word, though it is vague, is clear enough to keep away good and evil which excite desire and loathing. It means certainly a stasis and not a kinesis. How about the true? It produces also a stasis of the mind. You would not write your name in pencil across the hypothenuse of a right-angled triangle.

—No, said Lynch, give me the hypothenuse of the Venus of Praxiteles.

—Static therefore, said Stephen. Plato, I believe, said that beauty is the splendour of truth. I don't think that it has a meaning but the true and the beautiful are akin. Truth is beheld by the intellect which is appeased by the most satisfying relations of the intelligible: beauty is beheld by the imagination which is appeased by the most satisfying relations of the sensible. The first step in the direction of truth is to understand the frame and scope of the intellect itself, to comprehend the act itself of intellection. Aristotle's entire system of philosophy rests upon his book of psychology and that, I think, rests on his statement that the same attribute cannot at the same time and in the same connection belong to and not belong to the same subject. The first step in the direction of beauty is to understand the frame and scope of the imagination, to comprehend the act itself of esthetic apprehension. Is that clear?

—But what is beauty? asked Lynch impatiently. Out with another definition. Something we see and like! Is that the best you and Aquinas can do?

—Let us take woman, said Stephen.

—Let us take her! said Lynch fervently.

—The Greek, the Turk, the Chinese, the Copt, the Hottentot, said Stephen, all admire a different type of female beauty. That seems to be a maze out of which we cannot escape. I see however two ways out. One is this hypothesis: that every physical quality admired by men in women is in direct connection with the manifold functions of women for the propagation of the species. It may be so. The world, it seems, is drearier than even you, Lynch, imagined. For my part I dislike that way out. It leads to eugenics rather than to esthetic. It leads you out of the maze into a new gaudy lectureroom where MacCann, with one hand on *The Origin of Species* and the other hand on the new testament, tells you that you admired the great flanks of Venus because you felt that she would bear you burly offspring and admired her great breasts because you felt that she would give good milk to her children and yours.

—Then MacCann is a sulphuryellow liar, said Lynch energetically.

—There remains another way out, said Stephen, laughing.

—To wit? said Lynch.

—This hypothesis, Stephen began.

A long dray laden with old iron came round the corner of sir Patrick Dun's hospital covering the end of Stephen's speech with the harsh roar of jangled and rattling metal. Lynch closed his ears and gave out oath after oath till the dray had passed. Then he turned on his heel rudely. Stephen turned also and waited for a few moments till his companion's illhumour had had its vent.

—This hypothesis, Stephen repeated, is the other way out: that, though the same object may not seem beautiful to all people, all people who admire a beautiful object find in it certain relations which satisfy and coincide with the stages themselves of all esthetic apprehension. These relations of the sensible, visible to you through one form and to me through another, must be therefore the necessary qualities of beauty. Now, we can return to our old friend saint Thomas for another pennyworth of wisdom.

Lynch laughed.

—It amuses me vastly, he said, to hear you quoting him time after time like a jolly round friar. Are you laughing in your sleeve?

—MacAlister, answered Stephen, would call my esthetic theory applied Aquinas. So far as this side of esthetic philosophy extends Aquinas will carry me all along the line. When we come to the phenomena of artistic conception, artistic gestation and artistic reproduction I require a new terminology and a new personal experience.

—Of course, said Lynch. After all Aquinas, in spite of his intellect, was exactly a good round friar. But you will tell me about the new personal experience and new terminology some other day. Hurry up and finish the first part.

Who knows? said Stephen, smiling. Perhaps Aquinas would understand me better than you. He was a poet himself. He wrote a hymn for Maundy Thursday. It beings with the words *Pange lingua gloriosi*. They say it is the highest glory of the hymnal. It is an intricate and soothing hymn. I like it: but there is no hymn that can be put beside that mournful and majestic processional song, the *Vexilla Regis* of Venantius Fortunatus.

Lynch began to sing softly and solemnly in a deep base voice:

> *Impleta sunt quæ concinit*
> *David fideli carmine*
> *Dicendo nationibus*
> *Regnavit a ligno Deus.*

—That's great! he said, well pleased. Great music!

They turned into Lower Mount Street. A few steps from the corner a fat young man, wearing a silk neckcloth, saluted them and stopped.

—Did you hear the results of the exams? he asked. Griffin was plucked. Halpin and O'Flynn are through the home civil. Moonan got fifth place in the Indian. O'Shaughnessy got fourteenth. The Irish fellows in Clarke's gave them a feed last night. They all ate curry.

His pallid bloated face expressed benevolent malice and, as he had advanced through his tidings of success, his small fatencircled eyes vanished out of sight and his weak wheezing voice out of hearing.

In reply to a question of Stephen's his eyes and his voice came forth again from their lurkingplaces.

—Yes, MacCullagh and I, he said. He's taking pure mathematics and I'm taking constitutional history. There are twenty subjects. I'm taking botany too. You know I'm a member of the field club.

He drew back from the other two in a stately fashion and placed a plump woollengloved hand on his breast, from which muttered wheezing laughter at once broke forth.

—Bring us a few turnips and onions the next time you go out, said Stephen drily, to make a stew.

The fat student laughed indulgently and said:

—We are all highly respectable people in the field club. Last Saturday we went out to Glenmalure, seven of us.

—With women, Donovan? said Lynch.

Donovan again laid his hand on his chest and said:

—Our end is the acquisition of knowledge.

Then he said quickly:

—I hear you are writing some essay about esthetics.

Stephen made a vague gesture of denial.

—Goethe and Lessing, said Donovan, have written a lot on that subject, the classical school and the romantic school and all that. The *Laocoon* interested me very much when I read it. Of course it is idealistic, German, ultraprofound.

Neither of the others spoke. Donovan took leave of them urbanely.

—I must go, he said softly and benevolently. I have a strong suspicion, amounting almost to a conviction, that my sister intended to make pancakes today for the dinner of the Donovan family.

—Goodbye, Stephen said in his wake. Don't forget the turnips for me and my mate.

Lynch gazed after him, his lip curling in slow scorn till his face resembled a devil's mask:

—To think that that yellow pancakeeating excrement can get a good job, he said at length, and I have to smoke cheap cigarettes!

They turned their faces towards Merrion Square and went on for a little in silence.

—To finish what I was saying about beauty, said Stephen, the most satisfying relations of the sensible must therefore correspond to the necessary phases of artistic apprehension. Find these and you find the qualities of universal beauty. Aquinas says: *ad pulcritudinem tria requiruntur, integritas, consonantia, claritas.* I translate it so: *Three things are needed for beauty, wholeness, harmony and radiance.* Do these correspond to the phases of apprehension? Are you following?

—Of course, I am, said Lynch. If you think I have an excrementitious intelligence run after Donovan and ask him to listen to you.

Stephen pointed to a basket which a butcher's boy had slung inverted on his head.

—Look at that basket, he said.

—I see it, said Lynch.

—In order to see that basket, said Stephen, your mind first of all sep-

arates the basket from the rest of the visible universe which is not the basket.
The first phase of apprehension is a bounding line drawn about the object to
be apprehended. An esthetic image is presented to us either in space or in
time. What is audible is presented in time, what is visible is presented in
space. But, temporal or spatial, the esthetic image is first luminously apprehended as selfbounded and selfcontained upon the immeasurable background
of space or time which is not it. You apprehend it as *one* thing. You see it
as one whole. You apprehend its wholeness. That is *integritas*.

—Bull's eye! said Lynch, laughing. Go on.

—Then, said Stephen, you pass from point to point, led by its formal
lines; you apprehend it as balanced part against part within its limits; you
feel the rhythm of its structure. In other words the synthesis of immediate
perception is followed by the analysis of apprehension. Having first felt that
it is *one* thing you feel now that it is a *thing*. You apprehend it as complex,
multiple, divisible, separable, made up of its parts, the result of its parts and
their sum, harmonious. That is *consonantia*.

—Bull's eye again! said Lynch wittily. Tell me now what is *claritas* and
you win the cigar.

—The connotation of the word, Stephen said, is rather vague. Aquinas
uses a term which seems to be inexact. It baffled me for a long time. It would
lead you to believe that he had in mind symbolism or idealism, the supreme
quality of beauty being a light from some other world, the idea of which the
matter is but the shadow, the reality of which it is but the symbol. I thought
he might mean that *claritas* is the artistic discovery and representation of the
divine purpose in anything or a force of generalisation which would make the
esthetic image a universal one, make it outshine its proper conditions. But
that is literary talk. I understand it so. When you have apprehended that
basket as one thing and have then analysed it according to its form and
apprehended it as a thing you make the only synthesis which is logically and
esthetically permissible. You see that it is that thing which it is and no other
thing. The radiance of which he speaks is the scholastic *quidditas*, the *whatness*
of a thing. This supreme quality is felt by the artist when the esthetic image
is first conceived in his imagination. The mind in that mysterious instant
Shelley likened beautifully to a fading coal. The instant wherein that supreme
quality of beauty, the clear radiance of the esthetic image, is apprehended
luminously by the mind which has been arrested by its wholeness and fascinated by its harmony is the luminous silent stasis of esthetic pleasure, a
spiritual state very like to that cardiac condition which the Italian physiologist
Luigi Galvani, using a phrase almost as beautiful as Shelley's, called the
enchantment of the heart.

Stephen paused and, though his companion did not speak, felt that his
words had called up around them a thoughtenchanted silence.

—What I have said, he began again, refers to beauty in the wider sense
of the word, in the sense which the word has in the literary tradition. In the

marketplace it has another sense. When we speak of beauty in the second sense of the term our judgment is influenced in the first place by the art itself and by the form of that art. The image, it is clear, must be set between the mind or senses of the artist himself and the mind or senses of others. If you bear this in memory you will see that art necessarily divides itself into three forms progressing from one to the next. These forms are: the lyrical form, the form wherein the artist presents his image in immediate relation to himself; the epical form, the form wherein he presents his image in mediate relation to himself and to others; the dramatic form, the form wherein he presents his image in immediate relation to others.

—That you told me a few nights ago, said Lynch, and we began the famous discussion.

—I have a book at home, said Stephen, in which I have written down questions which are more amusing than yours were. In finding the answers to them I found the theory of esthetic which I am trying to explain. Here are some questions I set myself: *Is a chair finely made tragic or comic? Is the portrait of Mona Lisa good if I desire to see it? Is the bust of Sir Philip Crampton lyrical, epical or dramatic? Can excrement or a child or a louse be a work of art? If not, why not?*

—Why not, indeed? said Lynch, laughing.

—*If a man hacking in fury at a block of wood*, Stephen continued, *make there an image of a cow, is that image a work of art? If not, why not?*

—That's a lovely one, said Lynch, laughing again. That has the true scholastic stink.

10

Contemporary Theories
of Beauty
and the Aesthetics

The difficulties incurred in identifying art with beauty or with linking aesthetic judgments with a faculty of taste have led some philosophers to surmise that the concept of beauty, the phenomena of art, and the idea of the aesthetic are independent. If beauty is an objective quality which triggers a response, then the idea of beauty is different from a definition of art because many kinds of experiential objects may be beautiful or trigger an aesthetic response. If the aesthetic is identified with one's response then this term is neither necessarily connected with art nor with the qualities which trigger a response. Therefore it is sometimes claimed that the notion of the aesthetic should be defined in terms of a unique set of concepts, an attitude, or a unique kind of perception or experience. This leads to the position that we need not define the aesthetic purely in terms of a concept of beauty nor must one identify art with the aesthetic. Beauty, art, and the aesthetic are independent ideas, according to these views. Moreover, because of the historical failures of philosophers of art to develop a unique definition of all art phenomena, failures exemplified in Parts I and II of this book, some philosophers claim that a concept of the aesthetic rather than a definition of art is the feature to which philosophical attention should be addressed. This chapter presents some contemporary theories which focus on the concept of the aesthetic as the proper subject for philosophy of art.

The twentieth-century interest in the idea of the aesthetic attitude as a disinterested experience was made popular as early as 1912 in an article written by a British professor of Italian literature, Edward Bullough. Bullough argues, in brief, that the origin of an aesthetic experience is a disinterested detachment from whatever one is experiencing. To appreciate something aesthetically one places oneself or is placed at a "psychical distance" from the phenomenon to attain this detached point of view. This distancing is achieved by divorcing the experience from one's personal needs or desires so that one can view the object purely qualitatively. What Bullough calls *distance* is a factor in all art appreciation. Bullough notices that one can become over- or under-distanced so that one either loses all interest in the object, or one is so personally involved that the attitude is no longer contemplative.

To elaborate on the psychological phenomenon of distancing Virgil Aldrich proposes that the aesthetic attitude is achieved through a peculiar mode of perception which is different from ordinary observation. "Prehension," as he calls this mode, is a sensitive form of perception wherein one suspends one's normal observational expectations and experiences a phenomenon aesthetically. Aldrich's notion of prehension is an attempt to locate the source of disinterested aesthetic attitudes in a feature of perception, but unfortunately it is sometimes criticized as a contemporary replacement for the psychologically questionable faculty of taste.

Prehension, according to Aldrich, gives rise to the use of what he and Frank Sibley call *aesthetic concepts*. Aesthetic concepts are expressions one uses to talk about special nonreferential perceptual features. These terms include such phrases as "unified," "balanced," "integrated," "lifeless," "serene," "tragic," etc. These expressions are descriptive but they are distinguished from qualitative adjectives such as "large," "red," "thin," "loud," which refer to and describe specific perceptual features. Sibley claims that one must develop a trained sensibility to perceive these nonreferential aesthetic features and therefore to use and comprehend these aesthetic concepts. But Sibley does not go so far as to posit the notion of prehension or any other faculty as the source of this sensibility. George Seurat's painting, *Sunday Afternoon on the Island of La Grande Jatte* (Illustration 20) is the kind of work which might trigger a purely aesthetic experience since there is nothing social or political expressed in the work to distract the viewer from pure contemplation of it. The reader might want to examine other illustrations in the book to see whether they exhibit so-called aesthetic qualities which elicit such aesthetic responses.

The sculpture *Venus de Milo* (Illustration 1) provides the starting point for the contemporary phenomenologist Roman Ingarden's analysis of the aesthetic object and the aesthetic experience. Ingarden stresses two aspects of the aesthetic equally: the aesthetic object—the object for aesthetic contemplation—and the aesthetic experience itself. These elements together make up an aesthetic event. Ingarden points out that the object of an aesthetic experience need not be something existing in the real world. In reading, for example, the real object is printed words on the page, but the aesthetic object is the story itself which is expressed through, but is not identical with, the printed page. And even with the experience of real objects such as the *Venus de Milo*, in an aesthetic experience our mind overlooks the flaws of the marble and embellishes the perceived object to create an object for aesthetic contemplation.

Ingarden distinguishes four elements in an aesthetic experience which together distinguish these sorts of experiences from other forms of intention. First, the aesthetic experience is a process by which one's practical attitude is detached from the object in question. Second, the imagination constitutes the aesthetic object, that is, it creates the story from the printed page, or it sets apart *Venus de Milo* as an object distinct from the armless marble statue in the museum. Third, one now pursues or contemplates the object in a disinterested manner. Finally, one responds to the object in some sort of emotional or valuative way. Notice again that an aesthetic experience is always the experience *of* something, but that thing could be an imaginary object. In no case is the aesthetic object identified with a perceptual object even if the perceptual object, such as the statue *Venus de Milo*, triggers an aesthetic reaction. This is because in a true aesthetic experience the aesthetic reaction transforms the object in question into a nonpractical phenomenon for contemplation.

The status of the notion of the aesthetic attitude theories is very much in debate among contemporary philosophers. These theories and Bullough's thesis in particular are often criticized. It is sometimes argued by philosophers such as George Dickie that the aesthetic attitude theories exaggerate the psychological role of distancing as a peculiar state of mind. Some philosophers try to analyze audience response without appealing to special psychological phenomenon of psychical distance or a special mode of perception such as prehension. Yet the notion of beauty in art cannot be dismissed out of hand, because the concept still plays an important role in the analysis of art as Hanslick's analysis of the beautiful in music typifies. The reader should weigh the arguments on all sides of this important issue before evaluating the status of the aesthetic attitude and the aesthetic response as significant parts of the experience of art and as legitimate subjects for philosophy of art.

"Psychical Distance"
As a Factor in Art
and As an Aesthetic Principle

EDWARD BULLOUGH

I

1. The conception of "Distance" suggests, in connection with Art, certain trains of thought by no means devoid of interest or of speculative importance.

Edward Bullough, " 'Psychical Distance' As a Factor in Art and As an Aesthetic Principle," *British Journal of Psychology* 5 (1912).

Perhaps the most obvious suggestion is that of *actual spatial* distance, that is, the distance of a work of Art from the spectator, or that of *represented spatial* distance, that is, the distance represented within the work. Less obvious, more metaphorical, is the meaning of *temporal* distance. The first was noticed already by Aristotle in his *Poetics*; the second has played a great part in the history of painting in the form of perspective; the distinction between these two kinds of distance assumes special importance theoretically in the differentiation between sculpture in the round, and relief-sculpture. Temporal distance, remoteness from us in point of time, though often a cause of misconceptions, has been declared to be a factor of considerable weight in our appreciation.

It is not, however, in any of these meanings that "Distance" is put forward here, though it will be clear in the course of this essay that the above mentioned kinds of distance are rather special forms of the conception of Distance as advocated here, and derive whatever *aesthetic* qualities they may possess from Distance in its general connotation. This general connotation is "Psychical Distance."

A short illustration will explain what is meant by "Psychical Distance." Imagine a fog at sea: for most people it is an experience of acute unpleasantness. Apart from the physical annoyance and remoter forms of discomfort such as delays, it is apt to produce feelings of peculiar anxiety, fears of invisible dangers, strains of watching and listening for distant and unlocalized signals. The listless movements of the ship and her warning calls soon tell upon the nerves of the passengers; and that special, expectant, tacit anxiety and nervousness, always associated with this experience, make a fog the dreaded terror of the sea (all the more terrifying because of its very silence and gentleness) for the expert seafarer no less than for the ignorant landsman.

Nevertheless, a fog at sea can be a source of intense relish and enjoyment. Abstract from the experience of the sea fog, for the moment, its danger and practical unpleasantness, just as every one in the enjoyment of a mountain-climb disregards its physical labor and its danger (though, it is not denied, that these may incidentally enter into the enjoyment and enhance it); direct the attention to the features "objectively" constituting the phenomenon—the veil surrounding you with an opaqueness as of transparent milk, blurring the outline of things and distorting their shapes into weird grotesqueness; observe the carrying-power of the air, producing the impression as if you could touch some far-off siren by merely putting out your hand and letting it lose itself behind that white wall; note the curious creamy smoothness of the water, hypocritically denying as it were any suggestion of danger; and, above all, the strange solitude and remoteness from the world, as it can be found only on the highest mountain tops; and the experience may acquire, in its uncanny mingling of repose and terror, a flavor of such concentrated poignancy and delight as to contrast sharply with the blind and distempered anxiety of its other aspects. This contrast, often emerging with startling suddenness, is like a momentary switching on of some new current, or the passing ray of a brighter light, illuminating the outlook upon perhaps the most ordinary and familiar objects—an impression which we experience sometimes in instants of direst extremity, when our practical interest snaps like a wire from sheer over-tension, and we watch the consummation of some impending catastrophe with the marveling unconcern of a mere spectator.

It is a difference of outlook, due—if such a metaphor is permissible—to the insertion of Distance. This Distance appears to lie between our own self and its affections, using the latter term in its broadest sense as anything which affects our being, bodily or spiritually, for example as sensation, perception, emotional state or idea. Usually, though not always, it amounts to the same thing to say that the Distance lies between our own self and such objects as are the sources or vehicles of such affections.

Thus, in the fog, the transformation by Distance is produced in the first instance by putting the phenomenon, so to speak, out of gear with our practical, actual self; by allowing it to stand outside the context of our personal needs and ends—in short, by looking at it "objectively," as it has often been called, by permitting only such reactions on our part as emphasize the "objective" features of the experience, and by interpreting even our "subjective" affections not as modes of *our* being but rather as characteristics of the phenomenon.

The working of Distance is, accordingly, not simple, but highly complex. It has a *negative*, inhibitory aspect—the cutting-out of the practical sides of things and of our practical attitude to them—and a *positive* side—the elaboration of the experience on the new basis created by the inhibitory action of Distance.

2. Consequently, this distanced view of things is not, and cannot be, our normal outlook. As a rule, experiences constantly turn the same side towards us, namely, that which has the strongest practical force of appeal. We are not ordinarily aware of those aspects of things which do not touch us immediately and practically, nor are we generally conscious of impressions apart from our own self which is impressed. The sudden view of things from their reverse, usually unnoticed, side, comes upon us as a revelation, and such revelations are precisely those of Art. In this most general sense, Distance is a factor in all Art.

3. It is, for this very reason, also an aesthetic principle. The aesthetic contemplation and the aesthetic outlook have often been described as "objective." We speak of "objective" artists as Shakespeare or Velasquez, of "objective" works or art forms as Homer's *Iliad* or the drama. It is a term constantly occurring in discussions and criticisms, though its sense, if pressed at all, becomes very questionable. For certain forms of Art, such as lyrical poetry, are said to be "subjective"; Shelley, for example, would usually be considered a "subjective" writer. On the other hand, no work of Art can be

genuinely "objective" in the sense in which this term might be applied to a work on history or to a scientific treatise; nor can it be "subjective" in the ordinary acceptance of that term, as a personal feeling, a direct statement of a wish or belief, or a cry of passion is subjective. "Objectivity" and "subjectivity" are a pair of opposites which in their mutual exclusiveness when applied to Art soon lead to confusion.

Nor are they the only pair of opposites. Art has with equal vigor been declared alternately "idealistic" and "realistic," "sensual" and "spiritual," "individualistic" and "typical." Between the defense of either terms of such antithesis most aesthetic theories have vacillated. It is one of the contentions of this essay that such opposites find their synthesis in the more fundamental conception of Distance.

Distance further provides the much needed criterion of the beautiful as distinct from the merely agreeable.

Again, it marks one of the most important steps in the process of artistic creation and serves as a distinguishing feature of what is commonly so loosely described as the "artistic temperament."

Finally, it may claim to be considered as one of the essential characteristics of the "aesthetic consciousness"—if I may describe by this term that special mental attitude towards, and outlook upon, experience, which finds its most pregnant expression in the various forms of Art.

II

Distance, as I said before, is obtained by separating the object and its appeal from one's own self, by putting it out of gear with practical needs and ends. Thereby the "contemplation" of the object becomes alone possible. But it does not mean that the relation between the self and the object is broken to the extent of becoming "impersonal." Of the alternatives "personal" and "impersonal" the latter surely comes nearer to the truth; but here, as elsewhere, we meet the difficulty of having to express certain facts in terms coined for entirely different uses. To do so usually results in paradoxes, which are nowhere more inevitable than in discussions upon Art. "Personal" and "impersonal," "subjective" and "objective" are such terms, devised for purposes other than aesthetic speculation, and becoming loose and ambiguous as soon as applied outside the sphere of their special meanings. In giving preference therefore to the term "impersonal" to describe the relation between the spectator and a work of Art, it is to be noticed that it is not impersonal in the sense in which we speak of the "impersonal" character of Science, for instance. In order to obtain "objectively valid" results, the scientist excludes the "personal factor," that is, his personal wishes as to the validity of his results, his predilection for any particular system to be proved or disproved by his research. It goes without saying that all experiments and investigations are undertaken out of a personal interest in the science, for the ultimate support of a definite assumption, and involve personal hopes of success; but this does not affect the "dispassionate" attitude of the investigator, under pain of being accused of "manufacturing his evidence."

1. Distance does not imply an impersonal, purely intellectually interested relation of such a kind. On the contrary, it describes a *personal* relation, often highly emotionally colored, but of a *peculiar character*. Its peculiarity lies in that the personal character of the relation has been, so to speak, filtered. It has been cleared of the practical, concrete nature of its appeal, without, however, thereby losing its original constitution. One of the best-known examples is to be found in our attitude towards the events and characters of the drama: they appeal to us like persons and incidents of normal experience, except that that side of their appeal, which would usually affect us in a directly personal manner, is held in abeyance. This difference, so well known as to be almost trivial, is generally explained by reference to the knowledge that the characters and situations are "unreal," imaginary. . . . But, as a matter of fact, the "assumption" upon which the imaginative emotional reaction is based is not necessarily the condition, but often the consequence, of Distance; that is to say, the converse of the reason usually stated would then be true: namely, that Distance, by changing our relation to the characters, renders them seemingly fictitious, not that the fictitiousness of the characters alters our feelings toward them. It is, of course, to be granted that the actual and admitted unreality of the dramatic action reinforces the effect of Distance. But surely the proverbial unsophisticated yokel whose chivalrous interference in the play on behalf of the hapless heroine can only be prevented by impressing upon him that "they are only pretending," is not the ideal type of theatrical audience. The proof of the seeming paradox that it is Distance which primarily gives to dramatic action the appearance of unreality and not *vice versa*, is the observation that the same filtration of our sentiments and the same seeming "unreality" of *actual* men and things occur, when at times, by a sudden change of inward perspective, we are overcome by the feeling that "all the world's a stage."

2. This personal but "distanced" relation (as I will venture to call this nameless character of our view) directs attention to a strange fact which appears to be one of the fundamental paradoxes of Art: it is what I propose to call "the antinomy of Distance."

It will be readily admitted that a work of Art has the more chance of appealing to us the better it finds us prepared for its particular kind of appeal. Indeed, without some degree of predisposition on our part, it must necessarily remain incomprehensible, and to that extent unappreciated. The success and intensity of its appeal would seem, therefore, to stand in direct proportion to the completeness with which it corresponds with our intellectual and emotional peculiarities and the idiosyncrasies of our experience. The absence of such a concordance between the characters of a work and of the spectator is, of course, the most general explanation for differences of "tastes."

At the same time, such a principle of concordance requires a qualification, which leads at once to the antinomy of Distance.

Suppose a man who believes that he has cause to be jealous about his wife, witnesses a performance of *Othello*. He will the more perfectly appreciate the situation, conduct and character of Othello, the more exactly the feelings and experiences of Othello coincide with his own—at least he *ought* to on the above principle of concordance. In point of fact, he will probably do anything but appreciate the play. In reality, the concordance will merely render him acutely conscious of his own jealousy; by a sudden reversal of perspective he will no longer see Othello apparently betrayed by Desdemona, but himself in an analogous situation with his own wife. This reversal of perspective is the consequence of the loss of Distance.

If this be taken as a typical case, it follows that the qualification required is that the coincidence should be as complete as is compatible with maintaining Distance. The jealous spectator of *Othello* will indeed appreciate and enter into the play the more keenly, the greater the resemblance with his own experience—*provided* that he succeeds in keeping the Distance between the action of the play and his personal feelings: a very difficult performance in the circumstances. It is on account of the same difficulty that the expert and the professional critic make a bad audience, since their expertness and critical professionalism are *practical* activities, involving their concrete personality and constantly endangering their Distance. (It is, by the way, one of the reasons why Criticism is an art, for it requires the constant interchange from the practical to the distanced attitude and *vice versa,* which is characteristic of artists.)

The same qualification applies to the artist. He will prove artistically most effective in the formulation of an intensely *personal* experience, but he can formulate it artistically only on condition of a detachment from the experience *qua personal*. Hence the statement of so many artists that artistic formulation was to them a kind of catharsis, a means of ridding themselves of feelings and ideas the acuteness of which they felt almost as a kind of obsession. Hence, on the other hand, the failure of the average man to convey to others at all adequately the impression of an overwhelming joy or sorrow. His personal implication in the event renders it impossible for him to formulate and present it in such a way as to make others, like himself, feel all the meaning and fullness which it possesses for him.

What is therefore, both in appreciation and production, most desirable is the *utmost decrease of Distance without its disappearance.*

3. Closely related, in fact a presupposition to the "antinomy," is the *variability of Distance.* Herein especially lies the advantage of Distance compared with such terms as "objectivity" and "detachment." Neither of them implies a *personal* relation—indeed both actually preclude it; and the mere

inflexibility and exclusiveness of their opposites render their application generally meaningless.

Distance, on the contrary, admits naturally of degrees, and differs not only according to the nature of the *object,* which may impose a greater or smaller degree of Distance, but varies also according to the *individual's capacity* for maintaining a greater or lesser degree. And here one may remark that not only do *persons differ from each other* in their habitual measure of Distance, but that the *same individual differs* in his ability to maintain it in the face of different objects and of different arts.

There exist, therefore, two different sets of conditions affecting the degree of Distance in any given case: those offered by the object and those realized by the subject. In their interplay they afford one of the most extensive explanations for varieties of esthetic experience, since loss of Distance, whether due to the one or the other, means loss of esthetic appreciation.

In short, Distance may be said to be *variable both according to the distancing-power of the individual, and according to the character of the object.*

There are two ways of losing Distance: either to "under-distance" or to "over-distance." "Under-distancing" is the commonest failing of the *subject,* an excess of Distance is a frequent failing of Art, especially in the past. Historically it looks almost as if Art had attempted to meet the deficiency of Distance on the part of the subject and had overshot the mark in this endeavor. It will be seen later that this is actually true, for it appears that over-distanced Art is specially designed for a class of appreciation which has difficulty to rise spontaneously to any degree of Distance. The consequence of a loss of Distance through one or other cause is familiar: the verdict in the case of under-distancing is that the work is "crudely naturalistic," "harrowing," "repulsive in its realism." An excess of Distance produces the impression of improbability, artificiality, emptiness or absurdity.

The individual tends, as I just stated, to under-distance rather than to lose Distance by over-distancing. *Theoretically* there is no limit to the decrease of Distance. In theory, therefore, not only the usual subjects of Art, but even the most personal affections, whether ideas, percepts, or emotions, can be sufficiently distanced to be aesthetically appreciable. Especially artists are gifted in this direction to a remarkable extent. The average individual, on the contrary, very rapidly reaches his limit of decreasing Distance, his "Distance-limit," that is, that point at which Distance is lost and appreciation either disappears or changes its character.

In the *practice,* therefore, of the average person, a limit does exist which marks the minimum at which his appreciation can maintain itself in the esthetic field, and this average minimum lies considerably higher than the Distance-limit of the artist. It is practically impossible to fix this average limit, in the absence of data, and on account of the wide fluctuations from person to person to which this limit is subject. But it is safe to infer that, in art practice, explicit references to organic affections, to the material existence of the body, especially to sexual matters, lies normally below the Distance-limit, and can be touched upon by Art only with special precautions. Allusions to social institutions of any degree of personal importance—in particular, allusions implying any doubt as to their validity—the questioning of some generally recognized ethical sanctions, references to topical subjects occupying public attention at the moment, and such like, are all dangerously near the average limit and may at any time fall below it, arousing, instead of esthetic appreciation, concrete hostility or mere amusement.

This difference in the Distance-limit between artists and the public has been the source of much misunderstanding and injustice. Many an artist has seen his work condemned, and himself ostracized for the sake of so-called "immoralities" which to him were *bona fide* aesthetic objects. His power of distancing, nay, the necessity of distancing feelings, sensations, situations which for the average person are too intimately bound up with his concrete existence to be regarded in that light, have often quite unjustly earned for him accusations of cynicism, sensualism, morbidness, or frivolity. The same misconception has arisen over many "problem plays" and "problem novels" in which the public have persisted in seeing nothing but a supposed "problem" of the moment, whereas the author may have been—and often has demonstrably been—able to distance the subject matter sufficiently to rise above its practical problematic import and to regard it simply as a dramatically and humanly interesting situation.

The variability of Distance in respect to Art, disregarding for the moment the subjective complication, appears both as a general feature in Art, and in the differences between the special arts.

It has been an old problem why the "arts of the eye and of the ear" should have reached the practically exclusive predominance over arts of other senses. Attempts to raise "culinary art" to the level of a Fine Art have failed in spite of all propaganda, as completely as the creation of scent or liquor "symphonies." There is little doubt that, apart from other excellent reasons of a partly psycho-physical, partly technical nature, the actual, *spatial distance* separating objects of sight and hearing from the subject has contributed strongly to the development of this monopoly. In a similar manner *temporal remoteness* produces Distance, and objects removed from us in point of time are *ipso facto* distanced to an extent which was impossible for their contemporaries. Many pictures, plays, and poems had, as a matter of fact, rather an expository or illustrative significance—as for instance much ecclesiastical Art—or the force of a direct practical appeal—as the invectives of many satires or comedies—which seem to us nowadays irreconcilable with their aesthetic claims. Such works have consequently profited greatly by lapse of time and have reached the level of Art only with the help of temporal distance, while others, on the contrary, often for the same reason have suffered a loss of Distance, through *over*-distancing.

Special mention must be made of a group of artistic conceptions which present excessive Distance in their form of appeal rather than in their actual presentation—a point illustrating the necessity of distinguishing between distancing an object and distancing the appeal of which it is the source. I mean here what is often rather loosely termed "idealistic Art," that is, Art springing from abstract conceptions, expressing allegorical meanings, or illustrating general truths. Generalizations and abstractions suffer under this disadvantage that they have too much general applicability to invite a personal interest in them, and too little individual concreteness to prevent them applying to us in all their force. They appeal to everybody and therefore to none. An axiom of Euclid belongs to nobody, just because it compels every one's assent; general conceptions like Patriotism, Friendship, Love, Hope, Life, Death, concern as much Dick, Tom and Harry as myself, and I, therefore, either feel unable to get into any kind of personal relation to them, or, if I do so, they become at once, emphatically and concretely, *my* Patriotism, *my* Friendship, *my* Love, *my* Hope, *my* Life and Death. By mere force of generalization, a general truth or a universal ideal is so far distanced from myself that I fail to realize it concretely at all, or, when I do so, I can realize it only as part of my *practical actual being,* that is, it falls below the Distance-limit altogether. "Idealistic Art" suffers consequently under the peculiar difficulty that its excess of Distance turns generally into an *under*-distanced appeal—all the more easily, as it is the usual failing of the subject to *under-* rather than to *over*-distance.

Prehension

VIRGIL ALDRICH

The stage is set nicely for my task by certain remarks in an essay by Frank Sibley.[1] His main concern there, the logic of aesthetic terms, will occupy us at the end of the book. But he mentions aesthetic "perceptiveness" as a special "ability to *notice* or *discern* things," distinguishing this from mere subjective preference or liking on the one hand, and from the good eyesight of people with 20-20 vision on the other. This kind of perception is precisely what I am trying to isolate and characterize for what it is worth. First comes a statement of the framework of my philosophy of art, the sense of which

Excerpts from Virgil Aldrich, *Philosophy of Art* (Englewood Cliffs, N.J.: Prentice-Hall, 1963), pp. 19–24.

[1]"Aesthetic Concepts," *Philosophical Review,* LXVII (October 1959), 421–50. Reprinted in this volume.

will be detailed throughout the rest of the book. It will help to have a general impression of it to begin with.

What suggested to me the following theory of aesthetic perception and required me to stretch the concept of experience is the phenomenon that intrigued Gombrich and Wittgenstein: the phenomenon of the change of "aspects" in the duck-rabbit picture, the staircase drawing, and the cube diagram. For example, look at this figure

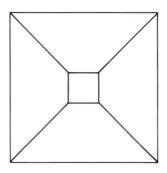

under these five titles: (1) square suspended in a frame, (2) lampshade seen from above, (3) lampshade seen from below, (4) looking into a tunnel, and (5) aerial view of a truncated pyramid. Call these "subject matters." You will notice that the space values of the figure are fixed according to which subject matter it is seen as. Call this a change of "aspects," and the phenomenon of the change itself "aspection." Although a condition of what you see is what you have in mind, the aspect is not just a thought or even just a subjective image; it is an object of perception of some sort. The figure objectively accommodates the various aspects.

That this is *not* so is suggested by the notion that the figure really or in itself is a physical object. So we get the notion of the projection of images that are only apparent, and thus of perceptual illusion. This is because the shape of a physical object does not change under aspection. Physical objects do not objectively accommodate aspects.

But reconsider the figure with a view to what it is simply or in itself. In the first place, you will find it difficult to get such a basic neutral awareness of it. It more readily appears as this or that. But, if pressed, we can report that what is simply there is a figure in printer's ink on white paper, the space values of which are indeterminate or not definite without presuppositions or ways of looking.

You may retort that anyone can see that it is a physical object. Well, what sort of seeing is *that?* Do I *simply* see it that way? I *can*, of course, see the figure as flat on the surface of the page and perhaps the page itself as a flat physical object, but this is an educated perception appealing implicitly to a standard of physical flatness. To see it that way is an achievement. You don't *simply* see it that way. In fact, I find it difficult to see the figure as flat on the page, but quite easy to see it protruding or receding in a white field as a lampshade or a tunnel. And to call it a physical object raises age-old questions as to whether it is visible at all. Physical objects are not simply seen. They are observed, and observation is under controls. Ask the scientist, if you distrust what philosophers have said about this.

Anyway, I shall say that what is simply there is a determinable somewhat—a figure in printer's ink on white paper—and shall call it, certainly not a physical object, but a "material thing." "Material" here suggests a potential for this or that formulation, perceptual and conceptual. This is the phenomenologically innocent use of "material." (Look at "matter" and "material" in these uses: "What's the matter?" "That's immaterial to me"; "Let's sit down and discuss the matter"; "That's material for a court-case"; "Can't a more interesting subject matter be found?" And think of Aristotle's use of "matter" for the potentiality of a thing's becoming this or that, realized in this or that form.) It is a use free of presuppositions, whereas "physical object" and "aesthetic object" are not, but are categories under which the material thing is realized as an aesthetic or physical object. "Thing" here is also an innocent word, unlike "object," which presupposes a category and a way of looking—a mode of perception.

What I am approaching is the phenomenon of categorial aspection. It is so pervasive that it usually escapes notice. The same material thing may be perceptually realized either as a physical or as an aesthetic object. This refers to two modes of perception different in category. In the figure above, on the other hand, it was an affair of seeing the material thing (the figure) as a number of other things. Categorical aspection involves a change of categorical aspects; the same material thing is perceived now as a physical object, now as an aesthetic object, neither of which involves seeing it as another *thing*. The difference between categorial aspects has to do with modes of perception and the kinds of space[2] in which their objects are realized. Moreover, such aspection is not as much under voluntary control as is the lampshade sort, since it involves an educated looking which is a gradual achievement.

Let us call "observation" the perceptual mode in which material things are realized in physical space. Then the very looking at things will be an incipient awareness of their space properties as fixed by metrical standards and measuring operations. Things seen this way will have a different structural cast from that of the same things in the aesthetic perception of them. Let us call the latter mode "prehension." The aesthetic space of things perceived thus is determined by such characteristics as intensities or values of colors and sounds, which, as we shall see later, comprise the medium presented by the material things in question. Take for example a dark city and a pale western sky at dusk, meeting at the sky line. In the purely prehensive or aesthetic view of this, the light sky area just above the jagged sky line pro-

---

[2]Virgil C. Aldrich, "Picture Space," *Philosophical Review*, LXVII (July 1958), 342–52.

trudes toward the point of view. The sky is closer to the viewer than are the dark areas of buildings. This is the disposition of these material things in aesthetic space with respect to their medium alone. It is precisely the medium in this sense that is discounted both in the observational view of them and in the plain, nonspecial view. Thus prehension is, if you like, an "impressionistic" way of looking, but still a mode of perception, with the impressions objectively animating the material things—there to be prehended.

Let us say, then, that under observation, the characteristics of the material thing are realized as "qualities" that "qualify" it, while for prehension, its characteristics are realized as "aspects" (objective impressions) that "animate" it. Such animation will occur in two ways or senses: (1) in the prehension that involves getting the aesthetic space values of the thing as structured simply by color and sound; this is, simply to see a material thing as an aesthetic object, a case of a categorial aspect—the sky line above is an example; and (2) in seeing the thing as something that it is not thought really to be; the figure is not mistaken for a lampshade while it is being seen as one, but it is animated by the image of something else. Representational works of art feature this second kind of animation. Both sorts of aspects or animation occur without any change in observable qualities of the thing as a physical object.

The presuppositionless terms in this account are: (1) "thing," which here specifies into "physical object" and "aesthetic object;" (2) "perception," which ramifies into "observation" and "prehension;" and (3) "characteristics," which are actualized as observed "qualities" that "qualify" the thing, or as prehended "aspects" that "animate" it. The presuppositions of the various controlled ways of looking at and talking about things are formulated in the categories specified for "physical object" and "aesthetic object," for "observation" and "prehension," and for "qualities" and "aspects."

A final crucial point: the distinction between "physical object" and "aesthetic object" is not anything like the distinction between "material" and "mental." Any object is a material thing appearing one way or another. There are no mental objects, fundamentally speaking. Materialists and idealists in metaphysics have concurred on this. But the point is that as "object" is a category word with presuppositions—physical or aesthetic—so is "subject." The diagram below illustrates it, and, in our thinking about art, should replace the unfortunate one given before on p. 8. It is a picture primarily of categorial aspection.

The message of this is simple enough, and is of tremendous importance for art. It means that the mind, as a potential for this or that sort of experience of material things, does not necessarily become subjective when it gives up observing them. The notion that it does become subjective was the unfortunate result of the traditional unilinear model. There is another access to material things—as objective in its own way as the observational is in its way—that the mind may take as prehending subject. In such a rapport, the

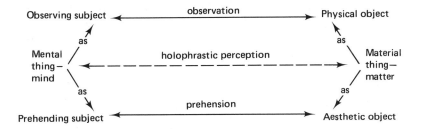

things will be realized as aesthetic objects, in the prehensive mode of perception. But since perception in either of these two determinate modes is an exclusive achievement—one excludes the other—a basic simple perception of things is presupposed, in the swim of which both material things and mental things are determinables, not realized as definitely this or that sort of objects and subjects. "Mind" and "matter" are therefore limiting concepts in the direction of polar opposites beyond categories. The nonspecial field of their fundamental rapport I call "holophrastic," a word that suggests something in which much is compacted both in that nonspecial kind of perception and in its nonspecial mode of expression in "ordinary language." . . .

Aesthetic Experience
and Aesthetic Object

ROMAN INGARDEN

I. The Difference between the Cognitive Perception of a Real Object and the Aesthetic Experience of an Aesthetic Object

The essential mistake of the views about an aesthetic experience consists in the opinion that the object of such an experience is *identical* with an element of the real world and the object of our activities or cognition. There are, indeed, some circumstances which seem to justify this opinion. May it not happen that we lift the window-blinds in our room some day in spring and catch the sight of the garden where the trees have opened into flower during

Excerpts from Roman Ingarden, "Aesthetic Experience and Aesthetic Object," *Philosophy and Phenomenological Research* 21 (1961). Reprinted with permission.

the night? We are suddenly dazzled and fascinated by the sight of apple trees abloom against the background of a fair sky. Are we not pleased with some real objects, which we find in the surrounding world, the same objects which we had seen before having experienced the feeling of ecstasy, and which we continue to see in spite of the fact that the wave of feeling and enchantment has passed away? And is it otherwise—we may be asked by someone—when we enter, for example, the rooms of the Louvre and see at once the perspective of several rooms at the end of which there appears against a dark background the snow-white Venus de Milo in all her wonderful slenderness and charm? Is it not just a piece of stone of a particular shape that we are pleased with and that our enthusiasm is directed to? The fact that this piece of stone is the work of an artist does not seem to alter, by any means, its reality [and to exclude the object we are pleased with from being studied by someone assuming a purely investigating attitude, e.g., when measuring the particular dimensions of the statue, testing the condition of the marble surface, etc.].

The facts mentioned do occur, indeed; nevertheless the theory suggested on their basis seems to be faulty. It is, namely, true that in cases similar to those described we *begin* with the perception of a real object. But the question is, first, whether, when starting from a real object, we remain within its limits while an aesthetic perception is taking place in ourselves, and, secondly, whether the starting from a real object is indispensable in every case of aesthetic perception.

The possibility of purely fictitious objects, which are devised by ourselves and by no means perceived, to be the objects of aesthetic perception, indicates that the second question should be answered in the negative. We may, e.g., imagine a very tragic situation to obtain for people, although we know by anticipation that it has never existed, and also that we have never perceived it in our intercourse with real persons. In spite of that we may assume toward this situation a positive or a negative aesthetic attitude. Another example may be furnished by every literary work of art. For it is neither among physical, psychical, nor psycho-physical objects, that we find literary works. Among physical objects there are only the so-called books, i.e., in their present form some sheets of paper bound together and covered with various drawings. However, a book is not yet a literary work, but only a means to "fix" the work, or rather to render it accessible to the reader. Among the experiences, on the other hand, there occur only the acts of "reading" and which do not constitute a literary work either. Nevertheless, the particular literary works may be the objects against the background of which aesthetic objects come to be constituted. Some doubts may be raised by the fact that when reading a literary work or listening to its being read aloud, as a matter of fact, we have first to do with a real object or with a real process (letters on the paper, real material of sounds). As we have already stated elsewhere, we do not remain within the limits of those objects when becoming acquainted with a work of art. But it isn't even necessary that we begin the reading with the perception of a real object, because the possibility is not excluded that we only imagine the "letters" or the corresponding sounds, e.g., when we are repeating a poem from memory. It should therefore be stated that it is not in every case of aesthetic perception that one must start from the perception of a real object.

A conjecture presents itself, that also in those cases, where we have before us a real object at the *beginning* of an aesthetic perception-process— e.g., in sense perception—the *reality* of the object in question is not indispensable for the accomplishment of this perception or for the given aesthetic object to be there. Then we are perceiving a piece of marble which we call the "Venus of Milo" and are fascinated with the peculiar charm of its shape. It may happen that our perception is an illusion, that in reality there is in the room of the Louvre no piece of marble or that it is quite different from what has appeared to our perception. All this would not in the least alter either our being enchanted or what has been *given* to us as the object of this experience. The reality of an object isn't thus necessary for the accomplishment of an aesthetic experience. And it is also not the reality in question that brings about our being or not being pleased with something in an aesthetic experience, because the occurrence of reality as a particular moment of the object perceived does not influence our *aesthetic* delight or aversion in any way. If this were not the case, all the objects which we perceive as real should be "beautiful," "fascinating," "pretty," or "ugly," which is not true.

However, this fact isn't sufficient in order to state that in every case in which we perceive an aesthetic object, grasping its beauty or its ugliness, *we do not remain* within the limits of the real object, with the perception of which our aesthetic experience has begun. For it may be that the reality of the object perceived is, indeed, in itself neither necessary nor such that it would entail the aesthetic values of the object of aesthetic experience, but instead of this some other qualities of the real object in question are both the source and the object of aesthetic experience. Those who think the objects of aesthetic experience to be simply some objects of particular qualities from among the real objects of sense perception usually argue just this way.

In order to decide this question let us consider, on the one hand, what we do when, in an investigating attitude, we aim at the obtaining of *knowledge* of a *real* object with the aid of sense perception, and, on the other hand, what we do when we experience a process which leads us finally to an object which presents itself in a direct experience, as having an aesthetic value. But we fail to explain the above question if we persist in the prejudice, often entertained, that the two opposed activities are some *momentary* experiences differing only by the feeling of "like" or "dislike" joining the momentary sense perception in the second case. For the cognition of a real object by sense perception (or with the aid of it) as well as the so-called aesthetic experience are processes extended in time, having their various *phases,* often composed of many acts of consciousness differing from one another.

We can *cognize,* in an investigating attitude, the piece of marble, which is called today the "Venus of Milo," only in the way that we accomplish the whole *series* of visual, tactile, or other perceptions which do not necessarily follow one another continuously. In each of these perceptions, we have not only to become clearly conscious of *what* is given to us (what kind of object, of what kind of properties), but also to realize if what is given to us is given in *such a way and in such circumstances* that we are right in acknowledging it to appertain to an object as its property, immanent in it. Thus, besides the perception itself, there comes here into account some *judgments* expressing its results, then the comparison of the results of particular perceptions, binding them with one another and a steady taking into consideration of the objective and subjective conditions in which the perception has been accomplished (e.g., the lighting of the interior, the neighborhood of other objects in the field of perception, and even the presence of such objects which, though not entering themselves the field of perception, cause a transitory change of the object in question, or at least the occurrence, in perception, of some of its apparent properties; our psychic condition during the perception—e.g., some emotional disturbances, the condition of our sense organs, etc.). These conditions are taken into account with the aim of considering their influence on the data of our perceptions. But the leitmotiv of these considerations—which are, indeed, constantly carried out by naturalists in their scientific observations and experiments—is, on the one hand, to *deny* to the object which is being cognized all the properties which, though given in some circumstances in perception as the properties of the object in question, do not pertain to it, their appearance among the data of perception being caused by some foreign factors and not by the nature of the object investigated. On the other hand, the aim of these considerations is to *ascribe* some properties to the object which we cognize on the basis of perception. Two cases may occur here: either some qualities are *given* in perception as the properties of an object and these qualities should be ascribed to the object, but only if they appear in the whole cognitive process as *independent* of irrelevant circumstances, i.e., circumstances of perception or cognition lying *beyond* the object perceived; or these qualities are not at all given in any of the perceptions of the object which is being cognized. On the basis of a number of checked perceptions we may, however, *infer* that these qualities, which are independent of any foreign circumstances of perception, are an *indispensable condition* supplementing the *appearance,* among the data of perception, of a particular quality as an (apparent) property of the cognized object. In this case also they should be ascribed to the object as its own properties. Thus, the whole process of cognition, composed of many different cognitive acts, is directed—if it proceeds regularly—by the idea of an exact *adjustment* of the cognitive results to the object to be cognized and of an exclusion of all those elements, which admit the slightest suspicion of having issued from factors *foreign* to the cognized object.

The matter—as it will be seen—presents itself quite differently in the pretty complicated process, which here will be called an "aesthetic experience." Those of us who have been in Paris and have looked at the piece of marble called the "Venus of Milo" know this piece to have various properties which, far from coming into account in an aesthetic experience, obviously hinder its accomplishment, in consequence of which we are inclined to *overlook* them, e.g., a dark stain on the nose of Venus, which impedes an aesthetic perception of its shape, or various rough spots, cavities, and holes in the breast, corroded probably by water, etc. In an aesthetic experience, we overlook these particular qualities of the stone and behave as if we didn't see them; on the contrary, we behave as if we saw the shape of the nose uniformly colored, as if the surface of the breast were smooth, with the cavities *filled up,* with a regularly formed nipple (without the damage actually to be found in the stone), etc. We *supplement* "in thought," or even in a peculiar perceptive representation, such details of the object as play a positive role in the attainment of the *optimum* of aesthetic "impression" possible in the given case; more exactly—details that give such a shape of the object of our aesthetic experience as distinguishes itself most fully by aesthetic values, which may appear, in the given conditions, *in concreto*. This kind of procedure would be most improper in the cognition, in an investigating attitude, of the properties of a real stone. Here, in an aesthetic perception, it "fits well." And this is by no means due to the persuasion, that all the details we "overlook" are only some "posterior damages" not to be taken into account, because they did not occur at the beginning when the statue issued from under the chisel of the artist. Such a way of posing the question would be proper only if we assumed the investigating attitude of art historians and if we wanted to learn, on the basis of the present condition of the stone-statue, what kind of statue it really *had been* as made by its creator. In this case we should also have to "supplement" the arms which are today broken off, etc. The reason for overlooking some details in an aesthetic perception is a different one: the details to be overlooked "shock" us; if they were perceived, they would introduce a *disharmonious* factor into the field of what is in perception *given* to us, they would bring *discordance* into the totality of an aesthetic object. Moreover, this object is, indeed, by no means identical with the given piece of marble. More exactly: it is *given* to us not as a piece of marble, but as the "Venus," i.e., as a woman or a goddess. Therefore we are right to speak of a head, of a breast, etc. We *see*—have *given*—a woman "body." And not only the mere body; in an aesthetic perception, we see the *Venus,* i.e., a woman or goddess in a situation and in a psychic condition, which expresses itself in her countenance, her movement, etc. At the same time, however, it is for us no *real* woman body and no *real* woman. If we met a living woman with such arms knocked off (suppose already "healed") we should, surely, experience a strong aversion, reacting, maybe, at the same time with pity, compassion, etc. But in an aesthetic perception of the "Venus of Milo" there is no trace of such experiences. We cannot say here that either the "stumps" are not seen at all, or that they are seen distinctly, our attention being specially paid to them during the perceptive process and their existence as if stressed. Neither can it be said that the missing arms are supplemented "in thought" or in imagination (though this is possible). These missing arms are, in this case, no hindrance for us. Many a time—as it is known—it has been called into question whether it would be "better" if those arms had not been knocked off—"better," of course, not for the piece of marble, nor for a living woman, but for the totality of an object aesthetically valuable, which *comes into existence* while an aesthetic experience is being accomplished; more exactly: "better" for the aesthetic *value* of the object which is being constituted only when an aesthetic experience is going on and which is given to us when constituted. In an aesthetic attitude, we somehow entirely forget the lack of arms and the missing arms. Things have taken such a happy turn that the whole object "seen" in this way does not lose anything, but, perhaps, rather profits by the fact that the arms do not appear in the field of vision. Thanks to this circumstance there appear some aesthetic values (e.g., a greater slenderness of the figure, the uniformity of the silhouette of the chest, etc.) which would not reveal themselves in this form if the arms had been actually preserved.

At any rate, this whole question proves that, in this case, there takes place no simple sense perception of a real stone or of a real woman, but that the sense perception is here solely a *basis* for the further peculiar psychic acts, built over it, which lead us to the "Venus of Milo" as an object of aesthetic experience. And correlatively: the object of aesthetic experience is *not identical with any real object,* and only some real objects, formed in a peculiar way, serve as a *starting point* and as a basis for some aesthetic objects to be built, a proper attitude of the perceiving subject being assumed. Besides, the so-called "aesthetic experience" is no *single* composite experience but a certain number of experiences connected with one another. In order to see the "Venus of Milo" in an aesthetic experience it is insufficient to "look" at her for a moment from a single point of view. One has to "perceive" her from different sides, in various perspective abridgments, from a nearer or a further distance; to be able, in every phase of aesthetic experience, on the basis of sense perception (nota bene a modified one) to look for those *visible properties* of the Venus of Milo, which reveal her aesthetic values accessible in the given aspect; then one has to grasp the qualities aesthetically valuable and to bind them synthetically with one another in order to succeed, in this way, in grasping the *whole* of the harmony of those qualities, and, at that time only—in a peculiar emotional contemplation—to *give oneself up to the charm* of the beauty of the constituted "aesthetic object." . . .

II. Phases and Elements of an Aesthetic Experience

As I have already stated, an aesthetic experience is not—contrary to what is often heard— a *momentary* experience, a momentary feeling of pleasure or displeasure, arising as a response to some data of sense perception, but a *composite process having various phases and a characteristic development* which contains many heterogeneous elements. That the opposed theory seems plausible is due to the fact that, many a time—in consequence of some irrelevant factors—the process does not attain its full development: it is either interrupted before the aesthetic object has been constituted and before the experience of it has culminated, or, in consequence of an artificial preparation, or of some professional habits, it does not commence from the beginning, but from the moment in which an aesthetic object is already constituted (e.g., when we look at a painting which we have already seen many times and which we have learned to see in the way it had been once constituted to us as an aesthetic object of peculiar properties). The duration and the complexity of this process depend, of course, on whether we have before us in a given case, a complicated or a simple aesthetic object. Sometimes it is simply a quality of color or a sound of voice which alone become such objects: than the process of aesthetic experience is correspondingly a more "fleeting" one, but even then it is not a momentary "feeling of pleasure" or "displeasure."

III. The Preliminary Emotion of the Aesthetic Experience

If an aesthetic process starts from a pure sense perception (which is not always the case), the most interesting part of the process and, at the same time, a very difficult one to grasp is the *transition* from the sense perception of a real object to the phases of the aesthetic experience. This is *change of attitude* from a practical one, assumed in everyday life, or from an investigating one, to an aesthetic attitude. What *causes this change of attitude* to occur? What happens when—instead of continuing to be employed with our everyday, practical or theoretical affairs—we *interrupt* (how often in a sudden and unexpected way) the "normal" course of our life and begin to occupy ourselves with something which, while not appertaining, seemingly, to our life, enriches it, at the same time, and confers upon it a new sense?

This transition may proceed in different ways with different people according to various circumstances. However, I do not think, I am far from the truth in indicating the following essential moments: namely, while perceiving a real object we are *struck* with a peculiar quality or with a multiplicity of qualities, or, at last, with a gestalt quality (e.g., a color or a harmony of colors, the quality of a melody, a rhythm, a shape, etc.) which not only focuses our attention on itself, but, in addition, is not indifferent to us. This initial quality evokes in us a special emotion which I shall call a *preliminary* emotion, because it is only this emotion which opens the proper process of aesthetic experience. As I have said, this quality "strikes" us, it imposes itself on us. Here I want to point out that the perception of this quality is *passive* and, in this phase of experience, a *fleeting* one, and, moreover, of such a kind that, if the whole process were in this phase suddenly interrupted, we ourselves probably would not know to answer the question what kind of quality it had been: we receive the impression of it, we experience it rather than perceive it. . . .

IV. Consequences of the Preliminary Emotion

. . . A preliminary emotion—and this is its most important function—causes a *change of our attitude:* a transition from a natural attitude of practical life into a specifically aesthetic one. The emotion (evoked by a quality or a so-called "gestalt" which excites us, containing, at the same time, a moment of desire, a longing for satiation with an intuitively given quality) brings the change about from a natural attitude directed to some existing *facts,* or to those to come in the range of the real world, to an attitude directed to *an intuitive intercourse with qualitative essences.* Both in sense, or inward, perception which is involved in our practical behavior (settling of daily life affairs, realizing the new state of things) and in the perception which we carry out for purely investigative purposes, we look for what *is.* In both cases *real* objects and facts are the matter of our perception. . . .

Under the influence of the preliminary emotion, the sense perception, among the data of which there had primarily occurred the quality evoking the emotion in question, is essentially modified: a. the conviction of the existence of the thing perceived, which conviction is normally included in an act of sense perception, is deprived of its binding power, is—to use an expression of Husserl—"neutralized"; b. the quality, which had primarily occurred as a property of a real thing given in this perception, becomes, as it were, freed from this formal structure; it remains for a moment a pure quality, usually to become in the further phases of the process of the aesthetic experience *a center of crystallization* for a new object: an aesthetic object. This is, perhaps, the most radical change of attitude that may be accomplished in our psychic life. Thus, it is no wonder that an aesthetic experience separates so much from the course of our daily lives and causes such a "check" of our daily activities that there occurs the phenomenon of "forgetting the world," and that either an exhaustion of the aesthetic experience itself or a stronger stimulus "from without"—i.e., from the real world—is necessary for the "return" we spoke of above to be accomplished.

However, it should not be supposed, on this basis, that an aesthetic experience is a purely passive, and noncreative "contemplating" of a quality (speaking more coarsely—a gaping at the quality), as opposed to an "active" practical life. On the contrary, it is a phase of a very *active,* intensive, and creative life of an individual, that these activities do not evoke any changes in the surrounding real world, nor are they "calculated" to do so. It is, moreover, true—as it will yet be proved—that the whole process of aesthetic experience includes, on the one hand, *active phases,* on the other hand, again, the fleeting phases of a passive experiencing, the moments of turning motionless and contemplative. . . .

V. The Final Phase of an Aesthetic Experience

The previous phases of the aesthetic experience are characterized by the fact that in a composite structure of this experience there may be distinguished the three kinds of elements: a. emotional (aesthetic excitement), b. creative (active)—constitution of an aesthetic object, c. passive—perception of the qualities already revealed and harmonized. The particular phases of the aesthetic experience are in various ways dominated by the particular elements, one time some of the elements prevailing, another time the others. This whole process is characterized by a peculiar *searching disquietude,* a changeability full of dynamism. In contrast with this, in the final phase of an aesthetic experience there ensues an *appeasement* in the sense that, on the one hand, there is a rather quiet *gazing upon* (contemplating) the qualitative harmony of the aesthetic object already constituted and a "taking in" of these qualities. On the other hand, along with this, there proceeds what I have named the second form of emotional response to a harmony of qualities. And namely, there arise some feelings in which an *acknowledgement of the value* of the constituted aesthetic object is taking place. Such experiences as being pleased with, admiration, rapture, are various *intentional feelings.*

Of course, not every aesthetic experience ends with the delineated culmination of a *positive* emotional response to the value of an aesthetic object, revealing itself in it. A *negative* emotional response under the form of aversion, abomination, indignation, boredom, etc., may be another final tone of an aesthetic experience. This is the case, *inter alia,* when an aesthetic object is not a *uniform harmony of qualities* "joined" to one another by the final harmony quality, i.e., when it is a "conglomeration" of the qualities not harmonized, rather than a coherent whole, its qualities neither "suggesting" nor postulating one another at all, on the contrary, postulating rather that they *do not coexist* within a *single* object. In such a case, the experience does not result in this "gazing" upon the harmony, nor in the satiation with the qualities, nor, at last, in this *intimacy and immediacy of a relation* with an aesthetic object, which are characteristic of the positive culmination of an aesthetic experience. It may rather be said that there is an apparent *distance* in relation to the object, and a feeling of condemnation (as an opposite to "acknowledgement") increases the said distance and compels us to reject the given aesthetic object altogether, to desist from looking at it—unless some other reasons, e.g., theoretical ones, incline us to occupy ourselves with it. On the basis of such a negative emotional response there may also be accomplished an intellectual estimation of the value of the given aesthetic object.

In *both* the cases considered—and this is to be stressed—there is a constitution of an aesthetic object. But an aesthetic experience may not attain this culmination, it may not begin at all; correlatively: no aesthetic object will be constituted. A certain real object, intended by its creator as a work of art, may be to us *completely indifferent* aesthetically. We may pass it by unaffected, not being excited to a preliminary emotion. And, but for outside information that the object in question is a work of art, it wouldn't even occur to our minds that an aesthetic attitude toward it is possible. In such cases we often evaluate a "work of art" *in a negative way*, criticizing it severely but, strictly speaking, we are not right in doing so. There is no real aesthetic evaluation in such a case and the "work of art" should simply be disregarded.

Aesthetic Concepts

FRANK SIBLEY

The remarks we make about works of art are of many kinds. In this paper I wish to distinguish between two broad groups. We say that a novel has a great number of characters and deals with life in a manufacturing town; that a painting uses pale colors, predominantly blues and greens, and has kneeling figures in the foreground; that the theme in a fugue is inverted at such a point and that there is a stretto at the close; that the action of a play takes place in the span of one day and that there is a reconciliation scene in the fifth act. Such remarks may be made by, and such features pointed out to, anyone with normal eyes, ears, and intelligence. On the other hand, we also say that a poem is tightly-knit or deeply moving; that a picture lacks balance, or has a certain serenity and repose, or that the grouping of the figures sets up an exciting tension; that the characters in a novel never really come to life, or that a certain episode strikes a false note. The making of such remarks as

Frank Sibley, "Aesthetic Concepts," *Philosophical Review*, 67 (1959). Reprinted by permission of *Philosophical Review* and the author.

these requires the exercise of taste, perceptiveness, or sensitivity, of aesthetic discrimination or appreciation. Accordingly, when a word or expression is such that taste or perceptiveness is required in order to apply it, I shall call it an *aesthetic* term or expression, and I shall, correspondingly, speak of *aesthetic* concepts or taste concepts.[1]

Aesthetic terms span a great range of types and could be grouped into various kinds and sub-species. But it is not my present purpose to attempt any such grouping; I am interested in what they all have in common. Their almost endless variety is adequately displayed in the following list: *unified, balanced, integrated, lifeless, serene, somber, dynamic, powerful, vivid, delicate, moving, trite, sentimental, tragic.* The list of course is not limited to adjectives; expressions in artistic contexts like "telling contrast," "sets up a tension," "conveys a sense of," or "holds it together" are equally good illustrations. It includes terms used by both layman and critic alike, as well as some which are mainly the property of professional critics and specialists.

I have gone for my examples of aesthetic expressions in the first place to critical and evaluative discourse about works of art because it is there particularly that they abound. But now I wish to widen the topic; we employ terms the use of which requires an exercise of taste not only when discussing the arts but quite liberally throughout discourse in everyday life. The examples given above are expressions which, appearing in critical contexts, most usually, if not invariably, have an aesthetic use; outside critical discourse the majority of them more frequently have some other use unconnected with taste. But many expressions do double duty even in everyday discourse, sometimes being used as aesthetic expressions and sometimes not. Other words again, whether in artistic or daily discourse, function only or predominantly as aesthetic terms; of this kind are *graceful, delicate, dainty, handsome, comely, elegant, garish.* Finally, to make the contrast with all the preceding examples, there are many words which are seldom used as aesthetic terms at all: *red, noisy, brackish, clammy, square, docile, curved, evanescent, intelligent, faithful, derelict, tardy, freakish.*

Clearly, when we employ words as aesthetic terms we are often making and using metaphors, pressing into service words which do not primarily function in this manner. Certainly also, many words *have come* to be aesthetic terms by some kind of metaphorical transference. This is so with those like "dynamic," "melancholy," "balanced," "tightly-knit" which, except in artistic and critical writings, are not normally aesthetic terms. But the aesthetic vocabulary must not be thought wholly metaphorical. Many words, including

---

[1] I shall speak loosely of an "aesthetic term," even when, because the word sometimes has other uses, it would be more correct to speak of its *use* as an aesthetic term. I shall also speak of "non-aesthetic" words, concepts, features, and so on. None of the terms other writers use, "natural," "observable," "perceptual," "physical," "objective" (qualities), "neutral," "descriptive" (language), when they approach the distinction I am making, is really apt for my purpose.

the most common (*lovely, pretty, beautiful, dainty, graceful, elegant*), are certainly not being used metaphorically when employed as aesthetic terms, the very good reason being that this is their primary or only use, some of them having no current non-aesthetic uses. And though expressions like "dynamic," "balanced," and so forth *have come* by a metaphorical shift to be aesthetic terms, their employment in criticism can scarcely be said to be more than quasi-metaphorical. Having entered the language of art description and criticism as metaphors they are now standard vocabulary in that language.[2]

The expressions I am calling aesthetic terms form no small segment of our discourse. Often, it is true, people with normal intelligence and good eyesight and hearing lack, at least in some measure, the sensitivity required to apply them; a man need not be stupid or have poor eyesight to fail to see that something is graceful. Thus taste or sensitivity is somewhat more rare than certain other human capacities; people who exhibit a sensitivity both wide-ranging and refined are a minority. It is over the application of aesthetic terms too that, notoriously, disputes and differences sometimes go helplessly unsettled. But almost everybody is able to exercise taste to some degree and in some matters. It is surprising therefore that aesthetic terms have been so largely neglected. They have received glancing treatment in the course of other aesthetic discussions; but as a broad category they have not received the direct attention they merit.

The foregoing has marked out the area I wish to discuss. One warning should perhaps be given. When I speak of taste in this paper, I shall not be dealing with questions which center upon expressions like "a matter of taste" (meaning, roughly, a matter of personal preference or liking). It is with an ability to *notice* or *discern* things that I am concerned.

In order to support our application of an aesthetic term, we often refer to features the mention of which involves other aesthetic terms: "it has an extraordinary vitality because of its free and vigorous style of drawing," "graceful in the smooth flow of its lines," "dainty because of the delicacy and harmony of its coloring." It is as normal to do this as it is to justify one mental epithet by other epithets of the same general type, *intelligent* by *ingenious, inventive, acute,* and so on. But often when we apply aesthetic terms, we explain why by referring to features which do *not* depend for their recognition upon an exercise of taste: "delicate because of its pastel shades and curving lines," or "it lacks balance because one group of figures is so far off to the

---

[2]A contrast will reinforce this. If a critic were to describe a passage of music as chattering, carbonated, or gritty, a painter's coloring as vitreous, farinaceous, or effervescent, or a writer's style as glutinous, or abrasive, he *would* be using live metaphors rather than drawing on the more normal language of criticism. Words like "athletic," "vertiginous," "silken" may fall somewhere between.

left and is so brightly illuminated." When no explanation of this kind is offered, it is legitimate to ask or search for one. Finding a satisfactory answer may sometimes be difficult, but one cannot ordinarily reject the question. When we cannot ourselves quite say what non-aesthetic features make something delicate or unbalanced or powerful or moving, the good critic often puts his finger on something which strikes us as the right explanation. In short, aesthetic words apply ultimately because of, and aesthetic qualities ultimately depend upon, the presence of features which, like curving or angular lines, color contrasts, placing of masses, or speed of movement, are visible, audible, or otherwise discernible without any exercise of taste or sensibility. Whatever kind of dependence this is, and there are various relationships between aesthetic qualities and non-aesthetic features, what I want to make clear in this section is that there are no non-aesthetic features which serve as *conditions* for applying aesthetic terms. Aesthetic or taste concepts are not in this respect condition-governed at all.

There is little temptation to suppose that aesthetic terms resemble words which, like "square," are applied in accordance with a set of necessary and sufficient conditions. For whereas each square is square in virtue of the *same* set of conditions, four equal sides and four right angles, aesthetic terms apply to widely varied objects; one thing is graceful because of these features, another because of those, and so on almost endlessly. In recent times philosophers have broken the spell of the strict necessary-and-sufficient model by showing that many everyday concepts are not of that type. Instead, they have described various other types of concepts which are governed only in a much looser way by conditions. However, since these newer models provide satisfactory accounts of many familiar concepts, it might plausibly be thought that aesthetic concepts are of some such kind and that they similarly are governed in some looser way by conditions. I want to argue that aesthetic concepts differ radically from any of these other concepts.

Amongst these concepts to which attention has recently been paid are those for which no *necessary* conditions can be provided, but for which there are a number of relevant features, A, B, C, D, E, such that the presence of some groups or combinations of these features is *sufficient* for the application of the concept. The list of relevant features may be an open one; that is, given A, B, C, D, E, we may not wish to close off the possible relevance of other unlisted features beyond E. Examples of such concepts might be "dilatory," "discourteous," "possessive," "capricious," "prosperous," "intelligent" (but see below). If we begin a list of features relevant to "intelligent" with, for example, ability to grasp and follow various kinds of instructions, ability to master facts and marshall evidence, ability to solve mathematical or chess problems, we might go on adding to this list almost indefinitely.

However, with concepts of this sort, although decisions may have to be made and judgment exercised, it is always possible to extract and state, from cases which have *already* clearly been decided, the sets of features or conditions which were regarded as sufficient in those cases. These relevant features which I am calling conditions are, it should be noted, features which, though not sufficient *alone* and needing to be combined with other similar features, always carry some weight and can count only in one direction. Being a good chess player can count only *towards* and not *against* intelligence. Whereas mention of it may enter sensibly along with other remarks in expressions like "I say he is intelligent because . . ." or "the reason I call him intelligent is that . . .," it cannot be used to complete such negative expressions as "I say he is *un*intelligent because . . ." But what I want particularly to emphasize about features which function as conditions for a term is that *some* group or set of them *is* sufficient fully to ensure or warrant the application of that term. An individual characterized by some of these features may not yet qualify to be called lazy or intelligent, and so on, beyond all question, but all that is needed is to add some further (indefinite) number of such characterizations and the point is reached where we have enough. There are individuals possessing a number of such features of whom one cannot deny, cannot but admit, that they are intelligent. We have left necessary-and-sufficient conditions behind, but we are still in the realm of conditions.

But aesthetic concepts are not condition-governed even in this way. There are no sufficient conditions, no non-aesthetic features such that the presence of some set or number of them will beyond question justify or warrant the application of an aesthetic term. It is impossible (barring certain limited exceptions, see below) to make any statements corresponding to those we can make for condition-governed words. We are able to say "If it is true he can do this, and that, and the other, then one just cannot deny that he is intelligent," or "if he does A, B, and C, I don't see how it can be denied that he is lazy," but we cannot make *any* general statement of the form "If the vase is pale pink, somewhat curving, lightly mottled, and so forth, it will be delicate, cannot be but delicate." Nor again can one say *any* such things here as "Being tall and thin is not enough *alone* to ensure that a vase is delicate, but if it is, for example, slightly curving and pale colored (and so forth) as well, it cannot be denied that it is." Things may be described to us in non-aesthetic terms as fully as we please but we are not thereby put in the position of having to admit (or being unable to deny) that they are delicate or graceful or garish or exquisitely balanced.

No doubt there are some respects in which aesthetic terms *are* governed by conditions or rules. For instance, it may be impossible that a thing should be garish if all its colors are pale pastels, or flamboyant if all its lines are straight. There may be, that is, descriptions using only non-aesthetic terms which are incompatible with descriptions employing certain aesthetic terms. If I am told that a painting in the next room consists solely of one or two bars of very pale blue and very pale grey set at right angles on a pale fawn ground, I can be sure that it cannot be fiery or garish or gaudy or flamboyant.

A description of this sort may make certain aesthetic terms *in*applicable or *in*appropriate; and if from this description I inferred that the picture was, or even might be, fiery or gaudy or flamboyant, this might be taken as showing a failure to understand these words. I do not wish to deny therefore that taste concepts may be governed *negatively* by conditions. What I am emphasizing is that they quite lack governing conditions of a sort many other concepts possess. Though on *seeing* the picture we might say, and rightly, that it is delicate or serene or restful or sickly or insipid, no *description* in non-aesthetic words permits us to claim that these or any other aesthetic terms must undeniably apply to it.

I have said that if an object is characterized *solely* by certain sorts of features this may count decisively against the possibility of applying to it certain aesthetic words. But of course the presence of just *a few* such features need not count decisively; other features may be enough to outweigh those which, on their own, would render the aesthetic term inapplicable. A painting might be garish even though much of its color is pale. These facts call attention to a further feature of taste concepts. One *can* find general features or descriptions which in some sense count in one direction only, only *for* or only *against* the application of certain aesthetic terms. Angularity, fatness, brightness, or intensity of color are typically not associated with delicacy or grace. Slimness, lightness, gentle curves, lack of intensity of color are associated with delicacy, but not with flamboyance, majesty, grandeur, splendor or garishness. This is shown by the naturalness of saying, for example, that someone is graceful *because* she's so light, but *in spite of* being quite angular or heavily built; and by the corresponding oddity of saying that something is graceful *because* it is so heavy or angular, or delicate *because* of its bright and intense coloring. This may therefore sound quite similar to what I have said already about conditions. There are nevertheless very significant differences. Although there is this sense in which slimness, lightness, lack of intensity of color, and so on, count only towards, not against, delicacy, these features can be said, at best, to count only *typically* or *characteristically* towards delicacy; they do not count towards in the same sense as condition-features count towards laziness or intelligence.

One way of reinforcing this is to notice how features which are characteristically associated with one aesthetic term may also be similarly associated with other and rather different aesthetic terms. "Graceful" and "delicate" may be on the one hand sharply contrasted with terms like "violent," "grand," "fiery," "garish," or "massive" which have characteristic non-aesthetic features quite unlike those for "delicate" and "graceful." But on the other hand they may also be contrasted with aesthetic terms which stand much closer to them, like "flaccid," "weakly," "washed out," "lanky," "anaemic," "wan," "insipid"; and the range of features characteristic of *these* qualities, pale color, slimness, lightness, lack of angularity and sharp contrast, is virtually identical with the range for "delicate" and "graceful." Similarly many of the features typically associated with "joyous," "fiery," "robust," or "dynamic" are identical with those associated with "garish," "strident," "turbulent," "gaudy," or "chaotic." Thus an object which is described very fully, but exclusively in terms of qualities characteristic of delicacy, may turn out on inspection to be not delicate at all, but anaemic or insipid. The failures of novices and the artistically inept prove that quite close similarity in point of line, color, or technique gives no assurance of gracefulness or delicacy. A failure and a success in the manner of Degas may be generally more alike, so far as their non-aesthetic features go, than either is like a successful Fragonard. But it is not necessary to go even this far to make my main point. A painting which has only the kind of features one would associate with vigor and energy but which even so fails to be vigorous and energetic *need* not have some other character, need not be instead, say, strident or chaotic. It may fail to have any particular character whatever. It may employ bright colors, and the like, without being particularly lively and vigorous at all; but one may feel unable to describe it as chaotic or strident or garish either. It is, rather, simply lacking in character (though of course this too is an aesthetic judgment; taste is exercised also in seeing that the painting has no character).

There are of course many features which do not in these ways characteristically count for (or against) particular aesthetic qualities. One poem has strength and power because of the regularity of its meter and rhyme; another is monotonous and lacks drive and strength because of its regular meter and rhyme. We do not feel the need to switch from "because of" to "in spite of." However, I have concentrated upon features which are characteristically associated with aesthetic qualities because, if a case could be made for the view that taste concepts are condition-governed, these would seem to be the most promising candidates for governing conditions. But to say that features are associated only *characteristically* with an aesthetic term is to say that they are not conditions; no description however full, even in terms characteristic of gracefulness, puts it beyond question that something is graceful in the way a description may put it beyond question that someone is lazy or intelligent.

. . . My arguments and illustrations so far have been rather simply schematic. Many concepts, including most of the examples I have used (*intelligent*, and so on,), are much more thoroughly open and complex than my illustrations suggest. Not only may there be an open list of relevant conditions; it may be impossible to give rules telling how many features from the list are needed for a sufficient set or in which combinations; impossible similarly to give rules covering the extent or degree to which such features need to be present in those combinations. Indeed, we may have to abandon as futile any attempt to describe conditions or formulate rules and content ourselves with giving only some very general account of the concept, making reference to samples or cases or precedents. We cannot master or employ these concepts therefore simply by being equipped with lists of conditions, readily applicable procedures or sets of rules, however complex. For to exhibit a mastery of one of these concepts we must be able to go ahead and apply the word correctly to new individual cases, at least to central ones; and each new case may be a uniquely different object, just as each intelligent child or student may differ from others in relevant features and exhibit a unique combination of kinds and degrees of achievement and ability. In dealing with these new cases mechanical rules and procedures would be useless; we have to exercise our judgment, guided by a complex set of examples and precedents. Here then there is a marked superficial similarity to aesthetic concepts. For in using aesthetic terms we learn from samples and examples, not rules, and we have to apply them, likewise, without guidance by rules or readily applicable procedures, to new and unique instances. Neither kind of concept admits of a "mechanical" employment.

Nevertheless it is at least noteworthy that in applying words like "lazy" or "intelligent" to new and unique instances we say that we are required to exercise *judgment*; it would be indeed odd to say that we are exercising *taste*. In exercising judgment we are called upon to weigh the pros and cons against each other, and perhaps sometimes to decide whether a quite new feature is to be counted as weighing on one side or on the other. But this goes to show that, though we may learn from and rely upon samples and precedents rather than a set of stated conditions, we are not out of the realm of general conditions and guiding principles. Samples and precedents necessarily embody, and are used by us to illustrate, the complex web of governing and relevant conditions. To profit by precedents we have to understand them; and we must argue consistently from case to case. This is the very function of precedents. Thus it is possible, even with these very loosely condition-governed concepts, to take clear or paradigm cases, to say "this is X because . . .," and follow it up with an account of features which clinch the matter.

Nothing like this is possible with aesthetic terms. Examples undoubtedly play a crucial role in giving us a grasp of these concepts; but we do not and cannot derive from these examples conditions and principles, however complex, which will guide us consistently and intelligibly in applying the terms to new cases. When, with a clear case of something which is in fact graceful or balanced or tightly-knit but which I have not seen, someone tells me why it is, what features make it so, it is always possible for me to wonder whether, in spite of these features, it really is graceful, balanced, and so on.

The point I have argued may be reinforced in the following way. A man who failed to realize the nature of taste concepts, or someone who, knowing he lacked sensitivity in aesthetic matters, did not want to reveal this lack might by assiduous application and shrewd observation provide himself with some rules and generalizations; and by inductive procedures and intelligent guessing, he might frequently say the right things. But he could have no great confidence or certainty; a slight change in an object might at any time unpredictably ruin his calculations, and he might as easily have been wrong as right. No matter how careful he has been about working out a set of consistent principles and conditions, he is only in a position to think that the object is very possibly delicate. With concepts like *lazy, intelligent,* or *contract,* someone who intelligently formulated rules that led him aright appreciably often *would* thereby show the beginning of a grasp of those concepts; but the person we are considering is not even beginning to show an awareness of what delicacy is. Though he sometimes says the right thing, he has not seen, but guessed, that the object is delicate. However intelligent he might be, we could easily tell him wrongly that something was delicate and "explain" why without his being able to detect the deception. (I am ignoring complications now about negative conditions.) But if we did the same with, say, "intelligent" he could at least often uncover some incompatibility or other which would need explaining. In a world of beings like himself he would have no use for concepts like delicacy. As it is, these concepts would play a quite different role in his life. He would, for himself, have no more reason to choose tasteful objects, pictures, and so on, than a deaf man would to avoid noisy places. He could not be praised for exercising taste; at best his ingenuity and intelligence might come in for mention. In "appraising" pictures, statuettes, poems, he would be doing something quite different from what other people do when they exercise taste. . . .

It must not be thought that the impossibility of stating any conditions (other than negative) for the application of aesthetic terms results from an accidental poverty or lack of precision in language, or that it is simply a question of extreme complexity. It is true that words like "pink," "bluish," "curving," "mottled" do not permit of anything like a specific naming of each and every varied shade, curve, mottling, and blending. But if we were to give special names much more liberally than either we or even the specialists do (and no doubt there are limits beyond which we could not go), or even if, instead of names, we were to use vast numbers of specimens and samples of particular shades, shapes, mottlings, lines, and configurations, it would still be impossible, and for the same reasons, to supply any conditions.

We do indeed, in talking about a work of art, concern ourselves with its individual and specific features. We say that it is delicate not simply because it is in pale colors but because of *those* pale colors, that it is graceful not because its outline curves slightly but because of *that* particular curve. We use expressions like "because of *its* pale coloring," "because of *the* flecks of bright blue," "because of *the* way the lines converge" where it is clear we are referring not to the presence of general features but to very specific and particular ones. But it is obvious that even with the help of precise names, or even samples and illustrations, of particular shades of color, contours and lines, any attempt to state conditions would be futile. After all, the very same feature, say a color or shape or line of a particular sort, which helps make one work may quite spoil another. "It would be quite delicate if it were not for that pale color there" may be said about the very color which is singled out in another picture as being largely responsible for its delicate quality. No doubt one way of putting this is to say that the features which make something delicate or graceful, and so on, are combined in a peculiar and unique way; that the aesthetic quality depends upon exactly this individual or unique combination of just these specific colors and shapes so that even a slight change might make all the difference. Nothing is to be achieved by trying to single out or separate features and generalizing about them.

I have now argued that taste concepts are not and cannot be condition- or rule-governed. Not to be so governed is one of their essential characteristics. In arguing this I first claimed in a general way that no non-aesthetic features are possible candidates for conditions, and then considered more particularly both the "characteristic" general features associated with aesthetic terms and the individual or specific features found in particular objects. I have not attempted to examine what relationship these individual features do bear to aesthetic qualities. An examination of the locutions we use when we refer to them in the course of explaining or supporting our application of an aesthetic term reinforces with linguistic evidence the fact that we are certainly not offering them as explanatory or justifying *conditions*. When we are asked why we say a certain person is lazy or intelligent or courageous, we are being asked in virtue of what we *call* him this; we reply with "because of the way he regularly leaves his work unfinished," or "because of the ease with which he handles such and such problems," and so on. But when we are asked to say why, in our opinion, a picture lacks balance or is somber in tone, or why a poem is moving or tightly organized, we are doing a different kind of thing. We may use similar locutions: "his verse has strength and and variety *because of the way* he handles the meter and employs the caesura," or "it is nobly austere *because* of the lack of detail and the restricted palette." But we can also express what we want to by using quite other expressions: "it is the handling of meter and caesura which is *responsible for* its strength and variety," "its nobly austere quality is *due to* the lack of detail and the use of a restricted palette," "its lack of balance *results from* the highlighting of the figures on the left," "those minor chords *make it* extremely moving," "those converging lines *give it* an extraordinary unity." These are locutions we cannot switch to with "lazy" or "intelligent;" to say what *makes* him lazy, what is *responsible for* his laziness, what it is *due to,* is to broach another question entirely.

One after another, in recent discussions, writers have insisted hat aesthetic judgments are not "mechanical": "Critics do not formulate general standards and apply these mechanically to all, or to classes of, works of art." "Technical points can be settled rapidly, by the application of rules," but aesthetic questions "cannot be settled by any mechanical method." Instead, these writers on aesthetics have emphasized that there is no "substitute for individual judgment" with its "spontaneity and speculation" and that "The final standard . . . [is] the judgment of personal taste." What is surprising is that, though such things have been repeated again and again, no one seems to have said what is meant by "taste" or by the word "mechanical." There are many judgments besides those requiring taste which demand "spontaneity" and "individual judgment" and are not "mechanical." Without a detailed comparison we cannot see in what particular way *aesthetic* judgments are not "mechanical," or how they differ from those other judgments, nor can we begin to specify what taste is. This I have attempted. It is a characteristic and essential feature of judgments which employ an aesthetic term that they cannot be made by appealing, in the sense explained, to conditions. This, I believe, is a logical feature of aesthetic or taste judgments in general, though I have argued it here only as regards the more restricted range of judgments which employ aesthetic terms. It is part of what "taste" means. . . .

Psychical Distance: In a Fog at Sea

GEORGE DICKIE

On a number of previous occasions[1] I have discussed Edward Bullough's theory of psychical distance, but always, for one reason or another, in a somewhat abbreviated way. In this article I try to bring together the material from all the earlier papers and integrate and supplement it in order to give a full-scale analysis of the theory.

Bullough's theory of psychical distance—first published sixty years ago—has had an enormous influence and following. Many aestheticians have simply accepted the theory as Bullough enunciated it, and many others have worked out their theories of the relation of spectators to art as developments from it. The theory has given strong impetus to what may be called "the aesthetic attitude" approach to aesthetic theory. The wide-spread appeal of the theory of psychical distance is shown by the fact that Bullough's article is reprinted in most of today's general aesthetics anthologies. I shall try to show that Bullough's theory is fundamentally wrong and that it has misled aesthetic theory.

George Dickie, "Psychical Distance: In a Fog at Sea," *British Journal of Aesthetics* 13 (1973), pp. 17–29.

---

[1]In *Aesthetics: An Introduction* (New York: Pegasus Press, 197), pp. 48–52; "Bullough and Casebier: Disappearing in the Distance," *The Personalist* (1972), pp. 127–31; "The Myth of the Aesthetic Attitude," *American Philosophical Quarterly* (1964), pp. 56–7; "Is Psychology Relevant to Aesthetics?" *The Philosophical Review* (1962), pp. 297–300; and "Bullough and the Concept of Psychical Distance," *Philosophy and Phenomenological Research* (1961), pp. 233–8. This paper was written during the tenure of a National Endowment for the Humanities Senior Fellowship.

Bullough conceives of psychical distance both as one of the essential elements of what he calls "aesthetic consciousness" and as a criterion of the beautiful.[2] Psychical distance is supposed to be a psychical component of a specific kind of consciousness which when "inserted" between a subject and his affections is productive of aesthetic experience. As Bullough puts it, aesthetic experience is ". . . due—if such a metaphor is permissible—to the insertion of Distance."[3] It is this act of "inserting" which attitude theorists presumably have in mind when they speak of people "distancing" some object or occurrence. Being *psychically distanced* is the psychological state, partially constitutive of "aesthetic consciousness," into which one is placed by an act of distancing or into which one is induced without an act of distancing by the properties of an object or occurrence. It seems clear that Bullough thinks that distancing is a kind of voluntary action; his present-day follower, Sheila Dawson, reads him that way and says that critics, actors, members of orchestras and the like "distance deliberately."[4] Presumably persons who frequently experience art are supposed to be capable of doing the act of distancing and, of course, all persons who have aesthetic experience, according to the distance theorists, will be in the state of being psychically distanced during the experience.

Bullough analyses the working of distance into two elements: "It has a *negative,* inhibitory aspect—the cutting-out of the practical sides of things and of our practical attitude to them—and a *positive* side—the elaboration of the experience on the new basis created by the inhibitory action of Distance."[5] The first aspect of distance is a psychological blocking of ordinary, practical actions and thoughts which is necessary for the positive side of distance, i.e. the experience of something as an object of aesthetic consciousness. The assumed necessity of the blocking comes out clearly when Bullough says that "by putting [an object] out of gear with practical needs and ends . . . the 'contemplation' of the object becomes alone possible."[6] There seems to have been a persistent belief among aestheticians that people are so concerned with "the reality of things" that they cannot appreciate the qualities of things unless this concern is somehow blocked. When the objects being experienced are works of art the belief takes the form of the persistent fear that people will mistake art for reality or will somehow entangle themselves with the art unless a specific kind of psychological process blocks them from doing so. . . .

It should be noted at this point that although Bullough explicitly says that distance has both negative and positive aspects, it is the alleged negative

[2] "'Psychical Distance' as a Factor in Art and an Aesthetic Principle." Reprinted in *Aesthetics,* E. M. Wilkinson ed. (Bowes and Bowes, London, and Stanford University Press, 1957), p. 96.

[3] *Ibid.,* p. 94.

[4] "'Distancing' as an Aesthetic Principle," *Australasian Journal of Philosophy* (1961), p. 158.

[5] *Op. cit.,* p. 95.

[6] *Ibid.,* p. 96.

and inhibitory psychological force which has come to be identified as psychical distance. Bullough himself devotes all his attention to distance as an inhibitory force, and what he at first calls the positive aspect of distance in effect becomes that which can happen after distance (the inhibition) occurs.

There is, however, more to Bullough's theory. Just as people can be more or less hungry, more or less tired, more or less happy, Bullough thinks people can be more or less distanced. "Distance," he writes, "may be said to be variable both according to the distancing-power of the individual, and according to the character of the object."[7] Ideally, according to Bullough, it is most desirable to attain "the utmost decrease of Distance without its disappearance."[8] Distance can be lost by its decreasing to the limit of the power of a particular person—he calls this "under-distancing"—or by a person having "an excess of Distance"[9]—he calls this "over-distancing." Bullough's theory has been criticized in a minor way by some who think he should not speak of distance as varying by degrees, but rather of a person either having distance or not having it.[10] I believe, however, that the theory is subject to a much more fundamental criticism which I will make later.

Bullough gets his theory off to a fast start by using an example of an actual threatening phenomenon. It seems initially plausible in such a case to think that a psychological force is needed to block our practical concerns for safety in order that we can aesthetically appreciate the threatening phenomenon. Bullough then turns to a discussion of psychical distance as it supposedly functions in the appreciation of art. In drama, the characters, he says, "appeal to us like persons and incidents of normal experience, except that that side of their appeal, which would usually affect us in a direct personal manner, is held in abeyance.[11] Most people, he notes, explain the holding in abeyance as the result of knowing the characters are fictional, but he denies that this is correct. He maintains that "Distance, by changing our relation to the characters, renders them seemingly fictitious, [it is] not . . . the fictitiousness of the characters [which] alters our feelings toward them."[12] Here is a clear instance of the fear that art is always in danger of being confused with reality and the consequent felt need for a psychological force to prevent the mistake. Bullough attempts to illustrate how the aesthetic appreciation of art can fail because of "under-distancing" and how it can occur when a person is properly distanced. Both of the hypothetical cases involve a jealous husband at a

---

[7]*Op. cit.,* p. 100.

[8]*Loc. cit.*

[9]*Loc. cit.*

[10]By myself some time ago in "Bullough and the Concept of Psychical Distance," *op. cit.,* pp. 233–8, and more recently by Allan Casebier in "The Concept of Aesthetic Distance," *The Personalist* (1971), pp. 70–91.

[11]*Ibid.,* p. 97.

[12]*Ibid.,* p. 98.

performance of *Othello*. On the one hand his jealousy may cause him to lose distance; "by a sudden reversal of perspective he will no longer see Othello apparently betrayed by Desdemona, but himself in an analogous situation with his own wife."[13] On the other hand the jealous husband can appreciate the play if he can maintain distance, although Bullough remarks that it will be very difficult for the jealous husband to maintain it.

Another hypothetical case which is frequently used to illustrate "under-distancing" is that of a spectator who loses distance and runs on to the stage to attack the villain and save the heroine. Bullough himself does not use this kind of case to illustrate his theory, but given his view that it is the spectator's being in a state of psychical distance which makes the stage characters seem fictitious to that spectator, it is perfectly plausible that if a spectator's being in a state of psychical distance ceased, he might (if the spectator were also chivalrous) attack a stage villain. This case is different from the fog and *Othello* cases since in them only thoughts supposedly are blocked or not blocked, whereas in the attacker-spectator case action supposedly is blocked (while the spectator is in a state of psychical distance) or not blocked (when the spectator is not in a state of psychical distance).

The *Othello* cases and the attacker-spectator resemble the fog case in that they, too, are desperate ones: in the first the enraged husband either loses distance and is not able to appreciate the play because plagued by jealous thoughts or is able to appreciate it only while struggling to maintain the necessary psychological state, which suppresses the jealous thoughts; and in the second the spectator loses distance and takes action. In both the *Othello* cases and the attacker-spectator case it also seems initially plausible to think that a psychological force is required to suppress the husband's jealousy and the spectator's impulse to assist the heroine. But even if a psychological force were required in such desperate cases, the enormous majority of the cases of the appreciation of art and nature are not desperate cases. Usually when we watch a play, look at a painting, listen to music or gaze at natural scenery, and appreciate them, there is no hint of impulses to action which have to be overcome. Nor do real life emotions such as jealousy and fear constantly occur and require blocking out. On Bullough's view, however, in order to have aesthetic experience we constantly have to overcome by distancing some such practical impulses to action as to join the actors on the stage or to plough the natural scenery into farmland or some such practical emotions as jealousy and fear. Bullough has taken several atypical cases of aesthetic appreciation, has tried to show that these desperate cases necessarily involve the occurrence of a psychological blocking force, and then has concluded that such a force is necessary for every case of aesthetic appreciation. But if one reverses Bullough's procedure and begins with "easy" cases, with the experience of works which are devoid of strong emotional content, then the idea that *all*

---

[13]*Ibid.*, p. 99.

aesthetic experiences require insulation from practical impulses and thoughts simply does not arise. Of course even with the reversed procedure someone might go on to conclude that desperate cases require the occurrence of distancing. But at least this weaker conclusion would show that "being distanced" is not a necessary condition for aesthetic appreciation.

Is there, however, any evidence that acts of distancing and states of being distanced ever actually occur in connexion with our experience of art? When the curtain goes up, when we walk up to a painting, or when we look at a sunset, do we ever commit acts of distancing and are we ever induced into a state of being distanced? I cannot recall committing any action which suspends practical activities or being in a psychological state which prevents practical activity. . . .

Even in cases such as being in a fog at sea, in which actual, practical dangers exist and in which we may be in a position to act practically, we are not, when we appreciate the qualities of the fog, restrained by a psychological force which "cuts out the practical side of things." If we appreciate some of the qualities of a fog at sea, we do not cease to be aware of the associated dangers (if we were aware of them to begin with) and we are or may be ready to act if the need arises and we know what to do. We may not at every moment while appreciating the qualities of the fog be thinking of the dangers, but this is not because the thought of the dangers have been removed by a special act or state of mind. In fact, thoughts of the danger might on some occasions for some people even heighten the enjoyment. The failure of the jealous husband at *Othello* to appreciate the play does not show that there is a case of someone who has lost or failed to achieve being psychologically restrained either. Later I shall try to give rather extensive descriptions of what I take to be actually going on in the *Othello* and the other cases which have been discussed. There does not, then, seem to be any real evidence to support the conclusion that acts of distancing or states of being distanced as described by Bullough and his followers actually occur. In fact reflection suggests that such acts and states do not occur in connexion with our experience of art.

If the distance theorists were simply asserting the existence of nonexistent acts and states, it would be bad enough. But their belief in the occurrence and necessity of psychological forces to restrain spectators causes them to have a distorted view of the experience of art, which in turn causes them to draw unwarranted normative conclusions about certain aspects of certain works of art. In addition, their belief in the existence of a special psychological state which controls the behaviour of spectators conceals from them the fact that it is institutional conventions which govern the behaviour of spectators. . . .

The theorists of psychical distance in concentrating so much of their attention on the psychological powers of individual persons have mistaken the functioning of an institutional convention against spectators participating in *some* works of art for the functioning of a psychological force the role of which is to prevent participation in all cases of aesthetic appreciation. Most theatre productions, for example, are presented with the tacit assumption (the institutional convention) that the spectators do not interact with the action of the play or communicate directly with the characters, but *Peter Pan* and many other plays are exceptions to the rule—they are presented under slightly different conventions. The conventions which govern the behaviour of spectators of art range all the way from dance situations in which the line between spectator and dancer is blurred to the extent that spectators may become dancers and dancers become spectators to the usual theatre situation in which the distinction between actor and spectator is rigidly maintained and the role of the spectator is rigidly defined. Between these extremes lie the cases already discussed and such things as hissing the villain and cheering the hero in old-fashioned melodrama and applauding *during* an act because of an especially good piece of performing. There have been many innovations in works of art and in the presentation of them, and the innovations continue to be made. This means that the conventions governing the presentation of art must be altered from time to time. Of course some people dislike any innovation especially if they hold theories which dress up the most frequently used conventions as psychological forces essential for "aesthetic consciousness." It is not that we are prevented from interacting with works of art by psychological forces within us; rather we are barred from interacting with many or most works by conventions governing particular art situations. Bullough's contention that such devices as picture frames, raised stages and the like help to cause a psychological phenomenon which restrains us from acting is wrong. Such devices serve, along with other purposes, as a signal (if any is needed) that a certain convention is to be observed. Other devices—such as Peter Pan's appeal or the stage manager of *Our Town* addressing the audience— serve to suspend the usual rule.

If there is no special psychological force which restrains spectators, what are the correct descriptions of the "desperate" cases which Bullough and his followers misdescribe? One possible explanation of a case in which a stage villain is attacked is that the attacker-spectator has ceased adhering to the non-participation convention because he has become deranged. In this case the attacker-spectator first knows of the convention, but for certain psychological reasons "loses sight of it." The spectator's attention to the play has been interrupted by his sudden deranged mistaking the play for real life. In another possible case an attacker-spectator might never have known of the non-participation convention, being entirely unfamiliar with the theatre and its conventions. In this case the spectator would never have attended to the play, that is he would from the beginning have mistaken the play for real life. One could go on for some time spinning out possible explanations for cases of attacker-spectators, but that is not necessary. What it is important to see is that such an attack is not an instance of practical behaviour but rather behaviour which is bizarre because it is either insane or uninformed.

In the case of the fog at sea a person can, as has already been shown, appreciate qualities of the fog without being psychologically restrained from practical concerns. In fact a person might even attend to and appreciate the fog qualities at the same time that he takes practical *action* against the dangers that the fog brings about. A sailor, for example, might appreciate the sight of the "milky opaqueness" of the fog while securing lines, an activity which is so routine that he does not have to watch his hands as he does it. Or a sailor might appreciate the sight of the fog and the feel of the dampness on his face as he peers from the bow for obstacles dead ahead. Such examples show that there is no necessary conflict between aesthetic appreciation and practical concerns. Of course many practical actions would conflict with the appreciation of the fog because they require complete attention—for example, one cannot gaze at a fog and watch a radar screen at the same time. Also some practical concerns might conflict with aesthetic appreciation in another way: for example a person might be so terrified in a fog at sea that he could not appreciate anything. If we ignore for the moment all the other kinds of cases and concentrate only on the terrified traveller kind, it can be seen that terrified travellers are not got to appreciate the qualities of fog by having them voluntarily restrain their fears or by getting them into a state in which their fears are hypnotically submerged. If, however, their fears can be allayed by the captain's display of lack of concern or by being shown that the radar scope shows no obstructions in the water, or by some other means which shows or seems to show that there is no danger, then perhaps the terrified travellers can be brought to appreciate the qualities of the fog. The terrified travellers do not require a special psychological force to restrain their fears, they require information which indicates to them that they have nothing to fear—then they would be able to focus attention on the qualities of the fog.

Consider the jealous husband at *Othello*. A jealous husband who fails to appreciate the play might fail to do so in several different ways. He might be a person whose thoughts of his own personal situation simply distract him from attending to the play once the play has reminded him of his problem. This kind of case is one which Bullough characterizes as being under-distanced. But the jealous husband has not been forced out of a special state of consciousness; his attention has just been distracted from one thing (the play) to another (his musings about his wife). The jealous husband is not in a special psychological relation to the play in this case; he is just not attending to it. Inattention is not a special kind of attention. In a second kind of case which Bullough would also classify as a case of being under-distanced a jealous husband might fail to appreciate *Othello* because, although he continues to attend to the action of the play, it makes him miserable because his own personal situation makes him abnormally sensitive to portrayals of jealousy. At this point it must be made clear that the word "appreciation" has several distinct meanings and that speaking simply of the appreciation of *Othello* may mask some important distinctions. In this second case the husband can appreciate *Othello* in the sense of fully understanding it and in the sense of finding it valuable, but he does not appreciate it in the sense of finding it enjoyable or pleasant. There are further ambiguities to be discerned in "enjoyable" and "pleasant," but it is not necessary for my purposes to do so. It is sufficient to note that much of the great art which we appreciate so keenly is not pleasant in the relevant sense. So the jealous husband can appreciate *Othello* without finding it pleasant. In fact his appreciation of the play may be keener than that of someone who has a more serene domestic life. Of course a jealous husband might find *Othello* so painful that his attention to it would be blocked out entirely or that he would leave the theatre. In this eventuality he could not appreciate the play in *any* sense because he could not attend to it, and he would be in a situation similar to that of the first case.

In a third and quite different kind of case a spectator at *Othello* might fail to appreciate the play because although he more or less attends to the action of the play, he constantly views the play either in relation to some real or imagined historical prototype, in relation to some social problem or to some other thing "external" to the play. These kinds of cases are called instances of "over-distancing" by Bullough and his followers. "Aesthetic consciousness," according to distance theorists, is destroyed in these kinds of cases by a concern with things outside the work of art in question. I think distance theorists greatly exaggerate the pernicious effects on appreciation of concerns with things external to works of art. This exaggeration is due to their imagining that appreciation requires being in a special mental state so delicate that the least external pressure destroys it. We almost always have, however, a background awareness of something external to a work we are appreciating. In this sense of awareness we recognize Othello's actions as jealous behaviour of a kind we meet with in real life, we recognize a visual design as a representation of a man or as a portrait of a particular man, and so on. There also are momentary distractions such as the awareness of coughing in the audience, the awareness of the hardness of the theatre seat, questioning thoughts of whether the stove got turned off at home, noticing the colour of the stage curtains, and so forth. Neither the background awareness nor the momentary distractions necessarily interfere with appreciation. It is, however, possible for concerns with external things to distract a spectator completely or substantially from a work of art. In such cases the correct thing to say is that the spectator's attention has been distracted from the work to such an extent that he is unable to appreciate it. It is not that the spectator is in a special relation *to the work*—the relation of having over-distanced it; he is out of relation to the work, that is he is wholly or partly not attending to it. . . .

To sum up, there is no reason to think that a psychological force to restrain either action or thoughts occurs or is required in the ordinary, non-desperate cases of aesthetic experience—the cases which constitute the enormous majority of such experiences. No such force occurs or is required in desperate cases either. In desperate cases which involve works of art no restraining force to prevent action occurs because, as Johnson says, we know throughout that we are observing works of art. Also, with desperate cases involving art no restraining force to prevent practical thoughts occurs either: we are either just able to concentrate our attention on the work or we are distracted from it in some way. In desperate cases which involve natural things no restraining force to prevent action or practical thoughts occurs either. In a given case we may or may not be able to concentrate our attention on the qualities of the natural thing, but there is no special kind of act or state of mind which can suspend action or anxieties.

THE AESTHETIC IN THE ARTS

The Beautiful in Music

EDUARD HANSLICK

So far we have considered only the negative aspect of the question, and have sought to expose the fallacy that the beautiful in music depends upon the accurate expression of feelings.

We must now, by way of completing the exposition, bring to light also its positive aspect, and endeavor to determine the nature of the beautiful in music.

Its nature is specifically musical. By this we mean that the beautiful is not contingent upon nor in need of any subject introduced from without, but that it consists wholly of sounds artistically combined. The ingenious co-ordination of intrinsically pleasing sounds, their consonance and contrast, their flight and reapproach, their increasing and diminishing strength—this it is which, in free and unimpeded forms, presents itself to our mental vision.

The primordial element of music is euphony, and rhythm is its soul: rhythm in general, or the harmony of a symmetrical structure, and rhythm in particular, or the systematically reciprocal motion of its several parts within a given measure. The crude material which the composer has to fashion, the vast profusion of which it is impossible to estimate fully, is the entire scale of musical notes and their inherent adaptability to an endless variety of melodies, harmonies, and rhythms. Melody, unexhausted, nay, inexhaustible, is preeminently the source of musical beauty. Harmony, with its countless modes of transforming, inverting, and intensifying, offers the material for constantly new developments; while rhythm, the main artery of the musical organism,

From Eduard Hanslick, *The Beautiful in Music*, trans. Gustav Cohen (Indianapolis: Bobbs-Merrill, 1957), selections from Chapter 3.

is the regulator of both, and enhances the charms of the timbre in its rich variety.

To the question: What is to be expressed with all this material? the answer will be: Musical ideas. Now, a musical idea reproduced in its entirety is not only an object of intrinsic beauty but also an end in itself, and not a means for representing feelings and thoughts.

The essence of music is sound and motion.

The arabesque, a branch of the art of ornamentation, dimly betokens in what manner music may exhibit forms of beauty though no definite emotion be involved. We see a plexus of flourishes, now bending into graceful curves, now rising in bold sweeps; moving now toward, and now away from each other; correspondingly matched in small and large arcs; apparently incommensurable, yet duly proportioned throughout; with a duplicate or counterpart to every segment; in fine, a compound of oddments, and yet a perfect whole. Imagine now an arabesque, not still and motionless, but rising before our eyes in constantly changing forms. Behold the broad and delicate lines, how they pursue one another; how from a gentle curve they rise up into lofty heights, presently to descend again; how they widen and contract, surprising the eye with a marvelous alternation of quiescence and mobility. The image thus becomes nobler and more exalted. If, moreover, we conceive this living arabesque as the active emanation of inventive genius, the artistic fullness of whose imagination is incessantly flowing into the heart of these moving forms, the effect, we think, will be not unlike that of music. . . .

The reason why people have failed to discover the beauties in which pure music abounds is, in great measure, to be found in the underrating by the older systems of aesthetics of the sensuous element and in its subordination to morality and feeling—in Hegel, to the "idea." Every art sets out from the sensuous and operates within its limits. The theory relating to the expression of feelings ignores this fact and, disdainfully pushing aside the act of hearing, it passes on immediately to the feelings. Music, say they, is food for the soul, and the organ of hearing is beneath their notice.

True, it is not for the organ of hearing as such, for the "labyrinth" or the "tympanum," that a Beethoven composes. But our imagination, which is so constituted as to be affected by auditory impressions (and in relation to which the term "organ" means something very different from a channel directed toward the world of physical phenomena), delights in the sounding forms and musical structures and, conscious of their sensuous nature, lives in the immediate and free contemplation of the beautiful.

It is extremely difficult to define this self-subsistent and specifically musical beauty. As music has no prototype in nature, and expresses no definite conceptions, we are compelled to speak of it either in dry, technical terms, or in the language of poetic fiction. Its kingdom is, indeed, "not of this world." All the fantastic descriptions, characterizations, and periphrases are either metaphorical or false. What in any other art is still descriptive is in music already figurative. Of music it is impossible to form any but a musical conception, and it can be comprehended and enjoyed only in and for itself.

The "specifically musical" must not, however, be understood only in the sense of acoustic beauty or symmetry of parts—both of which elements it embraces as of secondary importance—and still less can we speak of "a display of sounds to tickle the ear," or use similar phraseology which is generally intended to emphasize the absence of an intellectual principle. But, by laying stress on musical beauty, we do not exclude the intellectual principle; on the contrary, we imply it as essential, for we would not apply the term "beautiful" to anything wanting in intellectual beauty; and in tracing the essential nature of beauty to a morphological source, we wish it to be understood that the intellectual element is most intimately connected with these sonorific forms. The term "form" in musical language is peculiarly significant. The forms created by sound are not empty; not the envelope enclosing a vacuum, but a well, replete with the living creation of inventive genius. Music, then, as compared with the arabesque, is a picture, yet a picture the subject of which we cannot define in words, or include in any one category of thought. In music there is both meaning and logical sequence, but in a musical sense; it is a language we speak and understand, but which we are unable to translate. It is a highly suggestive fact that, in speaking of musical compositions, we likewise employ the term "thought," and a critical mind easily distinguishes real thoughts from hollow phrases, precisely as in speech. The Germans significantly use the term *Satz* ("sentence") for the logical consummation of a part of a composition, for we know exactly when it is finished, just as in the case of a written or spoken sentence, though each has a logic of its own.

The logic in music, which produces in us a feeling of satisfaction, rests on certain elementary laws of nature which govern both the human organism and the phenomena of sound. It is, above all, the primordial law of "harmonic progression" which, like the curve lines in painting and sculpture, contains the germ of development in its main forms, and the (unfortunately almost unexplained) cause of the link which connects the various musical phenomena.

All musical elements are in some occult manner connected with each other by certain natural affinities, and since rhythm, melody, and harmony are under their invisible sway, the music created by man must conform to them—any combinations conflicting with them bearing the impress of caprice and ugliness. Though not demonstrable with scientific precision, these affinities are instinctively felt by every experienced ear, and the organic completeness and logic, or the absurdity and unnaturalness of a group of sounds, are intuitively known without the intervention of a definite conception as the standard of measure, the *tertium comparationis*.[1]

---

[1]"Poetry may utilize the ugly (the unbeautiful) even in a fairly liberal measure, for, as it affects the feelings only through the medium of the ideas which it directly suggests, the knowledge that it is a means adapted to an end will, from the outset, soften its impression, even to the extent of creating a most profound sensation by force of contrast and by stimulating the imagination.

From this negative rationalness, inherent in music and founded on laws of nature, springs the possibility of its becoming invested also with positive forms of beauty.

The act of composing is a mental working on material capable of receiving the forms which the mind intends to give. The musical material in the hands of creative genius is as plastic and pliable as it is profuse. Unlike the architect, who has to mold the coarse and unwieldy rock, the composer reckons with the ulterior effect of past sounds. More ethereal and subtle than the material of any other art, sound adapts itself with great facility to any idea the composer may have in his mind. Now, as the union of sounds (from the interdependence of which the beautiful in music flows) is not effected by mechanically stringing them together but by acts of a free imagination, the intellectual force and idiosyncrasy of the particular mind will give to every composition its individual character. A musical composition, as the creation of a thinking and feeling mind, may, therefore, itself possess intellectuality and pathos in a high degree. Every musical work ought to bear this stamp of intellectuality, but the music itself must furnish evidence of its existence. Our opinion regarding the seat of the intellectual and emotional elements of a musical composition stands in the same realtion to the popular way of thinking as the idea of immanence does to that of transcendence. The object of every art is to clothe in some material form an idea which has originated in the artist's imagination. In music this idea is an acoustic one; it cannot be expressed in words and subsequently translated into sounds. The initial force of a composition is the invention of some definite theme, and not the desire to describe a given emotion by musical means. Thanks to that primitive and mysterious power whose mode of action will forever be hidden from us, a theme, a melody, flashes on the composer's mind. The origin of this first germ cannot be explained, but must simply be accepted as a fact. When once it has taken root in the composer's imagination, it forthwith begins to grow and develop, the principal theme being the center round which the branches group themselves in all conceivable ways, though always unmistakably related to it. The beauty of an independent and simple theme appeals to our aesthetic feeling with that directness which tolerates no explanation except, perhaps, that of its inherent fitness and the harmony of parts, to the exclusion of any alien factor. It pleases for its own sake, like an arabesque, a column, or some spontaneous product of nature—a leaf or a flower. . . .

The effect of music, however, is perceived and assimilated directly by the senses, and the verdict of the intellect comes too late to correct the disturbing factor of ugliness. It is for this reason that Shakespeare was justified in making use of the horrible, while Mozart was obliged to remain within the limits of the beautiful." (Grillparzer IX, 142.)

ILLUSTRATION 20
GEORGES SEURAT, *Sunday Afternoon on the Island of La Grande Jatte,* 1884-86.

11

Can a Work of Art
Be Defined?

Until the twentieth century almost everyone understood what counted as a work of art. Distinctions between art and other man-made things—artificts— were drawn explicitly from qualities of the works themselves. For example, painting and sculpture dealt primarily with nature, and all works called art had at least a modicum of recognizable, representational subject matter. Thus contemporary works such as Franz Kline's *White Forms* (Illustration 21) would not have counted as art.

Poetry followed certain rhyme schemes and patterns. Stylistic considerations dictated the length. E. E. Cummings's *when god lets my body be* (Illustration 22) is not poetry by any of these formal criteria. And James Joyce's Ulysses (Illustration 23), which flouts nineteenth-century novel form by replacing traditional plot structure and action with a stream of consciousness technique, would not, until recent times, have been accepted as a novel or even as literature.

From the Renaissance until our century, music has been written according to rules of harmony, melody, and rhythm, and according to patterns of certain prescribed forms such as the fugue, the sonata, and the symphony. In contrast, John Cage, a twentieth-century American who calls himself a composer, has compiled a work called *Collective Improvisations*. This work is not completely scored (written), and what the performers play are series of improvised sounds on instruments of their choice with no repeating patterns, rhythms, or melodies, for a time period of the performers' choosing. Such a composition would hardly have been classified as music before our era.

During the Renaissance a proper tragic drama was defined as a work in five acts where the unified action occurs in one location within a time period of twenty-four hours. These dramatic rules were not always obeyed, but it is unlikely that a work such as Brecht's *Measures Taken* would have been written prior to 1900. Aside from its nontraditional one-act structure, this work has no particular setting, scarcely a plot, and a confusing time sequence.

What works such as *Ulysses* might be trying to do or say would not have been taken into consideration by the pre-twentieth-century artworld. In fact it is unlikely that anyone calling herself or himself an artist would have produced such works. These phenomena would have been rejected as art simply because they did not conform to what was expected as proper art medium, proper formal structure, or proper subject matter.

The pre-twentieth-century artworld (e.g., artists, critics, viewers, curators, collectors, and philosophers) made judgments about art on at least two levels. First, as we have noted, since Aristotle works of art were automatically classified or distinguished from other artifacts on the basis of their medium, form, and subject matter. Second, works of art so set apart were evaluated in terms of whether they exhibited "proper" amounts of certain qualities or functioned in certain ways that were thought to be unique and peculiar to art. The idea was that if art is a unique cultural activity, then all kinds of art, e.g., painting, music, and literature, must have similar shared characteristics that are not exhibited by other phenomena. One could then define art in a general way in terms of these exhibited characteristics that were thought of as essential qualities of all works of art. These essential characteristics have been alternately defined as mimesis, beauty, expressiveness, symbolism, significant form, and even as the "spiritual food for mankind." And the history of aesthetics, is, in part, a running dispute about which qualities best define and apply most uniquely to art. In the first three parts of this book, we examined some of these definitions.

This whole enterprise, namely classifying art by medium, form, and subject matter, and defining and evaluating the essential unique exhibited qualities of these works, was brought into question when, in 1915, the French artist Marcel Duchamp introduced an ordinary urinal into an art museum, titled it *The Fountain* (Illustration 25), and allowed it to be called "art." The standard classifications of art works broke down when a urinal was admitted into a museum. More importantly, the claim that art is a unique cultural activity becomes questionable when literally anything is so titled, and it is at best difficult to imagine being able to define an inherent aesthetic quality of art that would apply both to a urinal and to, say, Constable's *Wivenhoe Park*.

Thus in our century the relatively simple distinctions between art and other artifacts have broken down, and traditional concepts for evaluating works of art have been challenged. The following examples acutely illustrate this breakdown.

John Cage, whom we mentioned earlier, has an unusual work entitled *4'33"*, in which no music (sound) is played.

We spoke earlier of Samuel Beckett's recent play *Breath*, a work thirty seconds long. The only action of the play is the stage curtain which is opened for thirty seconds on an empty stage and then closed.

A New York artist, Vito Acconci, some of whose works are in the

Museum of Contemporary Art in New York, regularly telephones newspapers to announce such happenings as his pulse beat or his breathing. Acconci calls these occurrences "art."

Confronted with events such as these, many contemporary philosophers have wondered whether it makes any sense to try to define art, and whether it is at all possible to distinguish any exhibited aesthetic features that are unique to such works. Ludwig Wittgenstein, a widely influential philosopher who died in 1951, analyzes attempts to develop definitions of art that apply exclusively to art. In the selection from his lectures with which we begin this chapter, Wittgenstein discusses some of the confusions that evolve from trying to identify art with other kinds of phenomena and with confusing aesthetic descriptions with other kinds of descriptions. Art, according to Wittgenstein, is, in some sense, a "special way of living." Artistic activity is a peculiar way of dealing with and describing the world that cannot be completely assimilated with other ways of dealing with the world. But Wittgenstein qualifies his remarks about art. Wittgenstein finds it impossible to isolate and define art uniquely, because art, artistic activities, and aesthetic judgments overlap with other ways of living.

Wittgenstein's suggestions are carried further by Morris Weitz in his essay, "The Role of Theory in Aesthetics." According to Weitz, what Wittgenstein might have meant in his oblique references to art is that one cannot isolate and define the essential features of art, because there are no isolatable features. There are similarities between all art forms. Both drama and the novel, for example, employ at least a modicum of representation. Music and the theatre are performance arts. Painting, sculpture, and music need not employ any mimetic elements. These are all what Wittgenstein would have called "family resemblances." But there is no one feature and no one definition which applies uniformly, universally, and uniquely to all art.

Moreover, what is counted as important to art overlaps with other human activities. Representation is important, for example, in historical research. Not all performances are "artistic." Three-dimensional shapes are not limited to sculpture and architecture. And expressiveness and communication is possible through nonartistic means. So there are family resemblances between art forms, other cultural phenomena, and nonaesthetic things.

Finally, Weitz argues, concepts of art are historically and culturally evolving concepts. What is called "art" and what exhibited features are essential to art has been defined differently in different ages and by different cultures so that it is impossible to give an exhaustive and permanent definition of art that will not be subject to disagreement and alteration. Therefore, according to Weitz, art is best conceived as an open concept, a concept whose texture changes as new art movements alter the notion of art and influence what is considered important in artistic activities.

The Wittgenstein-Weitz position is challenged by another contemporary philosopher, Maurice Mandelbaum. Mandelbaum agrees that one cannot define art in terms of one common exhibited feature that all works, if they are art, must have. But Mandelbaum argues that the family resemblance analogy does not point to the impossibility of defining art. He says that families, for example, have a common characteristic of ancestry that is the basis for resemblance. Games have the common attribute of being formulated to be played. Similarly Mandelbaum suggests that the essential feature of art might be definable as a relational quality or qualities that link art to the intentions of artists or to an audience. For example, works of art are generally defined as artifacts—objects created by persons, rather than as natural objects such as driftwood. (See Illustration 25.) This characteristic relates a certain class of objects to human experience. And works of art might have other such relational qualities. These sorts of qualities are what one calls nonexhibited features of art—features that define art in terms of its external relation to social or cultural mores (e.g., defining art as artifacts) or institutions (e.g., putting works in museums and thereby calling them "art"). If this is the case, then art, like families and games, would exhibit common, definable, relational, but nonexhibited features that would be the essential characteristics of art.

The American philosopher, George Dickie, also rejects the notion that art is an open concept. Dickie, in his well-known essay, "Defining Art," claims that art *can* be defined. Dickie agrees with Mandelbaum that one must abandon any attempt to define art in terms of exhibited features. Such definitions either are incomplete or they lead to confusions between what Dickie terms descriptive and evaluative senses of art. To take an example of what Dickie means, one will recall that Clive Bell argued that any work that exhibits the quality of significant form both exists as art and is not worthless, and any work which does not have this quality, such as Duchamp's urinal, is not art. Bell's identification of the existence of a work as art with its worth as art, according to Dickie, pushes us into declaring either that *The Fountain* is not art (because it does not exhibit significant form), or, if we call the urinal "art," then it has some redeeming aesthetic features. Most of us, however, Dickie claims, might want to accommodate the artworld position that *The Fountain* is classified as art without having to evaluate the urinal as having any artistic value.

To clear up confusions generated by definitions of art such as Bell's and to make sense out of the various strange things we currently label "art," Dickie takes up Mandelbaum's suggestion that one must analyze art in terms of its relational, nonexhibited, or external qualities rather than by trying to pinpoint unique exhibited features of all works. Dickie develops what he calls an institutional definition of art. This definition states that works of art are those artifacts so classified by social and cultural institutions of the artworld: by artists, curators, publishers, directors, art appreciators, and philosophers as "art." A work of art is any artifact that has been conferred the status of "art" and "candidate for appreciation" or "candidate for evaluation" by artworld institutions. Whether or not the artifact in question in fact has any aesthetic value is another, separate issue. Thus *The Fountain* has been conferred the status of art (i.e., classified as "art") by the artworld by being titled and placed in an art museum, even though later, from an evaluative point of view, most of us decide that it is pretty awful stuff, that is, bad art. Dickie's view of art is of great interest and controversy in contemporary art. Does this definition allow everything, and thus nothing, to be art? Ted Cohen's careful analysis and criticism of Dickie's position should be examined before one accepts or rejects Dickie's institutional theory of art.

Lectures on Aesthetics

LUDWIG WITTGENSTEIN

I

1. The subject (Aesthetics) is very big and entirely misunderstood as far as I can see. The use of such a word as "beautiful" is even more apt to be misunderstood if you look at the linguistic form of sentences in which it occurs than most other words. "Beautiful" [and "good"—] is an adjective, so you are inclined to say: "This has a certain quality, that of being beautiful."

2. We are going from one subject-matter of philosophy to another, from one group of words to another group of words.

3. An intelligent way of dividing up a book on philosophy would be into parts of speech, kinds of words. Where in fact you would have to distinguish far more parts of speech than an ordinary grammar does. You would talk for hours and hours on the verbs "seeing," "feeling," etc., verbs describing personal experience. We get a peculiar kind of confusion or confusions which comes up with all these words.[1] You would have another chapter on numerals—here there would be another kind of confusion: a chapter on "all," "any," "some," etc.—another kind of confusion: a chapter on "you," "I," etc.—another kind: a chapter on "beautiful," "good"—another kind. We get into a new group of confusions; language plays us entirely new tricks.

Excerpts from Ludwig Wittgenstein, *Lectures and Conversations on Aesthetics, Psychology, and Religious Beliefs,* ed. Cyril Barnett (Berkeley: University of California Press, 1972). Reprinted by permission of the University of California Press and Basil Blackwell.

[1]Here we find similarities—we find peculiar sorts of confusion which come up with *all* these words.—R.

4. I have often compared language to a tool chest, containing a hammer, chisel, matches, nails, screws, glue. It is not a chance that all these things have been put together—but there are important differences between the different tools—they are used in a family of ways—though nothing could be more different than glue and a chisel. There is constant surprise at the new tricks language plays on us when we get into a new field.

5. One thing we always do when discussing a word is to ask how we were taught it. Doing this on the one hand destroys a variety of misconceptions, on the other hand gives you a primitive language in which the word is used. Although this language is not what you talk when you are twenty, you get a rough approximation to what kind of language game is going to be played. Cf. How did we learn "I dreamt so and so?" The interesting point is that we didn't learn it by being shown a dream. If you ask yourself how a child learns "beautiful," "fine," etc., you find it learns them roughly as interjections. ("Beautiful" is an odd word to talk about because it's hardly ever used.) A child generally applies a word like "good" first to food. One thing that is immensely important in teaching is exaggerated gestures and facial expressions. The word is taught as a substitute for a facial expression or a gesture. The gestures, tones of voice, etc., in this case are expressions of approval. What *makes* the word an interjection of approval?[2] It is the game it appears in, not the form of words. (If I had to say what is the main mistake made by philosophers of the present generation, including Moore, I would say that it is that when language is looked at, what is looked at is a form of words and not the use made of the form of words.) Language is a characteristic part of a large group of activities—talking, writing, travelling on a bus, meeting a man, etc.[3] We are concentrating, not on the words "good" or "beautiful," which are entirely uncharacteristic, generally just subject and predicate ("This is beautiful"), but on the occasions on which they are said—on the enormously complicated situation in which the aesthetic expression has a place, in which the expression itself has almost a negligible place.

6. If you came to a foreign tribe, whose language you didn't know at all and you wished to know what words corresponded to "good," "fine," etc., what would you look for? You would look for smiles, gestures, food, toys. ([Reply to objection:] If you went to Mars and men were spheres with sticks coming out, you wouldn't know what to look for. Or if you went to a tribe where noises made with the mouth were just breathing or making music, and

---

[2]And not of disapproval or of surprise, for example?
     (The child understands the gestures which you use in teaching him. If he did not, he could understand nothing.)—R.

[3]When we build houses, we talk and write. When I take a bus, I say to the conductor: "Three-penny." We are concentrating not just on the word or the sentence in which it is used—which is highly uncharacteristic—but on the occasion on which it is said: the framework in which (nota bene) the actual aesthetic judgment is practically nothing at all.—R.

language was made with the ears. Cf. "When you see trees swaying about they are talking to one another." ["Everything has a soul."] You compare the branches with arms. Certainly we must interpret the gestures of the tribe on the analogy of ours.) How far this takes us from normal aesthetics [and ethics—T]. We don't start from certain words, but from certain occasions or activities.

7. A characteristic thing about our language is that a large number of words used under these circumstances are adjectives—"fine," "lovely," etc. But you see that this is by no means necessary. You saw that they were first used as interjections. Would it matter if instead of saying "This is lovely," I just said "Ah!" and smiled, or just rubbed my stomach? As far as these primitive languages go, problems about what these words are about, what their real subject is [which is called "beautiful" or "good"], don't come up at all.

8. It is remarkable that in real life, when aesthetic judgements are made, aesthetic adjectives such as "beautiful," "fine," etc., play hardly any role at all. Are aesthetic adjectives used in a musical criticism? You say: "Look at this transition," or [Rhees] "The passage here is incoherent." Or you say, in a poetical criticism [Taylor]: "His use of images is precise." The words you use are more akin to "right" and "correct" (as these words are used in ordinary speech) than to "beautiful" and "lovely."

9. Words such as "lovely" are first used as interjections. Later they are used on very few occasions. We might say of a piece of music that it is lovely, by this not praising it but giving it a character. (A lot of people, of course, who can't express themselves properly use the word very frequently. As they use it, it is used as an interjection.) I might ask: "For what melody would I most like to use the word 'lovely'?" I might choose between calling a melody "lovely" and calling it "youthful." It is stupid to call a piece of music "Spring Melody" or "Spring Symphony." But the word "springy" wouldn't be absurd at all, any more than "stately" or "pompous."

10. If I were a good draughtsman, I could convey an innumerable number of expressions by four strokes—

Such words as "pompous" and "stately" could be expressed by faces. Doing this, our descriptions would be much more flexible and various than they are as expressed by adjectives. If I say of a piece of Schubert's that it is melancholy, that is like giving it a face (I don't express approval or disapproval). I could instead use gestures or [Rhees] dancing. In fact, if we want to be exact, we do use a gesture or a facial expression. . . .

14. (If I give you the light and shadow on a body in a picture I can thereby give you the shape of it. But if I give you the highlights in a picture you don't know what the shape is.)

15. In the case of the word "correct" you have a variety of related cases. There is first the case in which you learn the rules. The cutter learns how long a coat is to be, how wide the sleeve must be, etc. He learns rules—he is drilled—as in music you are drilled in harmony and counterpoint. Suppose I went in for tailoring and I first learnt all the rules, I might have, on the whole, two sorts of attitude. (1) Lewy says: "This is too short." I say: "No. It is right. It is according to the rules." (2) I develop a feeling for the rules. I interpret the rules. I might say: "No. It isn't right. It isn't according to the rules." Here I would be making an aesthetic judgement about the thing which is according to the rules in sense (1). On the other hand, if I hadn't learnt the rules, I wouldn't be able to make the aesthetic judgement. In learning the rules you get a more and more refined judgement. (Although, if you haven't learnt Harmony and haven't a good ear, you may nevertheless detect any disharmony in a sequence of chords.) . . .

17. In what we call the Arts a person who has judgement develops. (A person who has a judgement doesn't mean a person who says "Marvellous!" at certain things.)[4] If we talk of aesthetic judgements, we think, among a thousand things, of the Arts. When we make an aesthetic judgement about a thing, we do not just gape at it and say: "Oh! How marvellous!" We distinguish between a person who knows what he is talking about and a person who doesn't.[5] If a person is to admire English poetry, he must know English. Suppose that a Russian who doesn't know English is overwhelmed by a sonnet admitted to be good. We would say that he does not know what is in it at all. Similarly, of a person who doesn't know metres but who is overwhelmed, we would say that he doesn't know what's in it. In music this is more pronounced. Suppose there is a person who admires and enjoys what is admitted to be good but can't remember the simplest tunes, doesn't know when the bass comes in, etc. We say he hasn't seen what's in it. We use the phrase "A man is musical" not so as to call a man musical if he says "Ah!" when a piece of music is played, any more than we call a dog musical if it wags its tail when music is played.[6]

18. The word we ought to talk about is "appreciated." What does appreciation consist in?

19. If a man goes through an endless number of patterns in a tailor's,

---

[4]In what we call the arts there developed what we call a "judge"—i.e. one who has judgment. This does not mean just someone who admires or does not admire. We have an entirely new element.—R.

[5]He must react in a consistent way over a long period. Must know all sorts of things.—T.

[6]Cf. the person who likes hearing music but cannot talk about it at all, and is quite unintelligent on the subject. "He is musical." We do not say this if he is just happy when he hears music and the other things aren't present.—T.

[and] says: "No. This is slightly too dark. This is slightly too loud," etc., he is what we call an appreciator of material. That he is an appreciator is not shown by the interjections he uses, but by the way he chooses, selects, etc. Similarly in music: "Does this harmonize? No. The bass is not quite loud enough. Here I just want something different. . . . " This is what we call an appreciation.

20. It is not only difficult to describe what appreciation consists in, but impossible. To describe what it consists in we would have to describe the whole environment.

21. I know exactly what happens when a person who knows a lot about suits goes to the tailor, also I know what happens when a person who knows nothing about suits goes—what he says, how he acts, etc.[7] There is an extraordinary number of different cases of appreciation. And, of course, what I know is nothing compared to what one could know. I would have—to say what appreciation is—e.g. to explain such an enormous wart as arts and crafts, such a particular kind of disease. Also I would have to explain what our photographers do today—and why it is impossible to get a decent picture of your friend even if you pay £1,000.

22. You can get a picture of what you may call a very high culture, e.g. German music in the last century and the century before, and what happens when this deteriorates. A picture of what happens in Architecture when you get imitations—or when thousands of people are interested in the minutest details. A picture of what happens when a dining-room table is chosen more or less at random, when no one knows where it came from.[8]

23. We talked of correctness. A good cutter won't use any words except words like "Too long," "All right." When we talk of a Symphony of Beethoven we don't talk of correctness. *Entirely different things* enter. One wouldn't talk of appreciating the *tremendous* things in Art. In certain styles in Architecture a door is correct, and the thing is you appreciate it. But in the case of a Gothic Cathedral what we do is not at all to find it correct—it plays an entirely different role with us.[9] The entire *game* is different. It is as different as to judge a human being and on the one hand to say "He behaves well" and on the other hand "He made a great impression on me."

24. "Correctly," "charmingly," "finely," etc. play an entirely different role. Cf. the famous address of Buffon—a terrific man—on style in writing;

---

[7]That is aesthetics.—T.

[8]Explain what happens when a craft deteriorates. A period in which everything is fixed and extraordinary care is lavished on certain details; and a period in which everything is copied and nothing is thought about.

A great number of people are highly interested in a detail of a dining-room chair. And then there is a period when a dining-room chair is in the drawing-room and no one knows where this came from or that people had once given enormous thought in order to know how to design it.—R.

[9]Here there is no question of *degree*.—R.

making ever so many distinctions which I only understand vaguely but which he didn't mean vaguely—all kinds of nuances like "grand," "charming," "nice."

25. The words we call expressions of aesthetic judgement play a very complicated role, but a very definite role, in what we call a culture of a period. To describe their use or to describe what you mean by a cultured taste, you have to describe a culture.[10] What we now call a cultured taste perhaps didn't exist in the Middle Ages. An entirely different game is played in different ages.

26. What belongs to a language game is a whole culture. In describing musical taste you have to describe whether children give concerts, whether women do or whether men only give them, etc., etc.[11] In aristocratic circles in Vienna people had [such and such] a taste, then it came into bourgeois circles and women joined choirs, etc. This is an example of tradition in music. . . .

35. In order to get clear about aesthetic words you have to describe ways of living. We think we have to talk about aesthetic judgements like "This is beautiful," but we find that if we have to talk about aesthetic judgements we don't find these words at all, but a word used something like a gesture, accompanying a complicated activity.[12]

36. [*Lewy:* If my landlady says a picture is lovely and I say it is hideous, we don't contradict one another.]

In a sense [and in *certain examples*—R] you do contradict one another. She dusts it carefully, looks at it often, etc. You want to throw it in the fire. This is just the stupid kind of example which is given in philosophy, as if things like "This is hideous," "This is lovely" were the only kinds of things ever said. But it is only one thing amongst a vast realm of other things—one special case. Suppose the landlady says: "This is hideous," and you say: "This is lovely"—all right, that's that.

II

1. One interesting thing is the idea that people have of a kind of science of Aesthetics. I would almost like to talk of what could be meant by Aesthetics.

2. You might think Aesthetics is a science telling us what's beautiful—

---

[10]To describe a set of aesthetic rules fully means really to describe the culture of a period.—T.

[11]That children are taught by adults who go to concerts, etc., that the schools are like they are, etc.—R.

[12]The judgment is a gesture accompanying a vast structure of actions not expressed by one judgment.—R.

"This is fine" is on a level with a gesture, almost—connected with all sorts of other gestures and actions and a whole situation and a culture. In Aesthetics just as in the arts what we called expletives play a very small part. The adjectives used in these are closer related to "correct."—T.

almost too ridiculous for words. I suppose it ought to include also what sort of coffee tastes well.[13]

3. I see roughly this—there is a realm of utterance of delight, when you taste pleasant food or smell a pleasant smell, etc., then there is the realm of Art which is quite different, though often you may make the same face when you hear a piece of music as when you taste good food. (Though you may cry at something you like very much.)

4. Supposing you meet someone in the street and he tells you he has lost his greatest friend, in a voice extremely expressive of his emotion.[14] You might say: "It was extrodinarily beautiful, the way he expressed himself." Supposing you then asked: "What similarity has my admiring this person with my eating vanilla ice and liking it?" To compare them seems almost disgusting. (But you can connect them by intermediate cases.) Suppose someone said: "But this is a quite different kind of delight." But did you learn two meanings of "delight"? You use the same word on both occasions.[15] There is some connection between these delights. Although in the first case the emotion of delight would in our judgement hardly count.[16]

5. It is like saying: "I classify works of Art in this way: at some I look up and at some I look down." This way of classifying might be interesting.[17] We might discover all sorts of connections between looking up or down at works of Art and looking up or down at other things. If we found, perhaps, that eating vanilla ice made us look up, we might not attach great importance to looking up. There may be a realm, a small realm of experiences which may make me look up or down where I can infer a lot from the fact that I looked up or down; another realm of experiences where nothing can be inferred from my looking up or down.[18] Cf. wearing blue or green trousers may in a certain society mean a lot, but in another society it may not mean anything.

6. What are expressions of liking something? Is it only what we say or interjections we use or faces we make? Obviously not. It is, often, how often I read something or how often I wear a suit. Perhaps I won't even say: "It's fine," but wear it often and look at it.[19]

7. Suppose we build houses and we give doors and windows certain dimensions. Does the fact that we *like* these dimensions necessarily show in

---

[13]It is hard to find boundaries.—R.

[14]Someone . . . who tells you he has lost his friend, in a restrained way.—R.

[15]But notice that you use the same word and not in the same chance way you use the same word "bank" for two things [like "river bank" and "money bank"—R.]—T.

[16]Although in the first case the gesture or expression of delight may be most unimportant in a way.—T.

[17]You might discover further characters of things which make us look up.—R.

[18]Some one might exaggerate the importance of the type of indication.—T.

[19]If I like a suit I may buy it, or wear it often—without interjections or making faces.—R. I may never smile at it.—T.

anything we say? Is what we like necessarily shown by an expression of *liking?*[20] [For instance—R] suppose our children draw windows and when they draw them in the wrong way we punish them. Or when someone builds a certain house we refuse to live in it or run away. . . .

9. You design a door and look at it and say: "Higher, higher, higher . . . oh, all right."[21] (Gesture) What is this? Is it an expression of content?

10. Perhaps the most important thing in connection with aesthetics is what may be called aesthetic reactions, e.g. discontent, disgust, discomfort. The expression of discontent is not the same as the expression of discomfort. The expression of discontent says: "Make it higher . . . too low! . . . do something to this."

11. Is what I call an expression of discontent something like an expression of discomfort *plus* knowing the cause of the discomfort and asking for it to be removed? If I say: "This door is too low. Make it higher," should we say I know the cause of my discomfort?

12. "Cause" is used in very many different ways, e.g.

(1) "What is the cause of unemployment?" "What is the cause of this expression?"

(2) "What was the cause of your jumping?" "That noise."

(3) "What was the cause of that wheel going round?" You trace a mechanism. . . .[22]

19. There is a "Why?" to aesthetic discomfort not a "cause" to it. The expression of discomfort takes the form of a criticism and not "My mind is not at rest" or something. It might take the form of looking at a picture and saying: "What's wrong with it?"

20. It's all very well to say: "Can't we get rid of this analogy?" Well, we cannot. If we think of discomfort—cause, pain—cause of pain naturally suggests itself.

21. The cause, in the sense of the object it is directed to is also the cause in other senses. When you remove it, the discomfort ceases and what not. . . .

34. Tracing a mechanism is one way of finding the cause; we speak of "the cause" in this case. But if cases of wheels made of butter and looking like steel were frequent we might say: "This ('this wheel') is not the only cause at all. This may only look like a mechanism."[23]

35. People often say that aesthetics is a branch of psychology. The idea is that once we are more advanced, everything—all the mysteries of Art—will be understood by psychological experiments. Exceedingly stupid as the idea is, this is roughly it.

---

[20]Our preferring these shows itself in all sorts of ways.—T.

[21]". . . *there:* thank God"—R. ". . . yes, that's right."—T.

[22]Cause: (1) Experiment and statistics. (2) Reason. (3) Mechanism.—T.

[23]We are constantly inclined to reduce things to other things. So excited by finding that it's sometimes concomitance, we wish to say it's all *really* concomitance.—T.

36. Aesthetic questions have nothing to do with psychological experiments, but are answered in an entirely different way.[24]

37. "What is in my mind when I say so and so?" I write a sentence. One word isn't the one I need. I find the right word. "What is it I want to say? Oh yes, that is what I wanted." The answer in these cases is the one that satisfied you, e.g. someone says (as we often say in philosophy): "I will tell you what is at the back of your mind: . . ."

"Oh yes, quite so."

The criterion for it being the one that was in your mind is that when I tell you, you agree. This is not what is called a psychological experiment. An example of a psychological experiment is: you have twelve subjects, put same question to each and the result is that each says such and such, i.e. the result is something statistical.

38. You could say: "An aesthetic explanation is not a causal explanation."

39. Cf. Freud: *Wit and the Unconscious.* Freud wrote about jokes. You might call the explanation Freud gives a causal explanation. "If it is not causal, how do you know it's correct?" You say: "Yes, that's right." Freud transforms the joke into a different form which is recognized by us as an expression of the chain of ideas which led us from one end to another of a joke. An entirely new account of a correct explanation. Not one agreeing with experience, but one accepted. You have to give the explanation that is accepted. This is the whole point of the explanation.

40. Cf. "Why do I say 'Higher!'?" with "Why do I say 'I have a pain'?"

The Role of Theory in Aesthetics

MORRIS WEITZ

Theory has been central in aesthetics and is still the preoccupation of the philosophy of art. Its main avowed concern remains the determination of the nature of art which can be formulated into a definition of it. It construes definition as the statement of the necessary and sufficient properties of what is being defined, where the statement purports to be a true or false claim

Morris Weitz, "The Role of Theory in Aesthetics," *Journal of Aesthetics and Art Criticism* XV (1956).

[24]I wish to make it clear that the important problems in aesthetics are not settled by psychological research.—T.

These problems are answered in a different way—more in the form "What is in my mind when I say so and so?"—R.

about the essence of art, what characterizes and distinguishes it from everything else. Each of the great theories of art—Formalism, Voluntarism, Emo-
tionalism, Intellectualism, Intuitionism, Organicism—converges on the attempt
to state the defining properties of art. Each claims that it is the true theory
because it has formulated correctly into a real definition the nature of art;
and that the others are false because they have left out some necessary or
sufficient property. Many theorists contend that their enterprise is no mere
intellectual exercise but an absolute necessity for any understanding of art
and our proper evaluation of it. Unless we know what art is, they say, what
are its necessary and sufficient properties, we cannot begin to respond to it
adequately or to say why one work is good or better than another. Aesthetic
theory, thus, is important not only in itself but for the foundations of both
appreciation and criticism. Philosophers, critics, and even artists who have
written on art, agree that what is primary in aesthetics is a theory about the
nature of art.

Is aesthetic theory, in the sense of a true definition or set of necessary
and sufficient properties of art, possible? If nothing else does, the history of
aesthetics itself should give one enormous pause here. For, in spite of the
many theories, we seem no nearer our goal today than we were in Plato's
time. Each age, each art-movement, each philosophy of art, tries over and
over again to establish the stated ideal only to be succeeded by a new or
revised theory, rooted, at least in part, in the repudiation of preceding ones.
Even today, almost everyone interested in aesthetic matters is still deeply
wedded to the hope that the correct theory of art is forthcoming. We need
only examine the numerous new books on art in which new definitions are
proffered; or, in our own country especially, the basic textbooks and anthologies to recognize how strong the priority of a theory of art is.

In this essay I want to plead for the rejection of this problem. I want
to show that theory—in the requisite classical sense—is *never* forthcoming
in aesthetics, and that we would do much better as philosophers to supplant
the question, "What is the nature of art?" by other questions, the answers
to which will provide us with all the understanding of the arts there can be.
I want to show that the inadequacies of the theories are not primarily occasioned by any legitimate difficulty such e.g., as the vast complexity of art,
which might be corrected by further probing and research. Their basic inadequacies reside instead in a fundamental misconception of art. Aesthetic
theory—all of it—is wrong in principle in thinking that a correct theory is
possible because it radically misconstrues the logic of the concept of art. Its
main contention that "art" is amenable to real or any kind of true definition
is false. Its attempt to discover the necessary and sufficient properties of art
is logically misbegotten for the very simple reason that such a set and, consequently, such a formula about it, is never forthcoming. Art, as the logic of
the concept shows, has no set of necessary and sufficient properties, hence a
theory of it is logically impossible and not merely factually difficult. Aesthetic

theory tries to define what cannot be defined in its requisite sense. But in recommending the repudiation of aesthetic theory I shall not argue from this, as too many others have done, that its logical confusions render it meaningless or worthless. On the contrary, I wish to reassess its role and its contribution primarily in order to show that it is of the greatest importance to our understanding of the arts. . . .

The problem with which we must begin is not "What is art?" but "What sort of concept is 'art'?" Indeed, the root problem of philosophy itself is to explain the relation between the employment of certain kinds of concepts and the conditions under which they can be correctly applied. If I may paraphrase Wittgenstein, we must not ask, What is the nature of any philosophical x? or even, according to the semanticist, What does "x" mean? a transformation that leads to the disastrous interpretation of "art" as a name for some specifiable class of objects; but rather, What is the use or employment of "x"? What does "x" do in the language? This, I take it, is the initial question, the begin-all if not the end-all of any philosophical problem and solution. Thus, in aesthetics, our first problem is the elucidation of the actual employment of the concept of art, to give a logical description of the actual functioning of the concept, including a description of the conditions under which we correctly use it or its correlates.

My model in this type of logical description or philosophy derives from Wittgenstein. It is also he who, in his refutation of philosophical theorizing in the sense of constructing definitions of philosophical entities, has furnished contemporary aesthetics with a starting point for any future progress. In his new work, *Philosophical Investigations,*[1] Wittgenstein raises as an illustrative question, What is a game? The traditional philosophical, theoretical answer would be in terms of some exhaustive set of properties common to all games. To this Wittgenstein says, let us consider what we call "games": "I mean board-games, card-games, ball-games, Olympic games, and so on. What is common to them all?—Don't say: 'there *must* be something common, or they would not be called "games" ' but *look and see* whether there is anything common to all.—For if you look at them you will not see something that is common to *all,* but similarities, relationships, and a whole series of them at that . . ."

Card games are like board games in some respects but not in others. Not all games are amusing, nor is there always winning or losing or competition. Some games resemble others in some respects—that is all. What we find are no necessary and sufficient properties, only "a complicated network of similarities overlapping and crisscrossing," such that we can say of games that they form a family with family resemblances and no common trait. If one asks what a game is, we pick out sample games, describe these, and add,

---

[1] L. Wittgenstein, *Philosophical Investigations* (Oxford, 1953), tr. by E. Anscombe; see esp. Part I, Sections 65–75. All quotations are from these sections.

"This and *similar things* are called 'games'." This is all we need to say and indeed all any of us knows about games. Knowing what a game is is not knowing some real definition or theory but being able to recognize and explain games and to decide which among imaginary and new examples would or would not be called "games."

The problem of the nature of art is like that of the nature of games, at least in these respects: If we actually look and see what it is that we call "art," we will also find no common properties—only strands of similarities. Knowing what art is is not apprehending some manifest or latent essence but being able to recognize, describe, and explain those things we call "art" in virtue of these similarities.

But the basic resemblance between these concepts is their open texture. In elucidating them, certain (paradigm) cases can be given, about which there can be no question as to their being correctly described as "art" or "game," but no exhaustive set of cases can be given. I can list some cases and some conditions under which I can apply correctly the concept of art but I cannot list all of them, for the all-important reason that unforeseeable or novel conditions are always forthcoming or envisageable.

A concept is open if its conditions of application are emendable and corrigible; i.e., if a situation or case can be imagined or secured which would call for some sort of *decision* on our part to extend the use of the concept to cover this, or to close the concept and invent a new one to deal with the new case and its new property. If necessary and sufficient conditions for the application of a concept can be stated, the concept is a closed one. But this can happen only in logic or mathematics where concepts are constructed and completely defined. It cannot occur with empirically-descriptive and normative concepts unless we arbitrarily close them by stipulating the ranges of their uses.

I can illustrate this open character of "art" best by examples drawn from its sub-concepts. Consider questions like "Is Dos Passos' *U.S.A.* a novel?" "Is V. Woolf's *To the Lighthouse* a novel?" "Is Joyce's *Finnegan's Wake* a novel?" On the traditional view, these are construed as factual problems to be answered yes or no in accordance with the presence or absence of defining properties. But certainly this is not how any of these questions is answered. Once it arises, as it has many times in the development of the novel from Richardson to Joyce (e.g., "Is Gide's *The School for Wives* a novel or a diary?"), what is at stake is no factual analysis concerning necessary and sufficient properties but a decision as to whether the work under examination is similar in certain respects to other works, already called "novels," and consequently warrants the extension of the concept to cover the new case. The new work is narrative, fictional, contains character delineation and dialogue but (say) it has no regular time-sequence in the plot or is interspersed with actual newspaper reports. It is like recognized novels, A, B, C . . . , in some respects but not like them in others. But then neither were B and C like A in some respects when it was decided to extend the concept applied to A to B and C. Because work N + 1 (the brand new work) is like A, B, C . . . N in certain respects—has strands of similarity to them—the concept is extended and a new phase of the novel engendered. "Is N 1 a novel?" then, is no factual, but rather a decision problem, where the verdict turns on whether or not we enlarge our set of conditions for applying the concept.

What is true of the novel is, I think, true of every sub-concept of art: "tragedy," "comedy," "painting," "opera," etc., of "art" itself. No "Is X a novel, painting, opera, work of art, etc.?" question allows of a definitive answer in the sense of a factual yes or no report. "Is this *collage* a painting or not?" does not rest on any set of necessary and sufficient properties of painting but on whether we decide—as we did!—to extend "painting" to cover this case.

"Art," itself, is an open concept. New conditions (cases) have constantly arisen and will undoubtedly constantly arise; new art forms, new movements will emerge, which will demand decisions on the part of those interested, usually professional critics, as to whether the concept should be extended or not. Aestheticians may lay down similarity conditions but never necessary and sufficient ones for the correct application of the concept. With "art" its conditions of application can never be exhaustively enumerated since new cases can always be envisaged or created by artists, or even nature, which would call for a decision on someone's part to extend or to close the old or to invent a new concept. (E.g., "It's not a sculpture, it's a mobile.")

What I am arguing, then, is that the very expansive, adventurous character of art, its ever-present changes and novel creations, makes it logically impossible to ensure any set of defining properties. We can, of course, choose to close the concept. But to do this with "art" or "tragedy" or "portraiture," etc., is ludicrous since it forecloses on the very conditions of creativity in the arts. . . .

The primary task of aesthetics is not to seek a theory but to elucidate the concept of art. Specifically, it is to describe the conditions under which we employ the concept correctly. Definition, reconstruction, patterns of analysis are out of place here since they distort and add nothing to our understanding of art. What, then, is the logic of "X is a work of art"?

As we actually use the concept, "Art" is both descriptive (like "chair") and evaluative (like "good"); i.e., we sometimes say, "This is a work of art," to describe something and we sometimes say it to evaluate something. Neither use surprises anyone.

What, first, is the logic of "X is a work of art," when it is a descriptive utterance? What are the conditions under which we would be making such an utterance correctly? There are no necessary and sufficient conditions but there are the strands of similarity conditions, i.e., bundles of properties, none of which need be present but most of which are, when we describe things as works of art. I shall call these the "criteria of recognition" of works of art. All of these have served as the defining criteria of the individual traditional theories of art; so we are already familiar with them. Thus, mostly, when we describe something as a work of art, we do so under the conditions of there being present some sort of artifact, made by human skill, ingenuity, and imagination, which embodies in its sensuous, public medium—stone, wood, sounds, words, etc.—certain distinguishable elements and relations. Special theorists would add conditions like satisfaction of wishes, objectification or expression of emotion, some act of empathy, and so on; but these latter conditions seem to be quite adventitious, present to some but not to other spectators when things are described as works of art. "X is a work of art and contains *no* emotion, expression, act of empathy, satisfaction, etc.," is perfectly good sense and may frequently be true. "X is a work of art and . . . was made by no one," or . . . "exists only in the mind and not in any publicly observable thing," or . . . "was made by accident when he spilled the paint on the canvas," in each case of which a normal condition is denied, are also sensible and capable of being true in certain circumstances. None of the criteria of recognition is a defining one, either necessary or sufficient, because we can sometimes assert of something that it is a work of art and go on to deny any one of these conditions, even the one which has traditionally been taken to be basic, namely, that of being an artifact: Consider, "This piece of driftwood is a lovely piece of sculpture." Thus, to say of anything that it is a work of art is to commit oneself to the presence of *some* of these conditions. One would scarcely describe X as a work of art if X were not an artifact, or a collection of elements sensuously presented in a medium, or a product of human skill, and so on. If none of the conditions were present, if there were no criteria present for recognizing something as a work of art, we would not describe it as one. But, even so, no one of these or any collection of them is either necessary or sufficient.

The elucidation of the descriptive use of "Art" creates little difficulty. But the elucidation of the evaluative use does. For many, especially theorists, "This is a work of art" does more than describe; it also praises. Its conditions of utterance, therefore, include certain preferred properties or characteristics of art. I shall call these "criteria of evaluation." Consider a typical example of this evaluative use, the view according to which to say of something that it is a work of art is to imply that it is a *successful* harmonization of elements. Many of the honorific definitions of art and its sub-concepts are of this form. What is at stake here is that "Art" is construed as an evaluative term which is either identified with its criterion or justified in terms of it. "Art" is defined in terms of its evaluative property, e.g., successful harmonization. On such a view, to say "X is a work of art" is (1) to say something which is taken to *mean* "X is a successful harmonization" (e.g., "Art *is* significant form") or (2) to say something praiseworthy *on the basis* of its successful harmonization. Theorists are never clear whether it is (1) or (2) which is being put forward. Most of them, concerned as they are with this evaluative use, formulate (2), i.e., that feature of art that *makes* it art in the praise-sense, and then go on to state (1), i.e., the definition of "Art" in terms of its art-making feature. And this is clearly to confuse the conditions under which we say something evaluatively with the meaning of what we say. "This is a work of art," said evaluatively, cannot mean "This is a successful harmonization of elements"— except by stipulation—but at most is said in virtue of the art-making property, which is taken as a (the) criterion of "Art," when "Art" is employed to assess. "This is a work of art," used evaluatively, serves to praise and not to affirm the reason why it is said.

The evaluative use of "Art," although distinct from the conditions of its use, relates in a very intimate way to these conditions. For, in every instance of "This is a work of art" (used to praise), what happens is that the criterion of evaluation (e.g., successful harmonization) for the employment of the concept of art is converted into a criterion of recognition. This is why, on its evaluative use, "This is a work of art" implies "This has P," where "P" is some chosen artmarking property. Thus, if one chooses to employ "Art" evaluatively, as many do, so that "This is a work of art and not (aesthetically) good" makes no sense, he uses "Art" in such a way that he refuses to *call* anything a work of art unless it embodies his criterion of excellence.

There is nothing wrong with the evaluative use; in fact, there is good reason for using "Art" to praise. But what cannot be maintained is that theories of the evaluative use of "Art" are true and real definitions of the necessary and sufficient properties of art. Instead they are honorific definitions, pure and simple, in which "Art" has been redefined in terms of chosen criteria.

But what makes them—these honorific definitions—so supremely valuable is not their disguised linguistic recommendations; rather it is the *debates* over the reasons for changing the criteria of the concept of art which are built into the definitions. In each of the great theories of art, whether correctly understood as honorific definitions or incorrectly accepted as real definitions, what is of the utmost importance are the reasons proffered in the argument for the respective theory, that is, the reasons given for the chosen or preferred criterion of excellence and evaluation. It is this perennial debate over these criteria of evaluation which makes the history of aesthetic theory the important study it is. The value of each of the theories resides in its attempt to state and to justify certain criteria which are either neglected or distorted by previous theories. Look at the Bell-Fry theory again. Of course, "Art is significant form" cannot be accepted as a true, real definition of art; and most certainly it actually functions in their aesthetics as a redefinition of art in terms of the chosen condition of significant form. But what gives it its aesthetic importance is what lies behind the formula: In an age in which literary and representational elements have become paramount in painting, *return* to the plastic ones since these are indigenous to painting. Thus, the role of the theory is not to define anything but to use the definitional form, almost epigrammatically, to pinpoint a crucial recommendation to turn our attention once again to the plastic elements in painting.

Once we, as philosophers, understand this distinction between the formula and what lies behind it, it behooves us to deal generously with the traditional theories of art; because incorporated in every one of them is a debate over and argument for emphasizing or centering upon some particular feature of art which has been neglected or perverted. If we take the aesthetic theories literally, as we have seen, they all fail; but if we reconstrue them, in terms of their function and point, as serious and argued-for recommendations to concentrate on certain criteria of excellence in art, we shall see that aesthetic theory is far from worthless. Indeed, it becomes as central as anything in aesthetics, in our understanding of art, for it teaches us what to look for and how to look at it in art. What is central and must be articulated in all the theories are their debates over the reasons for excellence in art— debates over emotional depth, profound truths, natural beauty, exactitude, freshness of treatment, and so on, as criteria of evaluation—the whole of which converges on the perennial problem of what makes a work of art good. To understand the role of aesthetic theory is not to conceive it as definition, logically doomed to failure, but to read it as summaries of seriously made recommendations to attend in certain ways to certain features of art.

Family Resemblances and Generalizations Concerning the Arts

MAURICE MANDELBAUM

In 1954 William Elton collected and published a group of essays under the title *Aesthetics and Language*. As his introduction made clear, a common

Maurice Mandelbaum, "Family Resemblances and Generalizations Concerning the Arts." *American Philosophical Quarterly* 2 (1965).

feature of these essays was the application to aesthetic problems of some of the doctrines characteristic of recent British linguistic philosophy.[1] While this mode of philosophizing has not had as pervasive an influence on aesthetics as it has had on most other branches of philosophy,[2] there have been a number of important articles which, in addition to those contained in the Elton volume, suggest the direction in which this influence runs. Among these articles one might mention "The Task of Defining a Work of Art" by Paul Ziff,[3] "The Role of Theory in Aesthetics" by Morris Weitz,[4] Charles L. Stevenson's "On 'What is a Poem' "[5] and W. E. Kennick's "Does Traditional Aesthetics Rest on a Mistake?"[6] In each of them one finds a conviction which was also present in most of the essays in the Elton volume: that it is a mistake to offer generalizations concerning the arts, or to put the matter in a more provocative manner, that it is a mistake to attempt to discuss what art, or beauty, or the aesthetic, or a poem, *essentially* is. In partial support of this contention, some writers have made explicit use of Wittgenstein's doctrine of *family resemblances*; Morris Weitz, for example, has placed it in the forefront of his discussion. However, in that influential and frequently anthologized article, Professor Weitz made no attempt to analyze, clarify, or defend the doctrine itself. Since its use with respect to aesthetics has provided the means by which others have sought to escape the need of generalizing concerning the arts, I shall begin my discussion with a consideration of it.

The *locus classicus* for Wittgenstein's doctrine of family resemblances is in Part I of *Philosophical Investigations*, sections 65–77.[7] In discussing what he refers to as language-games, Wittgenstein says:

> Instead of producing something common to all that we call language, I am saying that these phenomena have no one thing in common which makes us use the same word for all—but they are *related* to one another in many different ways.

---

[1]See William Elton (ed.), *Aesthetics and Language* (Oxford, Basil Blackwell, 1954), p. 1, n. 1 and 2.

[2]A discussion of this fact is to be found in Jerome Stolnitz, "Notes on Analytic Philosophy and Aesthetics," *British Journal of Aesthetics*, vol. 3 (1961), pp. 210–222.

[3]*Philosophical Review*, vol. 62 (1953), pp. 58–78.

[4]*Journal of Aesthetics and Art Criticism*, vol. 15 (1956), pp. 27–35, reprinted in this volume.

[5]*Philosophical Review*, vol. 66 (1957), pp. 329–362.

[6]*Mind*, vol. 67 (1958), pp. 317–334. In addition to the articles already referred to, I might mention "The Uses of Works of Art" by Teddy Brunius in *Journal of Aesthetics and Art Criticism*, vol. 22 (1963), pp. 123–133, which refers to both Weitz and Kennick, but raises other questions with which I am not here concerned.

[7]Ludwig Wittgenstein, *Philosophical Investigations*, translated by G. E. M. Anscombe (New York, Macmillan, 1953), pp. 31–36. A parallel passage is to be found in "The Blue Book": see *Preliminary Studies for the "Philosophical Investigations," Generally Known as The Blue and Brown Books* (Oxford, Basil Blackwell, 1958), pp. 17–18.

> And it is because of this relationship, or these relationships, that we call them all "language." ([Section] 65)

He then illustrates his contention by citing a variety of *games,* such as board games, card games, ball games, etc., and concludes:

> We see a complicated network of similarities overlapping and criss-crossing: sometimes overall similarities of detail. ([Section] 66)
>
> I can think of no better expression to characterize these similarities than "family resemblances"; for the various resemblances between members of a family: build, features, colour of eyes, gait, temperment, etc., etc. overlap and criss-cross in the same way.—And I shall say: "games" form a family. ([Section] 67)

In short, what Wittgenstein aims to establish is that one need not suppose that all instances of those entities to which we apply a common name do in fact possess any one feature in common. Instead, the use of a common name is grounded in the criss-crossing and overlapping of resembling features among otherwise heterogeneous objects and activities.

Wittgenstein's concrete illustrations of the diversity among various types of games may at first make his doctrine of family resemblances extremely plausible. For example, we do not hesitate to characterize tennis, chess, bridge, and solitaire as games, even though a comparison of them fails to reveal any specific feature which is the same in each of them. Nonetheless, I do not believe that his doctrine of family resemblances, as it stands, provides an adequate analysis of why a common name, such as "a game," is in all cases applied or withheld.

Consider first the following case. Let us assume that you know how to play that form of solitaire called "Canfield"; suppose also that you are acquainted with a number of other varieties of solitaire (Wittgenstein uses "patience," i.e., "solitaire," as one instance of a form of game). Were you to see me shuffling a pack of cards, arranging the cards in piles, some face up and some face down, turning cards over one-by-one, sometimes placing them in one pile, then another, shifting piles, etc., you might say: "I see you are playing cards. What game are you playing?" However, to this I might answer: "I am not playing a game; I am telling (or reading) fortunes." Will the resemblances between what you have seen me doing and the characteristics of card games with which you are familiar permit you to contradict me and say that I am indeed playing some sort of game? Ordinary usage would not, I believe, sanction our describing fortune-telling as an example of playing a game, no matter how striking may be the resemblances between the ways in which cards are handled in playing solitaire and in telling fortunes. Or, to choose another example, we may say that while certain forms of wrestling contests are sometimes characterized as games (Wittgenstein mentions

"*Kampfspiele*")[8] an angry struggle between two boys, each trying to make the other give in, is not to be characterized as a game. Yet one can find a great many resembling features between such a struggle and a wrestling match in a gymnasium. What would seem to be crucial in our designation of an activity as a game is, therefore, not merely a matter of noting a number of specific resemblances between it and other activities which we denote as games, but involves something further.

To suggest what sort of characteristic this "something further" might possibly be, it will be helpful to pay closer attention to the notion of what constitutes a family resemblance. Suppose that you are shown ten or a dozen photographs and you are then asked to decide which among them exhibit strong resemblances.[9] You might have no difficulty in selecting, say, three of the photographs in which the subjects were markedly round-headed, had a strongly prognathous profile, rather deep-set eyes, and dark curly hair.[10] In some extended, metaphorical sense you might say that the similarities in their features constituted a family resemblance among them. The sense, however, would be metaphorical, since in the absence of a biological kinship of a certain degree of proximity we would be inclined to speak only of resemblances, and not of a *family* resemblance. What marks the difference between a literal and a metaphorical sense of the notion of "family resemblances" is, therefore, the existence of a genetic connection in the former case and not the latter. Wittgenstein, however, failed to make explicit the fact that the literal, root notion of a family resemblance includes this genetic connection no less than

---

[8]Ludwig Wittgenstein, *Philosophical Investigations, §66,,* p. 31. For reasons which are obscure, Miss Anscombe translates *"Kampfspiele"* as "Olympic games."

[9]In an article which is closely related to my discussion, but which uses different arguments to support a similar point, Haig Khatchadourian has shown that Wittgenstein is less explicit than he should have been with respect to the levels of determinateness at which these resemblances are significant for our use of common names. See "Common Names and 'Family Resemblances'," *Philosophy and Phenomenological Research*, vol. 18 (1957–58), pp. 341–358. (For a related, but less closely relevant, article by Professor Khatchadourian, see "Art-Names and Aesthetic Judgments," *Philosohy*, vol. 36 [1961], pp. 30–48.)

[10]It is to be noted that this constitutes a closer resemblance than that involved in what Wittgenstein calls "family resemblances," since in my illustration the specific similarities all pertain to a single set of features, with respect to each one of which all three of the subjects directly resemble one another. In Wittgenstein's use of the notion of family resemblances there is, however, no one set of resembling features common to each member of the "family"; there is merely a crisscrossing and overlapping among the elements which constitute the resemblances among the various persons. Thus, in order to conform to his usage, my illustration would have to be made more complicated, and the degree of resemblance would become more attenuated. For example, we would have to introduce the photographs of other subjects in which, for example, recessive chins would supplant prognathous profiles among those who shared the other characteristics; some would have blond instead of dark hair, and protruberant instead of deep-set eyes, but would in each case resemble the others in other respects, etc. However, if what I say concerning family resemblances holds of the stronger similarities present in my illustration, it should hold *a fortiori* of the weaker form of family resemblances to which Wittgenstein draws our attention.

it includes the existence of noticeable physiognomic resemblances.[11] Had the existence of such a *twofold* criterion been made explicit by him, he would have noted that there is in fact an attribute common to all who bear a family resemblance to each other: they are related through a common ancestry. Such a relationship is not, of course, one among the specific features of those who share a family resemblance; it nonetheless differentiates them from those who are not to be regarded as members of a single family.[12] If, then, it is possible that the analogy of family resemblances could tell us something about how games may be related to one another, one should explore the possibility that, in spite of their great dissimilarities, games may possess a common attribute which, like biological connection, is not itself one among their directly exhibited characteristics. Unfortunately, such a possibility was not explored by Wittgenstein.

To be sure, Wittgenstein does not explicitly state that the resemblances which are correlated with our use of common names must be a sort that are directly exhibited. Nonetheless, all of his illustrations in the relevant passages

---

[11]Although Wittgenstein failed to make explicit the fact that a genetic connection was involved in his notion of "family resemblances," I think that he did in fact presuppose such a connection. If I am not mistaken, the original German makes this clearer than does the Anscombe translation. The German text reads:

> Ich kann diese Ähnlichkeiten nicht besser charakterisieren, als durch das Wort "Familienähnlichkeiten"; denn so übergreifen und kreuzen sich die verschiedenen Ähnlichkeiten, die zwischen den Gliedern einer Familie bestehen: Wuchs, Gesichtzüge, Augenfarbe, Gang, Temperament, etc., etc. (§67).

Modifying Miss Anscombe's translation in as few respects as possible, I suggest that a translation of this passage might read:

> I can think of no better expression to characterize these similarities than "family resemblances," since various similarities which obtain among the members of a family—their build, features, color of eyes, gait, temperament, etc., etc.—overlap and criss-cross in the same way.

This translation differs from Miss Anscombe's (which has been quoted above) in that it makes more explicit the fact that the similarities are similarities among the members of a single family, and are not themselves definitive of what constitutes a *family* resemblance.

[12]Were this aspect of the twofold criterion to be abandoned, and were our use of common names to be solely determined by the existence of overlapping and criss-crossing relations, it is difficult to see how a halt would ever be called to the spread of such names. Robert J. Richman has called attention to the same problem in 'Something Common'," *Journal of Philosophy,* vol. 59 (1962), pp. 821–830. He speaks of what he calls "the Problem of Wide-Open Texture," and says: "the notion of family resemblances may account for our extending the application of a given general term, but it does not seem to place any limit on this process" (p. 829).

In an article entitled "The Problem of the Model-Language Game in Wittgenstein's Later Philosophy," *Philosophy,* vol. 36 (1961), pp. 333–351, Helen Hervey also calls attention to the fact that "a family is so-called by virtue of its common ancestry" (p. 334). She also mentions (p. 335) what Richman referred to as the problem of "the wide-open texture."

involve aspects of games which would be included in a description of how a particular game is to be played; that is, when he commands us to "look and see" whether there is anything common to all games,[13] the "anything" is taken to represent precisely the sort of manifest feature that is described in rule-books, such as Hoyle. However, as we have seen in the case of family resemblances, what constitutes a *family* is not defined in terms of the manifest features of a random group of people; we must first characterize the *family* relationship in terms of genetic ties, and then observe to what extent those who are connected in this way *resemble* one another.[14] In the case of games, the analogue to genetic ties might be the purpose for the sake of which various games were formulated by those who invented or modified them, e.g., the potentiality of a game to be of absorbing non-practical interest to either participants or spectators. If there were any such common feature one would not expect it to be defined in a rule book, such as Hoyle, since rule books only attempt to tell us how to play a particular game: our interest in playing a game, and our understanding of what constitutes a game, is already presupposed by the authors of such books.

It is not my present concern to characterize any feature common to most or all of those activities which we call games, nor would I wish to argue on the analogy of family resemblances that there *must be* any such feature. If the question is to be decided, it must be decided by an attempt to "look and see." However, it is important that we look in the right place and in the right ways if we are looking for a common feature; we should not assume that any feature common to all games must be some manifest characteristic, such as whether they are to be played with a ball or with cards, or how many players there must be in order for the game to be played. If we were to rely exclusively on such features we should, as I have suggested, be apt to link solitaire with fortune-telling, and wrestling matches with fights, rather than (say) linking solitaire with cribbage and wrestling matches with weight-lifting. It is, then, my contention that Wittgenstein's emphasis on directly exhibited resemblances, and his failure to consider other possible similarities, led to a failure on his part to provide an adequate clue as to what—in some cases at least—governs our use of common names.[15]

---

[13]Ludwig Wittgenstein, *Philosophical Investigations,* §66, p. 31.

[14]Although I have only mentioned the existence of genetic connections among members of a family, I should of course not wish to exclude the effects of habitual association in giving rise to some of the resemblances which Wittgenstein mentions. I have stressed genetic connection only because it is the simplest and most obvious illustration of the point I have wished to make.

[15]I do not deny that directly exhibited resemblances often play a part in our use of common names; this is a fact explicitly noted at least as long ago as by Locke. However, similarities in origin, similarities in use, and similarities in intention may also play significant roles. It is such factors that Wittgenstein overlooks in his specific discussions of family resemblances and of games.

If the foregoing remarks are correct, we are now in a position to see that the radical denigration of generalization concerning the arts, which has come to be almost a hallmark of the writings of those most influenced by recent British philosophy, may involve serious errors, and may not constitute a notable advance.

In turning from Wittgenstein's statements concerning family resemblances to the use to which his doctrine has been put by writers on aesthetics, we must first note what these writers are *not* attempting to do. In the first place, they are not seeking to clarify the relationships which exist among the many different senses in which the word "art" is used. Any dictionary offers a variety of such senses (e.g., the art of navigation, art as a guile, art as the craft of the artist, etc.), and it is not difficult to find a pattern of family resemblances existing among many of them. However, an analysis of such resemblances, and of their differences, has not, as a matter of fact, been of interest to the writers of the articles with which we are concerned. In the second place, these writers have not been primarily interested in analyzing how words such as "work of art" or "artist" or "art" are ordinarily used by those who are neither aestheticians nor art critics; their concern has been with the writings which make up the tradition of "aesthetic theory." In the third place, we must note that the concern of these writers has not been to show that family resemblances do in fact exist among the various arts, or among various works of art; on the contrary, they have used the doctrine of family resemblances in a *negative* fashion. In this, they have of course followed Wittgenstein's own example. The position which they have sought to establish is that traditional aesthetic theory has been mistaken in assuming that there is any essential property or defining characteristic of works of art (or any set of such properties or characteristics); as a consequence, they have contended that most of the questions which have been asked by those engaged in writing on aesthetics are mistaken sorts of questions.

However, as the preceding discussion of Wittgenstein should have served to make clear, one cannot assume that if there is any one characteristic common to all works of art it must consist in some specific, directly exhibited feature. Like the biological connections among those who are connected by family resemblances, or like the intentions on the basis of which we distinguish between fortune-telling and card games, such a characteristic might be a relational attribute, rather than some characteristic at which one could directly point and say: "It is this particular feature of the object which leads me to designate it as a work of art." A relational attribute of the required sort might, for example, only be apprehended if one were to consider specific art objects as having been created by someone for some actual or possible audience.

The suggestion that the essential nature of art is to be found in such a relational attribute is surely not implausible when one recalls some of the many traditional theories of art. For example, art has sometimes been characterized as being one special form of communication or of expression, or as being a special form of wish-fulfillment, or as being a presentation of truth in sensuous form. Such theories do not assume that in each poem, painting, play, and sonata there is a specific ingredient which identifies it as a work of art; rather, that which is held to be common to these otherwise diverse objects is a relationship which is assumed to have existed, or is known to have existed, between certain of their characteristics and the activities and the intentions of those who made them.[16]

While we may acknowledge that it is difficult to find any set of attributes—whether relational or not—which can serve to characterize the nature of a work of art (and which will not be as vulnerable to criticism as many other such characterizations have been),[17] it is important to note that the difficulties inherent in this task are not really avoided by those who appeal to the notion of family resemblances. As soon as one attempts to elucidate how the term "art" is in fact used in the context of art criticism, most of the

---

[16]I know of no passage in which Wittgenstein takes such a possibility into account. In fact, if the passage from "The Blue Book" to which I have already alluded may be regarded as representative, we may say that Wittgenstein's view of traditional aesthetic theories was quite without foundation. In that passage he said:

> The idea of a general concept being a common property of its particular instances connects up with other primitive, too simple, ideas of the structure of language. It is comparable to the idea that *properties* are *ingredients* of the things which have the properties; e.g., that beauty is an ingredient of all beautiful things as alcohol is of beer and wine, and that we therefore could have pure beauty, unadulterated by anything that is beautiful (p. 17).

I fail to be able to identify any aesthetic theory of which such a statement would be true. It would not, for example, be true of Clive Bell's doctrine of "significant form," nor would it presumably be true of G. E. Moore's view of beauty, since both Bell and Moore hold that beauty depends upon the specific nature of the other qualities which characterize that which is beautiful.

However, it may be objected that when I suggest that what is common to works of art involves reference to "intentions," I overlook "the intentional fallacy" (see W. K. Wimsatt, Jr., and Monroe C. Beardsley, "The "Intentional Fallacy," *Sewanee Review,* vol. 54 [1946], pp. 468–488). This is not the case. The phrase "the intentional fallacy" originally referred to a particular method of criticism, that is, to a method of interpreting and evaluating given works of art; it was not the aim of Wimsatt and Beardsley to distinguish between art and non-art. These two problems are, I believe, fundamentally different in character. However, I do not feel sure that Professor Beardsley has noted this fact, for in a recent article in which he set out to criticize those who have been influenced by the doctrine of family resemblances he apparently felt himself obliged to define art *solely* in terms of some characteristic in the object itself (see "The Definition of the Arts," *Journal of Aesthetics and Art Criticism,* vol. 20 [1961], pp. 175–187). Had he been willing to relate this characteristic to the activity and intention of those who make objects having such a characteristic, his discussion would not, I believe, have been susceptible to many of the criticisms leveled against it by Professor Douglas Morgan and Mary Mothersill (ibid., pp. 187–198).

[17]I do not say *"all"* such definitions, for I think that one can find a number of convergent definitions of art, each of which has considerable merit, though each may differ slightly from the others in its emphasis.

same problems which have arisen in the history of aesthetic theory will again make their appearance. In other words, linguistic analysis does not provide a means of escape from the issues which have been of major concern in traditional aesthetics. . . .

In "The Role of Theory in Aesthetics" Professor Weitz places his primary emphasis on the fact that art forms are not static. From this fact he argues that it is futile to attempt to state the conditions which are necessary and sufficient for an object to be a work of art. What he claims is that the concept "art" must be treated as an open concept, since new art forms have developed in the past, and since any art form (such as the novel) may undergo radical transformations from generation to generation. One brief statement from Professor Weitz's article can serve to summarize this view:

> What I am arguing, then, is that the very expansive, adventurous character of art, its ever-present changes and novel creations, makes it logically impossible to ensure any set of defining properties. We can, of course, choose to close the concept. But to do this with "art" or "tragedy" or portraiture, etc. is ludicrous since it forecloses the very conditions of creativity in the arts.[18]

Unfortunately, Professor Weitz fails to offer any cogent argument in substantiation of this claim. The lacuna in his discussion is to be found in the fact that the question of whether a particular concept is open or closed (i.e., whether a set of necessary and sufficient conditions can be offered for its use) is not identical with the question of whether future instances to which the very same concept is applied may or may not possess genuinely novel properties. In other words, Professor Weitz has not shown that every novelty in the instances to which we apply a term involves a stretching of the term's connotation.

By way of illustration, consider the classificatory label "representational painting." One can assuredly define this particular form of art without defining it in such a way that it will include only those paintings which depict either a mythological event or a religious scene. Historical paintings, interiors, fête-champêtres, and still life can all count as "representational" according to any adequate definition of this mode of painting, and there is no reason why such a definition could not have been formulated prior to the emergence of any of these novel species of the representational mode. Thus, to define a particular form of art—and to define it truly and accurately—is not necessarily to set one's self in opposition to whatever new creations may arise within that

---

[18]Op. cit., p. 32.

particular form.[19] Consequently, it would be mistaken to suppose that all attempts to state the defining properties of various art forms are prescriptive in character and authoritarian in their effect.

This conclusion is not confined to cases in which an established form of art, such as representational painting, undergoes changes; it can also be shown to be compatible with the fact that radically new art forms arise. For example, if the concept "a work of art" had been carefully defined prior to the invention of cameras, is there any reason to suppose that such a definition would have proved an obstacle to viewing photography or the movies as constituting new art forms? To be sure, one can imagine definitions which might have done so. However, it was not Professor Weitz's aim to show that one or another definition of art had been a poor definition; he wished to establish the general thesis that there was a necessary incompatability, which he denoted as a logical impossibility, between allowing for novelty and creativity in the arts and stating the defining properties of a work of art. He failed to establish this thesis since he offered no arguments to prove that new sorts of instantiation of a previously defined concept will necessarily involve us in changing the definition of that concept.

To be sure, if neither photography nor the movies had developed along lines which satisfied the same sort of interest that the other arts satisfied, and if the kinds of standards which were applied in the other arts were not seen to be relevant when applied to photography and to the movies, then the antecedently formulated definition of art would have functioned as a closed concept, and it would have been used to exclude all photographers and all motion-picture makers from the class of those who were to be termed "artists." However, what would the defender of the openness of concepts hold that one should have done under these circumstances? Suppose, for example, that all photographers had in fact been the equivalent of passport photographers, and that they had been motivated by no other interests and controlled by no other standards than those which govern the making of photographs for passports and licenses: would the defender of open concepts be likely to have expanded the concept of what is to count as an art in order to have included photography? The present inclusion of photography among the arts

---

[19]To be sure, if no continuing characteristic is to be found, the fact of change will demand that the concept be treated as having been an open one. This was precisely the position taken by Max Black in a discussion of the concept "science." (See "The Definition of Scientific Method," in *Science and Civilization,* edited by Robert C. Stauffer [Madison, Wisconsin, 1949].) Paul Ziff refers to the influence of Professor Black's discussion upon his own views, and the views of Morris Weitz are assuredly similar. However, even if Professor Black's view of the changes in the concept "science" is a correct one (as I should be prepared to think that it may be), it does not follow that the same argument applies in the case of art. Nor does the fact that the meaning of "science" has undergone profound changes in the past imply that further analogous changes will occur in the future.

is justified, I should hold, precisely because photography arises out of the same sorts of interest, and can satisfy the same sorts of interest, and our criticism of it employs the same sorts of standards, as is the case with respect to the other arts. . . .

Defining Art

GEORGE DICKIE

In recent years it has been argued that the expression "work of art" cannot be defined and Morris Weitz has even argued that *being an artifact* is not a necessary condition for being a work of art.[1] More recently, however, Joseph Margolis has offered a definition[2] and Maurice Mandelbaum has made tentative suggestions about defining "art."[3]

I shall not repeat the well-known argument of Weitz, whose views I take to be representative of those who maintain that "art" cannot be defined, but shall state his main conclusion and comment on one of his arguments. Neither shall I repeat the arguments of Margolis or Mandelbaum, but I do want to note (1) that they agree that artifactuality is a necessary condition of art, and (2) that Mandelbaum points out the significance of the *nonexhibited* characteristics of art for the definition of "art."

Weitz's main conclusion is that there are no necessary and sufficient conditions for the definition of "art" or for any of the subconcepts of art, such as "novel," "tragedy," "painting," and so on. All of these notions are open concepts and their instances have "family resemblances."

Weitz rejects artifactuality as a necessary condition of art because we sometimes make statements such as "This driftwood is a lovely piece of sculpture."[4] We do sometimes speak this way of natural objects, but nothing

George Dickie, "Defining Art," *American Philosophical Quarterly* 6 (1969).

[1]Morris Weitz, "The Role of Theory in Aesthetics," *The Journal of Aesthetics and Art Criticism,* vol. 15 (1956), pp. 27–35; reprinted in *Philosophy Looks at the Arts,* ed. by Joseph Margolis (New York, 1962); Paul Ziff, "The Task of Defining a Work of Art," reprinted in *Aesthetics and the Philosophy of Criticism,* ed. by Marvin Levich (New York, 1963); William Kennick, "Does Traditional Aesthetics Rest on a Mistake," *Mind,* vol. 66 (1958), pp. 317–334.

[2]*The Language of Art and Art Criticism* (Detroit, 1965), pp. 37–47. Margolis' definition is not satisfactory, however; see Andrew Harrison's review in *Philosophical Books,* vol. 7 (1966), p. 19.

[3]"Family Resemblances and Generalization Concerning the Arts," *American Philosophical Quarterly,* vol. 2 (1965), pp. 219–228.

[4]Op. cit., p. 57.

follows from this fact. Weitz is confused because he takes the driftwood remark to be a descriptive statement and it is not. Weitz himself, quite correctly, distinguishes between an evaluative use and a descriptive use of "work of art,"[5] and once this distinction is understood it can be seen that the driftwood remark is an evaluation of the driftwood. But it is, of course, the descriptive sense of "work of art" which is at issue when the question of whether "art" can be defined is raised. I maintain that the descriptive use of "work of art" is used to indicate that a thing belongs to a certain category of artifacts. By the way, the evaluative sense can be applied to artifacts as well as nonartifacts, as when we say, "That painting is a work of art." Such remarks are not intended as tautologies.

Before going on to discuss the second condition of the definition of the descriptive sense of "art," it will be helpful to distinguish the generic concept of art from the various subconcepts which fall under it. It may very well be the case that all or some of the subconcepts of art, such as novel, tragedy, ceramics, sculpture, painting, and so on, may lack necessary and sufficient conditions for their application as subconcepts and it still be the case that "work of art," which is the genus of all these subconcepts, can be defined. For example, there may not be any characteristics which all tragedies have which would distinguish them from comedies, satyr plays, happenings, and the like within the domain of art. Even if this were the case, in the light of the foregoing, tragedies and all other works of art would have at least one characteristic in common, namely, artifactuality. Perhaps artifactuality and some one or more other features of works of art distinguish them from nonart. If all or some of the subconcepts of art cannot be defined and, as I think is the case, "art" can be, then Weitz is right in part. . . .

Assuming that artifactuality is the genus of art, the differentia is still lacking. This second condition will be a social property of art. Furthermore, this social property will, in Mandelbaum's terminology, be a nonexhibited, relational property.

W. E. Kennick contends that such an approach to the definition of "art" is futile. He argues from such facts as that the ancient Egyptians sealed up paintings and sculptures in tombs to the conclusion that "The attempt to define Art in terms of what we do with certain objects is as doomed as any other."[6] There are several difficulties with Kennick's argument. First, the fact that the Egyptians sealed up paintings and sculptures in tombs does not entail that they generally regarded them differently from the way in which we regard them. Indeed, they might have put them there for the dead to appreciate, or simply because they belonged to the dead person, or for some other reason. The Egyptian practice does not prove a radical difference between their

---

[5]Ibid., p. 56.
[6]Kennick, Op. cit., p. 330.

conception of art and ours such that a definition which subsumes both is impossible. Secondly, there is no need to assume that we and the ancient Egyptians (or any other group) share a common conception of art. I would be happy to be able to specify the necessary and sufficient conditions for the concept of art which we have (we present-day Americans, we present-day Westerners, we Westerners since the organization of the system of the arts in or about the 18th century—I am not sure of the exact limits of the "we"). Kennick nothwithstanding, we are most likely to discover the differentia of art by considering "what we do with certain objects," that is, "works of art." But, of course, there is no guarantee that any given thing we or an ancient Egyptian might possibly do with a work of art will throw light on the concept of art. Not every *doing* will reveal what is required.

Arthur Danto's stimulating article, "The Artworld,"[7] is helpful here. In speaking of Warhol's Brillo Carton and Rauschenberg's Bed, he writes, "To see something as art requires something the eye cannot de[s]cry—an atmosphere of artistic theory, a knowledge of history of art: an artworld."[8] What the eye cannot descry is a complicated nonexhibited characteristic of the artifacts in question. The "atmosphere" of which Danto speaks is elusive, but it has a substantial content. Perhaps this content can be captured in a definition. I shall first state the definition and then go on to defend it. *A work of art in the descriptive sense is (1) an artifact (2) upon which some society or some sub-group of a society has conferred the status of candidate for appreciation.*

The definition speaks of the conferring of the status of *candidate* for appreciation: nothing is said about actual appreciation and this leaves open the possibility of works of art which, for whatever reason, are not appreciated. Also, not every aspect of a work is included in the candidacy for appreciation, for example, the color of the back of a painting is not ordinarily an object of appreciation. The problem of *which* aspects of a work of art are to be included within the candidacy for appreciation is a question which I have pursued elsewhere.[9]

Just how is the status of candidate for appreciation conferred? An artifact's hanging in an art museum, a performance at a theater, and the like are sure signs that the status *has been conferred*. But many works of art never reach museum walls and some are never seen by anyone but the artist himself. The status, therefore, must be conferrable by a single person's treating an artifact as a candidate for appreciation, usually the artist himself, although not always, because someone might create an artifact without ever considering

---

[7]*The Journal of Philosophy,* vol. 61 (1964), pp. 571–584.

[8]Ibid., p. 580.

[9]In my "Art Narrowly and Broadly Speaking," *American Philosophical Quarterly,* vol. 5 (1968), pp. 71–77, where I analyze the notion of *aesthetic object.* The subject of the present essay is the concept of *art* which, although related to the notion of aesthetic object, is distinct from it.

it as a candidate for appreciation and the status be conferred by some other person or persons. But can status be conferred so easily? We associate status with ceremony—the wedding ceremony and the status of being married, for example. However, ceremony is not the only way of getting married, in some jurisdictions common-law marriage is possible—a status acquired without ceremony. What I want to suggest is that, just as two persons can acquire the status of common-law marriage within a legal system, an artifact can acquire the status of a candidate for appreciation within the system which Danto has called "the artworld."

A number of questions arise about this notion of status of candidate for appreciation and perhaps the whole matter can best be clarified by stating them and trying to answer them. Probably the first question is: what *kind* of appreciation? Surely the definition does seem to suggest that there is a special kind of "aesthetic" appreciation. Appreciation is not crucial, but something should be said about it to prepare the way for the crucial point. The kind of appreciation I have in mind is simply the kind characteristic of our experiences of paintings, poetry, novels, and the like. This remark seems to collapse the definition into circularity, but it does not because "work of art" (the term defined) does not appear in the explanation of appreciation, only subconcept terms appear. Another apparent problem is that works of art differ so much from one another—for example, comedies are very different from tragedies— that it seems unlikely that the appreciation characteristic of our experience of one kind of work has something in common with the appreciation characteristic of our experience of another kind of work. But paintings, poems, and plays are the *objects* of our appreciation and the fact that the objects differ considerably does not mean that the various appreciations differ. Indeed, if we mean by "appreciation" something like "in experiencing the qualities of a thing one finds them worthy or valuable," then there is no problem about the similarity of the various appreciations.

It can now be seen that appreciation will not serve to pick out the subclass of works of art from the class of artifacts—it is too broad: many artifacts which are obviously not works of art are appreciated. To pick out the class of works of art one must stress the conferring of the status of candidate rather than appreciation. When, for example, a salesman of plumbing supplies spreads his wares before us, he presents them for our appreciation all right, but the presenting is not a conferring of status of candidate, it is simply a placing before us. But what is the difference between "placing before" and "conferring the status of candidate?" The difference is analogous to the difference between my uttering "I declare this man to be a candidate for alderman" and the head of the election board uttering the same sentence while acting in his official capacity. When I utter the sentence it has no effect because I have not been vested with any authority in this regard. Of course the analogy is not a complete one—lines of authority in the politico-legal world are by and large explicitly defined and incorporated into law, while lines of authority (or something like authority) in the artworld are nowhere codified. The artworld carries on its business at the level of customary practice. Still there is a practice and this defines a social institution. To return to the plumbing line, the salesman's presentation is different from Duchamp's superficially similar act of placing a urinal which he christened "Fountain" in that now famous art show. The point is that Duchamp's act took place within a certain institutional setting and that makes all the difference. Our salesman of plumbing supplies could do what Duchamp did, that is, convert a urinal into a work of art, but he probably would not—such weird ideas seem to occur only to artists with bizarre senses of humor. Please remember that when I say "Fountain" is a work of art, I am not saying it is a good one. And in making this last remark I am not insinuating that it is a bad one either.

Duchamp's "ready-mades" raise the question—"If urinals, snowshovels, and hatracks can become works of art, why can't natural objects such as driftwood become works of art?" and, of course, driftwood and other natural objects can become works of art if any one of a number of things is done to them. One thing which would do the trick would be to pick it up, take it home, and hang it on the wall. Another thing which would do the trick would be to pick it up and enter it in an exhibition. (I was, by the way, assuming that Weitz's sentence about driftwood referred to a piece of driftwood in its ordinary situation on a beach and untouched by human hand.) This means that natural objects which become works of art acquire their artifactuality (are artifactualized) at the same time that the status of candidate for appreciation is conferred on them. But perhaps a similar thing ordinarily happens with paintings, poems, and such; they come to exist as artifacts at the same time that they have conferred on them the status of candidate for appreciation. (Of course, being an artifact and being a candidate for appreciation are not the same thing—they are two properties of a single thing which may be acquired at the same time.) A somewhat more complicated case would be an artifact from a primitive culture which played a role in a religious system and which had no artistic function in the sense developed here. Such an artifact might become a work of art in our culture in a way similar to that in which driftwood might become a work of art. However, such a religious object which becomes a work of art would be an artifact in two senses, but the driftwood in only one. (I am not suggesting that something cannot be a religious object and work of art at the same time—there are many counter-instances to this in our own culture.)

A question which frequently arises in connection with discussions of the concept of art is "How are we to conceive of paintings done by individuals such as Betsy the chimpanzee from the Baltimore Zoo?" It all depends on what is done with the paintings. (Note that I unhesitatingly call the objects paintings, although I am uncertain about their status as works of art.) For example, The Field Natural History Museum in Chicago recently exhibited some chimpanzee paintings. In the case of these paintings, we must say that they are not works of art. However, if they had been exhibited a few miles away at the Chicago Art Institute they would have been works of art. (If, so to speak, the director of the Art Institute had gone out on a limb.) It all depends on the institutional setting.

In concluding, it may be worthwhile to consider in what ways the definition offered here differs from some traditional definitions. (1) It does not attempt to smuggle a conception of good art into the definition of "art." (2) It is not, to use Margolis' term, "overloaded," as is the one Margolis cites as a horrible example: "Art is a human activity which explores, and hereby creates, new reality in a suprarational, visional manner and presents it symbolically or metaphoncally,[10] as a microcosmic whole signifying a macrocosmic whole."[11] (3) It does not contain any commitment to any metaphysical or unempirical theory, as contrasted with, for example, the view that art is unreal. (4) It is broad enough so that those things generally recognized as art can be brought under it without undue strain, as contrasted with, for example, the imitation definition which involves enormous strain in trying to show that every work of art is an imitation of something or other. (5) It takes into account (or at least attempts to) the actual practices of the artworld of the past and of the present day.

Now what I have been saying may sound like saying, "a work of art is an object of which someone has said, 'I christen this object a work of art'." And I think it is rather like that. So one *can* make a work of art out of a sow's ear, but of course that does not mean that it is a silk purse.[12]

The Return to Art Theory

GEORGE DICKIE

Theorizing about art begins with Plato, although it has never been the center of philosophical attention. Plato's claim that art is imitation is hardly a complete philosophy of art; at most it is a claim that imitation is a necessary

George Dickie, "The Return to Art Theory," *Modern Trends in Philosophy* Vol. II, reprinted by permission of the author and Yachdav Publishers, Co., Ltd., Tel-Aviv, Israel (1983).

---

[10]There are apparently two typographical errors here. Margolis quotes the word as "metaphonically" and the original text reads "metaphoncally." A reading of the original text indicates that it should have been "metaphorically."

[11]Op. cit., p. 44. The passage is quoted from Erick Kahler's "What is Art?," in *Problems in Aesthetics,* ed. by Morris Weitz (New York, 1959).

[12]Thanks are due to Monroe Beardsley, Marcia Eaton, William Hayes, Arnold Levison, and Maurice Mandelbaum who read this paper in manuscript and made many helpful suggestions.

condition for art. Perhaps just because of the lack of philosophical attention, the imitation "theory" persisted in the minds of everyone as the account of the nature of art without being examined or defended, or without even being held in a self-conscious way. It was not until the nineteenth century that the grip of the notion of imitation was broken, and theorizing about the nature of art began. Philosophers of art then began to explore the notion of expression and other ideas. From this time on until the middle of the twentieth century, the philosophy of art was a lively, if not very disciplined, area of philosophical activity.

In the 1950s first Paul Ziff,[1] then Morris Weitz,[2] and finally William Kennick[3] published articles purporting to show that theorizing about art's essential nature is philosophically misguided. The result of this attack was that theorizing about art by most analytic philosophers ceased abruptly. Philosophers outside the analytic sphere continued apace; for example, Suzanne Langer appears to have taken no notice of the articles by Ziff, Weitz, and Kennick and continued to pursue uninterruptedly her line that "Art is the creation of forms symbolic of human feeling."[4]

Throughout the period of the 1950s and 1960s analytic philosophers for the most part stopped trying to theorize about art. In the mid-1960s two articles appeared—one by Arthur Danto[5] and one by Maurice Mandelbaum[6]— which in different ways restored the confidence of at least some analytically inclined philosophers that it was reasonable (and respectable) to theorize about art. Danto helped to accomplish this new philosophical climate by ignoring the Ziff, Weitz, and Kennick articles (although it is certain that he was acquainted with them) and by beginning to theorize about art in a new and provocative, if not always very clear way. . . .

Danto's important methodological contribution is his invention of what may be called "The Visually Indistinguishable Objects Argument." Consider the following pairs of objects: a) Andy Warhol's *Brillo Box* and a brillo box which is visually indistinguishable from it, b) Duchamp's *Fountain* and a urinal which is visually indistinguishable from it, and c) the *Mona Lisa* and an accidentally produced object which is visually indistinguishable from it. (Only one such pair is needed to make the point, but there is safety in numbers as well as pedagogical point.) The argument assumes that the first member of each pair is a work of art but that the second member of each pair is not,

[1]"The Task of Defining a Work of Art," *Philosophical Review* 62 (1953), 58–78.

[2]"The Role of Theory in Aesthetics," *Journal of Aesthetics and Art Criticism* 15 (1956), 27–35.

[3]"Does Traditional Aesthetics Rest on a Mistake?" *Mind* 67 (1958).

[4]*Feeling and Form,* New York, 1953, p. 40.

[5]"The Artworld," *Journal of Philosophy* Oct. 15, 1964, 571–584.

[6]"Family Resemblances and Generalization Concerning the Arts," *American Philosophical Quarterly* 2 (1965), 219–228.

even though the members of each pair are visually indistinguishable. What the argument shows is that there is more to being a work of art than what is visually apparent. (The argument can with suitable changes be adapted for nonvisual art.) That is, it is the web of relations within which an object is enmeshed that makes it art; the visually indistinguishable object which is not a work of art lacks these relations.

Now there is nothing new about the notion of an essential context for a work of art; all the traditional theories of art imply a context but fail to exploit the fact. For the imitation theory, the context is the artist (the imitator) and subject matter (the imitated) within which is suspended the work of art (the imitation). For Suzanne Langer the context is the artist (the symbolizer) and subject matter (human feeling) within which is suspended the work of art (the forms which symbolize). For an expression theory, the context is the artist (the expresser) and his emotion (the expressed) within which is suspended the work of art (the vehicle of the expression). One could go on.

The important difference between the context suggested by Danto's articles and those of the traditional theories is the "thickness" of the Danto context. The contexts implicit in the traditional theories are by contrast "thin." I speak of the context *suggested* in Danto's articles because that is just what he does there; he does not really describe the context of artworks but makes scattered remarks which evoke the outlines of a "thick" context. In the first article, he alludes to "an atmosphere of artistic theory, a knowledge of the history of art: an artworld." In the second article, he remarks that "artwork" is an ascriptive term which attaches ". . . to objects in the light of certain conventions. . . ." In the third article, he writes, "Something is an artwork, then, only relative to certain art-historical presuppositions, . . ." None of these remarks is developed, but we are left with the impression of a context which is rich, structured, and historical. The contexts implied by the traditional theories by contrast lacks depth and complexity. There must be more to being art than simply being an imitation or symbolic of human feeling or an expression of emotion. For one thing, the contexts implied by these theories simply do not suffice to make art: for example, something can express an emotion or symbolize human feeling and not be art. Moreover, these theories make no mention of the persons for whom art is made, focusing wholly or mostly on the creator of art. Finally, these theorists do not exploit the cultural and historical background from which art emerges; they give the impression that art is the result of individual initiative unrelated in any essential way to its cultural background.

Although Danto does not develop his notion of a context in much detail, he does at least make a claim about one necessary condition of art. He asserts that works of art are always *about* something, claiming that "art *is* a language of sorts, . . ." It can perhaps be granted that a portrait of a particular person is about that person. Also, a representation of a woman can perhaps be said to be about a woman, although not about any particular person as a portrait is. What about Duchamp's *Fountain?* What is it about? Danto says that such works are comments about art itself, and perhaps this can be granted also. There are, however, many paintings—the typical nonobjective paintings—which do not seem to be *about* anything. Suppose one of these paintings consists of interpenetrating geometric figures of various colors and is titled *#3.* There does not seem to be any reason to say that such a painting is about art, as perhaps Duchamp's *Fountain* is. It clearly does not refer to any object or kind of object in the world, as a portrait or a representation of a woman does. It is not about geometric figures, although it consists of geometric figures. And, when one looks at an art such as music, the prospects of Danto's claim seem even dimmer. Some musical pieces and some musical passages are about something, but the enormous bulk of music is not *about* anything at all.

An important aspect of art is that it *can* be about something, and the imitation theory grasped and exploited this fact. Danto devotes a great deal of time criticizing the imitation theory. It is ironic that his own view is subject to the same criticism that destroys the imitation theory: namely, the theory overgeneralizes by taking the frequently occurring and important feature of representationality to be a defining characteristic of art.

If Danto's aboutness thesis is false, as it seems it is,[7] his "Visually Indistinguishable Objects" argument and what it implies about an essential context for works of art is of the greatest importance. I shall now give a brief account of my own views about art and of how they have developed in recent years.

Stimulated by Danto's and Mandelbaum's articles, I began to try to work out an *institutional* account of the essential context within which works of art have their place. The context or framework of art is said to be institutional because the context is conceived of as a cultural practice or institution which consists of a variety of roles which are fulfilled by persons behaving in certain established ways. The institutional theory has received its fullest expression in Chapters I and VII of my book *Art and the Aesthetic.*[8] There I offered the following definition of "work of art":

> A work of art in the classificatory sense is (1) an artifact (2) a set of the aspects of which has had conferred upon it the status of candidate for appreciation by

---

[7]In his recently published book, *The Transfiguration of the Commonplace* (Cambridge, Massachusetts, 1981), pp. 212, Danto continues to hold the aboutness thesis but adds a second condition for art to his theory. The two conditions are supposed to be necessary and sufficient for art.

[8](Ithaca: Cornell University Press, 1974), p. 204. Earlier, less complete, accounts occur in "Defining Art," *American Philosophical Quarterly,* July 1969, pp. 253–256 and in *Aesthetics: An Introduction* (Indianapolis, 1971), pp. 95–108.

some person or persons acting on behalf of a certain social institution (the artworld).

By speaking of the classificatory sense of "work of art," I meant to show that I was concerned with a basic, value-neutral sense of the notion, a notion which refers to the class which embraces masterpieces, good art, mediocre art, indifferent art, and worthless art. It is true that the expression "work of art" is sometimes used in an evaluative way to praise a piece of art or even a piece of nonart. There is however, I maintain, a basic, underlying conception of art which encompasses *all* art—good, bad, and indifferent.

The various elements of my definition and the theoretical explanations which accompanied the definition were subject to a number of misinterpretations as well as a number of telling criticisms. The criticisms can be accepted and the theory reworked and altered in a way which improves the theory while retaining its institutional character. It will be instructive to consider some of the misinterpretations as well as the criticisms.

Some readers mistakenly thought that I used the expression "the artworld" to refer to those powerful groups which have so much to say about which paintings get hung, which plays get produced, and the like. By "the artworld" I meant to refer to the complex of differentiated roles which must be fulfilled by persons in order for art to be created. The kind of powerful groups mentioned above are completely inessential to the function of the artworld as I am conceiving of it.

Many readers thought I understood the artworld to be a formally organized body of some kind. There are formally organized bodies which exist *within* the artworld: museums, artist guilds, and the like, but by "the artworld" I meant to refer to a broad, informal cultural practice, the complex of roles referred to in the last paragraph. This misunderstanding was in large part due to my use of such phrases as "conferred upon" and "acting on behalf," phrases which typically refer to the actions of formal organizations such as universities, states, and the like. I shall, henceforth, not use such terminology. Another misunderstanding caused by my use of this terminology is that I thought that it is the artworld acting as a whole which makes art, or that at least in some cases this happens. I intended to claim that the artworld is a kind of background against which individuals or groups of individuals create works of art. The artworld does not act as a whole itself. Also, my use of the word "persons" in the phrase "some person or persons" in the definition caused some to think that the word "persons" referred to the artworld as a whole and that the artworld acting as a whole creates art or at least has to accept an object as art. The artworld itself neither creates nor accepts; it is the background for creating art. I intended "persons" to refer to groups who create art as typically happens when movies are made.

I shall now turn to the discussion of changes which must be made in the theory in order to meet the criticisms raised against it. In *Art and the Aesthetic* little attention was devoted to the artifactuality condition and most of the space was given to the discussion of the complicated second condition which revolves around the notion of conferring. As a result of criticism by Monroe Beardsley, I have come to see that *conferring* is much too formal a notion to use to describe the informal institution that I take the artworld to be. In short, conferring is not an aspect of the creation of art. With the abandonment of conferring, the emphasis shifts to the artifactuality condition, and in the new version the whole development of the theory is through the artifactuality condition.

The question which now becomes crucial is "What are the minimal conditions which suffice for the creating of an artifact?" This question must be answered in order to deal with the question of how such things as Duchamp's *Fountain* are works of art (if they are), for Duchamp clearly did not make an artifact in any way very similar to the way in which a painter paints a picture or a sculptor makes a statue. In whatever way this question is decided, what is, I think, essential is that it is the making of an artifact which is central to the creation of art, however minimal that making may be. I will return to this question shortly.

The definition of "work of art" in *Art and the Aesthetic* speaks of a set of the artifact's aspects which is a candidate for appreciation. This part of the definition was an attempt to deal with the traditional problem of distinguishing the aspects of a work of art which are properly appreciated and/or criticized from those aspects which are not to be appreciated and/or criticized. For example, we intuitively distinguish the front of a painting from its back and focus our appreciation or criticism on it. What is the theoretical basis for our behavior? This is an important question for aesthetics, but I now think it can be and should be dealt with independently of the question of what art and art-making is. Consequently, I shall set this question to the side.

I shall now briefly outline the central feature of the new version of the institutional theory of art. (This new version is set forth in a more complete form in my forthcoming book *The Art Circle*.)

As already noted, the new version retains artifactuality as a necessary condition of art. To be an artifact, by the way, does not require being a physical thing, although of course many artifacts are physical. An artifact, as the dictionary tells us, is a man-made thing, and a man-made thing may be physical, but it may not be. Nonphysical things, for example, poems, are artifacts.

There is no problem or question about the artifactuality of traditional paintings, statues, poems, and the like; they have become artifacts by being crafted (made) in traditional ways. There is, however, a puzzle about how some recent works of art are the artifacts of their creators. Duchamp's *Fountain* is a good example of the problem. Duchamp took a urinal and without altering it entered it in an art exhibition under the title *Fountain*. The urinal itself was an artifact to begin with, but it was not an artifact of Duchamp's making, so its "original" artifactuality cannot possibly be the artifactuality of the work of art. The new version of the institutional theory maintains that *Fountain* is an artifact because of the way in which Duchamp *used* the urinal within the context of the artworld. He used the urinal as a medium analogously to the way in which a painter uses paint from a tube. *Fountain* is a kind of double artifact, but then so are most conventional works of art; for example, a typical painting is made by using already existing artifacts such as canvas and paints which are manufactured for the purpose. Duchamp's *Fountain* is perhaps the creation of an artifact in the most minimal way.

Reflection on the artifactuality of *Fountain* (not to be confused with the prior artifactuality of the urinal with which it is made) is particularly revealing. One might reflect on the artifactuality of a traditional painting or statue without noticing its essential artworld background, and thus fail to notice its context which is what the institutional theory is all about. Reflecting on the artifactuality of *Fountain,* however, almost forces one to take notice of its essential background; how could a physically unaltered object become an artifact unless it has been used within a context of some sort?

The claim that artifactuality is a necessary condition of art is not, of course, unique to the institutional theory. Each of the traditional theories of art makes this claim in one way or another. The institutional theory, however, very strongly emphasizes the context within which the production of the artifact takes place and claims that the artifactuality is essentially tied to the context, and it characterizes the context as institutional. What is meant by the claim that the essential background is institutional?

Everything at every moment exists within a context, i.e., the elements to which the thing stands in relation, and these elements range from stars to persons to bits of dust. Within this wholesale context there are specific contexts: all those elements to which a thing is gravitationally attracted, all those elements to which a thing is genetically related, all those elements to which a thing has legal commitments, and so on. These individual contexts have to be specified in some way.

The relevant context of works of art may be called "the artworld." The first thing to be noted about the artworld is that it is something which persists through time; it is a cultural pattern which the persons who fulfill the various artworld roles learn and pass on to others. In short, the artworld is a practice of human beings.

Not all practices, however, are institutional in nature. For example, the practice of dog-walking is not institutional, but the practice of promising is.

The relevant difference between these two practices is that the first is not rule-governed, while the second is. The various artworld activities, like promising, are rule-governed. Consider first the art-*making* part of the artworld. Earlier it was claimed that artifactuality is a necessary condition of art; this implies the rule: if one wishes to make a work of art, one must do so by creating an artifact. Art-*making* is not the only facet of the artworld; there are artworld publics which are also governed by rules. For example, at a traditional theater performance, members of the audience are forbidden from participating in the action of the play. In addition to rules which restrict audience behavior, there are conventions which are rule-like in that they guide audience attention; for example, the dimming of the lights which signals that the play is about to begin or recommence. There are many such rules and conventions which apply to the various artworld publics, that is, to theater audiences, art museum visitors, and the like. In addition to observing the rules and taking account of conventions, members of an artworld public have to have certain abilities (for example, the ability to see representations in visual designs) and sensitivities (for example, color vision), as well as a general background knowledge of the art form for which they are the public.

The core of the artworld consists of art-making (the artist's role) and "art-consuming" (the public's role). In addition to this essential core, there are supplementary artworld roles of various sorts: theater managers, museum curators, critics, art historians, and so on. At the very end of this line are the philosophers of art.

Earlier the artifact rule of art-making was mentioned. Now that the role of a public has been discussed, the second art-making rule can be stated: if one wishes to make a work of art, one must do so by creating a thing of a kind which is presented to an artworld public. These two rules are jointly sufficient for making works of art. The first thing to note about the second rule is that the notion of a public is made essential to the notion of a work of art. The second thing is that the rule does not require that a work of art actually be presented to anyone, but specifies only that it is a thing of a *kind* which is presented to a public. Many poems, paintings, and other works of art are never shown to anyone.

The artworld then is a historically developed, cultural institution (practice), and its large-scale divisions are artworld systems: theater, painting, literature, and so on. Within each system there are artist's roles and public's roles. Contained within each system is a body of works of art which have been produced by the system's artists and which are "aimed" at the system's public.

The institutional theory of art sees works of art as objects which exist and have a place within a web of cultural relations. The relations which make up this intricate web constitute a "thick" context as contrasted with the "thin" contexts of the traditional theories of art.

The Possibility of Art

TED COHEN

Among recent efforts to say what art is, one of the most salubrious is George Dickie's "Defining Art."[1] Like much of Dickie's best work, this essay is brief, direct, and convincing in the way it uncomplicates what philosophers have made murky. This time, however, I think he has tried to make things more simple and ingenuous than they can be. The definition Dickie presents and argues for is this:

> A work of art in the descriptive sense is (1) an artifact (2) upon which some society or some sub-group of a society has conferred the status of candidate for appreciation [p. 254*b*].

This definition is introduced early in Dickie's essay, and the rest of the essay is given to elucidating and defending it. Instead of summarizing here all Dickie has to say, I will quote relevant passages in the course of my criticism. At the beginning, however, it may be helpful to note three special features of Dickie's thesis.

(1) The somewhat checkered history of attempts to define art is usually seen as a series of specifications of art-making properties. These properties, though subtle and sometimes relational, have been understood to be properties the eye can descry. The definitions which require these properties of artworks are widely thought to have been discredited, if not by earlier examples, by the onslaught of problematic cases and counterexamples supplied by twentieth-century art. Each definition (for example, "Art is imitation, or expression, or significant form, or symbolic feeling") seems either to founder straightway, since many obvious artworks do not display the allegedly necessary property, or to retreat into insignificance, since the property it cites cannot be seen and is presumed to be present only because the objects are artworks. Dickie aims from the outset to specify a property which cannot be found merely by inspecting a putative artwork. He says:

> What the eye cannot descry is a complicated non-exhibited characteristic of the artifacts in question [p. 254*a*].

The idea is that the property required by the second condition of the definition is to be, as Dickie calls it, a social property, a non-exhibited status obtained within an institution.

Ted Cohen, "The Possibility of Art: Remarks on a Proposal by Dickie," *Philosophical Review* Vol. 82, No. 1, reprinted by permission of *Philosophical Review* and Ted Cohen.

---

[1]George Dickie, "Defining Art," *American Philosophical Quarterly*, 6 (1969), 253–256. All references to Dickie are to this essay and I will give page numbers parenthetically in the body of the text, using '*a*' and '*b*' to refer to the left and right columns of the pages.

(2) Since the eighteenth century there have been a number of definitions of art in terms of something like appreciation. Conceptions of appreciation have varied and so has the strategy of the definition. Usually some minimal requirement is given—for instance, that a thing be an artifact—and then it is held that appreciation of the thing is a necessary or sufficient condition of its being an artwork. The principal refinements have consisted in making the condition more subtle—requiring that a thing be likely to be appreciated, or that it be intended to be appreciated, or that it should be appreciated. Dickie's second condition is subtle enough to transform the character of this kind of definition. All questions of actual appreciation are waived. What is required is that a thing be a candidate for appreciation, and actually being appreciated is neither necessary nor sufficient for that.

(3) Dickie agrees with Morris Weitz in distinguishing two senses—or uses, as he sometimes says—of the term "work of art," an evaluative sense and a descriptive sense. Thus the initial qualification in the definition. Dickie is interested in the expression "work of art" only in its descriptive sense, and he has little to say about its evaluative sense. He does invoke the evaluative sense as an explanation of the propriety of remarks like "This driftwood is a work of art" which precludes their being counterexamples to the requirement that works of art be artifacts. Dickie holds that the descriptive and evaluative senses are distinct at least to this extent, that both artifacts and nonartifacts can be works of art in the descriptive sense. Furthermore, works of art in the descriptive sense need not be works of art in the evaluative sense. So being a work of art in one sense is neither necessary nor sufficient for being so in the other sense.

The third feature of the definition is less novel than the others. I mention it because I will claim, toward the end of my criticism, that Dickie's determination to keep out of the definition everything he takes to be a matter of merit has left his conception of art too spare.

The definition falls short, so to speak, both formally and materially, and it is the second condition which is defective. Despite the careful reference to candidacy for appreciation, and not to appreciation itself, we must be told something about appreciation—enough at least to give content to the notion of candidacy. Materially, what Dickie says about appreciation is too strong, even though very general; formally, it lacks a dimension without which it is not acute enough to discriminate art from other things.

What Appreciation Is

Dickie first says:

> The kind of appreciation I have in mind is simply the kind characteristic of our experiences of paintings, novels, and the like [p. 255a].

One may wonder whether there is such a kind of appreciation, and I believe there is not. It seems to me it is already too much to suppose that there is a kind of appreciation characteristic of our experiences of, say, Rembrandt, Cézanne, Pollock, Olitski, "and the like." But Dickie thinks this can be overcome.

> Indeed, if we mean by "appreciation" something like "in experiencing the qualities of a thing one finds them worthy or valuable," then there is no problem about the similarity of the various appreciations [p. 255a].

This suggestion fails to meet the one case Dickie speaks much about, that of Duchamp. Dickie calls Duchamp's "Fountain" a work of art with no hesitation, and I think he believes it a substantial achievement of his definition that it easily accommodates things like the works of Dada. But does it? I agree that whatever Dada's practitioners thought, their accomplishment was not simply the creation of Un-art. It was, however, the creation of something *different*. In understanding this I am inclined to follow Michael Fried, who has said this:

> the situation has been complicated still further by the calling into question, first by Dada and within the past decade by Neo-Dada figures such as Cage, Johns and Rauschenberg, of the already somewhat dubious concept of a "work of art." . . . It would, however, be mistaken to think of Dada—the most precious of movements—as opposed to art. Rather, Dada stands opposed to the notion of *value* or *quality* in art, and in that sense represents a reaction against the unprecedented demands modernist painting makes of its practitioners. (It is, I think, significant that Duchamp was a failed modernist—more exactly, a failed Cubist—before he turned his hand to the amusing inventions by which he is best known.) But there is a superficial similarity between modernist painting and Dada in one important respect: namely, that just as modernist painting has enabled one to see a blank canvas, a sequence of random spatters or a length of colored fabric as a picture, Dada and Neo-Dada have equipped one to treat virtually any object as a work of art—though it is far from clear exactly what this means.[2]

Whether or not one agrees with Fried, it seems clear that the "appreciation" of Dada was and is novel: If Fried is right, then to speak of Dada in terms of experiencing qualities one finds worthy or valuable is exactly wrong. Even if Fried is wrong, surely the one obvious point about Dada is that it is not the occasion for appreciation of the "kind characteristic of our experiences of paintings, novels, and the like." Of course Dickie has not said that Dada

---

[2]Michael Fried, the catalogue essay for *Three American Painters*, an exhibition of Noland, Olitski, and Stella, Fogg Art Museum, Harvard University, 1965, p. 47.

is, or is to be, appreciated in this way, but that it has acquired the status of being a candidate for such appreciation. But Dada in general, and certainly Duchamp's urinal, is virtually accompanied by an announcement that traditional appreciation (if there is such a thing) cannot occur. This suggests two things: (1) that being a candidate for appreciation in any but the emptiest sense of "appreciation" (where it signifies any kind of apprehension appropriate to anything which is an artwork) is not part of what it is to be an artwork, at least not for some works, and (2) that possibilities concerning what *can* be appreciated have some bearing on what can be made a candidate for appreciation. The second point is not considered by Dickie, and this is responsible for what I think of as a formal gap in his definition.

What Can Be a Work of Art

The second condition Dickie calls a "social property" of art (p. 253*b*). This idea, that part of what makes a thing a work of art is, so to speak, an institutionalized property, is the genuinely novel feature of Dickie's definition. The idea is present in recent works by Danto and Wollheim,[3] but I find it clearest in Dickie's essay and I shall confine myself to his definition. There are two broad areas for questions about how a thing acquires the social property which makes it art: in what circumstances and by whom can this property be bestowed, and what qualifies a thing to receive this bestowal. In the first area I have some more or less standard questions which are not altogether rhetorical for I, at least, do not see how to answer them on the basis of Dickie's remarks. The second area is more important since there I think Dickie does not see any questions to be answered.

If part of what makes a thing a work of art issues from an "institution" or "social practice," then we need to be told something of the details of the institution. There is merit enough in articulating the claim that artness is partly an institutional property—if that is true, and I do not mean to badger Dickie about the details. As he says,

> lines of authority in the politico-legal world are by and large explicitly defined and incorporated into law, while lines of authority (or something like authority) in the artworld are nowhere codified. The artworld carries on its business at the level of customary practice [p. 255*a*].

What Dickie says about this customary practice, however, leaves things more confusing than they might have been if he had simply referred such a practice and left it at that. Dickie sees a difference between a plumbing equipment

---

[3]Arthur Danto, "The Artworld," *Journal of Philosophy,* 61 (1964), 571–584; Richard Wollheim, *Art and Its Objects* (New York, 1968), esp. sec. 46, and "Minimal Art," *Arts Magazine,* 39 (1965), 26–32. Dickie cites Danto's paper as a stimulus to his own view.

salesman displaying his wares and Duchamp exhibiting his urinal, which he elucidates in this way:

> The difference is analogous to the difference between my uttering "I declare this man to be a candidate for alderman" and the head of the election board uttering the same sentence while acting in his official capacity [p. 255a].

But there is some ambiguity here: whose enfranchisement are we concerned with, some museum director's or Duchamp's? That Dickie means the former, or at least that he does not mean Duchamp, is suggested by this—

> The point is that Duchamp's act took place within a certain institutional setting and that makes all the difference. Our salesman of plumbing supplies could do what Duchamp did [p. 255b]—

and by his remark concerning a different case, "It all depends on the institutional setting" (p. 256a).

If Dickie is read this way, then his analogy is strikingly inept, for it is precisely not the case that our Dickie could do what the head of the election board did (make someone an aldermanic candidate). What the analogy suggests is that to make something art, one first must be an artmaker. I suspect that the analogy appeals to Dickie because it sets making-a-candidate-for-election beside making-a-candidate-for-appreciation. But it is clear that one needs status to bestow status in the political case. What about the case of art? What about the interchangeability of Duchamp and the plumbing supplier? What if a urinal merchant or a junk collector had attempted to carry out Duchamp's act, say with the very object Duchamp used, and had been turned away by the organizers of the show? Is that all there is to it: the urinal did not become art because it did not receive the requisite social property, though it received it later when Duchamp brought it around; and the only way in which Duchamp's being Duchamp figures is contingently (since the organizers knew him, they accepted his urinal)? Well, then what if Duchamp had been rejected as well? If he had then just sulked, that might be an end to it. But what if he displayed the rejected urinal in his own flat, set it out on a roped-off rug in the living room? Does that turn the trick? Then could the merchant do the same?

These are bewildering questions, and they become more annoying if we switch Duchamp and the salesman in the other direction. Suppose it is Duchamp who comes to your home, where perhaps you are in need of plumbing fixtures, and sets before you a number of objects, including the urinal. Now what? Dickie's account of appreciation does not help. Dickie notes (p. 255a) that the ordinary salesman is presenting his wares for appreciation, but insists that he is not conferring on them the status of candidate for appreciation. But he *could* be doing both things, couldn't he? Couldn't Duchamp? Suppose that Picasso came to your house hawking his paintings, and didn't care what you did with them. Or better, since you may believe that Picasso's paintings were already art before he got to your house, suppose that he came and was commissioned by you to do a sketch directly on the wall in order to disguise some cracks in the plaster. That would be art, wouldn't it? And if it is when Picasso does it, why not when the neighborhood painter and plasterer do it? And if Duchamp's urinal is art just as readily for having been brought to your house as for having gotten into the show, why not the salesman's?

Before his discussion of Duchamp and the salesman, Dickie offers an adroit remark to help in accepting the notion of a "conferral of status" when it is clear that for much art this cannot be said to occur overtly (some artists never exhibit).

> What I want to suggest is that, just as two persons can acquire the status of common-law marriage within a legal system, an artifact can acquire the status of a candidate for appreciation within the system which Danto has called "the artworld" [p. 254b].

Then how is it that Picasso's merest scribble and, perhaps, Duchamp's urinal have a status not possessed by just anyone's mere scribble or spare urinal? Perhaps it is like this: one of the ways the "artworld" breeds Art is by way of enfranchising Artmakers. Anyone who did "Nude Descending a Staircase" and the rest would be an Artmaker (however good), but only an Artmaker could make that urinal Art (if it is art). It is because he did "Nude" that Duchamp is an artist: it is because he is Duchamp that "Fountain" is not just a misplaced urinal.

This idea suggests that art and its institutions are inbred and self-justifying in ways that are hard to untangle, and I think that is plausible though I will not argue for it. It seems clear that Dickie does not agree with this. He says, after all, that the salesman could do what Duchamp did, and there is no suggestion that to do this the salesman must first acquire a power Duchamp already has. And, as noted, on this count the creation of an aldermanic candidate is a poor analogue (even Mayor Daley cannot make a man a candidate for alderman: he must make the election board make the man a candidate). The creation of a political candidate, like the act of christening, which Dickie refers to and which I will discuss later, seems an apt analogue of artmaking only so long as only one aspect is considered. In both artmaking and candidate-making there exist constraints in terms of the objects. The head of the election board cannot make just anyone a candidate. Typically there will be a minimum age, a residence requirement, a stipulation that there be no criminal record, a requirement that there be nominating petitions signed by some number of registered voters, and so on. Perhaps Dickie supposes his account of artmaking supplies an analogue for all this in the first condition, that the object be an artifact. But something is missing. There is nothing to

match the connection between the qualifications imposed on a would-be alderman and the point in making someone a candidate for alderman. The qualifications, which the election board is bound to impose, derive from
considerations of what aldermen do or are supposed to do. There is no doubt
a blending together of considerations of what aldermen do and what they do
well, but that need not be gone into. What connection of any kind is there
between being an artifact and being appreciated? Why is it that only artifacts
can be made candidates for appreciation, and, more important, why suppose
that every artifact can be made such a candidate? This problem, and the
failure of analogy in Dickie's failure to say anything about constraints in terms
of the artmaker (about who can make something art as only a deputized
official can make someone a political candidate), lead me to abandon Dickie's
own analogy. If we are to get to the subtleties implicit in Dickie's suggestion,
we need a different analogue for the act of making something art, one in
which a distinction appears, not between having a power and not having it
(as the head of the election board has a power not possessed by others), but
between exercising a power we all have and not exercising it (Like Duchamp's
act which Dickie thinks anyone could have carried out). I believe that Dickie
thinks we are all, or nearly all, in the artworld and that in the artworld
everyone is empowered to make art. A suitable analogue may illuminate what
limits the exercise of this power.

I take the act of conferring the status of candidate for appreciation to
be (or to be like) what Austin called an illocution, or what he earlier might
have called a performative.[4] The analogue chosen by Dickie, declaring someone a candidate in the uttering of certain words, is an illocution. To improve
on it, we need a different illocution. I will use the act of promising, though
it too is an imprecise analogue in some respects. There are a number of
obscurities in our understanding of the mechanics of promising, but that is a
help here, for it exposes the complexities that arise when we move from
formalized rituals and ceremonial acts like christening and political licensing
to less canonical ones like promising and, as Dickie thinks, making things
art. Before getting back to the definition of art, I need to use promising to
illustrate a point about illocutions which is not reflected in Dickie's conception
of what is required to make art.

The act of promising accomplished in the saying of "I promise . . ." in
appropriate circumstances is an illocution. Characteristically, this illocution
precipitates various effects and consequences Austin calls perlocutions. Among
possible perlocutions are, for instance, the recipient's feeling gratified in some
way, his attributing to the speaker an intention to do what is promised, his
acting in ways commensurate with or dependent on the speaker's doing what

---

[4]The outlines of Austin's conceptions of illocutions and perlocutions are, I hope, familiar enough
not to need rehearsing here, and it is only a general account that I am concerned with. For
Austin's detailed account see his William James Lectures, published as *How to Do Things with
Words* (Cambridge, Mass., 1962), esp. pp. 98 ff.

is promised. Though it oversimplifies things, I ask you to think of all these consequences or effects as one perlocution, a kind of generic response I will call "accepting" a promise. Promising is an illocution; having a promise accepted is a perlocution. In the case of promising and securing acceptance, the illocution and the perlocution are associated, I think, on two levels: as a relation between promising and acceptance in general, and as a constraint on promising in particular instances.

In general, the perlocution is something like the rationale, or part of the rationale, for the illocution. It constitutes a general reason, a reason *überhaupt,* for performing the illocution—it gives the act a point. As Kant noted, if there is no acceptance of promises, then the act of promising becomes not merely a vain effort, but it ceases to be that kind of act—it ceases to be promising. This is not to say that there must be acceptance in every case, that there is no such thing as an unaccepted promise. The perlocution is detachable from the illocution in particular cases. But something does follow with regard to individual cases.

In any particular case it must be possible, or at least appear to those concerned to be possible, that the perlocution transpire. It is, so to speak, in the nature of the illocution to effect the perlocution, and if it is obvious to those involved that this effect cannot occur, then the illocution is in some way and to some degree abortive. That is why I cannot promise you something we both know, and know one another knows that I cannot deliver. There may be *some* point in my giving my word knowing you know that I cannot keep it, but it cannot be a point usual in cases of giving one's word, and so I am not simply "giving my word—period."

Sometimes I cannot do an illocution because the illocutionary act is not open to do. I cannot christen a ship I have already christened nor marry you if you are already my wife. The illocution has been pre-empted. The pre-empting need not have been done by me: I cannot hire you if my partner has already signed you on, or arrest you if the sheriff has just booked you. But sometimes the illocution is no longer open because the associated perlocution has already been effected, whether or not by means of an illocution. For instance, I cannot argue the point with you if you are already persuaded, or warn you of a danger to which you are already alerted, or point out something you already see. Whether I can do these things is, perhaps, problematic if I am ignorant of what has already happened, but it seems clear that I cannot do them if I know that you are already persuaded, alert, or aware.

I take it as a kind of rule of thumb that the availability of at least some illocutions requires the openness of their associated perlocutions. The perlocution must be neither known to be already effected nor known to be clearly out of the question.

Let me import these points about perlocutions into Dickie's definition. I construe the act of conferring the status of a candidate for appreciation to be like an illocution, and I take the actual appreciation of a thing with this status to be like an associated perlocution. Being appreciated is neither a necessary nor a sufficient condition for something's being a candidate for appreciation, just as having what I say (about what I will do) accepted is neither necessary nor sufficient for its being a promise. But if what I say is a promise, then it must seem possible that it be accepted. And (supposing Dickie's definition correct), if I am to succeed in conferring the status of art on an object, it must seem possible that it be appreciated. My utterance is not a promise just because I say so, just because it has the form "I promise. . . ." (I cannot promise that I was on time yesterday, or that it will rain tomorrow.) And neither, I think, is x a work of art just because I say so. There are substantive constraints on what I can promise (however difficult it may be to formulate them), and there must be constraints on what I can make art. But what are they? Dickie names one—x must be an artifact.[5] But this is not enough. What of an artifact which clearly cannot be appreciated (in Dickie's sense)? I say that there are such things—for instance, ordinary thumbtacks, cheap white envelopes, the plastic forks given at some drive-in restaurants—and that if Dickie's definition were correct then these things could not be artworks because they could not receive the requisite status. Duchamp's urinal is like that. Things like that cannot acquire the status required by Dickie's second condition because it would be pointless or bizarre to give it to them.

Dickie's concrete mistake has been to suppose that Duchamp's "Fountain" has anything whatever to do with what Dickie calls appreciation. If such eccentric works are art, then if that requires that they have something in common with traditional art, it is not a candidacy for what they were designed to forestall and disdain. This material error is a symptom of a more formal, conceptual gap—namely, supposing that making something a candidate for appreciation can be altogether unilateral, so that any thing whatever could become a candidate upon someone's say-so. In fact, the untoward consequence of Dickie's suggestion is that it will rule out the very items Dickie is eager to accommodate. But then what about "Fountain"? Is Duchamp's "Fountain" a work of art, and Dickie's definition wrong because it misses this work, or is Dickie right and so "Fountain" not art? Neither of these choices is a healthy one. I am not clear about whether "Fountain" is a work of art, just like that. I am not as confident as either Dickie or Fried about this. If Fried is right, in the aftermath of Dada we are able to count nearly anything a work of art—but, he says, this leaves it unclear what it means to count something as a work of art. What is wrong with Dickie's definition, I think, is that as Dickie takes it, it is clear and it clearly applies to "Fountain." No definition should fit "Fountain" so comfortably. Why not takes some explaining.

To say that an illocution must be "pointless" if its associated perlocution

---

[5] I have completely recast Dickie's formulation, so that it calls for an illocution to be done and imposes one constraint on the circumstances appropriate to that kind of illocution. I should point out that Dickie has a different model in mind. He takes himself to be giving a definition by genus (artifactuality) and differentia (candidacy for appreciation).

is not open is not quite right. There can be a *point* in saying "I promise to love you forever" or "I promise never to feel anger again." Indeed, saying these things can be splendid ways, perhaps the only ways, of saying and doing some things. But that does not make these sayings promises (I think they cannot be promises because these things cannot be promised). Similarly, there can be a point, I suppose, in invoking a formula for bestowing the status of candidate for appreciation on a thing which cannot be an object of appreciation. But that will not give these things that status. In both kinds of cases, as with "pointless" illocutions in general, the effect is to draw attention from the thing said (or the putative object of appreciation) to the act of saying it (or the act of exhibiting it). If Austin is right, we cannot entirely separate the saying and the said without distortion, but we can identify, so to speak, the locus of significance and import: if the situation is normal and altogether unproblematic, the thing uttered (or the object of appreciation) engages us; if the situation is in certain ways remarkable, then however canonical the thing uttered seems, we will pass behind it to its genesis. What significance we can find in "Fountain" we find not in the urinal but in Duchamp's gesture. It is not that "Fountain" is simply a candidate for appreciation which cannot be appreciated (nor is "I promise to love you forever" simply a promise which cannot be accepted); its transparent resistance to appreciation is the sign that it is not simply a candidate for appreciation (as the fact that love cannot be promised is the sign that this utterance is not simply a promise).

It is not only the questionable conception of appreciation which undermines Dickie's definition. Let us ignore that for a while. At the end of his essay Dickie says:

> Now what I have been saying may sound like saying, "a work of art is an object of which someone has said, 'I christen this object a work of art.'" And I think it is rather like that. So one *can* make a work of art out of a sow's ear, but of course that does not mean that it is a silk purse [p. 256*b*].

What I have been arguing is that it cannot be this simple: even if in the end it is successful christening which makes an object art, not every effort at christening is successful. There are bound to be conditions to be met both by the namer and the thing to be named, and if they are completely unsatisfied, then saying "I christen . . ." will not be to christen. If making a thing art is like an ordinary illocution, then there are prior constraints. Austin's characteristic way of describing a kind of act or thing was to catalogue the dimensions in which it can be irregular. Thus a promise might be untoward, gauche, imprudent, impractical, ineffective, or unaccepted. As we move through various departures from the normal, pedestrian cases, passing through all the gross irregularities Austin called "infelicities," we come eventually to cases which are no longer promises. The boundary between non-promises and more or less failed promises is hard to locate, but (1) it exists, and (2) it is not identical with the boundary between utterances of the form "I promise . . ." and those without it, for this form is neither necessary nor sufficient. If artmaking is like an illocution, then a similar catalogue is in order, an account of the ways in which artmaking can be irregular. I do not blame Dickie for not yet supplying such a catalogue. I do complain that he has not noted the importance of such a catalogue, for if artmaking is simply a matter of informal illocutions, then the catalogue may be the only substantial definition we can get or need. There must be a boundary, however hard to chart, between making art, and trying but failing to make art. Dickie cannot account for this, because the difference is not simply the difference between objects which have been called art (or candidates for appreciation) and those which have not.

Duchamp's "Fountain" is a difficult case. It is difficult in the adjustment it demands of us, but neither of the two adjustments likely to be suggested is in order. One is to give up defining art, pointing to "Fountain" as an illustration of the inevitable failure of any definition. The other is to formulate a definition which covers "Fountain" as neatly as "Nude." Perhaps the most helpful part of Dickie's view is the implicit suggestion of a way to avoid this choice. Instead of either of these responses, I think we must give up the compulsion to *decide* about "Fountain," to rule it in or out; and I think we can do this by taking seriously the suggestion that whether "Fountain" is art depends upon whether and how a certain kind of act was performed.

Succeeding in getting "Fountain" under, or out from under, the term "art" is a delusive achievement: for the sake of a kind of ontological tidiness, most of what is interesting and instructive about "Fountain" is ignored. What we need to discuss are the ways in which "Fountain" is very much like normal art and the ways in which it is altogether unlike normal art, and then how this bears on the character of Duchamp's act of putting it forward and having it called art. When that discussion is done, nothing may be left to do. So it is with promising. Some cases are clearly promises, some clearly are not. Some are unclear. The unclear cases illuminate the clear ones as they bring out parts of the conception according to which the clear cases are clear. "I promise to wring your neck." Not a promise: I cannot promise what you do not want, knowing you do not want it. "I promise to keep all cigarettes out of your reach." This is not clear. Can I promise you something we agree you need even if we both know you do not want it? The hard thing to do is to hold on to the conviction that we know what art and promises are while refusing to suppose that we always can decide or need to decide.

Dickie and others have criticized earlier theories for having lost the good art/bad art distinction, often, as with Collingwood, willfully absorbing it into the very distinction between art and non-art. Ironically, Dickie has effectively reversed this: he has provided for room on the bad art side of the good art/bad art distinction for much of what is normally taken to be non-art. He says:

> Please remember that when I say "Fountain" is a work of art, I am not saying it is a good one. And in making this last remark I am not insinuating that it is a bad one either [p. 255*b*].

This is the view Dickie proposes to take of any object whatever. From this view the real difficulty, the philosophical anguish, will arise after the question of art has been settled, and that question is never more than a nominal problem encountered occasionally because "lines of authority (or something like authority) in the artworld are nowhere codified" (p. 255*a*) and so it may be hard to discover whether the thing has been christened. This view obscures too much. The works of the painters Fried discusses (Stella, Noland, Olitski) are clearly works of art, and the serious questions about them concern what kinds of paintings they are, and whether and why they are good. But there are very few such questions about "Fountain," most Dada works, and many contemporary works. The questions about them concern exactly whether and why they are art, and how they became anything like art. To make these questions easy is both to mistake the nature of these objects and to refuse to take seriously the question of the possibility of the creation of art.

ILLUSTRATION 21

FRANZ KLINE, *White Forms*, 1955.

Collection of the
Museum of Modern Art
New York.

ILLUSTRATION 22

when god lets my body be

e. e. cummings

when god lets my body be

From each brave eye shall sprout a tree
fruit that dangles therefrom

the purpled world will dance upon
Between my lips which did sing

a rose shall beget the spring
that maidens whom passion wastes

will lay between their little breasts
My strong fingers beneath the snow

Into strenuous birds shall go
my love walking in the grass

their wings will touch with her face
and all the while shall my heart be

With the bulge and nuzzle of the sea

ILLUSTRATION 23

Molly's Monologue from *Ulysses*

JAMES JOYCE

Yes because he never did a thing like that before as ask to get his breakfast
in bed with a couple of eggs since the *City Arms* hotel when he used to be
pretending to be laid up with a sick voice doing his highness to make himself
interesting to that old faggot Mrs Riordan that he thought he had a great leg
of and she never left us a farthing all for masses for herself and her soul
greatest miser ever was actually afraid to lay out 4d for her methylated spirit
telling me all her ailments she had too much old chat in her about politics

and earthquakes and the end of the world let us have a bit of fun first God help the world if all the women were her sort down on bathingsuits and lownecks of course nobody wanted her to wear I suppose she was pious because no man would look at her twice I hope Ill never be like her a wonder she didnt want us to cover our faces but she was a welleducated woman certainly and her gabby talk about Mr Riordan here and Mr Riordan there I suppose he was glad to get shut of her and her dog smelling my fur and always edging to get up under my petticoats especially then still I like that in him polite to old women like that and waiters and beggars too hes not proud out of nothing but not always if ever he got anything really serious the matter with him its much better for them to go into a hospital where everything is clean but I suppose Id have to dring it into him for a month yes and then wed have a hospital nurse next thing on the carpet have him staying there till they throw him out or a nun maybe like the smutty photo he has shes as much a nun as Im not yes because theyre so weak and puling when theyre sick they want a woman to get well if his nose bleeds youd think it was O tragic and that dyinglooking one off the south circular when he sprained his foot at the choir party at the sugarloaf Mountain the day I wore that dress Miss Stack bringing him flowers the worst old ones she could find at the bottom of the basket anything at all to get into a mans bedroom with her old maids voice trying to imagine he was dying on account of her to never see thy face again though he looked more like a man with his beard a bit grown in the bed . . .

ILLUSTRATION 24

MARCEL DUCHAMP, *The Fountain*, 1915.

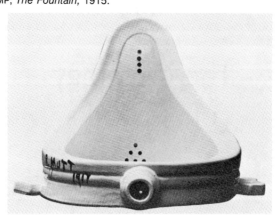

ILLUSTRATION 25

SUZANNE HARDING, *A Piece of Driftwood*, 1980.

12

The Ontology
of Artworks

Jeffrey Maitland, a contemporary aesthetician whose paper is included in this chapter, attacks the question of whether art can be defined from an entirely different point of view than philosophers in Chapter 11. Maitland suggests that the question of what is common and unique to art is, as Wittgenstein argued, unanswerable. Rather than appeal to an institutional analysis of art, however, Maitland proposes that the question, "What is a work of art?" should be reformulated in terms of an ontology of art. By this statement Maitland means that we should explore what sorts of phenomena works of art are, and we should examine what is peculiar to their ways of being or existing. Such explorations might yield what has heretofore escaped aestheticians: a definition or definitions of art in terms of its exhibited or inherent features.

Adopting an ontological perspective, Nicolas Wolterstorff, in his article "Toward an Ontology of Art Works," discusses what sorts of entities works of art are by examining all kinds of art forms. Wolterstorff notices that works of art are not alike in their modes of existing. For example, an oil painting is a one-of-a-kind object which cannot be reproduced in its original form. Such reproductions are "copies" or "fakes." Novels, on the other hand, can be reproduced in their original form any number of times. A piece of printed music such as Schöenberg's *Verkläerte Nacht* (Illustration 26) is not music until, and only when, it is performed. Wolterstorff argues that art forms are "norm-kinds" according to which one may group works in terms of their modes of presentation or reproduction in their original form. Wolterstorff analyzes how each form of art differs from other art forms in the ways in which works in each art form exist and present themselves. And thus one must define each form differently because of its unique ontological nature.

Maitland himself develops another kind of approach to an ontological point of view. Maitland concludes that all works of art have one shared distinct ontological characteristic: all works of art are what Maitland calls "performance presences." Maitland means, in brief, that art works of any kind do not merely exist as objects. Rather, works of art have an active "workly character." Because works of art are symbolic presentations of the artist's world or of his view of the world, all works of art are performances of the artist's perspective on this world. And thus, as such a presentation, the work of art actively interchanges with, or performs for, its viewers or audience. Whether Maitland has moved from an analysis of how works of art exist to setting up a criterion (performance presence) for evaluating art is left to the consideration of the reader. Nevertheless his analysis gives us new insights to the question, "What is a work of art?"

Toward an Ontology of Art Works

NICOLAS WOLTERSTORFF

What sort of entity is a symphony? A drama? A dance? A graphic art print? A sculpture? A poem? A film? A painting?

Are works of art all fundamentally alike in their ontological status?

These are the questions to be discussed in this paper.

A Phenomenology of the Distinctions Among Works of Art

In several of the arts there is application for the distinction between a performance of something and that which is performed. In music, for example, one can distinguish between a performance of *Verklärte Nacht* and that which is thereby performed, namely, Arnold Schöenberg's work *Verklärte Nacht*. Similarly, in dance one can distinguish between a performance of *Swan Lake* and that which is thereby performed, namely, the ballet *Swan Lake*.

Some people will be skeptical as to whether, in the cases cited and others of the same sort, we really do have two distinct entities—a performance and that which is performed. But assuming it to be true that the concept of a performance of something and the concept of something performed both have application to the arts, there are two sorts of considerations which force one to the conclusion that that which is performed on a given occasion is distinct from the performance of it.

In the first place, a thing performed and a performance thereof will

Excerpts from Nicolas Wolterstorff, "Toward an Ontology of Art Works," *Nous* 9 (1975).

always diverge in certain of their properties. For example, *having been composed by Schöenberg* is a property of *Verkläerte Nacht* but not of any performance of *Verkläerte Nacht*. On the other hand, *taking place at a certain time and place* is a property of every performance of *Verkläerte Nacht* but not of *Verkläerte Nacht* itself. It is worth noting that a work performed may diverge from performances thereof not only in "ontological" properties but also in "aesthetic" properties. For example, it may be that *having the voice part begin on A natural* is not a property of any performance of Schöenberg's *Pierrot Lunaire,* though it is a property of the work itself, indeed, an *essential* one.

A second sort of consideration, one which is actually a specific application of the first, also leads to the conclusion that in certain of the arts one must distinguish between those entities which are performances and those entities which are works performed. This second sort of consideration hinges on applications of the concepts of identity and diversity. That which is performed on one occasion may be identical with that which is performed on another; George Szell, for example, may twice over have conducted a performance of *Verkläerte Nacht*. Thus, there may be two distinct performances of one single musical work. But two distinct things cannot each be identical with some one thing. Thus, the two distinct performances cannot both be identical with the work performed. But if one of them, call it *A,* was identified with the work performed, then the other, call it *B,* would, by virtue of being a performance of the work performed, be a performance of performance *A*. Not only that, but performance *A* would be capable of being performed on many other occasions as well. Both of these consequences, however, seem impossible.

Let us henceforth call a work of art which can be performed, a *performance-work*. Most if not all performance-works are universals, in that they can be multiply performed.

It would seem that performances in the arts are as correctly called "works of art" as are performance-works. The ontological status of performances is relatively clear, however, while that of performance-works is immensely perplexing. Performances are occurrences or events. They take place at a certain time and place, begin at a certain time and end at a certain time, last for a certain stretch of time, and have temporal parts in the sense that each performance is half over at a certain time, three-quarters over at a certain time, one-eighth over at a certain time, etc. But what sort of entity is a performance-work? That is something which we shall have to discuss in considerable detail. What should already be clear, though, is that performance-works are not occurrences (events). Thus, already we can answer one of our opening questions. Works of art are not all alike in their ontological status.

In certain of the non-performing arts distinctions similar to the performance/performance-work distinction have application. Consider, for example, graphic-art prints. Here, a commonly applied distinction is that between a particular impression and the work of which it is an impression; between, for example, the tenth impression of *Obedient unto Death* and the print of which it is an impression, namely, Georges Rouault's *Obedient unto Death*. And consider those cases in which sculpture is produced from a mold. Here, a commonly applied distinction is that between a particular casting of, say, *The Thinker* and the sculptural work of which it is a casting, namely, Rodin's *The Thinker*. And consider thirdly those cases in the field of architecture in which many different buildings are produced according to one set of specifications. Here, a commonly applied distinction is that between a given example of, say, the Tech-Bilt House No. 1 and that of which it is an example, namely, the Tech-Bilt House No. 1.

It may be noticed that an impression of a work of graphic art, a casting of a work of sculptural art, and an example of a work of architectural art are all enduring physical objects. This is why we have grouped these particular arts together. In order to have a convenient terminology, let us call the entities of which there can be impressions, castings, or examples, *object-works*. And let us say that impressions, castings, and examples are *objects of* object-works. Thus, as a counterpart to the performance/performance-work distinction, we have the distinction between impressions, castings, and examples on the one hand and object-works on the other.

The considerations which impel us to distinguish between an object-work and those entities which are objects thereof are parallel to those which impel us to distinguish between an entity which is a performance-work and those entities which are performances thereof. One consideration is again that of divergence in properties. For example, *having a thumb-print in the lower left corner* may be a property of a given impression of Rouault's print *Obedient unto Death,* or even of all impressions thereof, though it is not a property of the print *Obedient unto Death*. A second consideration is again to be derived from applications of the concepts of identity and diversity. For example, there can be two different castings of the same sculptural work; and neither both of these castings together nor either one singly can be identified with the work. In the case of object-works there is yet a third sort of consideration which may be adduced, one hinging on applications of the concepts of existence and non-existence. Any one of the several objects of an object-work can be destroyed without the object-work thereby being destroyed. I could, for example, perform the horrifying operation of burning my impression of Rouault's *Obedient unto Death,* but I would not thereby put the print itself out of existence. Nor could I put the print out of existence by destroying any one of the other impressions, nor even by destroying the original etched plate.

It would seem that both object-works and the objects thereof are entitled to being called "works of art." Further, the ontological status of the latter is relatively unproblematic: They are physical objects. Of course, plenty of things about the nature of physical objects remains unclear. Yet we know what they are, and it is clear that impressions, castings, and examples are to be numbered among them. But what is an object-work? What is *its* ontological status? That is something which we shall have to discuss in detail.

There remain literary works, films, and paintings to consider. A literary work can be both written down and "sounded out." There can be both copies of it and utterances of it. Now, a copy is a physical object, whereas an uttering of something is a certain sort of event. Further, the *copy of* relation seems closely similar to the *example of,* the *impression of,* and the *casting of* relations. Accordingly, I shall say that a copy of a literary work is an object of it; and I shall add literary works to the group of entities to be called object-works. Furthermore, an utterance of a literary work is an event, very much like a performance. Accordingly, in the class of things to be called performance-works I shall include also literary works. Literary works, then, are both performance-works and object-works.

Saying this, however, makes one want to look back to see whether we do not have good ground for saying that works of music and drama are also both performance-works and object-works. In the case of dramatic works I think it is clear that we must say "No." A dramatic performance is a pattern of actions. The actions will in all but the most unusual cases include speech actions. But in all but the most unusual cases they will include other sorts of actions as well. More importantly, that pattern of actions which is a dramatic performance will always include actions of *role-playing.* For these reasons, a reading aloud or a recitation of the script of a drama is not yet a performance of the drama. A copy of the script for a drama is not a copy of the drama but instructions for proper performances thereof. The script may of course be a literary work in its own right. And that work can have both readings aloud and copies. But the drama is not the script. And a copy of the script is not a copy of the drama. The drama has no copies. All it has is performances. Dramas are only performance-works.

Music presents a somewhat less clear situation. The crucial question is this: Does a copy of the score stand to a work of music in a relationship similar enough to that in which a copy stands to a work of literature to justify us in calling the score-copy an object of the work? It seems to me not decisively clear one way or the other. What does seem clear is that a word can be both written down and uttered aloud, whereas a sound cannot be written down but only sounded out. The marks in a copy of a score are not instances of sounds but rather instructions for producing sounds. Of course, an instance of some sequence of words can also be treated as instructions for the utterance of that sequence; yet at the same time it is genuinely an instance of those words. Some words, especially those in primitive cultures, are never written down; some, especially those in technical languages, are never sounded out.

Yet most words have a dual manifestation. The same is not true of sounds. But suppose someone suggests that music should be thought of as being composed of *notes* rather than sounds, and then goes on to argue that notes, like words, can be both sounded out and written down. Obviously, this is a suggestion worthy of further investigation. Whether it is true or false is not at once clear. But nothing that is said hereafter will depend essentially on whether or not it is true. So I shall continue to suppose that music consists of sounds.

The film seems to have a dual status similar to that of words. One and the same film may have many copies, a copy being a physical object; and it may also have many showings, a showing being an occurrence (event). Thus, a film, like a literary work, has claim to being regarded as both an object-work and a performance-work. There is this difference worth noting though: A showing of a film will always occur by way of the showing of a certain copy of the film, whereas the utterance of a literary work need not occur by way of the reading of some copy of the work. One can recite it from memory.

As for paintings, it seems that neither the object/object-work distinction nor the performance/performance-work distinction has application, nor does it seem that any close counterpart to these distinctions has application. There is, of course, the distinction between the work and reproductions of the work. But this is a quite different distinction, as can be seen from the fact that one can also have reproductions of each of the various impressions of a print. What is lacking in painting is any counterpart to the print/impression distinction. All one has is a counterpart to the impression/reproduction distinction. The point may be put by saying that all the impressions of a print are originals, none is a reproduction. The conclusion must be that a painting is a physical object. But more will be said on this matter later in our discussion.

To say this is not, of course, to deny that reproductions of paintings along with reproductions of sculpture are, in some cases at least, entitled to being called "works of art" in their own right. So too are films, though they are for the most part "reproductive" of performances and of visible events and objects. And so too are recordings, though most recordings are 'reproductive' of sounds and of audible performances. It is interesting to note however, that in the case of visual-art reproductions and sculpture reproductions one again often has application for the print/impression or the work/casting distinction, and that in the case of recordings (records) one can distinguish between the recordings on the one hand and the various discs of the recording on the other and, in turn, between a given disc on the one hand and various playings of the disc on the other.

Though I have called what we have done thus far *phenomenology,* what I have said is of course not free from ontological commitment. In saying that the distinction between performances and that which is performed can be applied to the arts, I said something which entails that there are performance-works. And I said that of most if not all of these it is true that they can be multiply performed. A thorough nominalist would deny that there are any multiply performable entities. Similarly, he would deny the existence of "multiply-objectible" entities. I think it would be worthwhile to consider how the nominalist conviction that there are no such entities might most plausibly be developed; and I also think it would be worthwhile to consider whether any decisive arguments against such nominalism can be offered. But I shall not on this occasion attempt either of these. Rather, the question which I wish to discuss in detail is this: What is the ontological status of performance-works and object-works?

To simplify our terminology, I shall henceforth in this paper call only performance-works and object-works *art works*. And both performances of art works and objects of art works will be called examples of art works. I shall continue to use "work of art" to cover both art works and their examples, along with such things as paintings which are neither. Perhaps here is also a good place to remark that the fact that the performance/performance-work distinction or the object/object-work distinction applies to a certain art does not imply that it applies *throughout* that art. There may be works of that art which are neither. Those works of music, for example, which are *total* improvisations (as distinguished from those which are improvisations on a theme) are neither performances nor performance-works.[1] . . .

Art Works Are Kinds

We have seen some of the fundamental relations which hold between an art work and its examples. But we have not yet gained much insight into the ontological status of art works. We are left so far without any satisfying answer to our question: What *is* an art work? We must take a next step.

The proposal I wish to make is that performance-works and object-works are *kinds (types, sorts)*—kinds whose examples are the performances or objects of those works. A performance-work is a certain kind of performance; an object-work is a certain kind of object.

A phenomenon which tends at once to confirm us in the suggestion that art works are kinds whose examples are the examples of those works is the fact that kinds which are not art works are like art works in just the ways

---

[1]The general drift of the distinctions made above has been acquiring something of a consensus in recent years among those who have concerned themselves with the nature of works of art. See Harrison [2], MacDonald [3], Margolis [4], Stevenson [5], Wellek and Warren [7], and Wollheim [8] in References at end of this reading.

that (as we saw earlier) sets of their examples are unlike art works. Just as an art work might have had different and more or fewer performances and objects than it does have, so too the kind Man, for example, might have had different and more or fewer examples than it does have. If Napoleon had not existed, it would not then have been the case that Man did not exist. Rather, Man would then have lacked one of the examples which in fact it had. And secondly, just as there may be two distinct unperformed symphonies, so too may there be two distinct unexampled kinds—e.g., the Unicorn and the Hippogriff.

Not only does it seem that art works are *kinds*. What is even more striking is their many close similarities to those special kinds of kinds familiarly known as *natural* kinds.

It has long been noticed by philosophers that in the case of natural kinds there is a pervasive sharing of predicates and/or properties between kinds and their examples. Let us look at the pattern of such sharing, beginning with a proposal made by Richard Wollheim. Having excluded from consideration those properties which cannot be shared between kinds and examples, his suggestion is that the following is necessarily true: The *K* shares a certain property with all *Ks* if and only if it is impossible that something should be an example of the *K* and lack the property ([8]: 64–65).

What must be clearly perceived about this formula is that it speaks of *properties,* not of predicates. And in many if not most cases, a sharing of a predicate does not have, underlying it, a sharing of a property for which the predicate stands. That property which a grizzly possesses, of *being something that growls,* is not a property which the Grizzly could possess. Once one sees this, it becomes clear that the formula has an extremely limited application. Cases of shared predicates are common. Cases in which those predicates stand for properties which can be shared are relatively uncommon. Thus, the formula gives very little insight into the relation between kinds and their examples. Perhaps it's true that all grizzlies growl. And certainly it is true that the Grizzly growls (though at the same time it's true that something can be an example of the Grizzly while being mute). Yet this is not a counterexample to the formula; because what the Grizzly's growling consists of cannot be identical with what a grizzly's growling consists of. The tenability of the formula with respect to such cases is bought at the price of giving us no illumination with respect to them.

Even so, however, there are rather obvious counterexamples of other sorts to the formula. It could happen that a certain kind would share with all its examples the property of *having been referred to by someone or other.* Yet most kinds are such that something *could* be an example of them and still lack this property.

But now consider once again the sentence "The Grizzly growls." Is it not the case that "growls" is true of the Grizzly if it is impossible that some-thing should be a *properly* formed grizzly and not growl? A grizzly muted is a malformed grizzly, and so also is a grizzly born without a growl. What makes "growls" true of the Grizzly is that something cannot be a properly formed grizzly unless it growls. In botanical and zoological taxonomy books, one is not told about the features shared by all examples of a certain kind, but about the features which a thing cannot lack if it is to be a properly formed example of the kind. So already we have for natural kinds the same pattern which we earlier uncovered for art works: For any predicate P which is acceptable with respect to the K, if there is some property *being P* which P expresses in normal usage and which is such that it is impossible that something should be a properly formed example of the K and lack *being P,* then P is true of the K.

As in the case of art works, we must raise the question whether when we have a sharing of some predicate between a kind and its examples, we also have a sharing of some property for which that predicate stands. With respect to those cases which fit our general formula, I think the answer must be, "No, we do not." Predications in such cases are not univocal. But neither are they equivocal. They are analogical. When grizzlies growl, they emit from their throats certain characteristic sound-patterns which we English-speaking people call "growling." But the kind, Grizzly, does not do that. Its sound-emission cannot be caught on some record. Yet—the Grizzly growls. "Growls," when truly predicated of the Grizzly, would seem to stand for the property of *being such that something cannot be a properly formed example of it unless it growls.* Thus, there is a systematic non-univocality about "growls." The predicate "growls" stands naturally for two quite different properties, one holding of the Grizzly and one holding of at least every properly formed example thereof. In general, for those cases in which the sharing of predicates between a kind and its examples follows the general pattern which we have formulated, the predicates are used analogically in exactly the way in which they were seen to be used analogically in the corresponding cases for art works.

In concluding this section of our discussion, let us articulate an important assumption which we have been making throughout. Consider the kind: Red Thing. This does seem to be a genuine kind; it differs from the class of all red things in that it might have had different and more or fewer members than it does have. But now notice that there cannot be a distinction, among examples of this kind, between improperly formed examples and properly formed examples of the kind. For it is not possible that some of the examples of the Red Thing should be improperly formed examples of this kind (i.e., things improperly red), nor is it possible that some should be properly formed examples of the kind (i.e., things properly red). Or consider the two kinds: Properly Formed Orchid and Malformed Orchid. There seems no reason to doubt that there are such kinds as these. But neither of these can have properly formed examples, nor can either have improperly formed examples.

When a kind, the K, is such that it is possible that it should have properly formed examples and also possible that it should have improperly formed examples, let us say that the K is a *norm-kind*. We have assumed throughout our discussion that art works and natural kinds are both norm-kinds. . . .

How to Tell Correctness

Our discussion concerning the ontological status of art works has concentrated on music. The detailed application to the other arts of the points we have made can be left to the reader. But two final matters must be considered. One is this: Why can paintings and sculptures not be viewed as single-exampled kinds rather than as physical objects, thereby giving us a "unified theory" of art works? P. F. Strawson, after saying that "in a certain sense, paintings and works of sculpture" are types, adds this footnote:

> The mention of paintings and works of sculpture may seem absurd. Are they not particulars? But this is a superficial point. The things the dealers buy and sell are particulars. But it is only because of the empirical deficiencies of re-productive techniques that we identify these with the works of art. Were it not for these deficiencies, the original of a painting would have only the interest which belongs to the original manuscript of a poem. Different people could look at exactly the same painting in different places at the same time, just as different people can listen to exactly the same quartet at different times in the same place. ([6]: 231.)

The situation is not quite as Strawson represents it, however. Of course there is nothing impossible in a certain object-work's having but one object. But object-works are norm-kinds, and being such they have associated with them certain requirements for something's being a correct example of the work. What is different in the case of paintings is that there are no such associated requirements. There simply are no requirements for something's being a correct example of some kind of which *The Odalesque* is the premier example. Of course, one can pick out things which to a certain close degree *resemble* this painting. There is a kind corresponding to them, and the painting is an example of it. But this is not a norm-kind, and none of our names of paintings are names of such entities.

Secondly, a question which has been pressing for a long time is this: How do we tell what constitutes a correct example of some art work? By now, however, the question has almost answered itself. In the case of works produced by some artist, the answer is that we try to discover the relevant features of that artifact which the artist produced (or which he arranged to have produced) as a record of his selection and as a guide or production-item for the making of examples. Of course, we will often discover that we cannot find out with any surety what the relevant features of that artifact were (are). We may no longer have the poet's original copy of the poem nor any very reliable evidence as to what it was like in crucial respects. Or we may have several copies from the poet's hand and not know which he authenticated. Or we may have an original authenticated copy but it may contain mistakes made by the poet, and we may find it impossible to determine which of various possibilities he had in mind. Or we may have an original, authenticated, and correct copy, but we may no longer know how to interpret all the symbols. In all such cases and many others we simply have to acknowledge that we are to some extent uncertain as to what constitutes a correct example. To that extent, we are also uncertain as to the character of the work. Yet it is clear what we must look for: the features of that original artifact.

In the case of those art works sustained in the memory of a culture and for which there is no artifact functioning as guide or production-item, we simply have to find out what the culture would regard as a correct and what it would regard as an incorrect example of the work—which is the same as finding out what the culture takes the art work to be like in those respects.[2]

References

[1] Collingwood, R. G., *The Principles of Art* (Oxford: Oxford University Press, 1938).

[2] Harrison, Andrew, "Works of Art and Other Cultural Objects," *Proceedings of the Aristotelian Society* 68(1967–68): 105–28.

[3] MacDonald, Margaret, "Art and Imagination," *Proceedings of the Aristotelian Society* 53(1952–53): 205–26.

[4] Margolis, Joseph, *The Language of Art and Art Criticism* (Detroit: Wayne State University Press, 1965).

[5] Stevenson, C. L., "On 'What is a Poem?'," *Philosophical Review* 66(1957): 329–62.

[6] Strawson, P. F., *Individuals* (London: Methuen, 1959).

[7] Wellek, R., and Warren, A., *Theory of Literature* (New York: Harcourt, Brace and World, 1956).

[8] Wollheim, Richard, *Art and Its Objects* (New York: Harper and Row, 1968).

[9] Wolterstorff, Nicholas, *On Universals* (Chicago: University of Chicago Press, 1970).

[2]In thinking through the issues discussed in this paper, I have received a great deal of assistance from my colleagues in the Philosophy Department at Calvin College. I have also received valuable advice from the editor of *Noûs*, from a reader for *Noûs*, and from Kendall Walton.

Identity, Ontology, and the Work of Art

JEFFREY MAITLAND

Traditionally, when philosophers have asked, "What is art?" they were asking for what is unique and common to all art. Sometime ago, however, Morris Weitz insisted that ". . . the very expansive, adventurous character of art, its ever present changes of novel creations, make it logically impossible to ensure any set of defining properties."[1] Although few were convinced for long by Weitz's arguments, many for a time seemed agreed that the attempt to define art is, while not logically impossible, at least futile. But recently, some philosophers were struck with asking, "What is art?" in a rather different way. Instead of asking what is common and unique to art, one asks what sort of an object art is. As one might expect, many answers have been given to this ontological question in the contemporary as well as traditional literature. Some have argued that the work of art is an imaginary object, and others have argued that it is a material object. And, following Peirce, Richard Wollheim draws the type/token distinction and argues that the literary and musical work of art are to be identified with the type.

> Those physical objects which (as we have seen) can out of desperation be thought to be works of art in cases where there are no physical objects that can plausibly be thought of in this way are *tokens*. In other words, *Ulysses* and *Der Rosenkavalier* are types: my copy of *Ulysses* and tonight's performance of Rosenkavalier are tokens of those types.[2]

In reading around these disputes, however, I was impressed not so much by the diversity of answers, but with the similarity in the sort of argument upon which all these various views depend. I wondered how so many different thinkers[3] could disagree about the ontological status of art and yet appeal to the same argument. Part of my task, then, is to argue against a particular

Excerpts from Jeffrey Maitland, "Identity, Ontology and the Work of Art," *Southwestern Journal of Philosophy* 6 (1975).

---

[1]Morris Weitz, "The Role of Theory in Aesthetics," reprinted in *Philosophy Looks at the Arts*, ed., Joseph Margolis (New York, 1962), p. 55.

[2]Richard Wollheim, *Art and Its Objects* (New York, 1968), pp. 64–65.

[3]To name a few: Langer, Collingwood, C. I. Lewis, Sartre, Ingarden, and, of course, the philosopher singled out for treatment here, Richard Wollheim. I am not claiming that the argument examined in this paper exhausts the arguments used by all these philosophers. Perhaps one could say that the argument dealt with here is the most persistent as well as, apparently, the most convincing—thus the most important.

answer to the ontological question and to analyze and criticize the way in which many aestheticians arrive at their views. . . . Furthermore, because the argument I am attacking seems more plausible in the case of novels and poems than in painting and sculpture, it will be useful to limit the discussion at first to the literary work of art and, to the extent that my criticisms are correct for poems and novels, they will apply *a fortiori* to any attempt to use this argument for any other form of art. After showing what can and cannot be said about the work of art in the first section, I hope to offer, in the second, a more useful and important way of thinking about the work of art by asking the ontological question in a new way.

I

Let us begin by looking at Wollheim's way of dealing with the ontological question. He begins with the view that the work of art is a physical object:

> That there is a physical object that can be identified as *Ulysses* or *Der Rosen-kavalier* is not a view that can long survive the demand that we should pick out or point to that object. . . . For instance it would follow that if I lost my copy of *Ulysses, Ulysses* would become a lost work. Again, it would follow that if the critics disliked tonight's performance of *Rosenkavalier,* then they dislike *Rosenkavalier.* Clearly, neither of these inferences is acceptable.[4]

Wollheim goes on to argue:

> But, it might now be maintained, of course it is absurd to identify *Ulysses* with my copy of it . . . , but nothing follows from this of a general character about the wrongness of identifying works of art with physical objects. . . . For instance, it is obviously quite wrong to say that *Ulysses* is my copy of it. Nevertheless, there is a physical object, of precisely the same order of being as my copy, though significantly not called a "copy," with which such an identification would be quite correct. This object is the author's manuscript: that, in other words, which Joyce wrote when he wrote *Ulysses.*[5]

Arguing against this identification, Wollheim says:

> The critic who admires *Ulysses* does not necessarily admire the manuscript. . . . And—here we come to an objection directly parallel to that which seemed fatal to identifying *Ulysses* with my copy of it—it would be possible for the manuscript to be lost and *Ulysses* to survive.[6]

Looking more closely, we find Wollheim sometimes concluding that no physical object can be identified *as Ulysses* and, at other times, that no physical

---

[4]*Art and Its Objects,* p. 5.

[5]Ibid., pp. 5–6.

[6]Ibid., p. 6.

object can be identified *with Ulysses*. But let us set these ambiguities aside for the moment in favor of following Wollheim's argument through to the conclusion that the literary work of art is a type.

To continue then, after considering one feature after another as possible candidates for the work of art, Wollheim says, "A final and desperate expedient to save the physical object hypothesis is to suggest that all those works of art which cannot plausibly be identified with physical objects are identical with classes of such objects."[7] Wollheim raises a few objections to this identification, and then argues:

> But perhaps a more serious, and certainly more interesting, objection is that in this suggestion what is totally unexplained is why the various copies of *Ulysses* are all said to be copies of *Ulysses* and nothing else. . . . For the ordinary explanation of how we come to group copies . . . as being of this book . . . is by reference to something else, something other than themselves, to which they stand in some special relation.[8]

This "something other" to which the copies stand in a special relation is a type. Thus, the work of art *Ulysses* is identical to a type, and my copy of *Ulysses* is a token of that type.[9]

But something odd has happened here. Wollheim does not raise, as he says in the above quote, a serious *objection* to the view that *Ulysses* is identical to the class of its copies. No doubt, the claim that *Ulysses* is identical to the class of its copies fails to explain how we come to group all these copies as copies of *Ulysses*. But this does not constitute an objection to the view. Indeed, instead of arguing against the view, Wollheim is actually asking a new question, quite different from the one with which he began his argument. Recall that he wants to deal with the traditional question, "What is art?" by asking the ontological question, "What sort of an object is art?" Yet, at this point in the argument, the ontological question is simply abandoned in favor of a new question, a platonic question, *viz.*, "In virtue of what are all these copies of *Ulysses* said to be copies of *Ulysses?*" Thus, by failing to keep these questions separate, one answer is given where two are required.

Notice how the argument progresses. Wollheim begins *Art and Its Objects* with the ontological question. He apparently tries to answer this question by constructing an argument which shows that *Ulysses* cannot be identical to a physical object, my copy, the printed page, the manuscript, and so forth. He then makes the unwarranted assumption (I will show why this assumption is unwarranted later) that since *Ulysses* is not identical to any of these things,

---

[7]Ibid., p. 7.
[8]Ibid., p. 8.
[9]See pp. 64–72 of *Art and Its Objects* for a statement of this view.

it must be identical to "something other." By subtly shifting from the ontological question (which becomes in the argument, "with what is the work of
art, *Ulysses,* identical?") to the platonic question, Wollheim is deceived into
thinking that he has raised an objection to a particular answer to the ontological question and is still pursuing the same course of reasoning. That is,
he thinks he is dealing with the ontological question when, in fact, he is
dealing with the platonic question, which he then tries to answer. Thus, while
it may be that the type/token distinction solves the difficulties raised by the
platonic question, it does not, on that account, show that the literary work
of art is *identical* to a type. While the type may be that in terms of which I
identify this particular copy as a copy of *Ulysses,* that which I appreciate as
the work of art, *Ulysses* is *not identical* to a type. Wollheim originally was
interested in what sort of an object the literary work of art is. But, we now
discover that he has set that question aside in favor of a certain sort of logical
problem—a problem that arises with any number of objects besides novels
and poems (e.g., Coke bottles, traffic tickets, newspapers). Thus, Wollheim's
view leaves us still wondering what art is.[10]

Furthermore, confusing these questions brings about a rather peculiar
result for Wollheim's final view. Obviously, when I read and appreciate *Ulysses,* I do it by holding my copy in my hands, turning the pages, savoring
passages here and there, and so on. That is, in reading and appreciating
Ulysses, I read and appreciate one object. Yet, Wollheim's view forces us to
see this activity as the reading and appreciating of two objects. Since, on
Wollheim's view, the literary work of art is not my copy of *Ulysses* (my copy
is a token), *Ulysses* must be identical to something other than my copy. This
something other than my copy is a type, or as Wollheim sometimes calls it,
a generic *entity.* Thus, it follows that when I read and appreciate *Ulysses,* I
must be reading and appreciating two objects—my copy of *Ulysses* and the
work of art, *Ulysses,* which is a generic entity. If Wollheim simply restricted
his attention to the platonic question, he would not be forced to this odd

---

[10]After having mistakenly arrived at the view that the literary work of art is identical to a type,
Wollheim is naturally left wondering what sort of thing a type is. Since one of the major projects
of *Art and Its Objects* is to answer the question, "What is art?" by answering the question, "What
sort of an object (if any) is art?" one would expect a rather detailed account of what sort of a
thing a type is. Yet, Wollheim says, "The question is very difficult, and, unfortunately, to treat
it with the care and attention to detail it deserves is beyond the scope of this essay." He does
not, however, simply leave this question hanging and does attempt to give some sort of answer
to it. He says that the question, "What sort of thing is a type? . . . is essentially a logical problem.
It is that of determining the criteria of identity and individuation appropriate to, say, a piece of
music or a novel." (*Art and Its Objects,* p. 64) Indeed, the problem of identity and individuation
which arises here comes from asking the platonic question. Perhaps the type/token distinction
solves these problems. But clearly it is not an answer to the ontological question: while the type
may be that in terms of which I *identify* this particular copy as a copy of *Ulysses,* that which I
appreciate as the work of art *Ulysses* is *not identical to* a type.

conclusion. By asking the ontological question first, however, and then answering it by answering the platonic question, he is forced to see types as special kinds of objects—the "something other" to which novels and poems are identical. Yet, to now answer only the platonic question would be tantamount to setting aside the very question with which he begins his entire investigation, *viz.,* "What is art?"

Since the answer to the platonic question is irrelevant as an answer to "What is art?" I want now to return again to the ontological question to see if it can be asked as an identity question. Earlier, I noted in passing that Wollheim concludes both that *Ulysses* cannot be identified *as* my copy and *with* my copy. It is clear by now that he also means to conclude that *Ulysses* is not *identical* to my copy. As it turns out, the family of expressions centering around "identity" (e.g., "identified as," "identified with," "identical to") have a variety of different uses. Let us now examine some of these uses and decide which conclusions follow from Wollheim's argument and which ones do not.

Clearly, Wollheim thinks he has shown ". . . There is no object existing in space and time (as physical objects must) that can be picked out and thought of as . . . a novel."[11] Can we imagine situations where my copy of *Ulysses* can be identified as the work of art? Well, suppose it happens that a number of us are discussing *Ulysses* in a room barren of other art objects. A number of objects are in the room: a table, chairs, a rug, . . . and my copy of *Ulysses.* Is there some object that can be identified as the work of art, *Ulysses?* The answer, of course, is "Yes, my copy." How could my copy, in this situation, fail to be the object in question?

As it turns out, expressions involving "identified with" are systematically ambiguous. In some instances, for example, we might be interested in identifying a poem *with* its genre, or kind. In other cases, "identified with" has a quite different use. For example, we might use an authorized copy of a novel to sort out deviant and unauthorized copies of the novel. If my copy is the only authorized copy, we might say, "The novel is to be identified with (identified by means of) my copy." In yet another case, if a number of us own copies of a novel, and I own the only authorized, mistake-free copy, we could quite legitimately identify the novel with my copy. And, finally, "identified with" expressions are often used interchangeably with "identical with" or "identical to." Thus, for example, someone might wonder whether Clark Kent is identical to Superman or, in aesthetics, someone might wonder whether *Ulysses* is identical to my copy.

Later, I will return to the differences between these identity questions in order to show how confusing their uses tends to beg the question in favor

---

[11]*Art and Its Objects,* p. 4.

of an ontology of special objects (i.e., that special object, the "something other" to which the work of art is identical). The point of marking out some of these differences now, however, is to indicate that the only use of "identified with" that is relevant to the argument is the "identical to" use. From this it follows that the argument entitles us *only* to the conclusion that the literary work of art is not identical to the printed page, my copy, and so forth. The argument does not prove that *Ulysses* cannot be identified *as* my copy or, in certain cases, that *Ulysses* cannot be identified *with* my copy. Distinguishing among identity expressions also yields a possible explanation as to why Wollheim so readily shifts from the ontological to the platonic question: platonic difficulties can often be voiced through an identity expression. As I pointed out previously, a type may be that in terms of which or by means of which a particular copy can be *identified* as a copy of *Ulysses* (platonic use). But that which I appreciate as the work of art, *Ulysses,* is not *identical* to a type (ontological use).

More importantly, however, many theorists have assumed that the argument warrants quite a different conclusion than the one stated above. That is, Wollheim as well as many other philosophers have thought that since the work of art is not identical to its copies, it must be identical to "something else," "something other than themselves." R. G. Collingwood, for example, in comparing hearing music to hearing a lecture draws this unwarranted conclusion: ". . . just as what we get out of the lecture is something *other* than the noises we hear proceeding from the lecturer's mouth, so what we get out of the concert is something *other* than the noises made by the performers."[12] Collingwood's argument is that since the work of art is not identical to the noises, it must be identical to something other than the noises. This something other, on his view is, of course, an imaginary object. . . . To extend the list of theorists who have used this argument to prove this unwarranted conclusion is unnecessary. Notice, however, that the argument apparently justifies the same sort of gratuitous conclusion for all the arts. Since poems are not identical to the printed page, and music is not identical to sounds, and dance is not identical to bodily movement, and paintings are not identical to the painted canvas, and so on, it seems to follow that these works of art must be something over and above the stuff of which they are made. Once we are tempted by the move from "the work of art is not identical to the stuff of which it is made or to any of its aspects" to "the work must be something over and above the stuff and its various features," we naturally find ourselves searching for that special object with which the work of art is identical. Thus, it is easy to see how so many philosophers can use the same argument to prove such diverse views as to the nature of the work of art.

---

[12]R. G. Collingwood, *The Principles of Art* (New York, 1938), p. 141 (my italics).

At most, the argument proves that certain views concerning that with which the work of art is identical are false. . . . Wollheim . . . does not show there must be something other with which *Ulysses* is identical, only that *Ulysses* is not identical to my copy of it. For someone to point out that destroying my copy of *Ulysses* does not destroy the work of art is simply a way of saying there are other copies of *Ulysses* around; it is not also to say that *Ulysses* is something other than my copy.

Quite simply, I want to argue that not all cases where *x* is not identical to *y* are cases where *x* is something over and above *y*, and that the work of art and its object is one of these cases. Let me bring the point home with a borrowed example. Suppose a woman makes a pair of gloves for her husband from a ball of wool and later unpicks the gloves and makes a wool cap. Since the cap was made from a ball of wool which at previous time was a pair of gloves, if we say *that* which is made from the wool is identical to the wool, we must also say that the gloves are identical to the cap. By Leibniz's law, that which is made from the wool cannot be identical to the wool, because whatever is true of what is made from the wool must then also be true of the wool. But this is not the case with the gloves and the cap, because the wool preexists and survives them. We may say, then, that the cap is made of the wool, but not that it is identical to the wool. To say that the cap is something over and above the wool would be to claim that somehow the cap is something other than the wool of which it is made, or that somehow the wool does not fully exhaust the cap. Such might be the case, for example, if the woman added new wool, or some decorative elements which were not wool and not originally part of the gloves. But clearly this is not the case in our example. Thus, we must conclude that the cap is not identical to the wool, and yet that the cap is not something over and above the wool. "The 'is' of material constitution is not the 'is' of identity."[13]

I think it is fair to say that aestheticians have been correct in arguing that a novel is not identical to its copies, that a painting is not identical to the painted canvas, and so forth. However, if what I have argued is correct, we must refuse to agree with their claim that the work of art is something over and above its stuff or objects. In this way, we can avoid a materialistic theory of art, because the work of art is not identical to the stuff of which it is made. And, because the work of art is not something over and above its

---

[13]David Wiggens, "On Being in the Same Place at the Same Time," *The Philosophical Review,* Jan., 1968, p. 91. I am grateful to William Rowe for reading an earlier version of this paper. He helped me to see some of its shortcomings and suggested I look at Wiggens' work on identity. I was happy to discover that Wiggens had also spotted the mistaken tendency to move from claiming "such and such is not identical to the stuff of which it is constituted" to "such and such must be something over and above the stuff of which it is constituted." *See also* Wiggens' *Identity and Spatio-Temporal Continuity* (London, 1967).

stuff, there is no point in arguing that the work of art is a mental object or some peculiar logical object (e.g., a generic entity).[14] Thus, what the work of art *is* is neither mental nor physical even though it may be composed of material stuff and/or mental elements (as, for example, in conceptual art).

Earlier, I distinguished among a number of uses of identity expressions in order to show that Wollheim was mistaken in excluding some of these from our talk about the work of art. Now, I want to return to these distinctions to show why philosophers, and in particular Wollheim, are so readily disposed to bifurcate the work of art from its stuff and objects. Part of the puzzle and difficulties concerning art that we are led into by Wollheim are manufactured through a set of interconnected confusions that dispose one to look for the work of art in something other than the copies. As we have just seen, the tendency to bifurcate the work of art and its stuff is in part due to not being clear about the differences between the expressions "not identical to" and "over and above." But the disposition to seek for the work of art outside its stuff and object is also nurtured by a failure to understand how some identity expressions function: both the "identified as" and the "identified with" expressions assume two objects, whereas the "identical to" expression does not presuppose two objects ("identified with" expressions when used interchangebly with the "identical to" formulations also do not assume two objects). If one asks, for example, "Is Clark Kent *identical* to Superman?" two objects are not assumed since Clark and Superman are one and the same person. But to ask, "Can T. S. Eliot be identified *with x?*"—where *x* is a particular school of philosophy or poetics or where *x* is a photograph—clearly assumes two objects. And, again, two objects are assumed in the following question: "Can T. S. Eliot be identified *as x?*"—where *x* is a poet.

Notice, then, how the argument, in Wollheim's hands, trades on confusing these identity expressions: First, one is brought to see the work of art *as* (say) my copy of it (this, as we have seen, is a perfectly legitimate identification); but, then, by emphasizing the "identical to" expression, one concludes quite correctly that the work of art is not identical *to* my copy; then, because the "identical to" expression (which does not assume two objects and is connected to a true conclusion) is confused with two other identity expressions (these do assume two objects and thereby dispose one to seek the work of art in something other than its copies), one is easily led to think

---

[14]The conclusion that the work of art is not identical to its stuff or objects and is not over and above its stuff or object also avoids one of the peculiar results of Wollheim's view: that in reading and appreciating *Ulysses* I am reading and appreciating two things. We can see how this is so by returning for a moment to the wool gloves and cap example. As we have seen, the cap is not identical to the wool of which it is made and the cap is not something over and above the wool. Hence, when I am touching the cap, I am touching the wool. But it does not follow that in touching the cap and wool, I am touching *two objects*. Analogously, *Ulysses* is not identical to my copy of it, and *Ulysses* is not something other than my copy. And, when I am reading my copy of *Ulysses*, I am reading *Ulysses*. But it does not follow that I am reading *two objects*.

that *Ulysses* cannot be identified *as* or *with* my copy of it, and, finally, that *Ulysses* must be some sort of object other than my copy—and thus identical to this other object, whatever and wherever it might be.

II

We are now at the point where we can claim that the work of art is not identical to the stuff of which it is made or to its objects and that the work of art is not over and above its stuff or objects. Yet, do we know what the work of art is? Is this a satisfactory answer?

In a way, it is a satisfactory answer for it allows us to say certain things about works of art that were forbidden by many aesthetic theories. For example, I can buy *Ulysses* at the book store and send it through the mail; paintings hang on walls, not in minds. However, in another way, this conclusion all by itself is not a satisfying answer. To be sure, it is a conclusion that had to be untangled from a thicket of confusion and as such serves to remind us where thought need not go anymore. But this is a negative conclusion and does not give any way of thinking about art. We do not yet know what the work of art is.

Well, what is the work of art then? In order to answer the question, we must not formulate it as "What sort of an object is art?" We have already seen how the argument does not support the variety of answers to this question. However, the ontological question must not be abandoned. Rather, it must be asked in a new way, in a way that will not prejudice us into thinking that the work of art is some sort of an *object*. Indeed, as long as we persist in viewing art as an object, we will fail to understand the nature of art. Thus, I want to ask the ontological question about art again.

Let us ask the ontological question in the following way: "What is it that is appreciated when one appreciates a work of art?" Consider, would knowing that the work of art is one kind of object rather than another help us to answer this question? To claim that what one appreciates in appreciating a work of art is a mental object or physical object or a type does not begin to answer the question I am asking. I care about some works of art more than others. And I have been fortunate enough, on occasion, to deeply appreciate some pieces of music. To tell me that what I appreciated on these occasions was some sort of object would be like telling a lover that what he loved was a skin bag. What we appreciate, create, and care about are works of art. But what is a work of art?

Let me change examples for a moment and ask the ontological question about something more familiar. I live in a house and care about the house in which I live. What is it that I live in when I live in my house? What is a house? A quite natural reply to this question might be, "Something made of bricks, metal, and wood." Yet, even though knowledge of constitution and construction of a house is not altogether unrelated and irrelevant to the ontological question, it still does not speak to the question. Knowing that a house was constructed in a certain way with bricks, metal, and wood would not, *all by itself,* be enough. That is, in order to answer the question, I would need to have lived in such a house for the knowledge of constitution and construction to be useful. Consider, for example, the difference between a room with hardwood floors and a similar room with old and worn linoleum. If one wanted to characterize the *lived* difference between these two rooms to someone who had not lived with either floor, it would be pointess to simply say that one had a hardwood floor and the other had linoleum. Thus, the question I am asking is prior to that of constitution and construction.

Moreover, houses do not just take up a certain amount of measureable space. They occupy the space they take up in vastly different ways. Imagine, for example, two houses which pretty much take up the same amount of measureable space, but one house has an attic and many more rooms than the other. Clearly, these two houses occupy their space differently and dwelling in each would not be the same dwelling. In an important sense, we could say that their mode of existence is different.

Suppose that as building inspectors we are interested in establishing whether a number of prefabricated houses are the same kind of house. In order to identify a particular house as an exemplification of its kind, we might have recourse to the blueprint. The blueprint, then, functions as a type (in Wollheim's sense) in terms of which we can correctly *identify* token houses. But the house itself is not *identical* to the type or blue print. I do not live in a blueprint. Thus, to characterize a house as a material object or as a type would not tell us what a house is—it would not elucidate the lived space of the house; it would not elucidate house dwelling.

As it turns out, there are many different kinds of houses and dwellings. There is no reason to think that there exists some one feature or set of features common and unique to all houses. A useful and interesting way of answering the question would not consist in trying to say something about houses in general—such as all houses are a shelter from the elements. It is true that all houses are shelters and we could even suppose for the moment that the only things that are shelters are houses. But, again, this answer does not speak to the question. Everyone knows that a house is not a home—perhaps it is equally true that a shelter is not a house. Elucidating the mode of existence of the house requires not beginning with houses in general. Instead, we must limit our descriptions and characterizations to houses of a particular kind set within certain landscapes. We may, in the end, arrive at some general notion of the mode of existence of the house because what a house is, is revealed in each house. But the notion of the house that results from this sort of investigation would be open and richly textured.[15]

Against this background, let us ask the ontological question again about art. What is it that we appreciate when we appreciate the work of art? Again, simply to say that the work of art is an object of a certain sort or constituted and constructed in a certain way would not answer the question. For example, to know that a painting was done in acrylics rather than oils or that it is a stain painting rather than an oil painting, does not give us, *all by itself,* any useful information for understanding how the painting is aesthetically situated—not unless we first have some feeling for the aesthetic difference acrylics or the staining technique can make. That is, this information will not be helpful until we have learned to appreciate stain paintings or paintings done with acrylics. Appreciation is always the appreciation of the work of art, and the question of the mode of existence of the work of art is prior to questions of constitution, construction, and techniques. How the constitution, construction, and techniques are *at work* in and serve the work of art, however, is part of what we have to uncover when we seek art's ontological status, i.e., art's mode of existence.

Imagine hanging two objects of exactly the same dimensions on a wall: one is a painting and one is a plywood board. To be sure, both *take up* the same amount of space, but there is surely an important difference in how this space is *occupied.* The painting is present in the room and, to the appreciator, in a vastly different way than the plywood board is present. And, of course, how one painting occupies the space it takes up can be remarkably different from another painting: think of the differences between a painting by Stella and one by Rauschenberg. Similarly, two pieces of music might take up the same amount of time, but the difference in the way that time is used (e.g., how it flows or does not move) can be enormous. Compare, for example, a piece by Mozart to one by Xenakis or Feldman. It is possible to go on in this way for all the arts. We might try to describe the timeless character of Faulkner's worlds or of Feldman's music, the craggy cliffs of Ruggles' sonorities, how Varese's music is a revolving and evolving lamination of sound, and so on. But to fill in these rather bare suggestions for all the arts is beyond what one person can do. Nevertheless, elucidating the various modes of existence of the various arts and of particular works of art, and bringing us into closer contact with the work of art's unique *presence* is a very important part of the critic's (as well as the philosopher's) task.

What, then, is the work of art? It is that which we appreciate when we appreciate the work of art. What we appreciate is not simply some sort of

---

[15]For an interesting attempt to elucidate lived space, *see* Gaston Bachelard's *The Poetics of Space* (Boston, 1971.)

object (as a mental object, physical object, or a type) but a work of art. And yet, as we have seen, the work of art is not something over and above its object or stuff. In order to call attention to what the work of art is, to what Heidegger[16] calls the workly character of the work of art, I have settled on the notion of a performative presence. By saying that the work of art is a performative presence, I am trying to move from seeing art simply as an object or some subjective experience. The work of art is more a *doing* than a being or having. When we appreciate a work of art we appreciate its performative presence, what is *at work* in the work. A Rauschenberg painting is a different sort of performative presence than a Stella or a Van Eyck. Paintings perform differently than music, but music can have color, paintings are lyrical, and poetry sings. A plywood board and a painting of the same dimensions both are different presences, but only the painting is a performative presence.

Just as a performative utterance, in J. L. Austin's sense, is the doing of something rather than merely the saying of something, so, too, a poem is the *doing* of something. The poet does not simply utter statements *about* the world or make his art correspond to or represent reality. The poet's words do something: they make present a world, or as in the case of metapoetry, they make present the conditions of poetry itself. The same point can be made about the novel. Robbe-Grillet, for example, attempts to redirect attention to the performative presencing of the novel by cautioning against seeing Kafka's works as *no more* than allegories. On such a view,

> . . . literature would always consist and in a systematic way, in speaking of *something else.* . . . Now, on the contrary, if there is one thing of which an unprejudiced reading convinces us it is the absolute reality of the things Kafka describes. The visible world of his novels is certainly for him the real world. . . . The hallucinatory effect derives from their extraordinary clarity and not from mystery or mist. Nothing is more fantastic, ultimately, than precision. Perhaps Kafka's staircases lead *elsewhere,* but they are *there,* and we look at them, step by step, following the detail of the banisters and the risers. Perhaps his gray walls hide something, but it is on them that the memory lingers, on their cracked whitewash, their crevices. . . . In the whole of Kafka's work, man's relations with

---

[16]Martin Heidegger, "The Origin of the Work of Art," in *Poetry, Language, Thought,* tr. Albert Hofstadter (New York, 1971). In his analysis of the work of art, Heidegger once again has thought his way beyond traditional metaphysics. He clearly sees that art cannot be investigated fruitfully if made identical to some sort of mental or physical object. With this insight, he moves well beyond the object-ridden language of traditional aesthetics. Furthermore, implicit in Heidegger's analysis is the clear understanding that the work of art is not something over and above its object. We are interested, Heidegger says, in the work-being of art, not its object-being.

I have chosen to speak of the performative character of art where Heidegger has chosen to speak of the workly character of the work. As far as I can see these expressions both call attention to the proximal reality of art in the same way.

the world, far from having a symbolic character, are constantly direct and immediate.[17]

Robbe-Grillet surely overstates his point in the last sentence. He ought to say that Kafka's art will be lost if it is reduced to allegory. Novels can, indeed, perform by being allegorical, by being about something, by saying something. But what the novel is cannot be understood as *simply* and *wholly* symbolic.

Similarly, a painting is the doing of something in paint, rather than merely the applying of paint to a canvas or the attempt to represent something. Much of twentieth-century painting has forcefully and clearly directed attention to the performative presencing of art by acknowledging and insisting on the conditions of painting in the work of art itself. What is done and achieved in paint, whether it is the making present of the conditions of painting or making present a world or a dreamscape, is painting's performative character. And because what is achieved in two paintings or in two poems is different, the way these works of art are *there* or *present* for us is different. Thus, when we appreciate a work of art, we appreciate what is at work in the work—we appreciate the work of art's performative presencing.

The work of art is not present for appreciation as a thing, but as a performative presence. Art is not identical to its stuff or objects and is not something over and above its stuff or object. Just as a lover does not love skin and bones and just as a house dweller does not live in metal, wood, and bricks, so, too, one who appreciates a work of art does not appreciate an object—he appreciates a work of art. When we appreciate the work of art we are interested in art's performative presence or work-being rather than its object-being. Art's center, its proximal reality, the place from which it opens out for appreciation, is how art works and performs.

Appreciation, creation, evaluation are *of* the work of art. The question as to what the work of art is, then, is philosophically fundamental and prior to the questions we might raise about the activities of appreciation, creation, interpretation, and evaluation. In criticism as well, the question as to what the work of art is, is the first question with which we must deal. Harold Rosenberg, for example, claims ". . . I should like to point out that in dealing with *new* things there is a question that precedes that of good or bad. I refer to the question, 'What is it?'—the question of identity."[18] Rosenberg's way of characterizing Action Painting's mode of existence is as an event. To this characterization, Mary McCarthy replied, "You cannot hang an event on the wall, only a picture."[19] To criticize Rosenberg in this way, however, is to

---

[17]Alain Robbe-Grillet, *For A New Novel* (New York, 1965), pp. 164–165.

[18]Harold Rosenberg, *The Tradition of the New* (New York, 1965), Preface to the second edition.

[19]Ibid.

confuse, in Heidegger's language, the work-being of art with its object-being. To admonish Rosenberg in this way, moreover, is to seriously misunderstand what Rosenberg is doing and in effect to rule out that part of criticism upon which the rest of criticism depends. Perhaps one cannot hang an event on the wall, but one can hang a work of art on the wall, and the performative presence of Action Painting is perhaps best understood and appreciated through event language. Ontology, then, is at least one area where philosophy and criticism converge.

Since art is a performative presence, the concept of "performative presence" is as open and richly textured as the concept of "art"—but not so open as to invite anything under any circumstances to enter. The mode of existence, the performative presence, will vary from particular painting to particular painting, from style to style, and from art form to art form.

No doubt, common achievements and overlapping strands of similarities can be discovered. Many diverse works count as art. The twentieth century has created, in fact, a variety of borderline cases. Indeed, with some of these works the notion of border-lineness is an extremely important part of the work, if not the essential element to be appreciated. That is, border-lineness is an important way in which these works exist or perform for us.

Understanding art as a performative presence, moreover, comes much closer to meeting the traditional demand long obscured in "What is art?" To be sure, the concept of "performative presence" does not pick out an essence in the sense of some one thing or set of things common to all art. And it is not the ascription of a property in the way in which "this is red" is the ascription of the property red. The performative presence of art is what art is, and is thus an answer to the ontological question. Yet, this questioning and answering calls attention to itself by calling for a way of thinking about art and for investigations into the ontology of art. What is needed is an ontology of music, an ontology of poetry, an ontology of painting, an ontology of dance, and so on. These ontological investigations would not try to say what sort of object art is, but would try to uncover the performative presencing of the arts.[20]

Let us not forget, however, that as appreciators what we are interested in is the work of art, not simply the concept of art. The concept we have grows and expands from our appreciative encounters with proximal realities of art—with art's ever-changing performative presence. Consequently, as

---

[20]These investigations have been undertaken by Heidegger in *Poetry, Language, Thought* and also by Bachelard in *The Poetics of Space* and *The Poetics of Reverie. See also* Stanley Cavell's ontology of film, *The World Viewed* (New York, 1971), and Michael Fried's work on Modernist painting.

I do not mean to imply that these investigations are not in any way undertaken by the tradition—only that these investigations were obscured by the wrong kinds of questions. The expression theorists, for example, tried to put their finger on the performative presence of art. But expression, at least expression as it is usually understood, is not the whole story. There is more to physiognomy than the expression of emotion.

aestheticians, a large and important part of our task consists in uncovering the immense number of variations in the performative presencing of the arts.

ILLUSTRATION 26

ARNOLD SCHÖNBERG, *Verklärte Nacht,* facsimile of part of the musical score, from *Arnold Schönberg* by Egon Wellesz, trans. W. H. Kerridge (Freeport, N.Y.: Books for Libraries Press, 1925; rpt. 1969), pp. 70–71.

13

New Approaches
in Art Theory

This chapter includes three new themes for philosophical consideration: a theory for the aesthetic appreciation of the environment, a feminist view of aesthetics, and the issue, Do art works have rights? These themes are relatively unrelated to each other. Each idea is so new it is yet to be fully developed as an aesthetic theory. But each raises new questions for the student in philosophy of art.

According to Allen Carlson, the subject matter for aesthetic experiences need not be limited to works of art. Keeping in mind theories of the aesthetic such as those presented in Part III, Carlson asks how and whether one can similarly extend aesthetic appreciation to nature. How does one appreciate a piece of driftwood (Illustration 25) or a landscape such as *Door County* (Illustration 27)? Carlson suggests what he calls an environmental approach to the aesthetic appreciation of nature. One needs to attend to nature not just as background for human experiences but also as a foreground focus for appreciation. To do this one must become involved perceptually with nature. An aesthetic experience of nature is a perceptual and an environmental experience, in contrast to an aesthetic experience of art which is both nonenvironmental and only minimally perceptual. And Carlson intimates that aesthetics should be the study of many modes of aesthetic appreciation and not limit itself merely to the subject matter of art.

Lucy Lippard and Estella Lauter introduce the reader to a fresh approach to art theory by analyzing some aesthetic notions from a feminist perspective. They raise the following questions: Is there a women's art? What are the philosophical parameters of a feminist aesthetic? And what sorts of theories about art apply to feminist works of art? Both Lippard, a modern art critic, and Lauter, a theorist and artist, feel that women's art is an existing phenomenon in the artworld. The play, *For Colored Girls* . . . (Illustration 28) is a clear example of feminist drama. However, feminist art, as a distinct art movement, is not clearly recognized by the artworld. And a feminist aesthetic oriented to define gender differences in art needs to be worked out fully. Nevertheless both essays provoke new thoughts about the nature of art and aesthetic theory in light of changing views about women in society.

The question of human rights is a persistent theme in political and social philosophy. But until recently "rights" have not been a topic for aesthetic inquiry. However, Alan Tormey's recent article, "Aesthetic Rights," has provoked a storm of controversy over whether or not works of art have rights. Tormey claims that art works are endowed with interests for which there are corresponding obligations. For example, it is in the interest of a great painting not to be defaced. Therefore there is a corresponding obligation not to paint moustaches on *Lady Delmé*. These interests of art works outlive the artist and are obligations to the work, not to the person who created the work. If art works do have these obligation-related interests, Tormey argues that art works, like persons, have rights, e.g., the right not to be defaced. Tormey is unclear about what aesthetic rights entail, and if there are such aesthetic rights, Tormey's theory needs to spell this out. For example, the existence of feminist art might demand a special view of rights. And if artworks have rights, one wonders whether the theory can be extended to other things. If one can have an aesthetic experience of the environment, does the environment have rights as well? Tormey's theory is provocative, but it needs careful examination. What sorts of things do *not* have rights, according to this view?

Appreciation and the Natural Environment

ALLEN CARLSON

I

With art objects there is a straightforward sense in which we know both what and how to aesthetically appreciate. We know *what* to appreciate in that, first, we can distinguish a work and its parts from that which is not it nor a part of it. And, second, we can distinguish its aesthetically relevant aspects from its aspects without such relevance. We know that we are to appreciate the sound of the piano in the concert hall and not the coughing which interrupts it; we know that we are to appreciate that a painting is graceful, but not that it happens to hang in the Louvre. In a similar vein, we know *how* to appreciate

Allen Carlson, "Appreciation and the Natural Environment," *Journal of Aesthetics and Art Criticism* (1979). Reprinted with permission.

in that we know what "acts of aspection" to perform in regard to different works. Ziff says:

> . . . to contemplate a painting is to perform one act of aspection; to scan it is to perform another; to study, observe, survey, inspect, examine, scrutinise, etc., are still other acts of aspection. . . . I survey a Tintoretto, while I scan an H. Bosch. Thus I step back to look at the Tintoretto, up to look at the Bosch. Different actions are involved. Do you drink brandy in the way you drink beer?[1]

It is clear that we have such knowledge of what and how to aesthetically appreciate. It is, I believe, also clear what the grounds are for this knowledge. Works of art are our own creations; it is for this reason that we know what is and what is not a part of a work, which of its aspects are of aesthetic significance, and how to appreciate them. We have made them for the purpose of aesthetic appreciation; in order for them to fulfill this purpose this knowledge must be accessible. In making an object we know what we make and thus its parts and its purpose. Hence in knowing what we make we know what to do with that which we make. In the more general cases the point is clear enough: In creating a painting, we know that what we make is a painting. In knowing this we know that it ends at its frame, that its colors are aesthetically important, but where it hangs is not, and that we are to look at it rather than, say, listen to it. All this is involved in what it is to be a painting. Moreover, this point holds for more particular cases as well. Works of different particular types have different kinds of boundaries, have different foci of aesthetic significance, and perhaps most important demand different acts of aspection. In knowing the type we know what and how to appreciate. Ziff again:

> Generally speaking, a different act of aspection is performed in connection with works belonging to different schools of art, which is why the classification of style is of the essence. Venetian paintings lend themselves to an act of aspection involving attention to balanced masses; contours are of no importance, for they are scarcely to be found. The Florentine school demands attention to contours, the linear style predominates. Look for light in a Claude, for color in a Bonnard, for contoured volume in a Signorelli.[2]

I take the above to be essentially beyond serious dispute, except as to the details of the complete account. If it were not the case, our complementary

---

[1] Paul Ziff, "Reasons in Art Criticism," *Philosophy and Education,* ed., I. Scheffler (Boston, 1958). Reprinted in *Art and Philosophy,* ed., W. E. Kennick (New York, 1964), p. 620.

[2] Ibid. Ziff is mainly concerned with the way in which knowledge of types yields different acts of aspection. For an elaboration of this point and its ramifications concerning what is and is not aesthetically significant in a work, see K. Walton, "Categories of Art," *Philosophical Review* (1970), 334–67. How our knowledge of art (and the artworld) yields the boundaries between art and the rest of reality is interestingly discussed in A. Danto, "The Artistic Enfranchisement of Real Objects: the Artworld," *Journal of Philosophy* (1964), 571–84.

institutions of art and of the aesthetic appreciation of art would not be as they are. We would not have the artworld which we do. But the subject of this paper is not art nor the artworld. Rather: it is the aesthetic appreciation of nature. The question I wish to investigate is the question of what and how to aesthetically appreciate in respect to natural environment. It is of interest since the account which is implicit in the above remarks and which I believe to be the correct account for art cannot be applied to the natural environment without at least some modification. Thus initially the questions of what and how to appreciate in respect to nature appear to be open questions.

II

In this section I consider some paradigms of aesthetic appreciation which *prima facie* seem applicable as models for the appreciation of the natural environment. In this I follow tradition to some extent in that these paradigms are ones which have been offered as or assumed to be appropriate models for the appreciation of nature. However, I think we will discover that these models are not as promising as they may initially appear to be.

The first such paradigm I call the object model. In the artworld non-representational sculpture best fits this model of appreciation. When we appreciate such sculpture we appreciate it as the actual physical object which it is. The qualities to be aesthetically appreciated are the sensuous and design qualities of the actual object and perhaps certain abstract expressive qualities. The sculpture need not represent anything external to itself; it need not lead the appreciator beyond itself: it may be a self-contained aesthetic unit. Consider a Brancusi sculpture, for example, the famous *Bird In Space* (1919). It has no representational connections with the rest of reality and no relational connections with its immediate surroundings and yet it has significant aesthetic qualities. It glistens, has balance and grace, and expresses flight itself.

Clearly it is possible to aesthetically appreciate an object of nature in the way indicated by this model. For example, we may appreciate a rock or a piece of driftwood in the same way as we appreciate a Brancusi sculpture: we actually or contemplatively remove the object from its surroundings and dwell on its sensuous and design qualities and its possible expressive qualities. Moreover, there are considerations which support the plausibility of this model for appreciation of the natural environment. First, natural objects are in fact often appreciated in precisely this way: mantel pieces are littered with pieces of rock and driftwood. Second, the model fits well with one feature of natural objects: such objects, like the Brancusi sculpture, do not have representational ties to the rest of reality. Third and most important, the model involves an accepted, traditional aesthetic approach. As Sparshott notes, "When one talks of the aesthetic this or that, one is usually thinking of it as entering into a subject/object relation."[3]

In spite of these considerations, however, I think there are aspects of the object model which make it inappropriate for nature. Santayana, in discussing the aesthetic appreciation of nature (which he calls the love of nature), notes that certain problems arise because the natural landscape has "indeterminate form." He then observes that although the landscape contains many objects which have determinate forms, "if the attention is directed specifically to them, we have no longer what, by a curious limitation of the word, is called the love of nature."[4] I think this limitation is not as curious as Santayana seems to think it is. The limitation marks the distinction between appreciating nature and appreciating the objects of nature. The importance of this distinction is seen by realizing the difficulty of appreciating nature by means of the object model. For example, on one understanding of the object model, the objects of nature when so appreciated become "ready-mades" or "found art." The artworld grants "artistic enfranchisement" to a piece of driftwood just as it has to Duchamp's urinal or to the real Brillo cartons discussed by Danto.[5] If this magic is successful the result is art. Questions of what and how to aesthetically appreciate are answered, of course, but in respect to art rather than nature; the appreciation of nature is lost in the shuffle. Appreciating sculpture which was once driftwood is no closer to appreciating nature than is appreciating a totem pole which was once a tree or a purse which was once a sow's ear. In all such cases the conversion from nature to art (or artifact) is complete; only the means of conversion are different.

There is, however, another understanding of how the object model applies to the objects of nature. On this understanding natural objects are simply (actually or contemplatively) removed from their surroundings, but they do not become art, they remain natural objects. Here we do not appreciate the objects *qua* art objects, but rather *qua* natural objects. We do not consider the rock on our mantel a ready-made sculpture, we consider it only an aesthetically pleasing rock. In such a case, as the example of non-representational sculpture suggests, our appreciation is limited to the sensuous and design qualities of the natural object and perhaps a few abstract expressive qualities: Our rock has a wonderfully smooth and gracefully curved surface and expresses solidity.

---

[3]F. E. Sparshott, "Figuring the Ground: Notes on Some Theoretical Problems of the Aesthetic Environment," *Journal of Aesthetic Education* (1972), 13.

[4]George Santayana, *The Sense of Beauty* (New York, 1961), p. 100.

[5]Danto, op. cit., p. 579.

The above suggests that, even when it does not require natural objects to be seen as art objects, the object model imposes a certain limitation on our appreciation of natural objects. The limitation is the result of the removal of the object from its surroundings which the object model requires in order even to begin to provide answers to questions of what and how to appreciate. But in requiring such a removal the object model becomes problematic. The object model is most appropriate for those art objects which are self-contained aesthetic units. These objects are such that neither the environment of their creation nor the environment of their display are aesthetically relevant: the removal of a self-contained art object from its environment of creation will not vary its aesthetic qualities and the environment of display of such an object should not affect its aesthetic qualities. However, natural objects possess what we might call an organic unity with their environment of creation: such objects are a part of and have developed out of the elements of their environments by means of the forces at work within those environments. Thus the environments of creation are aesthetically relevant to natural objects. And for this reason the environments of display are equally relevant in virtue of the fact that these environments will be either the same as or different from the environments of creation. In either case the aesthetic qualities of natural objects will be affected. Consider again our rock: on the mantel it may seem wonderfully smooth and gracefully curved and expressive of solidity, but in its environment of creation it will have more and different aesthetic qualities—qualities which are the product of the relationship between it and its environment. It is here expressive of the particular forces which shaped and continue to shape it and displays for aesthetic appreciation its place in and its relation to its environment. Moreover, depending upon its place in that environment it may not express many of those qualities, for example, solidity, which it appears to express when on the mantle.

I conclude that the object model, even without changing nature into art, faces a problem as a paradigm for the aesthetic appreciation of nature. The problem is a dilemma: either we remove the object from its environment or we leave it where it is. If the object is removed, the model applies to the object and suggests answers to the questions of what and how to appreciate. But the result is the appreciation of a comparatively limited set of aesthetic qualities. On the other hand if the object is not removed, the model seemingly does not constitute an adequate model for a very large part of the appreciation which is possible. Thus it makes little headway with the what and how questions. In either case the object model does not provide a successful paradigm for the aesthetic appreciation of nature. It appears after all not a very "curious limitation" that when our attention is directed specifically toward the objects in the environment it is not called the love of nature.

The second paradigm for the aesthetic appreciation of nature I call the scenery or landscape model. In the artworld this model of appreciation is illustrated by landscape painting; in fact the model probably owes its existence to this art form. In one of its favored senses "landscape" means a prospect— usually a grandiose prospect—seen from a specific standpoint and distance; a landscape painting is traditionally a representation of such a prospect.[6] When aesthetically appreciating landscape paintings (or any representative paintings, for that matter) the emphasis is not on the actual object (the painting) nor on the object represented (the actual prospect); rather it is on the representation of the object and its represented features. Thus in landscape painting the appreciative emphasis is on those qualities which play an essential role in representing a prospect: visual qualities related to coloration and overall design. These are the qualities which are traditionally significant in landscape painting and which are the focus of the landscape model of appreciation. We thus have a model of appreciation which encourages perceiving and appreciating nature as if it were a landscape painting, as a grandiose prospect seen from a specific standpoint and distance. It is a model which centers attention on those aesthetic qualities of color and design which are seen and seen at a distance.

It is quite evident that the scenery or landscape model has been historically significant in our aesthetic appreciation of nature.[7] For example, this model was evident in the eighteenth and nineteenth centuries in the use of the "Claude-glass," a small, tinted, convex mirror with which tourists viewed the landscape. Thomas West's popular guidebook to the Lake District (first published in 1778) says of the glass:

> . . . where the objects are great and near, it removes them to a due distance, and shews them in the soft colours of nature, and most regular perspective the eye can perceive, art teach, or science demonstrate . . . to the glass is reserved the finished picture, in highest colouring, and just perspective.[8]

---

[6]This favored sense of "landscape" is brought out by Yi-Fu Tuan. See *Topophilia: A Study of Environmental Perception, Attitudes, and Values* (Englewood Cliffs, 1974), pp. 132–33, or "Man and Nature: An Eclectic Reading," *Landscape,* Vol. 15 (1966), 30.

[7]For a good, brief discussion of this point, see R. Rees, "The Scenery Cult: Changing Landscape Tastes over Three Centuries," *Landscape,* Vol. 19 (1975). Note the following remarks by E. H. Gombrich in "The Renaissance Theory of Art and the Rise of Landscape," *Norm and Form: Studies in the Art of the Renaissance* (London, 1971), pp. 117–18: ". . . I believe that the idea of natural beauty as an inspiration of art . . . is, to say the least, a very dangerous oversimplification. Perhaps it even reverses the actual process by which man discovers the beauty of nature. We call a scenery 'picturesque' . . . if it reminds us of paintings we have seen. . . . Similarly, so it seems, the discovery of Alpine scenery does not precede but follows the spread of prints and paintings with mountain panoramas."

[8]Thomas West, *Guide to the Lakes* (London: 1778) as quoted in J. T. Ogden, "From Spatial to Aesthetic Distance in the Eighteenth Century," *Journal of the History of Ideas,* Vol. XXXV (1974), 66–67.

In a somewhat similar fashion, the modern tourist reveals his preference for this model of appreciation by frequenting "scenic viewpoints" where the actual space between the tourist and the prescribed "view" often constitutes "a due distance" which aids the impression of "soft colours of nature, and the most regular perspective the eye can perceive, art teach, or science demonstrate." And the "regularity" of the perspective is often enhanced by the positioning of the viewpoint itself. Moreover, the modern tourist also desires "the finished picture, in highest colouring, and just perspective"; whether this be the "scene" framed and balanced in his camera's viewfinder, the result of this in the form of a kodachrome slide, and/or the "artistically" composed postcard and calendar reproductions of the "scene" which often attract more appreciation than that which they "reproduce." R. Rees has described the situation as follows:

> . . . the taste has been for a view, for scenery, not for landscape in the original Dutch—and present geographical—meaning of term, which denotes our ordinary, everyday surroundings. The average modern sightseer, unlike many of the Romantic poets and painters who were accomplished naturalists, is interested *not* in natural forms and processes, but in a prospect.[9]

It is clear that in addition to being historically important, the landscape model, like the object model, gives us at least initial guidelines as to what and how to appreciate in regard to nature. We appreciate the natural environment as if it were a landscape painting. The model requires dividing the environment into scenes or blocks of scenery, each of which is to be viewed from a particular point by a viewer who is separated by the appropriate spatial (and emotional?) distance. A drive through the country is not unlike a walk through a gallery of landscape paintings. When seen in this light, this model of appreciation causes a certain uneasiness in a number of thinkers. Some, such as ecologist Paul Shepard, seemingly believe this kind of appreciation of the natural environment so misguided that they entertain doubts about the wisdom of *any* aesthetic approach to nature.[10] Others find the model to be ethically suspect. For example, after pointing out that the modern sightseer is interested only in a prospect, Rees concludes:

> In this respect the Romantic Movement was a mixed blessing. In certain phases of its development it stimulated the movement for the protection of nature, but in its picturesque phase it simply confirmed our anthropocentism by suggesting that nature exists to please as well as to serve us. Our ethics, if the word can

---

[9]R. Rees, "The Taste for Mountain Scenery," *History Today,* Vol. XXV (1975), 312.

[10]Paul Shepard, *The Tender Carnivore and the Sacred Game* (New York, 1973), pp. 147–48. Shepard made this position more explicit at a lecture at Athabasca University, Edmonton, Alberta, November 16, 1974.

be used to describe our attitudes and behaviour toward the environment, have lagged behind our aesthetics. It is an unfortunate lapse which allows us to abuse our local environments and venerate the Alps and the Rockies.[11]

What has not been as generally noted, however, is that this model of appreciation is suspect not only on ethical grounds, but also on aesthetic grounds. The model requires us to view the environment as if it were a static representation which is essentially "two dimensional." It requires the reduction of the environment to a scene or view. But what must be kept in mind is that the environment is not a scene, not a representation, not static, and not two dimensional. The point is that the model requires the appreciation of the environment not as what it is and with the qualities it has, but rather as something which it is not and with qualities it does not have. The model is in fact inappropriate to the actual nature of the object of appreciation. Consequently it not only, as the object model, unduly limits our appreciation—in this case to visual qualities related to coloration and overall design, it also misleads it. Hepburn puts this point in a general way:

> Supposing that a person's aesthetic education . . . instills in him the attitudes, the tactics of approach, the expectations proper to the appreciation of art works only, such a person will either pay very little aesthetic heed to natural objects or else heed them in the wrong way. He will look—and of course look in vain— for what can be found and enjoyed only in art.[12]

I conclude that the landscape model, as the object model, is inadequate as a paradigm for the aesthetic appreciation of nature. However, the reason for its inadequacy is instructive. The landscape model is inadequate because it is inappropriate to the nature of the natural environment. Perhaps to see what and how to appreciate in respect to the natural environment, we must consider the nature of that environment more carefully. In this regard there are two rather obvious points which I wish to emphasize. The first is

---

[11]Rees, "Mountain Scenery," op. cit., p. 312. Ethical worries are also expressed by Tuan, *Topophilia*, op. cit., Chapter 8, and R. A. Smith and C. M. Smith, "Aesthetics and Environmental Education," *Journal of Aesthetic Education* (1970), 131–32. Smith and Smith put the point as follows: "Perhaps there is a special form of arrogance in experiencing nature strictly in the categories of art, for the attitude involved here implies an acceptance, though perhaps only momentarily, of the notion that natural elements have been arranged for the sake of the man's aesthetic pleasure. It is possible that this is what Kant had in mind when he said that in the appreciation of natural beauty one ought not assume that nature has fashioned its forms for our delight and that, instead, "it is we who receive nature with favour, and not nature that does us a favour.' "

[12]R. W. Hepburn, "Aesthetic Appreciation of Nature," *Aesthetics and the Modern World*, ed. H. Osborne (London, 1968), p. 53. Hepburn implicitly argues that our aesthetic appreciation of nature is enhanced by our "realizing" that an object is what it is and has the qualities which it has. See pp. 60–65.

that the natural environment is an environment; the second is that it is natural.

When we conceptualize the natural environment as "nature" I think we are tempted to think of it as an object. When we conceptualize it as "landscape" we are certainly led to thinking of it as scenery. Consequently perhaps the concept of the "natural environment" is somewhat preferable. At least it makes explicit that it is an environment which is under consideration. The object model and the landscape model each in its own way fail to take account of this. But what is involved in taking this into account? Here I wish initially to follow up some remarks made by Sparshott. He suggests that to consider something environmentally is primarily to consider it in regard to the relation of "self to setting," rather than "subject to object" or "traveler to scene."[13] An environment is the setting in which we exist as a "sentient part"; it is our surroundings, our setting, the environment is that which we take for granted, that which we hardly notice—it is necessarily unobtrusive. If any one part of it becomes obtrusive, it is in danger of being seen as an object or a scene, not as our environment. As Sparshott says, "When a man starts talking about 'environmental values' we usually take him to be talking about aesthetic values of a background sort."[14]

The aesthetic values of the environment being primarily background values has obvious ramifications for the questions of what and how to appreciate. In regard to what to appreciate this suggests the answer "everything," for in an essentially unobtrusive setting there seems little basis for including and excluding. I will return to this shortly. In regard to how to appreciate, the answer suggested is in terms of all those ways in which we normally are aware of and experience our surroundings. Sparshott notes that "if environmental aspects are background aspects, eye and ear lose part of their privilege" and goes on to mention smell, touch, and taste, and even warmth and coolness, barometric pressure and humidity as possibly relevant.[15] This points in the right direction, but as Sparshott also notes, it seems to involve a difficulty: that "the concept of the aesthetic tugs in a different direction"—the direction of the subject/object relation involving primarily the visual scrutiny of an aesthetic object.[16] However, I do not think this difficulty need be as serious as Sparshott seems to think. I suspect the apparent tension here is not due to the concept of the aesthetic being necessarily tied

---

[13]Sparshott, op. cit., pp. 12–13. Sparshott also considers other possible relations which are not directly relevant here. Moreover, I suspect he considers the "traveler to scene" relation to be more significant than I do.

[14]Ibid., pp. 17–18.

[15]Ibid., p. 21.

[16]Ibid., pp. 13–14, p. 21.

to the subject/object relation or to the visual, but rather is due to its being antithetical to the appreciation of anything only as unobtrusive background. To confirm this we need to consider the concept of the aesthetic as it is elaborated by John Dewey in *Art as Experience.*[17] Dewey's concept is such that anything which is aesthetically appreciated must be obtrusive, it must be foreground, but it need not be an object and it need not be seen (or only seen). Moreover, to assume that that which is aesthetically appreciated need be an object or only seen is to confine aesthetic appreciation to either the object model or the landscape model, which, as we have noted, impose unacceptable limitations on the aesthetic appreciation of the natural environment.

I suggest then that the beginning of an answer to the question of *how* to aesthetically appreciate an environment is something like the following: We must experience our background setting in all those ways in which we normally experience it, by sight, smell, touch, and whatever. However, we must experience it not as unobtrusive background, but as obtrusive foreground! . . . We cannot appreciate everything; there must be limits and emphasis in our aesthetic appreciation of nature as there are in our appreciation of art. Without such limits and emphases our experience of the natural environment would be *only* "a meld of physical sensations" without any meaning or significance. It would be a Jamesian "blooming buzzing confusion" which truly substituted "confusion for order" and which, I suspect . . . would not be wholly satisfying. Such experience would be too far removed from our aesthetic appreciation of art to merit the label "aesthetic" or even the label "appreciation." Consider again the case of art. In this case, as noted in Section I, the boundaries and foci of aesthetic significance of works of art are a function of the type of art in question, *e.g.,* paintings end at their frames and their colors are significant. Moreover, I suggested that our knowledge of such matters is due to art works being our creations. Here it is relevant to note the second point which I wish to emphasize about natural environments: they are natural. The natural environment is not a work of art. As such it has no boundaries or foci of aesthetic significance which are given as a result of our creation nor of which we have knowledge because of our involvement in such creation.

The fact that nature is natural—not our creation—does not mean, however, that we must be without knowledge of it. Natural objects are such that we can discover things about them which are independent of any involvement by us in their creation. Thus although we have not created nature, we yet know a great deal about it. This knowledge, essentially common sense/scientific knowledge, seems to me the only viable candidate for playing the role in regard to the appreciation of nature which our knowledge of types of art, artistic traditions, and the like plays in regard to the appreciation of art.

---

[17]John Dewey, *Art as Experience* (New York, 1958), especially Chapters I–III.

Consider the aesthetic appreciation of an environment. . . . We experience the environment as obtrusive foreground—the smell of the hay and of the horse dung, the feel of the ant, the sound of the cicadas and of the distant traffic all force themselves upon us. We experience a "meld of sensations" but, as noted, if our state is to be aesthetic appreciation rather than just the having of raw experience, the meld cannot be simply a "blooming buzzing confusion." Rather it must be what Dewey called a consummatory experience: one in which knowledge and intelligence transform raw experience by making it determinate, harmonious, and meaningful. For example, in order for there to be aesthetic appreciation we must recognize the smell of the hay and that of the horse dung and perhaps distinguish between them; we must feel the ant at least as an insect rather than as, say, a twitch. Such recognizing and distinguishing results in certain aspects of the obtrusive foreground becoming foci of aesthetic significance. Moreover, they are natural foci appropriate to the particular natural environment we are appreciating. Likewise our knowledge of the environment may yield certain appropriate boundaries or limits to the experience. For example, since we are aesthetically appreciating a certain kind of environment, the sound of cicadas may be appreciated as a proper part of the setting, while the sound of the distant traffic is excluded much as we ignore the coughing in the concert hall.

What I am suggesting is that the question of *what* to aesthetically appreciate in the natural environment is to be answered in a way analogous to the similar question about art. The difference is that in the case of the natural environment the relevant knowledge is the common sense/scientific knowledge which we have discovered about the environment in question. This knowledge gives us the appropriate foci of aesthetic significance and the appropriate boundaries of the setting so that our experience becomes one of aesthetic appreciation. If to aesthetically appreciate art we must have knowledge of artistic traditions and styles within those traditions, to aesthetically appreciate nature we must have knowledge of the different environments of nature and of the systems and elements within those environments. In the way in which the art critic and the art historian are well equipped to aesthetically appreciate art, the naturalist and the ecologist are well equipped to aesthetically appreciate nature.[18]

The point I have now made about what to appreciate in nature also has ramifications for how to appreciate nature. When discussing the nature of an environment, I suggested that Tuan's description seems to indicate a general act of aspection appropriate for any environment. However, since natural environments differ in type it seems that within this general act of aspection there might be differences which should be noted. To aesthetically appreciate an environment we experience our surroundings as obtrusive foreground al-

---

[18]I have in mind here individuals such as John Muir and Aldo Leopold. See, for example, Leopold's *A Sand County Almanac.*

lowing our knowledge of that environment to select certain foci of aesthetic
significance and perhaps exclude others, thereby limiting the experience. But
certainly there are also different kinds of appropriate acts of aspection which
can likewise be selected by our knowledge of environments. Ziff tells us to
look for contours in the Florentine school and for color in a Bonnard, to
survey a Tintoretto and to scan a Bosch. Consider different natural environments. It seems that we must survey a prairie environment, looking at the
subtle contours of the land, feeling the wind blowing across the open space,
and smelling the mix of prairie grasses and flowers. But such an act of aspection
has little place in a dense forest environment. Here we must examine and
scrutinize, inspecting the detail of the forest floor, listening carefully for the
sounds of birds and smelling carefully for the scent of spruce and pine. Likewise, the description of environmental appreciation, in addition to being a
model for environmental acts of aspection in general, is also a description of
the act of aspection appropriate for a particular kind of environment—one
perhaps best described as pastoral. Different natural environments require
different acts of aspection; and as in the case of what to appreciate, our
knowledge of the environment in question indicates how to appreciate, that
is, indicates the appropriate act of aspection.

The model I am thus presenting for the aesthetic appreciation of nature
might be termed the environmental model. It involves recognizing that nature
is an environment and thus a setting within which we exist and which we
normally experience with our complete range of senses as our unobtrusive
background. But our experience being aesthetic requires unobtrusive background to be experienced as obtrusive foreground. The result is the experience
of a "blooming buzzing confusion" which in order to be appreciated must
be tempered by the knowledge which we have discovered about the natural
environment so experienced. Our knowledge of the nature of the particular
environments yields the appropriate boundaries of appreciation, the particular
foci of aesthetic significance, and the relevant act or acts of aspection for that
type of environment. We thus have a model which begins to give answers to
the questions of what and how to appreciate in respect to the natural environment and which seems to do so with due regard for the nature of that
environment. And this is important not only for aesthetic but also for moral
and ecological reasons.

In this paper I have attempted to open discussion on the questions of
what and how to aesthetically appreciate in regard to nature. In doing so I
have argued that two traditional approaches, each of which more or less
assimilates the appreciation of nature to the appreciation of certain art forms,
leave much to be desired. However, the approach which I have suggested,
the environmental model, yet follows closely the general structure of our
aesthetic appreciation of art. This approach does not depend on an assimilation of natural objects to art objects or of landscapes to scenery, but rather
on an application of the general structure of aesthetic appreciation of art to

something which is not art. What is important is to recognize that nature is an environment and is natural, and to make that recognition central to our aesthetic appreciation. Thereby we will aesthetically appreciate nature for what it is and for the qualities it has. And we will avoid being the person described by Hepburn who "will either pay very little aesthetic heed to natural objects or else heed them in the wrong way," who "will look—and of course look in vain—for what can be found and enjoyed only in art."[19]

What Is Feminist Art?

LUCY LIPPARD

I became involved in the women's movement for endless reasons, but the most public one is the fact that, as a working critic for five years, I had been guilty of the same lack of seriousness toward women's work as the museums and galleries. Although I had once been an artist's wife, serving tea and smoothing the way for visitors, and had had my own infuriating experiences in that anonymous role, I continued to go to men's studios and either disregard or matronize the women artists who worked in corners of their husband's spaces, or in the bedroom, even in the kitchen. I was, I think now, unconsciously responding to her sense of inferiority and insecurity as well as to my own (my "reputation" supposedly depended on male support and respect. . . .).

Now, three years later, a lot has changed, but there is still an immense amount of changing yet to be done. One no longer hears as a matter of course comments from dealers like "I can't have a woman in the gallery, they're too difficult," or "Collectors won't buy women's work." Nor does the art press dare use the term "feminine" in a value-judgmental context, something that once caused many women literally to be afraid of using delicate line, sewn materials, household imagery, or pastel colors—especially pink. One well-known stain painter was accused in a review of "painting her monthlies." This won't happen anymore, or if it does, such a statement might come from an artist who, exploring her own experience, is doing just that!

Totally aside from the political necessities fulfilled by women's shows, they also provide a fascinating field of speculation for the question asked so

From Lucy Lippard, *From the Center: Feminist Essays on Women's Art* (New York: E. P. Dutton & Co., Inc., 1976).

[19]Hepburn, op. cit., p. 53.

often over the last two or three years: Is there a women's art? And if so, what is it like? One of the difficulties in drawing any conclusions so early in the game is the fact that art is inevitably influenced by other art publicly made visible, which now means primarily art by men. However, the overwhelming fact remains that a woman's experience in this society—social and biological—is simply not like that of a man. If art comes from inside, as it must, then the art of men and women must be different too. And if this factor does not show up in women's work, only repression can be to blame.

For every time I can be specific about this differentiation, there are endless times in which it remains just out of reach. Perhaps it is impossible to pin it down until women's place in society is indeed equalized and women's work can be studied outside of the confines of oppressive conditioning. Nevertheless, generalizations are made in every field, especially art, and often profitably. It seems most important that our eyes and spirits be attuned to the glimpses we are afforded of women's sensibility and imagery. There are some things I've noticed that I can't seem to deny. For example, in 1966 I was organizing a show around the work of Eva Hesse and Frank Viner—a kind of offbeat, not quite Minimal, not quite funky style I called "Eccentric Abstraction" that later developed into so-called anti-form. I found a lot of women doing this kind of sensuous geometric work—far more than I'd encountered on similar searches for other styles, and in addition, I, a woman, was doing the show because this kind of work appealed to me personally. I wondered briefly about that at the time, and did still more so four years later when I became involved in the women's movement. When I went to a great many women's studios in the winter of 1970/71, I noticed that these and other elements often recurred. It might have been attributable to my own taste, or to something more universal. When I first heard Judy Chicago's and Miriam Schapiro's theories about the high incidence of central-core imagery, of boxes, ovals, spheres, and "empty" centers in women's art, I vehemently resisted them. I was still resisting them when we visited the women's show I organized for the Aldrich Museum, and they ran from work to work shouting "there it is!" There it was. I was astounded, because I'd had no intentions of focusing on that idea, no knowledge that I had been doing so.

Here, in any case, for your own consideration, are some of these elements that recur: a uniform density, or overall texture, often sensuously tactile and repetitive or detailed to the point of obsession; the preponderance of circular forms, central focus, inner space (sometimes contradicting the first aspect); a ubiquitous linear "bag" or parabolic form that turns in on itself; layers, or strata, or veils; an indefinable looseness or flexibility of handling; windows; autobiographical content; animals; flowers; a certain kind of fragmentation; a new fondness for the pinks and pastels and ephemeral cloud colors that used to be tabu unless a woman wanted to be accused of making "feminine" art. Theories and refutations and new theories and new refutations will continue to surround this issue, but it is a rewarding debate that can only help women artists and critics to develop a sense of our individual esthetic directions, and perhaps in the process to define more clearly the web formed by the multiple threads of these individual developments.

What Is Female Imagery?

A PANEL DISCUSSION

The women participating in this discussion are: Susan Hall, figurative painter; Lucy Lippard, art critic; Linda Nochlin, art historian; Joan Snyder, abstract painter; Susana Torre, architect.

What is female imagery?

NOCHLIN: My first reaction is anger, because the term is so constricting. I'm human, undefined by preconceptions, an androgynous being that isn't slated to give birth to any particular imagery. But my second reaction is to try and think it through. I do live in a society, and who I am is determined by the structure of experience a woman is supposed to have. My experience is filtered through a complex interaction between me and the expectations that the world has of me.

I've been reading Dorothy Richardson, who, I think, invented the stream-of-consciousness style at the beginning of this century. She consciously set out to create a female style and imagery, the quality of female existence in a certain time and place. She captured a middle-class Englishwoman's experience and sensibility. That's female imagery, not something Jungian—predetermined and absolute.

LIPPARD: How about visual imagery?

NOCHLIN: That's where it gets hard for me. It's not a specific image, iconography, or subject that has to do exclusively with women. It has more to do with process, or modalities of approaching experience, but even then I get stuck. It has to be invented, like any iconography.

HALL: There's a scale of negative and positive physical charges in men and women. Somebody said that man is sixty percent positive physically—projected out toward the world—and forty percent negative, mentally. Woman is just the reverse. So together they form a bond. Then there are many subtle combinations of masculine and feminine. I thought about these related to painting, from Helen Frankenthaler to Georgia O'Keeffe. And I realized that in order to be an artist at all you have to have, physically, a certain kind of energy, a certain kind

Susan Hall, Lucy Lippard, Linda Nochlin, Joan Snyder, and Susana Torre, "What Is Female Imagery?" *Ms.*, 3 (1975).

of momentum. It would be very difficult on this level for the superfeminine inward woman to do art work because she would need that physically charged energy.

SNYDER: I think there is a female sensibility. I know what it *isn't*. But I can't pinpoint what it is, though I've boasted I can walk into the Whitney Annual and pick out the women's work.

Women have been working in the closet for so long that we're now seeing new and original work by women that we don't see by men. The sociologist in me would like to explore the lives of artists to understand why they're making their art. The quality of people's lives has a lot to do with the art they make. One of the dangers women are facing right now is that we've been accepted into the art world and are acting out male artists' life-styles. That's an enormous danger to any kind of sensibility. Whether or not we're going to change anything has a lot to do with how we respond—or what our needs are, I guess.

LIPPARD: Of course, "female imagery" was first used, and should continue to be used, to mean female *sexual* imagery. That wasn't understood and it all got confused. I prefer "female sensibility" because it's vaguer, even more impossible to pin down. There is a lot of sexual imagery in women's art—circles, domes, eggs, spheres, boxes, biomorphic shapes, maybe a certain striation or layering. But that's too specific. It's more interesting to think about fragments, which imply a certain antilogical, antilinear approach also common to many women's work. I like fragments, networks, everything about everything. Men's work isn't so much cliché-aggressive, all angles and phallic, as it's closed—the "this is *my* image" number. Women are, for all kinds of reasons, more open, into themselves in a very different way.

TORRE: I read in *Architectural Design* that the only way in which a woman can experience herself as a person is through a creative act of her own. "Creative" doesn't necessarily mean artmaking: political action can be an act of creation, too. That's crucial for women. Feminism shouldn't be an interpretation of this world, but a transformation of it. Right now, the issue of sensibility is secondary to the issue of consciousness. Female consciousness is different from male consciousness, and it's still in the process of being structured. It's impossible to give a tight definition of something that's in the process of becoming, but we can talk tentatively about a particular stage of this process in various areas—female imagery, for instance.

The image is an incredibly powerful medium. It can express in synthesis levels of consciousness that are not rationally apparent but can mesmerize people. I see the making of a female imagery as a tool for generating further consciousness in other women, and people in general. As an architect, it seems to me that women more than men should be able to find, through the daily appropriation of space, a closer correlation between spaces and biological and cultural rituals. We are less removed from spatial experience than men.

NOCHLIN: I was part of the 1950s—cosmopolitan, asexual, ideologically male-dominated. I never looked at an artist's work as masculine or feminine. Now my whole perception of reality has been irrevocably altered; feminism has made me question all the presuppositions and ideologies about art I've been handed over the years. Why is one form considered "good" and another "not good"? I often see women's styles as being partly conditioned by opposition, as having meaning in the context of being opposed to existing styles. The painter Florine Stettheimer, for instance, did conventionally "advanced academic" work at the turn of the century. She knew what the avant-garde was doing—Marcel Duchamp and other innovators were her friends. But eventually she said No to both the academic and the avant-garde modes and went on to invent something of her own, something private, something that was called "feminine." She's being appreciated more fully now; we're ready to look at her work in its totality, not just as negatively "bizarre, feminine form," but as a conscious step, radical in the 1920s and 1930s.

I'm looking at Gertrude Stein differently, too, as one of the innovators of our century in many fields. I hadn't thought of her as a woman expressing a woman's experience before. Yet Florine Stettheimer and Gertrude Stein aren't in any way alike. I find analogies in how they invent in opposition to what's prevailing, but I don't find a common thread and I don't think that's necessary. I don't find a common thread in American art from the late nineteenth century, either. But I'm interested in exploring the quality and the style and seeing what possibilities there are for inventing or adapting languages or forms in women's work. I don't want to pin it down because women aren't any more alike in an easily definable way than men. Perhaps we should talk of female *styles,* always in the plural.

HALL: Things only become clear to me after I've finished a series of paintings, because I don't want to paint something that was that clear and specific to begin with. I'm conscious of a diffused kind of process.

LIPPARD: That's the way I work and I find a lot of women work. But I wonder if that's *because* of our alienation from logic and rationality or whether it comes from somewhere else.

HALL: When I'm involved in something difficult, what interests me is seeing ways of moving beyond it. All the power struggles in the art world, all the problems with galleries, are just challenges. We have to meet them and move on to the other side, whatever that is.

LIPPARD: I have such *doubts* about writing on women artists in the art magazines and doing shows that get women into more shows within the current rotten structure. I've been dragging them into something most of them know very little about, because most women artists have been so isolated from the workings of the art world. There's this conflict about getting a piece of the pie, even if it's poisonous, and knowing it's really their choice and not mine.

SNYDER: I think women tend to be more autobiographical in their work than men. If anybody was really looking at my own work, I'd be very embarrassed because they'd know all about me. My work is an open diary. That's what I often miss in men's work—an autobiographical or narrative aspect. Some women artists are making statements that make me say, "Oh, right, I know exactly what she's talking about." I can't do that with most of my male artist contemporaries. Men talk about art a lot and I don't think women talk about art as much as they talk about life.

LIPPARD: You made this beautiful claim—which maybe all of us feel but are scared to make: that you can tell women's art from men's art. How?

SNYDER: It has to do with a kind of softness, layering, a certain color sensibility, a more expressive work than any man is going to do right now, and a repetitious-ness—use of grids, obsessive in a way. When I look at women's art, I look for ideas and images that not only move me visually, but tell me something about who the artist is, what she is, what she's trying to say. I'm not interested in art so mysterious that it doesn't tell me a thing.

In 1968 I did flock paintings, using flesh colors and sensuous, vagina-type shapes, stretching membranes, little seeds, floating objects. They were sensuous paintings and they were about me. And then I needed to make them more layered, maybe to tell a story. Now when I look back, to try to figure out where my grids came from, I see that I started doing them about a month before I got married. When I made the decision to put structure into my life, structure appeared in my painting.

LIPPARD: I do feel that women are more interested in people, probably because you live vicariously if you're isolated. So women become more interested in soap opera and fiction. But women also care more about variety than men, and variety connects to fragmentation and to the autobiographical aspect, too—as a sort of defiance. We play so many roles in our lives, while most men play only one or two. The beginning of any woman's career has always been the business of sitting back and listening to men and thinking, "Well, I have an identity, too; it isn't very interesting, maybe. I've never met Mark Rothko and I never did this and I never did that, but I have my little things." Those "little things" are the secrets that women turn in on and depend on.

In a way, the women's movement gave me permission to like the art I always identified with, but didn't allow myself to like because if I had, I might not have been so successful. This wasn't at all conscious. I loved and identified with the art I was seeing, too, but I was leaving some important things out. By the time the women's movement hit, I was feeling almost male. I lived alone with my kid in another country for a while then, writing fiction, and when I came back, I wasn't ashamed of being a woman anymore. The idea of identifying with women's work was very exciting to me—the whole thing of caring. A lot of women's work, and the best of men's work, has an indefinable aspect of *caring* about it.

Another totally separate thing is that the cliché of women's art is getting as bad as the cliché of men's art. Before the movement, women were denying their identity, trying to be neutral, and intentionally making art that couldn't be called "feminine." When somebody said, "You paint like a man," or "You write like a man," you were supposed to be happy, and you *were* happy, because you knew you were at least making neutral art instead of feminine art—god forbid. So now we're bending over backward in the other direction, insisting that there are clichés that define women's art. Women now make "women's art" instead of "men's art" or "neutral art." It may be easier to find out what women's art is, or what female imagery is, quick, this second, because the work of women who've been isolated and closeted, which has come out in the last three years, is personal, still has the blush of innocence on it.

That level we may never see again. I want to catch those ephemeral moments before we all move into a different, and I hope, more powerful and clearer level.

Moving to the Ends of Our Own Rainbows: Steps Toward a Feminist Aesthetic

ESTELLA LAUTER

Any coherent aesthetic position nowadays must be multidimensional. It must encompass at least a definition of art, a set of standards for its evaluation and a theory about its relationship to the "artworld." Such a position is developed by both formal and informal means—by critics, historians, philosophers, curators, publishers, gallery owners, patrons and artists—and it changes constantly in the daily process of decision-making. Thus it is always difficult to say precisely what the "aesthetic" of a movement, school or era is. The task of defining a feminist aesthetic is doubly difficult because feminism is scarcely past the phase of early adulthood in its development. Still, the subject arises with some urgency, lest the substantial aesthetic expressions of women in this century be swallowed by history, as the achievements of women in previous centuries have been.

Further trouble arises immediately in the definition of feminism as it relates to the arts. The term "feminist" is used loosely to define any position that is favorable to women and more restrictively to designate commitment to certain values: e.g. equal rights, equal pay for equal work, control over one's body in matters of reproduction. One may embrace such values with radical, reformist or integrationist intensity. Since relatively few artists take the time to become activists, specific political commitments are nearly impossible to pin down and may turn out to be irrelevant to the interpretation of works of art. Thus a feminist aesthetic must be drawn from women who are not directly inspired by politics as well as from those who are. The identifying mark of feminist art, then, is simply its articulation of the artist's consciousness of what it means to be a woman.

In the midst of these difficulties, my objectives here must be quite limited. I propose to review the statements of one feminist critic, Lucy Lippard, who has been the most influential apologist for feminist visual art since the publication of her book, *From the Center: Feminist Essays on Women's Art,* in 1976.[1] From her work, I think it is possible to extrapolate a feminist aesthetic theory with potentially broad application across the arts. At least, it may be possible to clarify how women are "movin to the ends of/our/own rainbows"[2] of aesthetic consciousness.

Let us begin to construct a feminist aesthetic with a definition of art. At the bottom of it is the notion that art is gendered. In societies where gender differences are pronounced, issues of gender are bound to appear in the arts. They may not appear in every work, and they may not appear in the same way. One cannot walk into a gallery or read a poem and know immediately which work was created by a woman. Gender conditioning is a complex affair which produces different results in artists. It has worked on some women to restrict their artistic expression to certain media (say, embroidery at one extreme and hard edge painting in reaction to it at the other), and on others to allow them to revalue previously denigrated aspects of human experience. The belief that art is gendered, however, underlies most of the exhibits and books devoted to women artists in the decade of the Seventies.

Lucy Lippard was among the first to say that gender differences were apparent in both the subject matter and the form of visual works by women. As early as 1973 in response to the first major all-women's exhibit in America (the "Women Choose Women" show at the Brooklyn Museum), she noted the following recurrent elements in the contemporary work on display:

> . . . a uniform density, or overall texture, often sensuously tactile and repetitive or detailed to the point of obsession; the preponderance of circular forms, central focus, inner space (sometimes contradicting the first aspect); a ubiquitous linear "bag" or parabolic form that turns in on itself; layers, or strata, or veils; an indefinable looseness or flexibility of handling; windows; autobiographical content; animals; flowers; a certain kind of fragmentation; a new fondness for the pinks and pastels and ephemeral cloud colors that used to be tabu unless a woman wanted to be accused of making "feminine" art. [Lippard, p. 49]

Lippard attributed these patterns generally to the differences in women's social and biological experiences in American society, saying that if women's art did not differ from men's it could only be because of repression [Lippard, p. 48. Subsequent page numbers given here refer to Lippard's book.] Gender, then seemed to be an essential factor in determining the focus of attention, the "regional" qualities of color, texture, and shape, and the means of achieving formal unity.

---

[1]Lucy Lippard, *From the Center: Feminist Essays on Women's Art* (N.Y.: Dutton, 1976).

[2]The words are Ntozake Shange's closing lines in *For Colored Girls Who Have Considered Suicide When the Rainbow is Enuf* (N.Y.: Macmillian, 1977), p. 64.

Later, Lippard modified this position. While still affirming the idea that certain recurrent images in art by women have "biological and sexual sources," she began to see that there is "no technique, form, or approach used exclusively by women" [p. 69]. Furthermore, she began to think that the overtly sexual imagery tended to occur in "early, or immature, or naive, not yet acculturated work" [p. 69]. From the beginning, Lippard had been nervous about the concept of "female imagery," preferring the broader term "female sensibility" [pp. 49–81]. She was intrigued by "a certain antilogical, antilinear approach common to many women's work" [p. 81], particularly as it was expressed in fragments or networks and in the penchant for autobiography [p. 89]. She even ventured the guess that the openness of women's art was related to the greater variety of roles women play [p. 89]. Instead of working out these hypotheses in greater detail, however, Lippard gradually retreated from them. Without abandoning the idea that gender is an essential element of art, she began to think less about its specific manifestations in form and content and more about the effect of women on the evolution of art.

This idea becomes the focus of Lippard's most recent essay on feminist art, wherein she contends that:

> Feminism's greatest contribution to the future of art has probably been precisely its *lack* of contribution to modernism. Feminist methods and theories have instead offered a socially concerned alternative to the increasingly mechanical "evolution" of art about art.[3]

Feminist art, regardless of its political stripe, she argues, challenges the modernist idea of the work of art as an object—a closed system accessible only by relatively rare and highly trained acts of empathy. Art by women of the Seventies is characterized by an "atmosphere of outreach virtually abandoned by modernism" [Lippard, "Sweeping Exchanges," p. 362. Subsequent page numbers here refer to this book.] Thus, the specific images, forms, and media that women have developed become "*surface* phenomena," and the warfare in the artworld over who did what first and whether or not men can create the same phenomena is beside the point. Along the way, feminists have fallen into certain traps:

> . . . the adoption of certain clichés in images (fruit and shell, mirror and mound), materials (fabrics and papers), approaches ("non-elitist"), and emotions (non-transformative pain, rage and mother-love); a certain naiveté (also carrying with it a certain strength) that comes from the wholesale rejection of all other art, especially abstraction and painting; a dependence and, at the other extreme, an unthinking acceptance of literally anything done by a woman. [p. 363]

---

[3]Lippard, "Sweeping Exchanges: The Contribution of Feminism to the Art of the 1970s," *Art Journal* (Fall/Winter, 1980), p. 362.

The artists who have avoided these traps (and Lippard does not mention them by name) have done so chiefly by becoming collaborative, by engaging in consciousness-raising dialogue about the social and aesthetic realities of their lives and art, and by developing a new respect for their audience. The impulse toward formal originality, the sine qua non of Twentieth Century art, is replaced by a concern with re-structuring the relationships between art and life. The impulse toward self-expression is replaced by the broader task of "speaking for those who cannot speak" on their own behalf [p. 363].

Lippard singles out three models of interaction between feminist artists and their constituencies. Cooperative, collective, collaborative or anonymous art, of the kind epitomized in traditional quiltmaking, is high on Lippard's list of valued "structures" that could change the meaning of art in society by changing our definition of the artist. Public consciousness-raising events or performances, such as Judy Chicago's massive tribute to women, "The Dinner Party," model the idea that art can be socially effective. And group or public rituals, such as the performance based on the group experience of braiding and burning a spiral of cornstalks that Mary Beth Edelson staged at the University of Iowa in 1978,[4] bring art into direct relationship with communal needs.

Aside from existing in a more or less pure form in the examples I have given, these models also inform the aesthetics of work in traditional fine art media, posters, video, publications, and all manner of performances. Ntozake Shange's choreopoem excerpted in this anthology is a case in point. It grew out of the experience of five women who met for two years at the Bacchanal, a woman's bar outside Berkeley, to read poems and "make a woman's theater for about twenty patrons."[5] From these humble origins, the poems became a full-scale Broadway production whose every performance reenacted a ritual of survival for black women and accomplished an act of consciousness-raising for the black men and "uncolored" members of the audience.

Shange's work is an example of the idea of "inclusiveness" that Lippard identifies as characteristic of feminist art. As a collage of poems, dance, music, and theater elements, it challenges the boundaries of several forms. It does so, however, not to make a statement about the nature of art, but to respond to the imperatives of Shange's female heritage and to take responsibility for expressing it.

Many of Lippard's own examples of her models are less recognizable as works of art. She has in mind events that take place outside the normal boundaries of the artworld, in "schools, streets, shopping malls, prisons, hospitals or neighborhoods" [p. 364]. She has in mind documentary pieces about women in prison done by an international group living in Paris; or "Desert People" costume rituals performed by an Israeli woman to com-

---

[4]Cited in Mary Beth Edelson's *Seven Cycles: Public Rituals* (N.Y.: AIR Gallery, 1980), p. 51.
[5]Shange, p. ix.

municate the plight of the Bedouin tribes; or even the photography of a man in a poor New England milltown who uses his art as a consciousness-raising tool.

Presumably, Lippard would agree with Morris Weitz that art has no necessary and sufficient principles.[6] Even traditional artmaking skills, for example, are no longer sufficient in an arena of art that must accept the changes made by the context and the audience in the subject and form of the work. All previous definitions are superceded (without being replaced) by the concept of "inclusiveness." The structures of such art are more like webs or networks than like artifacts, and they are nothing if not expandable. They could encompass any subject, style, form, medium, situation and audience and change endlessly in response to new environments. Feminist art is *like* the collage, both because it "offers a way of knitting the fragments of our lives together" and because it "potentially leaves nothing out" [p. 365]; all the previous forms of art may legitimately become part of its structures.

The key to Lippard's concept of quality as well as to her definition of feminist art is her idea of "dialogue." The work of art must be designed to affect the audience both aesthetically and politically, and it must do so by creating the possibility of dialogue. The conception and performance or ex-ecution of art are no longer sufficient; the response of the audience is part of the work. The extent to which the audience is *moved* to speak back to the work is the measure of its quality. In this respect, Lippard's theory of art resembles the theories of Plato, Aristotle, Horace, and Longinus more than the post-modernist theories of our own time.[7] The kinds of response, the nature of the dialogue, and the relationship of either to the work that generates them remain to be detailed. Nevertheless, Lippard has established the first ground rule for evaluation within a feminist aesthetic.

Neither the work's status as art nor its quality is dependent upon the artworld, according to Lippard's theory. Until her article appeared in the *Art Journal* it is doubtful that anyone in the artworld knew of the eight projects she cites as examples of feminist art of the Seventies. Although Lippard does not address the issue of evaluation directly, she implies that it is up to the artist and the audience together to decide if the work in question is art and if it is good. If members of the artworld are part of the audience, Lippard might say, so much the better for the pocketbook of the artist. If not, she seems confident that the art will continue to be made.

Clearly she hopes that feminist art will change the artworld. She imagines this change in several ways: in terms of the feminist challenges to the modernist artworld's definition of art, separation of art and life, and its inexorable march

---

[6]"The Role of Theory in Aesthetics," *The Journal of Aesthetics and Art Criticism* XV (1956), 27–35.

[7]See Jane P. Tompkins's groundbreaking essay, "The Reader in History: The Changing Shape of Literary Response" in her *Reader-Response Criticism: From Formalism to Post Structuralism* (Baltimore: Johns Hopkins, 1980), pp. 201–226, esp. pp. 202–206.

of progress. If feminist art succeeds in making its point that art is a network of relationships with an audience—a network whose social aspects are as important as its aesthetic aspects, and one which may mine historical styles as well as create new ones—the effect on the artworld could be enormous. Presumably the curator and the critic, along with all the other functionaries, would join the artist in facilitating the audience's social aesthetic response, and the activity of judgment would be a far less important, more complex affair than it presently is.

Since feminist art "speaks" and invites response by its very lack of pretension and by its availability to people who are not highly trained in viewing art, it will not require much support from the artworld. Witness the success of "The Dinner Party," for example. Regardless of its success in changing the artworld, then, feminist art could continue to develop independently on the fringes of the established marketplace for a very long time.

Lippard's fledgling theory based in the visual arts may have far-reaching implications for other arts. Thus, we might notice that the features of style which are said to define female writing amount to the same kind of challenge to the modernist idea of art as object that Lippard posits for feminist visual art. Consider the following description of contemporary writing by women:

> As women strain to break through the limits of English, certain patterns begin to emerge, recurrences of similar syntactic ways of ordering perception that is always moving and often contradictory. One observation may negate another. The natural imagery of growth, proliferation, and evolution replaces nature as object and product. Flux, not stasis, perceptive categories give way to active, process verbs and concrete nouns, the language of touch; verbs of specific action replace the abstract more general verbs. On the discourse level, we find a discursive, conjunctive style instead of the complex, subordinating, linear style of classification and distinction. It is not that there is no classification taking place, but rather that the syntactic structure must accommodate itself to the shifting perspectives of the writer's observing mind.[8]

At the basic level of linguistic choice, contemporary women writers challenge the idea that the work is finished and separate from both the author and the reader. It is, above all else, a process to be completed by the reader. If feminist criticism takes this idea seriously, it should lead to new developments of reader response theory that go well beyond the modernist biases of its main practitioners. It should also lead to entirely new bases of evaluation and a reconsideration of the relationship of feminist writers and critics to the literary artworld.

Lippard's theory is powerful because it hooks up with a widely accepted

---

[8]Julia Penelope Stanley and Susan J. Wolfe (Robbins), "Toward a Feminist Aesthetic," *Crysalis: A Magazine of Women's Culture* #6 (1978), p. 67.

psychological theory regarding female development. Women are said to have "more flexible ego boundaries" than men partially as a result of our biosexual experiences of menstruation, coitus, pregnancy, childbirth, and lactation.[9] The "inclusiveness" of both traditional and contemporary art by women, the tendency to measure its worth by the response it draws from others (particularly from other women), and the disregard for the artificial boundaries of the artworld may be deeply rooted in the biological difficulties of maintaining rigid boundaries between the individual female body and other bodies. We experience the relationship between inside and outside differently than the masculine-based culture prescribes. Instead of being pathological, this difference may be the basis of a new aesthetic and cultural renaissance. For if we are witnessing the development of an aesthetic that is rooted in the realities of female biology, we can expect it to appeal eventually to a very broad audience, regardless of its affiliations with the artworld.

Instead of being a description of a limited art movement in the late Twentieth Century, Lippard's steps toward a feminist aesthetic promise to take us to an unsuspected end of the rainbow of aesthetic consciousness.

Aesthetic Rights

ALAN TORMEY

The thesis that I shall attempt to establish here is that art works are the bearers of a special class of *rights*; that art works have, in virtue of their status *as* art works, certain determinable entitlements to be dealt with, or not to be dealt with, in particular ways.

The argument will require consideration both of some of the logical implications of the concept of a right and of a dimension of our aesthetic experience. It should be understood, however, that this does not threaten a wholly stipulative or normative enterprise. I will not be arguing that we *should* grant rights of a special sort to art works, but rather that certain aspects of our aesthetic experience, under one possible set of descriptions, suggest that we do in fact regard art works as invested with rights of a kind analogous to those that we normally concede to persons.

Alan Tormey, "Aesthetic Rights," *Journal of Aesthetics and Art Criticism* XXXI (1973). Reprinted with permission.

---

[9]See Nancy Chodorow, "Family Structure and Feminine Personality," in Michelle Z. Rosaldo and Louise Lamphere, eds., *Women, Culture and Society* (Stanford: Stanford, 1974), pp. 58–60.

Rights

The first step then will be to provide a sketch of what may be plausibly defended as a set of sufficient conditions for the possession of rights. Like Bentham, I shall not be concerned so much with what rights are, but with what it is to *have* a right.

Now, one *prima facie* obstacle must be confronted at once. Rights, it will be objected, may be possessed or claimed only by rational beings, or only by actual or potential rational beings, or only by humans and higher animals, or, at the very outside—by a magnanimous stretching of good will and a tolerance for distant analogy—by all sentient creatures.[1] But even the most generous of extensions must exclude material objects or mere "things" from the class of legitimate claimants of rights. There are sufficient difficulties, we shall be reminded, over the inclusion of animals, idiots, infants, and embryos without introducing a plea for insensate objects. But I can only reiterate here that I am not entering a plea for a plaintiff; rather I shall be arguing that there are some irreducible facts about our aesthetic experience and our transactions with art works that can be adequately accounted for only if we recognize that art works are tacitly held to be *de facto* bearers of certain rights.

Fortunately for our purposes, it is unnecessary to discuss all of the reasons that have been advanced for setting the limits of rights or entitlements at one point on the ontological scale rather than another. But it will be necessary to remove the ground from the objection that art works logically *could* not be possessors of rights, since they are "mere" objects or insensate entities. This general objection to the possibility of insensate entities possessing rights can best be understood as a purported consequence of the argument, frequently encountered in philosophical discussions of rights, that a limiting and necessary condition of the possession of rights is the possession of interests, viz., that only those entities that can claim, or have claimed for them, certain interests (general welfare, freedom from harm or destruction, avoidance of mistreatment or injustice, freedom to pursue one's goals, etc.) can be said to have rights, since rights are most plausibly construed as entitlements to the pursuit or protection of interests. And it is presumably on these grounds that rights are to be assigned or withheld. But it is not entirely clear just how the possession of interests itself is to be established and limited. Persons, or at least persons considered as members of a social structure, are clearly interest bearers. But persons are not the exclusive bearers of interests. We also speak, for instance, of corporate interests where it is clear that the

---

[1] There are useful reviews of the relevant arguments in H. J. McClosky, "Rights," *Philosophical Quarterly* 15 (April 1965): 115–27, and S. I. Benn, "Rights," in *Encyclopedia of Philosophy*, ed. P. Edwards 7: (New York: Macmillan Co., 1967), 195–99.

possessor of those interests—the company or the nation—is itself insensate, and where *its* interests are frequently distinguishable from those of its sensate constituents. There are (perhaps always deplorable) occasions where, for example, the interests of a nation may be furthered only at the expense of the interests of that nation's population. And in this flexible but perfectly ordinary sense of "interest," what is to prevent us from speaking of the interests not only of corporations and nations but also of roles, offices, and professions, as well as those of species (as distinct from individuals) or of unborn generations? Even if we accept the arguments for the dependence of rights on interests—and I believe that we should accept them—there can be no justification for automatically eliminating a potential bearer of rights on the ground of its ontological status alone, since interests may attach to a variety of ontologically disparate entities, some of which are neither concrete nor sensate.

It is one thing, however, to remove an objection and another to support a thesis; and I will argue later that art works are genuine interest-bearers; but first we must consider the other side of the conceptual coin. If rights are construed, roughly, as entitlements, they may be thought of not only as entailing interests on the part of the claimant or possessor but also, in the standard case, obligations on the part of those—necessarily rational—beings from whom a respect for those interests can legitimately be required or expected.[2] And this is a general requirement. Where the rights of X entail corresponding obligations for Y, X *need* not be a rational being, but Y must be. And this asymmetry is evident from the examples of infants and animals, who have rights but no obligations, even though their rights impose obligations on other, more rational, creatures. It is significant that this is a logical asymmetry, and thus remains unaltered even where both X and Y are rational beings. All that is altered in this case is that there is now the possibility of a symmetrical exchange of roles. Y may also have rights that impose obligations on X. We shall be concerned in what follows specifically with instances where only Y is rational and sensate.

Even if the possession of interests is a necessary condition for having a right then, it is not sufficient in the absence of a related obligation imposed or generated by that interest. And not all interests are obligation-imposing. It may be in the interests, say, of someone to learn of the intentions and projects of a business rival, but this hardly imposes an obligation on the rival

---

[2] I take "entitlement" to include both "entitlement *to*" (e.g., perform actions, pursue policies) and "entitlement *to be*" (e.g., treated in particular ways or protected from certain treatments). There are both active and passive entitlements then, but only the later will be relevant here. The conception of a passive entitlement comes close I believe to Bentham's thesis that to have a right is to be the beneficiary of someone's duty or obligation. (See *Works, III,* and also David Lyons, "Rights, Claimants, and Beneficiaries," *American Philosophical Quarterly* 6 (July 1969): 173–85.

to reveal his plans. And if there are any interests that impose no obligations whatever on any rational being, those interests cannot be the foundation for any claim to rights. But in the presence of what we may call obligation-generating interests we are, *ceteris paribus,* justified in speaking of rights. Succinctly, then, I shall regard it as a sufficient condition for *having* a right that something have entitlements, where an entitlement is construed as the possession of an obligation-generating interest.

All this is admittedly, and intentionally, merely a sketch. It is not of course a definition of "right" nor should it be seen as more than the schematic formulation of one set of sufficient conditions for something's having a right. But it is enough for my purposes, and I shall therefore assume that, if it can be shown of some entity, X, that it is the possessor of interests that are genuinely obligation-generating (i.e., interests that entitle its possessor either to pursue, unopposed, certain goals of its own choosing or to be treated in certain prescriptible ways by obligation bearers), then we have every reason to speak of that entity as having corresponding rights. It remains to argue that art works are entities that fulfill these conditions, and that exercise will occupy the next section. Briefly, I hope to show, by isolating certain aspects of our aesthetic experience and by arguing for a particular description of them, that their occurrence under these (or analogous) descriptions points strongly to the conclusion that we do in fact regard art works as entities which fulfill the relevant conditions outlined in the first part, and that, in effect, we tacitly ascribe rights to them.[3]

Aesthetic Pain

The following are descriptions of possible experiences:

1. Hearing a violinist play the Debussy Sonata for Violin and Piano with a strident tone and faulty intonation.
2. Watching an inexperienced and awkward ballerina attempt *Giselle.*
3. Looking at a grotesquely proportioned building.
4. Seeing the *Annunciation* of Pinturicchio in Spello after someone has painted a moustache on the Virgin.
5. Reading a trite and worthless novel.

I will first discuss these examples, hoping to fix some of the parameters of the concept of aesthetic pain. (The relevance of this discussion to the issue

---

[3]There is no "is-ought" confusion here. I am not about to argue, again, that art works ought to have or be given rights, but that reflection on our aesthetic experience under at least one possible set of descriptions reveals that, in fact, we tacitly attribute or ascribe rights to them.

of aesthetic rights will then be more explicitly considered in part III of this essay.) "Aesthetic pain" is not a standard expression in contemporary critical parlance and will, I recognize, raise some noteworthy eyebrows. Part of my intention here is to demonstrate its usefulness and to show that it has, or can be given, a philosophically respectable role to play in critical discourse.

To begin with, if the adjunctive locution "aesthetically painful" is applicable at all, I think it should be allowed to apply to the experiences described in (1) and (2). A presumptive reason for considering these to be aesthetically painful experiences is that they would normally evoke, in the perceptive experient, some form of avoidance behavior: for example, in the first case, eliminating the sound source where possible, and in the second, closing one's eyes or averting one's gaze. Such experiences will also frequently be accompanied by expressions (winces or grimaces) that would be commonly taken to be expressions of pain. Now, such reactions might be sufficient to justify the attribution of "painful" to the experience, but they do nothing to sanction the addition of "aesthetically." Are such experiences then *aesthetically* painful merely because they occur in the process of attending to an aesthetic object? Clearly not, for if that were the case, any pain that one might experience while attending to a performance would be aesthetically painful, and it would be absurd to apply that concept to a concurrent toothache.

If we are to distinguish a dimension of our experience as aesthetically painful, it must be one that is somehow occasioned or brought about by properties of the aesthetic object or the aesthetic situation attended to.[4] But, now, which are the relevant properties? It seems clear that not all of the properties attributable to a performance are essential to its being an *instantiation* of a particular work. Some will be accidental or nonessential properties: for example, the overall decibel level of a musical performance is to a large extent a function of the acoustical ambience in which the performance takes place, and variations in this function leave the relation between performance and work largely unaffected. But if, unluckily, the level should be excessively high, the sound may prove intolerably painful for the listener. And this experience, although *caused* by a property of the aesthetic object could not reasonably be called *aesthetically* painful. Something other than a merely accidental or nonessential property of the object must be involved.

---

[4]Where a performance is involved, "aesthetic object" should be understood to refer to the entire complex of performance-plus-work. Also, largely for reasons of style and economy, I have used the "material mode" throughout much of this paper, speaking, for example, of experiences and properties. It should be understood that nothing that is logically essential hinges on this, and that the argument could be consistently recast substituting references to criterial conditions for the application of predicates of varying logical types for references to properties and experiential qualities.

I want to suggest that, in (1) and (2), what is responsible for the aesthetic painfulness of the experience is the recognition of *incongruity* between performance and work, and it is our awareness of an aesthetic distortion *of* the work *in* the performance that gives rise to the distinctive experience that I have labeled "aesthetic pain."[5]

Having suggested that the source of aesthetic pain in (1) and (2) lies in the recognition of an incongruity between performance and work, I will now consider the remaining examples.

Our third case ushers in a new set of problems. So far, we have considered only examples from the performing arts, and the concept of an aesthetically painful experience has been explicated entirely by reference to performances and their properties. What then of the visual arts: of sterile sculptures, bizarre buildings, and screeching canvases? Are they also sources of the aesthetically painful?

There are special difficulties here that will be mentioned shortly, but, in general, I would argue that the visual arts are not, *per se*, sources of experience that we should call aesthetically painful. Many works of visual art are plainly ugly or disproportioned, but the ugly and the painful are distinct, and it is just here that we have use for the distinction. Unless it is shown that attentively viewing an ugly object analytically guarantees the occurrence of a painful experience, we must respect, as independent, questions concerning the presence of ugliness and the occurrence of aesthetic pain. There are works of art that one may find unrelievedly ugly or discordant, but it has been a truism since Plato that one may be fascinated by the ugly and the discordant; and contemporary criticism, at least, has found room for these properties as potential bearers of aesthetic merit. And it is difficult to understand how aesthetic merit could reasonably be credited to any property if it were responsible for the engendering of aesthetically painful experiences. One might of course object to this by arguing, on the ground of some espoused aesthetic theory, that the presence of qualities like ugliness and discordance must always count *against* and never *for* the attribution of aesthetic value. But even if we accept this argument it follows only that a wholly ugly or discordant object

---

[5]It may occur to some to object that "incongruity" is suspect in this context, since the ontological status of essentially repeatable works of art is notoriously problematic. This is not the place to sort out all of the ontic puzzles surrounding these objects, and in any case, it is unnecessary to do so, for my argument is consistent with all but the decision to regard a work as *identical* with the set of its performances; and there are good reasons, apart from its intuitive implausibility, for rejecting this possibility. (See, for example, Richard Wollheim, *Art and Its Objects:* "If a novel or opera just is its copies or its performances, then we cannot, for purposes of identification, refer from the latter to the former." [New York: Harper & Row, 1968], p. 8.)

By speaking of the *instantiation* of such works I do, however, (intentionally) suggest that there is a resemblance between members of this class of art works and *concepts,* which are also capable of instantiation, and also with varying degrees of success.

is wholly worthless, not that it is also aesthetically painful to behold. The contemplation of an ugly or aesthetically worthless object may induce a reaction that we would be willing to call "aesthetic displeasure" or "aesthetically displeasing"; but to be displeased by something is not to be pained by it. Something other than the simple presence of "bad-making" features in an art work is required for an explanation of the possibility of aesthetic pain. And what this suggests, I believe, is that there are no properties of an art work, *denoted by single-place predicates,* that are sufficient for the occasioning of aesthetic pain, and that some relation property, such as incongruity, is a necessary condition for its occurrence.

And here we encounter an interesting result: for there is no analog in the visual arts to the possibility of incongruity between a musical or theatrical performance and the work performed. To criticize the performance of a painter is to criticize the painting. And if the source of aesthetic pain is located in the recognition of incongruities between work and instantiation, then we should anticipate an absence of this quality in our experience of the visual arts.[6]

I mentioned earlier that there were special problems here. One concerns the fact that some works of visual art are undeniably capable of inducing pain in the viewer. There are works of op art, for example, that cause noticeable retinal discomfort through their contrast in intensities and rapidly oscillating spatial ambiguities. And there are works of post-painterly art that contain areas of such extent and intensity of color that prolonged viewing may be mildly painful. But the question recurs: are these experiences *aesthetically* painful? The answer, one might assume, lies in relating the discomfiting properties of these visual art objects to the accidental (nonessential) decibel level of a musical performance, also a potential pain inducer. And since we have already argued for the irrelevance of the latter to the occurrence of aesthetic pain, we should now be able to reply to the question negatively by closing the analogy. But the elegance of this solution is unfortunately marred by a stubborn discrepancy. It is not at all clear that the pain inducing properties of, say, a work of op art are accidental or nonessential to it in the way that an intolerably high decibel level is a nonessential property of a performance.[7] The best criterion we have for determining whether a property is artistically or aesthetically "essential" is to ask if an alteration in the property in question

---

[6]There is an important exception to this in the class of visual art works that *do* admit instantiations: etchings, woodcuts, lithographs, and serigraphs, for example, of which *prints* are the instantiations. The possibility of incongruity between work and instantiation arises here, just as it does with performable art works. Consider, for instance, the effect of printing Dürer's *Melancolia* in psychedelic orange ink!

[7]I should say "of most performances." Possible exceptions may be discovered in the performances of a number of hard rock groups.

would also be an alteration in the *work* itself. And it seems reasonably clear that, in the op art instance, the answer must be yes. But even if the pain-inducing properties of a visual art object are essential properties, we have yet to determine whether an encounter with that object may be aesthetically painful. And in spite of the fact that pain may be induced here by properties that are essential to the character and identity of the work, I think it is reasonable to argue that the pain is nonetheless non-aesthetic. . . .

. . . If we consider our fourth example, we should be able to isolate a new variable. Here, a work of art, itself a radiantly attractive fresco, is marred by the intrusion of an extraneous feature. It is not just that the Virgin is unlikely to have *had* a moustache; the crude and darkly comic addition to Pinturicchio's masterpiece is experienced as a form of interference with our perception of the work. Moreover, it is an affront to the art object itself, a kind of aesthetic violence and injustice. And here we have an insight into the connection among examples (1), (2), and (4). All three exemplify the relation of an art work to *something* (an attempted instantiation, an extraneous addition) that is seen as a marring or a distortion of the work itself. And it is the recognition that violence or injustice has been done *to* an art work of value that I believe is the source of the distinctive experience of what I have chosen to call "aesthetic pain." Now, if this is correct it should also explain why it is that mere artistic worthlessness is insufficient to account for aesthetic pain. (Three-inch plastic replicas of Michelangelo's *Moses* and jigsaw puzzles of Leonardo's *L'Ultima Cena* would, I think, be found merely worthless aesthetically if it were not that we saw them as mocking travesties of valued objects.) . . .

Our fifth and final example, reading a trite and worthless novel, also I believe supports these conclusions. The judgment that an art work is *itself* bad or worthless is easily distinguished from the judgment that an art work of value has been *treated* in such a way as to marr, mask, or distort its aesthetic merits. There is a world of difference between the banality of the average nineteenth-century *roman sentimental* and the noxiousness of the *Reader's Digest's* truncation of *The Brothers Karamazov*. And there is a difference too between the offensiveness of the merely crude or obscene *in* art and the offensiveness of the inept or the intentionally destructive treatment *of* significant art; and we are entitled to the linguistic apparatus to identify these distinctions, whether they are presently a part of canonical criticism or not.

The incongruity between performance and work in (1) and (2) and the interference of extraneous with essential properties in (4) can both be subsumed under a category with greater scope and explanatory power. It is a commonly painful experience to observe the distortion or the debasing of *any* valued object, and where that object is an art work, the values that are debased are aesthetic values; and where we are witness to the debasement I would argue that we are justified in employing the adjunctive locution "aesthetically painful" to describe our experience.

Some Conclusions

We may return now to the question of aesthetic rights. It will, incidentally, not be crucial for the argument concerning rights that there should be general acquiescence in employing the expression "aesthetic pain" to characterize the sort of experiences that are discussed in the preceding section. There may be other, less troublesome, expressions that could be substituted, though I believe the case for adopting "anesthetic pain" is a strong one. What is necessary is that it be acknowledged that some of our transactions with art works are logically subject to a class of descriptions that admit predicates like "injustice," "violence," "marring," "debasing," "distortion," and "affront," predicates which, in the last section, occur in the description of various aesthetic situations—specifically, situations in which a valued art work has been treated or handled in an objectionable way. If art works are vulnerable to this variety of mistreatment (whose *recognition* I have argued is the source of aesthetic pain), this furnishes excellent presumptive evidence that we commonly regard them as invested with interests that are obligation-generating. And we correspondingly expect or require performers, curators, publishers, viewers, and audiences to fulfill varying obligations to the works that come into their provenance. Our aesthetic experience or, rather, one set of descriptions of that experience then suggests that we do in fact conceive of art works as endowed with obligation-generating interests, and since these are the conditions, outlined in part J, sufficient for the possession of rights, there can be no further reason to deny that artworks have such rights.

But this is perhaps the place to confront a lingering objection. I should be forced to admit that this entire enterprise has been misguided if it could be successfully argued that in speaking of the interests of art works we are trading on the shiftiness of an ellipsis. The objection comes to this: Surely, it is persons who have the relevant interests, and to speak of the interests of art works or of their entitlements to the protection of those interests is merely to short-circuit the proper locutions which should refer to the interests and entitlements of artists, performers, critics, and all those persons who stand to gain or lose something through their encounters with art works. "Aesthetic rights" is simply a misleading way of referring to *my* rights (or yours) with regard to the corpus of extant art works. This is a forceful objection and, I believe, the most formidable obstacle in the way of accepting the conclusion that I have attempted to press. But let us consider some examples of obligation statements relating to art works: "You ought not to paint moustaches on Renaissance frescoes"; or "One ought always to exhibit the *Night Watch* in a soft and diffuse light"; or (more generally) "One ought not to make a mockery of great art." Now, if the objection is correct, the interests that are furthered or protected by fulfilling these obligations are the interests of the artists themselves or of their admirers. But is this true? What interest of Pinturicchio do I damage by painting a moustache on his Virgin? Since he is no longer vulnerable to personal affront, only his reputation could be at stake. But is the marring of his fresco a threat to his reputation as a painter? Only, I should think, if we took the moustache to have been painted by Pinturricchio himself. But if it is not the interests of the artist himself that are threatened here, then surely (the objection continues) it must be the interests of all those actual and potential viewers of the work that we are enjoined to protect. But this will not do either. Consider again the locutions that we have used to describe the relevant aesthetic situations. It is the *work* itself that is affronted, distorted, defamed, maligned, insulted, or done violence to—not the artist, the performer, or the public, even though their interests may suffer and their rights also can be infringed as a *result* of the mistreatment of the art work. But these are logically distinct possibilities; and it is my contention that anything that can be victimized by actions that fall under descriptions of the sort just catalogued is the legitimate bearer of rights. Succinctly, anything that is, logically, subject to mistreatments of this kind has interests of the obligation-generating sort, and thus, has rights.

Postscript

The conclusion that we have reached is that art works have rights that are logically distinct from the rights of persons who are concerned with them. This conclusion is, to say the least, striking; and it will not be amiss to suggest an analogy that may help to soften the impact. One of the central and often repeated reasons for valuing art works is also a common reason for valuing persons, viz., their uniqueness or individuality. True, the loss of a single portrait by Hals or a single sculpture by Moore may hardly matter given the enormous wealth of remaining art works. But the same could be said of the loss of a single person, and yet both may be valued not because they are indispensable but because they are, as individuals, irreplaceable. Art works, no more than persons, are fully interchangeable entities, and it is their logical similarity with respect to their *identity* that may account for our treating art works as quasi-persons, and thus, in accordance with Kantian injunctions, for our apparent willingness to regard them as endowed with rights.

ILLUSTRATION 27

SUZANNE HARDING, *Door Country, 1977.*

ILLUSTRATION 28

sorry

NTOZAKE SHANGE

lady in blue
one thing i dont need
is any more apologies
i got sorry greetin me at my front door
you can keep yrs
i dont know what to do wit em
they dont open doors
or bring the sun back
they dont make me happy
or get a mornin paper
didnt nobody stop usin my tears to wash cars
cuz a sorry

i am simply tired
of collectin
            i didnt know
            i was so important toyou'
i'm gonna haveta throw some away
i cant get to the clothes in my closet
for alla the sorries
i'm gonna tack a sign to my door
leave a message by the phone
            'if you called
            to say yr sorry
            call somebody
            else
            i dont use em anymore'
i let sorry/didnt meanta/& how cd i know abt that
take a walk down a dark & musty street in brooklyn
i'm gonna do exactly what i want to
& i wont be sorry for none of it
letta sorry soothe yr soul/i'm gonna soothe mine

you were always inconsistent
doin somethin & then bein sorry
beatin my heart to death

talkin bout you sorry
well
i will not call
i'm not goin to be nice
i will raise my voice
& scream & holler
& break things & race the engine
& tell all yr secrets bout yrself to yr face
& i will list in detail everyone of my wonderful lovers
& their ways
i will play oliver lake
loud
& i wont be sorry for none of it

i loved you on purpose
i was open on purpose
i still crave vulnerability & close talk
& i'm not even sorry bout you bein sorry
you can carry all the guilt & grime ya wanna
just dont give it to me
i cant use another sorry
next time
you should admit
you're mean/low-down/triflin/& no count straight
                    out
steada being sorry alla the time
enjoy bein yrself

The Contributors

SAINT THOMAS AQUINAS (1225?–1274) was an Italian scholastic philosopher, often called the Angelic Doctor (Lat. *Doctor Angelicus*) and Prince of Scholastics (Lat. *Princeps Scholasticorum*). He entered the Dominican order and studied under Albertus Magnus (1248–52), was canonized by Pope John XXXII (1323); and was proclaimed doctor of the church (1567) by Pius V. He is known particularly as a systematizer of Catholic theology and philosophy.

VIRGIL ALDRICH is professor of philosophy at the University of Utah. Long active in aesthetics, his book *Philosophy of Art* is widely read.

ARISTOTLE (385/4–322 B.C.), along with his teacher, Plato, is surely one of the most famous Western philosophers of all time. He wrote the *Poetics* about 330 B.C. It is one of the most influential works ever written in aesthetics.

RUDOLF ARNHEIM is well known in the field of philosophy and psychology of art. He is the author of *Visual Thinking, Entropy and Art, Toward a Psychology of Art, Genesis of a Painting,* and *Film as Art.*

ANTONIN ARTAUD (1896–1948) was a French dramatist and director whose concept of the "Theatre of Cruelty" was enormously influential, although Artaud himself spent a great deal of his life in mental asylums and seldom was able to test his theatrical principles on stage. *The Theatre and its Double* is his most famous work.

MONROE C. BEARDSLEY is professor of philosophy at Temple University. He is one of the best-known writers in aesthetics in the Anglo-American world. His major work *Aesthetics: Problems in the Philosophy of Criticism* was published in 1958 and has had an enormous influence on the subject.

CLIVE BELL (1881–1964) was a highly influential critic and a member of the famous Bloomsbury group which included such figures as Virginia Woolf, John Maynard Keynes, and G. E. Moore.

CHARLES BIEDERMAN is one of the founders and earliest Constructionist artists. His book *Art As the Evolution of Visual Knowledge* is an outstanding and unusual contribution to the history of aesthetics and aesthetic theory.

HIERONYMUS BOSCH (c. 1450–1516) was perhaps the greatest master of fantasy who ever lived. His obsessive and haunted world is that of Gothic twilight; it is the best surviving expression of some aspects of the waning of the Middle Ages, although it is now largely incomprehensible. His paintings are in many major museums.

BERTOLT BRECHT (1898–1956) is considered the father of modern theatre. His theory of the epic theatre has influenced almost every contemporary Western playwright. Although born in Germany, he spent World War II in Hollywood writing screenplays. After the war he returned to East Germany where he directed the Berliner Ensemble. Among his major plays are *The Life of Galileo, Mother Courage and Her Children, The Good Woman of Setzuan,* and *The Caucasian Chalk Circle.*

EDWARD BULLOUGH (1880–1934) was professor of Italian literature at Cambridge University. He is most famous, however, for his aesthetic writings and his coining of the term "psychical distance."

EDWARD CASEY graduated from Northwestern University and is professor of philosophy at Yale University. His book *Imagining* is an outstanding contribution to the phenomenology of that subject.

JOHN CAGE is a contemporary American composer. His revolutionary ideas have strongly influenced much of very modern music. His most famous is the theory of indeterminism which specifies randomness as the guiding principle in the writing and performance of his music.

ALLEN CARLSON is associate professor of philosophy at the University of Alberta, Canada.

SAMUEL TAYLOR COLERIDGE (1772–1834) was an English poet and critic. He was an intimate friend of Wordsworth and joined with him to produce the *Lyrical Ballads* which included Coleridge's *Ancient Mariner,* the *Nightingale,* and *Love.* In addition to being a well-known poet, Coleridge introduced German idealistic philosophy to England and is considered the father of modern Shakespearean criticism.

TED COHEN is Chairman of the Department of Philosophy at the University of Chicago. In addition to writing in aesthetics, Cohen has also done extensive work on Kant and J. L. Austin.

R. G. COLLINGWOOD (1889–1943). Collingwood was Waynflete Professor of Metaphysics at Oxford University, England. He published extensively in philosophy as well as history. In addition to *The Principles of Art,* Collingwood also wrote *An Essay on Philosophical Method, An Essay on Metaphysics, The New Leviathan, The Idea of Nature,* and *The Idea of History.*

JOHN CONSTABLE (1776–1837) was, with Turner, the major English landscape painter of the nineteenth century. He first exhibited in 1802, but achieved only limited recognition. In 1824 his *Hay Wain* and a *View on the Stour* were awarded a Gold Medal at the Paris Salon; the great success of these and other works imported into France had an appreciable effect on the development of the Barbizon School and on the painting of the Romantic movement.

e. e. cummings (1894–1962) was an American painter and poet who is best known for his stylistic experimentation and, in particular, his lack of punctuation in poetry. Despite these oddities, many of his poems are considered among the finest American verse.

ARTHUR DANTO is professor of philosophy at Columbia University. He has published widely in all areas of philosophy including important works in the analytical tradition. Danto was also a member of the abstract expressionistic school of painting in New York in the 1950s.

GEORGE DICKIE is professor of philosophy at the University of Illinois, Chicago Circle Campus. His work in aesthetics over the last two decades culminated in the publication of his book *Art and the Aesthetic: An Institutional Analysis* (1974).

MARCEL DUCHAMP (1887–1968) was one of the original Dadaists. Before the invention of Dada he had shocked New York with his *Nude Descending a Staircase* in the Armory Show of 1913. Most of his works are in Philadelphia.

T. S. ELIOT (1888–1965) was a well-known American poet and literary critic who spent the better portion of his life in England. His most famous works include *The Waste Land* and *Ash Wednesday*. He was also a playwright.

SIGMUND FREUD (1856–1939), Austrian psychologist, inventor of psychoanalysis, was a brilliant and lucid writer on many subjects. He wrote some essays on aesthetic matters, but he is best known for his theory of the nature of the unconscious.

E. H. GOMBRICH, Director of the Warburg Institute, London, is the author of *The Story of Art, Art and Illusion,* and *Meditations on a Hobby Horse.*

NELSON GOODMAN is one of the most distinguished contemporary philosophers. Professor Goodman received his undergraduate and graduate degrees from Harvard. He has held special appointments at many universities, and has given the Alfred North Whitehead Lecture at Harvard and the John Locke Lectures at Oxford. He is the author of many scholarly essays and a number of books including *Fact, Fiction and Forecast* and *The Structure of Appearance.*

EDUARD HANSLICK (1825–1904) was born in Prague and became professor of music at the University of Vienna and music critic for the famous journal *Weiner Zeitung.* Aesthetically, he championed Brahms and scorned Wagner.

SUZANNE HARDING received her Ph.D. in aesthetic education from Loyola University where she is art director. She has had a number of exhibitions of her photography and has won several awards in photography.

FRANCIS HUTCHESON (1694–1746) was one of the first British empiricist philosophers who wrote on beauty and morals. His influence on aesthetics and ethics cannot be underestimated.

ROMAN INGARDEN (1893–1970) was a Polish philosopher who, in his early years, was a student of Husserl's at Freiburg. Among his phenomenological writings on aesthetic questions, the best known is perhaps *Das Literarische Kunstwerk* (1930; second revised edition 1959).

PHILLIP JOHNSON is a well-known American architect and is considered one of the fathers of the postmodern movement in architecture.

JAMES JOYCE (1882–1941) was an Irish writer, born in Dublin, and educated at Belvedere College and Royal University at Dublin. He is the author of *Dubliners, A Portrait of the Artist as a Young Man, Ulylsses, Exiles* (drama), and *Finnegans Wake.*

WASSILY KANDINSKY (1866–1944) was born in Moscow but trained as a painter in Munich, after abandoning a legal career. He painted his first purely abstract work in 1910, and was therefore one of the founders of "pure" abstract painting. In 1911 he was one of the founders of the *Blaue Reiter* group, and in 1912 he published a book which was translated into English (in 1914) as *The Art of Spiritual Harmony.*

IMMANUEL KANT (1724–1804) is one of the greatest philosophers in the Western tradition. Kant's three critiques—the *Critique of Pure Reason,* the *Critique of Practical Reason,* and the *Critique of Judgment*—are perennial sources of philosophical scholarship and analysis.

FRANZ KLINE (1910–1962) was one of the leading representatives of the post-war American art movement which had so great an influence in the 1950s and 1960s. He was an exponent of Abstract Expressionism who was deeply influenced by Oriental calligraphy and whose color schemes were normally limited to black, white, and grey.

SUSANNE LANGER is one of the most influential present-day theorists of art. Her ideas are elaborately set forth in *Philosophy in a New Key, Feeling and Form, Mind: An Essay on Human Feeling,* and *Problems of Art.* She taught at Connecticut College where she is Professor Emeritus of Philosophy.

ESTELLA LAUTER teaches aesthetics at the University of Wisconsin, Green Bay. She has published criticisms of visual arts and poetry in interdisciplinary journals and has recently completed two books, *Women as Mythmakers* and *Feminist Archetypal Theory* (edited with Carol Schreier Rupprecht).

LUCY LIPPARD is both one of our finest critics of contemporary art and a perceptive supporter of women artists. Her essays, written since the publication of *Changing* in 1971, delineate the growth of Lippard's feminism and the present status of women's art.

JEFFREY MAITLAND teaches philosophy at Purdue University. He is the author of several articles in aesthetics and is an expert on Martin Heidegger.

MAURICE MANDELBAUM is professor of philosophy at Johns Hopkins University. He has written many books and essays in aesthetics and other topics in philosophy.

KARL MARX (1818–1883) was a German political philosopher. Marx was expelled from Prussia in 1849, settled in London, and devoted himself to the philosophical development of his theory of socialism and to agitation for social reforms. His great work, *Das Kapital* (vols. 1867, 1885, 1895), was carried to completion by his collaborator, Friedrich Engels. His other most notable work, also written in collaboration with Engels, was the *Communist Manifesto* (1847).

MAURICE MERLEAU-PONTY (1908–1961) was professor of philosophy at the College de France from 1953 and was influential also as a commentator on current affairs. Among his numerous works, *The Phenomenology of Perception,* published in English translation in 1962, is perhaps best known to English readers.

LEONARD B. MEYER (1918–   ), professor of music, University of Chicago, is the author of *Emotion and Meaning in Music* (1956) and the recently published *Music, the Arts and Ideas.*

MICHELANGELO (1475–1564) is probably the most famous artist of all time. Michelangelo was born near Florence and was a student of Domenico Ghirlandaio. He worked under the patronage of Lorenzo de' Medici and later under Pope Julius II and Pope Leo X. Michelangelo was a painter, a sculptor, and an architect. His best-known works include four pietas, the ceiling in the Sistine Chapel in the Vatican, and his architectural design of the dome of St. Peters.

FRIEDRICH NIETZSCHE (1844–1900), the noted German philosopher, has been called a nihilist and is sometimes considered an early existentialist. His tempestuous life and works have long been subject to misunderstanding. *The Birth of Tragedy* (1872) and *The Will To Power* (1901) contain Nietzsche's thoughts on art.

HAROLD OSBORNE is a British aestheticist. In addition to *Aesthetics* and *Art Theory,* he is the author of the *The Theory of Beauty* (1952) and *Aesthetics and Criticism* (1955). He is also editor of the *British Journal of Aesthetics.*

PABLO PICASSO (1881–1973). No man has changed the nature of art more radically than Picasso. Like Giotto, Michelangelo, and Bernini he stands at the beginning of a new epoch. Most museums of Modern Art throughout the world have examples of his works. *Guernica,* a huge composition prompted by the Spanish Civil War, expresses in complicated iconography and personal symbolical language, the artist's abhorrence of violence and war.

PLATO (427–348 B.C.). Surely one of the most famous and influential thinkers of all time, Plato's philosophical writings are of perennial interest. The issues he raised and the solutions he proposed are as central today as they were to him and his fellow Athenians.

PLOTINUS (204–269), the founder of the Roman School of Neo-Platonism, produced an original synthesis of Plato's philosophy, stressing the notion of emanation from the One to everything else, including art and beauty. His works were arranged by his disciple and biographer, Porphyry, into sets of nine essays each—hence, the term, *Enneads.* His influence on artistic creation is noteworthy in the history of aesthetics.

ALEXANDER POPE (1688–1744). An English poet, Pope came to public notice with the publication of *Pastorals* in Tonson's *Miscellany* and gained sure reputation with his brilliant mock-heroic poem *The Rape of the Lock.*

SIR HERBERT READ (1893–1968)—English critic, poet, and essayist—was the author of many books on all phases of art, including *The Art of Sculpture.*

SIR JOSHUA REYNOLDS (1723–1792)—famous portrait painter and intimate friend of Dr. Samuel Johnson—was the first president of the Royal Academy, an office which provided him the opportunity to deliver his *Discourses,* a summation of eighteenth-century aesthetics.

GILBERT RYLE (1900–1976) was a leading figure in analytic philosophy at Oxford University. He was a long-time editor of the journal *Mind.* In addition to his most famous work, *The Concept of Mind,* he wrote a number of influential articles and short books.

RICHARD SALIARIS is a graduate from the American College of Switzerland and the Oxford School of Design. He lives and paints in Athens, Greece, where he has had many exhibitions of his works.

GEORGE SANTAYANA (1863–1952). Poet, critic, philosopher and essayist, as his first of many books George Santayana wrote *The Sense of Beauty,* a work on aesthetics which has become one of the more important contemporary books on the subject.

JEAN-PAUL SARTRE (1905–1980), a writer of novels and plays as well as works of philosophy and criticism, was the most widely known of those who have been called Existentialists. His *L'Etre et le Neant* was published in 1943, and in English translation in 1957.

ARNOLD SCHÖNBERG (1874–1951). Schöenberg was an Austrian composer; his departure from accepted forms of composition identified him with the ultramodern school of music. Works include string sextet *Verklärte Nacht* (1899) and the symphonic poem *Pelleas and Melisande.*

GEORGES SEURAT (1859–91). Seurat studied at the Ecole des Beaux-Arts. He was also much influenced by the aesthetic theories based on the observations of a scientist, Charles Henry, and the conclusions of David Sutter's writings on the phenomena of vision. These led him to evolve first the theory of Divisionism and then a method of painting by use of colour contrasts. Areas of shadow are broken down into the complementaries of adjacent areas of light, the light itself being broken down into local color, the color of the light and of reflections. Where the Impressionists stressed the flickering quality of light and figures caught in movement, Seurat aimed at a static quality.

WILLIAM SHAKESPEARE (1564–1616). Surely the most famous writer in the English language, Shakespeare wrote thirty-six plays, as well as a number of sonnets. *Hamlet* is one of his most-performed works.

NTOZAKE SHANGE is a contemporary black woman playwright.

DONALD SHERBURNE is professor of philosophy at Vanderbilt University and editor of the interdisciplinary journal, *Soundings*. He is a well-known scholar on Whitehead and has written several articles in aesthetics.

F. N. SIBLEY is professor of philosophy at the University of Lancaster. A writer in the analytical tradition, he has published several highly influential articles on the concept of the aesthetic.

BERYL LAKE STEELE is a member of the faculty at the University of Surrey, England.

ROBERT A. M. STERN, a professor and well-known architect, is one of the foremost designers of postmodern architecture and a leader in the movement.

ALAN TORMEY is professor of philosophy at the University of Maryland. He is the author of *The Concept of Expression* as well as many essays on the philosophy of art.

COUNT LEO NIKOLAEVICH TOLSTOY (1828–1910). Tolstoy's importance as a novelist is unquestionable. In *What Is Art?* he investigated the moral, social, and religious significance of art.

PAUL VALERY (1871–1945) was a distinguished poet as well as a critic and philosopher. He was elected to the French Academy in 1925, and from 1937 was professor of poetry at the College de France.

ELISEO VIVAS is Professor Emeritus at Northwestern University. Venezuelan by birth, he was educated in the United States. In addition to articles and books on aesthetics, Vivas is the author of *The Moral Life* and *Ethical Life* and is a well-known ethicist.

MORRIS WEITZ is professor of philosophy at Brandeis University. He has been a leading figure in American aesthetics for many years. His essays and books have influenced much discussion in leading journals.

NATHANAEL WEST (1903–1940) was an American novelist whose satiric novels of the 1930s were widely read only after his death, when he was posthumously recognized as one of America's finest early twentieth-century writers.

OSCAR WILDE (1856–1900) was an Irish poet, wit, and dramatist. At Oxford, he won the Newdigate prize and became an apostle of a cult affecting the doctrine of art for art's sake. Wilde gained notoriety with his aesthetic eccentricities. He wrote works of fiction, including *The Picture of Dorian Gray,* and a number of plays, including *Lady Windermere's Fan* (1892), *A Woman of No Importance* (1893), *The Importance of Being Earnest* (1895), and *Salome.* Tried on a charge of sodomy, convicted, and imprisoned, he ended his life in disgrace and poverty.

LUDWIG WITTGENSTEIN (1889–1951) was one of the most influential philosophers in Britain during this century despite the fact that he was Austrian by birth and wrote mostly in German. His most famous works are the *Tractatus Logico-Philosophicus* and the *Philosophical Investigations.*

NICHOLAS WOLTERSTORFF is professor of philosophy, Calvin College. He is the author of *On Universals* (1970), *Reason Within the Bounds of Religion* (1976), and *Art in Action*.

WILLIAM BUTLER YEATS (1865–1939) was an Irish poet and dramatist. Although he is best known for his poetic works, Yeats was the leader of the Irish literary revival in the theater and wrote many plays according to his mystical theories of drama. He sometimes thought of himself as having mediumistic powers. Some of his most famous poems include *The Wilde Swans at Coole* and *The Tower*.